W9-DFI-523

A+ Guide to Software: Managing, Maintaining, and Troubleshooting

Second Edition

Jean Andrews, Ph.D.

Australia • Canada • Mexico • Singapore • Spain • United Kingdom • United States

A+ Guide to Software: Managing, Maintaining, and Troubleshooting, Second Edition
is published by Course Technology.

Senior Product Manager:
Laura Hildebrand

Senior Editor:
William Pitkin III

Marketing Manager:
Jason Sakos

Associate Product Managers:
Tim Gleeson and Nick Lombardi

Editorial Assistant:
Christy Urban

Copyeditor:
Chris Smith

Manufacturing Coordinator:
Trevor Kallop

Production Editor:
Jennifer Goguen

Quality Assurance:
Nicole Ashton

Cover Design:
Julie Malone

Compositor:
GEX Publishing Services

Printed in Canada

3 4 5 6 7 8 9 TC 06 05 04 03

For more information, contact Course Technology, 25 Thomson Place, Boston, Massachusetts, 02210.

Or find us on the World Wide Web at:
www.course.com

ISBN 0-619-18627-5

Brief Contents

TABLE OF CONTENTS v

A+ TABLE OF CONTENTS xiii

INTRODUCTION xx

CHAPTER ONE
Introducing and Comparing Operating Systems 1

CHAPTER TWO
How an OS Works with Hardware and Other Software 43

CHAPTER THREE
Understanding the Boot Process and Command Line 95

CHAPTER FOUR
Installing and Using Windows 9x 157

CHAPTER FIVE
Supporting and Troubleshooting Windows 9x 217

CHAPTER SIX
Understanding and Supporting Windows NT 267

CHAPTER SEVEN
Installing and Using Windows 2000 Professional 303

CHAPTER EIGHT
Managing and Troubleshooting Windows 2000 331

CHAPTER NINE
Installing and Using Windows XP Professional 373

CHAPTER TEN
Managing and Supporting Windows XP 409

CHAPTER ELEVEN
Supporting Hard Drives 445

CHAPTER TWELVE
Windows on a Network 483

CHAPTER THIRTEEN
Windows on the Internet 537

CHAPTER FOURTEEN
Linux, Macs, and Notebooks 575

APPENDIX A
Error Messages and Their Meanings 613

APPENDIX B
ASCII Character Set and Ansi.sys 617

APPENDIX C
The Hexadecimal Number System and Memory Addressing 621

APPENDIX D
The Professional PC Technician 631

GLOSSARY 643

INDEX 657

Table of Contents

A+ TABLE OF CONTENTS xiii

INTRODUCTION xx

CHAPTER ONE
Introducing and Comparing Operating Systems 1
What an Operating System Does 2
Operating System Components 4
How an OS Relates to Users 5
Comparing Operating Systems 7
DOS (Disk Operating System) 12
Windows Operating Systems 13
Windows 9x 13
Windows NT 17
Windows 2000 24
Windows XP 29
Other Operating Systems 32
Unix 32
Linux 33
OS/2 34
Macintosh Operating System (Mac OS) 34
Chapter Summary 37
Key Terms 38
Review Questions 38
Hands-on Projects 39
Case Project 41

CHAPTER TWO
How an OS Works with Hardware and Other Software 43
How an OS Relates to Hardware 44
The Motherboard 46
The CPU 48
Memory or RAM 48
Buses on the Motherboard 49
System Resources on the Motherboard 52
BIOS on the Motherboard and Other Circuit Boards 64
CMOS Setup Chip 66
Hard Drives and Other Secondary Storage Devices 66
How an OS Relates to Other Software 71
Real (16-Bit) and Protected (32-Bit) Operating Modes 71
How an OS Uses BIOS and Device Drivers 74
How an OS Launches Applications 80
How Application Software Is Loaded and Initialized 81
Loading Application Software Using the Windows Desktop 86

Chapter Summary 88
Key Terms 90
Review Questions 90
Hands-on Projects 92
Case Project 94

CHAPTER THREE
Understanding the Boot Process and Command Line 95
Booting Up Your Computer 96
Startup BIOS Controls the Beginning of the Boot 96
Loading the MS-DOS Core of Windows 9x 102
Emergency Startup Disks 105
Windows 9x Startup Disks 105
Accessing a Command Prompt 110
How DOS and Windows 9x View and Manage Memory 112
Physical Memory and Memory Addresses 114
Areas of the Memory Map 115
Utilities that Manage Memory 119
Some Default Settings Used by Windows 122
Managing Floppy Disks and Hard Drives 123
How Data is Logically Stored on a Floppy Disk 123
The Formatting Process for a Floppy Disk 124
How a Hard Drive Is Logically Organized to Hold Data 128
Using Fdisk to Partition a Drive 135
Formatting Each Logical Drive 137
Using Commands to Manage a Floppy Disk or Hard Drive 138
Using Batch Files 147
Chapter Summary 148
Key Terms 150
Review Questions 151
Hands-on Projects 152
Case Project 155
Prepare a Hard Drive for the Installation of Windows 9x 155

CHAPTER FOUR
Installing and Using Windows 9x 157
Windows 9x Versions and Architecture 158
How Windows 98 Differs from Windows 95 158
Windows Me 159
Windows 9x Architecture 160
Installing Windows 9x 164
What's on the Windows 9x CD 165
Preparing for Installation 166
Installing Windows 9x as a Clean Installation 167
Installing 9x as an Upgrade 168
Installation Process from the Setup Screen 171
Instructions for Specific Upgrades 178
Downloading and Installing Updates for Windows 9x 180

Using Windows 9x 180
Keystroke Shortcuts in Windows 180
Managing the Windows 9x Desktop 182
Using Windows Explorer to Manage Floppy Disks and Hard Drives 186
Installing Hardware with Windows 9x 190
Adding New Hardware 190
Plug and Play and Hardware Installations 196
Installing Applications in Windows 9x 198
Preparing for Software Installation 198
Performing Software Installations 199
Troubleshooting Software Installations 199
Supporting DOS Applications Under Windows 9x 200
Managing Memory with Windows 9x 204
Memory Management with Device Drivers in Windows 9x 204
Windows 9x Swap File 206
Virtual Machine Manager 207
Getting Help from Microsoft 208
Chapter Summary 209
Key Terms 212
Review Questions 213
Hands-on Projects 214
Case Project 215

CHAPTER FIVE
Supporting and Troubleshooting Windows 9x 217
Booting Windows 9x 218
Files Used to Customize the Startup Process 218
The Windows 9x Startup Process 220
Loading an Application at Startup 224
Troubleshooting the Windows 9x Boot Process 224
Error Messages Received While Loading Windows 9x 225
Microsoft Windows 9x Startup Menu 226
Using the Startup Disk for Troubleshooting 232
The Windows 9x Registry 233
How the Registry Is Organized 234
Recovering from a Corrupted Registry 235
Modifying the Registry 237
Tools Used to Monitor, Control, and Troubleshoot Windows 9x 239
System Applet in Control Panel 242
System Monitor 243
System Configuration Utility 243
Tools to Manage Security 245
Managing a Hard Drive 246
Device Manager 250
Dr. Watson 251
Windows Help and the Microsoft Web Site 252
Troubleshooting Hardware in Windows 9x 253
Troubleshooting Legacy Devices and Drivers 255

Troubleshooting Applications in Windows 9x 256
Problems with a Software Program Itself 257
Uninstalling Software 258
Troubleshooting Problems with Windows Performance 259
Chapter Summary 259
Key Terms 262
Review Questions 262
Hands-on Projects 263

CHAPTER SIX
Understanding and Supporting Windows NT 267

A Break with the Past: A New Windows Architecture 268
The Modular Concept of Windows NT 268
Windows NT Modes 272
Installing Windows NT 275
Hard Drive Partitions 276
A Choice of File Systems 277
Preparing to Install Windows NT 279
Installing Windows NT as the Only OS 281
Installing Windows NT as the Second OS on the Hard Drive 283
Supporting Windows NT 285
Memory in Windows NT 285
Installing Hardware and Software 286
Windows NT Networking 289
Understanding the Windows NT Boot Process 292
Troubleshooting Windows NT 294
Troubleshooting the Windows NT Boot Process 295
Chapter Summary 299
Key Terms 300
Review Questions 300
Hands-on Projects 302
Case Project 302

CHAPTER SEVEN
Installing and Using Windows 2000 Professional 303

Windows 2000 Architecture 304
New Features 304
Basic Disks and Dynamic Disks 306
Installing Windows 2000 Professional 307
Plan the Installation 307
Clean Installation 314
Clean Install When the Hard Drive Has an Operating System Installed 316
Upgrade Installation 317
After the Installation: Backing Up the System State 318
Using Windows 2000 319
Managing the Desktop 320
Installing Hardware and Applications 323
Installing Hardware 323
Installing Applications 325

Chapter Summary 326
Key Terms 327
Review Questions 327
Hands-on Projects 328
Case Project 330

CHAPTER EIGHT
Managing and Troubleshooting Windows 2000 331
Understanding the Boot Process 332
Customizing the Boot Process 332
Troubleshooting the Boot Process 335
Tools for Maintenance and Troubleshooting 344
Using the Backup Tool to Restore the System State 345
Windows 2000 Support Tools 345
Windows File Protection 347
Command Window 348
Disk Properties Window 349
Computer Management 350
Microsoft Management Console 354
Performance Monitoring and Optimization 360
Managing Virtual Memory 365
Dr. Watson and Memory Dumps 366
Windows Update 367
Chapter Summary 368
Key Terms 369
Review Questions 369
Hands-on Projects 370

CHAPTER NINE
Installing and Using Windows XP Professional 373
Features and Architecture of Windows XP 374
Windows XP Features 374
Windows XP Architecture 376
Installing Windows XP 377
Planning the Installation 377
Installation Process 381
After the Installation 387
Using Windows XP 391
Customizing the Windows XP Desktop 393
Managing Audio and Video 396
Multiple Logins and Remote Assistance 398
Installing Hardware and Applications 398
Installing Hardware 398
Installing Applications 401
Chapter Summary 404
Key Terms 405
Review Questions 406
Hands-on Projects 407

CHAPTER TEN

Managing and Supporting Windows XP **409**

Security Using Windows NT/2000/XP 410
User Accounts and Profiles 410
Disk Quotas 416
EFS (Encrypted File System) 418
Internet Connection Firewall 421
The Windows NT/2000/XP Registry 422
How the Registry Is Organized 422
Editing the Registry 426
Other Maintenance and Troubleshooting Tools 428
Help on the Web 431
Troubleshooting the Boot Process 433
System Restore 435
Windows XP Startup Disk 436
Automated System Recovery 437
Error Messages and Their Meanings 439
Chapter Summary 440
Key Terms 442
Review Questions 442
Hands-on Projects 443

CHAPTER ELEVEN

Supporting Hard Drives **445**

Supporting Hard Drives 446
Disk Compression 446
Disk Caching 449
Troubleshooting Hard Drives 451
Making Backups 457
Volume Types and Fault Tolerance 466
Viruses and Other Computer Infestations 467
Understanding Computer Infestations 468
Protecting Against Computer Infestations 474
Chapter Summary 477
Key Terms 478
Review Questions 478
Hands-on Projects 479

CHAPTER TWELVE

Windows on a Network **483**

Networking Basics 484
How Network Communication Works 484
Understanding Network Layers 485
The OSI Model Applied to a Local Network 487
Addressing on a Network 490
MAC Addresses 491
IP Addresses 493
Host Names and NetBIOS Names 499
Assigning or Changing a Computer Name 500

Connecting to a Network and Sharing Resources 502
Connecting to a NetBEUI Network 502
Connecting to a TCP/IP Network 506
Sharing Resources on the Network 511
How Computers Find Each Other on a LAN 523
Network Drive Maps 525
Direct Cable Connection 527
Remote Access to a Network 528
Allowing Inbound Connections 528
Remote Control 529
Chapter Summary 530
Key Terms 532
Review Questions 533
Hands-on Projects 534

CHAPTER THIRTEEN
Windows on the Internet 537
The OSI Model Applied to a TCP/IP Network 538
IP Address and Port Identifies a Service 538
TCP/IP Protocols at Each Layer 540
TCP/IP Utilities 544
Connecting to the Internet Using a Dial-up Connection 546
How Dial-up Networking Works 546
Creating a Dial-up Connection in Windows 9x 547
Creating a Dial-up Connection in Windows 2000 551
Dial-up Networking Problems 553
DSL and Cable Modem Connections 555
Cable Modem 555
DSL 557
Sharing Internet Connections 557
Supporting Internet Clients 559
Supporting Web Browsers 560
Supporting E-Mail 564
Supporting FTP 566
Chapter Summary 569
Key Terms 571
Review Questions 571
Hands-on Projects 572

CHAPTER FOURTEEN
Linux, Macs, and Notebooks 575
Introducing the Mac OS 576
Starting Up a Mac 576
Using the Mac 579
Supporting Hardware 583
Introducing Linux 588
Root Account and User Accounts 588
Directory and File Layout 589
Linux Commands 591
Using the vi Editor 595
Window Managers 597

Supporting Notebooks 598
Windows 98 Notebook Features 599
Windows 2000 Notebook Features 600
Windows XP Notebook Features 601
Power Management 602
Online Resources for Notebooks 607
Chapter Summary 607
Key Terms 609
Review Questions 609
Hands-on Projects 610

APPENDIX A
Error Messages and Their Meanings 613

APPENDIX B
ASCII Character Set and Ansi.sys 617

APPENDIX C
The Hexadecimal Number System and Memory Addressing 621
Learning to "Think Hex" 622
Place Value 622
How Exponents Are Used to Express Place Value 626
Binary Number System 626
Memory Addressing 627
Displaying Memory with DOS DEBUG 628

APPENDIX D
The Professional PC Technician 631
What Customers Want: Beyond Technical Know-how 631
Support Calls: Providing Good Service 632
Planning for Good Service 632
Making an On-site Service Call 633
Phone Support 634
When You Can't Solve the Problem 637
Recordkeeping and Information Tools 638
Professional Organizations and Certifications 639
Why Certification? 640
Protecting Software Copyrights 640
What Does the Law Say? 641
What Are Your Responsibilities under the Law? 641

GLOSSARY 643

INDEX 657

A+ Operating System Technologies Examination Objectives

OBJECTIVES	CHAPTERS	PAGE NUMBERS
Domain 1 Operating System Fundamentals		
1.1 Identify the major desktop components and interfaces, and their functions. Differentiate the characteristics of Windows 9x/ME, Windows NT 4.0 Workstation, Windows 2000 Professional, and Windows XP.		
■ Contrasts between Windows 9x/ME, Windows NT, Windows 2000 and XP	1	3, 7–32
■ Major Operating System components		
■ Registry	5, 10	234–235, 434–438
■ Virtual Memory	2, 4, 6	72, 206–208, 285
■ File System	2, 3	67–68, 123–133
■ Major Operating System Interfaces		
■ Windows Explorer	4	186–189
■ My Computer	2, 4, 12	51, 186, 501
■ Control Panel	4	190–192
■ Computer Management Console	8	354–357
■ Accessories/System Tools	7, 8	318, 343, 345
■ Command line	8	348
■ Network Neighborhood/My Network Places	12	504, 511
■ Task Bar/systray	4, 7, 9	183–184, 320–322, 395
■ Start Menu	4, 5, 7	184–185, 237–238, 259, 320–322
1.2 Identify the names, locations, purposes, and contents of major system files.		
■ Windows 9x –specific files		
■ Io.sys	3	102–103
■ MSDOS.sys	3	102–103
■ Autoexec.bat	3	102–103
■ Command.com	3	102–103
■ Config.sys	3	102–103
■ HIMEM.SYS	3	102–103, 119–122
■ EMM386.exe	3	119–122
■ win.com	3, 5	104, 231
■ SYSTEM.INI	5	218–219
■ WIN.INI	5	218–219
■ Registry data files		
■ System.dat	5	234
■ User.dat	5	234
■ Windows NT-based specific files		
■ BOOT.INI	6	292–294
■ NTLDR	6	292–294
■ NTDETECT.COM	6	292–294
■ NTBOOTDD.SYS	6	292–294
■ NTUSER.DAT	6	292–294
■ Registry data files	10	434–438
1.3 Demonstrate the ability to use command-line functions and utilities to manage the operating system including the proper syntax and switches.		
■ Command/CMD	3, 8	102–103, 348
■ DIR	3	140

A+ Operating System Technologies Examination Objectives

OBJECTIVES	CHAPTERS	PAGE NUMBERS
■ ATTRIB	3	144–145
■ VER	3	146
■ MEM	3	120–122
■ SCANDISK	3	146
■ DEFRAG	3	146
■ EDIT	3	147
■ XCOPY	3	142–143
■ COPY	3	142
■ FORMAT	3	139–140
■ FDISK	3	139
■ SETVER	3	123
■ SCANREG	3	146
■ MD/CD/RD	3	143–144
■ Delete/Rename	3	143–144, 140
■ DELTREE	3	143
■ TYPE	3	140
■ ECHO	3	104
■ SET	3	104
1.4 Identify basic concepts and procedures for creating, viewing and managing disks, directories and files. This includes procedures for changing file attributes and the ramifications of those changes (for example, security issues).		
■ Disks		
■ Partitions		
■ Active Partition	6	276
■ Primary Partition	3	130–131
■ Extended Partition	3	130–131
■ Logical partition	3	130–131
■ Files Systems		
■ FAT16	6	277–279
■ FAT32	6	277–279
■ NTFS4	6	277–279
■ NTFS5.x	6	277–279
■ Directory Structures (root directory, subdirectories, etc)		
■ Create folders	4	188–189
■ Navigate the directory structure	4	188–189
■ Maximum depth	4	188–189
■ Files		
■ Create files	4	187
■ File naming conventions (Most common extensions, 8.3, maximum length)	2, 3, 4	68–69, 138–139, 189
■ File attributes – Read Only, Hidden, System, and Archive attributes	4	189
■ File Compression	8	349–350
■ File Encryption	10	430–433
■ File permissions	10	422–425
■ File types (text vs binary file)	13	568
1.5 Identify the major Operating System Utilities, their purpose, location, and available switches.		
■ Disk Management Tools		

A+ Operating System Technologies Examination Objectives

OBJECTIVES	CHAPTERS	PAGE NUMBERS
■ Defrag.exe	3, 5	146, 246–248
■ Fdisk.exe	3	135–136
■ Backup/Restore Utility (MSbackup, NTBackup, etc)	5, 7, 8, 11	240, 318–319, 345 461–466
■ ScanDisk	3, 5	146, 230, 248–249
■ CHKDSK	3	145
■ Disk Cleanup	8	350
■ Format	8	351–353
■ System Management Tools		
■ Device manager	2, 5	51, 250–251
■ System Manager	5, 8	239–249, 363–365
■ Computer Manager	8	350–351
■ MSCONFIG.EXE	5	243–245
■ REGEDIT.EXE (View information/Backup registry)	10	438–439
■ REGEDT32.EXE	10	438–439
■ SYSEDIT.EXE	5	218–219
■ SCANREG	3, 5	146, 235–236
■ COMMAND/CMD	8	348
■ Event Viewer	8	357–360
■ Task Manager	8	361–363
■ File Management Tools		
■ ATTRIB.EXE	3	144–145
■ EXTRACT.EXE	3	147
■ Edit.com	3	147
■ Windows Explorer	4	186–189
Domain 2 Installation, Configuration and Upgrading		
2.1 Identify the procedures for installing Windows 9x/ME, NT 4.0 Workstation, 2000 Professional, and XP and bringing the operating system to a basic operational level.		
■ Verify hardware compatibility and minimum requirements	4, 7, 9	166–170, 307, 377–379
■ Determine OS installation options		
■ Installation type (typical, custom, other)	4, 6	171, 282
■ Network configuration	6, 7, 9	279–284, 309–310, 380
■ File system type	4, 6, 7, 9	166–170, 276–279, 308–309, 379
■ Dual Boot Support	6, 7, 9	283–284, 311, 386–387
■ Disk preparation order (conceptual disk preparation)		
■ Start the installation	4, 6, 9	166–173, 279–284, 381
■ Partition	7	311–318
■ Format drive	7	311–318
■ Run appropriate set up utility		
■ Setup	7	314
■ Winnt	6, 7	284, 314, 317
■ Installation methods		
■ Bootable CD	6, 7	284, 314, 317
■ Boot floppy	6, 7, 9	281, 314, 381
■ Network installation	7	314, 317
■ Drive Imaging	7, 11	309, 465
■ Device Driver Configuration		
■ Load default drivers	7	311–313

A+ Operating System Technologies Examination Objectives

OBJECTIVES	CHAPTERS	PAGE NUMBERS
■ Find updated drivers	7	311–313
■ Restore user data files (if applicable)	7, 9	310–311, 388–389
■ Identify common symptoms and problems	4	173–175
2.2 Identify steps to perform an operating system upgrade from Windows 9x/ME, Windows NT 4.0 Workstation, Windows 2000 Professional, and Windows XP. Given an upgrade scenario, choose the appropriate next steps.		
■ Upgrade paths available	4, 7, 9	178–180, 311, 380
■ Determine correct upgrade startup utility (e.g. WINNT32 vs WINNT)	7, 9	316–317, 384
■ Verify hardware compatibility and minimum requirements	7	311–314
■ Verify application compatibility	7	313–314
■ Apply OS service packs, patches, and updates	4, 6, 7, 8, 9	180, 284, 318, 367, 387, 443–445
■ Install additional Windows components	7, 9	318–319, 387
2.3 Identify the basic system boot sequences and boot methods, including the steps to create an emergency boot disk with utilities installed for Windows 9x/ME, Windows NT 4.0 Workstation, Windows 2000 Professional, and Windows XP.		
■ Boot Sequence		
■ Files required to boot	5, 6	220–224, 292–294
■ Boot steps (9x, NT-based)	5, 6	220–224, 292–294
■ Alternative Boot Methods		
■ Using a Startup disk	5, 6, 8, 10	224–233, 295–299, 342–344, 448–449
■ Safe/VGA-only mode	5, 6, 8, 10	224–233, 295–299, 335–338, 445–447
■ Last Known Good configuration	6, 8, 10	295–299, 335–338, 445–447
■ Command Prompt mode	5, 6, 10	224–233, 295–299, 703–704
■ Booting to a system restore point	10	447–448
■ Recovery Console	8	338–342
■ Boot.ini switches	8	332–334
■ Dual Boot	6, 7	283–284, 311
■ Creating Emergency Disks with OS Utilities	5, 6, 8, 10	224–233, 296–299, 342–344, 448–449
■ Creating emergency repair disk (ERD)	6, 8, 10	296–299, 342–344, 448–449
2.4 Identify procedures for installing/adding a device, including loading/adding/configuring device drivers, and required software.		
■ Device Driver Installation		
■ Plug and Play (PNP) and non-PNP devices	4, 5, 7	190, 196–198, 255–256, 323–325
■ Install and configure device drivers	4, 6, 7	190–194, 286–288, 323–325
■ Install different device drivers	4, 7, 9	190–194, 323–325, 398–401
■ Manually install a device driver	4	194–195
■ Search the Internet for updated device drivers	9	398–401
■ Using unsigned drivers (driver signing)	9	398–401
■ Install Additional Windows components	7	318–319
■ Determine if permissions are adequate for performing the task	10	426–428

A+ Operating System Technologies Examination Objectives

OBJECTIVES	CHAPTERS	PAGE NUMBERS
2.5 Identify procedures necessary to optimize the operating system and major operating system subsystems.		
■ Virtual Memory Management	4, 6, 8	206–208, 285, 365–366
■ Disk Defragmentation	3, 5, 8	146, 350, 246–248
■ Files and Buffers	3	102, 123
■ Caches	11	449–451
■ Temporary file management	8	350
Domain 3 Diagnosing and Troubleshooting		
3.1 Recognize and interpret the meaning of common error codes and startup messages from the boot sequence, and identify steps to correct the problems.		
■ Common Error Messages and Codes		
■ Boot failure and errors		
■ Invalid boot disk	5	224–226
■ Inaccessible boot device	5	224–226
■ Missing NTLDR	6	296
■ Bad or missing Command interpreter	5	224–226
■ Startup messages		
■ Error in CONFIG.SYS line XX	5	224–226
■ Himem.sys not loaded	A	615
■ Missing or corrupt Himem.sys	A	615
■ Device/Service has failed to start	8	357
■ A device referenced in SYSTEM.INI, WIN.INI, Registry is not found	A	615
■ Event Viewer – Event log is full	8	357–360
■ Failure to start GUI	5, 6, 8, 10	224–233, 295–299, 335–344, 445–452
■ Windows Protection Error	4	163
■ User-modified settings cause improper operation at startup	8	336
■ Registry corruption	5, 8, 10	235–236, 341–342, 447–448
■ Using the correct Utilities		
■ Dr. Watson	5, 8, 10	240, 251–252, 366–367, 441
■ Boot Disk	5, 6, 8, 10	232–233, 296–299, 342–344, 448–449
■ Event Viewer	8	357–360
3.2 Recognize when to use common diagnostic utilities and tools. Given a diagnostic scenario involving one of these utilities or tools, select the appropriate steps needed to resolve the problem.		
■ Startup disks		
■ Required files for a boot disk	3, 10	102, 448–449
■ Boot disk with CD-ROM support	3, 4	105–107, 194–195
■ Startup Modes		
■ Safe mode	5, 8, 10	228–232, 336–337, 445–447
■ Safe Mode with command prompt	5, 8	228–232, 336–337,
■ Safe mode with networking	5, 8, 10	228–232, 336–37, 445–447
■ Step-by-Step/Single step mode	5	228–232
■ Automatic skip driver (ASD.exe)	5	239

A+ Operating System Technologies Examination Objectives

OBJECTIVES	CHAPTERS	PAGE NUMBERS
■ Diagnostic tools, utilities and resources		
■ User/installation manuals	8	367
■ Internet/web resources	8	367
■ Training materials	8	367
■ Task Manager	8, 10	361–363, 442
■ Dr. Watson	5, 8, 10	240, 251–252, 366–367, 441
■ Boot Disk	5, 6, 8, 10	232–233, 296–299, 342–344, 448–449
■ Event Viewer	8	357–360
■ Device Manager	5, 9	250–251, 399–401
■ WinMSD	6	286
■ MSD	4	197–198
■ Eliciting problem symptoms from customers	5	253
■ Having customer reproduce error as part of the diagnostic process	5	253
■ Identifying recent changes to the computer environment from the user	5	253
3.3 Recognize common operational and usability problems and determine how to resolve them.		
■ Troubleshooting Windows-specific printing problems		
■ Print spool is stalled	12	521–523
■ Incorrect/incompatible driver for print	12	521–523
■ Incorrect parameter	12	521–523
■ Other Common problems		
■ General Protection Faults	4, 8	163, 345–346, 357–360
■ Bluescreen error (BSOD)	10	451–452
■ Illegal operation	8	345–346, 366–367
■ Invalid working directory	2	83–84
■ System lock up	5, 8	256–258, 345–346
■ Option (Sound card, modem, input device) or will not function	5	256–258
■ Application will not start or load	5, 8	256–258, 345–346
■ Cannot log on to network (option – NIC not functioning)	12	510
■ Applications don't install	5, 8	256–258, 345–346
■ Network connection	8, 12	357–360, 510
■ Viruses and virus types		
■ What they are	11	467–477
■ TSR (Terminate Stay Resident) programs and virus	11	467–477
■ Sources (floppy, emails, etc.)	11	467–477
■ How to determine presence	11	467–477
Domain 4 Networks		
4.1 Identify the networking capabilities of Windows. Given configuration parameters, configure the operating system to connect to a network.		
■ Configure protocols		
■ TCP/IP		
■ Gateway	12	506–510
■ Subnet mask	12	506–510
■ DNS (and domain suffix)	12, 13	499–500, 506–510, 561

A+ Operating System Technologies Examination Objectives

OBJECTIVES	CHAPTERS	PAGE NUMBERS
■ WINS	12	499–500
■ Static address assignment	12	493–494, 506–510
■ Automatic address assignment (APIPA, DHCP)	12	497
■ IPX/SPX (NWLink)	12	488
■ Appletalk	12	488
■ NetBEUI/ NetBIOS	12	489
■ Configure Client options		
■ Microsoft	12	484
■ Novell	12	484
■ Verify the configuration	12	488–490
■ Understand the use of the following tools		
■ IPCONFIG.EXE	12	493
■ WINIPCFG.EXE	12	492
■ PING	12	510
■ TRACERT.EXE	13	544–545
■ NSLOOKUP.EXE	13	545–546
■ Share resources (Understand the capabilities/limitations with each OS version)	12	502–505, 511–521
■ Setting permissions to shared resources	12	514–521
■ Network type and network card	12	484–487
4.2 Identify the basic Internet protocols and terminologies. Identify procedures for establishing Internet connectivity. In a given scenario configure the operating system to connect to and use Internet resources.		
■ Protocols and terminologies		
■ ISP	12	497
■ TCP/IP	12, 13	490–491, 538–543
■ E-mail (POP, SMTP, IMAP)	13	564–566
■ HTML	13	560
■ HTTP	13	540
■ HTTPS	13	560
■ SSL	13	560
■ Telnet	13	545
■ FTP	13	566–569
■ DNS	12, 13	499–500, 506–510, 561
■ Connectivity technologies		
■ Dial-up networking	13	546–555
■ DSL networking	13	555
■ ISDN networking	13	555
■ Cable	13	555–557
■ Satellite	13	555
■ Wireless	13	555
■ LAN	13	555, 557–559
■ Installing and Configuring browsers		
■ Enable/disable script support	13	561
■ Configure Proxy Settings	12	498–499
■ Configure security settings	12	498–499
■ Firewall protection under Windows XP	10, 13	433–434, 557

Introduction

A+ Guide to Software: Managing, Maintaining, and Troubleshooting, Second Edition was written to be the very best tool on the market today to prepare you to support operating systems used on personal computers. This book takes you from the just-a-user level to the I-can-fix-this level for the most common PC operating system concerns. This book achieves its goals with an unusually effective combination of tools that powerfully reinforce both concepts and hands-on real-world experience. It also provides thorough preparation for CompTIA's newly revised 2003 A+ Operating System Technologies Exam.

This book includes:

- **CoursePrep® A+ Test Preparation software** will be available for this book approximately 90 days after the final A+ Exams are released. This software simulates the actual A+ exam environment for added practice before exam day. If you would like to be waitlisted for a copy of this CD-ROM, please contact your sales representative or customer service. Once the CD is available, it will automatically be included in the back of this book. The test prep software will be available for download free of charge at *www.course.com*. Go to the site and enter in this book's ISBN (0-619-18627-5) and click on the student download link to get the software. If prompted, the user name and password is: testprep. This password is case sensitive and does not contain a space between the two words.
- **Comprehensive review and practice end-of-chapter material**, including a chapter summary, key terms, review questions, and hands-on projects.
- **Step-by-step instruction** on installation, maintenance, optimizing system performance, and troubleshooting.
- A **wide array of photos and screen shots** support the text, displaying in detail exactly how to best understand, purchase, install and maintain your software.
- Several **in-depth**, **hands-on projects** at the end of each chapter designed to make certain that you not only understand the material, but can execute procedures and make decisions on your own.

In addition, the carefully structured, clearly written text is accompanied by graphics that provide the visual input essential to learning. And for instructors using the book in a classroom, a special CD-ROM is available that includes an Instructor's Manual, an Online Testing system, and a PowerPoint presentation.

The book begins with a survey and comparison of all major operating systems. Then you learn to work from the command prompt using MS-DOS commands needed for drastic troubleshooting situations. Next you will install and learn to use each major Microsoft operating system. The chapters are organized so that you can install and learn to use and support Windows 98, then proceed to Windows NT, then to Windows 2000, and finally, to Windows XP. You will learn about the special concerns of Windows on a network, on the Internet, and on notebook computers. You will also be introduced to Linux and the Mac OS.

This book provides thorough preparation for CompTIA's newly revised A+ OS Exam. This book maps completely to the revised certification exam objectives. This certification credential's popularity among employers is growing exponentially, and obtaining certification increases your ability to gain employment and improve your salary. To get more information on A+ Certification and its sponsoring organization, the Computing Technology Industry Association, see their Web site at *www.comptia.org*.

FEATURES

To ensure a successful learning experience, this book includes the following pedagogical features:

- **Learning Objectives:** Every chapter opens with a list of learning objectives that sets the stage for you to absorb the lessons of the text.
- **Comprehensive Step-by-Step Troubleshooting Guidance:** Troubleshooting guidelines are included in almost every chapter.
- **Step-by-Step Procedures:** The book is chock-full of step-by-step procedures covering subjects from understanding how the latest operating system technologies work to installation and maintenance.
- **Art Program:** Numerous detailed photographs, three-dimensional art, and screenshots support the text, displaying operating system screens exactly as you will see them in your work.
- **A+ Table of Contents:** This table of contents indicates every page that relates to the each certification objective. This is a valuable tool for quick reference.

Tip icons include pointers from the author's experiences that provide additional insight in the topic at hand.

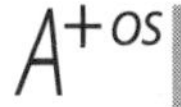

A+ icons: All of the content that relates to CompTIA's A+ Certification exams, whether it's a page or a sentence, is highlighted with an A+ icon. The icon notes the exam name and the objective number. This unique feature highlights the relevant content at a glace, so you can pay extra attention to the material.

Caution icons highlight critical safety information. Follow these instructions carefully to protect yourself, the PC and its data.

Note icons highlight additional information about the subject being discussed.

- **End-of-Chapter Material:** Each chapter closes with the following features, which reinforce the material covered in the chapter and provide real-world, hands-on testing of the chapter's skill set:
- **Chapter Summary:** This bulleted list of concise statements summarizes all major points of the chapter.
- **Review Questions:** You can test your understanding of each chapter with a comprehensive set of review questions.
- **Key-Terms:** The content of each chapter is further reinforced by an end-of-chapter key-term list. The definitions of all terms are included at the end of the book in a full-length glossary.

Hands-On Projects: You get to test your real-world understanding with hands-on projects involving a full range of hardware problems. Each hands-on activity in this book is preceded by the Hands-On icon and a description of the exercise that follows.

- **CoursePrep® A+ Test Preparation software:** 50 test preparation questions mimic the A+ testing environment so you can practice for exam day.
- **Web site:** For updates to this book and information about our complete line of A+ PC Repair products, please visit our Web site at *www.course.com/pcrepair*.

SUPPLEMENTS

For instructors using this book in a classroom environment, the following teaching materials are available on a single CD-ROM:

INSTRUCTOR'S RESOURCES

The following supplemental materials are available when this book is used in a classroom setting. All of the supplements available with this book are provided to the instructor on a single CD-ROM.

Electronic Instructor's Manual: The Instructor's Manual that accompanies this textbook includes additional instructional material to assist in class preparation, including suggestions for classroom activities, discussion topics, and additional projects.

Solutions to all end-of-chapter material, including the Review Questions, and where applicable, Hands-on Projects, and Exercises.

ExamView®: This textbook is accompanied by ExamView, a powerful testing software package that allows instructors to create and administer printed, computer (LAN-based), and Internet exams. ExamView includes hundreds of questions that correspond to the topics covered in this text, enabling students to generate detailed study guides that include page references for further review. The computer-based and Internet testing components allow students to take exams at their computers, and also save the instructor time by grading each exam automatically.

PowerPoint Presentations: This book comes with Microsoft PowerPoint slides for each chapter. These are included as a teaching aid for classroom presentation, to make available to students on the network for chapter review, or to be printed for classroom distribution. Instructors, please feel at liberty to add your own slides for additional topics you introduce to the class.

Figure Files: All of the figures in the book are reproduced on the Instructor's Resources CD, in bit-mapped format. Similar to the PowerPoint presentations, these are included as a teaching aid for classroom presentation, to make available to students for review, or to be printed for classroom distribution.

Daily Lesson Planner: This free teaching tool enables instructors to use our A+ products with even greater ease! It includes detailed lecture notes and teaching instructions that incorporate all of the components of the A+ Total Solutions. User name and password required for download. It is available on the Instructor's CD and online at *www.course.com/pcrepair.*

ACKNOWLEDGEMENTS

Thank you to the wonderful people at Course Technology who continue to provide support, warm encouragements, patience, and guidance. Laura Hildebrand, Kristen Duerr, Jennifer Goguen, and Nick Lombardi of CT: You've truly helped make this second edition fun! Thank you, Nicole Ashton, John Bosco, and John Freitas for your careful attention to the technical accuracy of the book.

Thank you to all the people who took the time to voluntarily send encouragements and suggestions for improvements to the previous editions. Your input and help is very much appreciated. The reviewers all provided invaluable insights and showed a genuine interest in the book's success. Thank you to Paul Danzer (Housatonic Community College), Russell Davis (Pittsburgh Technical Institute), Berry Smith (Virginia College at Huntsville), Alexander Uskuraitis (The Chubb Institute), and Henry Yoder (Pittsburgh Technical Institute). Thank you to Tony Woodall of Omega Computers for your outstanding research efforts.

This book is dedicated to the covenant of God with man on earth. Part of the proceeds from this book goes to Joy Land, a home for children in Hyderabad, A.P., India.

Jean Andrews, Ph.D.

PHOTO CREDITS

Figure 1-10, 2-4, 2-5, 2-6, 2-8, 2-19, 2-20, 2-27, and 4-25 courtesy of Jennifer Dark.

Required Materials

The following hardware, software, and other equipment are needed to do the hands-on projects at the end of chapters:

- You need a working PC that you can install an operating system on.
- Operating systems needed are Windows 98, Windows NT Workstation, Windows 2000 Professional, and Windows XP Professional.

The logo of the CompTIA Authorized Curriculum Program and the status of this or other training material as "Authorized" under the CompTIA Authorized Curriculum Program signifies that, in CompTIA's opinion, such training material covers the content of the CompTIA's related certification exam. CompTIA has not reviewed or approved the accuracy of the contents of this training material and specifically disclaims any warranties of merchantability or fitness for a particular purpose. CompTIA makes no guarantee concerning the success of persons using any such "Authorized" or other training material in order to prepare for any CompTIA certification exam.

The contents of this training material were created for the CompTIA Operating System Technologies exam covering CompTIA certification exam objectives that were current as of September, 2003.

How to Become CompTIA Certified:

This training material can help you prepare for and pass a related CompTIA certification exam or exams. In order to achieve CompTIA certification, you must register for and pass a CompTIA certification exam or exams.

In order to become CompTIA certified, you must:

(1) Select a certification exam provider. For more information please visit *http://www.comptia.org/certification/general_information/test_locations.asp*.

(2) Register for and schedule a time to take the CompTIA certification exam(s) at a convenient location.

(3) Read and sign the Candidate Agreement, which will be presented at the time of the exam(s). The text of the Candidate Agreement can be found at *http://www.comptia.org/certification/general_information/candidate_agreement.asp*.

(4) Take and pass the CompTIA certification exam(s).

For more information about CompTIA's certifications, such as their industry acceptance, benefits, or program news, please visit *http://www.comptia.org/certification/default.asp*.

CompTIA is a non-profit information technology (IT) trade association. CompTIA's certifications are designed by subject matter experts from across the IT industry. Each CompTIA certification is vendor-neutral, covers multiple technologies, and requires demonstration of skills and knowledge widely sought after by the IT industry.

To contact CompTIA with any questions or comments:
Please call + 1 630 268 1818
questions@comptia.org

CHAPTER

1

INTRODUCING AND COMPARING OPERATING SYSTEMS

In this chapter, you will learn:

- What an operating system does
- How DOS began and how it is used today
- About the various Windows operating systems and the differences between them
- Advantages and disadvantages of common non-Windows operating systems

Personal computers have changed the way we work, play, and do business. Everyone, no matter how young or old they are or how they make their living, encounters a personal computer in some way almost daily. So, in a very real sense, we are all computer users. You might use a personal computer to write documents, build spreadsheets, make a purchase using the Web, or e-mail your friends. No matter how experienced a computer user you are, this book can take you from the just-a-user stage to understanding what happens behind the scenes when you click on that Web site link or install that new screen saver. Not only will you understand what happened, but you'll also be able to customize your operating system (OS) and applications, troubleshoot and solve problems with the OS, and optimize your system for best performance. The goals of this book are to enable you to compare different operating systems and make wise buying decisions about them and to empower you to understand, troubleshoot, customize, and optimize a Windows operating system. In addition, this book prepares you to pass the A+ Operating System Technologies exam, one of the two exams required by CompTIA (*www.comptia.org*) for A+ Certification. Its companion book, *A+ Guide to Managing and Troubleshooting Hardware* (Course Technology 2002, ISBN 0-619-12002-9), prepares you for the Hardware Service Technician exam, the other exam required by CompTIA for A+ certification. To begin using this book, nothing more is expected of you than to be a knowledgeable computer user.

This book is organized to make it easy for you to learn by doing. The operating systems are covered in such a way that you can install one and learn to use, support, and troubleshoot it before moving on to the next. This first chapter starts this process by introducing you to many different operating systems and some things they all have in common. In this chapter, you will learn what an operating system does and how it relates to the user. Operating systems continue to evolve as hardware and software technologies improve. As you read about various OSs in this chapter, you will see the evolution from DOS to Windows 9x and to Windows NT/2000/XP. You will also be introduced to alternate OSs (Unix, Linux, OS/2, and Mac OS).

What an Operating System Does

An **operating system** is a computer program that controls a computer. A computer is like an automobile; it doesn't work unless a driver controls it. In Figure 1-1, the passenger and chauffeur make the automobile a functioning tool that can be used to accomplish a task. Without their intelligence, skill, and direction, the car is nothing more than an interconnected assemblage of electronic and mechanical devices. Software performs a similar function for hardware. Software is the intelligence of the computer; it senses what hardware is present, decides how it is configured and used, and then uses that hardware to perform tasks.

The operating system is the most important and primary software used to control a computer, much like a chauffeur driving a car. Applications such as Microsoft Word or Lotus Notes depend on the operating system to be the middleman between them and the hardware. You can think of an application as a passenger in a car who depends on a chauffeur to drive the car. However, sometimes a user drives an application such as when you are using Microsoft Excel to build a spreadsheet. In this case, you're the passenger depending on the chauffeur (two layers of software—application and operating system) to drive your car (hardware).

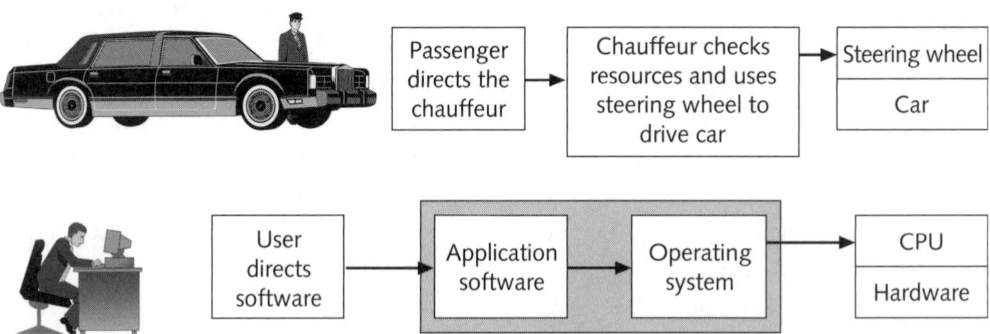

Figure 1-1 A user interacts with a computer much as a passenger interacts with a chauffeured car

A+ OS 1.1

A computer might have several applications installed to meet various needs of the users, but it only needs one operating system. There are many operating systems on the market, each designed to support different types of hardware systems and user needs:

- *DOS.* The first OS among IBM computers and IBM-compatible computers was DOS, the disk OS. Because DOS was written for early PCs, it has significant limitations today. DOS was the OS used by early versions of Windows. Two of them were Windows 3.1 and Windows 3.11 (collectively referred to as 3.x). Windows 3.x did not perform OS functions but simply served as a user-friendly intermediate program between DOS and applications and the user.
- *Windows 9x.* The more recent Windows 95, Windows 98, and Windows Me, which we collectively call Windows 9x, are true operating systems with a DOS core and provide a user-friendly interface. Windows 98 is the most popular OS for desktop computers for home use. (Many people chose to not upgrade from Windows 98 to Windows Me because they did not consider it a significant enough upgrade.)
- *Windows NT, Windows 2000, and Windows XP.* Windows NT comes in two versions, Windows NT Workstation for workstations, and Windows NT Server to control a network. Windows 2000 is an upgrade of Windows NT, and Windows XP is an upgrade of Windows 2000. Windows 2000 also comes in several versions, some designed for the desktop and others designed for high-end servers. Windows 2000 Professional is popular as an OS for the corporate desktop. Windows 2000 Server, Advanced Server, and Datacenter Server are network server OSs. Windows XP currently comes in two main versions: Windows XP Home, and Windows XP Professional. Windows XP is expected to first replace Windows 9x and then replace Windows 2000.
- *Unix.* Unix is a popular OS used to control networks and to support applications used on the Internet.
- *Linux.* Linux is a scaled-down version of Unix that is provided, in basic form, free of charge and includes open access to the programming code of the OS. It is often used for server applications.
- *OS/2.* OS/2, developed by IBM and Microsoft, is used less commonly for home desktop PC use but is used in certain types of networks. Windows NT was developed using some of the core components of OS/2 and was intended by Microsoft to replace OS/2.
- *Mac OS.* Mac OS is available only for Apple Macintosh computers and is often used for graphics applications and in educational settings.

You will learn more about each of these OSs later in this chapter. Although there are important differences between them, OSs share four main functions including:

- *Managing hardware*
  - Managing the BIOS (programs permanently stored on hardware devices)
  - Managing memory, which is a temporary place to store data and instructions as they are being processed

  - Diagnosing problems with software and hardware
  - Interfacing between hardware and software (that is, interpreting application software needs to the hardware and interpreting hardware needs to application software)
- *Managing files*
  - Managing files on hard drives, floppy drives, CD-ROM drives, and other drives
  - Creating, storing, retrieving, deleting, and moving files
- *Providing a user interface*
  - Performing housekeeping procedures requested by the user, often concerning secondary storage devices, such as formatting new disks, deleting files, copying files, and changing the system date
  - Providing a way for the user to manage the desktop, hardware, applications, and data
- *Managing applications*
  - Installing and uninstalling applications
  - Running applications and managing the interface to the hardware on behalf of an application

In short, an operating system controls the hardware components that make up a computer and also provides an interface that a user or an application can use. Figure 1-2 illustrates that an OS must relate to the user, to applications, and to various hardware components. You can also see that the OS must relate to these hardware devices by way of the **CPU (central processing unit)**, also called a **microprocessor**, the most important microchip in the system that is responsible for processing all data and instructions.

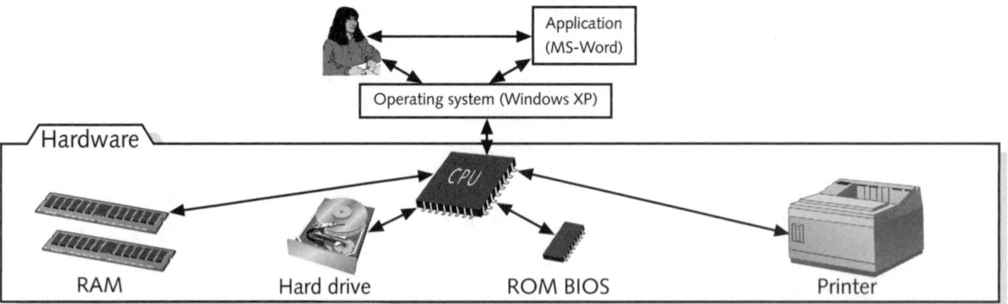

Figure 1-2 Users and applications depend on the OS to relate to all hardware components

Operating System Components

An operating system is made up of several internal components, which you will learn about throughout this book. Every operating system has two main components: the shell and the kernel (see Figure 1-3). A **shell** is that portion of the OS that relates to the user and to applications. The shell provides a command, menu, or icon interface to the user using various interface tools such as Windows Explorer, the Control Panel, or My Computer.

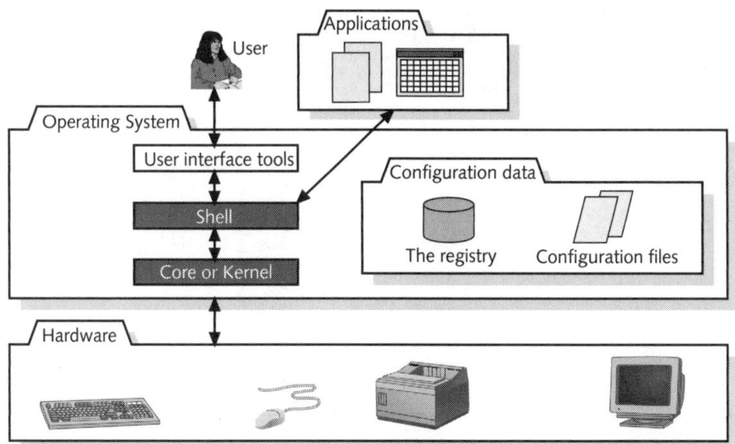

Figure 1-3 Inside an operating system, different components perform various functions

The core, or **kernel**, of the OS is responsible for interacting with hardware. It has more power to communicate with hardware devices than the shell so that applications operating under the OS cannot get to hardware devices without the shell passing those requests to the kernel. This structure provides for a more stable system.

An operating system needs a place to keep hardware and software configuration information, user preferences, and application settings that are used when the OS is first loaded and are accessed as needed by hardware, applications, and users. This information can be kept in a database or text files. Windows uses a database for most of this information called the **registry**. In addition, some data is kept in text files called **initialization files**, which often have an .ini or .inf file extension.

How an OS Relates to Users

When a PC is first turned on, the operating system is executed. After the OS is in control, it either automatically executes an application software program or turns to the user for its next instruction. If you are working with the OS, you will see an interface on the monitor screen. This interface can be command-driven, menu-driven, or icon-driven.

A+ OS 1.1

Command-Driven Interfaces

With a command-driven interface, you key in command lines to tell the OS to perform operations. For example, in Figure 1-4, the VER command reports the operating system version. DOS and Unix use command-driven interfaces, and other OSs may provide access to a command-driven interface. For instance, the command-driven interface of a command window under Windows 9x provides the C prompt, which can look like this:

`C:\Windows>` or `C:\>`

To access this window, sometimes called a DOS box, click Start, Programs, MS-DOS Prompt. Computer technicians who are good typists and are very familiar with DOS-like commands often prefer this kind of OS interface. What shows in the prompt depends on the current drive and directory.

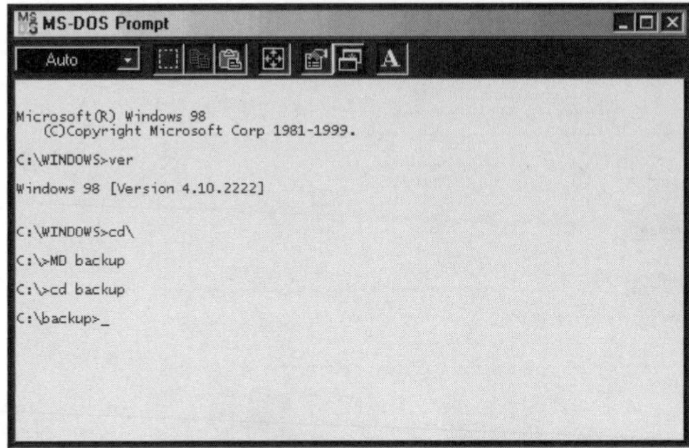

Figure 1-4 An operating system command-driven interface: a DOS box

Menu-Driven Interfaces

Some OSs allow you to choose from a list of options displayed on the screen. An example of such a menu-driven interface is Explorer in Windows 98. From the drop-down menus, you can format disks, rename files, copy and delete files, and perform many other operations to manage files and storage devices (see Figure 1-5). Note that Explorer uses icons as well as menus.

Icon-Driven Interfaces

Today's OSs are more likely to use an icon-driven interface than a command-driven one. With an icon-driven interface, sometimes called a **GUI (graphical user interface)**, you perform operations by selecting icons (or pictures) on the screen. When an OS is first executed, the initial screen that appears, together with its menus, commands, and icons, is called the **desktop**. Figure 1-6 shows the Windows 2000 default desktop, which has an icon-driven interface. You double-click an icon with the mouse to execute an applications software program or right-click an icon to see its shortcut menu. Just about all OSs today offer a combination of menu and icon-driven interfaces such as the Control Panel window in Figure 1-6, which includes both menus and icons.

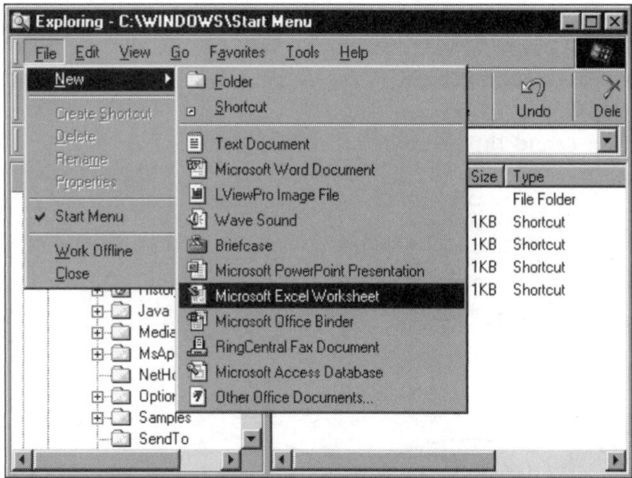

Figure 1-5 A menu-driven interface: Explorer in Windows 98

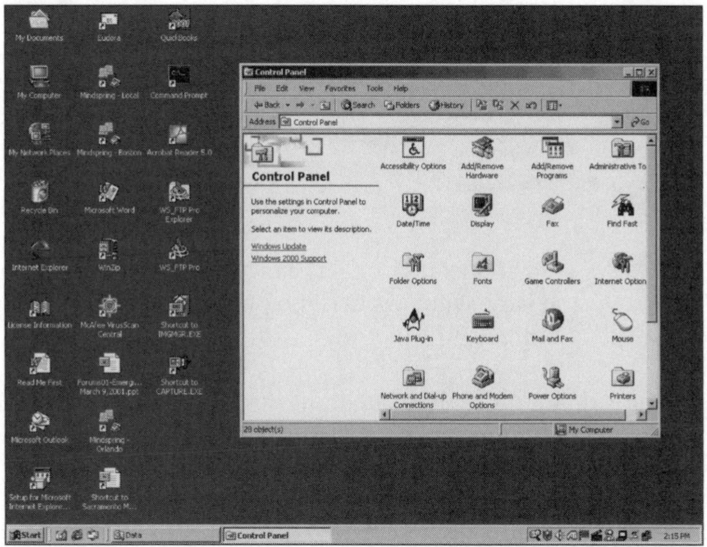

Figure 1-6 An icon-driven interface: Windows 2000 desktop

Comparing Operating Systems

A+ OS 1.1 The goal of this section is to help you understand what each OS does best and how to compare features of each in order to make wise buying decisions and technical comparisons. It's impossible to adequately do that without including in our discussions some technical terms. Most of these terms are covered in detail in the next chapter, but, for now, we offer some basic definitions. To understand the differences between OSs, you need to understand the following terms:

- Each process that a CPU is aware of is called a **thread**.

A+ OS 1.1

- **Single-tasking** occurs when the CPU or an OS can run only one program at a time. The CPU is aware of and is actively running only one thread. In Figure 1-7, DOS is a single-tasking OS, which can manage only one application at a time, passing a single thread to the CPU. All older CPUs used when DOS was written could only handle a single thread.

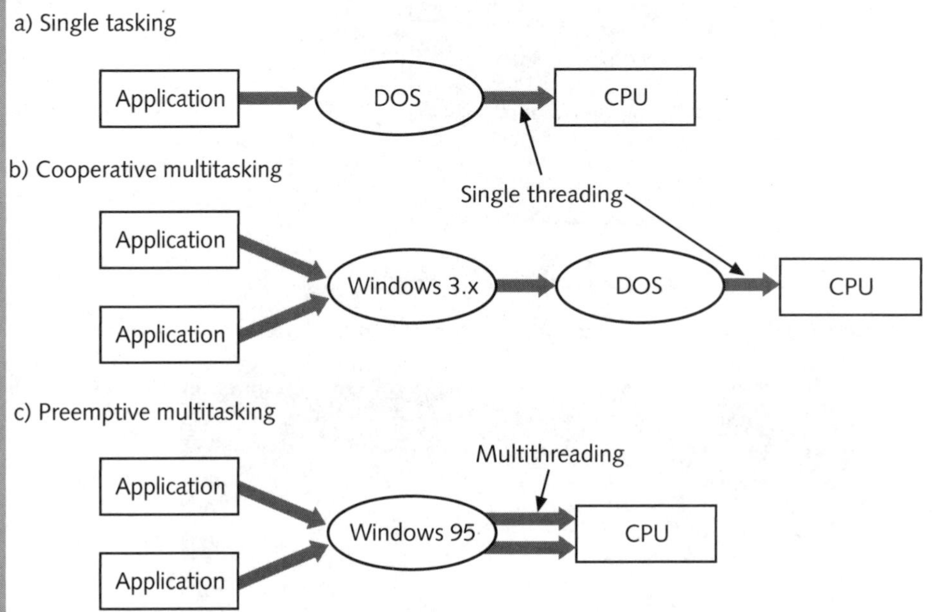

Figure 1-7 Windows 3.x used cooperative multitasking with a single thread to the CPU Windows 95 and later Windows OSs use preemptive multitasking with multithreading to the CPU

- **Multitasking** is doing more than one thing at the same time. In Figure 1-8 you can see two applications open on the Windows 98 desktop, and you can move from one to the other by clicking your mouse on each window. In one sense, the OS is multitasking because it is supporting two applications at the same time. However, both applications can't use the CPU at the same time. For example, if you command Microsoft Excel to print a large spreadsheet and, before the printing is done, command Microsoft Word to save a large document, both applications will be requesting resources from the OS at the same time. The OS manages this multitasking by sharing its resources between the two applications, doing part of one task and part of the other, switching back and forth until both tasks are done. The OS and the CPU that the OS is using are not multitasking in the true sense of the word because they are only doing one thing at a time. All OSs today support some form of multitasking so that two or more applications can be open at a time. The type of multitasking they use partly depends on the CPU. Some CPUs can actually multitask (perform two commands at the same time, each from a different thread), but, in order to

A+ OS 1.1

get a true multitasking system, you need two CPUs, each processing a thread at the same time. Having two or more CPUs in the same system is called **multiprocessing**.

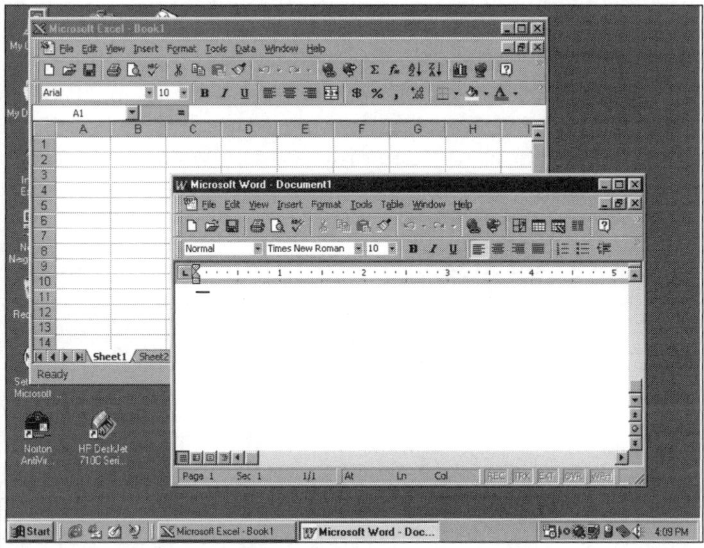

Figure 1-8 A multitasking environment allows two or more applications to run simultaneously

- **Cooperative multitasking** (see Figure 1-7) was used by Windows 3.x, which was designed for the older i386 and i486 CPUs by Intel that could only handle a single thread. Cooperative multitasking is sometimes called **task switching** because it is not true multitasking, in that the CPU is only aware of one program running at a time. But Windows 3.x is switching back and forth between applications so that more than one application can be loaded at the same time. Also, Windows 3.x used DOS as the underlying OS. Windows 3.x passed one thread to DOS, which passed it to the CPU. DOS and the CPU were not aware that more than one application was open. Using Windows 3.x, you could observe cooperative multitasking when you had two applications open, each in its own window. You didn't need to close one application before opening another. However, with cooperative multitasking, if one program was doing something (for example, when you saw the hourglass on the screen while the software was attempting to print or save a file) you could not click on another application and immediately switch to it.
- **Preemptive multitasking**, also shown in Figure 1-7, is another type of pseudo-multitasking whereby the OS allots CPU time to an application for a specified period, and then preempts the processing to give the CPU to another application. The end result is that the computer appears to be doing true multitasking. If two threads are running, the CPU can be aware of both, but still only

A+ OS 1.1

one is active. Windows 95 was the first version of Windows to provide preemptive multitasking, and it requires the cooperation of the CPU. The OS and the CPU are managing two programs at once using multithreading.

- **Environment** refers to the type of support the OS provides to the applications software. For example, in order for applications software to offer you a window with mouse movement, buttons to click, and icons to view, it must be supported by a GUI environment, such as Windows. Such an application is said to need a "GUI environment" to work. Another example is the DOS environment that offers to its applications software only a "single-tasking environment" in which a software package does not expect another applications software package to be running concurrently with it.
- **16-bit mode** and **32-bit mode**, also called **real mode** and **protected mode**, respectively, have to do with whether the CPU processes 16 or 32 bits at a time. OSs, applications, and CPUs all operate in either 16-bit (real) or 32-bit (protected) modes. 16-bit OSs support cooperative multitasking, and 32-bit OSs support preemptive multitasking.
- **FAT (file allocation table)** is a table on a hard drive or floppy disk that tracks the locations of files on a disk. A disk is composed of **tracks**, which are concentric circles on the disk surface, shown in Figure 1-9. Each track is divided into several segments, each called a **sector**. A **cluster** is the smallest unit of space on a disk for storing data and is made up of one or more sectors. The FAT contains a list of clusters, and which clusters are used for each file stored on the disk. The most recent version of FAT, FAT32, is a more efficient method of organization for large drives than FAT16 (the earlier version).

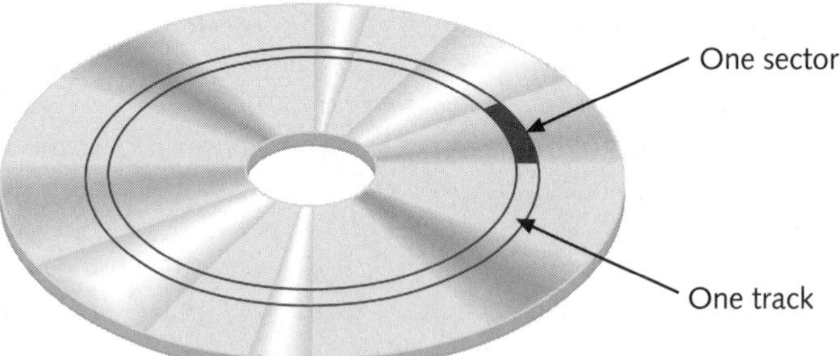

Figure 1-9 A hard drive or floppy disk is divided into tracks and sectors. Several sectors make one cluster

- A computer provides several ports on the back of the computer case to connect different devices, such as a keyboard, mouse, or printer
- **RAM (random access memory)** is temporary memory stored on chips inside the computer. These chips are stored on memory modules, some of which are shown in Figure 1-10. Memory is a place for the CPU to store programs and data while it is processing both, and the information stored in

A+ OS 1.1

RAM disappears when the computer is turned off. Because of hardware limitations at the time, DOS divided memory into categories called base memory, upper memory, and extended memory. Windows 9x still uses this same arrangement, although it makes better use of these categories, and is not as limited by them. Windows NT/2000/XP uses an altogether new and more efficient arrangement called memory paging. The goal of each OS is the same: provide as much memory as possible for software to use so as not to hinder software performance.

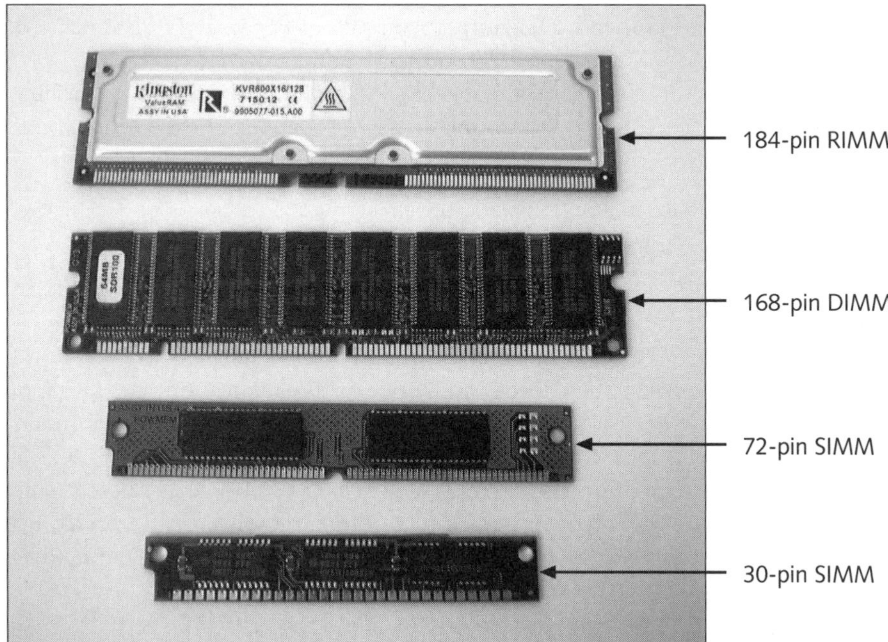

Figure 1-10 Types of RAM modules

A+ OS 1.1

Now that you've learned some basic terms relating to OSs, let's compare several OSs keeping in mind several criteria:

- What kind of interface does the OS provide for the user?
- Can the OS support some form of multitasking?
- How many and what kinds of applications are written to work with the OS?
- What are the hardware requirements to make efficient use of the OS?
- What computer ports and other hardware devices and features does the OS support?
- How does the OS perform in a network?

The following sections compare the most well-known OSs used in PCs and the OS used in Macintoshes, including their advantages and disadvantages. When choosing an OS, consider all the criteria discussed in these sections. Your choice will be determined by

A+ OS 1.1 the size and type of your microcomputer system, your familiarity with the various OSs, and the applications software you plan to use. As you read these sections, keep in mind the four main functions of an operating system (managing hardware, providing a user interface, working with files, and running applications), and notice how each OS performs these functions differently.

DOS (Disk Operating System)

DOS was the first OS used by IBM microcomputers. For years DOS remained the unchallenged standard for OSs used by IBM and IBM-compatible machines. It is a simple operating system, and simple often means reliable. PC technicians should be familiar with DOS because it can be very effective in troubleshooting situations when a more complex OS fails.

To see what the DOS command-driven interface looks like, refer back to Figure 1-4.

With Windows 3.x, DOS ran in the background as the true OS and used Windows 3.x as a middle layer, or "go-between" program, between the application and DOS, providing the operating environment for application software packages. In this environment, users could interact with applications directly through Windows or directly through DOS. Windows 3.x supported cooperative multitasking because it managed more than one open application by passing segments to DOS, which then, in turn, interfaced with hardware. However, DOS and Windows applications tended to conflict with each other when sharing hardware devices.

A point of historical interest: Windows 3.11, called Windows for Workgroups, was the first Windows environment designed to interface with a network without depending on separate application software to do the job. Windows 3.x (3.1 and 3.11) is no longer in general use and has been replaced by Windows 9x.

DOS is still used in some proprietary systems where older hardware and software (sometimes called **legacy** hardware or software) are still doing the job and there is little reason to upgrade either. However, the primary use of DOS today is as a troubleshooting tool. Windows 9x has a DOS core, and when the Windows 9x GUI interface fails to load, the only recourse is to fall back to the tried-and-true DOS portion of the OS stored on floppy disks or the hard drive. Also, Windows NT, 2000, and XP all offer some form of a recovery tool that includes a command prompt where you issue DOS-like commands. You'll learn about these in future chapters.

Table 1-1 summarizes the advantages and disadvantages of DOS.

Table 1-1 Advantages and disadvantages of DOS

Advantages	Disadvantages
• DOS runs on small, inexpensive microcomputers with a minimum amount of memory and hard drive space. • Text-based DOS programs are faster and more compact than comparable graphics-intensive GUI programs. • Some older applications are still in use today that were written for DOS and older hardware because of the low overhead of DOS compared to more modern OSs. • DOS is still a viable option for some specialized applications using a dedicated computer that does not involve heavy user interaction—for example, a microcomputer dedicated to controlling an in-house phone system. • DOS can be used to boot up and troubleshoot a computer when a more sophisticated OS is too cumbersome and has too much overhead.	• Memory management is awkward and sometimes slow. • DOS has no icon-driven interface. • DOS does only single-tasking; that is, it supports only one application running at a time. • DOS was not designed for use on networks. A separate applications software program is necessary for a DOS machine to access a network. • The last standalone version is DOS 6.22, which does not take advantage of the many new CPU features now available. (However, Windows 9x has a newer DOS core.) • Hardly any new software is being written for DOS.

Windows Operating Systems

A+ OS 1.1

In this section, you will learn about Windows 9x, NT, 2000, and XP. The previous section on DOS introduced DOS's relationship to Windows, specifically to Windows 3.x, which is not discussed in detail in this section because it is not commonly used anymore. As you read this section, you will learn about the evolution of Windows OSs and some of the corresponding changes in technology.

Windows 9x

A+ OS 1.1

Windows 95, Windows 98, and Windows Me (referred to collectively as Windows 9x) take us two steps closer to a new OS but do not completely eliminate DOS. Windows 95 is the marriage of Windows for Workgroups (Windows 3.11) with an updated version of DOS sometimes known as DOS 7.0, together with some completely new additions and improvements to the OS. Windows 95 also introduced an improved and more automated method of installing new hardware devices, called Plug and Play. Windows 98 added several new features to the OS and Windows Me added even more, but both retain the fundamental DOS core and are a blend of low-end and high-end technologies. These operating systems fulfill the Microsoft commitment to be **backward-compatible** with older software and hardware while still taking advantage of newer technology.

A+ OS 1.1

As an example of a Windows 9x interface, Figure 1-11 shows a desktop for Windows 98 Second Edition. A window is open, showing the Control Panel, which provides a centralized location from which to administer hardware, software, and system settings, and the Start and Programs menus are open. These features will appear much the same on other Windows 9x desktops.

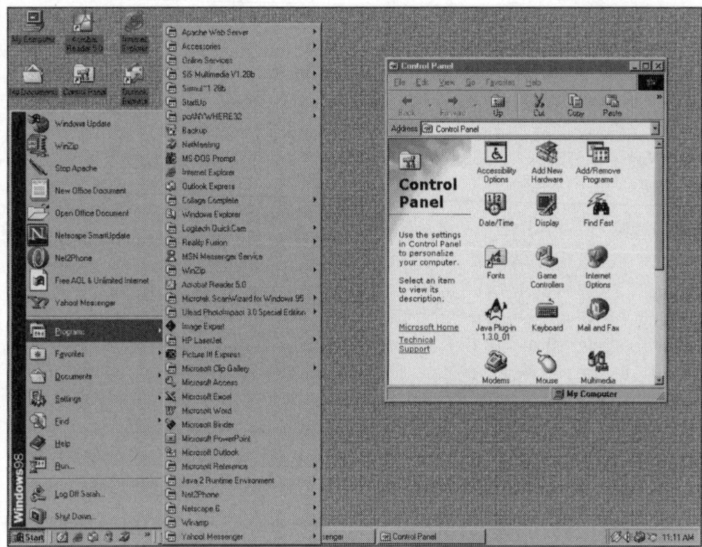

Figure 1-11 The Windows 98 SE desktop

Table 1-2 lists the hardware requirements of Windows 9x. Note that Table 1-2 gives the *recommended* minimum to run each version of Windows 9x. You may find different values in other documentation, because these OSs may run under lower specifications than the recommended minimums. System requirements can also change depending on whether you are installing on a new system or upgrading an older system, as well as which features you choose to install. Also, sometimes Microsoft lists the minimum requirements to *install* an OS, which might be different than the requirements to *run* an OS. (Requirements in Table 1-2 are for running the OS.) Keep these differences in mind when reviewing the lists of minimum hardware requirements for OSs throughout this chapter.

Table 1-2 Recommended minimum hardware requirements for Windows 9x

Description	Windows 95	Windows 98	Windows Me
Processor	486 or higher	Pentium	Pentium 150 MHz
RAM	8 MB	24 MB	32 MB
Free hard drive space	50 MB	195 MB	320 MB

A+ OS 1.1

Table 1-3 summarizes the advantages and disadvantages of Windows 9x.

Table 1-3 Advantages and disadvantages of Windows 9x

Advantages	Disadvantages
• Windows 9x offers a very user-friendly and intuitive GUI interface. • Windows 9x offers almost complete backward-compatibility for applications written for DOS and earlier versions of Windows. • Windows 9x is a mix of older and newer OS technology and allows both older and newer software and hardware to run. • Windows 9x offers the ability for one PC to talk with another over phone lines without additional software. It works well for low-end network use, such as when two users want to exchange files. • Disk access time under Windows 9x is improved over DOS and Windows 3.x. • Plug and Play features make installing some new hardware devices easier than with earlier OSs. • Windows 9x supports preemptive multitasking. While the hourglass is showing on the window of an application, you can make another application active by clicking on its window. • Because it is the most popular OS today, many users are comfortable with it and are reluctant to change.	• Because of its hardware requirements, Windows 9x cannot be used on some older PCs. • Because of the attempt to bridge older and newer technology, there are some problems with failures and errors created in this hybrid environment.

How Windows 9x Differs from Windows 3.x and DOS

Windows 9x is an OS that bridges two worlds. In Figure 1-12, you see that Windows 3.x and DOS constitute a 16-bit world, with memory management centered around base, upper, and extended memory limitations. Windows 9x still has a DOS-based core, uses many 16-bit programs, and must manage memory in fundamentally the same way as DOS does. However, Windows 95 introduced 32-bit programming, an early form of memory paging, networking, and many other features available in Windows NT/2000/XP. Windows 9x includes hundreds of device drivers, some of which can be loaded and unloaded as needed. (**Device drivers** are software programs stored on the hard drive that are designed to run an input/output hardware device, such as a monitor or a mouse. You will learn more about device drivers in the next chapter.)

Windows 9x claims to be completely backward-compatible with older software and with hardware designed to work in a DOS and Windows 3.x environment. Windows 9x uses cooperative multitasking when supporting 16-bit applications and preemptive multitasking when supporting 32-bit applications.

A+ OS 1.1

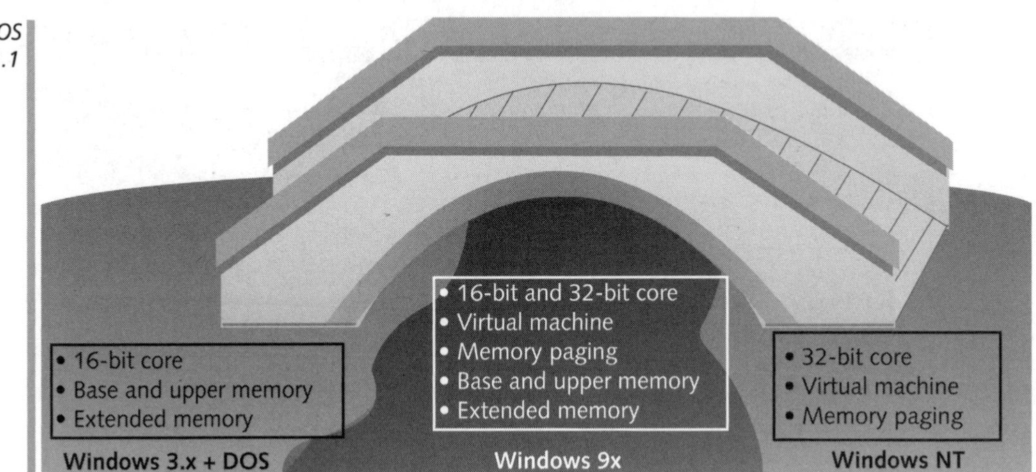

Figure 1-12 Windows 9x is the bridge from DOS to Windows NT

Windows 98 Upgrades

Microsoft has produced two upgrades for Windows 98: Windows 98 Second Edition (Windows 98 SE) and Windows Millennium Edition (Windows Me). Each upgrade has significant enhancements over its predecessor.

Windows 98 SE includes several patches, or fixes, for the first edition of Windows 98, updates of existing components, and some new components. Most new features involve improved networking and Internet access. Improved support for ATM networks includes the addition of Point-to-Point Protocol (PPP) over ATM, which allows a dial-up connection over an ATM network. Security for a dial-up connection over regular phone lines was also upgraded. ATM is a high-speed network technology used by wide area networks.

A new feature is Internet Connection Sharing (ICS), which makes it possible for a Windows 98 PC to access the Internet through another computer on a local network so that only one computer requires a direct connection to an ISP. This feature means that several PCs on a small home network can share the same access to an ISP without incurring additional charges and without installing third-party software. Support for modems that use a USB port and support for a wake-on-LAN connection are also included. (A **LAN**, or **local area network**, is a small computer network that is usually confined to one building or other geographically small area.) Wake-on-LAN means that a PC can go into a low-power state and then return to standard power when the network card detects activity from another computer on the network.

Windows Me takes us one step closer to the merging of Windows 9x and Windows 2000 because it contains features from each OS, although, at its core, it is still a Windows 9x upgrade. It's designed for home users and not for businesses. It focuses on enhancements

A+ OS 1.1

to multimedia features such as support for video cameras, digital cameras, scanners, and a jukebox recorder. It includes a compression utility for video files and a video editor. True to its goal as a home PC operating system, the OS is very user-friendly, including more informative error messages and troubleshooting utilities. The more technical differences among Windows 95, Windows 98 and Windows Me are covered in Chapter 4.

To learn which version of Windows is installed, right-click the My Computer icon and select Properties from the shortcut menu. The System Properties windows opens. Click the General tab.

When deciding to upgrade from one version of Windows 9x to another, if you have the hardware power to support it, you are better off upgrading from Windows 95 to Windows 98 because of the many tools and features that add to the stability of Windows 98. The upgrade from Windows 98 to Windows Me is not as important unless you need the added support for multimedia devices.

Windows NT

A+ OS 1.1

Windows NT (New Technology) breaks with previous versions of Windows. Although older applications written for DOS and DOS with Windows might work under Windows NT, Windows NT developers do not guarantee compatibility between the OSs. Windows NT takes an aggressive and altogether new approach toward managing hardware resources and interfacing with applications software. It completely eliminates the underlying relationship with DOS.

Windows NT supports preemptive multitasking and multiprocessing (two or more CPUs). Windows NT is designed to work within a powerful networked environment. Computers called servers are configured to store programs and data used remotely by other computers called clients. With client/server arrangements, an organization's resources can be used more effectively, since computers are networked together to share these resources. Windows NT Workstation is designed to run on clients, and Windows NT Server to run servers. Table 1-4 summarizes the advantages and disadvantages of Windows NT.

Goals of Windows NT

Windows NT was conceived when IBM and Microsoft collaborated in building OS/2. While IBM took over OS/2, Microsoft redesigned and added to the original code, calling the new OS Windows NT. The next two evolutions of the OS were called Windows 2000 and Windows XP. Windows NT/2000/XP have many of the same objectives as Unix and are considered the primary competitors to Unix in the client/server industry. Because Windows NT/2000/XP also function on a LAN, they are considered competitors of NetWare software by Novell, which is popular for managing LANs. Finally, Windows NT/2000/XP compete for some of the standalone PC market, contending with Windows 9x. In this discussion about the goals of Windows NT, the

A+ OS 1.1 information given also applies to Windows 2000/XP. For an OS to contend for so many markets, it needs to meet many goals, including those discussed below.

Table 1-4 Advantages and disadvantages of Windows NT

Advantages	Disadvantages
• Windows NT is designed to run in powerful client-server environments and targets both the client and the server market. • Windows NT offers a completely new file management system, different from earlier Windows OSs. • Windows NT Workstation offers both networking over a LAN and dial-up connections over phone lines. • Windows NT Server offers powerful security both as a file server and for network administration. • Windows NT supports preemptive multitasking and multiprocessing.	• The hardware requirements of Windows NT eliminate it as a plausible option for older, low-end PCs. • Windows NT is not compatible with some older hardware and software. • Windows NT does not use some of the technologies or have the newer features used by Windows 2000 and XP, including Safe Mode, Plug and Play, USB support, Device Manager, and FAT32. • Windows NT is largely outdated and replaced by Windows 2000.

Room to Grow Windows NT is designed for expandability, so it can more easily accommodate new hardware and software. The main way that NT does this is by using a modular approach to performing tasks. For example, DOS and Windows 9x allow applications to have direct access to memory, but Windows NT/2000/XP does not allow an application direct access to memory or other hardware devices. Applications are required to pass their requests to NT, which processes them and gives to the application as much memory as it requests if that memory is currently not used by other applications. Because of this layer of protection between software and hardware, when hardware requirements change, Windows NT manages the change; the application is insulated from the change. (However, a disadvantage to this approach is that Windows NT must have an interface to all new device drivers before any application operating under Windows NT can use a new device.)

Portability to Different Platforms Because of Windows NT's modular approach, it easily ports to different platforms or hardware configurations, including different CPU technologies. The Windows NT installation CD-ROM comes with three directories ready to accommodate three different CPU technologies. (For Intel-based CPUs, the directory on the CD is \i386.) Windows NT can accommodate several CPU technologies because it isolates parts of the OS from other parts in a modular fashion. The part of the OS that interacts with the hardware is the **HAL (hardware abstraction layer)**, which is the layer between the OS and the hardware. The HAL is available in different versions, each designed to address the specifics of a particular CPU technology. The HAL is the only part of the OS that has to change when platforms change. The other components of the OS need not be changed when the platform changes.

A+ OS 1.1

Compatibility with Other OSs and Legacy Software Because Windows NT had its beginnings in OS/2, Microsoft is committed to Windows NT being compatible with software written for OS/2. Generally, Windows NT does not support legacy devices (older computer devices that do not use current technology). As long as DOS applications don't attempt to access resources directly, they too can run under Windows NT.

Security Windows NT provides security similar to that on Unix systems, which is greater than that found in Windows 9x. Windows NT security features include the following:

- The requirement that a user have a logon ID and password to gain access to the PC
- Security between users on the same PC, so that one user can block another user from data or software
- Auditing trails to identify security breaches
- Memory protection between different applications loaded at the same time

Performance and Reliability Although no OS is fault proof, Windows NT/2000/XP provides a much more stable environment than do many OSs, including Windows 9x. Windows NT/2000/XP is less likely to hang, or "lock up," than are other PC OSs. If an application stalls, other applications also loaded are less likely to be affected. When using powerful workstations, Windows NT/2000/XP outperforms Windows 9x.

Windows NT vs. Windows 9x

When comparing Windows NT and Windows 9x, remember the following two important points. First, if Windows NT is installed on a PC that is not as powerful as the type of computer it is designed to run on, Windows NT does not perform as well as Windows 9x would on that PC. However, on a powerful workstation PC with a configuration recommended for Windows NT, Windows NT usually performs faster and better than Windows 9x. The second important point is that Windows NT is not another evolution of DOS, Windows 3.x, and Windows 9x. In fact, the opposite is true. Windows NT was developed before Windows 95. Windows 95 and its upgrade, Windows 98, were built as a bridge between the old (DOS with Windows 3.x) and the new (Windows NT).

While Windows 9x and Windows NT Workstation differ dramatically in underlying architecture and structure, they share many features, including a similar user interface, some of the same utilities (such as Internet Explorer and Microsoft Messaging), and other features such as system policies, user profiles, and hardware profiles. Windows NT Workstation offers higher performance, reliability, and security than does Windows 9x. On the other hand, Windows 9x has less demanding hardware requirements, offers broad application and device compatibility, and works well on notebook PCs because of better power management features and Plug and Play capability.

The key to appreciating the advantage that Windows NT has over Windows 9x is in the platforms and settings that Windows NT targets. Windows NT is designed to satisfy the needs of powerful workstations networked in a corporate environment. Windows 9x,

A+ OS 1.1

however, is used on low-end PCs dominating the home market, where multimedia application software and ease of installation are more of an issue than network security and high-end performance.

One major difference between Windows 9x and Windows NT is that Windows NT is a full 32-bit operating system, operating in protected mode as soon as it receives control from BIOS. (You will learn more about the relationship between BIOS and the OS in the next chapter.) Windows 9x begins the boot process in real mode and loads some real-mode components before shifting to protected mode. Windows 9x supports real-mode device drivers; Windows NT does not allow them. Table 1-5 lists the major differences between Windows NT and Windows 9x.

Table 1-5 Comparing Windows NT to Windows 9x

Feature	Windows 9x	Windows NT
Hardware requirements	Low, requiring a 486 PC with 8–16 MB of RAM	High, requiring a Pentium with 16–32 MB of RAM
Hardware compatibility	Supports most legacy devices	Supports most current devices, but does not claim backward-compatibility with legacy devices
Software compatibility	Fully backward-compatible with older DOS and Windows 3.x applications	No support for any application that attempts to access hardware directly
Installation	Offers Plug and Play capability	Does not offer Plug and Play and offers less device driver support
Power management	Built-in power management for laptops	None
Performance	Offers multitasking for 32-bit and 16-bit applications	Also offers preemptive multitasking for 32-bit applications and cooperative multitasking for 16-bit applications. Has significantly better performance on systems with at least 32 MB of RAM
Reliability and stability	Much better than Windows 3.x	Very high reliability and stability; all applications run in protected memory space
Security	Allows violation of the logon process controlled from a server	Very high security down to the file level

Windows NT Workstation includes the following features:

- *Desktop performance.* Supports a powerful multitasking environment and multiple microprocessors for true multitasking

A+ OS 1.1

- *Hardware profiles.* Can maintain separate hardware profiles for different hardware configurations on the same PC.
- *Internet Explorer.* Provides a built-in Web browser (Internet Explorer).
- *Peer Web services.* Provides a personal Web server.
- *Security.* Provides security for individual files, folders, and other resources. User access to a PC's resources can be controlled by user IDs and passwords on the standalone PC or managed from a network controller.
- *Stability.* Uses protective processing, which prevents applications from causing errors in other applications or in Windows NT itself.

Many of these same features, including Internet Explorer, hardware profiles, and user access, are available from Windows 9x as well. The minimum hardware requirements for Windows NT on an IBM-compatible PC are listed below. However, even though Windows NT does run on this minimum hardware configuration, remember that you need a powerful high-end PC to experience the full benefits of Windows NT.

- Pentium-compatible processor or higher
- 16 MB of RAM (32 MB is recommended)
- 125 MB of hard disk space

While the minimum requirements listed above refer to IBM-compatible machines, Windows NT can run on other computers as well, providing the same interface and functionality. The main difference between Windows NT running on an IBM-compatible CPU and Windows NT on other computers is in the HAL. The hardware platforms supported by Windows NT are listed below. This book focuses only on the Intel-based CPUs of IBM-compatible machines.

- Intel x86-based (486 or higher) processor
- MIPS R4x00-based processor
- Alpha AXP-based processor
- PReP-compliant PowerPC-based processor

Hardware Supported by Windows NT Many hardware devices are not supported by Windows NT. For this reason, before you decide to install Windows NT, determine if all components on your PC will work under Windows NT. For instance, you might have to replace a network card, modem, video card, and so on, before Windows NT works. To determine if a hardware component is supported by Windows NT, see the **hardware compatibility list (HCL)** for Windows NT that comes with the software. The most recent copy is available on the Microsoft Web site at *www.microsoft.com/hcl*. On the list, which you can search by hardware category and/or company name, are all hardware devices supported by Windows 98, Windows NT, Windows 2000, and Windows XP. For instance, Figure 1-13 shows the partial results of a search for video cards compatible with

A+ OS 1.1

Windows NT 4.0. If a device is not on the list, ask the manufacturer if there is a driver specifically for Windows NT (not just Windows 9x). If no driver exists, this device will not work under Windows NT.

The Windows NT Desktop Beginning with Windows NT 4.0, the Windows NT desktop took on a similar look and feel to Windows 9x. Figure 1-14 shows the Windows NT desktop with the Start menu and Control Panel, both of which work just as they do in Windows 9x, although some Control Panel icons are different.

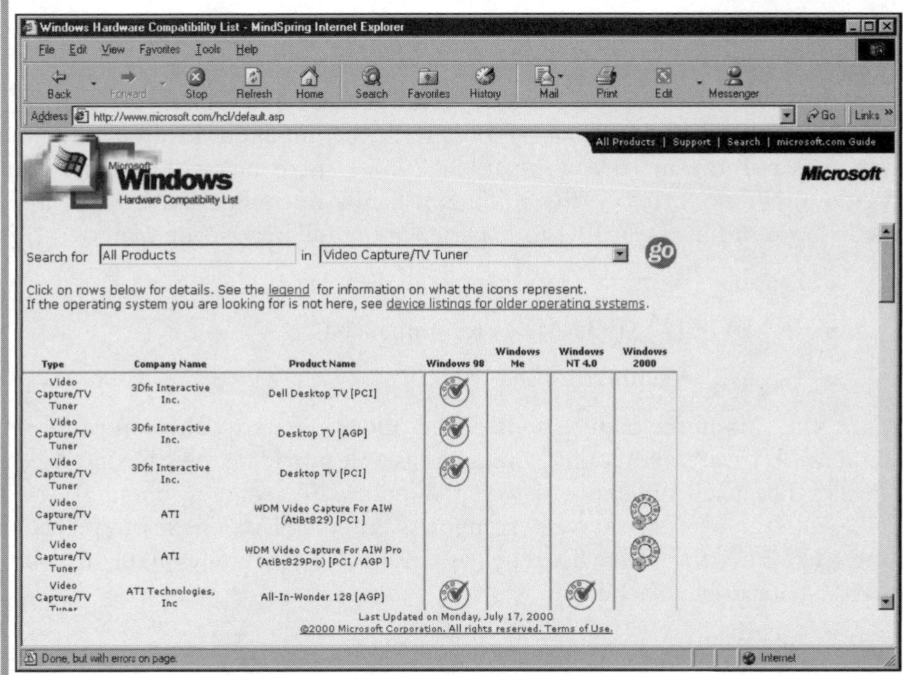

Figure 1-13 Some video capture cards compatible with Windows NT from the HCL

The Windows NT Command Prompt Another similarity between Windows NT and Windows 9x is the command prompt that allows the user to enter DOS-like commands. To access the command prompt, click Start, point to Programs, and then click Command Prompt (as in Figure 1-14). The Command Prompt window opens, as in Figure 1-15. From the command prompt, you can enter DOS-like commands. In Windows 9x, the DOS prompt is actually accessing a version of DOS. In Windows NT, however, the Command Prompt interface is provided as a convenience for those wanting to use familiar DOS-like commands. There are no actual DOS programs underlying and running under Windows NT.

A+ OS 1.1

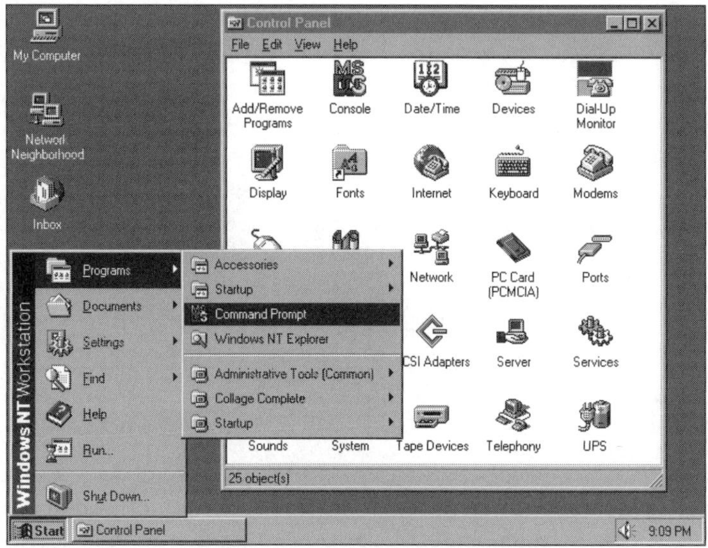

Figure 1-14 The Windows NT desktop is similar to that of Windows 9x

```
Command Prompt
Microsoft(R) Windows NT(TM)
(C) Copyright 1985-1996 Microsoft Corp.

D:\>ver

Windows NT Version 4.0

D:\>dir
 Volume in drive D has no label.
 Volume Serial Number is 4634-6C7F

 Directory of D:\

09/18/97  04:02p        <DIR>          WINNT
09/18/97  04:08p        <DIR>          Program Files
09/18/97  04:37p        <DIR>          TEMP
09/18/97  04:51p        <DIR>          COLLWIN
10/24/97  11:33a        <DIR>          NUTSBOLT
11/14/97  08:58p            45,088,768 pagefile.sys
               6 File(s)     45,088,768 bytes
                            261,087,232 bytes free

D:\>_
```

Figure 1-15 The Windows NT command prompt uses DOS-like commands

Choosing Between Windows 9x and Windows NT Although there is still a large installed base of Windows NT, it is now outdated, having been superseded by Windows 2000 and Windows XP. In most situations, you would not choose to install it on a new system or upgrade from Windows 9x to Windows NT. Rather, you would be making the decision to choose between Windows 9x and Windows 2000 or Windows 9x and Windows XP. However, if you happen to be in a situation where you are forced to decide between Windows 9x and Windows NT as your PC OS, consider the following:

- Does Windows NT support all the hardware devices on your PC? (Check the hardware compatibility list.)

A+ OS 1.1

- Is the PC powerful and big enough to support Windows NT? (See the hardware requirements listed earlier in the chapter, and then allow extra resources for your applications.)
- Will the software you intend to use on the PC work better under Windows 98 or Windows NT? Running older DOS and Windows 16-bit applications might be a problem in a Windows NT environment. Verify that your current, older software works under Windows NT, or plan to replace the current software with 32-bit versions. Be aware, however, that some 32-bit programs written for Windows 9x might not work under Windows NT because of differences in the API calls to the operating system. An **API (application program interface)** is a method by which one program calls another program to perform a task.

Windows 2000

A+ OS 1.1

Windows 2000 is actually a suite of operating systems, each designed for a different sized computer system. The Windows 2000 desktop (see Figure 1-16) looks much the same as that of Windows 9x and NT. Windows 2000 is built on the Windows NT architecture and was designed to ultimately replace both Windows 9x for low-end systems and Windows NT for midrange and high-end systems. For the most part, Windows 2000 has already replaced Windows NT, and Windows XP is slowly replacing Windows 2000.

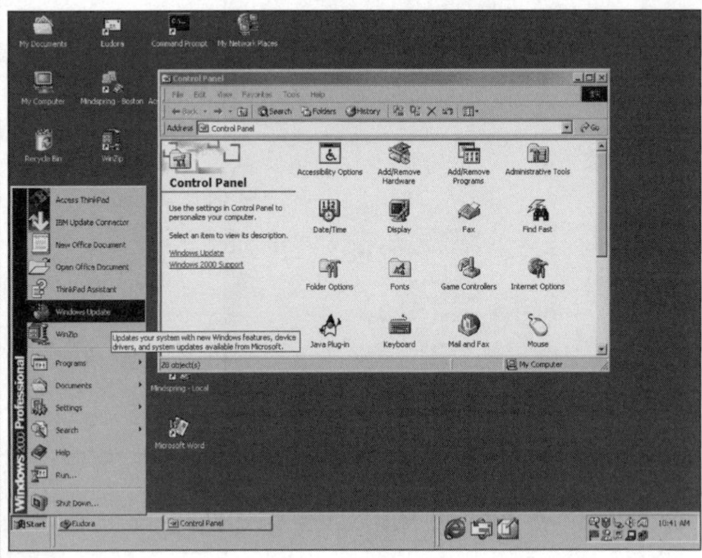

Figure 1-16 The Windows 2000 Professional desktop

Windows 2000 includes four operating systems:

- *Windows 2000 Professional* was designed to replace both Windows 9x and Windows NT Workstation as a personal computer desktop or notebook OS. It is an improved version of Windows NT Workstation, using the same new

A+ OS 1.1

1

technological approach to hardware and software, and includes all the popular features of Windows 9x, including Plug and Play.

- *Windows 2000 Server* is the improved version of Windows NT Server and is designed as a network operating system for low-end servers.
- *Windows 2000 Advanced Server* is a network operating system that has the same features as Windows 2000 Server but is designed to run on more powerful servers.
- *Windows 2000 Datacenter Server* is a network operating system that is another step up from Windows 2000 Advanced Server. It is intended to be used in large enterprise operations centers.

Hardware and software must qualify for all the Windows 2000 products just as they must qualify for Windows NT. For hardware, check the Hardware Compatibility List at *www.microsoft.com/hcl*. For software applications, search the list of compatible software applications list at *www.microsoft.com/windows2000/professional/howtobuy/upgrading/compat/default.asp*.

Table 1-6 compares the hardware specifications for Windows 2000 products.

Table 1-6 Comparing Windows 2000 products

Description	Windows 2000 Professional	Windows 2000 Server	Windows 2000 Advanced Server	Windows 2000 Datacenter Server
Minimum processor required (CPU)	133 MHz Pentium-compatible	133 MHz Pentium-compatible	133 MHz Pentium-compatible	133 MHz or higher
Minimum hard drive size	2 GB	2 GB	2 GB	2 GB
Minimum hard drive free space	650 MB	1 GB	1 GB	1 GB
Minimum RAM	64 MB	128 MB minimum supported; 256 MB minimum recommended	128 MB minimum supported; 256 MB minimum recommended	256 MB
Maximum RAM supported	4 GB	4 GB	8 GB	64 GB
Maximum CPUs in one system	2	4	8	32

A+ OS 1.1

Windows 2000 and Windows 98

Windows 2000 was built on Windows NT and is basically the next evolution of Windows NT with the added user-friendly features of Windows 98. For the corporate desktop or home market, in most cases you would choose to use Windows XP rather than Windows 2000. However, if you must select between Windows 2000 and Windows 98, Windows 2000 is a better choice for the corporate desktop and Windows 98 is the better choice for the home PC. Because of the power management improvements that Windows 2000 has over Windows 98, Windows 2000 is the best choice for notebook computers. For the business environment, Windows 2000 offers better support for very large hard drives, more security, and better reliability. For home users, Windows 98 works best with games, music, and video, and offers the best support for the most hardware and software products.

Table 1-7 summarizes the advantages and disadvantages of Windows 2000.

Table 1-7 Advantages and disadvantages of Windows 2000

Advantages	Disadvantages
• Windows 2000 provides powerful support to a network, including advanced security for the network and the ability to organize access to network resources in a centralized location on the network called an Active Directory. • Windows 2000 is backward-compatible with all Windows NT and Windows 9x applications and most Windows 3.x and DOS applications. • Windows 2000 is really four operating systems, each targeting a different sized computer and different computing needs, thus making the OS suite extremely versatile.	• Just as with Windows NT, Windows 2000 hardware requirements disqualify it as an option for an older, low-end PC operating system. • Windows 2000 is not scalable. Rather than having one OS that can easily handle a major computer system upgrade, the user must purchase one version of Windows 2000 for a small system and another to handle the upgraded system. • Although the perception of Windows as a high-end network operating system is changing, traditionally Windows has not been as stable as the Unix operating system for large enterprise use.

Reliability Windows 2000 is more reliable than Windows 98. The Windows File Protection feature of Windows 2000 prevents Windows system files and device drivers from being overwritten by faulty application installation programs or deleted by users, which prevents corruption and improves system reliability. By contrast, Windows 98 does not always ask for your permission before allowing an application to alter or overwrite a critical system file. Also, Windows 2000 has some new tools to help application developers build installation disks for their products and troubleshoot application problems.

Security Windows 2000 offers better security than previous operating systems. The **NTFS (NT file system)** developed for Windows NT and used by Windows 2000 and Windows XP gives better security. Windows 2000 has its own data encryption system and uses Kerberos (a security standard) to encrypt a user ID and password as the user logs on to the network from a Windows 2000 workstation. None of these features are available under Windows 98.

A+ OS 1.1

Personalized Start Menu Windows 2000 includes a personalized Start menu that shows only the applications used most often so that the menus are not cluttered with applications seldom used. See Figure 1-17. The down arrows indicate that there are more applications in the list but they are hidden from view. To see these applications, hold your cursor over the menu for a brief moment.

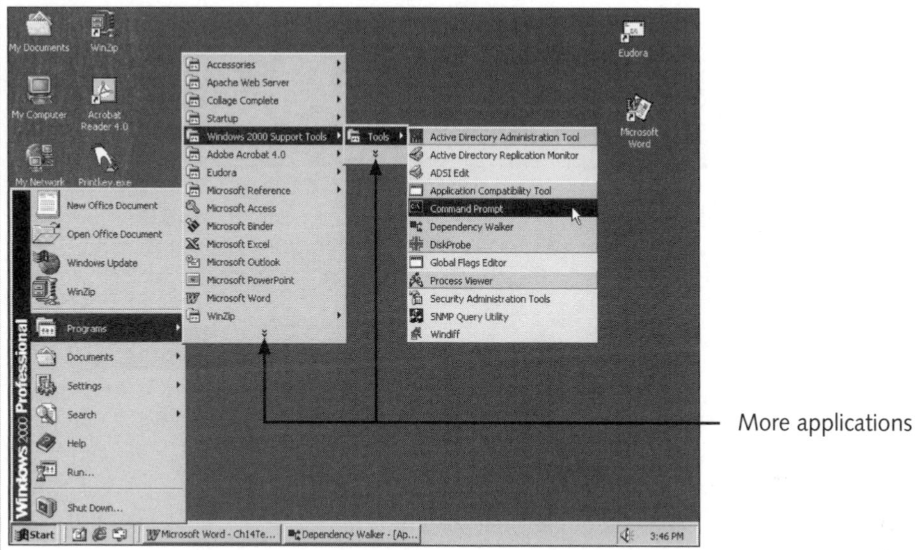

Figure 1-17 The Windows 2000 personalized Start menu does not initially show applications that are not often used

Power Use Windows 2000 and Windows 98 use the **Advanced Configuration and Power Interface (ACPI)**, which enables a computer to power down unused devices to conserve power, and gives the user much more control over power to the system. The Windows 2000 ACPI features are improved over those of Windows 98. Both require the cooperation of an ACPI-compliant motherboard. For example, on a PC with an ACPI motherboard, to set the Power Options of Windows 2000, open the Control Panel shown in Figure 1-18. Double-click the Power Options icon. The Power Options Properties dialog box opens. Click the Advanced tab (see Figure 1-19). From the list of power options, select what will happen when you press the power button on your computer case. For example, you can set the computer to change to Standby mode when you press the power button. On the Hibernate tab, you can also control when and how the system goes into hibernation, a state whereby little power is used but open applications are restored the next time you power up.

ACPI specifications were developed by Compaq, Intel, Microsoft, Phoenix, and Toshiba to allow for reliable power management through hardware and software cooperation. For more information about ACPI, see *www.acpi.info/index.html*. You'll also learn more about ACPI later in this book.

A+ OS 1.1

Because Windows 2000 uses NT technology, it does not support older device drivers written for DOS or Windows 9x, nor does it support all legacy devices or software. If you have a legacy application or device, you might have to use Windows 98. To determine if your hardware is supported under Windows 2000, see the Microsoft Web site *www.microsoft.com/hcl*. For software applications, search the list of compatible software applications list at *www.microsoft.com/windows2000/professional/howtobuy/upgrading/compat/ default.asp*.

Figure 1-18 Windows 2000 Control Panel

Added Notebook Computer Features The following features are available for notebook computers using Windows 2000, but are not a part of Windows 98:

- A feature called Offline Files and Folders allows you to download files and folders from a network to the PC so you can work on them offline. When the PC is later connected to the network, the files and folders can be uploaded to the network so that any changes are kept current on the network.
- The technology is included in Windows 2000 to allow a notebook user to work from home and connect to the corporate network over the Internet in a secure connection. To do this, Windows 2000 encrypts data before it is transmitted over the Internet.
- The power management features of Windows 2000 are enhanced and improved over those of Windows 98.

In summary, Windows 2000 Professional is designed as a desktop client computer operating system for a large network in a corporate or educational environment. Windows 98 is best used on a PC in a home or on a small network. Finally, for a notebook computer, Windows 2000 is the best choice.

A+ OS 1.1

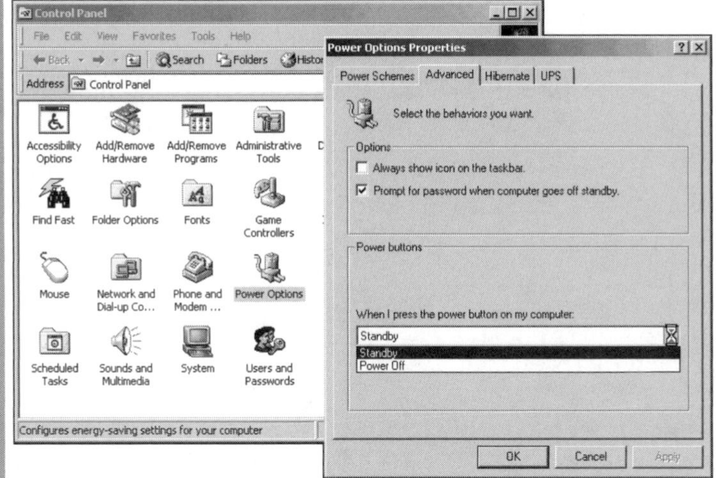

Figure 1-19 Windows 2000 offers several features to control power available from the Power Options icon of Control Panel

Windows 2000 and Windows NT

Windows 2000 is the upgrade of Windows NT. It contains the same core technology and provides a number of new capabilities. Windows 2000 supports the FAT16, FAT32, and NTFS file systems. The Windows 2000 registry is organized and edited the same way as the Windows NT registry. Utilities, such as Event Viewer and Dr. Watson, also work the same way with minor changes. Windows 2000 provides an encrypted file system for added security and support for virtual private networks (secure connections over the Internet between a person and a business or between two businesses). Windows 2000 Help and Troubleshooter utilities are much more comprehensive than the Windows NT or Windows 98 utilities. Windows 2000 supports multiple monitors, IEEE 1394 (FireWire), USB, and ACPI. (You will learn about FireWire in the next chapter.)

Added Features Recall that Windows NT does not support Plug and Play. Windows 2000 uses an advanced version of Plug and Play that does all the work for configuring a system and does not use the Plug and Play features of a motherboard.

Many of the specific differences between Windows NT and Windows 2000 are beyond the scope of this chapter and are covered in detail later in this book in the chapters on each operating system.

Windows XP

A+ OS 1.1

Windows XP attempts to accomplish integration of 9x and 2000, while providing added support for digital and networking technologies. The two main versions are Windows XP Home and Windows XP Professional, though editions for the advanced server market will

A+ OS 1.1

likely be available by the time this book is published. Both editions have these features, among others:

- A new user interface, which is shown in Figure 1-20. Notice how different it looks from the desktops for earlier Windows versions such as Windows 9x and Windows 2000.
- The ability for two users to log on simultaneously, both with their own applications open

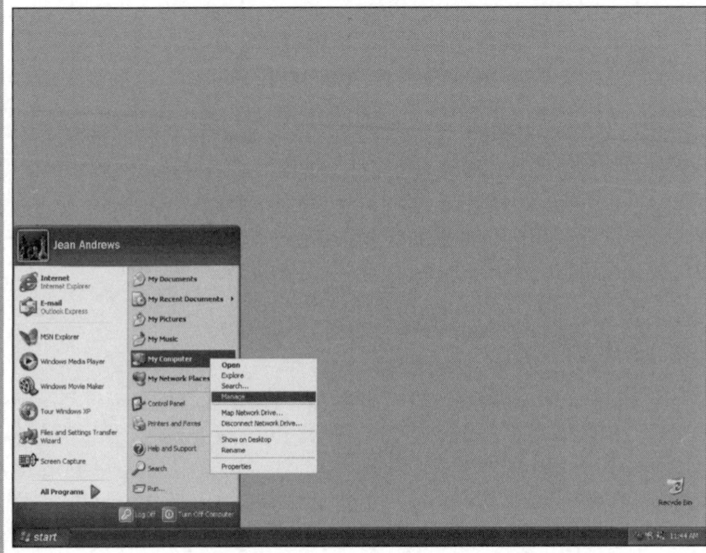

Figure 1-20 The Windows XP desktop and Start menu

- Windows Media Player for Windows XP, which provides a centralized application for working with digital media
- Windows Messenger for instant messaging, conferencing, and application sharing
- An expanded Help feature
- Advanced security features

Here are some of the features that Windows XP Professional adds to the home edition:

- Features for remote access, including remote desktop and roaming user profiles
- Additional security features
- Multilingual capabilities
- Support for new higher performance processors

There is also Windows XP 64-bit Edition designed to be used with a high-end CPU such as the Intel Itanium. This version of Windows XP is designed mostly for servers or heavily technical workstation users who need greater amounts of memory and higher performance

A+ OS 1.1

than standard desktop users, for example, for scientific and engineering applications. For instance, an aircraft designer who needs to simulate how various conditions affect aircraft materials might use Windows XP on a system supporting resource-intensive simulation and animation applications.

Windows Internet Explorer, Windows Media Player, a firewall, and other Microsoft products are tightly integrated with the Windows XP operating system. Some users see this as a disadvantage and others see it as an advantage. Full evaluation of the integration of Microsoft software with the Windows XP operating system is beyond the scope of this overview.

The minimum requirements for Windows XP Professional are:

- A minimum of 64 MB of RAM, with 128 MB recommended
- At least 1.5 GB of free hard drive space, with 2 GB recommended
- A CPU that runs at least 233 MHz, with a 300 MHz CPU recommended. Remember that Windows XP can support two CPUs.

Remember that the requirements of an OS will vary depending on which version you have installed and what applications and hardware you have installed with it.

Windows XP provides several enhancements over Windows 2000 and other earlier versions. Table 1-8 summarizes the advantages and disadvantages of Windows XP.

Table 1-8 Advantages and disadvantages of Windows XP

Advantages	Disadvantages
• Provides better integration of Windows 9x and NT than did Windows 2000. • Offers significant GUI enhancements over earlier versions of Windows. • Adds features but uses only slightly more total memory for the OS than does Windows 2000. • Adds advanced file sorting options, such as sorting pictures by resolution or sound files by artist. • Includes built-in support for compressed files. • Has improved troubleshooting tools and is generally more stable than previous Windows OSs.	• Requires nearly a gigabyte of hard drive space for the operating system itself, and at least a 233 MHz processor with 64 MB of RAM. • Programs used with Windows XP may require more than the minimum system specifications for the operating system. • Nearly eliminates support for device drivers not approved by Microsoft. • Security concerns with centralized storage of online information in Microsoft Passport, a repository of the user IDs and passwords you use on the Internet.

A+ OS 1.1

Windows XP and Previous Windows OSs

Windows XP is replacing all previous versions of Windows in the home market and for the corporate desktop. If your hardware and applications qualify, select Windows XP Home Edition for a home PC over Windows 98/Me. For a corporate environment, use Windows XP Professional over Windows NT/2000. The only exception to this is compatibility issues with older hardware and software.

Other Operating Systems

As a PC technician you are likely to see a variety of operating systems on all kinds of personal computers. Windows and non-Windows operating systems share many of the same functions and goals. In this section, you will learn about Unix, Linux, OS/2, and Mac OS. Pay close attention to the advantages and disadvantages of each as well as comparisons between the technologies.

Unix

Unix originally was written for mainframe computers in the early 1970s; only in the past few years has it become available for many different kinds of computers, including PCs, and it is also a popular OS for networking. Unix computers are often used for Internet support. Problems with Unix stem mostly from the lack of consistency from one vendor's version to another. Hardware requirements for Unix vary widely depending on the version installed.

Table 1-9 summarizes the advantages and disadvantages of the Unix OS, including comparisons of Unix and Windows.

Table 1-9 Advantages and disadvantages of Unix

Advantages	Disadvantages
• Unix was written for powerful microcomputer systems and has strong multitasking capability, including preemptive multitasking. • Unix manages large quantities of memory well. • Unix performs very well in a networking environment. • Unix does not require as much memory or processor time as Windows does. • Unix systems generally do not crash as frequently as Windows systems. • Design and implementation of Unix include support for remote management.	• Unix industry standards are not uniform, making it difficult for Unix developers, administrators, and users to move from one Unix vendor to another. • Unix requires a powerful, large microcomputer system. • Few business applications software packages have been written for Unix for PCs, although there are several very powerful database packages available under Unix, such as Informix and Oracle. • Unix does not provide the user-friendly GUI that Windows OSs include. • Unix does not include some of the customized applications development and Web publishing features that Windows has.

Linux

A variation of Unix that has recently gained in popularity is Linux (pronounced "Lih-nucks"), an OS originally created by Linus Torvalds when he was a student at the University of Helsinki in Finland. Basic versions of this OS are available for free, and all the underlying programming instructions (called source code) are also freely distributed. Like Unix, Linux is distributed by several different companies, whose versions of Linux are sometimes called **distributions**. Popular distributions of Linux include SuSE (*www.suse.com*), RedHat (*www.redhat.com*), Caldera (*www.caldera.com*), Mandrake (*www.linux-mandrake.com*), and TurboLinux (*www.turbolinux.com*). Linux can be used both as a server platform and a desktop platform, but its greatest popularity has come in the server market. Hardware requirements for Linux vary widely, depending on the distribution and version installed.

For more information on Linux, see *www.linux.org* as well as the Web sites of the different distributors of Linux.

Table 1-10 summarizes the advantages and disadvantages of Linux.

Table 1-10 Advantages and disadvantages of Linux

Advantages	Disadvantages
• Linux rarely crashes. • Basic versions can be downloaded and installed free. • Linux distributions that include technical support and software packages are available at a lower cost than other operating systems. • Linux generally handles network connections better than Windows. • Source code is available to users, enabling customization of the development environment. • Linux on an inexpensive PC is an excellent training tool toward learning Unix.	• Linux can be difficult to install, particularly for users who are not familiar with Unix commands. • Linux does not provide a GUI, though a Windows-like office suite can be installed. • Documentation can be spotty. • Linux can be difficult for casual users to operate. • Optimizing a Linux system can take a significant investment of time and research. • Not many applications are available for Linux on the desktop.

Network services such as a Web server or e-mail server often are provided by a computer running the Linux operating system. Linux is well suited to support various types of servers. Because Linux is very reliable and does not require a lot of computing power, it is sometimes used as a desktop OS, although it is not as popular for this purpose because it is not easy to use. As a PC support technician, you should know a little about Linux, including a few basic commands, which are covered in a later chapter.

Because many users prefer a Windows-style desktop, several applications have been written to provide a GUI shell for Unix and Linux. These shells are called X Windows. A typical X Windows screen is shown in Figure 1-21.

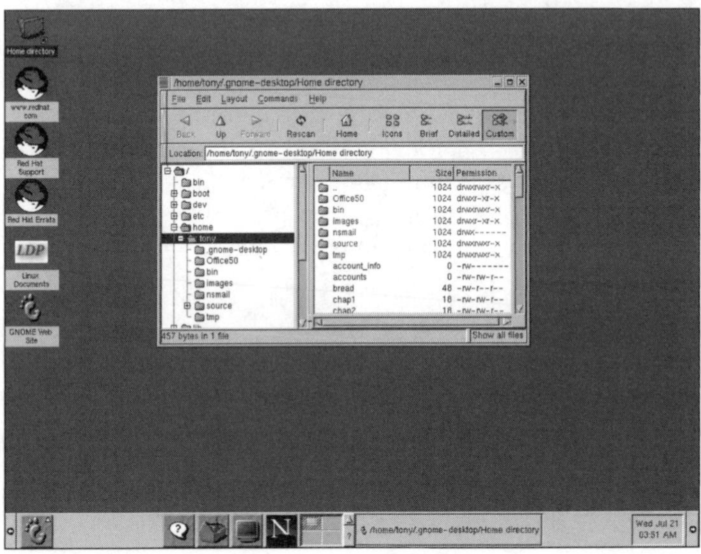

Figure 1-21 X Windows software provides a GUI shell for Linux and Unix users

OS/2

OS/2, written by IBM in cooperation with Microsoft Corporation, was designed as a replacement for DOS. OS/2 requires at least a 486 processor, 12–16 MB of RAM, and 100–300 MB of free hard drive space (depending on which features are installed). Many airline ticketing systems, worldwide and local banks, prisons, railroad systems, and U.S. government branches use OS/2. OS/2 never gained popularity for individual PC users. Although some people have predicted the downfall of OS/2 for years, its use continues, and applications are still being written for it. Recently, IBM adapted OS/2 for use with Web business solutions, including support for Web server software, Web protocols, and database interaction. Table 1-11 summarizes the advantages and disadvantages of OS/2.

Macintosh Operating System (Mac OS)

The Mac OS is available only on Macintosh computers. Both were first introduced in 1984. Several versions of the Macintosh OS have been written since, the latest being Mac OS X (ten), which offers easy access to the Internet and allows any Macintosh computer to become a Web server for a small network. Because it is easy to use, the Mac OS has been popular in educational environments from elementary school through the university level. It also provides excellent support for graphics and multimedia applications. Mac OS X requires at least 128 MB of RAM and 1.5 GB of hard drive space.

The Mac OS X interface is significantly different from that of the Mac OS 9, including two new features called the dock and the toolbar, as shown in Figure 1-22. When a Mac is turned on, a program called the Finder is automatically launched. This is the program that provides the desktop, which functions as the GUI for the Mac OS. Generally, under normal Mac OS operation, you cannot quit the Finder program.

Table 1-11 Advantages and disadvantages of OS/2

Advantages	Disadvantages
• OS/2 supports preemptive multitasking. • OS/2 can handle large quantities of memory directly and quickly. • OS/2 runs many DOS applications better than Windows and Unix. • OS/2 has an icon-driven interface. • OS/2 works well in a networking environment. • Software designed for OS/2 sometimes runs more efficiently than comparable Windows programs.	• Relatively few application software packages are written for OS/2. • Many microcomputer users are not familiar with OS/2 and avoid it for that reason. • OS/2 requires a powerful computer system and large amounts of RAM and hard drive space to run efficiently.

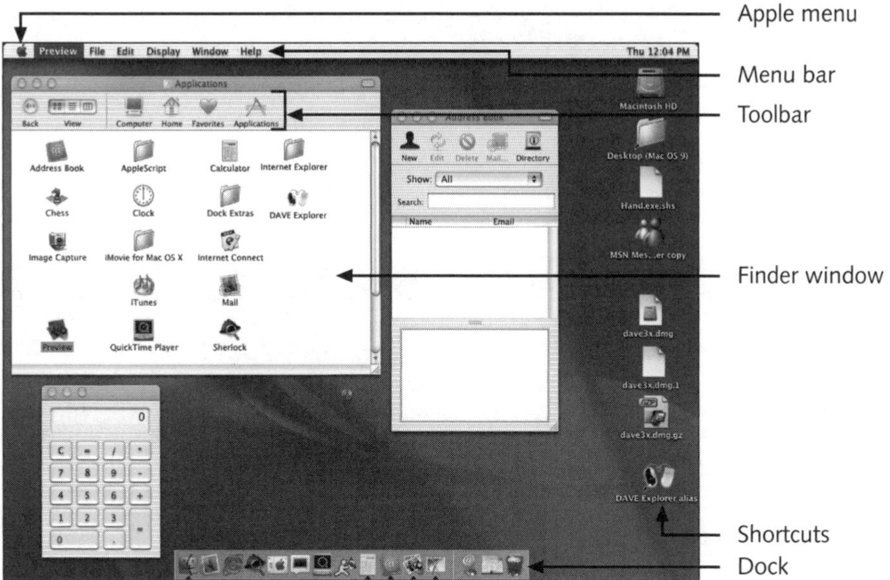

Figure 1-22 The Mac OS desktop is intuitive and easy to use

Windows are used to navigate among files and applications in the Mac. The Mac windows function similarly to windows in Microsoft operating systems, in that they can be minimized or maximized, icons can be moved around within them, and the window on top is active when several are open. You can work within one window, using buttons and menu options to navigate between applications and views, or you can open each application or view in a new Finder window.

Before Apple introduced the iMac, most of the Mac OS was permanently stored in Apple ROM, and only Apple had access to that code. This prevented other companies from manufacturing computers that ran Macintosh software. With the iMac, Apple moved most of the OS code into an upgradeable file called Mac OS ROM, stored on the hard drive but still stores some startup code in a smaller ROM chip. The Mac OS X ROM file contains programs called managers that perform specific system functions like keeping track of windows, organizing menus, allocating system resources, and many others. Another important difference between Mac OS X and earlier versions is that the Mac OS X provides support for preemptive multitasking and is thus less likely to freeze than were earlier versions when several applications are running simultaneously.

The Mac OS X tries to make user interaction with the OS as smooth and as minimal as possible by providing superior Plug and Play capabilities, so that new hardware devices can be added easily and are automatically recognized by the OS. Additionally, the Mac OS does not allow users to interact directly with the OS code as some other OSs do. This can be an advantage because the Mac OS automatically performs certain functions that the user has to perform with other OSs.

Although the initial cost of setting up a Macintosh system is generally higher than for a comparable IBM-compatible system, the cost of support and maintenance is generally lower for the Mac.

Table 1-12 summarizes the advantages and disadvantages of the Macintosh OS.

Table 1-12 Advantages and disadvantages of the Macintosh operating system

Advantages	Disadvantages
• The Mac OS has an excellent icon-driven interface, and it is easy to learn and use. • The Mac OS has supported a GUI interface and Plug and Play devices since it was first developed. • The Mac OS manages large quantities of memory. • Many applications exist for the Mac OS to create and edit graphics, build Web sites, and manage multimedia. • Mac OS systems are generally less prone to crashing than Windows systems.	• Historically, the Macintosh was not viewed as a professional computer but rather was relegated to education and game playing. Then the Mac gained a significant place in the professional desktop publishing and graphics markets. Most recently, the availability of more powerful IBM-compatible PCs and OSs to handle the high demands of graphics has reduced the demand for the Mac. • Because IBM-compatible PCs have a larger share of the market than Macintosh computers, software compatible with the Mac OS is not always as readily available.

Chapter Summary

- An operating system controls the different hardware components that make up a computer and also provides an interface that a user or an application can use.
- Operating system functions include managing BIOS (programs permanently stored on hardware devices) and memory, interfacing between hardware and software, and performing tasks requested by the user (such as formatting disks and copying or deleting files).
- The two main components of an operating system are the shell and the kernel.
- The Windows registry and initialization files are used to store system information such as configuration settings, application settings, and user preferences.
- Users interact with an OS by a command-driven, menu-driven, or icon-driven interface.
- A thread is a process that the CPU is aware of.
- Multitasking is the ability of a CPU to run more than one program at a time. In cooperative multitasking, the CPU switches back and forth between applications. In preemptive multitasking, the CPU allots a specific period of time to an application and then preempts that application to provide CPU time to another application.
- OSs, applications, and CPUs all operate in either 16-bit (real) mode or 32-bit (protected) mode, depending on how many bits the CPU can process at once.
- The most well-known OSs for microcomputers are DOS, Windows, Unix, Linux, Mac OS, and OS/2.
- DOS was replaced by Windows as the most popular OS, but decisions made when DOS was designed still affect Windows 9x today.
- Windows 95, Windows 98, and Windows Me are collectively referred to as Windows 9x.
- Windows 9x is a bridge between older and newer OS technologies. It can support both 16-bit and 32-bit applications.
- The two upgrades Microsoft released for Windows 98 are Windows 98 SE and Windows Me.
- Windows NT breaks with previous versions of Windows by severing the connection between Windows and DOS and not allowing applications to have direct access to system resources.
- Windows NT is the first fully 32-bit Windows OS. Windows 2000 and XP are also 32-bit.
- Windows 2000 is actually a suite of operating systems: Windows 2000 Professional, Windows 2000 Server, Windows 2000 Advanced Server, and Windows 2000 Datacenter Server.
- Windows NT does not support Plug and Play, does not have a Safe Mode, and does not have a Device Manager. Windows 9x, Windows 2000, and Windows XP support all these.
- Windows XP attempts to accomplish integration of 9x and 2000, while providing added support for digital and networking technologies. The two main versions are Windows XP Home and Windows XP Professional.

- Unix was originally written for mainframe computers in the early 1970s. Today, it is available for other types of computers, such as servers and PCs. It is often used for Internet support.
- Linux is a variation of Unix that was created by Linus Torvalds. Basic versions of the OS are available for free download, and the underlying source code is openly distributed.
- OS/2 was written by IBM in cooperation with Microsoft and is now distributed and maintained by IBM. Systems that use OS/2 include airline ticketing systems, worldwide and local banks, and railroads. OS/2 is generally not very popular with PC users.
- Mac OS is only available on Macintosh computers. It has been widely used in educational markets and with graphics-intensive applications.

KEY TERMS

16-bit mode
32-bit mode
ACPI (Advanced Configuration and Power Interface)
API (Application Program Interface)
backward-compatible
cluster
cooperative multitasking
CPU (central processing unit)
desktop
device driver
distributions
environment
FAT (file allocation table)
GUI (graphical user interface)
HAL (hardware abstraction layer)
HCL (hardware compatibility list)
initialization files
kernel
LAN (local area network)
legacy
microprocessor
multiprocessing
multitasking
NTFS (NT file system)
operating system
preemptive multitasking
protected mode
RAM (random access memory)
real mode
registry
sector
shell
single-tasking
task switching
thread
track

REVIEW QUESTIONS

1. List three well-known OSs.
2. What are the four main things an OS does?
3. Name three types of user interfaces.
4. Which Microsoft operating system only supports single-tasking?
5. What is the difference between cooperative multitasking and preemptive multitasking?
6. Which Microsoft OS first supported preemptive multitasking?
7. Which operating system was the first one used by IBM microcomputers?

8. Windows ______________ used DOS as its underlying OS, Windows ______________ is a true OS but bases its core functions on DOS, and Windows ______________ was the first Windows version to fully sever the connection with DOS and create an altogether new OS core.
9. Which Windows OS uses only 16-bit processing? Some 16-bit and some 32-bit? 32-bit only?
10. A software program stored on the hard drive designed to be used by the OS to run an input/output hardware device is called a ______________.
11. Windows Me is an upgrade of Windows ______________.
12. Why does Windows NT not guarantee backward compatibility with applications written with older Windows versions?
13. Which Windows operating system does not support Plug and Play?
14. What kind of multitasking does Windows NT support?
15. What information can you find on the HCL?
16. Name the four OSs in the Windows 2000 suite.
17. Which is a better choice for networks: Windows 9x or Windows 2000?
18. What file systems used to organize a hard drive does Windows 2000 support?
19. What is the name of the Windows database used to hold configuration information?
20. Which is the best choice for notebook computers: Windows 9x, NT, or 2000? Why?
21. Under what circumstances would Windows 98 be a better choice for a home computer user than Windows 2000?
22. Name at least two advantages of Windows XP over earlier versions of Windows.
23. Name two Windows OSs that support USB ports. Name one Windows OS that does not support USB.
24. In documentation, why is there sometimes a discrepancy in the hardware requirements listed for an OS?
25. What was Unix originally written for? How is it used today?
26. How is true multitasking achieved?
27. Which OS offers basic versions for free download and includes open access to its source code?
28. Name an OS that does not use a GUI.
29. What are two features on the Mac OS X desktop that were not present in Mac OS 9?
30. What are two popular uses for Mac OS?

HANDS-ON PROJECTS

Use the HCL

Make a list of the hardware devices installed on your computer. Check for the HCL on Microsoft's Web site (*www.microsoft.com/hcl*) and determine which versions of Windows you can use with the hardware you presently have installed. Print the results of your search of the HCL for your hardware devices. (If you are unsure what hardware devices are installed, use Device Manager. For Windows 9x, click **Start**, **Settings**, **Control Panel**, double-click the **Systems** icon, and then click the **Device Manager** tab. Installed hardware devices are listed.)

Compare Interfaces

This exercise assumes that you are using Windows 95 or a later version of Windows. In this exercise, you will take screenshots of the three different types of interfaces and compare them. First, take a screenshot of your desktop, which is an example of an icon-driven interface.

1. Minimize all programs you have running so that you see your desktop with its icons showing.
2. Press the **Print Screen** key on your keyboard. (The actual label on the key may be different, depending on the keyboard you are using.) This will copy an image of your screen onto the clipboard.
3. On your **Start** menu, select **Programs**, then **Accessories**, then **Paint**. This will start the Microsoft Paint program.
4. Click **Edit**, **Paste** or you can press the **Ctrl** key and the **V** key simultaneously to paste the image of your screen into Paint.
5. Save the screenshot with the name **icon_interface**.
6. Print the screenshot by choosing the **File** menu within Paint, then **Print**. You now have a printed screenshot of an icon-driven interface.
7. Next, from your **Start** menu, point to **Programs** and click **MS-DOS Prompt**. (In Windows 2000 and XP, click **Start**, point to **(All) Programs**, then **Accessories**, and click **Command Prompt**.) Take a screenshot of the Command Prompt window using the procedure in Steps 2–4 above. Save the screenshot with the name **command_interface**, and then print it.
8. Finally, right-click your **Start** menu and select **Explore** to open Windows Explorer. Take a screenshot of Explorer using the method in Steps 2–4, save it as **menu_interface**, and then print the screenshot.

Compare the printouts of the three different types of interface. What are the similarities and differences between them? Besides menus, what other type of interface is Explorer an example of?

Choosing an OS

Read the three scenarios below and determine which OS you think should be installed in each situation. Use the information given in this chapter and Web sites on the Internet to research the OSs you are considering.

A. You have two computers in your home, one running Windows 95 and one running Windows NT, and you are installing a third computer. The computers in your home have not previously been networked, and you intend to network them when you install the third one. You would like to be able to use the programs you already have installed as well as newer programs, and you want to be able to install new hardware devices easily. Which OS should you choose for the new computer? Will you keep the present OSs on the existing computers?

B. You have been asked to set up the computer for the new graphic artist at your company who is an expert using Adobe PageMaker (*www.adobe.com*) on a Macintosh computer. In addition to running this graphics software, this person will need to use the same software programs as the other members of the office, Microsoft Office (*www.microsoft.com*). Which OS would you choose for this person?

C. You are setting up a new network for a small business that has about 20 employees, and you are planning to install the same OS on everyone's computer. You need a highly efficient network that can process information quickly and can work well with the company's extensive database of customer and product information. Which OS will you choose for each personal computer on the network?

Discuss your choices for scenarios A, B, and C with your instructor and classmates, including the following questions:

1. Which OS did you choose, and why?
2. What are the advantages and disadvantages of your choice?
3. What other OSs could you have chosen for the same scenario, and how would that have changed the situation?
4. Other than the information in the chapter, what additional information do you want to know before you feel confident you can make a good decision?

Researching on the Internet: Windows Updates

Visit Microsoft's Windows Web site at *www.microsoft.com/windows.* Which versions of Windows are considered current, and which are listed as previous versions? Are there any mentioned in this chapter that are not listed? Make a list of the Windows versions and their status, making use of the links on the Windows site as necessary.

Case Project

In the case projects in this book, you will install and uninstall several different operating systems. First, you need to determine what operating system you presently have installed. For Windows, on the desktop right-click the **My Computer** icon and then choose **Properties** from the shortcut menu. The System Properties window will open, showing the OS and version.

Whenever you are installing, uninstalling, or reconfiguring hardware or software, it is a good idea to keep detailed notes of what you are doing in case you need to backtrack. This information can also be useful for troubleshooting and technical support. You will be keeping a notebook for the case projects throughout this book. As your first entry in the notebook, write down the information shown on the General tab of the System Properties window about the system that is presently installed on your computer.

This project assumes that you are beginning with a computer that has Windows 95 or later installed. If you are beginning with a blank PC, make an initial entry in your notebook about the specifications of the OS you are planning to install, such as the OS and version, the minimum hardware requirements for it, and the hardware you have in the system on which you will be installing the OS.

CHAPTER

2

How an OS Works with Hardware and Other Software

In this chapter, you will learn:

- How an OS relates to hardware
- How an OS relates to other software
- How an OS launches applications

In the last chapter you were introduced to many different operating systems used on personal computers. In this chapter, you'll go behind the scenes to see how these operating systems relate to the hardware they manage and the applications they support. You'll see how an OS controls several of the more significant hardware devices using the resources made available to it for interaction with these devices. You'll also see how an OS serves an application, providing the interface the application needs to command and use hardware devices.

How an OS Relates to Hardware

Just as a chauffeur controls a car at the direction of a passenger, software controls hardware at the direction of a user (see Figure 2-1). There are several layers of software needed. You see these in Figure 2-1 as applications software, the operating system, and BIOS and device drivers. Device drivers and BIOS are software written to interface with specific hardware devices. **BIOS (basic input/output system)** is permanently stored on microchips. You'll see two of these microchips later in the chapter. The BIOS that the OS uses to help manage the system is called **system BIOS** and is stored on a BIOS chip on the motherboard. Device drivers are stored on the hard drive until needed and are generally first added to the system as part of the device installation process. Device drivers can come from a device manufacturer, or an OS can use its own device drivers. That distinction is made in Figure 2-2.

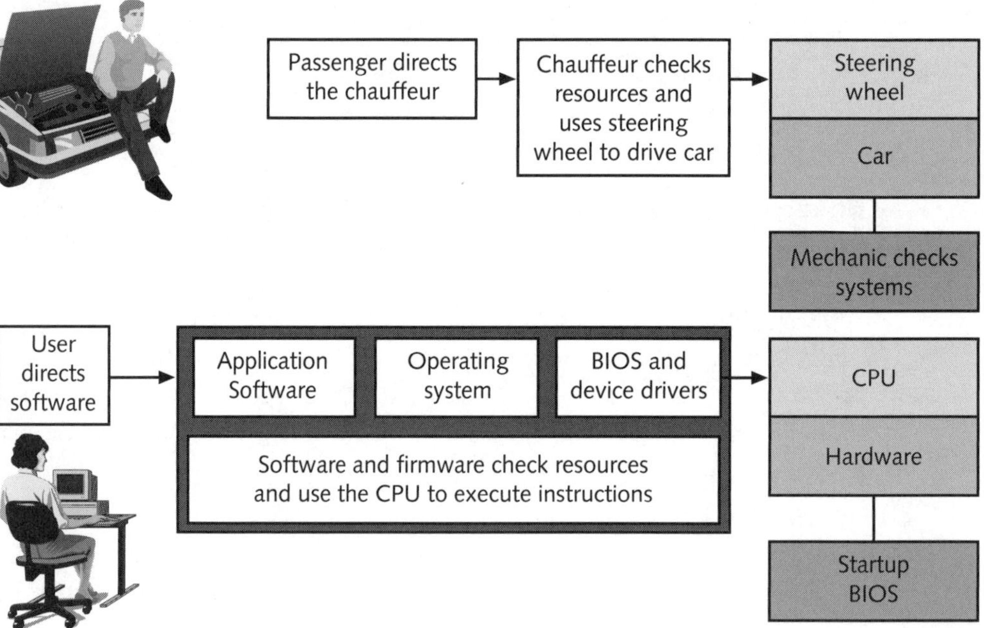

Figure 2-1 Software interacts with hardware much as a chauffeur and a mechanic interact with a car

One advantage of using BIOS and device drivers to interface with hardware is that it frees the OS or application software from having to know the specifics of how to communicate with the device. For example, different printers understand data and commands according to different sets of rules and standards called protocols. Application software and the OS can pass print requests to the printer driver, which communicates with the printer, as in Figure 2-3. With the device drivers doing the interpreting, application software developers do not have to include the specific protocol and standards for every printer that might be used by the applications they write.

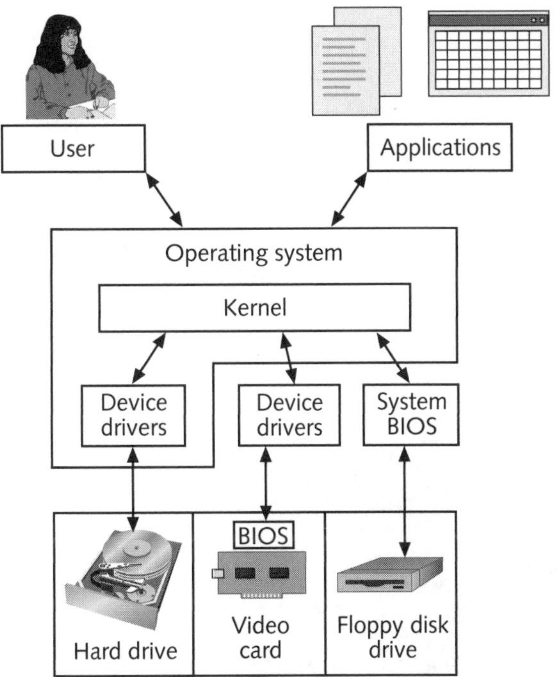

Figure 2-2 An OS relates to hardware by way of BIOS or device drivers

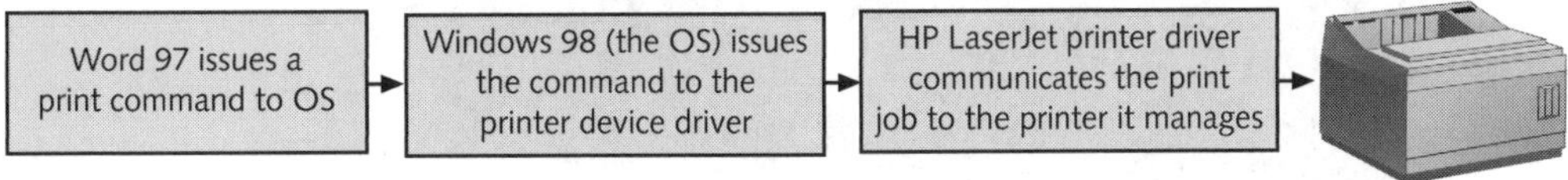

Figure 2-3 Any specific protocols and commands sent to the printer are the responsibility of the printer device driver

The application software does not even need to know which printer is being used, because Windows keeps track of the default printer. The application sends print jobs to Windows for printing. Windows uses the default printer unless the user selects a different one from the Windows printer list. Windows knows which device driver to call to execute the print job because the device driver was assigned to that printer when the printer was installed. You'll learn more about BIOS and device drivers later in the chapter.

It's difficult to describe what a chauffeur does unless you first know a little about a car. In the same way, it's difficult to describe what an application, operating system, BIOS, and device drivers do unless you know something about computer hardware, so first, you'll learn about several hardware components common to most systems.

The Motherboard

The **motherboard**, shown in Figure 2-4, is the largest circuit board inside a computer case and is also the most complex. Because the CPU is central to all operations by hardware or software, all devices must somehow connect to the CPU, and they all do this by way of the motherboard. In order to allow for and manage this communication, the motherboard has several slots, connections, embedded wires, microchips, and ports that you will learn about in this section. When you look on the back of a computer case, you can see some ports that are connected directly to the motherboard that provide a way for external components to connect to the CPU.

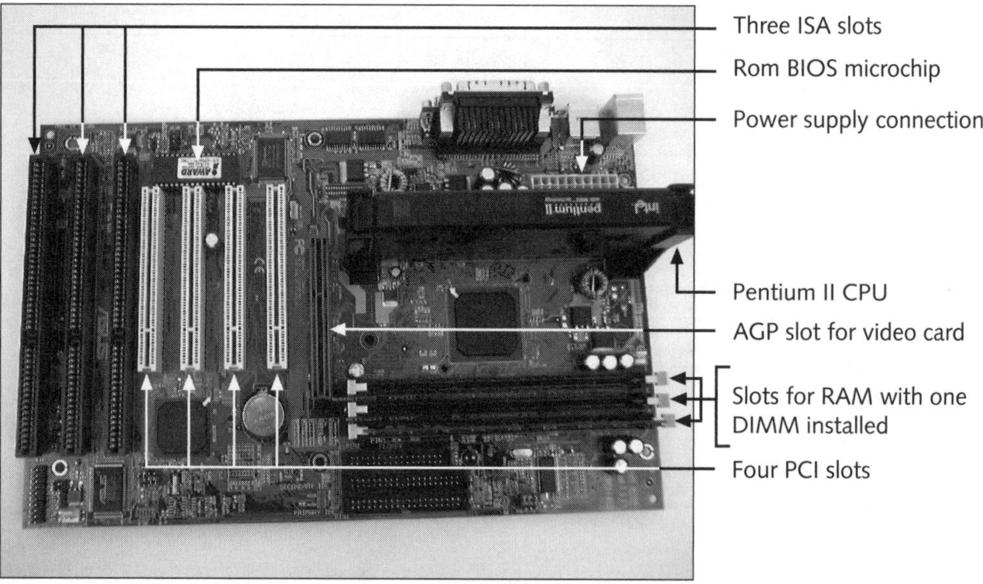

Figure 2-4 The motherboard is the largest circuit board inside the computer case and houses the CPU

Figure 2-5 shows the ports provided to the outside of the case by this motherboard: a keyboard port, mouse port, two serial ports, two USB ports, and parallel port. A **serial port** is called a serial port because data travels serially (one bit follows the next). This port is often used for an external modem or serial mouse (a mouse that uses a serial port). A **parallel port** carries data in parallel and is most often used by a printer. A **USB (universal serial bus)** port is a newer port used by many input/output devices such as a keyboard, printer, scanner, or mouse. In later chapters, you'll learn how the OS configures and manages each of these ports and the devices that use them.

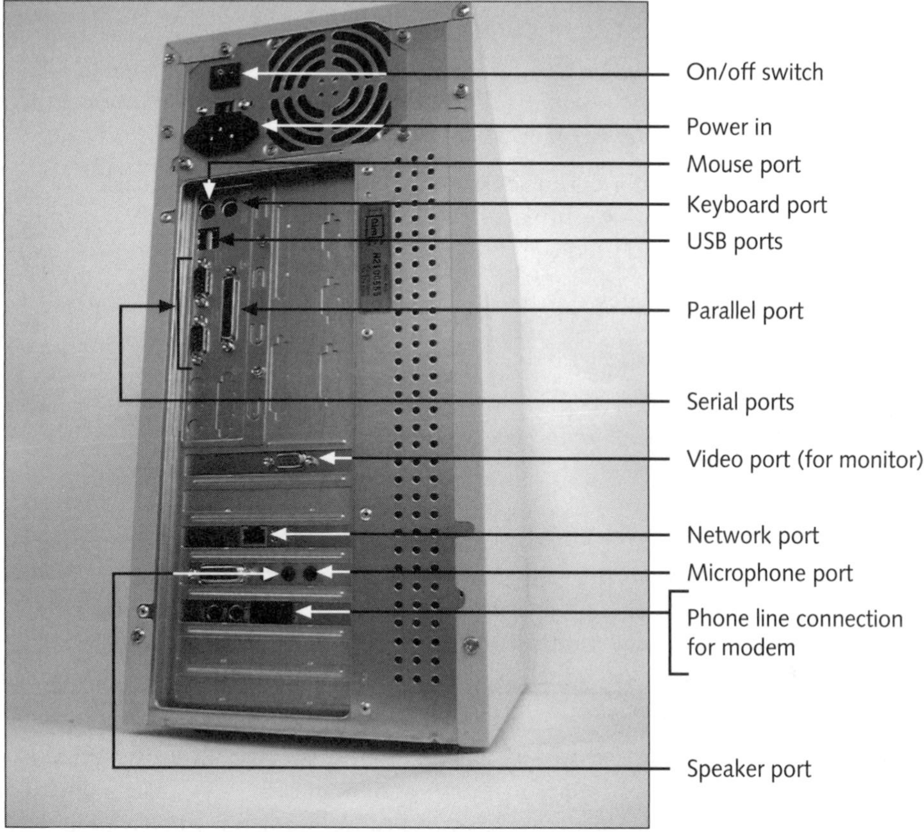

Figure 2-5 Input/output devices connect to the computer case by ports usually found on the back of the case

Listed below are the major components found on all motherboards, some of which are labeled in Figure 2-4 and are discussed in detail in the sections that follow.

- Central processing unit (CPU), the computer's most important chip
- Random access memory (RAM) used to temporarily hold data and instructions as they are processed
- Traces or wires on the motherboard used for communication
- Expansion slots to connect expansion cards to the motherboard
- ROM BIOS memory chip used to permanently store instructions that control basic hardware functions (explained in more detail later in the chapter)
- CMOS configuration chip (also explained later in the chapter)
- Power supply connections to provide electricity to the motherboard and expansion cards

The CPU

The CPU is central to all processing done by a computer. Every command from the OS is passed to the CPU, which controls all the hardware components in the computer. For this reason, in Figure 2-1, the steering wheel of a car is compared to the CPU of a computer.

The CPU is installed in a slot or socket on the motherboard (refer back to Figure 2-4). All CPUs today operate in one of two modes: 16-bit or 32-bit, which are sometimes called real mode and protected mode. There are several differences between these two modes, but fundamentally, 16-bit mode or **real mode** means that the CPU processes 16 bits of data at one time and in 32-bit mode or **protected mode**, it processes 32 bits at a time.

A new CPU, the Intel Itanium operates in 64-bit mode. Windows XP 64-bit Edition is designed to use this type of CPU.

An operating system must be using the same mode the CPU is using. All CPUs for personal computers today, when they are first turned on, begin processing in real mode and must be instructed to change over to protected mode. Every operating system, therefore, begins processing in real mode. Only DOS stays in real mode. The other OSs quickly switch to protected mode, which is much faster than real mode. You'll learn more about real mode and protected mode in the next sections.

The speed of a CPU is partly determined by how much data it can process at one time and how much data it can send or receive at one time. Every CPU has lines coming to it that are embedded on the motherboard collectively called a **bus** (see Figure 2-6). These lines are devoted to different purposes. Some lines on the bus are designated to carry data and they are called the **data bus** or **data path**. Early CPUs used a 16-bit data path and processed 16 bits at one time. Today's CPUs can use one size for the data path but another for internal processing. For example, the Pentium III CPU uses a 64-bit data path coming to and from the CPU, but internally it processes 32 bits at a time. Other lines on a bus are used for addresses, control signals, and voltage.

Memory or RAM

RAM (random access memory) is microchips used to temporarily hold data and instructions while the CPU processes both. These microchips are stored on tiny circuit boards called memory modules. Memory modules can be SIMMs, DIMMs, or RIMMs. The most common module for today's motherboards is a DIMM (refer back to Figure 2-4). A memory module is installed in memory slots on the motherboard designed to hold a particular type and speed of module.

Figure 2-6 On the bottom of the motherboard, you can see bus lines ending at the CPU socket

Using Windows 9x, you can see what type of CPU and how much memory you have installed. Right-click the My Computer icon on your desktop, select Properties from the shortcut menu, and click the General tab (see Figure 2-7). Also shown is the version of Windows you are using.

Memory is useless to the system until it has been assigned addresses that the operating system, device drivers, and BIOS can use to communicate with it. These **memory addresses** are numbers that are assigned to each usable cell of memory, and the assignments are normally done when the OS is first loaded. How memory addresses are assigned and used is covered later in the chapter.

Buses on the Motherboard

All hardware devices are directly or indirectly connected to the motherboard because they are all dependent on the CPU on the motherboard for processing their data. Each bus provides a way for devices to connect to it and, ultimately, to the CPU. Sometimes a bus provides a port on the outside of the computer case for an external device to connect to by way of a cable or cord, or the bus might provide a slot on the motherboard into which a circuit board fits. In any case, a device always connects to a single bus on the motherboard. A motherboard can have several different buses; each type of bus has data lines, address lines, and control lines. An operating system relates to the bus, so the OS must support it in order for it to be used by the system.

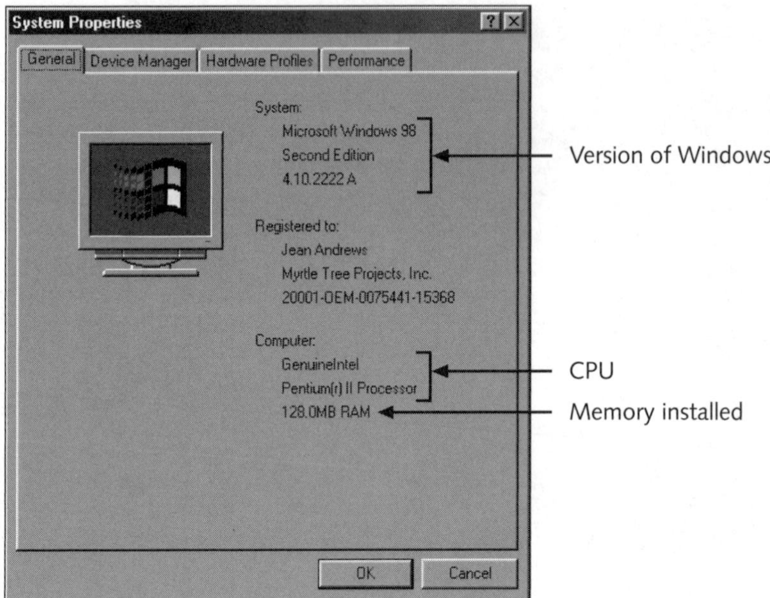

Figure 2-7 Use the System Properties window to see how much memory is installed

Some common buses and the expansion slots they support are listed and described below:

- The first motherboards of the 1980s only had one bus, the **system bus**, which supported several **ISA (Industry Standard Architecture)** slots. The first ISA slot had only eight lines for data and was called the 8-bit ISA slot. It had 20 address lines and ran at 4.77 MHz, which means that data was transferred on the bus at a rate of 4,770,000 transfers per second. Today's system buses run up to 400 MHz, have a 64-bit wide data path and a 36-bit or more wide address path. These system buses, sometimes called **memory buses**, **front-side buses**, or **local buses**, always connect directly to the CPU and memory, but are much too fast to support the slow ISA slots, which connect to the system bus by way of slower I/O buses that act as middle men.
- Later, the 8-bit ISA slot was improved by adding an additional 8 lines for data, and this version is known as the 16-bit ISA slot. This slot runs at 8.33 MHz and has 24 lines for the address bus. All operating systems for personal computers today support the 16-bit ISA slot although its use is diminishing in favor of faster I/O buses. You can see three ISA slots in Figure 2-8. An 8-bit expansion card, as shown in the figure, can use the first part of the 16-bit slot.
- The **PCI (Peripheral Component Interconnect) bus** was invented for devices that are faster than the 16-bit ISA bus but can't run as fast as the system bus between memory and the CPU. The PCI bus runs in sync with the system bus at one-third or one-half the speed. All Windows OSs support PCI.

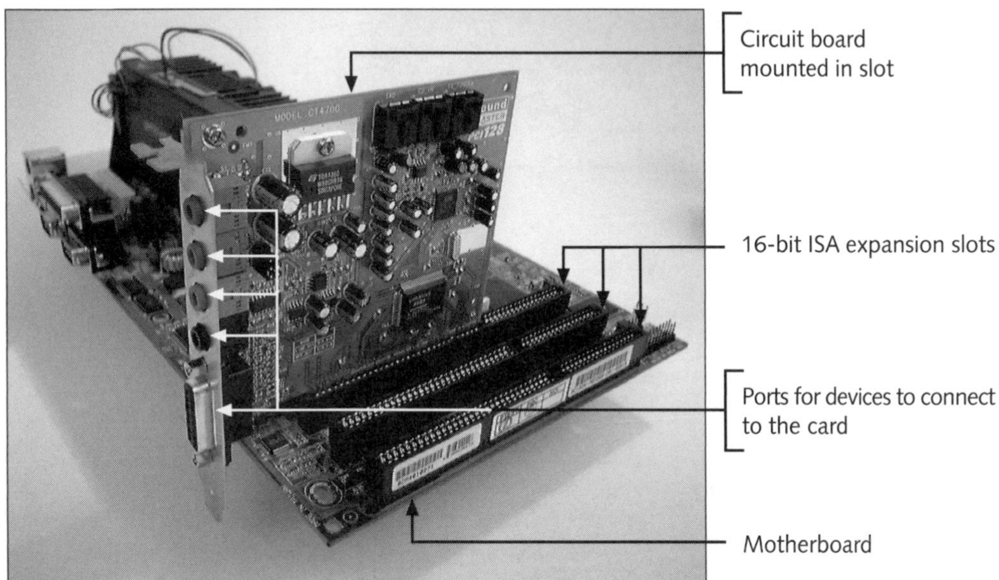

Figure 2-8 This 8-bit ISA sound card is mounted in the 8-bit part of a 16-bit ISA slot on a motherboard

- The **AGP (Accelerated Graphics Port) bus** was designed to accommodate a fast video card, which is a circuit board that controls the monitor. Windows 98 and Windows 2000/XP support AGP. A motherboard will only have a single AGP slot to accommodate one monitor.
- The USB is designed to provide ports off the motherboard for slower external devices such as a mouse, keyboard, scanner, video camera, or digital telephone. You saw two USB ports on the back of a computer case in Figure 2-5. The USB bus supports up to 127 devices, which can be daisy chained together and connected to a single USB port on a motherboard. Windows 95 with the USB update, Windows 98/Me, and Windows 2000/XP support USB.
- FireWire, sometimes called IEEE 1394 or simply 1394, is a very fast bus designed to connect fast external devices to a port off the motherboard called a FireWire or 1394 port. The bus was designed by the Institute of Electrical and Electronic Engineers (IEEE), led primarily by Apple Computer, which named the bus FireWire. Windows 98/Me and Windows NT/2000/XP support FireWire.

A+ OS 1.1 1.5

Device Manager under Windows 9x and Windows 2000/XP (Windows NT does not have a Device Manager) is the primary tool used to manage bus resources and the devices that use them. To access Device Manager using Windows 9x, right-click the My Computer icon on the desktop, select Properties from the shortcut menu, and click on the Device Manager tab. (For Windows 2000, from the System Properties window, click on the Hardware tab, and then click Device Manager.) The Device Manager tab of the System Properties window for Windows 98 is shown in Figure 2-9. You can see two PCI devices, a modem and a network card, and the AGP video card listed in the window. Also showing is the USB controller.

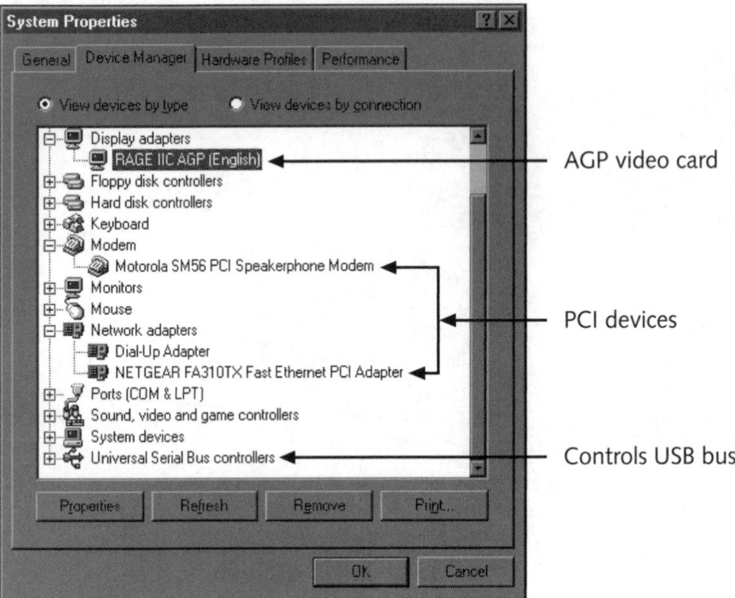

Figure 2-9 Device Manager will usually tell you what bus a device is using, in the device name

System Resources on the Motherboard

Just as a chauffeur has resources or tools to control a car (such as controls on the console) and the car has resources to alert the chauffeur that it needs attention (such as the oil warning light), software has resources to control hardware and hardware has resources to alert software that it needs attention. Think of a system resource as a tool used by either hardware or software to communicate with the other.

There are four types of system resources: memory addresses, I/O addresses, interrupt request numbers (IRQs), and direct memory access (DMA) channels. Table 2-1 lists these system resources used by software and hardware and defines each.

As you can see from Table 2-1, all four resources are used for communication between hardware and software. Hardware devices signal the CPU for attention using an IRQ. The OS addresses a device by one of its I/O addresses. The OS looks at memory as a hardware device and addresses it with memory addresses, and DMA channels are used to pass data back and forth between a hardware device and memory. As you read about these system resources, you might be interested in examining your own computer to see how the system resources are used. To do that, for Windows 98, go to Device Manager, select Computer, and then click Properties. The Computer Properties window displays. For Windows 2000, go to Device Manager and, from the menu, click View, Resources by type (see Figure 2-10).

Table 2-1 System resources used by software and hardware

System Resource	Purpose
Memory addresses	Numbers that are assigned to physical memory located either in RAM or ROM chips. Software can access this memory by using these addresses. On the motherboard, memory addresses are transferred on the address bus.
IRQ	A control line of a motherboard bus that a hardware device can use to signal the CPU that the device needs attention. Some lines have a higher priority for attention than others. Each IRQ line is assigned a number (0 to 15) to identify it.
I/O addresses	Numbers assigned to hardware devices that software uses to command a device. Each device "listens" for these numbers and responds to the ones assigned to it. On the motherboard, I/O addresses are transferred on the same address lines used by memory addresses.
DMA channel	A number designating a channel through which the device can pass data to memory without involving the CPU. Think of a DMA channel as a shortcut for data moving to/from the device and memory. Physically, DMA channels are lines on the motherboard.

Working from a command prompt, you can view system resources using the MSD utility. You will learn how to do that in a hands-on project at the end of this chapter.

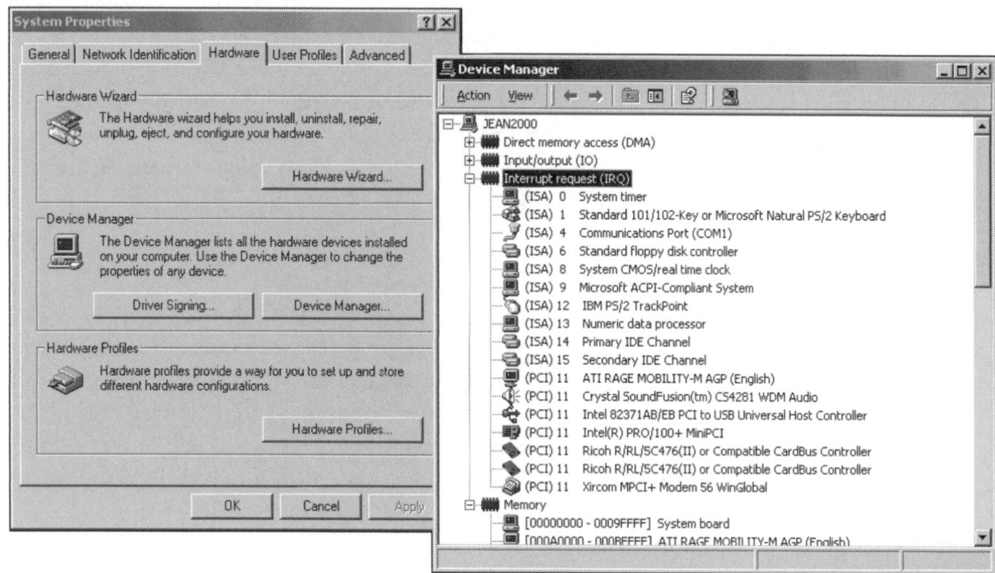

Figure 2-10 Windows 2000 Device Manager shows the current assignments for system resources

Interrupt Request Number (IRQ)

When a hardware device needs the CPU to do something, such as when the keyboard needs the CPU to process a keystroke after a key has been pressed, the device needs a way to get the CPU's attention and the CPU must know what to do once its attention is turned to the device. These interruptions to the CPU are called **hardware interrupts**, in which the device initiates an interrupt by placing voltage on the designated IRQ line assigned to it, somewhat like a passenger on a trolley car pulls a cord to signal the driver to stop the trolley. This voltage on the line serves as a signal to the CPU that the device has a request that needs processing. Often, a hardware device that needs attention from the CPU is referred to as "needing servicing." Many processes that the CPU carries out are initiated by interrupts and are said to be "interrupt-driven." Later in this chapter you will see how software can also issue an interrupt to the CPU so that the software can have access to a device.

Notice in Figure 2-10 that IRQ 11 is being shared by several devices on this Windows 2000 system. You can look to the left of the IRQ number and see that some of these IRQs are being managed by the ISA bus controller, and the others are managed by the PCI bus controller. ISA-managed IRQs cannot be shared, but PCI-managed IRQs can be shared. Also notice that IRQ 15 is used by the secondary IDE channel, and IRQ 14 is used by the primary IDE channel. IDE channels are used to connect hard drives, CD-ROM drives, Zip drives, and DVD drives to the motherboard. You'll learn more about IDE later in the chapter.

With interrupts, the hardware device or the software initiates communication by sending a signal to the CPU, but a device can be serviced in another way, called polling. With **polling**, software is constantly running that has the CPU periodically check the hardware device to see if service is needed. Not very many devices use polling as the method of communication; most hardware devices use interrupts. A joystick is one example of a device that does use polling. Software that is written to manage a joystick has the CPU check the joystick periodically to see if the device has data to communicate, which is why a joystick does not need an IRQ to work.

I/O Addresses

Another system resource that is made available to hardware devices is input/output addresses, or I/O addresses. **I/O addresses**, or **port addresses**, sometimes simply called **ports**, are numbers that the CPU can use to access hardware devices, in much the same way it uses memory addresses to access physical memory. The address bus on the motherboard sometimes carries memory addresses and sometimes carries I/O addresses. If the address bus has been set to carry I/O addresses, then each device is "listening" to this bus. See Figure 2-11. If the address belongs to it, then it responds; otherwise it ignores the request for information. In short, the CPU "knows" a hardware device as a group of I/O addresses. If it wants to know the status of a printer or a floppy drive, for example, it passes a particular I/O address down the address bus on the motherboard.

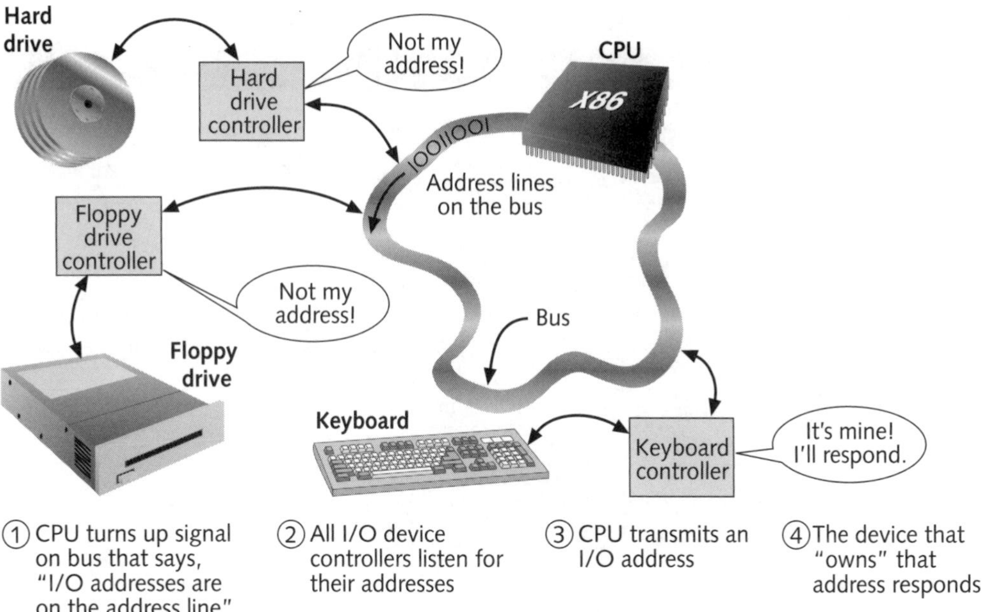

Figure 2-11 I/O address lines on a bus work much like an old telephone party line; all devices "hear" the addresses, but only one responds

A few common assignments for I/O addresses are listed in Table 2-2. Because IBM made many address assignments when the first PC was manufactured in the late 1970s, common devices such as a hard drive, a floppy drive, or a keyboard have no problem with I/O addresses. Their controllers can simply be programmed to use these standard addresses. Devices such as scanners or network cards that were not assigned I/O addresses in the original IBM list can be configured to use more than one group of addresses, depending on how they are set up during either the installation process or during the boot process. **Booting** is the process a computer goes through when it is first turned on. Figure 2-12 shows how I/O addresses are assigned on a Windows 98 computer.

COM and LPT Assignments

In Table 2-2, notice the COM and LPT assignments. COM1 and COM2 are preconfigured assignments that can be made to serial devices such as modems, and LPT1 and LPT2 are preconfigured assignments that can be made to parallel devices such as printers. For example, rather than assigning an IRQ and some I/O addresses to a modem, the modem is configured to use the assignments previously made to COM2, making it easier to configure the modem and to avoid conflicts with other devices that also need an IRQ and some I/O addresses.

Table 2-2 IRQs and I/O addresses for devices

IRQ	I/O Address	Device
0	0040-005F	System timer
1	0060-006F	Keyboard controller
2	00A0-00AF	Access to IRQs above 7
3	02F8-02FF	COM2
3	02E8-02EF	COM4
4	03F8-03FF	COM1
4	03E8-03EF	COM3
5	0278-027F	Sound card or parallel port LPT2
6	03F0-03F7	Floppy drive controller
7	0378-037F	Printer parallel port LPT1
8	0070-007F	Real-time clock
9-10		Available
11		SCSI or available (SCSI is a bus system often used for fast hard drives)
12	238-23F	System-board mouse
13	0F8-0FF	Math coprocessor
14	1F0-1F7	IDE hard drive
15	170-170	Secondary IDE hard drive or available

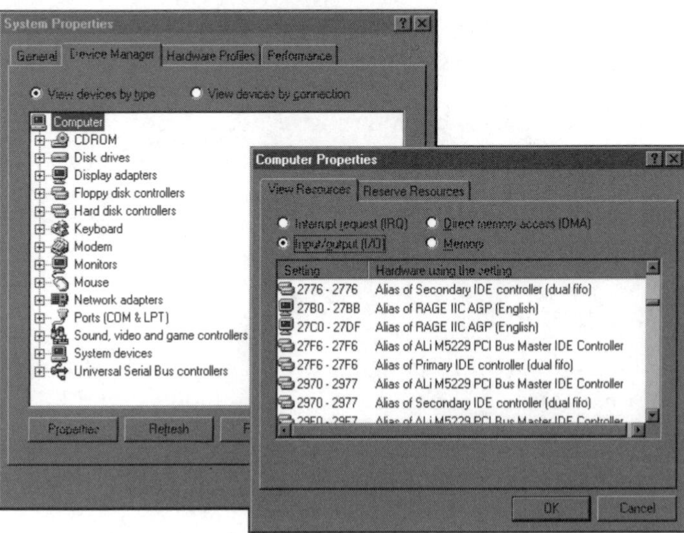

Figure 2-12 Use Device Manager to view I/O address assignments on a Windows 98 PC

It is common for a system to assign COM1 or COM2 to a serial port and LPT1 or LPT2 to a parallel port, which you saw in Figure 2-5. When an external modem connects to a serial port that has been assigned COM1, the modem is using the system resources assigned to COM1. If a printer is connected to the parallel port assigned to LPT1, it is using the system resources assigned to LPT1. You will learn more about COM and LPT assignments in later chapters.

Memory Addresses

An operating system relates to memory as a long list of cells that it can use to hold data and instructions, somewhat like a one-dimensional spreadsheet. Each memory location or cell is assigned a number beginning with zero. These number assignments are made when the OS is first loaded and are called memory addresses. Think of a memory address as a seat number in a theatre (see Figure 2-13). Each seat is assigned a number regardless if it has someone sitting in it. The person sitting in a seat can be data or instructions, and the OS does not refer to the person by name but only by the seat number. For example, the OS might say, "I want to print the data in memory addresses 500 through 650."

These addresses are most often displayed on the screen as hexadecimal (base 16 or hex) numbers in segment/offset form (for example, C800:5, which in decimal is 819,205). Let's first look at how memory addresses are assigned, and then we'll turn our attention to how the CPU makes use of them.

Figure 2-13 Memory addresses are assigned to each location in memory and these locations can store data or instructions

See Appendix C for more information on the hexadecimal number system and how it applies to memory addresses.

How Memory Addresses Are Assigned Remember that the CPU uses lines coming to and from it to receive and send data. It has another group of lines called the address bus that is uses to send and receive the memory addresses that it uses to access memory. For example, if it wants to read the data in memory address 819,205, it must send the value 819,205 to memory to say to memory, "Send me the data stored in cell 819,205." It does this by sending the binary value for 819,205 on the address bus, which is 11001000000000000101. Each line on the address bus must hold one of the bits for this number. In this case, 20 lines are required. Therefore, the largest memory address the CPU can use is limited by the number of lines on the motherboard devoted to the address bus.

Windows offers a calculator that can quickly convert numbers in binary, digital, and hexadecimal. You can use it to follow along with the conversions used here. Enter a number in one number system, and then click another number system to make the conversion. To access the calculator in Windows 9x or Windows NT/2000/XP, click Start, Programs, Accessories, Calculator.

Early CPUs had only 20 lines on the bus available to them to handle addresses, so the largest memory address the CPU could use was 11111111111111111111, which is 1,048,575 or 1,024K or 1 MB of memory. This 1 MB of memory was used by DOS and divided up according to the scheme shown in Table 2-3.

Table 2-3 Division of memory under DOS

Range of Memory Addresses	Range Using Hex Terminology	Type of Memory
0 to 640K	0 to A0000	Conventional or base memory
640K to 1024K	A0000 to FFFFF	Upper memory (A through F ranges)
Above 1024K	100000 and up	Extended memory

The first 640K of memory was used by DOS and applications, and the addresses from 640K up to 1024K were used by the BIOS and device drivers, which are discussed later in the chapter. Then newer CPUs and motherboards were developed with 24 address lines and more so that memory addresses above 1024K became available, and were called **extended memory**. Windows 9x still uses these same divisions of memory although it makes the most use of extended memory. Memory addresses are expressed using hexadecimal notation. Because the hex numbers in upper memory begin with A through F, the divisions of upper memory are often referred to as the A range, B range, C range, and so on, up to the F range.

Table 2-3 applies to DOS and Windows 9x only. Windows NT/2000/XP uses an altogether different memory-mapping design, in which there is no conventional, upper, or extended memory; it's all just memory.

Using Windows 9x Device Manager, you can see how the first 1 MB of memory addresses are assigned (see Figure 2-14). To view the list, select Computer and click Properties, then click Memory. Notice in the figure that the system BIOS has been assigned memory addresses in the F range of upper memory. This F range is always reserved for motherboard BIOS and is never requested by other programs. When the CPU is first turned on and needs a program to know how to boot up, it begins with the instructions stored on the ROM BIOS chip that are assigned to these memory addresses.

How Memory Addresses Are Used Once memory addresses have been assigned to memory, they can be used for communication with all software layers. As you saw in Figure 2-2, BIOS, device drivers, the OS, and application software are working when a computer is running. During output operations, application software must pass information to the OS, which in turn passes that information to a device driver or to the BIOS. The BIOS and device drivers managing input devices must pass information to the OS, which passes it to the application software. These layers of software all identify the data they want to share by referring to the memory address of the data (see Figure 2-15).

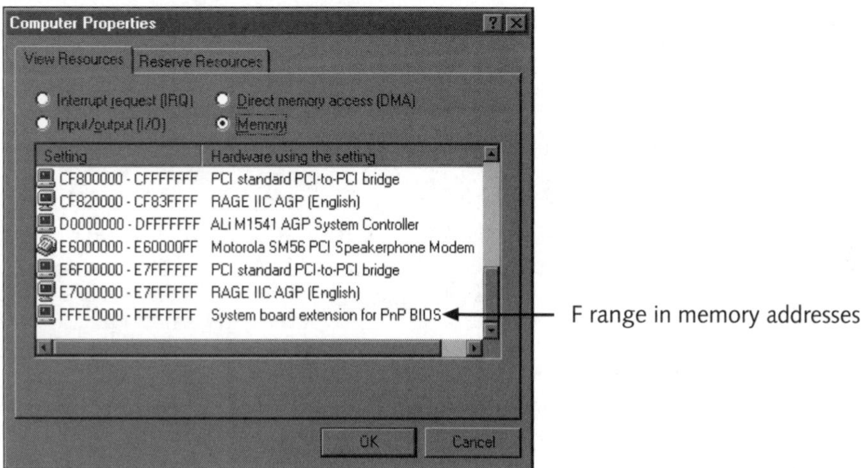

Figure 2-14 Computer Properties window shows how the first megabyte of memory addresses are assigned

Direct Memory Access (DMA) Channels

Another system resource used by hardware and software is a **DMA (direct memory access) channel**, a shortcut method whereby an I/O device can send data directly to memory, bypassing the CPU. Some devices, such as a hard drive or sound card, are designed to use DMA channels, and others, such as the mouse, are not. Those that use the channels might be able to use only a certain channel, say channel 3, and no other. Alternately, the BIOS might have the option of changing a DMA channel number to avoid conflicts with other devices. Conflicts occur when more than one device uses the same channel. DMA channels are not as popular as they once were because their design makes them slower than newer methods. However, slower devices such as floppy drives, sound cards, and tape drives may still use DMA channels.

Figure 2-15 Applications, the OS, and drivers pass data among them by communicating the address of memory holding the data

Using Device Manager, Figure 2-16 shows the current DMA assignments for this Windows 98 system. Notice that DMA1 is used by a sound card, and a floppy drive is using DMA2. DMA3 is available for a printer, and DMA4 is designated for access by the DMA controller for the higher DMA channels.

Using System Resources

Now let's look at examples of how the system resources help carry out hardware and software interrupts. This will help show you how the resources work together.

Hardware Interrupts Once the CPU is interrupted by an IRQ, the job of the IRQ is over and the CPU must handle the interruption. To do that, the CPU must use a program designed to interface with the device. This program to process an interrupt is called the **request handler** or **interrupt handler**. The program is either a part of the total BIOS in a system or is a device driver that had previously been installed on the hard drive.

To see how the process of handling an interrupt works, we'll use the example of a keyboard that uses an IRQ to request attention from the CPU. Figure 2-17 shows the process it uses, which works like this:

Step 1. A key is pressed on the keyboard. The keyboard controller puts voltage on its assigned IRQ 1 to the CPU, saying, "I need attention." The CPU sees the IRQ, acknowledges it, and turns its attention to servicing it. By sending the acknowledgment, it is requesting that the device controller send a number called an interrupt (abbreviated INT) that tells the CPU what service the device needs.

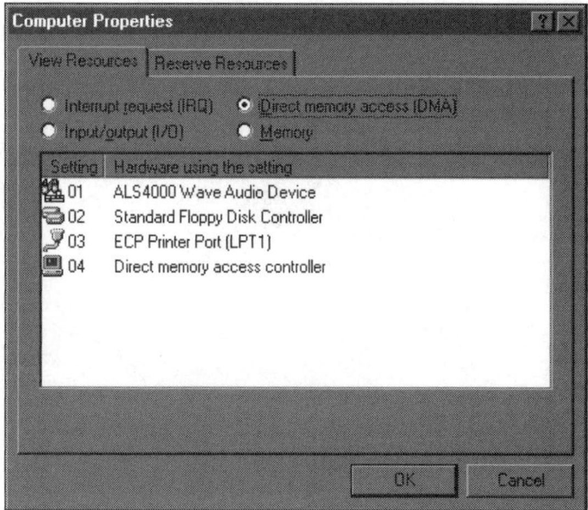

Figure 2-16 How DMA channels are currently assigned on this Windows 98 system

Step 2. The keyboard controller sends INT 9 to the CPU, saying that it has a pressed key to process. The CPU uses this value to locate the program to handle this interrupt.

Step 3. The CPU looks to a table in RAM called the **interrupt vector table**, or **vector table**, that contains a list of memory address locations of interrupt handlers. The INT value passed to the CPU by the controller points to the correct row in the table where the memory addresses in which the instructions to service the keyboard (a portion of system BIOS) are stored.

Step 4. The CPU looks to the location in memory of the request handler and begins to follow the instructions there.

Step 5. The CPU, following the interrupt handler instructions, processes the keystroke.

The BIOS and operating system initialize the interrupt vector table during booting, but later another program can modify the vector table to change the interrupt handler location to execute another program instead. This is a common method that a virus uses to propagate itself.

Software Interrupts In the hardware interrupt example, two of the four system resources were used (memory addresses and an IRQ). The keyboard controller used an IRQ to initiate communication. When the software initiates communication, such as when the user of word-processing software gives the command to save a file to the hard drive, this is known as a **software interrupt**, which is demonstrated in Figure 2-18. Both hardware and software interrupts use the same numeric INT (interrupt) values to communicate their requests to the CPU. The interrupt value for a call to the hard drive for I/O interaction is INT 13.

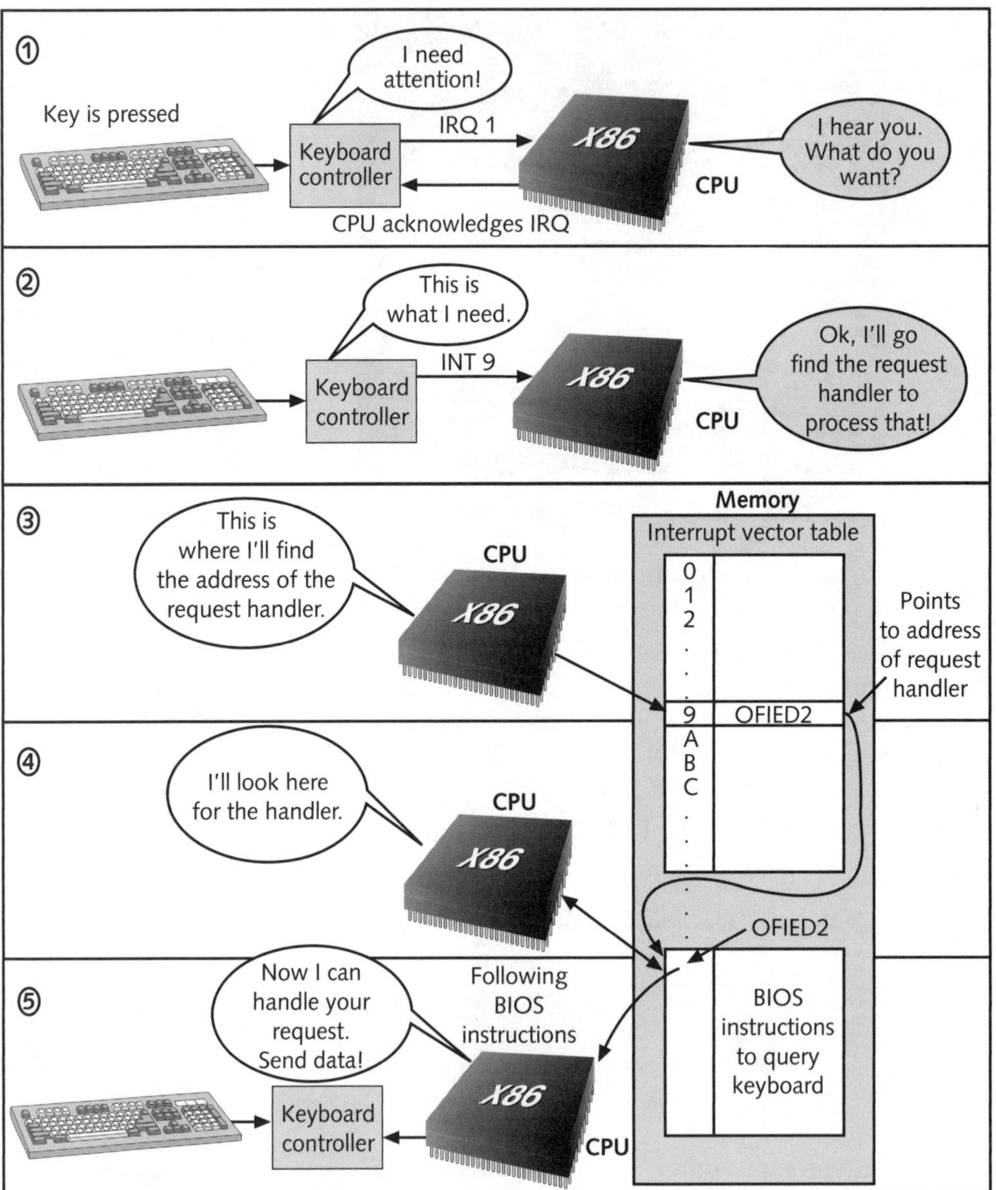

Figure 2-17 The story of a hardware interrupt, where the request handler is BIOS

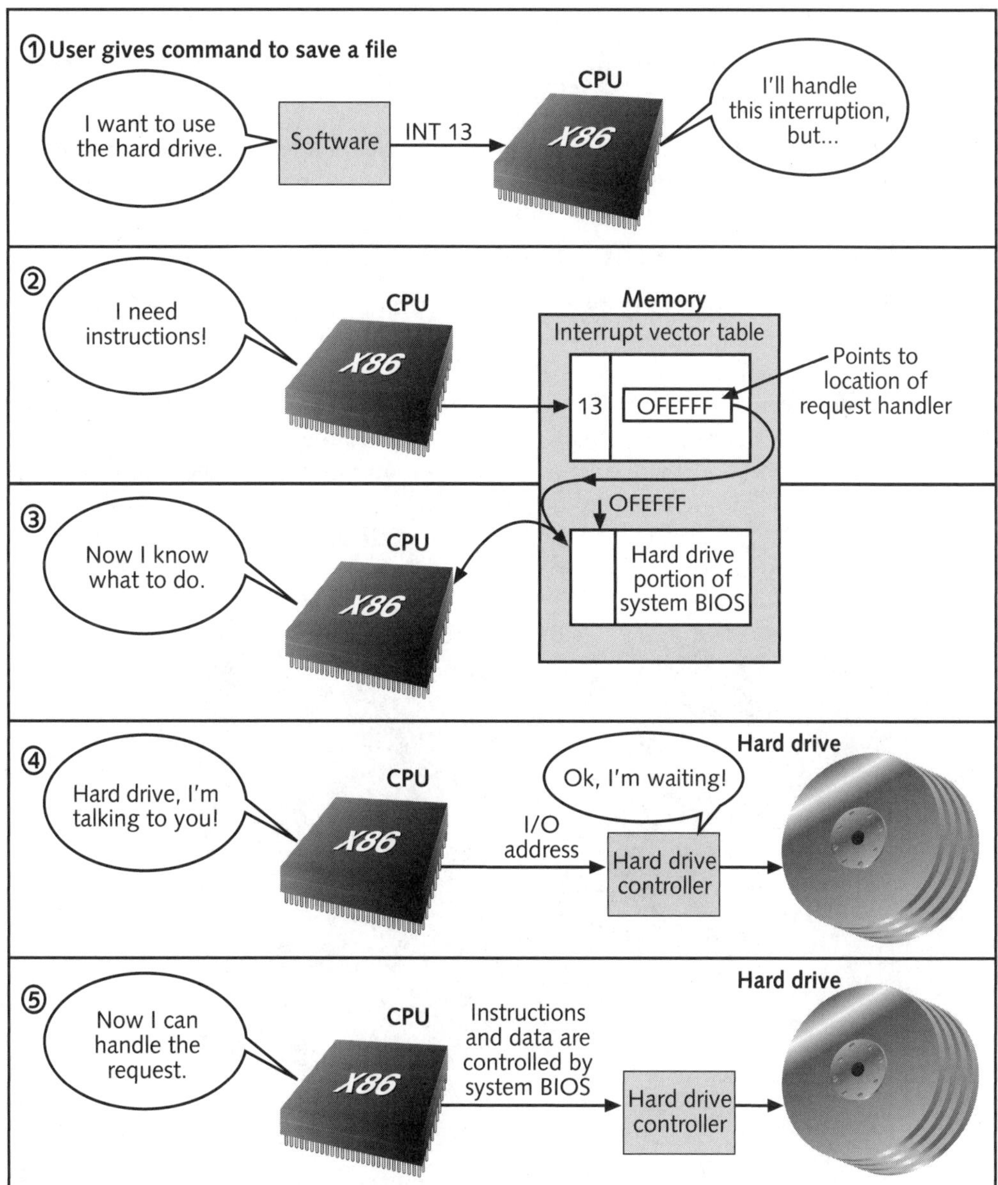

Figure 2-18 The story of a software interrupt

The software interrupt process as shown in Figure 2-18 works like this:

Step 1. The CPU receives the software interrupt, INT 13.

Step 2. The CPU turns to the interrupt vector table, using the INT value to locate the correct request handler.

Step 3. Next, the CPU locates the handler in memory.

Step 4. The CPU alerts the hard drive that instructions are forthcoming by sending one of the hard drive's I/O addresses over the address bus.

Step 5. The CPU follows the instructions of the request handler, in this case, system BIOS, to manage the hard drive.

BIOS on the Motherboard and Other Circuit Boards

A+ OS 2.4

The BIOS is a hybrid of two worlds. It's technically both hardware and software; it's the intersection point of the two and must communicate with both, as shown in Figure 2-2. Because this software is permanently stored on a microchip, it is called **firmware**, and the chip is called a ROM (read-only memory) BIOS chip. The motherboard and other hardware devices contain ROM BIOS chips. The motherboard contains a vital ROM BIOS chip (Figure 2-19) that contains the programming necessary to start the computer, called **startup BIOS**, and other fundamental BIOS programs to control I/O devices such as the floppy disk drive and keyboard (called system BIOS). In addition, some complex hardware devices contain BIOS software embedded directly on the card.

Figure 2-19 The ROM BIOS chip on the motherboard contains the programming to start up the PC as well as perform many other fundamental tasks

Advanced Configuration and Power Interface (ACPI)

Some BIOSs on the motherboard and operating systems support a power saving feature using the standards developed by Intel, Microsoft, and Toshiba, called the Advanced Configuration and Power Interface (ACPI) standards. Using ACPI, a system can be powered up by an external device such as a keyboard. Windows 9x and Windows 2000 support

A+ OS 2.4

ACPI, as do most newer motherboard BIOS. Microsoft calls an ACPI-compliant BIOS a "good" BIOS. To see if your BIOS is ACPI compliant, check this Microsoft URL:

www.microsoft.com/windows2000/professional/howtobuy/upgrading/compat

Plug and Play

Another feature of both the BIOS and the OS is **Plug and Play (PnP)**, a standard designed to make the installation of new hardware devices easier. If the BIOS is a Plug and Play BIOS, it will begin the process of configuring hardware devices in the system. It gathers information about the devices and then passes that information to the operating system. If the operating system is also Plug and Play compliant, it will use that information to complete the hardware configuration process. For a system to be fully Plug and Play, the BIOS, the operating system and all devices must be Plug and Play.

Windows 9x and Windows 2000/XP support Plug and Play, but Windows NT does not. However, Windows 2000/XP Plug and Play is more advanced than the Windows 9x version and does not use the startup BIOS to help with Plug and Play configurations. Therefore, on a Windows 2000/XP system, it is not important if the motherboard BIOS is Plug and Play.

The Plug and Play standard applies to the operating system, to BIOS on the motherboard and to BIOS on devices. Plug and Play under Windows or the motherboard BIOS does not assign resources to a device if the device does not allow it. For example, if a legacy sound card requires a certain group of upper memory addresses that are hard-coded into its on-board BIOS, there's nothing that Plug and Play can do about that. (Hard-coded is computer jargon for something being coded so that it cannot be changed.) Plug and Play simply tries to work around the problem as best it can. If two non-Plug and Play hardware devices require the same resource and their BIOS does not provide for accepting a substitute, these two devices cannot coexist on the same PC.

Newer devices that contain BIOS that is Plug and Play compliant are more cooperative. At startup, they simply send a request and then wait for the OS to assign the resources they need to work. Startup BIOS that is Plug and Play does some of the up-front work for Windows 9x, but Windows 2000 does all its Plug and Play configuration without the help of BIOS. How Windows 9x and BIOS cooperate to use Plug and Play during startup is covered later in the chapter.

A Plug and Play hardware device will have something like Windows 9x Ready or Windows 9x Compliant written on the box.

ESCD (extended system configuration data) Plug and Play BIOS is an enhanced version of Plug and Play that creates a list of all the things you have done manually to the configuration that Plug and Play does not do on its own. This ESCD list is written to the BIOS chip so that the next time you boot, the startup BIOS can faithfully relay that information

A+ OS 2.4 to Windows 9x. The BIOS chip for ESCD BIOS is a special RAM chip called Permanent RAM, or PRAM, that can hold data written to it without the benefit of a battery, which the CMOS setup chip requires.

CMOS Setup Chip

Another chip on the motherboard, called the **CMOS configuration chip**, **CMOS setup chip**, or **CMOS RAM chip**, contains a very small amount of memory, or RAM, enough to hold configuration or setup information about the computer. This chip is responsible for remembering the current date and time, which hard drives and floppy drives are present, how the serial and parallel ports are configured, and so forth. When the computer is first turned on, it looks to this CMOS chip to find out what hardware it should expect to find. The CMOS chip is powered by a trickle of electricity from a small battery located on the motherboard or computer case, usually close to the CMOS chip itself so that, when the computer is turned off, the CMOS chip still retains its data.

The program to change CMOS setup is stored in the ROM BIOS chip and can be accessed during the startup process. The keystrokes to enter CMOS setup are displayed somewhere on the screen during startup in a statement such as "Press the Del key to enter setup." Different BIOSs use different keystrokes. The CMOS setup does not normally need to be changed except when there is a problem with hardware, a new floppy drive is installed, or a power-saving feature needs to be disabled or enabled. The CMOS setup can also hold a power-on password to help secure a system. Know that this password is not the same password that can be required by a Windows OS at startup.

Hard Drives and Other Secondary Storage Devices

A hard drive is an example of a **secondary storage** device, which is a device that can hold data and instructions, but the data and instructions can only be stored there and not processed there by the CPU. Before the instructions can be processed, they must be copied from a secondary storage device to a **primary storage** device, which is memory. In other words, you store files that contain data and programs on a hard drive, but to use these data and programs, they must be copied into memory. You'll learn more about this process later in the chapter.

Another difference between secondary and primary storage devices is that secondary devices hold data permanently, and primary devices hold data temporarily. What is stored on your hard drive remains there even when the PC is turned off, but what is stored in memory is lost as soon as you turn off your PC. The most common secondary storage devices are hard drives, floppy disk drives, CD-ROM drives, DVD drives, and Zip drives. Figure 2-20 shows a hard drive subsystem.

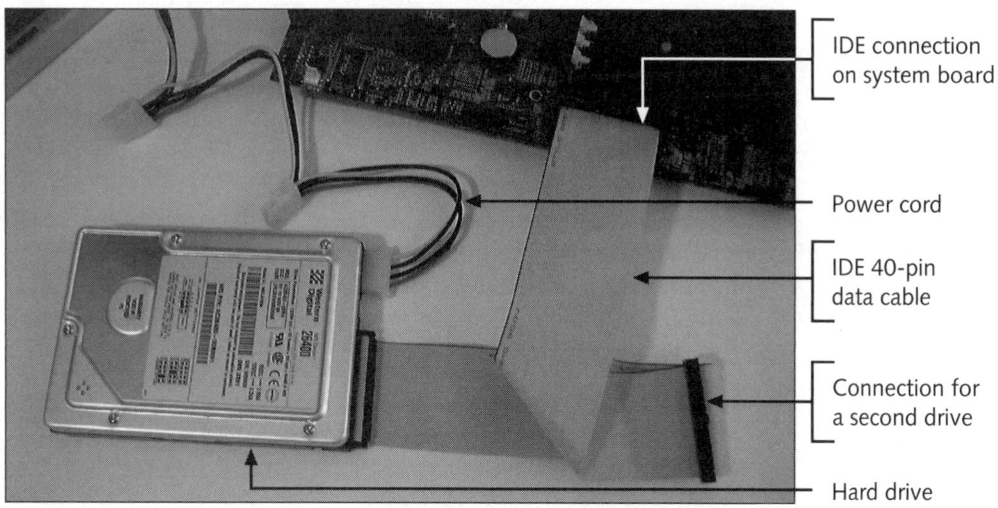

Figure 2-20 A PC's hard drive subsystem

Most motherboards offer two **EIDE (Enhanced Integrated Drive Electronics)** connections. **IDE (Integrated Drive Electronics)** is a group of standards that governs how a hard drive works, and EIDE is a group of standards that govern how a secondary storage device such as a hard drive, CD-ROM drive, or Zip drive can interface with a system. In the industry, we most often use the term IDE for both IDE and EIDE. The connections for the two IDE channels on the motherboard are called the primary and secondary channels. Each cable or channel can accommodate two IDE devices, such as a hard drive and a CD-ROM drive, for a total of four IDE devices in one system. Power to the hard drive comes through a power cable from the PC's power supply.

A+ OS 1.1

The operating system is responsible for storing the files and folders on a secondary storage device such as a hard drive, using organizational methods called a **file system**. Windows uses several different file systems, all of which are discussed in later chapters. The most common file system for hard drives is the FAT file system.

Regardless of the file system used, every OS manages a hard drive by using directories (Windows calls these folders), subdirectories, and files. A **directory table** is a list of files and subdirectories. When a hard drive is first installed and formatted, there is a single directory table on the drive called the **root directory**. For logical drive C, the root directory is written as C:\.

A physical hard drive can be divided into logical drives, sometimes called volumes. You will learn more about logical drives and volumes in Chapter 7.

A+ OS 1.1 1.4 This root directory can hold files or other directories as shown in Figure 2-21, which can have names such as C:\Tools. These directories called **subdirectories**, **child directories**, or **folders**, can, in turn, have other directories listed in them. Any directory can have files and/or other directories listed in it, for example, C:\wp\data\myfile.txt in Figure 2-21. The C: identifies the drive. If the directory had been on a floppy disk, it would have been either A: or B:. When you write the drive and directories pointing to the location of the file as in this example, the drive and directories are called the **path** to the file. The first part of the file before the period is called the **filename** (myfile), and the part after the period is called the **file extension** (txt), which, for Windows and DOS, always has three characters or fewer. The file extension identifies the type file, such as .doc for Microsoft Word document files or .xls for Microsoft Excel spreadsheet files.

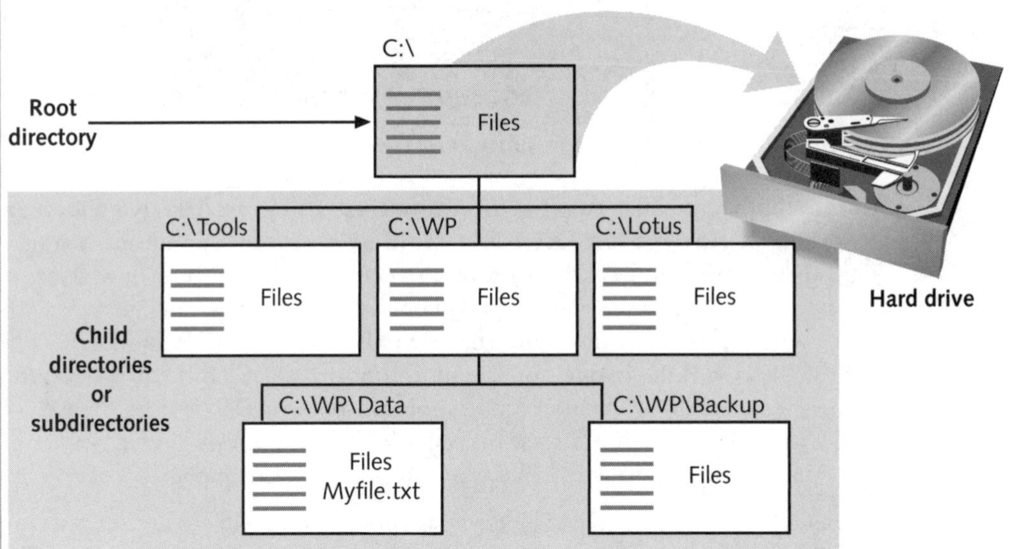

Figure 2-21 A hard drive is organized into groups of files stored in directories. The first directory is called the root directory. All directories can have sub- or child directories. Under Windows, a directory is called a folder.

A+ OS 1.4 File Naming Conventions

Because Windows 9x is built on a DOS core, you need to understand how to name files under DOS. Under DOS, a filename can contain up to eight characters and the file extension can contain up to three characters, which are separated by a period, like this: *filename.ext.* Characters used can be the letters a through z, the numbers 0 through 9, or the following characters: _, ^, $, ~, !, #, %, &, - {, } , (,), @, ‘, `. Be sure to not use a space, period, *, ?, or \ in a filename or file extension. Acceptable file extensions for program files are .com, .sys, .bat, and .exe. A **program file** contains a list of instructions for the OS to follow. For example, the DOS utility program to display information about the system is Msd.exe.

A+ OS 1.4

Under Windows 95 and later Windows OSs, filenames can be as long as 255 characters and may contain spaces. Before Windows 95, these long filenames were used only by the Macintosh OS. When using long filenames in Windows 9x, remember that the DOS portion of the system can only understand eight-character file names with three-character extensions. When the DOS part of the system is operating, it will truncate long filenames and assign new eight-character ones. Windows NT/2000/XP has no DOS core and therefore does a better job of managing long filenames.

File Organization

By creating different directories on a hard drive, you can organize your program files and data files by placing programs in one directory and files created by those programs in a second directory. This organization is comparable to keeping paper records in separate folders. You can also organize files on other secondary storage media such as floppy disks or Zip drives.

When representing directories, Windows uses a backslash, like this: C:\Tools. However, Unix uses a forward slash to represent directories. The root directory in Unix is written / and subdirectories are written as /etc or /bin. Also, Windows does not care if directory names and filenames are uppercase or lowercase, but Unix is case sensitive: /Bin is a different directory than /bin.

The FAT File System

The FAT (file allocation table) file system, introduced in Chapter 1, is based on a table that is a very long list of all the entries on a hard drive that can hold data. Two FAT file systems used by Windows for hard drives are FAT16 and FAT32. The 16 or 32 stands for the size of each number in the table—16 bits or 32 bits, although, for FAT32, only 28 of them are used to hold a number. There is one entry in the FAT for each cluster on the hard drive. A cluster is the smallest unit of space on the hard drive used to hold data that is addressed by the OS. An OS puts files on the hard drive in increments of whole clusters. All clusters on a hard drive are assigned a single number, beginning with zero. The OS identifies a cluster by this cluster number and knows how many bytes or characters of data a cluster can hold. All clusters on a logical drive hold the same number of bytes.

Figure 2-22 shows that the OS relates to the hard drive by using the two tables, the FAT and the directory table. A logical drive such as drive C has only one FAT, but can have several directory tables, one for each subdirectory on the drive. The directory table tells the OS the name of a file and the first cluster number for that file. All the other cluster numbers for the file are kept in the FAT. For example, suppose a file named Mydata.txt begins at cluster 5 and requires three clusters to hold the file. The OS reads the file using the following steps. The first three are numbered in Figure 2-22:

A+ OS 1.2

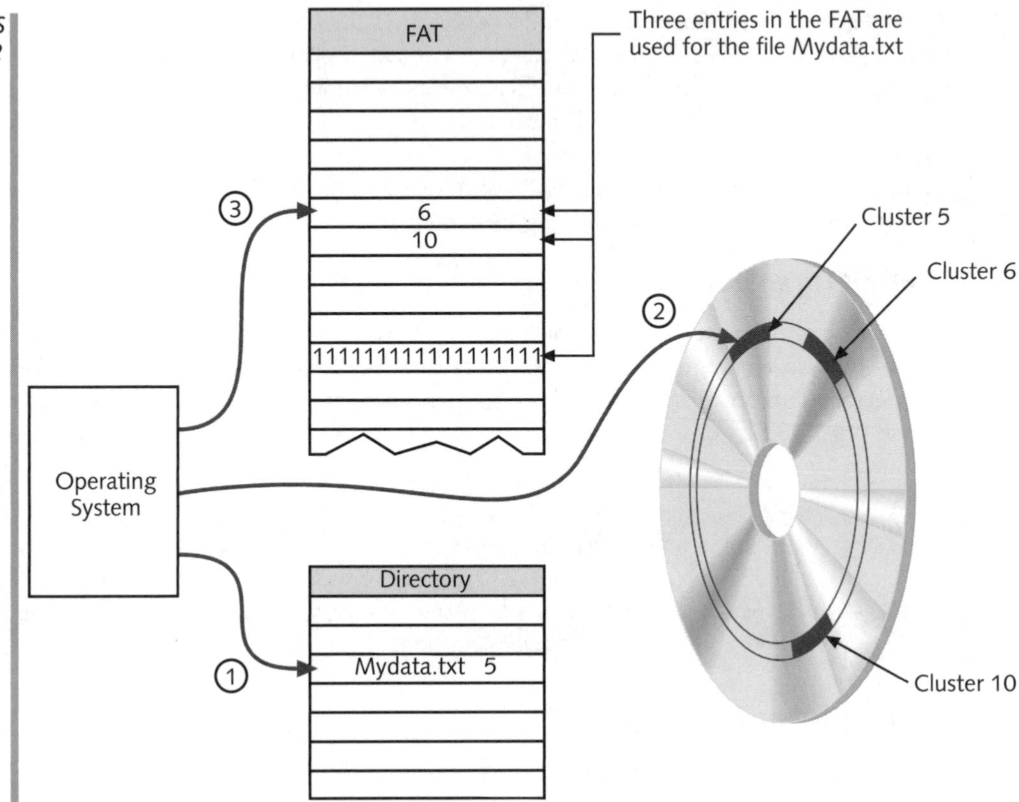

Figure 2-22 How an OS reads a file from the hard drive

1. The OS goes to the directory and reads the name of the file (Mydata.txt) and the first cluster number (5).
2. The OS retrieves the contents of cluster 5 on the hard drive which is the first segment of the file.
3. The OS turns to the FAT and looks at the fifth position in the FAT and reads 6 which says the next segment of the file is in cluster 6.
4. It retrieves the second segment of the file from cluster 6 on the hard drive.
5. The OS turns to the sixth position in the FAT and reads 10, which says the next segment of the file is in cluster 10.
6. It retrieves the third segment of the file from cluster 10 on the hard drive.
7. The OS turns to the 10th position in the FAT and reads all 1s in the FAT entry, which says this is the last cluster in the file. (If the FAT is FAT16, then an entry of 16 ones is written in the FAT. If it is FAT32, then an entry of 28 ones is written.)

There are other organizational tables and entries that an OS uses to manage a hard drive besides the FAT and directory tables. You will learn about them in the next chapter.

How an OS Relates to Other Software

Now that you have learned about several of the more important hardware devices and how system resources on the motherboard are used to enable their interaction with software, we turn our attention to the OS and how it interfaces with other software, including BIOS, device drivers, and applications. Because the CPU operates in two modes, real mode and protected mode, the OS must be able to operate in each mode, which also affects the mode that an application uses. Therefore, we begin our discussion of software by looking more carefully at each of these modes.

Real (16-Bit) and Protected (32-Bit) Operating Modes

Remember that the two modes a CPU can operate in are real mode (sometimes called 16-bit mode) and protected mode (sometimes called 32-bit mode). There are several differences between real mode and protected mode which are discussed in this section, but the fundamental difference is that in real mode, a CPU processes 16 bits at a time and in protected mode, it processes 32 bits at a time.

In real mode, illustrated in Figure 2-23, a CPU assumes that only one application or program is running at a time, which is called single tasking, so it gives that program direct access to all hardware devices including memory. It uses a 16-bit data path and 1 MB of memory addresses, unless a **memory extender** is used, which is an OS utility program that provides an OS with memory addresses above 1 MB, called extended memory. The DOS and Windows 9x memory extender is Himem.sys, which you will learn to use in the next chapter.

Real mode is limited to 16-bit data processing because originally only 16 lines on the motherboard bus were devoted to transmitting data to and from the CPU.

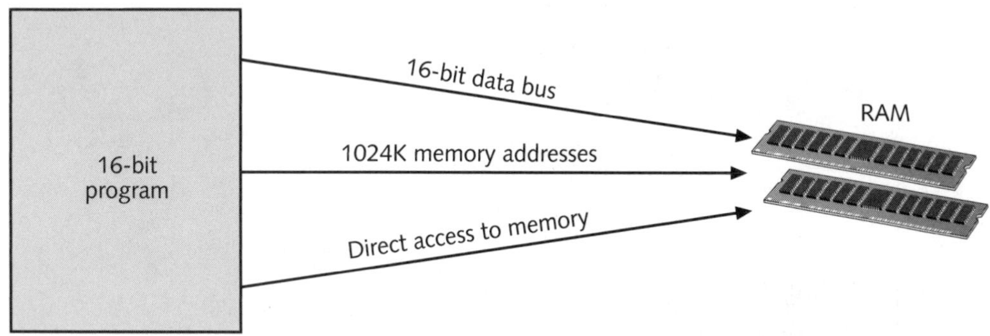

Figure 2-23 Real mode, or MS-DOS mode, provides single-tasking; 1024K of memory addresses; direct access to RAM using a 16-bit data path

In protected mode, more than one program can run at the same time, which is a type of multitasking. In protected mode, each program can be safely contained within its own range of resources. Here lies the meaning behind the two terms, real and protected. Real mode means that the software has "real" access to the hardware, and protected mode means that more than one program can be running and each one is "protected" from the other(s).

A+ OS 1.1 In protected mode, as shown in Figure 2-24, more than one program can run, and the programs have access to memory addresses of 4096 MB or 4 GB, depending on the motherboard, CPU, and OS being used, or sometimes more. In protected mode, the OS does not allow a program direct access to RAM, but works as the mediator between memory and programs. This allows the OS some latitude in how it uses RAM. If the OS is low on RAM, it can store some data on the hard drive. This method of using the hard drive as though it were RAM is called **virtual memory**, and data stored in virtual memory is stored in a file on the hard drive called a **swap file** or **page file**. The OS manages the entire process, and the applications know nothing about this substitution of hardware resources for RAM. The programs running in protected mode just see memory addresses and have no idea where they are located.

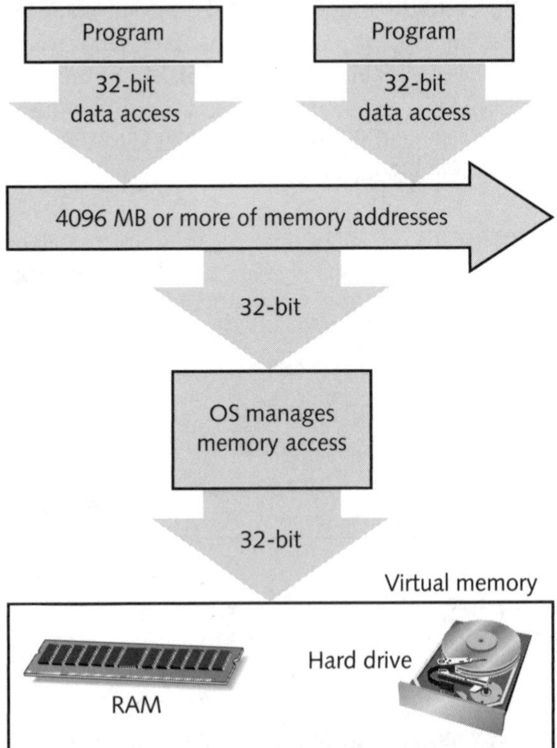

Figure 2-24 Protected mode is multitasking program access to more than 1024K of memory addresses using 32-bit data segments where the OS manages direct memory access

Even after protected mode became available, hardware and software needed to be backward compatible (able to support older technology), so real mode is still supported by today's CPUs and operating systems. In fact, the CPU starts in real mode and must be told to switch to protected mode. For this reason, an OS starts in real mode and commands the CPU to switch to protected mode before allowing user interaction or loading an application. DOS and the MS-DOS mode of Windows 9x operate in real mode. Windows 9x and Windows NT/2000/XP start out in real mode and then switch to protected mode. Table 2-4 summarizes the differences between real mode and protected mode.

Table 2-4 A CPU and an OS operate in either real mode or protected mode

Real mode	Protected mode
16-bit data path	32-bit data path
Only one program runs at a time.	Several programs can be loaded and running.
The CPU can access up to 1 MB of memory unless a memory extender is used.	The CPU can access 4 GB or more of memory.
Programs have direct access to hardware.	Programs access hardware by way of the operating system.

How Real and Protected Modes Are Used by an OS

The OS must be in sync with the CPU, using the same mode it is using. Not only must the OS be in sync with the CPU, but applications must be compiled to run in either real or protected mode. In addition, there is a mode that is a hybrid of real and protected mode that was used by older software written for Windows 3.x, where the mode is real but the intent is to run more than one program in a pseudo-protected environment. This unique situation that occurred with Windows 3.x is important because it helps to make clear the different ways in which an OS can manage applications.

Windows 3.x was not really an OS, but neither did it act like normal application software. It was installed by DOS and used DOS as its operating system, and, therefore, is considered to be a DOS application. Windows 3.x provided an operating *environment*, which refers to the overall support that it provided to application software, and applications were installed under Windows 3.x. The two primary things that Windows 3.x provided that DOS did not were a graphical user interface (GUI) and a limited form of multitasking.

16-bit and 32-bit Software

Applications and device drivers written for Windows 3.x are called 16-bit Windows software. Data access is 16 bits at a time, and each program is written so that it should not infringe on the resources of other applications that might be running. Software written for Windows 95 and higher are called 32-bit drivers or 32-bit applications. In short, there are three general types of software that run on PCs:

- 16-bit DOS software designed to run in real mode as the only program running and expecting direct access to hardware. Under DOS, an application might attempt to serve as its own device driver. These programs could use only the first 1 MB of memory.

- 16-bit Windows software designed for Windows 3.x to run where other programs might also be running. These applications might or might not attempt to directly access hardware resources and could most likely use extended memory.
- 32-bit Windows software designed to run in protected mode with other software and that can be loaded in extended memory. These applications never attempt to access hardware directly.

Nearly all applications and device drivers written today are 32-bit, although 16-bit software still exists, and you must know how to support it in a Windows environment. You will learn more about supporting 16-bit applications and drivers in Chapter 4.

DOS, with or without Windows 3.x, is a real mode OS. Windows 9x is a hybrid operating system. Some of Windows 9x uses 16-bit data access (called 16-bit programs) and some uses 32-bit data access (called 32-bit programs). The Windows 9x 16-bit components exist primarily for backward-compatibility with older hardware and software. Because the 32-bit programs access twice as much data at one time as 16-bit programs do, the 32-bit programs are faster. This fact largely explains why Windows 9x is faster than DOS. Windows NT/2000/XP are true 32-bit OSs; all OS programs are written using 32-bit coding methods.

A 32-bit OS will allow a 16-bit program to run by providing it with an environment that appears to the program to be a 16-bit environment. This technique is called **virtual real mode**. How each of the Windows operating systems provides a virtual real mode is covered in later chapters.

After Windows 9x is loaded, you can switch to real mode by using the Shut Down menu. Click Start, Shut Down, and then select Restart in MS-DOS mode from the menu. You will get a C prompt and a full screen from which you can run DOS commands or applications. Windows Me, Windows 2000, and Windows XP do not support accessing real mode while the OS is loaded, although recovery procedures using these operating systems sometimes are done in real mode, as you will see in later chapters.

How an OS Uses BIOS and Device Drivers

Looking back at Figure 2-2, you can see that an operating system uses programs designed to interact with specific hardware devices. There are two kinds of programs used for this purpose, BIOS and device drivers. In Figure 2-2, you can see that some device drivers belong to the OS and others do not. You can also see that the total BIOS in a system can be located in several places in the system. The OS communicates with simple devices, such as floppy drives or keyboards, through BIOS, and with more complex devices, such as digital cameras or CD-ROM drives, through device drivers. We first look at the BIOS and then turn our attention to device drivers.

How an OS Uses System BIOS

System BIOS contains the programming instructions to run the simple hardware devices that are common to every system, specifically the keyboard and floppy disk drive. In addition, system BIOS can be used to access the hard drive. In the case of the hard drive, an OS has a choice of using system BIOS or device drivers. Most often it will use device drivers because they are faster. One reason device drivers are faster than system BIOS is that device drivers are executed from RAM, and BIOS is stored in ROM, and RAM access is faster than ROM access. However, sometimes the OS will use system BIOS to access the hard drive when older software requires it.

There is a good way to determine whether the BIOS or a device driver is controlling a device. If the device is configured using CMOS setup, most likely system BIOS controls it. If the device is configured using the OS, most likely a driver controls it.

For example, in Figure 2-25, the setup main menu for an Award BIOS system shows the ability to configure, or set, the system date and time, the Supervisor Password (power-on password), floppy drive diskettes, the hard drive, and the keyboard. Figure 2-26 shows another setup window for this same BIOS that can configure serial ports, an infrared port, and a parallel port. All these devices can be controlled by system BIOS. On the other hand, there is no setup window in this BIOS to control the DVD drive or Zip drive that are installed on this system. The BIOS is not aware of these devices; this means they are controlled by device drivers.

```
                       AwardBIOS Setup Utility
  Main        Advanced  Power      Boot   Exit

  System Time               [11:42:09]          Item Specific Help
  System Date               [04/04/2000]
  Legacy Diskette A         [1.44M, 3.5 in.]   <Enter> to select field;
  Legacy Diskette B         [None]             <+>, <-> to change value
  Floppy 3 Mode Support     [Disabled]

► Primary Master            [Auto]
► Primary Slave             [Auto]
► Secondary Master          [Auto]
► Secondary Slave           [Auto]
► Keyboard Features

  Language                  [English]
  Supervisor Password       [Disabled]
  User Password             [Disabled]
  Halt On                   [All Errors]
  Installed Memory          128MB

F1   Help  ↑↓ Select Item  -/+    Change Values     F5   Setup Defaults
ESC  Exit  ⇄  Select Menu  Enter  Select Sub Menu   F10  Save and Exit
```

Figure 2-25 Use the BIOS setup main menu for Award BIOS to configure some of the devices controlled by system BIOS

CMOS setup windows are accessed during startup. A system displays a message at the bottom of the screen saying something like, "Press Del to enter setup." Pressing the indicated key launches a program stored on the ROM BIOS microchip to change the contents of CMOS RAM. This BIOS setup program provides windows like those in Figures 2-25 and 2-26.

```
                    Award BIOS Setup Utility
                Advanced

          I/O Device Configuration              Item Specific Help

 Onboard FDC Swap A & B         [No Swap]     <Enter> to select if
 Floppy Disk Access Control     [R/W]         switch drive letter
                                              assignments or not.
 Onboard Serial Port 1:         [3F8H/IRQ4]
 Onboard Serial Port 2:         [2F8H/IRQ3]
 UART2 Use Infrared             [Disabled]

 Onboard Parallel Port:         [378H/IRQ7]
 Parallel Port Mode:            [ECP + EPP]
 ECP DMA Select:                [3]

F1   Help ↑↓ Select Item  -/+    Change Values      F5   Setup Defaults
ESC  Exit ⇄  Select Menu  Enter  Select Sub Menu    F10  Save and Exit
```

Figure 2-26 Use this Award BIOS setup window to configure several I/O devices, including the serial, parallel and infrared ports

How Device Drivers Control Hardware

Device drivers, which are software designed to interface with specific hardware devices, serve the same functions as BIOS programs, but they are stored on the hard drive rather than on ROM chips, as BIOS is. Some device drivers are provided by the OS, and some are provided by the manufacturer of the specific hardware device with which they are designed to interface. In either case, unlike BIOS, device drivers are usually written for a particular OS and must be rewritten to be used with another.

When you purchase a printer, DVD drive, Zip drive, digital camera, scanner, or other hardware device, bundled with the device is a set of floppy disks or CDs that contain the device drivers (see Figure 2-27). You must install these device drivers under the operating system so it will have the necessary software to control the device. In most cases, you install the device and then install the device drivers. There are a few exceptions, such as a digital camera using a serial port to download pictures. In this case, you install the software to drive the digital camera before you plug in the camera. See the device documentation to learn what to do first. Device driver installations are covered in later chapters.

Figure 2-27 A device such as this CD-ROM drive comes packaged with its device drives stored on a floppy disk or CD. Alternately, you can use device drivers built into the OS.

You can find device drivers in a number of sources. Some come with and are part of the operating system, some come with hardware devices when they are purchased, and some are provided for download over the Internet from a device manufacturer's Web site.

There are two kinds of device drivers: 16-bit real-mode drivers and 32-bit protected-mode drivers. Windows 9x supports both, but Windows NT/2000/XP uses only 32-bit drivers.

Device Drivers Under Windows 9x Windows 9x comes with 32-bit drivers for hundreds of hardware devices. Windows automatically loads these drivers into extended memory (memory above 1024K) at startup or when the device first needs them. However, not all older devices are supported by Windows drivers, so a system might sometimes need to use an older 16-bit real-mode device driver. These 16-bit drivers are loaded by entries in the **Config.sys**, **Autoexec.bat**, and **System.ini** files, text files used to configure DOS and Windows 3.x that are supported by Windows 9x for backward-compatibility. These drivers use upper memory addresses. When the driver is installed, the driver installation program makes appropriate entries in these files.

Under DOS, when a program such as a device driver stays in memory until it is required by the CPU, it is called a **terminate-and-stay-resident (TSR)** program. The term is seldom used today, except when talking about real mode programs.

Windows uses Autoexec.bat and Config.sys in order to be backward-compatible with DOS, and uses System.ini in order to be backward-compatible with Windows 3x. However, using 16-bit drivers can slow performance, so to get the most out of Windows 9x, you should use 32-bit protected-mode drivers designed for Windows 9x. When selecting a driver to install, be sure the driver claims to be Windows 9x compatible, which means that it is a 32-bit driver and you can install the driver using the Add New Hardware Wizard. If the driver must be installed using a setup program provided by the driver manufacturer and cannot be installed using the Add New Hardware Wizard, then it is a 16-bit driver.

Windows 9x keeps information about 32-bit drivers in the Windows **registry**, a database of hardware and software settings, Windows configuration settings, user parameters, and application settings. Windows 32-bit drivers are sometimes called dynamic drivers because they can be loaded into memory when the device is accessed and then unloaded to conserve memory when the device is disconnected or turned off. Drivers that always remain in memory are called static drivers.

Sometimes, to address bugs, make improvements, or add features, manufacturers release device drivers that are more recent than those included with Windows. Whenever possible, it is best to use the latest driver available for a device provided by the device manufacturer. You can usually download these updated drivers from the manufacturer's Web site. For example, suppose you have just borrowed a printer from a friend but you forgot to borrow the CD with the printer drivers on it. You can go to the printer manufacturer's Web site, download the drivers to a folder on your PC, and install the driver under Windows. Figure 2-28 shows you a Web page from the Hewlett-Packard (HP) Web site showing a list of downloadable drivers for ink-jet printers. You will learn how to install and update drivers and troubleshoot problems with drivers in later chapters.

Sixteen-bit drivers under Windows 9x can cause slow performance, so use 32-bit drivers whenever possible. Sometimes it can be difficult to determine whether a device driver is 16-bit or 32-bit. One way to identify whether Windows 9x is using a 16-bit driver is to go into Device Manager and look for an exclamation point beside the device, which indicates that the driver has a problem. This might indicate that the driver is a 16-bit driver. If a driver is loaded from Config.sys or Autoexec.bat, it is a 16-bit driver; if it is loaded from the registry, it is a 32-bit driver. System.ini can contain both types. Table 2-5 summarizes basic information about device drivers under Windows 9x.

2

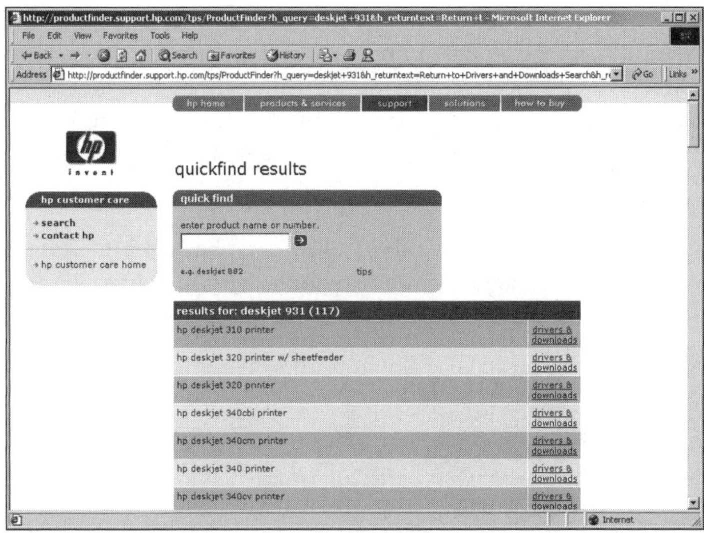

Figure 2-28 Download the latest device drivers from a manufacturer's Web site

Table 2-5 Two types of device drivers and how to use them under Windows 9x

Characteristic	16-bit Device Drivers	32-bit Device Drivers
Operating mode	Real mode	Protected mode
Use of memory	May use upper memory addresses	Stored in extended memory
How loaded	Loaded by a command line in Config.sys, Autoexec.bat, or System.ini	Automatically loaded from the registry by Windows 9x at startup or when the device is used
How changed	Edit the Config.sys or Autoexec.bat files	From Device Manager, select the device and use the Properties, Driver tab
How to identify the type	In Device Manager, look for an exclamation point beside the device name	Look to see how the driver is loaded, from the registry, System.ini, Autoexec.bat or Config.sys. Also, look for no exclamation point beside the device name in Device Manager.
When to use this type	Use a 16-bit driver under Windows only when a 32-bit driver is not available. When operating under DOS, 16-bit drivers are required.	When you can, always use 32-bit drivers because they are faster and give fewer configuration problems.

Device Drivers Under Windows 2000 Windows 2000 installs protected-mode drivers in the same way as Windows 9x, but Windows 2000 does not claim to support 16-bit device drivers. For Windows 2000, always check the hardware compatibility list (HCL) to determine if a driver will work under Windows 2000. Go to this Microsoft Web site and search for your device:

www.microsoft.com/windows2000/professional/howtobuy/upgrading/compat

If the device does not install properly or produces errors, check the manufacturer's Web site for a driver that the manufacturer says is compatible with Windows 2000.

How an OS Launches Applications

Most application software fits into eight categories: word processing, spreadsheets, database management, graphics, communications, games, mathematical modeling, and software development tools. Each software category contains many different products. For example, some popular database management packages include Access, Paradox, and Filemaker, and two popular word-processing packages include Word and WordPerfect. Some application software manufacturers produce suites of software, which combine a word-processing program and spreadsheet program, and usually include a database management program, a presentation package, an e-mail package, and a World Wide Web browser package. Suites have many advantages, including providing similar user interfaces. The programs are designed to make it easy to move data from one suite program to another, and files within a suite's programs can be linked, so that updates to data or text are automatically recorded in all linked files.

Application software is designed to work on top of a particular OS. "On top of" here means that the application depends on the OS, such as Windows 98 or Windows 2000, in order to run. An application depends on an OS to provide access to hardware resources, manage its data in memory and in secondary storage, and perform many other background tasks. For example, consider a situation in which Windows 98 loads an application and executes it. The application cannot run or even load itself without Windows 98, much as a document cannot be edited without a word-processing program. Windows 98 stays available to the application for the entire time the application is running. The application passes certain functions to Windows 98, such as reading from a CD-ROM or printing.

An application written to work with one OS, such as Windows 98, does not necessarily work with another, such as a Macintosh system. There are, however, some exceptions. For instance, OS/2 is written so that any application designed to work with DOS also works with OS/2, an early selling point for OS/2. However, to take full advantage of an operating system's power and an application's power, buy application software written specifically for your OS.

Application software is downloaded from the Internet, or comes written on floppy disks or on CD-ROMs, and usually must be installed on a hard drive in order to run. During the installation, the install program creates folders on the hard drive and copies files to them. For Windows, it also makes entries in the Windows registry and puts files in the folder and subfolders that it later uses as software components to perform various tasks. It can also place icons on the desktop and add entries to the Start menu. Because the install program does all the work for you, installing a software package usually is very easy and is covered in later chapters for each of the Windows operating systems.

How Application Software Is Loaded and Initialized

A+ OS 2.4

Starting application software seems like a simple task. For example, in Windows 98, you click the shortcut icon on the desktop, and the application window opens, ready for you to use it. But much happens behind the scenes between your click and the appearance of the application awaiting your next command. Software or programs are stored in program files on a secondary storage device, such as a hard drive or CD, until needed. Before they can be executed, they must first be copied or loaded into RAM and assigned memory addresses, as Figure 2-29 shows.

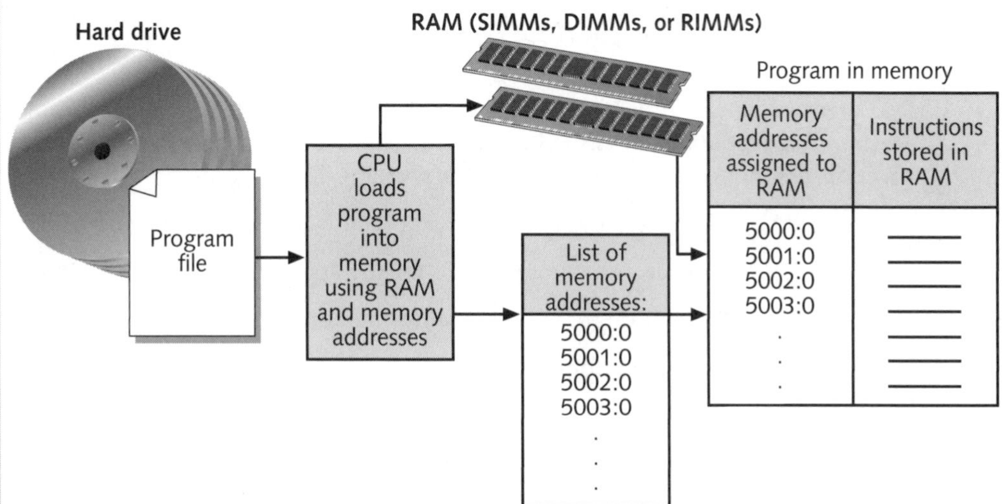

Figure 2-29 RAM is a hardware resource, and memory addresses are a system resource; both are used when loading software into memory for execution

Even the operating system programs must be copied from the hard drive into memory before these programs are executed. The process from a bird's eye view goes like this and is illustrated in Figure 2-30: The OS program files are copied into memory and assigned memory addresses and then executed. The OS copies a program file into memory, which is executed. The program requests data from the hard drive, which is copied into memory, and then the program uses that data. In Figure 2-30, you can see that memory is used by the OS, the applications, and data. In addition, BIOS and device drivers are also using memory and are executed from memory as the OS needs them.

A+ OS 2.4

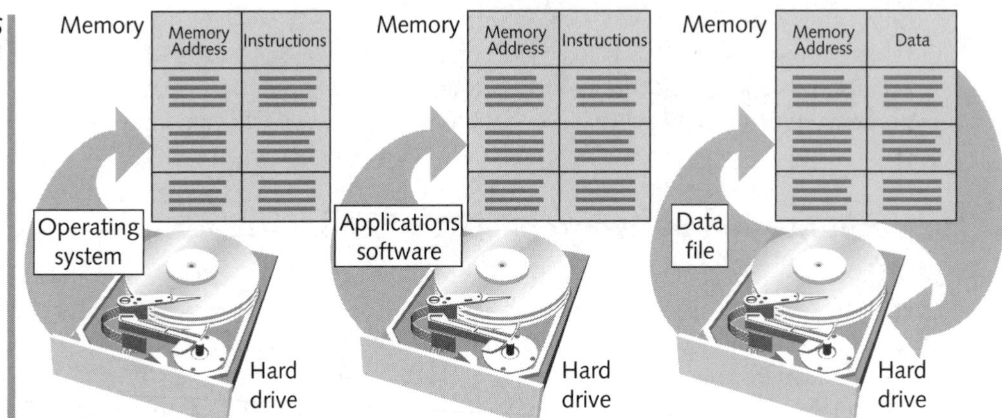

Figure 2-30 Both the operating system and application software must be loaded into memory before execution, and existing data must also be copied from secondary storage into memory to be processed. After processing, data must be saved back to secondary storage.

Understanding the process of loading and initializing software is important to people responsible for supporting PCs. Listed below are the major steps that must take place. This section describes the process in detail for several OSs.

1. The OS receives the command to execute the application.
2. The OS locates the program file for the application.
3. The OS loads the program file into memory.
4. The OS gives control to the program.
5. The program requests memory addresses from the OS for its data.
6. The program initializes itself and possibly requests that data from secondary storage be loaded into memory.
7. The program turns to the user for its first instruction.

We begin with Windows 98 in MS-DOS mode as our OS. Before we discuss the specific command to load software in real mode, let's first look at the command prompt the user sees and what information it provides. If you booted a Windows 98 PC from a floppy disk into command prompt mode, the MS-DOS prompt would look like this:

```
A:\>
```

This prompt is called the A prompt. The MS-DOS prompt (A:\>) displayed immediately after booting means that the OS was copied from drive A, which is where the startup disk containing enough of the OS to load in real mode is stored. Drive A then becomes the default drive and default directory, sometimes called the current working drive and directory, which the OS automatically uses to save and retrieve files. The colon following the letter identifies the letter as the name of a drive, and the backslash identifies the directory

A+ OS 2.4 on the drive as the root or main directory. The > symbol is the prompt symbol that the OS uses to say, "Enter your command here." To make the hard drive (drive C) the default drive, enter C: at the A prompt.

The prompt now changes to

```
C:\>
```

Recall that when a hard drive is first formatted for use by an OS, the format procedure creates a single directory on the drive, called the root directory. This directory is written in the OS command lines as a single backslash (\) (or forward slash in the case of Unix) with no other directory name following. In the preceding OS prompt, the backslash indicates that it is the root directory.

A+ OS 3.3 Launching the Program File

At the command prompt, when you type a single group of letters with no spaces, the OS assumes that you want to execute a program with the filename that you just typed, stored in a program file in the current directory. The OS first attempts to find the program file by that name, then copies the file into RAM, and then it executes the program. Let's use the program Mem.exe, a Windows 9x utility to display how memory is currently allocated, as our example. The program file Mem.exe is stored on the hard drive in C:\Windows\command folder. Note what happens in Figure 2-31 when you type *mem* at the A: prompt, like this:

```
A:\>mem
```

The OS says it cannot find the program to execute. It looked only on the floppy disk (drive A) for Mem.com, Mem.exe, or Mem.bat, the three file extensions that MS-DOS recognizes for programs. If the OS doesn't find any of these files in the current directory, it stops looking and displays the error message:

```
Bad command or file name
```

To help the OS locate the program file, we must first change the default drive to the hard drive by giving the command:

```
A:\> C:
```

Notice in Figure 2-31 that the prompt changes to C:\>, indicating that the logical drive C on the hard drive is the default drive. Now we change the default directory on the hard drive to \Windows\Command using the **CD (change directory) command** like this:

```
C:\>CD\windows\command
```

(Remember that DOS and Windows commands are not case sensitive, so it makes no difference whether you type CD, Cd, or cd.) The prompt now looks like this:

```
C:\WINDOWS\COMMAND>
```

Next in Figure 2-31, we enter the *mem* command again, and this time the OS locates and executes the program file.

A+ OS 3.3

```
A:\>mem
Bad command or file name

A:\>c:

C:\>cd\windows\command

C:\WINDOWS\COMMAND>mem

Memory Type           Total     Used     Free
----------- --------- ----    ------
Conventional             640K     160K       480K
Upper                      0K       0K         0K
Reserved                   0K       0K         0K
Extended (XMS)       130,036K   2,112K   127,924K

Total memory         130,676K   2,272K   128,404K

Total under 1 MB         640K     160K       480K

Largest executable program size      479K (490, 816 bytes)
Largest free upper memory block        0K         (0 bytes)
MS-DOS is resident in the high memory area.

C:\WINDOWS\COMMAND>
```

Figure 2-31 Finding a program file

There is another way to tell the OS where to look to find program files. As part of the boot procedure, you can give the OS a list of paths in which to look for executable program files beyond the default directory, by using the **Path** command. You can cause the Path command to be executed automatically during the boot process by storing the command in the Autoexec.bat file (to be discussed in the next chapter). You can also execute the Path command at any time after booting. The last Path command you execute overrides any previous ones. To see the list of paths that are presently active, type Path at the command prompt, and then press Enter. This command is shown in Figure 2-32. To enter a new list of paths, type Path followed by each path name, separating one path from the next by a semicolon, as shown in the second Path command in Figure 2-32.

A+ OS 2.4 3.2

2

```
C:\>path
PATH=F:\;A:\;G:\

C:\>path F:\;A:\G:\C:\;C:\Windows\Command

C:\>path
PATH=F:\;A:\G:\C:\;C\WINDOWS\COMMAND

C:\>
```

Figure 2-32 The Path command

In Figure 2-32, the first Path command displays the list of active paths, which are three logical drives, F, A, and G. The second Path command changes this list, giving the OS the same three logical drives as well as the drive C root directory and the C:\Windows\Command directory. The last Path command displays the new list of active paths.

When you tell the OS to execute a program, you can also include the path to that program file as part of the command line. For example, if the Mem.exe file is stored in the directory C:\Windows\Command, you can execute the program by typing the following:

```
A:\> C:\Windows\Command\Mem.exe
```

Here, you are telling the OS that the name of the program file is Mem.exe and that its location is in the directory \Windows\Command on drive C. With this method, the directory and drive that contains the Mem program need not be the defaults, nor do you need to use the Path command.

In summary, using the MS-DOS mode of Windows 9x, the OS searches for executable program files using the following rules:

1. If no path is given before the filename, the OS looks in the current directory.
2. If there is a path given in front of the filename in the command line, the OS looks in that path.
3. If no path is given, and the file is not in the current directory, the OS looks in the paths given to it by the last Path command executed.

Although the Path command and Autoexec.bat are not necessary in Windows 9x, you can use them. If you have an Autoexec.bat file in your root directory when Windows 9x starts, it reads the Path command stored in that file. You can also store DOS commands in batch files and execute them from Windows 9x by double-clicking the filename of the batch file in Explorer.

If you don't have an Autoexec.bat file with a Path command, Windows 9x uses a default path of C:\Windows; C:\Windows\Command. Not all paths to program files must appear in the Path command, as they must in DOS.

A+ OS 2.4 3.2

Copying the Program into Memory

Recall that once the OS finds the program file, it copies the file into memory (RAM) in a location that the OS chooses (see Figure 2-33). After it copies the program into memory, the OS goes to the first address in memory occupied by the program to receive its first instruction. If the program requests some memory for its data (and most will), the OS decides which memory addresses to give the program (usually the memory after the program).

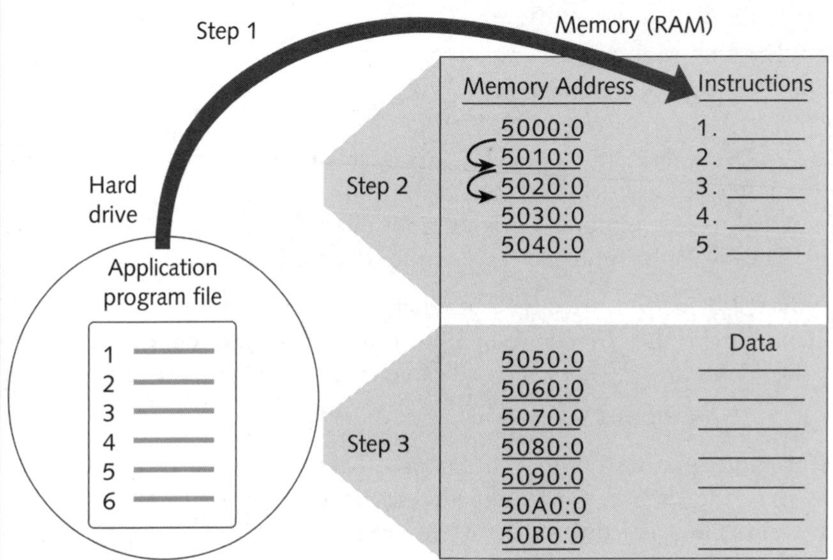

Figure 2-33 Applications software is stored in files but executed from memory

If the program wants to write or read data to or from memory, the OS manages these tasks. If the program needs to print, display something on the screen, or read from or write to the hard drive or a floppy disk, the OS does the work and returns to the program when finished. In other words, the OS is the "software behind the software," doing the background tasks for an application or utility program.

Loading Application Software Using the Windows Desktop

A+ OS 2.4 3.2

In graphical mode, once an application is installed, Windows 9x and Windows NT/2000/XP offer four ways to execute software:

- Place a shortcut icon directly on the desktop for the applications you use often and want to get to quickly. These shortcuts contain the command line used to execute the application. To view this command line, right-click an application icon. A drop-down menu then appears. From the menu, select Properties. The icon's Properties box appears (see Figure 2-34). From this box, you can view the complete command line that the icon represents. How to create shortcuts for each Windows OS is covered in later chapters.

A+ OS 2.4 3.2

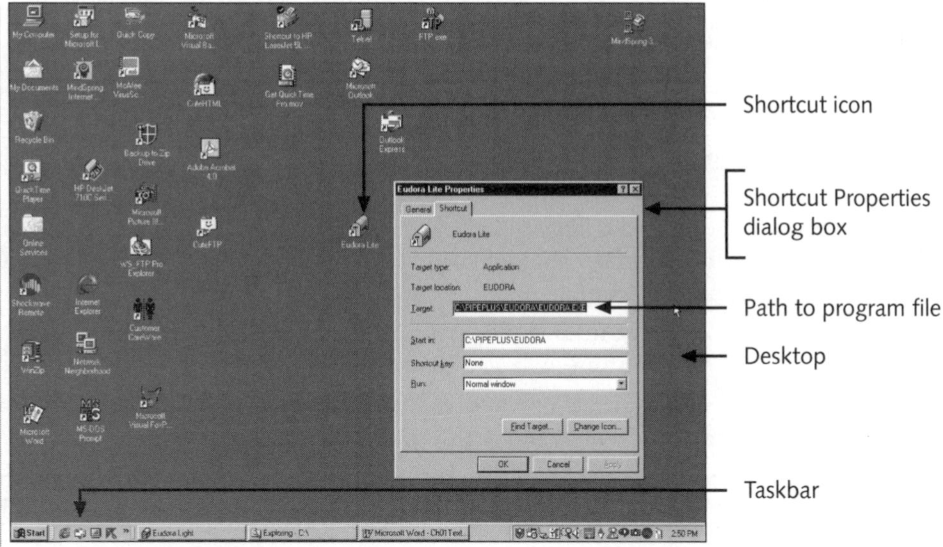

Figure 2-34 Windows has icons on the desktop that point to program files on the hard drive

- Click the Start button, select Programs, and select the program from the list of installed software.
- Use the Run command: Click the Start button on the Windows taskbar, and then click Run to display the Run dialog box (see Figure 2-35). In this box, enter a command line or click Browse to search for a program file to execute.

Figure 2-35 The Windows Run dialog box allows you to enter DOS-like commands

- Execute a program or launch an application file by double-clicking the filename in Windows Explorer or My Computer.

2

Chapter Summary

- Four types of software are BIOS or firmware, device drivers, operating systems (OSs), and application software. Sometimes device drivers are considered part of the OS.
- Application software relates to the OS, which relates to BIOS and device drivers to control hardware.
- The motherboard is the largest circuit board inside the computer case and holds the CPU, the most important microchip inside a computer that is responsible for all processing done by the system.
- Ports on the motherboard include serial, parallel, and USB ports. It is expected that motherboards in the future will also have FireWire ports.
- A CPU can operate in real or protected mode. In real mode, it processes 16 bits at a time, and in protected mode, it processes 32 bits at a time.
- RAM (memory) temporarily holds data and programs while the CPU processes both. Common RAM modules installed on the motherboard are SIMMs, DIMMs and RIMMs.
- A motherboard has several buses, each designed for a different purpose and running at a different speed. Some buses are the 8-bit and 16-bit ISA buses, the system bus, the PCI bus, the AGP bus used for a single video card, the USB bus that provides USB ports for slower I/O devices, and IEEE 1394 (FireWire) used for faster I/O devices.
- Four system resources that aid in the communication between hardware and software are I/O addresses, IRQs, DMA channels, and memory addresses.
- An IRQ is a line on a bus that a device uses to alert the CPU that it needs servicing.
- A DMA channel provides a shortcut for a device to send data directly to memory, bypassing the CPU.
- Memory addresses are numbers, often written in hexadecimal and in segment/offset form, assigned to RAM and ROM so that the CPU can access both.
- The CPU sends a device's I/O address over the address bus when it wants to communicate with the device.
- The 8-bit ISA bus had a limited number of system resources available to it, which were increased when the 16-bit ISA bus was invented.
- COM and LPT are preconfigured assignments of system resources that can be used by a device. For example COM1 is IRQ 4 and I/O addresses 03F8 through 03FF.
- A hardware interrupt is initiated by a hardware device sending an IRQ to the CPU. A software interrupt is initiated by the software sending an interrupt number (INT) to the CPU.
- For DOS and Windows 9x, the three types of logical primary memory are conventional (or base) memory, upper memory, and extended memory. These assignments are rooted in how the 20-line memory address bus of early PCs limited memory to 1024K. Windows 9x makes the most use of extended memory.

- Software manages memory by means of memory addresses that point to locations in RAM. The number of memory addresses is partly limited by the number of wires on the bus devoted to these addresses.
- RAM and ROM BIOS on the motherboard and other circuit boards need memory addresses assigned to them so the CPU can access them.
- The size of the data segment that software can access at one time is determined by the number of wires on the bus assigned for the data path.
- When a PC is first turned on, the startup BIOS is in control. It later loads the OS and then turns control over to it.
- BIOS and an OS can support two common standards, ACPI to conserve power and Plug and Play to make device installations easier.
- BIOS manages a CMOS RAM chip on the motherboard that contains configuration settings for the motherboard. A program in BIOS lets you change CMOS setup at startup.
- Real mode is used by DOS and is limited to running a single program and using a 16-bit data path and 1024K of memory addresses.
- Most hard drives and other secondary storage devices use IDE technology, which can support up to four drives in a system. There are two IDE connections on the motherboard, for two cables. Each cable can connect two drives.
- A file system is a method by which the OS organizes the files on a hard drive. The most popular file system for Windows is FAT, which can be either FAT16 or FAT32.
- Using FAT, clusters are listed in the FAT and filenames are listed in a directory table.
- Directories (folders) can contain files and other child directories or subdirectories (folders).
- Under DOS a filename can contain eight characters with a three-character extension. Using Windows, a long filename can contain up to 255 characters, including spaces.
- Protected mode allows more than one program to run at a time, can use a 32-bit data path, and has more than 1024K of memory addresses. In protected mode, the OS manages access to RAM and does not allow a program direct access to it.
- Virtual memory is "fake" memory, whereby data is stored in a swap file on the hard drive. The OS makes applications think that they are using real memory.
- Device drivers are either written using 16-bit or 32-bit code. Most drivers today are 32-bit protected-mode drivers loaded from the registry by Windows.
- Older 16-bit device drivers are loaded from Autoexec.bat, Config.sys, or System.ini by Windows 9x to be backward-compatible with DOS and Windows 3.x.
- Using MS-DOS mode of Windows 9x, a program can be executed from a command prompt. A Path command is required if the program is not in the default directory and the path is not included before the filename in the command line.
- From the Windows desktop, programs can be launched from the Start menu, a shortcut icon on the desktop, the Run dialog box, or Windows Explorer or My Computer.

Key Terms

AGP (Accelerated Graphics Port) bus
Autoexec.bat
BIOS (basic input/output system)
booting
bus
CD (change directory) command
child directory
CMOS configuration chip
CMOS RAM chip
CMOS setup chip
Config.sys
data bus
data path
directory table
DMA (direct memory access) channel
EIDE (Enhanced Integrated Drive Electronics)
extended memory
file extension
file system
filename
firmware
folder
front-side bus
hardware interrupt
IDE (Integrated Drive Electronics)
I/O addresses
interrupt handler
interrupt vector table
IRQ (interrupt request number)
ISA (Industry Standard Architecture)
local bus
memory address
memory bus
memory extender
motherboard
page file
parallel port
path
PCI (Peripheral Component Interconnect) bus
Plug and Play (PnP)
polling
port
port address
primary storage
program file
protected mode
RAM (random access memory)
real mode
registry
request handler
root directory
secondary storage
serial port
software interrupt
startup BIOS
subdirectory
swap file
system BIOS
system bus
System.ini
Terminate-and-stay-resident (TSR)
USB (universal serial bus)
vector table
virtual memory
virtual real mode

Review Questions

1. How does firmware differ from a software program stored on the hard drive?
2. Name one way BIOS and device drivers are the same. Name one way they are different.
3. Which Windows operating system does not support Plug and Play?
4. Memory above 1024K is called ________________.
5. Real mode operates using a ________________-bit data path, and protected mode uses a ________________-bit data path.

6. Real mode allows programs direct access to ________________, but protected mode does not.
7. List four system resources that software uses to manage hardware.
8. What Windows 9x utility allows you to see the IRQ assignments made to devices?
9. What must happen to a program that is stored on a hard drive before it can be executed?
10. Name three types of memory modules.
11. Name one system resource that a video card most likely will not need.
12. Where in memory are 32-bit device drivers stored?
13. Is a mouse more likely to be controlled by a device driver or by system BIOS?
14. Name one device that is likely to be controlled by system BIOS.
15. How is a software interrupt initiated?
16. How is a hardware interrupt initiated?
17. Describe a request handler. Where in memory can you find a list of addresses where request handlers are located?
18. When the mouse initiates a hardware interrupt to the CPU, how does the CPU know where to find a program to service the mouse?
19. If memory addresses are used by the CPU to access memory, then what are I/O addresses used for?
20. What is the I/O address range for the keyboard?
21. Why are DMA channels not as popular as they once were with high-speed devices?
22. Name a device that uses polling in order to be serviced by the CPU.
23. Which Windows OS uses Plug and Play but does not depend on BIOS Plug and Play to aid in the configuration process?
24. What is the name of the memory extender program used by DOS and Windows 9x?
25. When an OS uses part of a hard drive to act like memory, what is the file on the hard drive called that is used for this virtual memory?
26. List three text files that Windows 9x supports for loading device drivers in order to remain backward compatible with DOS and Windows 3.x.
27. Using Device Manager, what do you look for to indicate that a device driver is likely to be 16-bit software?
28. What makes a BIOS a "good" BIOS according to Microsoft?
29. If the command prompt is A:\> and you want the default drive to be drive C, what command do you use?
30. What is the command to change the default directory to \Windows?
31. If you enter the command MEM at the command prompt, what filenames with extensions does the OS look for to execute a program?
32. List four ways an application can be launched from the Windows desktop.
33. Describe how you can change the contents of the CMOS RAM setup chip.

HANDS-ON PROJECTS

Using Microsoft Diagnostics with Windows 9x

DOS and Windows offer the Microsoft Diagnostics utility. This utility examines your system, displaying useful information about ports, devices, memory, and the like. The MSD.EXE utility can be found in the \TOOLS\OLDMSDOS directory on your Windows 9x installation CD. Using Windows Explorer, copy it to your hard drive, storing it in a folder named \Tools.

For Windows 9x, boot your PC to a MS-DOS prompt in real mode. From the DOS prompt, execute this command: **C:\TOOLS\MSD**. You should see a screen similar to that in Figure 2-36.

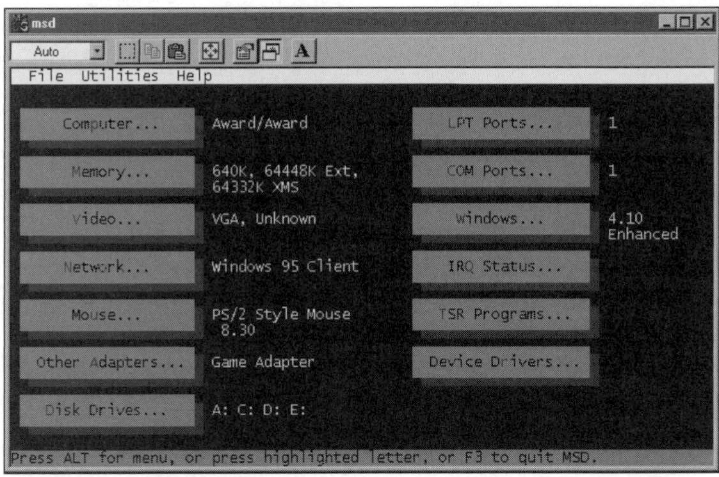

Figure 2-36 MSD opening screen

Browse carefully through all the menu options of this utility and answer the following questions about your system:

1. List the following or print the appropriate MSD screen: manufacturer, version number, and date of your system BIOS, video BIOS, and mouse device driver.
2. What kind of video card is installed?
3. How much memory is currently installed on this PC?
4. What version of the OS are you running?
5. What CPU is the PC using?

Exit MSD. Save the information you noted to compare with the information that will be obtained from MSD in Windows 2000.

You will need Windows 2000 installed on a PC to do the rest of this project. Copy the MSD.exe program to a folder on your Windows 2000 PC named \Tools. From within Windows 2000, open a command prompt. (Click **Start**, **Programs**, **Accessories**,

Command Prompt). From the Command prompt, start MSD using this command: \Tools\MSD. Browse through all menu options and answer the same questions about your system as you did for Windows 9x above.

Observing Windows 9x in Real Mode

Using Windows 9x, boot into MS-DOS real mode and then do the following.

1. From the command prompt, make drive C, root directory the default drive and directory. The prompt should be C:\>.
2. Use the DIR command to get a list of files on C:\. Does the hard drive contain Autoexec.bat and Config.sys files in the root directory? If so, print them using a local printer (not a network printer). Use one of the following methods:

```
C:\> TYPE filename.ext > PRN
C:\> PRINT filename.ext
C:\> COPY filename.ext PRN
C:\> COPY filename.ext LPT1
```

3. At the DOS prompt, enter the following Prompt command that is used to customize the DOS command prompt. The space between $P and $G can contain any text, for example $PThisIsAPrompt$G:

```
PROMPT $P   $G
```

   What prompt did you get?
4. By examining the prompt, guess what $P in the command line accomplishes and what $G accomplishes. Test your theory by changing the PROMPT command, leaving first $P and then $G out of the command line.

Without the appropriate PATH command, you cannot execute software stored on one drive or directory while you are in another. If you still have the Msd.exe program stored in the \Tools directory of your hard drive, you can test this theory. Do the following:

5. Make drive C, the root directory, the default drive and directory.
6. Enter the Msd command. Does the command work? What error message do you see?
7. What are the current paths your system knows? To find that out, enter the Path command without any paths following.

Using Device Manager

Using Device Manger under Windows 9x or Windows 2000, answer these questions about your computer. (To access Device Manager using Windows 9x, right-click the **My Computer** icon on the desktop, select **Properties** from the shortcut menu, and click the **Device Manager** tab. For Windows 2000, from the System Properties window, click on **Hardware** tab, and then click **Device Manager**.)

1. Does your computer have a network card installed? If so, what is the name of the card?
2. What are three settings that can be changed under Device Manager?
3. What are all the hardware devices that Device Manager recognizes as present?

CASE PROJECT

To prepare for installing a new operating system on a hard drive, you need to know the search order of drives that startup BIOS uses to search for an OS. The order might be C and then A or some other order. Enter the CMOS setup of your PC and search for the setup screen that sets the boot order. Change the order so that BIOS looks to the floppy drive (drive A) to load the OS before it looks to drive C. Answer these questions:

1. What keystroke did you press at startup to enter CMOS setup?
2. What BIOS does your motherboard use (include brand and version)?
3. What is the name of the setup menu that contains the boot sequence order?
4. What was the boot sequence order when you first entered setup?
5. What is the new boot sequence order?

CHAPTER

3

UNDERSTANDING THE BOOT PROCESS AND COMMAND LINE

In this chapter, you will learn:

- To understand the process of booting to a command prompt
- How to create and use Windows 9x rescue disks to troubleshoot and solve problems when booting Windows
- How DOS and Windows 9x view and manage memory
- How DOS and Windows 9x use and manage floppy disks and hard drives

An OS relates to hardware and other software by using system resources on the motherboard and operating modes that apply to the CPU and other software. Recall that an OS and a CPU can operate in either real mode or protected mode and that a 32-bit OS such as Windows 9x can provide an environment for 16-bit software as well as 32-bit software. This chapter focuses on using the command line in real mode under Windows 9x, which is called MS-DOS mode. Real mode can be used to boot the computer and troubleshoot problems with Windows when it cannot boot to the Windows desktop. It is important to learn to use the command line because it is the tried-and-true tool for the worst of operating system problems. Also, Windows 9x uses DOS-like core components and, therefore, understanding and learning to use MS-DOS mode commands helps you to understand this foundation of Windows. In addition, when troubleshooting problems with booting Windows 2000/XP, a command prompt provided by the Recovery Console is sometimes the only tool that is available in the worst-case situations. Many of the commands in this chapter also work at the command prompt provided by the Recovery Console. In short, knowing how to use the command prompt is essential to PC troubleshooting.

We begin the chapter by learning how a PC first boots up and loads the operating system. Then, you will learn how to create floppy disks that can be used to boot to a command prompt. Next we will turn our attention to how memory, floppy disks, and hard drives are managed in MS-DOS mode. Finally, we will look at some essential steps to use when troubleshooting a failed boot.

There are three ways to access a command prompt on a computer running Windows: by booting to it from a bootable disk, by accessing a command prompt window from within Windows, or through the Recovery Console in Windows 2000 or Windows XP. You will learn about the Recovery Console in Chapter 8.

BOOTING UP YOUR COMPUTER

Understanding what happens when you first turn on your PC and boot up to an operating system command prompt or desktop is essential to learning to troubleshoot problems with the operating system. This section looks at the details of that process.

The term "booting" comes from the phrase "lifting yourself up by your bootstraps" and refers to the computer bringing itself up to an operable state without user intervention. Booting can refer to either a soft boot or hard boot. A **hard boot**, or **cold boot**, involves initially turning on the power with the on/off switch. A **soft boot**, or **warm boot**, involves using the operating system to reboot. For DOS, pressing the three keys Ctrl, Alt, and Del at the same time performs a soft boot. For Windows 9x and Windows NT/2000/XP, one way to soft boot is to click Start, click Shut Down, select Restart from the Shut Down menu, and then click OK. You can also press Ctrl + Alt + Del and then select Shut Down from the Close Program dialog box that appears.

A hard boot is more stressful on your machine than a soft boot because of the initial power surge through the equipment. Also, a soft boot is faster. Always use the soft boot method to restart unless the soft boot method doesn't work. If you must power down, avoid turning off the power switch and immediately turning it back on without a pause, because this can damage the machine. Some PCs have a reset button on the front of the case. Pressing the reset button starts the booting process at an earlier point than does the operating-system soft boot and is, therefore, a little slower but might work when the OS soft boot fails. For newer motherboards, pressing the reset button restarts the system without actually powering off and thus avoids the stress to the system caused by the initial power surge when the power first comes on.

Startup BIOS Controls the Beginning of the Boot

A successful boot process depends on the hardware, the BIOS, and the operating system all performing without errors. If errors occur, they might or might not stall or lock up the boot process. The boot process can be divided into four main steps: BIOS checking hardware, loading the OS, the OS initializing itself, and finally loading and executing an application. We will look at a brief overview of all four before we examine the first three parts in detail. (The fourth part, loading and executing an application, was covered in the last chapter.) Startup BIOS is in control for the first step; control is turned over to the OS in the second step.

Step 1: POST. Startup BIOS tests essential hardware components. This test is called the **power-on self test (POST)**. The ROM BIOS startup program surveys hardware resources and needs, and assigns system resources to meet those needs (see Figure 3-1). The ROM BIOS startup program begins the startup process by reading configuration information stored in DIP switches, jumpers, and the CMOS chip, and then comparing that information to the hardware—the CPU, video card, floppy disk drive, hard drive, and so on. Some hardware devices have BIOSs of their own that request resources from startup BIOS, which attempts to assign these system resources as needed.

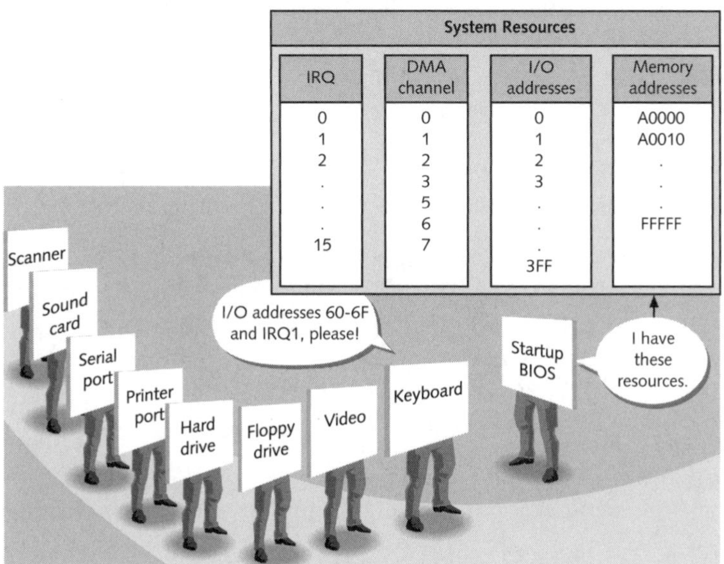

Figure 3-1 Boot Step 1: ROM BIOS startup program surveys hardware resources and needs and assigns system resources to satisfy those needs

Step 2: The ROM BIOS startup program searches for and loads an OS. Most often the OS is loaded from logical drive C on the hard drive. Configuration information on the CMOS chip tells startup BIOS where to look for the OS. Most newer BIOSs support loading the OS from the hard drive, a floppy disk, a CD, or a Zip drive. The BIOS turns to that device, reads the beginning files of the OS, copies them into memory, and then turns control over to the OS. This part of the loading process works the same for any operating system; only the OS files being loaded change.

Step 3: The OS configures the system and completes its own loading. The OS checks some of the same things that startup BIOS checked, such as available memory and whether that memory is reliable. Additionally, the OS continues beyond that by loading the software to control a mouse, CD-ROM, scanner, and other peripheral devices. These devices generally have device drivers stored on the hard drive.

Step 4: The user executes application software. When you tell the OS to execute an application, the OS first must find the application software on the hard drive, CD-ROM, or other secondary storage device, copy the software into memory, and then turn control over to it. Finally, you can command the application software, which makes requests to the OS, which, in turn, uses the system resources, system BIOS, and device drivers to interface with and control the hardware. At this point, the user is like the passenger in the back seat of the car with the chauffeur at the wheel. The trip has begun!

We now look at the first three steps in detail, beginning with the POST.

Power-on Self Test (POST) and Assignment of System Resources

When you turn on the power to a PC, the CPU begins the boot process by initializing itself and then turning to the ROM BIOS for instructions. The ROM BIOS then performs POST. Listed below are the key steps in this process.

- When the power is first turned on, the system clock begins to generate clock pulses.
- The CPU begins working and initializes itself (resetting its internal values).
- The CPU turns to memory address FFFF0h, which is the memory address always assigned to the first instruction in the ROM BIOS startup program.
- This instruction directs the CPU to run POST.
- POST first checks the BIOS program operating it and then tests CMOS RAM.
- A test determines that there has not been a battery failure.
- Hardware interrupts are disabled (this means that pressing a key on the keyboard or using another input device at this point will not affect anything).
- Tests are run on the CPU, and it is initialized further.
- A check determines if this is a cold boot. If so, the first 16 KB of RAM is tested.
- Hardware devices installed on the computer are inventoried and compared to configuration information.
- Video cards, memory, keyboard, floppy disk drives, hard drives, ports, and other hardware devices are tested and configured, and IRQ, I/O addresses, and DMA are assignments made. The OS will later complete this process.
- Some devices are set up to go into "sleep mode" to conserve electricity.
- The DMA controller is checked.
- Interrupt vectors are moved into the interrupt vector table.
- The interrupt controller is checked.

- CMOS setup (a BIOS program to change CMOS configuration data) is run if requested.
- BIOS begins its search for an OS.

During POST, before the CPU has checked the video system, errors are communicated by beeps. Short and long beeps indicate an error; the coding for the beeps depends on the BIOS. After POST checks and verifies the video controller card (note that POST does not check to see if a monitor is present or working), POST can use the monitor to display its progress. After checking video, POST checks RAM by writing and reading data. A running count of RAM is displayed on the monitor during this phase.

Next, the keyboard is checked, and if you press and hold any keys at this point, with some BIOSs an error occurs. Secondary storage, including floppy disk drives and hard drives, is also checked. The hardware that POST finds is checked against the data stored in the CMOS chip, jumpers, and/or DIP switches to determine if they agree.

System resources are assigned to devices by more than one method. Jumpers and DIP switches might be set to request a resource (for example, a jumper might be set "on" if IRQ 5 is requested or "off" if IRQ 7 is requested), or the resources needed might simply be hard-coded into the BIOS as part of the ROM programming that cannot be changed.

On earlier computers, system resources were always assigned to the device during the boot process (see Figure 3-1). Think of the process as a dialog. First, the startup BIOS recognizes that a hardware device is present. The BIOS asks the device, "What resources do you need?" The device says, "I need this IRQ, these I/O addresses, this DMA channel, and these addresses in upper memory for my BIOS." For legacy hardware, a device is the sole owner of these resources, and problems occur when more than one device attempts to use the same resource. (However, remember from our earlier discussion of IRQs that some newer buses allow more than one device to share the same IRQ and newer protected-mode BIOSs don't require upper memory addresses.) Today, more flexible Plug and Play devices simply say, "I need one IRQ, some I/O addresses, and this many memory addresses for my BIOS. Please tell me the resources I can use."

If a computer takes full advantage of the Windows 9x OS, its BIOS is Plug and Play BIOS, meaning that BIOS configures the Plug and Play devices before it loads Windows 9x. A Plug and Play device allows BIOS to select the device's computer resources, such as an IRQ, an I/O address, and DMA channels. BIOS first enables the devices that are not Plug and Play, and then tries to make the Plug and Play devices use the leftover resources. BIOS then turns this information over to Windows 9x when it loads, which completes the assignment of resources. Also recall that Windows 2000 and Windows XP use an advanced version of Plug and Play that does not use the BIOS Plug and Play, and that Windows NT does not support Plug and Play.

A+ OS 2.3

How the BIOS Finds and Loads the OS

Once POST and the first pass at assignment of resources is complete, the next step is to load an OS. Most often the OS is loaded from logical drive C on the hard drive. The

A+ OS 2.3

minimum information required on the hard drive to load an OS is listed below. You can see some of these items labeled in Figure 3-2.

- A sector at the very beginning of the hard drive, called the **Master Boot Record (MBR)**, which contains a program needed to locate the beginning of the OS on the drive
- A **partition table**, which contains a map to the logical drives on the hard drive, including how many partitions and logical drives there are, which drive is the boot drive (the active partition), and where each logical drive begins and ends
- At the beginning of the boot drive (usually drive C) the OS boot record that loads the first program file of the OS; for Windows 9x, that program is **Io.sys**
- For Windows 9x, **Msdos.sys** is needed next, followed by **Command.com**. These two files, plus Io.sys, are the core components of the real-mode portion of Windows 9x; Windows NT/2000/XP has a different set of startup files.

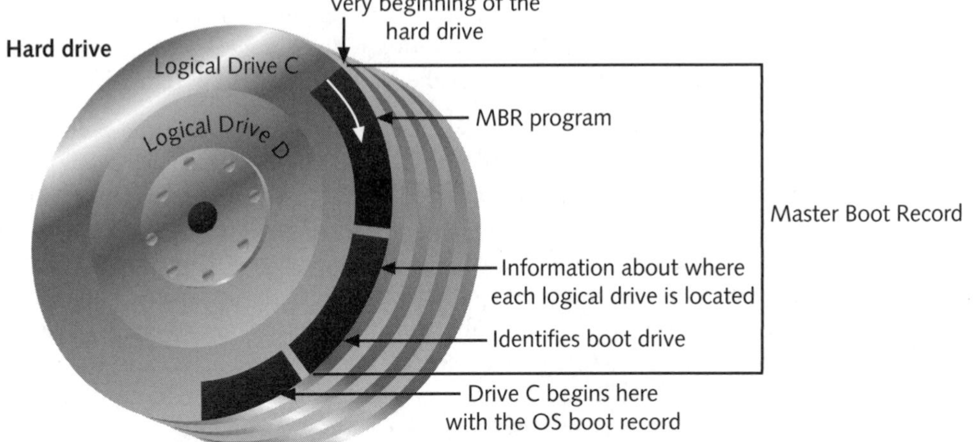

Figure 3-2 A hard drive might contain more than one logical drive; the partition table at the beginning of the drive contains information about the location of each logical drive, indicates which drive is the boot drive, and holds the Master Boot Record that begins the boot process for the operating system

One logical drive on the hard drive, usually drive C, is designated as the boot drive, and the OS is stored on it. At the beginning of this logical drive is the OS boot record, which contains the bootstrap loader, a program that knows the names of the files that contain the core programs of the OS.

The process by which the BIOS loads the OS begins with BIOS looking to CMOS setup to find out which secondary storage device should have the OS (see Figure 3-3). Recall that you saw how to change this boot sequence on your PC in a case project at the end of Chapter 2. Setup might instruct the BIOS to first look on drive C, and, if no OS is found there, then try drive A; or the order might be A then C. If BIOS looks first to drive A and does not find a disk in the drive, it turns to drive C. If it first looks to drive A and finds a disk

A+ OS 2.3

in the drive, but the disk does not contain the OS (for Windows 9x, that means the OS boot record, Io.sys, Msdos.sys, and Command.com), then this or a similar error message appears:

```
Non-system disk or disk error, press any key to continue
```

3

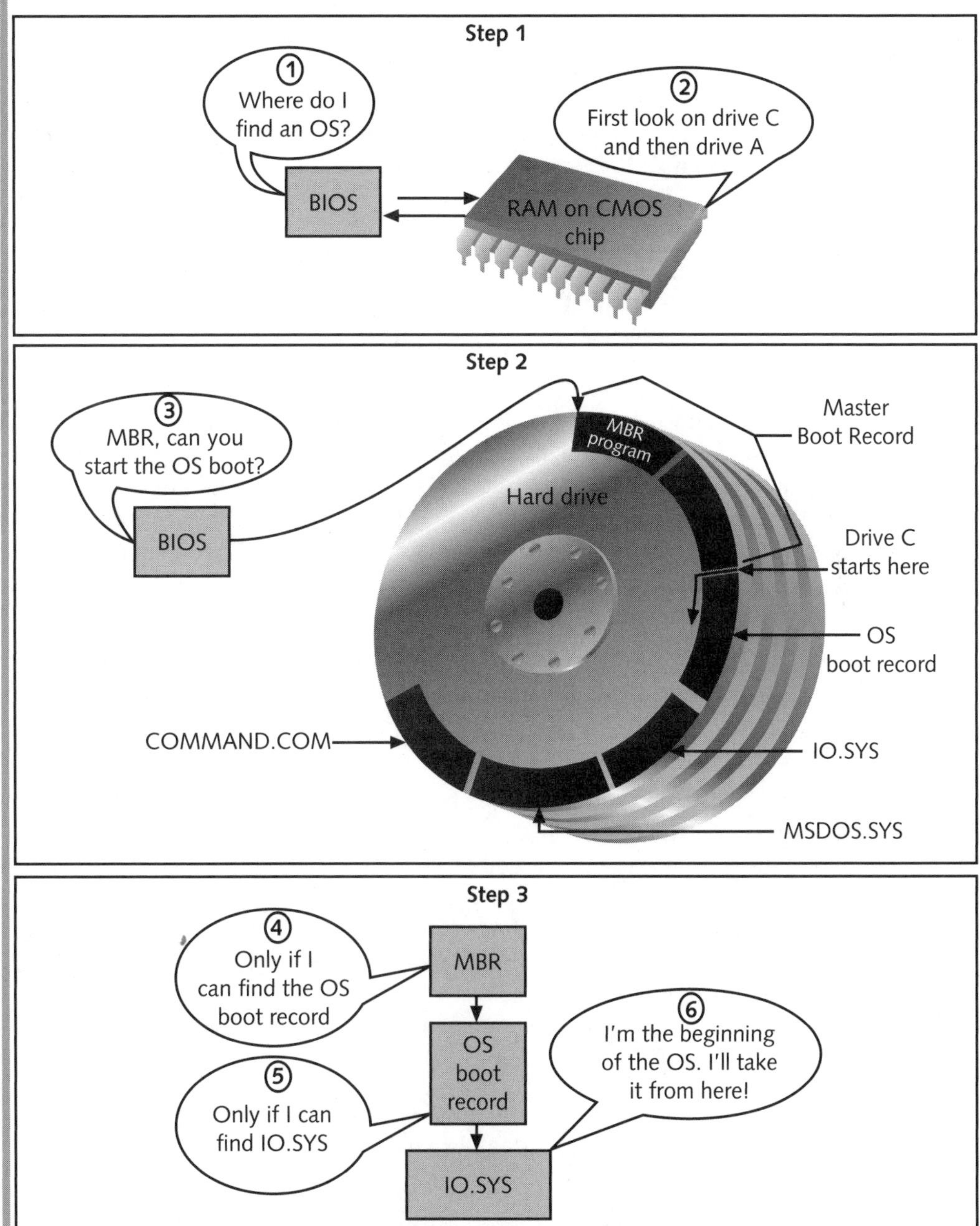

Figure 3-3 Boot Step 2: BIOS searches for and begins to load an operating system (in this example, Windows is the OS)

A+ OS 2.3 You must replace the disk with one that contains the OS or simply remove the disk to force the BIOS to continue on to drive C to find the OS.

Loading the MS-DOS Core of Windows 9x

A+ OS 1.2 1.3 2.5 3.2 This section describes what first happens during booting when only the MS-DOS core of Windows 9x is loaded, which brings the OS to a real-mode command prompt similar to a DOS command prompt. It's important for a PC technician to understand this real-mode DOS core because it is often used as a troubleshooting tool when the hard drive fails. You can boot to a command prompt in several ways, including booting from a Windows startup disk or using the Windows startup menu. How to prepare a startup disk is covered later in the chapter. How to use the Windows startup menu is covered in Chapter 5.

In Step 2 of Figure 3-3, the BIOS locates the MBR on the hard drive, which looks to the partition table to determine where the logical boot drive is physically located on the drive. It then turns to the OS boot record of that logical drive.

The OS boot record is a very short program; it loads just one hidden file, which makes up the DOS core, into memory (see Figure 3-3, Step 3 and Figure 3-4). (A **hidden file** is a file that is not displayed in the directory list.) The OS boot record program knows the filename, which is Io.sys. The Io.sys file contains the basic I/O software for real mode and requires that the Msdos.sys file be present. Msdos.sys is a text file that contains some parameters and switches that can be set to affect the way the OS boots. You will learn about the contents of Msdos.sys and how to change it to affect the boot process in Chapter 5.

The three OS files that are necessary in Windows 9x to boot to a command prompt are Io.sys, Msdos.sys, and Command.com. Config.sys and Autoexec.bat are not required but are used if they are present.

Once Io.sys is loaded into memory, the boot record program is no longer needed, and control is turned over to Io.sys. This program looks for Msdos.sys, reads it, and uses the settings in it. Io.sys then looks on the hard drive for a file named Config.sys. This configuration file contains commands that tell Io.sys how many files it can open at any one time (Files=) and how many file buffers to create (Buffers=). (A buffer is a temporary holding area for files.) Config.sys also includes the commands to load device drivers (Device=) as well as other information. An example of a typical command in Config.sys is the following command, which gives real-mode Io.sys access to memory above 1 MB, called extended memory:

```
Device=himem.sys
```

Several drivers can be loaded into memory from commands in Config.sys. Io.sys puts these programs in memory wherever it chooses. However, a program can request that it be put in a certain memory location.

A+ OS 1.2 1.3

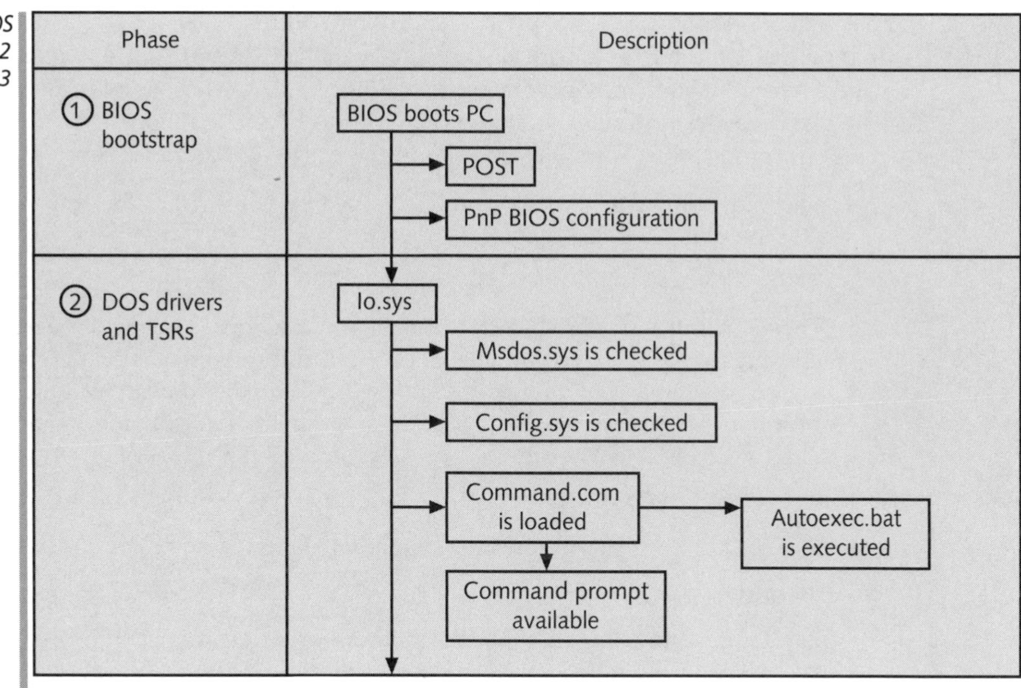

Figure 3-4 Boot Step 3: Operating system completes the boot process; MS-DOS core is loaded and command prompt presented to user

Sometimes Config.sys is used to create a RAM drive. A **RAM drive** is an area of memory that looks and acts like a hard drive, but because it is memory, it is much faster. It is sometimes used to speed up access to often-used software. Windows creates a RAM drive when booting from the startup disk, to hold files after they have been uncompressed, because this eliminates the need to have access to the hard drive and there is not room for them on the floppy disk. An example of a command in Config.sys to create a RAM drive is:

```
device=ramdrive.sys 2048
```

The command tells the OS to create a RAM drive that is 2048K in size.

After Config.sys is executed, Io.sys looks for another OS file, named Command.com. This file has three parts: more code to manage I/O, programs for internal OS commands such as Copy and Dir, and a short program that looks for the Autoexec.bat file.

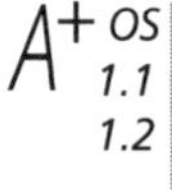
A+ OS 1.1 1.2

Some OS commands are **internal commands**, meaning they are embedded in the Command.com file, and others are **external commands**, meaning they have their own program files. An example of an external command is Format, stored in the file Format.com.

A+ OS 1.1 1.2 1.3

Command.com looks for Autoexec.bat and, if it's found, executes it. The filename **Autoexec.bat** stands for "automatically executed batch file." A **batch file** is a text file that contains a series of commands that are executed in order. Autoexec.bat lists OS commands that are executed automatically each time the OS is loaded. The following commands are examples of commands that might be found in the Autoexec.bat file:

- The Path command lists two paths, separated by semicolons. You learned about the Path command in Chapter 2.

  ```
  PATH C:\;C:\Windows;
  ```

- The Set command is used to create and assign a value to an environmental variable that can later be read by an application. A software installation program might add a Set command to your Autoexec.bat file. Later, the software will use the environmental variable in the program. An example of a Set command assigning a path to the variable Mypath is:

  ```
  Set Mypath=C:\VERT
  ```

- The Restart command causes the system to reboot.

  ```
  Restart.com
  ```

- The Temp command lets applications know where temporary files are to be stored. By default, DOS stores temporary files in C:\Temp, Windows 9x uses C:\Windows\Temp, Windows NT uses C:\Temp, and Windows 2000/XP uses C:\Winnt\Temp. Add the Temp command to Autoexec.bat if applications are putting temporary files in strange locations.

  ```
  Temp=C:\Temp
  ```

- The Echo command turns on and off the displaying of commands and messages. Use it in a batch file to control output to screen.

  ```
  Echo off
  ```

The boot process into real mode with a command prompt is completed after Autoexec.bat has finished executing. At this point, Command.com is the program in charge, providing you with a command prompt and waiting for your command. On the other hand, if a program or menu was executed from Autoexec.bat, it might ask you for a command.

The command prompt will indicate the drive that loaded the OS. If the OS files were loaded from a floppy disk, the command prompt will be A:\>, and if the OS was loaded from the hard drive, the command prompt will be C:\>. This drive and root directory are now the default drive and default directory, sometimes called the current working drive or directory.

If you want to complete loading Windows, use the Win command. Enter this command at the C prompt:

```
C:\> WIN
```

Note that commands used at a command prompt are not case sensitive, that is, you can enter *WIN*, *Win*, or *win*.

EMERGENCY STARTUP DISKS

A+ OS 3.2

Although you normally boot from a hard drive, problems with the hard drive sometimes make it necessary to boot from a floppy disk. A floppy disk that has enough software on it to load an operating system is called a **bootable disk**, or **system disk**. A bootable disk that has some utility programs on it to troubleshoot a failed hard drive is called a **rescue disk**, **emergency startup disk (ESD)**, or **startup disk**. Having a rescue disk available for an emergency is very important, and a PC technician should always have one or more on hand. For DOS, you have to create your own rescue disk, making sure it includes the necessary system files and any utilities that you might need in an emergency.

Beginning with Windows 95, the OS provided an automated method to create a rescue disk. This rescue disk is created under the Control Panel, Add/Remove Programs group. The files on the rescue disk vary with the version of Windows 9x. You can also create your own bootable disk or add your own utilities to the rescue disk created by Windows. In addition, in some situations, you will need a startup disk, which you can use to boot up a PC for the first time after a new hard drive has been installed when the hard drive has nothing written on it.

In this section, you will learn several ways to create these startup disks and then, in the remainder of the chapter, you will learn to use many of the utilities that Windows puts on these disks.

Windows 9x Startup Disks

A+ OS 3.2

Windows 9x can create a startup disk for you, complete with everything you need to troubleshoot a failed hard drive or prepare a new hard drive for use. The disk does not need to be created on the same computer that will use it, although in most cases you should use the same version of Windows as used by the computer that will be using the disk. Follow these directions to create a startup disk for Windows 9x.

1. Click **Start** on the Taskbar, point to **Settings**, and then click **Control Panel**.
2. In the Control Panel window, double-click the **Add/Remove Programs** icon.
3. Click the **Startup Disk** tab, and then click the **Create Disk** button (see Figure 3-5).
4. Windows might need the Windows CD to create the disk. Insert the CD if it is requested. The startup disk will then be created.

A+ OS 3.2

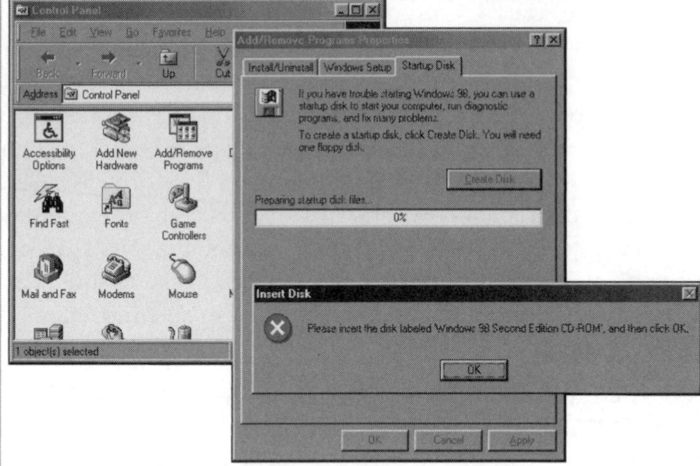

Figure 3-5 Windows might use the Windows CD to create a startup disk

Table 3-1 lists the files included on the startup disk for Windows 98, Second Edition (Windows 98 SE). Other versions of Windows 9x contain some, but not all, of these files.

Table 3-1 Files on the Windows 98 startup disk

File	Description
Aspi2dos.sys	Real-mode Adaptec CD-ROM driver
Aspi4dos.sys	Real-mode Adaptec CD-ROM driver
Aspi8dos.sys	Real-mode Adaptec CD-ROM driver
Aspi8u2.sys	Real-mode Adaptec CD-ROM driver
Aspicd.sys	Real-mode Adaptec CD-ROM driver
Autoexec.bat	Batch file that contains commands executed at startup
Btcdrom.sys	Mylex/BusLogic CD-ROM driver
Btdosm.sys	Mylex/BusLogic CD-ROM driver
Command.com	Command interpreter
Config.sys	Loads device drivers
Drvspace.bin	Used to access compressed hard drive
Ebd.cab	Cabinet file containing other utility program files
Ebd.sys	Identifies the startup disk
Extract.exe	Used to uncompress the Ebd.cab file
Fdisk.exe	Partitions the hard drive
Findramd.exe	Locates the RAM drive during startup
Flashpt.sys	Mylex/BusLogic CD-ROM driver
Himem.sys	Extended Memory Manager
Io.sys	System boot file

A+ OS 3.2

Table 3-1 Files on the Windows 98 startup disk (continued)

File	Description
Msdos.sys	Contains boot parameters.
Oakcdrom.sys	Generic device driver for CD-ROM drives.
Ramdrive.sys	Creates a RAM drive at startup.
Readme.txt	Information about the startup disk.
Setramd.bat	Searches for a drive letter to assign the RAM drive.

3

The file Ebd.cab is a compressed file, called a **cabinet file**, that contains several compressed files that are listed in Table 3-2. You will learn to use many of these commands later in the chapter. During startup, the contents of the cabinet file are uncompressed and copied to the RAM drive because there is not enough space for them on the floppy disk and the startup disk assumes the hard drive might not be accessible. You can also use the Extract command to extract specific files when the RAM drive is not active.

Table 3-2 Files contained in the cabinet file, Ebd.cab

File	Description
Attrib.exe	Changes file attributes.
Chkdsk.exe	Determines the status of a disk and repairs it.
Debug.exe	Debugging utility used to view contents of memory.
Edit.com	Text editor used from a command prompt.
Extract.exe	Extracts files from a cabinet file.
Format.com	Formats a hard drive.
Mscdex.exe	Microsoft utility to interface with a CD-ROM driver.
Scandisk.exe	Checks and repairs hard drives.
Scandisk.ini	Contains parameters for Scandisk.exe.
Sys.com	Copies system files to a disk making it bootable.

Creating Your Own Bootable Rescue Disk for Windows 9x

Using Windows Explorer, you can create a system disk (Windows terminology for a bootable disk) and then copy program files to the disk that you might need in an emergency. The first step is to format the disk, which writes tracks on the disk and puts a file system on the disk. More details of what happens during the format operation are covered later in the chapter. To format a floppy disk in Windows 9x, follow these steps.

1. Click the **Start** button on the Taskbar, point to **Programs**, and then click **Windows Explorer**. Right-click either drive A or drive B. The shortcut menu in Figure 3-6 appears.

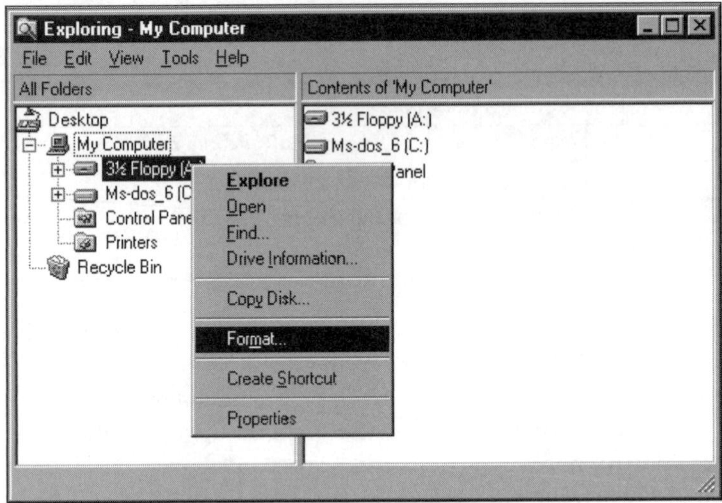

Figure 3-6 Menu for managing a floppy disk

2. Click **Format** on the menu. The dialog box shown in Figure 3-7 opens. Notice that you have three format options: Quick format (does not overwrite existing tracks), Full format (writes new tracks and sector markings), and an option to copy just the system files to the disk; these are the files needed to make the disk bootable (Io.sys, Msdos.sys, and Command.com are copied to the disk).

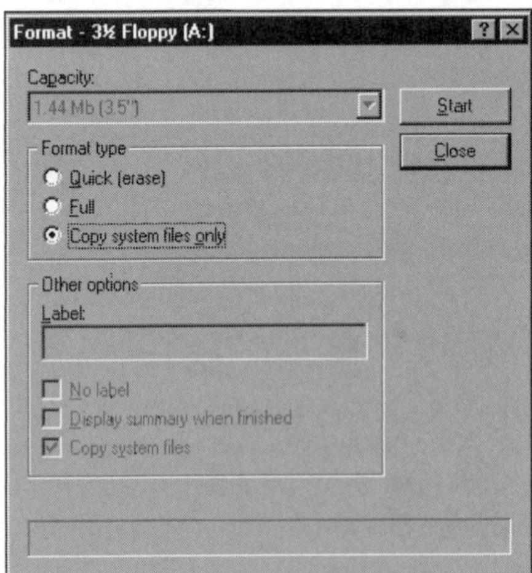

Figure 3-7 Format a disk in Microsoft Windows 9x

3. If the disk has been preformatted at the factory, you can select the third option, to copy system files only, but if the disk has never been formatted, select **Full**. Then click **Start**.

3

From a command prompt, you can create your own bootable rescue disk and manually copy OS utility files to it. To make a bootable rescue disk for Windows 9x, from the command prompt, type:

```
Format A:/S
```

The command erases any files currently on the disk in drive A, and the /S switch copies the two hidden files, Io.sys and Msdos.sys, and Command.com to the disk in drive A, making the disk bootable.

You might also want to put some utility programs on the disk to help in troubleshooting. In addition to the files listed in Tables 3-1 and 3-2, other files you might need are xcopy.exe, MSD.exe, Mem.exe, and More.com. You will learn about these files later in the chapter.

Editing Autoexec.bat and Config.sys

You can change Config.sys and Autoexec.bat to configure your OS environment or troubleshoot boot problems. Use any text editor to edit the files. For example, from a command prompt, use EDIT, a full-screen text editor, and from Windows, use Notepad, WordPad, or Sysedit. From Windows, Sysedit is the preferred method and is covered in Chapter 5.

If you make a mistake when editing Autoexec.bat or Config.sys, you can cause a boot problem. Before editing these files on your hard drive, always make a rescue disk. If you are editing one of these files on a rescue disk, you can make a backup copy of the file before you edit it or have a second rescue disk ready just in case.

Do not use word-processing software, such as Word or WordPerfect, to edit Autoexec.bat or Config.sys, unless you use the ASCII text mode, because word-processing applications place control characters in their document files that prevent the OS from interpreting the file correctly.

You need to know how to edit the Autoexec.bat and Config.sys files at the command prompt. Follow these directions to use Edit.com to edit the Autoexec.bat file on a rescue disk:

1. Boot to the command prompt and make drive A the default drive, as follows:

   ```
   C:\> A:
   ```

2. If the default directory is not the root directory, make it so, using the CD (Change Directory) command, as follows:

   ```
   A:\DOS> CD\
   ```

The prompt at the root directory of drive A should look like this:

```
A:\>
```

No matter what the default directory was (in this example, it was \DOS), the backslash (\) in the prompt indicates that the root is now the default.

3. If Autoexec.bat exists on the floppy disk, back it up, as follows:

   ```
   A:\> Copy Autoexec.bat Autoexec.bk
   ```

4. Edit the file, as follows:

   ```
   A:\> Edit Autoexec.bat
   ```

Your screen should be similar to the one shown in Figure 3-8. After you have made your changes, to exit from the editor, press the **Alt** key to activate the menus, and choose **Exit** from the File menu. When asked if you want to save your changes, respond **Yes** to exit the editor and save any changes.

5. You can reboot your computer (**Crtl+Alt+Del**) to execute the new Autoexec.bat file, or you can type Autoexec.bat at the command prompt. If the computer stalls during the boot, use another startup disk to reboot. You can also press the **F5** key to bypass the startup files during the boot.

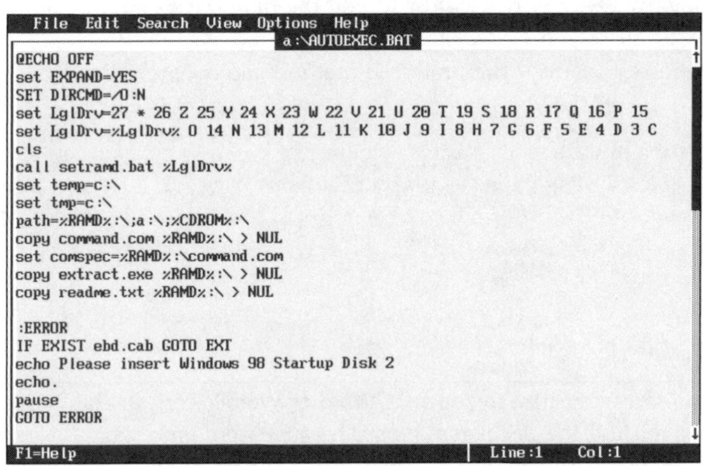

Figure 3-8 Edit Autoexec.bat

Accessing a Command Prompt

A+CORE 1.1 2.3

There are several ways to get to the command prompt. From the Windows desktop, you can access a command prompt by clicking Start, Programs, MS-DOS Prompt. A command prompt window, sometimes called a **DOS box**, appears, as shown in Figure 3-9. In it you can enter DOS-like commands discussed in this chapter. To exit the window, type Exit at the command prompt. This DOS box is not actually operating in real mode, but is operating in the virtual real mode provided by Windows. In fact, Windows sees this DOS box as the window provided for the 16-bit program Command.com. Every Windows OS offers this command window.

A+CORE 1.1 2.3

You can also get a DOS box by this alternate method: click Start, Run, and enter Command.com in the Run dialog box. Because you are not using true real mode and Windows is still running in the background, some commands entered from a DOS box might not work correctly or might even produce errors. There is a way to force Windows 9x to create a real-mode environment for a 16-bit program, and it is covered in Chapter 4.

You can use other means to get a true real-mode environment. The easiest way is to click Start, click Shutdown, and select Restart in MS-DOS mode from the Shutdown dialog box. This method only works for Windows 95 and Windows 98. Windows Me, Windows NT, Windows 2000, and Windows XP do not support accessing real mode in this way. For Windows Me and Windows XP, create a MS-DOS startup disk, insert it in the floppy disk drive, and boot from that disk. Recall that the startup BIOS boot sequence must be drive A first and then drive C for you be able to do this. Windows NT and Windows 2000 do not offer the option to create a MS-DOS startup disk, but, in a pinch, you can use one created on another PC to boot a Windows NT/2000 computer to a DOS prompt.

For Windows 9x, you can also boot to a command prompt by holding down the Ctrl key or the F8 key while booting, which causes the OS to display a startup menu. From the menu, select Command prompt only.

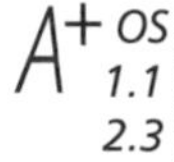

1.1 2.3

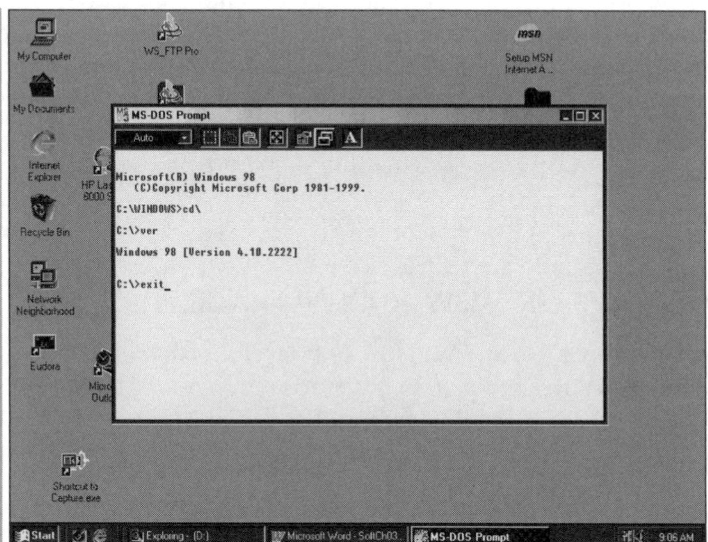

Figure 3-9 A MS-DOS Prompt window operates in the virtual real mode provided by Windows 9x

In some situations, it is appropriate to use a startup disk created by one OS to boot a failed system that has a different OS installed. For example, suppose Windows NT/2000/XP refuses to boot. Using a different PC, you can create a startup disk under Windows 98 and then use it to boot the Windows NT/2000/XP PC. If you can successfully boot to an A

A+ OS 1.1 2.3 prompt, you have demonstrated that the hard drive or files stored on it is the source of the problem. However, it is best to use recovery procedures and disks native to the OS installed.

Suppose there is an important data file on the Windows NT/2000/XP computer and you don't have the proper recovery disks for the OS. You might be able to use the Windows 98 startup disk to recover the file. There are special considerations for Windows NT/2000/XP. These OSs support more than one file system, and a Windows 9x startup disk supports only FAT16 or FAT32. If a Windows NT/2000/XP hard drive has a different file system installed, such as NTFS (New Technology File System), then the Windows 9x startup disk will not be able to read that file system. In this situation, you can work from an A prompt (A:\>), but you will not be able to access the hard drive. The solution is to create rescue disks under these operating systems that can read the file system.

When Windows 9x (including Windows Me) creates a startup disk, it copies files to the disk from the \Windows\Command\EBD folder. You can also copy these files to a formatted disk to manually create a startup disk.

Looking at the list of files in Tables 3-1 and 3-2 that are stored on a Windows 98 startup disk, you can see several files needed to manage memory and hard drives, two hardware devices that are essential to successfully booting a PC into Windows. Before we discuss how to use a startup disk to troubleshoot a failed Windows boot, let's look at these programs on the startup disk and how the MS-DOS portion of Windows 9x uses them to manage memory and hard drives. These same methods also affect the way Windows 9x manages memory and a hard drive, even when the desktop is loaded, so this knowledge also applies to future chapters.

How DOS and Windows 9x View and Manage Memory

Memory management under DOS and Windows 9x can seem complicated because of the way the process has evolved over the past 20 years or so. Like an old house that has been added to and remodeled several times, the present-day design is not as efficient as that of a brand new house. Decisions made by IBM and Microsoft in the early 1980s still significantly affect, and in some cases limit, the way memory is used under Windows 9x. Because Windows NT, followed by Windows 2000 and Windows XP, have had the luxury of being designed from the ground up, they are free of those limitations.

Recall from Chapter 2 that earlier versions of DOS operated completely in real mode, which initially allowed access to only the first 1 MB of memory addresses. Later, DOS added a memory extender, **Himem.sys**, that allowed access to memory addresses above 1 MB. Early versions of Windows 3.x working with DOS could keep more than one program loaded at the same time by swapping them in and out of memory; this was called standard mode but was actually real mode with some fancy maneuvering. Later versions of Windows 3.x let 16-bit programs share memory (more than one program could access the same memory and share its data) in a "virtual DOS machine" in 386 enhanced mode. Windows 3.x could also perform virtual memory management by creating a swap file stored on the hard drive and using it as if it were memory.

Windows 95 was the first OS in the evolution of Windows operating systems to support 32-bit protected-mode applications software. Most of the OS code is written in 32-bit protected mode. It still allows 16-bit real-mode device drivers, and 16-bit software can run in a **virtual DOS machine (VDM)**, just as with Windows 3.x, or can run in real mode. A VDM is an environment that a 32-bit protected-mode OS provides for a real-mode program to operate in.

Windows NT made a break with the past. All its code is written in protected mode, and it does not allow other software to operate in real mode, but only in a virtual real mode, which it tightly controls. This makes Windows NT a much more stable OS than Windows 9x.

Table 3-3 summarizes the evolution of operating systems and software as it applies to memory. Notice that Windows NT is the first Microsoft OS to resolve many issues involving real mode, particularly the 1024K limitation imposed by real mode. With DOS and Windows 3.x, this limitation directly affected managing memory resources and, in some cases, can still be significant with Windows 9x.

Table 3-3 Summary of how operating systems have evolved in managing memory

Operating System	Real Mode	Protected Mode
DOS	Operates totally in real mode, but later offered Himem.sys, a device driver that allows programs access to extended memory.	NA
DOS with Windows 2.x	Operated totally in real mode but managed the process of switching programs in and out of memory.	NA
DOS with Windows 3.x	Real mode was called standard mode. Allows only one 16-bit application at a time in memory.	Protected mode is called 386 enhanced mode. Multiple applications can share memory.
Windows 9x	Allows real-mode drivers to be loaded during startup; 16-bit DOS applications are allowed a real-mode session.	Switches back and forth between real mode and protected mode as necessary; supports both 16-bit and 32-bit applications in a virtual machine.
Windows NT/2000/XP	NA	All work is done in protected mode. Supports 32-bit applications. 16-bit applications can operate in a virtual machine only.

Physical Memory and Memory Addresses

To understand how memory use evolved, beginning with DOS and moving to Windows NT, you must understand basic memory concepts. Recall from Chapter 2 that a memory address is a number the CPU assigns to ROM or RAM to track the memory it can use. A CPU has a limited number of memory addresses that it can assign to physical memory, determined by the number of memory address lines available on the memory bus.

Some older 16-bit programs work only when they can use certain memory addresses, such as a hexadecimal number like C80000. This address is part of the physical memory's ROM programming; no other address works for it. An example of this kind of memory is a ROM chip on an older video card. Some memory, usually ROM chips on expansion boards, must be assigned one of two, or sometimes three, sets of addresses. You make the choice by setting jumpers or DIP switches on the board or, in more recent cases, when you run an installation program for the board. New Plug and Play boards don't have this restriction. Their ROM code can be assigned any values chosen by the OS or system BIOS. Plug and Play cards are required to use whatever memory addresses are assigned to them. The system is free to assign any address it chooses to this physical memory.

Both RAM and ROM must be assigned memory addresses so the CPU can access this memory. System BIOS stored on motherboard ROM chips must be assigned addresses by the CPU so that the CPU can access that programming. The assigning of addresses to both RAM and ROM occurs during booting, and is sometimes called memory mapping. In Figure 3-10, the memory addresses available to the CPU are listed on the left, and the physical RAM and ROM that need these addresses are on the right. These RAM modules are located on the motherboard, and ROM chips are found on a sound card, network card, and video card in this example. RAM is holding several device drivers, applications, and the OS.

Programming stored on ROM chips is not usually copied into RAM, despite what many people believe. It is simply assigned memory addresses by the CPU. These ROM programs become part of the total memory available to the CPU, and do not use up part of total RAM. The resources they use are memory addresses. The RAM memory is still available to be assigned other addresses. There is an exception, called shadowing ROM, when programs stored on ROM are copied to RAM to improve performance.

Finally, memory management in DOS and Windows 9x presents limitations not so much because of the operating systems themselves, but because applications, device drivers, and BIOS used the standards presented to the industry when DOS was first introduced and these standards are still in effect today. Compared to that of other operating systems, memory management in DOS and Windows 9x is handicapped because DOS has existed longer than most other operating systems. Therefore, DOS must maintain compatibility with software and devices that have been around for a long time. Also, Microsoft made the commitment with Windows 9x that it, too, would be compatible with older software and BIOS written for DOS and Windows 3.x using DOS. Probably the greatest limitation of Windows 9x today is this commitment to maintain backward-compatibility with older software and hardware.

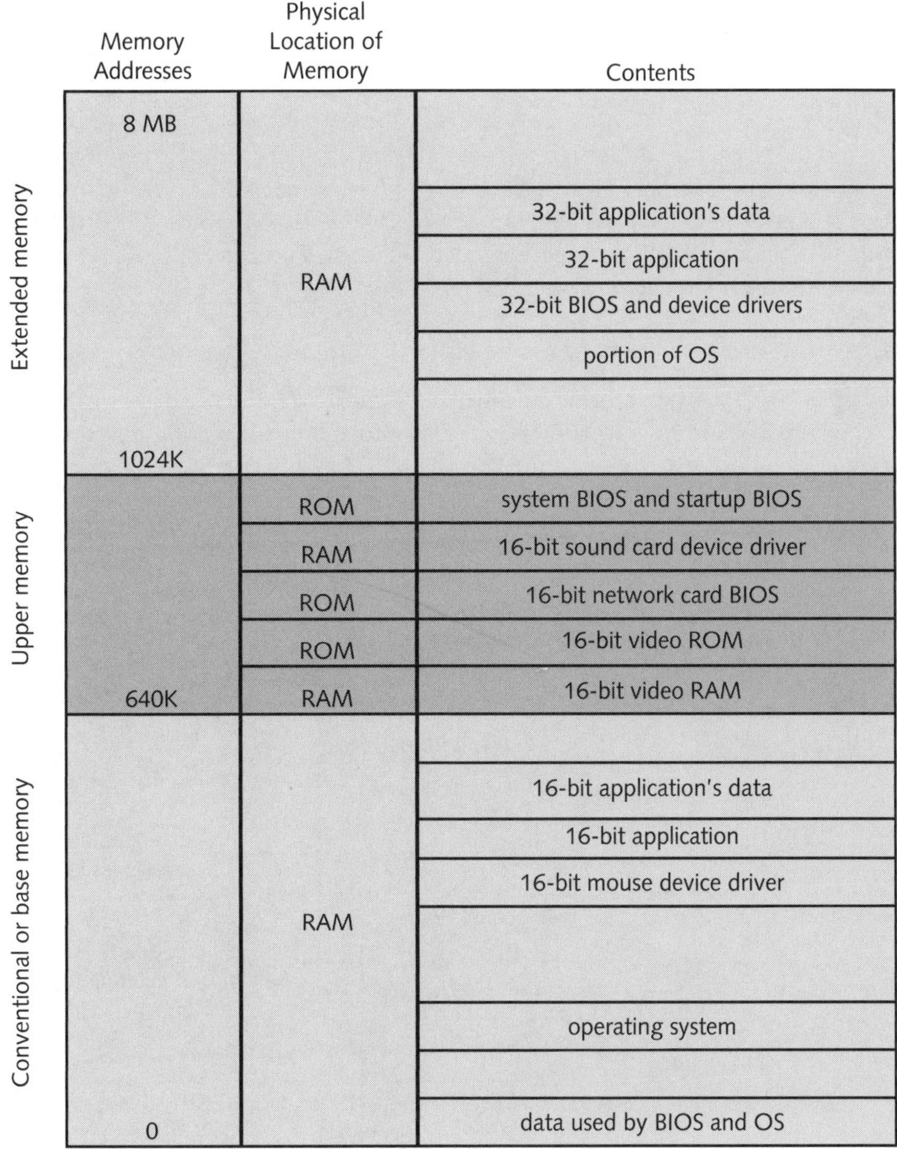

Figure 3-10 Memory map showing how ROM and RAM, on and off the motherboard, might be mapped to memory addresses

Areas of the Memory Map

A+ OS 1.1

There are several types of memory that the OS manages: conventional, upper, and extended memory. These memory types are logical divisions or categories rather than physical ones, and the divisions are determined by their memory addresses rather than by their physical location. The following sections cover this logical memory management. A segment of

A+ OS 1.1

RAM can be assigned memory addresses in the upper memory range today but be assigned a range of addresses in extended memory tomorrow. It's still just RAM, no matter what address it's assigned. The difference is the way the CPU can use this memory because of the addresses assigned to it.

To get a clear picture of this memory-addressing schema, consider the memory map shown in Figure 3-11. The first 640K of memory addresses are called **conventional memory**, or base memory. The memory addresses from 640K up to 1024K are called **upper memory**. Memory above 1024K is called extended memory. The first 64K of extended memory is called the **high memory area (HMA)**.

Conventional Memory

In the early 1980s, when IBM and Microsoft were designing the original PCs, they decided to make 640K of memory addresses available to the user, thinking that this was plenty for anything the user would ever want to do. This 640K of addresses was intended to hold the OS, the applications software, and the data being processed. At that time, 640K of memory addresses was more than enough to handle all the applications available. Today, 640K of memory addresses is inadequate, for the following reasons:

- Many applications are very large programs, requiring a considerable number of memory addresses to hold the programs as well as the data.

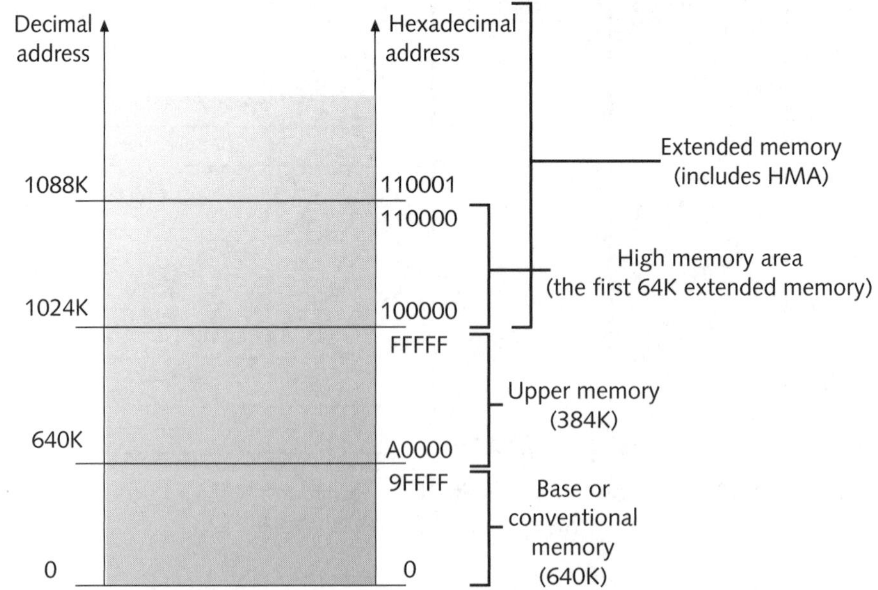

Figure 3-11 Memory address map showing the starting and ending addresses of conventional, upper, and extended memory, including the high memory area

A+ OS 1.1

- Often more than one application runs at the same time, each of which requires its own memory area for the program and data. Also, sometimes computers in a network serve more than one user at a time. In the early 1980s, a PC was expected to be used by a single user, operating one application at a time.
- Users expect software to provide a friendly graphical user interface, or GUI. Graphical user interfaces provide icons, graphics, and windows on a screen, all requiring large amounts of memory.

3

The problem caused by restricting the number of memory addresses available to the user to only 640K could have been easily solved by simply providing more addresses to the user in future versions of DOS. However, another original design decision ruled this out. The next group of memory addresses, the 384K above conventional memory, called upper memory, were assigned to utility operations for the system. The system requires memory addresses to communicate with peripherals. The programs (such as BIOS on a video card or on the motherboard) and data are assigned memory addresses in this upper memory area. For example, the video BIOS and its data are placed in the very first part of upper memory, the area from 640K to 768K. All video ROM written for DOS-based computers assumes that these programs and data are stored in this area. Also, many DOS and Windows applications interact directly with video ROM and RAM in this address range.

Programs almost always expect data to be written into memory directly above the addresses for the program itself, an important fact for understanding memory management. Thus, if a program begins storing its data above its location in conventional memory, eventually it will "hit the ceiling," the beginning of upper memory assigned to video ROM. The major reason that applications have 640K memory limit is that video ROM begins at 640K. If DOS and Windows 9x allowed applications into these upper memory addresses, all DOS-compatible video ROM would need to be rewritten, and many DOS applications that access these video addresses would not work. Know that 32-bit device drivers and applications under Windows 9x don't have this problem because they can run from extended memory and turn to the OS to access video.

Windows NT/2000/XP are not backward-compatible with older hardware and software because they do not manage memory in the same way. You will learn more about how these operating systems manage memory later in this book.

Upper Memory

The memory map in Figure 3-11 shows that the memory addresses from 640K up to (but not including) 1024K are called upper memory. In the hexadecimal number system (see Appendix C for an explanation of this system), upper memory begins at A0000 and goes through FFFFF. Video ROM and RAM are stored in the first part of upper memory, hex A0000 through CFFFF (the A, B, and C areas of memory). Sixteen-bit BIOS programs for other legacy expansion boards are assigned memory addresses in the remaining portions of upper memory. BIOS on the motherboard (system BIOS) is assigned the top part of upper memory, from F0000 through FFFFF (the F area of upper memory). Upper memory often has unassigned addresses, depending on which boards are present in the system. Managing

A+ OS 1.1 memory effectively involves gaining access to these unused addresses in upper memory and using them to store device drivers and TSR (terminate-and-stay-resident) programs.

Figure 3-12 shows that video memory addresses fall between A0000 and CFFFF. For VGA and Super VGA video, the A and B areas hold data sent to the video card, and the C area contains the video BIOS.

Extended Memory and the High Memory Area

Memory above 1 MB is called extended memory. The first 64K of extended memory is called the high memory area, which exists because a bug in the programming for the older 286 CPU (the first CPU to use extended memory) produced this small pocket of unused memory addresses. Beginning with DOS 5, the OS capitalized on this bug by storing portions of itself in the high memory area, thus freeing some conventional memory where DOS had been stored. This method of storing part of DOS in the high memory area is called "loading DOS high." You will see how to do this later in the chapter.

Extended memory is actually managed by the OS as a device (the device is memory) that is controlled by a device driver. To access extended memory, you need the device driver (called a memory extender) that controls it, and you must use applications that have been written to use the extended memory. The amount of extended memory you can have on your computer is limited by the amount of RAM that can be installed on your motherboard and the number of memory addresses the CPU and the memory bus can support.

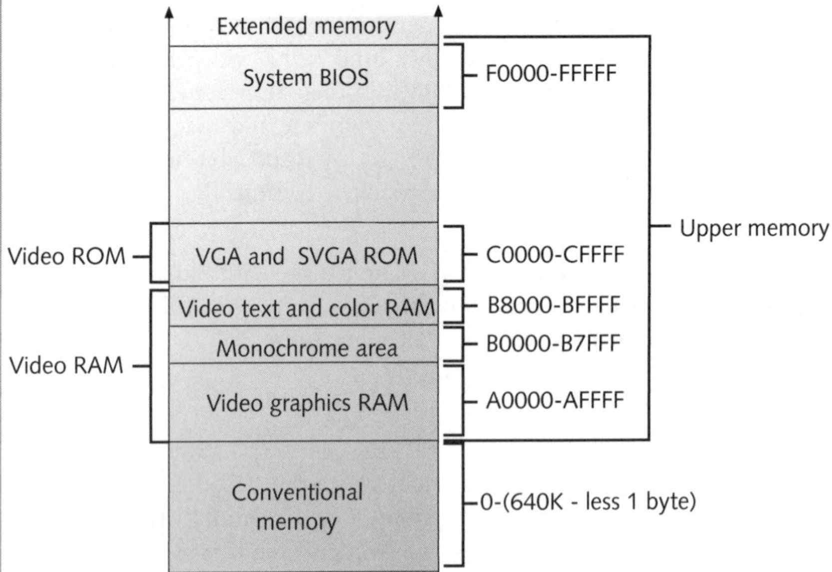

Figure 3-12 Memory map of upper memory showing starting and finishing addresses and video ROM and RAM assignments

Utilities that Manage Memory

A+ OS 1.2 The two utilities used by Windows 9x to manage memory above 640K are Himem.sys and Emm386.exe. Himem.sys is the device driver for all memory above 640K. The program file **Emm386.exe** contains the software that loads device drivers and other programs into upper memory. Himem.sys is automatically loaded by Windows 9x during the boot process but can also be loaded by an entry in Config.sys. Emm386.exe is not loaded automatically by Windows 9x, but you can load it by an entry in Config.sys.

Using Himem.sys

Himem.sys is considered a device driver because it manages memory as a device. It can be executed by the Device= command in Config.sys. Figure 3-13 shows an example of a very simple Config.sys file on a floppy disk that loads Himem.sys. The Config.sys file is being edited by the Edit.com text editor utility.

To create the file on a floppy disk, you can use either of these two methods:

- Make drive A the default drive and enter this command:

  `A:\> Edit Config.sys`

- Make drive C the default drive and enter this command:

  `C:\> Edit A:Config.sys`

Figure 3-13 Config.sys set to use memory above 640K

The second line in the Config.sys file, device=A:\util\mouse.sys, tells DOS to load into memory a device driver that is found on the floppy disk in the \Util directory, which allows you to use the mouse while in MS-DOS mode.

The third line in the Config.sys file, device=A:\util\ansi.sys, tells DOS to load the device driver Ansi.sys into memory. Ansi.sys helps control the keyboard and monitor, providing color on the monitor and an additional set of characters to the ASCII character set. For more information about ASCII and ANSI, see Appendix B.

A+ OS 1.2 1.3

Using Emm386.exe

In DOS and Windows 9x, Emm386.exe manages the memory addresses in upper memory. Before we see how to use it, let's begin by examining memory when upper memory addresses are not available. To do that, we use the MEM command, which lets us view how memory is currently allocated. Use the /C option to get a complete list and include the |MORE option to page the results on your screen. Figure 3-14 was produced using this command:

```
MEM /C |MORE
```

In Figure 3-14, the first column shows the programs currently loaded in memory. The second column shows the total amount of memory used by each program. The columns labeled Conventional and Upper Memory show the amount of memory being used by each program in each of these categories. This PC is not making use of upper memory for any of its programs. At the bottom of the screen is the total amount of free conventional memory (544,720 bytes) that is available to new programs to be loaded. Making this value as high as possible is the subject of this section.

```
Modules using memory below 1 MB:

  Name           Total              Conventional          Upper Memory
  --------  ----------------     ----------------      ----------------
  MSDOS       18,672   (18K)       18,672   (18K)             0     (0K)
  HIMEM        1,168    (1K)        1,168    (1K)             0     (0K)
  DBLBUFF      2,976    (3K)        2,976    (3K)             0     (0K)
  IFSHLP       2,864    (3K)        2,864    (3K)             0     (0K)
  WIN          3,616    (4K)        3,616    (4K)             0     (0K)
  COMMAND      8,416    (8K)        8,416    (8K)             0     (0K)
  SAVE        72,768   (71K)       72,768   (71K)             0     (0K)
  Free       544,720  (532K)      544,720  (532K)             0     (0K)

Memory Summary:

  Type of Memory          Total          Used          Free
  ----------------   -----------   -----------   -----------
  Conventional           655,360       110,640       544,720
  Upper                        0             0             0
  Reserved                     0             0             0
  Extended (XMS)     133,156,864        69,632   133,087,232
  ----------------   -----------   -----------   -----------
-- More --
```

Figure 3-14 MEM report with /C option on a PC not using upper memory

Creating and Using Upper Memory Blocks Figure 3-15 shows an example of a Config.sys file that is set to use upper memory addresses. The first line loads the Himem.sys driver. The second line loads the Emm386.exe file. Emm386.exe assigns addresses in upper memory to memory made available by the Himem.sys driver. The NOEMS switch at the end of the command line says to Windows, "Do not create any simulated expanded memory." Expanded memory is an older type of memory above 1 MB that is no longer used by software. The command to load Emm386.exe must appear after the command to load Himem.sys in the Config.sys file.

A+ OS 1.2 1.3

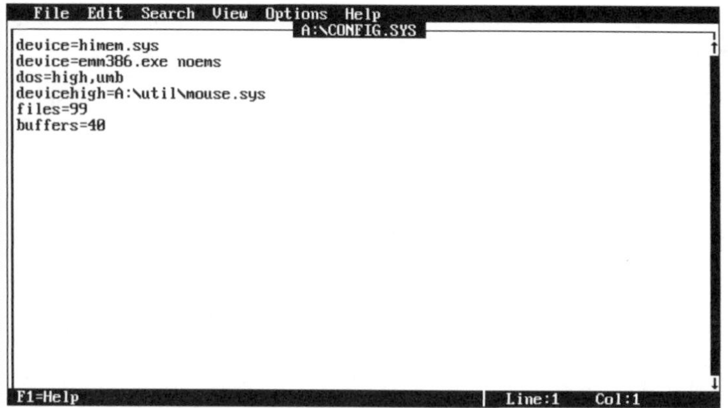

Figure 3-15 Config.sys set to use upper memory

The command DOS=HIGH,UMB serves two purposes. The one command line can be broken into two commands like this:

```
DOS=HIGH
DOS=UMB
```

The DOS=HIGH portion tells the OS to load part of the DOS core into the high memory area ("loading DOS high"). Remember that the high memory area is the first 64K of extended memory. This memory is usually unused unless we choose to store part of DOS in it with this command line. Including this command in Config.sys frees some conventional memory that would have been used by the OS.

The second part of the command, DOS=UMB, creates upper memory blocks. An **upper memory block (UMB)** is a group of consecutive memory addresses in the upper memory area that has had physical memory assigned to it. The OS identifies blocks that are currently not being used by system ROM or expansion boards, and the memory manager makes these blocks available for use. This command, DOS=UMB, enables the OS to access these upper memory blocks. After the UMBs are created, they can be used in these ways:

- `Devicehigh=` command in Config.sys
- `Loadhigh` command in Autoexec.bat
- `Loadhigh` command at the command prompt (explained below)

The next line in the Config.sys file in Figure 3-15 uses a UMB. The command Devicehigh=A:\Util\Mouse.sys tells the OS to load the mouse device driver into one of the upper memory blocks created and made available by the previous three lines. This process of loading a program into upper memory addresses is called loading high.

Loading Device Drivers High Using the Devicehigh= command in Config.sys, rather than the Device= command, causes the driver to load high. With the Devicehigh= command, the OS stores these drivers in UMBs using the largest UMB first, then the next largest, and so on until all are loaded. Therefore, to make sure there is enough room to hold

A+ OS 1.2 1.3

them all in upper memory, order the Devicehigh= command lines in Config.sys so that the largest drivers are loaded first.

You can determine the amount of memory a device driver allocates for itself and its data by using the MEM command with the /M filename option:

```
MEM /M filename
```

The filename is the name of the device driver without the file extension.

You can also use a UMB from Autoexec.bat using the Loadhigh (LH) command. For example, to load high Mscdex.exe, a utility to access a CD-ROM drive, use either command:

```
LH Mscdex.exe
Loadhigh Mscdex.exe
```

In either case, the program is loaded into the largest UMB available and does not use up more precious conventional memory. Note that before the Loadhigh command will work, the program files Himem.sys and Emm386.exe must be available to the OS and these three lines must be added to Config.sys and executed by booting the computer:

```
Device=HIMEM.SYS
Device=EMM386.EXE NOEMS
DOS=UMB
```

If the Himem.sys and Emm386.exe files are not in the root directory of the boot device, you must include the path to the file name in the Device= line, like this:

```
Device=C:\DOS\HIMEM.SYS
```

When a program is loaded high, two things can go wrong. Either the program might not work from upper memory, causing problems during execution, or there might not be enough room in upper memory for the program and its data. If the program causes the computer to hang when you attempt to run it, or if it simply refuses to work correctly, remove it from upper memory.

Some Default Settings Used by Windows

A+ OS 1.2 1.3

You have just seen how Windows MS-DOS mode uses Config.sys and Autoexec.bat. Most of the settings that once were put into Config.sys under DOS are now embedded into the Windows 9x Io.sys file. If Config.sys or Autoexec.bat are present, the entries in those files override the default entries in Io.sys. The entries in Io.sys cannot be changed and are listed in Table 3-4.

A+ OS 1.3 2.5

Table 3-4 Entries in Io.sys that once were in Config.sys

Entry	Description
Buffers=30	The number of file buffers to create.
DOS=HIGH	The DOS core of Windows 9x is loaded into the high memory area (HMA).
Files=60	The number of files that can be open at one time under 16-bit applications.
Himem.sys	Himem.sys is loaded to manage extended memory in Windows 9x.
Lastdrive=Z	The last letter that can be assigned to a logical drive.
Setver.exe	A program that tells DOS applications that the version of DOS they are looking for is the version they are using. The program allows some older DOS applications to run that might otherwise hang.
Shell=Command.com /P	Loads Command.com and executes Autoexec.bat.
Stacks=9,256	The number of frames of instructions that can be held in memory in a queue at one time. Used for backward compatibility with older applications.

Managing Floppy Disks and Hard Drives

A+ OS 1.1

When a hard drive (sometimes called the HDD) is first installed, it has nothing written on it except empty track markings put there at the factory. A floppy disk is completely blank and does not even have these track markings. The OS must prepare both these media for use by putting track markings on a floppy disk and putting a file system on both floppy disk and hard drive. In addition, the OS is responsible for managing the file system, including creating, deleting, copying and moving directories and files. This section looks at the commands to do all this from a command prompt under Windows 9x. Except for writing a new file system to a hard drive, these same functions can also be done from within Windows using Windows Explorer.

Before we get into how to use specific commands, you will learn about how data is organized on floppy disks and hard drives, a subject that was first introduced in the last chapter.

How Data is Logically Stored on a Floppy Disk

A+ OS 1.1

When a floppy disk is first formatted, sector and track markings are written to the disk. Recall from Chapter 1 that tracks are concentric circles on the disk and a segment of a track, called a sector, always holds 512 bytes of data. All floppy disks, no matter what size or density, and hard drives are divided into tracks and sectors, and each sector holds 512 bytes of data.

A+ OS 1.1

You learned in the last chapter that a cluster, sometimes called a file allocation unit, is a group of sectors that is the smallest unit on a disk used to hold a file or a portion of a file. "Sector" refers to how data is physically stored on a disk, while "cluster" describes how data is logically organized. The BIOS manages the disk as physical sectors, but the OS considers the disk only as a long list of clusters that can each hold a fixed amount of data (see Figure 3-16). The OS keeps that list of clusters in the file allocation table (FAT).

There are several variations of floppy disks including the older 5¼ inch floppy disk, the 3½inch double-density floppy disk, and the most current floppy disk, the 3½ inch high-density disk, which holds 1.44 MB of data. Let's see how this disk holds that data.

The 3½ inch high-density floppy disk has 80 tracks and 18 sectors per track on each side. Each side has 80 tracks × 18 sectors, or 1,440 sectors. This type of disk has only one sector per cluster, making 1,440 × 2 sides, or 2,880 clusters. Because each cluster holds 512 bytes (one sector) of data, a 3½ -inch high-density floppy disk has 2,880 × 512 = 1,474,560 bytes of data. Divide this number by 1,024 to convert bytes to kilobytes. The storage capacity of this disk is 1,440 kilobytes. Divide by 1,000 to convert kilobytes to megabytes, and the storage is 1.44 MB.

There is a discrepancy in the computer industry regarding the definition of a megabyte. Sometimes 1 megabyte = 1,000 kilobytes; at other times, we use the relationship of 1 megabyte = 1,024 kilobytes.

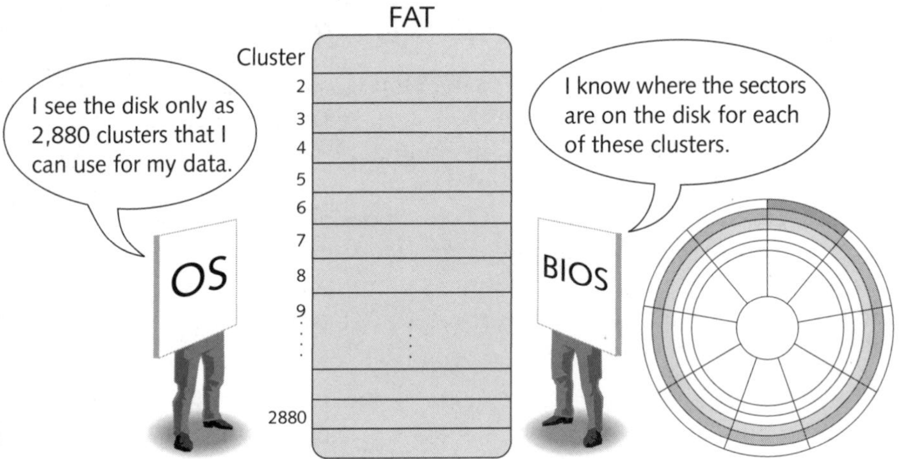

Figure 3-16 Clusters or file allocation units are managed by the OS in the file allocation table (FAT), but BIOS manages these clusters as one or two physical sectors on the disk

The Formatting Process for a Floppy Disk

A+ OS 1.1

The formatting of all floppy disks is similar, no matter what their size or density. During formatting, the Format command without added options performs the following steps:

- Creates the tracks and sectors by writing tracks as necessary and marks the place on each track where the first sector begins

A+ OS 1.1

- Creates the boot record (discussed below)
- Creates two copies of the file allocation table (FAT) (discussed in detail below)
- Creates the root directory

These basic steps are described in detail next. Later in this chapter you will learn how to add options to the formatting process.

3

Creating the Tracks and Sectors

The Format command prepares a disk for use. The first step in the formatting process erases any data on the disk. In its simplest form, without adding any parameters, the Format command always overwrites all data on the disk.

The Boot Record

At the beginning of each floppy disk, the first sector contains basic information about how the disk is organized, including the number of sectors, the number of sectors per cluster, the number of bits in each FAT entry, and other basic information that an OS or BIOS needs in order to read the data on the disk. This information is stored in the first sector on the disk called the **boot sector,** or **boot record**. At the end of the boot record is a small program, called the **bootstrap loader**, that can be used to boot from the disk. Table 3-5 shows the layout of the boot record and its contents. The boot record indicates which version of DOS or Windows was used to format the disk, and is always located at the beginning of the disk at track 0, sector 1 (bottom of the disk, outermost track). This uniformity of layout and content allows any version of DOS or Windows to read any DOS or Windows disk. You will learn more about hard drive boot records later in the chapter.

Table 3-5 Contents of the floppy disk boot record

1. Bytes per sector
2. Sectors per cluster
3. Number of FATs
4. Size of the root directory
5. Number of sectors
6. Medium descriptor byte
7. Size of the FAT
8. Sectors per track
9. Number of heads (always 2)
10. Number of hidden sectors
11. Program to load the OS

The ninth item in Table 3-5 is the number of heads. A head refers to the read/write head that is a part of the physical components of the drive. Because the disk always has only one top and one bottom with a read/write head assigned to each, the number of heads is

A+ OS 1.1

always two. The last item in Table 3-5 is the program that searches for and loads Io.sys if it is present on the disk. If Io.sys, Msdos.sys, and Command.com are on the disk, the disk is said to be bootable.

All boot records, however, are the same, whether or not the disk is bootable. When the PC is looking for a bootable disk during POST, if a disk is in the drive, the program stored in the boot record is executed. If this program does not find Io.sys, the disk is not bootable and a message appears, such as the following:

```
Non-system disk or disk error...Replace and strike any key
when ready...Disk boot failure
```

POST stops until the user intervenes. Only the program in the boot record can determine if the disk is bootable.

The File Allocation Table (FAT)

When formatting a floppy disk, after the boot record is created, the next step is to write two copies of the FAT to the disk. Recall from Chapter 2 that the FAT lists the location of files on the disk in a one-column table. Because the width of each entry in the column is 12 bits, the FAT is called a 12-bit FAT or **FAT12**. The FAT lists how each cluster or file allocation unit on the disk is currently used. A file is stored in one or more clusters that do not have to be contiguous on the disk. If a file is not stored in consecutive clusters, it is called a **fragmented file**. In the FAT, some clusters might be marked as bad (the 12 bits to mark a bad cluster are FF7h). These bits can be entered in the FAT when the disk is formatted or added later with the Recover command. An extra copy of the FAT is kept immediately following the first. If the first is damaged, sometimes you can recover your data and files by using the second copy.

The Root Directory

After creating the file allocation tables, the formatting process sets up the root directory. Recall that the root directory, or main directory, is a table listing all the files assigned to this table. The root directory contains a fixed number of rows to accommodate a predetermined number of files and subdirectories; the number of available rows is dependent upon the disk type. A 3½-inch high-density floppy disk has 224 entries in the root directory.

The root directory will later contain information about each file and subdirectory stored in it. Each directory entry is 32 bytes long, although only 22 bytes are used. Table 3-6 lists how the 22 bytes are used.

Notice that the root directory contains only the starting cluster number. To find out what other clusters store the file, look in the file allocation table. By dividing the size of the file by the number of bytes per cluster and rounding up to the nearest whole number, you can determine how many clusters the file occupies.

A+ OS 1.1

Table 3-6 Root directory information for each file

Root Directory Bytes	Usage
8	Name of file
3	File extension
1	Attribute byte (special meaning for each bit)
10	Not used
2	Time of creation or last update
2	Date of creation or last update
2	Starting cluster number in binary
4	Size of file in binary

Also note that there is no place for the period (often referred to as "dot") that we normally see between the filename and the file extension in OS command lines. The period is not stored in directories but is only used in OS command lines to indicate where the filename ends and the file extension begins. For the long filenames in Windows 9x and Windows NT/2000/XP, more room in the directory is required. This is provided by using more than one entry in the directory for a single file, enough to accommodate the length of the filename. Both the long filename and the DOS version short filename are stored in the directory.

Time and date of creation or last update are stored in a coded form that is converted to a recognizable form when displayed on the screen. The date and time come from the system date and time, which the OS gets from the real-time clock during the boot. At the command prompt, you can change these with the Date and Time commands. Using the Windows desktop, change the date and time in the Control Panel. The earliest possible date allowed for both is 1/1/1980.

The file attributes are used for various purposes. One file attribute byte is broken into bits; each bit has a specific meaning. The first two bits are not used. The meanings of the other six bits are listed in Table 3-7, beginning with the leftmost bit in the byte and moving to the right. You can use several OS commands to change the file attributes; you'll learn about many of them later in this chapter.

Table 3-7 Meaning of each bit in the directory attribute byte for each file (reading from left to right across the byte)

Bit	Description	Bit=0	Bit=1
1, 2	Not used		
3	Archive bit	Not to be archived	To be archived
4	Directory status	File	Subdirectory
5	Volume label	Not volume label	Is volume label
6	System file	Not system file	Is system file
7	Hidden file	Not hidden	Hidden
8	Read-only file	Read/write	Read-only

A+ OS 1.1

Bit 3, the archive bit, is a switch used to indicate whether the file has been changed since the last backup and should be backed up next time a backup is made. You will learn more about this process in Chapter 11.

The root directory and all subdirectories contain the same information about each file. Only the root directory has a limitation on the number of entries. Subdirectories can have as many entries as disk space allows. Because long filenames require more room in a directory than short filenames, assigning long filenames reduces the number of files that can be stored in the root directory.

In summary, the Format command writes tracks and sectors on the disk, and creates a boot record, an empty file allocation table, and an empty root directory. If you include the /S option in the Format line, you add Io.sys, Msdos.sys, and Command.com, which together make a disk bootable. The three files are referenced in the FAT and in the root directory. The two hidden files have their file attribute bit 7, the hidden bit, set to 1 (hidden). When you make a Windows 9x rescue disk or use Windows Explorer to format a disk making the disk a system disk, these three files are copied to the disk to make the disk bootable.

How a Hard Drive Is Logically Organized to Hold Data

A+ OS 1.1

Recall that today's hard drives come from the factory already low-level formatted (that is, with track and sector markings already in place). During installation, after the hard drive is physically installed, the next step is to partition the drive into manageable areas. The high-level divisions are called partitions, and within the partitions, the drive is further divided into logical drives or volumes. This section discusses the different types of divisions, how they are organized and used by the OS, and how to use OS commands to partition and format a hard drive for first use.

Preparing a hard drive to hold data requires the following three steps:

1. *Low-level format.* This physically formats the hard drive and creates the tracks and sectors. For hard drives today, this has already been done by the time you buy the drive, and does not involve an OS.
2. *Partitioning the hard drive.* Even if only one partition is used, this step is still required. The DOS and Windows 9x Fdisk program sets up a partition table at the beginning of the hard drive. Within each partition, Fdisk also creates logical drives, assigning letters to these drives. Windows NT/2000/XP uses the Diskpart program at the command prompt or the Disk Management utility from within Windows to create and delete partitions and logical drives.
3. *High-level format.* This must be done by the OS for each logical drive on the hard drive. As each logical drive is formatted, the OS creates an OS boot record, a root directory, and two copies of VFAT for the logical drive, just as it does for a floppy disk. DOS and Windows 9x uses the Format.com program to do the job, and Windows NT/2000/XP uses Diskpart or Disk Management.

A+ OS 1.1

Although you might have a 10 GB hard drive that is only a single physical drive, an OS can divide this single physical drive into more than one logical drive. Figure 3-17 shows the several divisions of a hard drive.

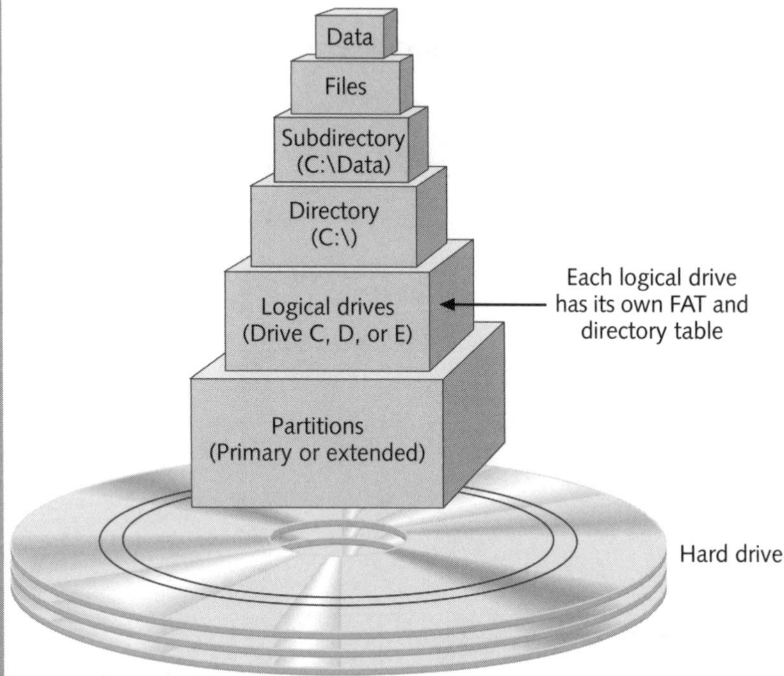

Figure 3-17 A hard drive is divided and organized at several levels

When partitioning the drive using Fdisk, Diskpart, or Disk Management, two kinds of divisions take place. First, the physical drive is divided into one or more partitions, and then each partition is further divided into logical drives or volumes. (A logical drive is sometimes called a logical partition; don't let the two uses of the term "partition" confuse you; partitions and logical partitions are divisions at different levels.) Figure 3-18 shows a typical example; the hard drive is divided into two partitions. The first partition contains one logical drive (drive C), and the second partition is divided into two logical drives (D and E). The partition table at the very beginning of the drive records all these divisions. The partition table is located in the first sector of the hard drive on head 0, track 0, sector 1, which is the MBR that was introduced earlier. Table 3-8 lists the contents of a partition table. Don't confuse this first physical sector of the hard drive with sector 1 as Windows knows it. The OS's sector 1 comes after the physical sector 1 and is the first sector in the logical drive C.

A+ OS 1.1 1.4

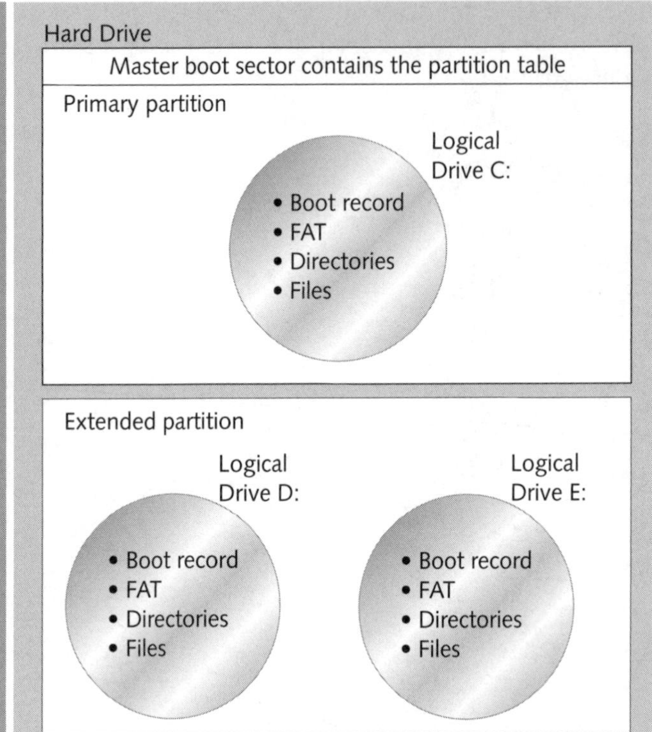

Figure 3-18 A hard drive is divided into one or more partitions that contain logical drives

The partition table is exactly 512 bytes long. During POST, the partition table program, which is stored at the beginning of the Master Boot Record, executes and checks the integrity of the partition table itself. If it finds any corruption, it refuses to continue execution, and the disk is unusable. Sometimes the MBR is the target of a **boot sector virus**, which can cause problems with the boot process and data retrieval. The DOS and Windows 9x Fdisk /MBR command or the Windows 2000/XP Fixmbr command is used to repair damage to the MBR.

If the table entries are valid, the partition table program looks in the table to determine which partition is the active partition, and it executes the bootstrap loader program in the boot record of that partition.

Using DOS or Windows 9x, a hard drive can have only one primary partition and one extended partition, although the partition table can contain four partitions. Also, the **primary partition** can only have a single logical drive. In that case, the one logical drive in the primary partition is the only logical drive on the hard drive that can boot the operating system and is the active partition. The **extended partition** can have several logical drives. Using Windows NT/2000/XP, the drive can have up to four partitions, but only one of them can be an extended partition.

A+ OS 1.1 1.4

3

Table 3-8 Hard drive partition table in the MBR

Item	Bytes Used	Description
1	446 bytes	Program that calls the boot program on the OS boot record.
2	16-byte total 1 byte 3 bytes 1 byte 3 bytes 4 bytes 4 bytes	Description of first partition. Is this the bootable partition? (Yes = 90h, No = 00h) Beginning location of the partition. System indicator; possible values are: 0 = Not a DOS partition 1 = DOS with a 12-bit FAT 4 = DOS with a 16-bit FAT 5 = Not the first partition 6 = Partition larger than 32 MB Ending location of partition. First sector of the partition table relative to the beginning of the disk. Number of sectors in the partition.
3	16 bytes	Describes second partition, using same format as first partition.
4	16 bytes	Describes third partition, using same format as first partition.
5	16 bytes	Describes fourth partition, using same format as first partition.
6	2 bytes	Signature of the partition table, always AA55.

How Many and What Kind of Logical Drives?

After the hard drive is formatted and ready for use, you are not usually aware that the several logical drives on the hard drive all belong to the same hard drive. For example, Figure 3-19 shows three drives, C, D, and E, that are logical drives on one hard drive. If you right-click the icon for one drive, such as drive D in the figure, and select Properties from the shortcut menu, you can see the amount of space allotted to this logical drive and how much of it is currently used. Also note that in the figure drive D is formatted using the FAT32 file system. It is possible for one logical drive to be formatted with one file system and other logical drives on the same hard drive be formatted using a different file system such as FAT16 or NTFS. You'll see examples of this in future chapters.

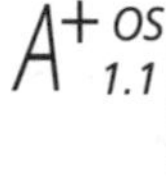

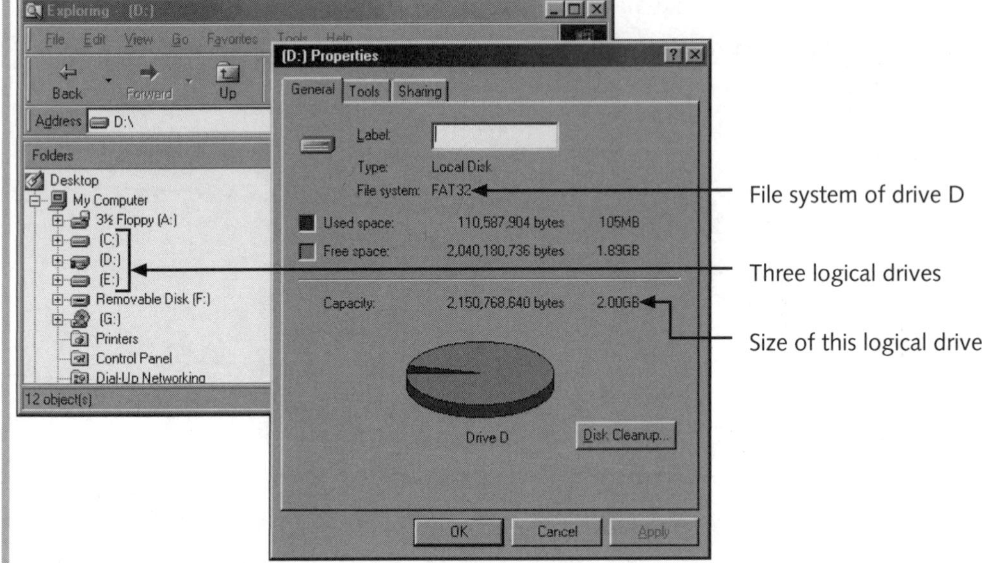

Figure 3-19 This hard drive contains three logical drives

DOS and all versions of Windows support the FAT16 file system. Windows 95 offers a slightly improved file system called VFAT that supports long filenames, and Windows 95, Service Release 2 (sometimes called Windows 95b or Windows 95 OSR2), introduced the FAT32 file system. FAT32 is supported by this and all later versions of Windows 9x, Windows 2000, and Windows XP. Windows NT introduced the NTFS file system, which is also supported by Windows 2000 and Windows XP. You'll learn about the different versions of NTFS in later chapters. The next sections discuss FAT16, VFAT, and FAT32. With these file systems, the primary goal is to reduce the size of one cluster so as to not waste space on the hard drive for short files that don't need large clusters.

FAT16

DOS and all versions of Windows support the FAT16 file system, which uses 16 bits for each cluster entry in the FAT. Using FAT16, the smallest cluster size is four sectors. Each cluster is 512 bytes/sector × 4 sectors/cluster, or 2,048 bytes. A one-character file takes up 2,048 bytes of space on a hard drive. For larger drives, the number of sectors in one cluster is even larger.

Virtual File Allocation (VFAT)

Windows 95 and Windows for Workgroups feature some improved methods of hard drive access, called **VFAT**, or **virtual file allocation table**. These enable Windows to use 32-bit protected-mode device drivers for hard drive access. In Windows for Workgroups, VFAT is called 32-bit file access. Windows 95 supports filenames up to 255 characters. Recall that the filename and extension are stored in the root directory or in a subdirectory list. Each entry in the directory is 32 bytes long, and each 32-byte entry is called a block. Long filenames

A+ OS 1.1

require more than one block in the directory. The FAT is not affected, but still uses 16 bits per cluster entry. VFAT has been rendered outdated by FAT32.

Some DOS-based disk utility programs can damage the entries in a directory in these additional blocks because they are not programmed to manage the extra blocks used to hold long filenames. Even a simple DEL command under DOS can leave the extra blocks in the directory used to hold the long filename unavailable for later use. The Windows 9x ScanDisk utility can recover these unreleased blocks.

3

FAT32

Beginning with Windows 95 OSR2, Microsoft offered a FAT that contains 32 bits per FAT entry instead of the older 12-bit or 16-bit FAT entries. Actually, only 28 of the bits are used to hold a cluster number; the remaining 4 bits are reserved.

FAT32 is recommended for hard drives larger than 512 MB and is efficient for drives up to 16 GB. In this range, the cluster size is 8K. After that, the cluster size increases to about 16K for drives in the 16 GB to 32 GB range. You are then reaching a hard drive size that warrants a more powerful file management system than FAT32, such as NTFS, supported by Windows NT/2000/XP, discussed in later chapters.

If you are currently using FAT16 and are considering switching to FAT32, you can use PartitionMagic by PowerQuest Corporation (*www.powerquest.com*), to scan your hard drive and tell you how much of the drive is used for slack space. Knowing this can help you decide if the change will yield you more usable drive space. In Chapter 5 you will learn how use a Windows utility to convert a FAT16 drive to FAT32.

How Many Logical Drives?

When you partition a hard drive and create logical drives, you decide how many logical drives you want and how large each drive will be. Some people prefer to use more than one logical drive to organize their hard drives, especially if they plan to have more than one OS on the same drive. However, the main reason you need multiple logical drives is to optimize space and access time to the drive. The larger the logical drive, the larger the cluster size, and the more slack or wasted space. When deciding how to allocate space to logical drives, the goal is to use as few logical drives as possible and still keep cluster size to a minimum. For Windows 9x, use FAT32 in order to get the smaller cluster size.

Table 3-9 gives the information you need to decide how to divide your drive. Notice that the largest logical drive possible using FAT16 is 2 GB (this limitation is rooted in the largest cluster number that can be stored in a 16-bit FAT entry). However, you can see from the table that, to make a drive that big, the cluster size must be huge. Also, the largest hard drive that FAT16 can support is 8.4 GB; if the drive is larger than that, you must use FAT32.

A+ OS 1.2 2.1

Table 3-9 Size of some logical drives compared to cluster size for FAT16, FAT32, and NTFS

File System	Size of Logical Drive	Size of Cluster
FAT16	Up to 128 MB	4 sectors per cluster
	128 to 256 MB	8 sectors per cluster
	256 to 512 MB	16 sectors per cluster
	512 MB to 1 GB	32 sectors per cluster
	1 GB to 2 GB	64 sectors per cluster
FAT32	512 MB to 8 GB	4 sectors per cluster
	8 GB to 16 GB	8 sectors per cluster
	16 GB to 32 GB	16 sectors per cluster
	More than 32 GB	32 sectors per cluster
NTFS	Up to 512 MB	1 sector per cluster
	512 MB to 1 GB	2 sectors per cluster
	More than 1 GB	4 sectors per cluster

When to Partition a Drive

There are several reasons to partition a drive. When you first install a new hard drive, you must partition it to prepare it for use. Also, if an existing hard drive is giving errors, you can repartition the drive and reformat each logical drive to begin fresh. If you suspect that a virus has attacked the drive, you can repartition it to begin with a clean drive. Also, if you want to wipe a hard drive clean and install a new OS, you can repartition a drive in preparation for formatting it with a new file system.

When installing Windows 9x, before you can use the Windows 9x CD for Windows 9x upgrades, you can boot from a bootable disk and use Fdisk to partition the hard drive and install enough of a previous version of Windows on it to boot from it. (When using the Windows 98 Upgrade CD, you will also need the first Window 3.x setup disk or Windows 95 setup CD because Windows 98 upgrade setup asks for it during the Windows 9x installation.) During a Windows 9x installation, if the drive is not partitioned, the install procedure automatically executes Fdisk to partition the drive.

You can use Fdisk to partition a drive or use third-party software such as PartitionMagic. Fdisk is simply and easy to use, but PartitionMagic has some advantages over Fdisk. A major one is that when Fdisk partitions a drive, it erases all data on the existing partitions that it changes or overwrites, but PartitionMagic protects data when it changes the partitions on the drive. Also, PartitionMagic has a more user-friendly GUI interface.

There are times that you should not use Fdisk to partition a drive. If the drive has already been partitioned by third-party software such as Disk Manager or Storage Dimensions' SpeedStor, you should use the same third-party product to repartition the drive. This is because these products implement a type of drive translation that is used to enable a large hard drive to exist in a system whose system BIOS does not support such large drives. To know if a large hard drive has been partitioned to do disk translation, look for entries in the

Config.sys file that point to third-party software to manage the drive. Examples of these command lines are Dmdrvr.bin, Sstor.sys, Harddrive.sys, and Evdisk.sys. If you find lines with these filenames mentioned, use the same third-party software to repartition the drive.

Using Fdisk to Partition a Drive

A+ OS 1.5

Windows 9x and DOS use Fdisk to partition a drive. To use Fdisk, boot from a startup disk that has the Fdisk.exe utility on it and enter Fdisk at the command prompt. The Fdisk opening menu, shown in Figure 3-20 appears. Select option 1 to create the first partition. The menu in Figure 3-21 appears. Use option 1 to create the primary DOS partition. If you plan to install Windows 9x later, be sure this partition is at least 150 MB, preferably more. Make this first partition the **active partition**, which is the partition that is used to boot the OS. Fdisk automatically makes this partition drive C.

In order for a hard drive to be bootable, it must have an active primary partition, which Fdisk will designate as drive C.

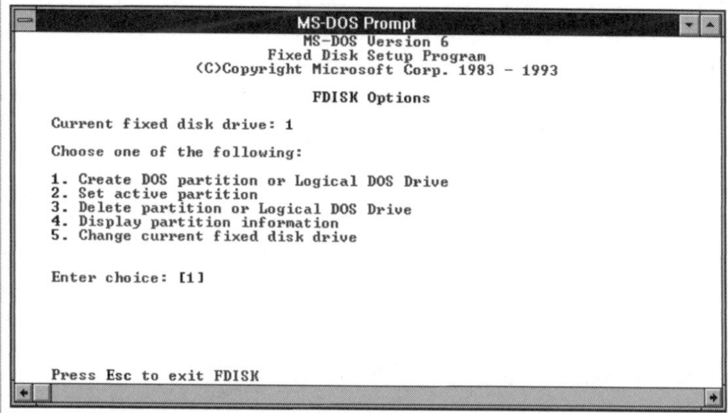

Figure 3-20 Fixed disk setup program (FDISK) menu

Next, use option 2 shown in Figure 3-21 to create an extended DOS partition using the remainder of the hard drive, then use option 3 to create logical drives in the extended partition.

When you are creating logical drives, you decide how large you want each drive to be. If you have at least 512 MB available for the drive, a message appears asking Do you wish to enable large disk support (Y/N)? If you respond Y, then Fdisk assigns the FAT32 file system to the drive, otherwise it uses FAT16.

A+ OS 1.5

```
MS-DOS Prompt

                Create DOS Partition or Logical DOS Drive

Current fixed disk drive: 1

Choose one of the following:

1. Create Primary DOS Partition
2. Create Extended DOS Partition
3. Create Logical DOS Drive(s) in the Extended DOS Partition


Enter choice: [1]



Press Esc to return to FDISK Options
```

Figure 3-21 FDISK menu to create partitions and logical drives

Fdisk also assigns a drive letter to the logical drive. For a primary partition, drive C is assigned to the one volume and drives D, E, and so forth are assigned to volumes in the extended partition. However, if a second hard drive is installed in a system, Fdisk takes this into account when assigning drive letters. Drive D is assigned to the one volume in the primary partition of the second hard drive, leaving drive letters E, F, G, H and so forth for the volumes in the extended partitions of both hard drives. For example, in a two-hard drive system where each hard drive has three logical drives, the drive letters for the first hard drive will be C, E, and F and the drive letters for the second hard drive will be D, G, and H.

When Fdisk is completed, the hard drive has a partition table, an active and extended partition, and logical drives within these partitions. As seen in Figure 3-20, you can choose option 4 of Fdisk to display partition information (see Figure 3-22). After you exit the Fdisk window, reboot the PC before you format the logical drives.

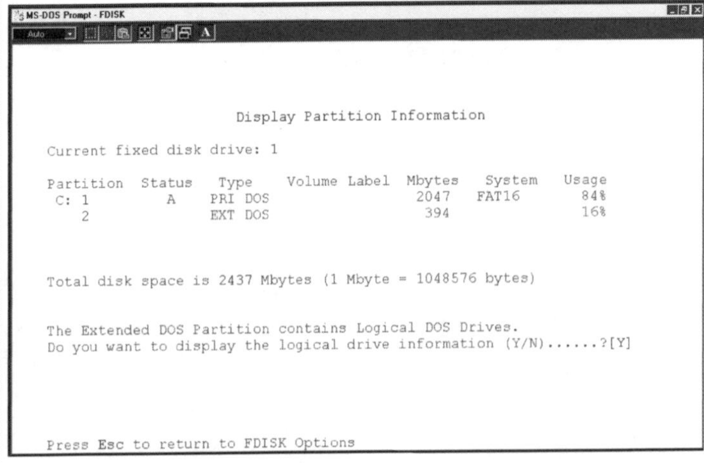

Figure 3-22 FDISK displays partition information

Formatting Each Logical Drive

A+ OS 2.1

Now that the hard drive is partitioned and logical drives are created and assigned drive letters, the next step is to format each logical drive. For the configuration in Figure 3-25, the three commands used to format these three logical drives are:

```
Format C:/S
Format D:
Format E:
```

In the Format command line, the /S option makes the drive bootable, and the drive letter tells the OS which drive to format. Other options for the Format command are covered in the next section.

The OS format for each logical drive creates these file system items at the beginning of each logical drive, which are similar to the file system items used on floppy disks:

- Boot record
- FAT
- Root directory

The Boot Record

A boot record is used during the boot process to inform the OS how a logical drive is organized. If the logical drive is the boot device, the boot program at the end of the boot record will load the first Windows hidden file, Io.sys which requires that Msdos.sys and Command.com be present. Table 3-10 shows the complete record layout for the boot record. The medium descriptor byte tells the OS what type of disk this is. The values of this descriptor byte are given in Table 3-11.

Table 3-10 Layout of the boot record on each logical drive

Description	Number of Bytes
Machine code	11
Bytes per sector	2
Sectors per cluster	1
Reserved	2
Number of FATs	1
Number of root directory entries	2
Number of logical sectors	2
Medium descriptor byte	1
Sectors per FAT	2
Sectors per track	2
Heads	2
Number of hidden sectors	2
Total sectors in logical volume	4

A+ OS 2.1

Table 3-10 Layout of the boot record on each logical drive (continued)

Description	Number of Bytes
Physical drive number	1
Reserved	1
Extended boot signature record	1
32-bit binary volume ID	4
Volume label	11
Type of file system (FAT12, FAT16, or FAT32)	8
Program to load operating system (boot strap loader)	Remainder of the sector

Table 3-11 Disk type and descriptor byte

Disk Type	Descriptor Byte
3½-inch double-density floppy disk, 720K	F9
3½-inch high-density floppy disk, 1.44 MB	F0
Hard disk	F8

The FAT and the Root Directory

The purpose of the FAT and how it is used have already been discussed in detail and will not be repeated here. The layout of the root directory is the same for hard drives as for floppy disks, which were discussed earlier in the chapter. Recall that the total number of bytes for each file entry in a directory is 32. Refer back to Table 3-6 for a list of entries in the root directory.

Although earlier versions of Windows did limit the number of entries in the root directory, Windows 98 does not. Note, however, that the OS manuals recommend that you keep only about 150 entries in any one directory. Having any more entries slows access to the directory.

Using Commands to Manage a Floppy Disk or Hard Drive

A+ OS 1.4

You can use several OS commands to manage a floppy disk and hard drive. A number of commands are described in this section with some of their more common options. For more information about these and other OS commands, type the command name at a command prompt followed by /? (slash and a question mark).

There are two wildcards you can use with filenames to execute a command on a group of files or a file for which you do not know the entire name. The question mark (?) is a wildcard for one character, and the asterisk (*) is a wildcard for more than one character. For example, if you wanted to find all files in a directory that start with A and have a three-letter file extension, you would use the following command:

```
dir a*.???
```

A+ OS 1.4

One other thing you need to be aware of when using commands at the command line is how DOS restricts the length of filenames. DOS allows only eight characters for a filename and three for the extension; this is often called the 8.3 format. For filenames that do not meet this format, such as the filename Mydocument.doc, DOS will display the filename with the first few letters and a tilde (~) character:

3

```
Mydocum~.doc
```

If you have two documents that would have the same name if truncated in this manner, DOS will also add an identifying number. For example, if you have a document named Mydocument.doc and one named Mydocumentnew.doc, in a list of files, DOS will truncate these as follows:

```
Mydocu~1.doc
Mydocu~2.doc
```

If you are entering a long file or folder name in a command line, you can enclose the file name in double quotes, like this: "My long file name.doc".

A+ OS 1.3

Fdisk /Status /MBR

As you learned earlier, the Fdisk command creates partitions and logical drives on a hard drive, displays partition information, and restores a damaged Master Boot Record. Table 3-12 shows options for this command.

Table 3-12 Options for the Fdisk command

Fdisk Command Option	Description
/MBR	Repairs a damaged MBR program stored at the beginning of the partition table
/Status	Displays partition information for all hard drives in the system.

Many real-mode commands, such as Fdisk/MBR, have equivalent commands in the Windows 2000 Recovery Console, which you will learn about in Chapter 8. The Recovery Console is also available with Windows XP.

Format Drive: /S /V:Volumename /Q /U /Autotest

Recall that the Format command is used to format a disk or a hard drive. For a hard drive, first run Fdisk to partition the drive and create each logical drive. Then use Format to format each logical drive. Table 3-13 shows options for this command.

Table 3-13 Options for the Format command

Format Command Option	Description
/V	Allows you to enter a volume label only once when formatting several disks. The same volume label is used for all disks. A volume label is displayed at the top of the directory list to help you identify the disk.

A+ OS 1.3

Table 3-13 Options for the Format command (continued)

Format Command Option	Description
/S	Stores the system files on the disk after formatting. Writes the two hidden files and Command.com to the disk, making the disk bootable.
/Q	Recreates the root directory and FATs if you want to quickly format a previously formatted disk that is in good condition. /Q does not read or write to any other part of the disk.
/F:size	Specifies the size of a floppy disk. If the size is not specified, the default for that drive is used. The common values for size are: /F:360 is 360K, double-density 5¼-inch disk /F:1.2 is 1.2 MB, high-density 5¼-inch disk /F:720 is 720 K, double-density 3½-inch disk /F:1.44 is 1.44 MB, high-density 3½-inch disk
/U	Allows for an unconditional format of the disk, which does a more thorough job of formatting the disk by erasing all data. Use this option when you have been getting read/write errors on the disk.
/Autotest	Does not prompt the user before and during the format.

Dir

Use this command to list files and directories. Some examples are:

DIR /P	List one screen at a time.
DIR /W	Use wide format, where details are omitted and files and folders are listed in columns on the screen.
DIR *.txt	Use wildcard character.
DIR Myfile.txt	Check that a single file is present.

Type

The Type command displays on screen the contents of text file. Some examples are:

`Type Myfile.txt`	Displays file contents
`Type Myfile.txt >PRN`	Redirects output to printer
`Type Myfile.txt |More`	Displays output one screen at a time

Del or Erase

The Del or Erase command erases files or groups of files. Where the command does not include drive and directory information, like the following examples, the OS uses the default drive and directory when executing the command.

For example, to erase all the files in the A:\DOCS directory, use the following command:

```
C:\> ERASE A:\DOCS\*.*
```

To erase all the files in the current default directory, use the following command:

```
A:\DOCS> DEL *.*
```

To erase all files in the current directory that have no file extension, use the following command:

```
A:\DOCS> DEL *.
```

To erase the file named Myfile.txt, use the following command:

```
A:\> DEL MYFILE.TXT
```


Undelete

The Undelete command attempts to recover files that have been deleted. Following are some variations of the Undelete command. The Undelete command is not included in Windows 9x.

To list the files that can be undeleted, without actually undeleting them, use the following command:

```
A:\>UNDELETE /list
```

To recover deleted files without prompting for confirmation on each file, use the following command:

```
A:\>UNDELETE /all
```

Recover

The Recover command attempts to recover a file from damaged sectors on a disk. Always specify the drive, path, and filename of the file you want to recover with the Recover command. If you want to recover several files, use the command on one file at a time. The Recover command is not available in Windows 9x.

To recover the file named Myfile.txt on a floppy disk, use the following command:

```
RECOVER A:\DOCS\MYFILE.TXT
```

Whatever portion of the file that the Recover command can read is stored in the root directory and named A:FILE0000.REC (or the next available number). Copy this file to another disk before trying to recover the second file.

Because the Recover command might mark clusters as bad in the FAT, first use the Diskcopy or Copy command (described below) before using Recover. Data that might have been saved by other methods can sometimes be destroyed by the Recover command.

Diskcopy

The Diskcopy command makes an exact duplicate (sector by sector) of one floppy disk (called the source disk) to another disk of the same size and type (called the target disk).

To duplicate a floppy disk using only a single drive, use the following command:

```
C:\>DISKCOPY A: A:
```

The OS prompts you as many times as necessary to insert the source disk and then insert the target disk to make the exact copy. Data is copied from one disk to the other, byte by byte, including any hidden files, bad sectors, fragmented files, or other contents; everything is copied as is. For this reason, the copy can be faulty if the target disk has bad sectors. Diskcopy ignores the fact that a sector is marked as bad in the FAT and copies to it anyway. The Diskcopy command copies formatting information, so the target disk does not need to be formatted before executing the copy.

A+ OS 1.3

Copy

The Copy command copies a single file or group of files. The original files are not altered.

To copy a file from one drive to another, use the following command:

```
A:\>COPY drive:\path\filename.ext drive:\path\filename.ext
```

The drive, path, and filename of the original source file immediately follow the Copy command, and the drive, path, and filename of the destination file follow the source filename. If you do not specify the filename of the copy, the OS assigns the original name of the file. If you omit the drive or path of the source or the destination, then the OS uses the current default drive and path.

To copy the file Myfile.txt from the root directory of drive C to drive A, use the following command:

```
C:\>COPY MYFILE.TXT A:
```

Because a drive or path is not indicated before the filename Myfile.txt, the OS assumes that the file is in the default drive and path.

To copy all files in the C:\DOCS directory to the floppy disk in drive A, use the following command:

```
C:\>COPY C:\DOCS\*.* A:
```

To make a backup file named System.bak of the System.ini file in the \Windows directory of the hard drive, use the following command:

```
C:\WINDOWS> COPY SYSTEM.INI SYSTEM.BAK
```

If you use the Copy command to duplicate multiple files, the files are assigned the names of the original files. When duplicating multiple files, no filename can be listed in the destination portion of the command line.

Xcopy /C /S /Y /D:

The Xcopy command is more powerful than the Copy command. It follows the same general command-source-destination format as the Copy command, but it offers several more options, as outlined next, with a couple of useful examples.

Use the /S option with the Xcopy command to copy all files in the directory \DOCS, as well as all subdirectories under \DOCS and their files, to the disk in drive A. Use the following command:

```
C:\>XCOPY C:\DOCS\*.* A: /S
```

A+ OS 1.3

To copy all files from the directory C:\DOCS created or modified on March 14, 2002, use the /D switch, as in the following command:

```
XCOPY C:\DOCS\*.* A: /D:03/14/02
```

Use the /Y option to overwrite existing files without prompting and use the /C option to keep copying even when there is an error.

3

Deltree

The Deltree command deletes the directory tree beginning with the subdirectory you specify, including all subdirectories and all files in all subdirectories in that tree. Use it with caution!

```
C:\>DELTREE [drive:]path
```

Mkdir [drive:]path or MD [drive:]path

The Mkdir (abbreviated MD, for make directory) command creates a subdirectory entry in a directory. To create a directory named \GAME on drive C, use this command:

```
MKDIR C:\GAME
```

The backslash indicates that the directory is under the root directory. To create a directory named CHESS under the \GAME directory, use this command:

```
MKDIR C:\GAME\CHESS
```

The OS requires that the parent directory GAME already exist before it creates the child directory CHESS.

Figure 3-23 shows the result of the Dir command on the directory \GAME. Note the two initial entries in the directory table, the . (dot) and the .. (dot, dot) entries. These two entries are created by the Mkdir command when the OS initially sets up the directory. You cannot edit these entries with normal OS commands, and they must remain in the directory for the directory's lifetime. The . entry points to the subdirectory itself, and the .. entry points to the parent directory, in this case, the root directory.

```
C:\>DIR \GAME /P

 Volume in drive C has no label
 Volume Serial Number is 0F52-09FC
 Directory of C:\GAME

.            <DIR>      02-18-93   4:50a
..           <DIR>      02-18-93   4:50a
CHESS        <DIR>      02-18-93   4:50a
NUKE         <DIR>      02-18-93   4:51a
PENTE        <DIR>      02-18-93   4:52a
NETRIS       <DIR>      02-18-93   4:54a
BEYOND       <DIR>      02-18-93   4:54a
        7 file(s)           0 bytes
                      9273344 bytes free

C:\>
```

Figure 3-23 Dir of the \GAME directory

A+ OS 1.3

Chdir [drive:]path or CD [drive:]path or CD..

The Chdir (abbreviated CD, for change directory) command changes the current default directory. In its easiest-to-follow form, you simply state the drive and the entire path that you want to be current:

```
CD C:\GAME\CHESS
```

The command prompt now looks like this:

```
C:\GAME\CHESS>
```

To move from a child directory to its parent directory, use the .. variation of the command:

```
C:\GAME\CHESS> CD..
C:\GAME>
```

Remember that .. always means the parent directory. You can move from a parent directory to one of its child directories simply by stating the name of the child directory:

```
C:\GAME> CD CHESS
C:\GAME\CHESS>
```

Do not put a backslash in front of the child directory name; doing so tells DOS to go to a directory named CHESS that is directly under the root directory.

Rmdir [drive:]path or RD [drive:]path

The Rmdir command (abbreviated RD, for remove directory) removes a subdirectory. Before you can use the Rmdir command, three things must be true:

- The directory must contain no files.
- The directory must contain no subdirectories.
- The directory must not be the current directory.

The . and .. entries are present when a directory is ready for removal. For example, to remove the \GAME directory in the above example, the CHESS directory must first be removed:

```
C:\> RMDIR C:\GAME\CHESS
```

Or, if the \GAME directory is the current directory, use this command:

```
C:\GAME> RD CHESS
```

Once you remove the CHESS directory, you can remove the \GAME directory. You must first leave the \GAME directory like this:

```
C:\GAME>CD..
C:\> RD \GAME
```

A+ OS 1.3 1.5

Attrib

The Attrib command displays or changes the read-only, archive, system, and hidden attributes assigned to files. To display the attributes of the file MYFILE.TXT, use this command:

```
ATTRIB MYFILE.TXT
```

A+ OS 1.3 1.5

To hide the file, use this command: `ATTRIB +H MYFILE.TXT`

To remove the hide status of the file, use this command: `ATTRIB -H MYFILE.TXT`

To make the file a read-only file, use this command: `ATTRIB +R MYFILE.TXT`

To remove the read-only status of the file, use this command: `ATTRIB -R MYFILE.TXT`

To turn the archive bit on, use this command: `ATTRIB +A MYFILE.TXT`

To turn the archive bit off, use this command: `ATTRIB -A MYFILE.TXT`

Unformat

The Unformat command might be able to reverse the effect of an accidental format. To unformat a disk, use this command:

```
UNFORMAT C:
```

Path

As discussed in Chapter 2, the Path command lists where the OS should look to find executable program files. This command is discussed here again to make the list of commands more complete. A sample Path command is

```
PATH C:\;C:\DOS;C:\WINDOWS;C:\UTILITY
```

Each path is separated from the next with a semicolon. You should put the most-used paths at the beginning of the line, because the OS searches the paths listed in the Path command line from left to right. The Path command goes in the Autoexec.bat file and can be executed from the OS prompt.

Sys Drive:

The Sys command copies the system files needed to boot to a disk or hard drive. Use the command if the system files on a drive are corrupted. You can access the drive, but you cannot boot from it. The command to copy system files to the hard drive is:

```
SYS C:
```

A+ OS 1.5

Chkdsk [drive:] /F /V

The Chkdsk command reports information about a disk. Use the /F option to have Chkdsk fix errors it finds, including errors in the FAT caused by clusters marked as being used but that do not belong to a particular file (called lost allocation units) and clusters that are marked in the FAT as belonging to more than one file (called cross-linked clusters). To check the hard drive for errors and repair them, use this command:

```
CHKDSK C: /F
```

To redirect the output from the Chkdsk command to a file that you can later print, use this command:

```
CHKDSK C: >Myfile.txt
```

The /V option of the Chkdsk command displays all path and filename information for all files on a disk:

```
CHKDSK C: /V
```

Chkdsk is useful when using a startup disk; otherwise, use Scandisk or disk error-checking from the Windows desktop.

A+ OS 1.3 1.5

Scandisk Drive: /A /N /P

The Scandisk command scans a hard drive for errors and repairs them if possible. Scandisk checks the FAT, long filenames, lost and cross-linked clusters, directory tree structure, bad sectors, and compressed structure if the drive has been compressed using Windows DriveSpace or DoubleSpace. The /A parameter is used to scan all nonremovable local drives. Use this command only to display information without fixing the drive:

```
SCANDISK C: /P
```

Use this command to display information and fix errors:

```
SCANDISK C:
```

Use this command to start and stop Scandisk automatically:

```
Scandisk C: /N
```

If you use the above command, Scandisk will still stop to report errors.

A+ OS 1.3 1.5 2.5

Defrag Drive: /S

The Defrag command examines a hard drive or disk for fragmented files (files written to a disk in noncontiguous clusters) and rewrites these files to the disk or drive in contiguous clusters. Use this command to optimize a hard drive, improving the hard drive performance.

Use the /S:N option to sort the files on the disk in alphabetical order by filename.

```
DEFRAG C: /S:N
```

Use the /S:D option to sort the files on the disk by date and time.

```
DEFRAG C: /S:D
```

A+ OS 1.3

Ver

Use the Ver command to display the version of the operating system in use.

A+ OS 1.3 1.5

Scanreg /Restore /Fix /Backup

The Scanreg command restores or repairs the Windows 98 registry. It uses backups of the registry that Windows 98 Registry Checker automatically makes each day. To restore the registry from a previous backup, use this command:

```
SCANREG /RESTORE
```

A menu appears asking you which backup to use.

To repair a corrupted registry, use this command:

```
SCANREG /FIX
```

To create a new backup of the registry, use this command:

```
SCANREG /BACKUP
```

Don't use this last command if you are having problems with the registry.

A+ OS 1.5

Extract filename.cab file1.ext /D

The Extract command extracts files from a cabinet file such as the Ebd.cab file on the Windows 98 startup disk. To list the files that are contained in the cabinet file, use this command:

```
EXTRACT EBD.CAB /D
```

To extract the file Debug.exe from the Ebd.cab file, use this command:

```
EXTRACT EBD.CAB DEBUG.EXE
```

To extract all files from the Ebd.cab cabinet file, use this command:

```
EXTRACT EBD.CAB *.*
```

Debug

The Debug program is an editor that can view and manipulate the components of a file system on floppy disks and hard drives, including the FAT, directories, and boot records. It can also be used to view the contents of memory and hexadecimal memory addresses. To access Debug, enter the command Debug at the command prompt.

A+ OS 1.3 1.5

Edit [path][filename]

The Edit program (Edit.com) is a text editor that was used earlier in the chapter to edit Autoexec.bat and Config.sys files. It is a handy quick and dirty way to edit text files while working at a command prompt. To edit the file Autoexec.bat on a floppy disk, use this command:

```
EDIT A:\AUTOEXEC.BAT
```

If the file does not already exist, Edit creates the file.

With older versions of DOS, Qbasic.exe was required for Edit.com to work correctly.

Using Batch Files

Suppose you have a list of OS commands that you want to execute several times. Perhaps you have some data files to distribute to several PCs in your office, and, having no LAN, you must walk from one PC to another, doing the same job repeatedly. A solution is to store the list of commands in a batch file on disk and then execute the batch file at each PC. Windows requires that the batch file have a .bat file extension. For example, store these five OS commands on a disk in a file named MYLOAD.BAT:

```
C:
MD\UTILITY
MD\UTILITY\TOOLS
CD\UTILITY\TOOLS
COPY A:\TOOLS\*.*
```

From the command prompt, you execute the batch file, just as you do other program files, by entering the name of the file, with or without the file extension:

```
A:\>MYLOAD
```

All the commands listed in the file will execute, beginning at the top of the list. The batch file above will create a subdirectory under the C drive called Utility\Tools; change to that directory as the default directory, and copy all files from the \Tools directory in drive A into that new subdirectory. Look at any good book on DOS to find examples of the very useful ways you can elaborate on batch files, including adding user menus.

CHAPTER SUMMARY

- For DOS, the three types of memory are conventional (or base) memory, upper memory, and extended memory. These assignments are rooted in how the 20-line memory address bus of early PCs limited memory to 1024K.
- When the OS loads from a hard drive, the BIOS first executes the Master Boot Record (MBR), which executes the OS boot record, which, for Windows 9x, attempts to find Io.sys on the hard drive.
- Io.sys, which uses Msdos.sys, and Command.com, form the core of real-mode Windows 9x. These three files are necessary to boot to a command prompt. Config.sys and Autoexec.bat are not required, but are used if they are present. Other files are needed to load the GUI desktop and run GUI applications.
- Autoexec.bat and Config.sys are two files that contain commands used to customize the 16-bit portion of the Windows 9x load process.
- A floppy disk that has enough software on it to load an operating system is called a bootable disk, or system disk. A bootable disk that has some utility programs on it to troubleshoot a failed hard drive is called a rescue disk, emergency startup disk (ESD), or startup disk.
- Create a startup disk in Windows 9x using the Control Panel, Add/Remove Programs icon.
- The boot process can be divided into four parts: POST, loading the OS, the OS's initializing itself, and loading and executing an application.
- Startup BIOS is in control of the beginning of the boot process, after which it turns control over to the OS.
- The MBR is a small program at the very beginning of the hard drive that is needed to locate the beginning of the OS on the drive.
- A hard drive can be partitioned into one or more logical drives. The partition table contains a map to the logical drives on the hard drive, including an indication of which drive is the boot drive.
- A hidden file is a file not displayed in the directory list. One example is Io.sys, which contains the basic I/O software for real mode.

- A RAM drive is an area of memory that looks and acts like a hard drive, only it performs much faster. It is sometimes used to speed up access to often-used software or to hold program files when the hard drive is not accessible.
- The file Command.com has three parts: code to manage I/O, programs for internal OS commands such as Copy and Dir, and a short program that looks for the Autoexec.bat file.
- You can access a command prompt window, sometimes called a DOS box, in Windows 9x by clicking Start, Programs, and MS-DOS Prompt. You can also access it by clicking Start, Run and typing Command.com in the Run dialog box.
- The Himem.sys memory extender was added by DOS to allow access to memory addresses above 1 MB. Himem.sys, along with Emm386.exe, is used by Windows 9x to manage memory above 640K. Emm386.exe contains the software that loads 16-bit device drivers and other programs into upper memory.
- Windows 95 was the first version of Windows to support 32-bit protected mode application software. Windows NT was the first version of Windows in which all of the OS code was written in 32-bit protected mode and 16-bit applications could only operate in virtual real mode.
- You can use a UMB (upper memory block) from Autoexec.bat with the Loadhigh (LH) command.
- The MEM command with the appropriate parameters shows exactly where in upper memory the UMBs are located and what software has been assigned addresses in upper memory.
- When a hard drive is first installed, it has nothing written on it except the track and sector markings put there at the factory. A floppy disk is completely blank and does not even have the track and sector markings. The OS is responsible for formatting and managing both hard drives and floppy disks.
- Tracks are concentric circles on a disk. A segment of a track is called a sector and always holds 512 bytes of data.
- On a floppy disk, the Format command creates tracks and sectors, the boot record, two copies of the file allocation table (FAT), and the root directory.
- Basic information about how a floppy disk is organized is stored in the first sector of the disk, called the boot sector or the boot record. At the end of a boot record is a small program, called the bootstrap loader that can be used to boot from the disk.
- The FAT lists the location of files on a disk in a one-column table. For the file systems FAT12, FAT16, and FAT32, the number after FAT indicates how many bits wide each entry in the column is. FAT12 is a file system for floppy disks.
- VFAT is an improvement over FAT16 that was introduced in Windows 95; it supports long filenames. FAT32, which made VFAT obsolete, was introduced in Windows 95 Second Edition. NTFS was introduced with Windows NT.
- After a drive is physically installed, the next step is to partition the drive into manageable areas. The high-level divisions are called partitions, and within the partitions, the drive is further divided into logical drives or volumes.

- The Fdisk command is used to partition a hard drive. If a drive has been partitioned using third-party software such as Disk Manager or Speed Stor, you may not be able to use Fdisk. You must use the third-party software to change the partitions on the drive.
- The largest drive that FAT16 can support is 8.4 GB. FAT32 is recommended for hard drives larger than 512 MB and is efficient for drives up to 16 GB.
- The Format command is used to format floppy disks and logical drives. The /S option with the Format command makes a drive bootable. The Unformat command attempts to reverse the effect of an accidental format.
- The Del or Erase command deletes files or groups of files. The Undelete command attempts to recover files that have been erased. The Recover command attempts to recover a file from damaged sectors on a disk.
- The Diskcopy command makes an exact duplicate of one floppy disk on another disk of the same size and type. The Copy command copies a single file or group of files. The Xcopy command is more powerful that the Copy command and supports copying subdirectories.
- The Sys command copies the system files needed to boot to a disk or drive.
- Mkdir creates a subdirectory, Chdir changes the current directory, and Rmdir removes a subdirectory.
- The Attrib command displays or changes the read-only, archive, system, and hidden attributes assigned to files.
- The Path command specifies where the OS should look to find executable program files.
- Chkdsk and Scandisk both check drives for errors and repair them. Scandisk does a more thorough scan and basically replaces Chkdsk.
- The Scanreg command restores or repairs the Windows 98 registry.

Key Terms

active partition
Autoexec.bat
batch file
boot record
boot sector
boot sector virus
bootable disk
bootstrap loader
cabinet file
cache
cold boot
Command.com
conventional memory
DOS box
emergency startup disk (ESD)
Emm386.exe
extended partition
external command
FAT12
fragmented file
hard boot
hidden file
Himem.sys
HMA (high memory area)
internal command
Io.sys
MBR (Master Boot Record)
Msdos.sys
partition table
POST (power-on self test)
primary partition
RAM drive
rescue disk
soft boot
startup disk
system disk
UMB (upper memory block)
upper memory
VDM (virtual DOS machine)
VFAT (virtual file allocation table)
warm boot

Review Questions

1. What is the difference between a hard boot and a soft boot?
2. What are the four main parts of the boot process?
3. Give the memory address that is always assigned to the first instruction in the ROM BIOS startup program.
4. Name the program that is needed to locate the beginning of the OS on a drive.
5. Which file systems for a hard drive does Windows 98 support?
6. Which version of Windows introduced the VFAT file system? The FAT32 file system?
7. What three OS files are necessary to boot to MS-DOS mode? What is the function of each? What additional two files are not required but are used if they are present?
8. Name at least three program files that are included in the Ebd.cab file.
9. Why is it important not to edit Autoexec.bat with word-processing software such as Microsoft Word or WordPerfect?
10. Give two ways to access a command prompt from Windows 9x.
11. What Windows OS allows applications to run in either real mode or protected mode? What Windows OS was the first to force 16-bit applications to run in virtual real mode?
12. What are the three types of memory that Windows 9x manages? What are the memory address ranges for each?
13. What is the hexadecimal address range for upper memory?
14. Name the two utilities that Windows uses to manage memory above 640K. Give a brief description of each.
15. How many bytes are contained in a sector?
16. What is the name of the first sector on a floppy disk? What information is contained in this sector?
17. How many bytes long is each entry in the root directory?
18. What is the /S switch used for with the Format command? The /V switch? The /F:size switch?
19. What Windows OS introduced the NTFS file system?
20. Name the Windows 98 command that is used to partition a hard drive. When should you not use this command?
21. The ________________ command changes the operating system name assigned to a hard drive, and the ________________ command erases files or groups of files.
22. What command line would you use to list files that can be undeleted without actually undeleting them?
23. Explain the difference between the Diskcopy command, the Copy command, and the Xcopy command.

24. What command is used to create a subdirectory? To change the current directory? To remove a subdirectory?
25. The ______________ command displays or changes the read-only, archive, system, and hidden characteristics of files.
26. Name the file that DOS uses to access memory addresses above 1 MB.
27. What command is used to list where the OS should look to find executable program files?
28. Explain the difference between the Chkdsk and Scandisk commands.
29. What is a hidden file? Name a Windows 9x file that is hidden.
30. What improvement did VFAT offer when it was introduced? Which file system replaced it?
31. What is the purpose of the Ebd.cab file on the Windows 98 startup disk?
32. FAT32 is recommended for hard drives larger than ______________ and is efficient for drives up to ______________.
33. When using Fdisk, what is the question that the software asks you that will cause it to use the FAT32 file system?

HANDS-ON PROJECTS

Observing the Boot Process

1. Using an operational computer, if your computer has a reset button, press it, and then watch what happens. If your computer does not have a reset button, turn it off, wait a few seconds, and then turn it back on. Write down every beep, light that goes on or off, and message on the screen that you notice. Compare your notes to others' to verify that you are not overlooking something.
2. Answer these questions from observing the boot process:
   a. What type of video card are you using?
   b. Who is the BIOS vendor and what version of the BIOS are you using?
   c. As the computer boots, memory is counted. Observe the memory count and record the amount of memory detected. What number system is used to count this memory?
3. Unplug the keyboard and reboot the computer. Write down what happens that is different.
4. Plug the keyboard back in, unplug the monitor, and reboot. After you reboot, plug the monitor in. Did the computer know the monitor was missing?
5. Put a floppy disk that is not bootable in drive A and reboot. Write down what you observe. If you booted to the desktop as normal, what caused the PC to not look to the floppy disk to load the OS?

Observing Windows 9x in Real Mode

Using Windows 9x, boot into MS-DOS real mode and then do the following.

1. From the command prompt, make a bootable disk using either of the two following commands. If the disk is already formatted, but has no files stored on it, use this command:

   ```
   C:\> Sys A:
   ```

To format the disk and also make it bootable, use this command:

   ```
   C:\> Format A:/S
   ```

2. Your disk should now contain a boot record, the two hidden files, and Command.com. Use the Dir command to see them: DIR A:. Compare the bytes available on the disk to a disk that is not bootable. Calculate how many bytes must be in the two hidden files.
3. Does the hard drive contain Autoexec.bat and Config.sys files in the root directory? If so, print them using a local printer (not a network printer). Use one of the following methods:

   `C:\> TYPE filename.ext>PRN` or `C:\> COPY filename.ext LPT1`

4. Test your bootable disk by inserting it in drive A and doing a soft boot. What prompt do you see on the screen?
5. At the DOS prompt, enter the Prompt command that is used to customize the DOS command prompt, where the space between P and $ can contain any text:

   ```
   PROMPT $P    $G
   ```

   What prompt did you get?
6. By examining the prompt, guess what $P in the command line accomplishes and what $G accomplishes. Test your theory by changing the Prompt command, leaving first $P and then $G out of the command line.
7. Using Edit, create an Autoexec.bat file on your bootable disk. Create a Prompt command to include your first name. Test the command by booting from this disk.
8. Without the appropriate Path command in your active Autoexec.bat file, you cannot execute software stored on drive C from the A prompt. Test this theory by trying to execute some application software that you know is stored on your hard drive. For example, if you have MSD on your hard drive, try to execute the software at the A prompt by using the following command:

   ```
   A:\> MSD
   ```

   What error did you get? Why?

3

Creating a Startup Disk Using Windows 9x

Using directions in the chapter, create a startup disk in Windows 9x, and then test it by rebooting the computer with the disk still in the drive. Answer these questions using the Readme.txt file on the startup disk:

1. What command line is recommended to check your hard drive for errors?
2. At what point in the boot process is the RAM drive created?
3. If you reboot your PC after booting from the startup disk, will the RAM drive remain in memory?
4. Using a second disk, create a system disk using Windows Explorer. Compare the contents of the two disks.

How Large Is a Cluster?

Remember that each entry in a FAT tracks the use of one cluster. The number of sectors per cluster varies from one file system to another. The Chkdsk command displays the size of one cluster. There is another way to determine the size of a cluster with a simple test. Do the following:

1. Use the Dir command and note how much space is available on your hard drive.
2. Using Edit or Notepad, create a text file containing only a single character.
3. Use the Dir command again, note how much disk space is available and compare the two values, before and after a single one-character file is written to the disk. The difference in the two values is the size of one cluster, which is the smallest amount that can be allocated to a file.
4. Verify your calculations using Chkdsk.

Challenging Project

Using Windows 9x, create your own bootable disk that loads the 16-bit real-mode drivers to use a mouse. Test the mouse by booting from the disk and using the mouse with the EDIT text editor.

CASE PROJECT

Prepare a Hard Drive for the Installation of Windows 9x

This project requires that you completely erase everything on your hard drive. If you have important data on the drive, don't do this project!

Do the following to prepare a hard drive for a new installation of Windows 9x, which you will perform in the next chapter:

1. Boot from a Windows 9x startup disk and, using Fdisk, create primary and extended partitions on the drive. The primary partition will contain drive C. If there is room on the drive, create two logical drives in the extended partition.
2. Format all three logical drives, placing system files on drive C.
3. Verify that you can boot to drive C and get a C prompt and that all three drives are accessible.
4. Use the Dir command to print a directory of each drive to a local printer. Use these or similar commands: DIR C:>PRN, DIR D:>PRN, and DIR E:>PRN
5. Using Scandisk, scan each logical drive disk surface for errors.

CHAPTER

4

INSTALLING AND USING WINDOWS 9X

In this chapter, you will learn:

- About the different versions and architecture of Windows 9x
- How to install and use Windows 9x
- How to install hardware and applications with Windows 9x
- How to manage hard drives, floppy disks, and memory with Windows 9x
- How to get help from Microsoft

As a PC support technician, you need to know how to install, use, and troubleshoot the Windows OSs in common use today. You need to have a general knowledge of how hardware works and a detailed knowledge of how Windows and other types of software work. In Chapter 2, you learned how hardware and software work together, and in Chapter 3 you were introduced to the DOS portion of Windows 9x. This chapter covers how Windows 9x is structured, how it is used, and how it works with various software programs and hardware devices. This information lays the foundation for the next chapter, in which you will learn how to troubleshoot Windows 9x, as well as later chapters on using and troubleshooting other Windows OSs.

Windows 9x Versions and Architecture

Windows 9x has had several releases, including Windows 95, Windows 95 Service Release 2 (SR2), Windows 98, Windows 98 Second Edition (SE), and Windows Me (Millennium Edition). Each of these OSs uses the same basic architectural structure, and each release has improvements over previous versions plus new features. We next discuss the major differences between these releases and then look at the Windows 9x architecture.

How Windows 98 Differs from Windows 95

Windows 98 is basically the same operating system as Windows 95, with the same core components and the same fundamental services to software, hardware, and the user. However, it does offer some added features and improved performance over Windows 95. Some of the added features, including FAT32 and support for USB and DVD, became available with Windows 95 Release 2. Windows 98 also includes some new system tools to monitor and improve system performance, new hardware support, and additional Web tools.

FAT32 is not compatible with Windows NT or disk compression, including the use of DoubleSpace under Windows 98. To use disk compression or to have a file system compatible with Windows NT, use FAT16. Windows 2000/XP supports FAT32.

Windows 95 and Windows 98 load, run, and install very much the same way. As we continue through this chapter and the next, any significant differences between the two versions will be noted. Table 4-1 summarizes the changes that took place from Windows 95 to Windows 98. Some of the terms in the table may be unfamiliar to you but are covered later in the book.

Table 4-1 Features new to Windows 98

Feature	Description
Troubleshooting utilities	Windows 95 had a few troubleshooting utilities, but the 15 utilities that come with Windows 98 are more interactive.
Update Wizard	The Update Wizard connects to the Microsoft Web site and automatically downloads any new drivers or fixes.
Maintenance Wizard	The Maintenance Wizard can be used to regularly schedule several maintenance tasks, which include running Disk Defragmenter and ScanDisk.
DriveSpace 3	An improved version of DriveSpace for Windows 95, it includes a third level of data compression, called UltraPack, which takes up less space per file than does the regular compression utility, called HiPack.
Power management	Windows 98 supports some power management features, if both hardware and software are present to use them.
Registry Checker	Backs up and restores the registry.

Table 4-1 Features new to Windows 98 (continued)

Feature	Description
Web tools and features	Several Windows 98 features take on an Internet look and feel. Windows 98 also supports viewing TV and interactive programs. You'll need a special TV interface card to do it.
FAT32	FAT32 is a file system that allows for a smaller cluster size on large drives than does the earlier FAT16.
New hardware support	With 1,200 device drivers, Windows 98 supports many more hardware devices than did Windows 95. Also, Windows 98 supports USB, DVD drives, multiple video cards supporting multiple monitors, and faster data throughput for CD-ROM drives.
Win32 Driver Model (WDM)	A new device driver model, also used by Windows NT, makes it possible for the same device driver to be used by both operating systems, making it easier for device manufactures to supply drivers for their devices.

Windows Me

Windows Me, the last Windows 9x upgrade, has a desktop that looks more like Windows 2000 than Windows 98 SE, and, just like Windows 2000, it does not include the option to boot to the DOS command prompt in the Start menu. That means that you cannot boot Windows Me from the hard drive in true real mode, although you do have a MS-DOS Command Prompt window. If you want to get a true real-mode command prompt using Windows Me, create a blank formatted floppy disk and copy Io.sys and Command.com from the \Windows\Command\EBD folder to the disk, and then boot from this disk.

Windows Me does not allow real-mode device drivers and TSRs to be loaded from Config.sys and Autoexec.bat as do earlier versions of Windows 9x. If you want to run these 16-bit programs, your only option is to load them after Windows Me loads. One way to do this is to include them in a batch file that is listed in the Properties tab of the MS-DOS Command Prompt shortcut.

Troubleshooting tools new to Windows Me include:

- System Restore, which automatically backs up the registry and other system files when the system is idle, after about every 10 hours of operating time. When needed, the System Restore Wizard can be used to choose between earlier versions of the saved system.
- System File Protection, which is similar to Windows 2000 System File Protection, prevents system files from being deleted. For example, if you attempt to delete files in the Program Files folder where applications are normally stored, the utility will work in the background to compress and save these files in case you need them later. The utility also prevents an application installation from overwriting newer DLL files with older or nonstandard versions.

Windows 9x Architecture

A+ OS 2.3

Like other OSs, Windows 9x has a shell and a kernel. The two most important parts of the shell are the **user component** and the GDI. The user component manages input from the keyboard and other user devices, output from the user interface, and the **GDI (Graphics Device Interface)**. The GDI is a component of the OS responsible for presenting the graphical interface to the user and providing graphics support to output devices. The purposes of each component are listed in Table 4-2.

Table 4-2 Core components of Windows 9x

Component Name	Main Files Holding the Component	Functions
Kernel	Kernel32.dll, Krnl386.exe	Handles the basic OS functions such as managing memory, file I/O, and loading and executing programs.
User	User32.dll, User.exe	Controls the mouse, keyboard, ports, and desktop, including the position of windows, icons, and dialog boxes.
GDI	GDI32.dll, GDI.exe	Draws screens, graphics, and lines, and prints them.

A+ OS 1.1

Figure 4-1 shows the three core portions of the Windows 9x OS. In Figure 4-1, you can see that the basic Windows 9x core component, the kernel, uses mostly 32-bit code. The 16-bit code is only retained to provide entry points into the kernel from 16-bit application programs. The user portion uses mostly 16-bit code, primarily because it uses less memory than the 32-bit equivalent and does not have a need for significant speed. The GDI core uses a mix of 16-bit and 32-bit code in order to maintain compatibility with 16-bit application programs.

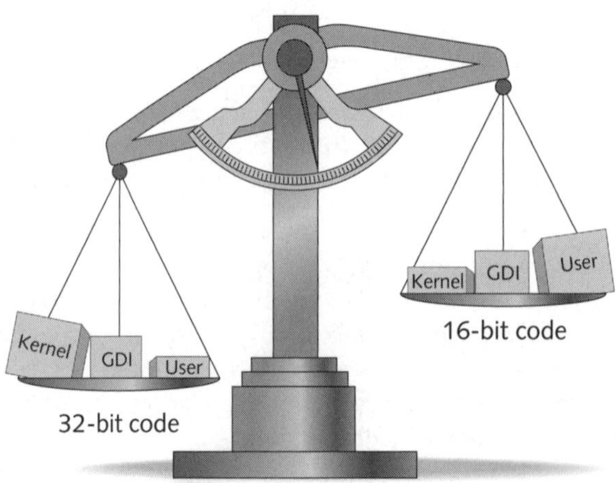

Figure 4-1 Windows 9x uses some 32-bit and some 16-bit code in its three core components

A+ OS 1.1

The Windows 9x core relates to users, software, and hardware by way of several modules, as seen in Figure 4-2. Just as DOS and Windows 3.x each provided a shell for the user to interface with the OS, Windows 9x provides a group of user interface tools and a shell for applications. Configuration data that was stored in Windows 3.x ini files is stored in the Windows 9x registry, a database that also contains the initialization information for applications, a database of hardware and software settings, Windows configuration settings, user parameters, and application settings. (You will read about the registry in several places in this chapter and will learn about it in more detail in the next chapter.)

4

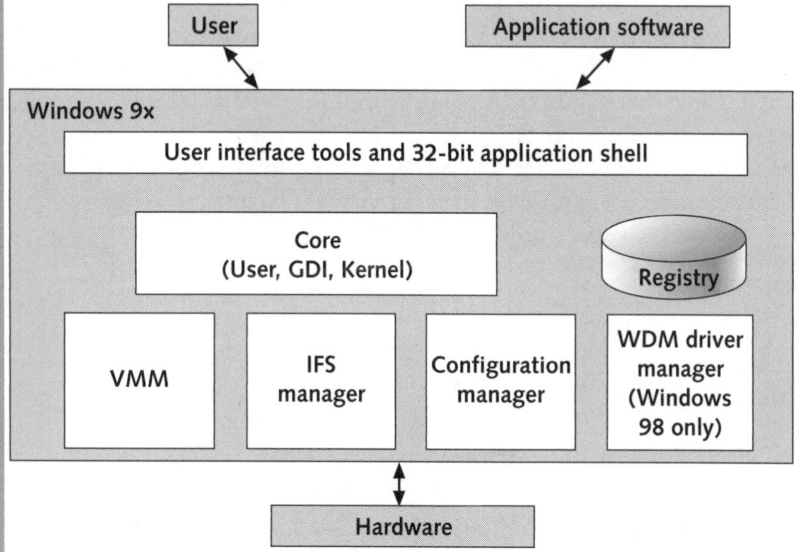

Figure 4-2 The Windows 9x architecture as it relates to the user, application software, and hardware

Virtual Machines

Before we look at the different components in Figure 4-2, you need to understand how these components relate to applications and hardware. Recall from earlier chapters that DOS allows applications direct access to hardware, but, beginning with Windows 95, the Windows operating system manages hardware for applications. Applications call on the OS to access hardware or other software by using an **application programming interface (API) call**. When applications are first loaded by Windows 9x, the methods to access hardware and software are made available to the software through an interface called a **virtual machine**. An application sees a virtual machine as a set of resources made available to it through these predefined APIs. An OS can provide a virtual machine to a single application that commands all the resources of that virtual machine, or the OS can assign a virtual machine to be shared by two or more applications. Think of virtual machines as multiple logical machines within one physical machine, similar in concept to several logical drives within one physical drive.

Figure 4-3 shows several virtual machines that Windows 9x can provide. In the figure, the system virtual machine (system VM) is the most important VM under Windows 9x and is where all the OS processes run. It can also support 32-bit and 16-bit Windows application programs, but DOS programs run in their own virtual machines.

A DOS program expects to directly control the hardware of the entire PC, memory included. If a DOS program begins to use memory addresses not assigned to it, errors occur in a multitasking environment. Windows 9x solves this problem by providing the DOS program with its own virtual machine. In effect, the application program says, "I want all of memory and all of this and all of that." Windows 9x says, "OK, here they are," and gives the program its own PC, including all the virtual memory addresses it wants from 0 to 4 GB as well as its own virtual hardware! As far as the DOS program is concerned, it can go anywhere and do anything within its own PC. The DOS application program does not try to communicate with any other application program or to access the data of another program, because it thinks there are no other programs; it controls its entire world, and it's the only program in it. That's a virtual machine.

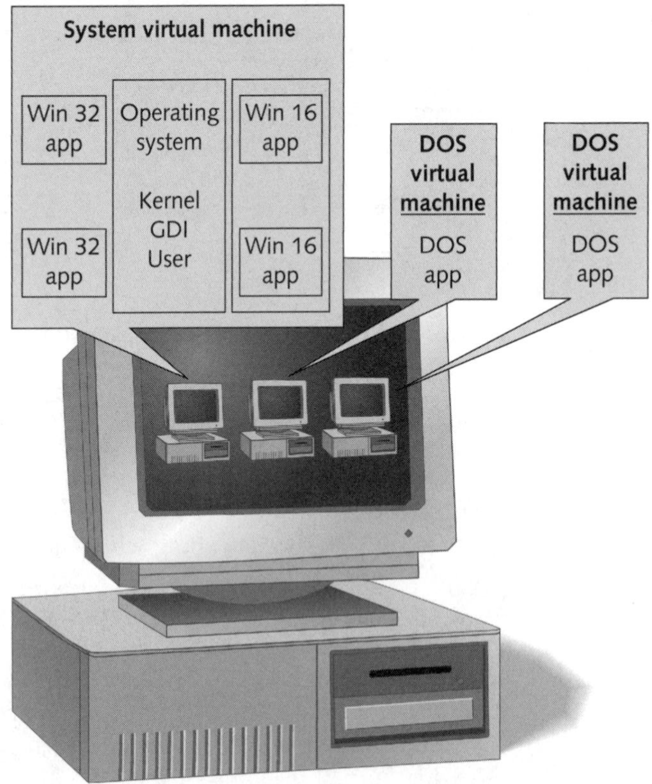

Figure 4-3 Windows 9x uses the virtual machine concept

One important result of running DOS programs in individual virtual machines is that when a DOS program makes an error, the virtual machine it is using hangs, but other programs and the OS are isolated from the problem and thus are not affected by it.

Windows 16-bit application programs offer a slightly different challenge to Windows 9x. These programs make some of the same mistakes that DOS programs do and can cause the system to hang. However, they also sometimes expect to access other programs and their data. The 16-bit Windows programs don't expect to control the hardware directly and are content to route their requests to Windows. Windows 9x places these programs within the system virtual machine because they communicate with hardware through the OS, but Windows 9x puts these programs together in their own memory space so they can share memory addresses.

A+ OS 3.1 3.3

The result of this arrangement is that, when a 16-bit Windows program causes an error called a Windows Protection Error or a General Protection Fault, it can disturb other 16-bit programs, causing them to fail. However, it does not disturb DOS programs in their own virtual machine or 32-bit programs that don't share their virtual memory addresses. (You will learn more about virtual memory addresses later in the chapter.)

Components of Windows 9x

We now turn our attention back to the OS components that create, configure, and manage the virtual machines used by software and the OS. Figure 4-2 serves as a simple but complete reference point for all the components of Windows 9x, illustrating how they relate to the user, hardware, and software, and to each other. As you can see, Windows 9x architecture uses a modular approach that divides functions into separate program groups, making each component easier to update and to implement.

One component in Figure 4-2 is the **Virtual Machine Manager (VMM)**, the component responsible for managing virtual machines and all the resources needed by each application running in them. One hardware device that all applications require is memory, and the VMM manages memory and virtual memory for applications. **Virtual memory** uses hard drive space so that it acts like memory. Windows stores virtual memory in a file called a swap file, discussed later in the chapter. The purpose of virtual memory is to increase the amount of memory available. Of course, because a hard drive is much slower than RAM, virtual memory works at a considerably slower speed than real memory. For example, a hard drive may have a data access time of 10 ms (10/1,000 second or 10 milliseconds), whereas RAM speed may be 60 ns (60/1,000,000,000 second or 60 nanoseconds).

Another component, called the **Installable File System (IFS)** manager, is responsible for all disk access. The **Configuration Manager** is responsible for the Plug and Play features of Windows 9x and other hardware configuration tasks such as providing system resources to hardware devices. In Figure 4-2, the only component that is found in Windows 98 but not Windows 95 is the **Win32 Driver Model (WDM)** driver manager, the component responsible for managing device drivers. The WDM makes it possible for device drivers written for Windows 98 to also work with Windows NT.

Keep in mind that Windows 9x is a compromise OS, attempting to bridge the 16-bit world and the 32-bit world. It makes many compromises between these two worlds.

A+ OS 2.1

Although Windows 9x supports 16-bit device drivers and applications, it's preferable to use 32-bit drivers and 32-bit applications for four main reasons:

- 32-bit drivers and applications are generally much faster than 16-bit software.
- 32-bit drivers and applications can be stored in extended memory, releasing more of the first megabyte of memory.
- 32-bit drivers can be dynamically loaded, meaning that they are loaded into memory when they are needed and then removed when not needed, thus conserving memory. In contrast, 16-bit drivers must be stored in conventional or upper memory and remain there as long as the OS is running.
- 32-bit applications can share data with other 32-bit applications and are generally better designed, making better use of OS resources.

When Windows 9x is installed over DOS, it searches for 16-bit drivers and replaces them with 32-bit drivers if it can.

INSTALLING WINDOWS 9X

A+ OS 2.1

In the previous chapter, you learned how to boot a computer to a C prompt on a working hard drive. In this chapter, you will learn how to install Windows 9x from that point. Remember as you proceed that there are separate installation CDs for installing Windows 9x on a PC without Windows (Microsoft labels the OS as Windows 9x for a New PC) and for installing Windows 9x on a PC with an earlier version of Windows (Microsoft labels the OS as Windows 9x Upgrade). The CDs for installing Windows 9x on a new PC are significantly more expensive than the upgrade CDs. To use the upgrade CDs, you must have a previous version of Windows installed on your hard drive.

A problem arises if you have just replaced a failed hard drive with a new hard drive and you want to do a fresh installation using a Windows 9x Upgrade CD. During the OS installation, the upgrade CD will ask you to provide a Microsoft floppy disk or CD from an earlier version of Windows. If you cannot provide the CD or floppy, the upgrade installation will terminate and you must use the more expensive version, Windows 9x for a New PC.

First, let's look at what's on the Windows 9x installation CD and how to prepare your hard drive for installation.

What's on the Windows 9x CD

A+ OS 2.1

The Windows 9x installation CD contains all the files you will need to complete installation of the OS, as well as some system administration tools, instructions and tutorials, and other utilities. The CD includes a setup wizard that guides you through the process of installation and does not require you to work with the OS files themselves.

The Windows 9x installation CD includes files you can use for the following tasks:

- Installing the OS
- Customizing configuration of the operating system
- Configuring and optimizing your desktop
- Network administration
- Diagnosing and troubleshooting system errors
- File management

Figure 4-4 shows the opening screen of the Windows 98 CD. It provides links to find information on software available with Windows 98, play video clips showing the multimedia features of Windows 98, browse the CD for a particular file or program, and add or remove software.

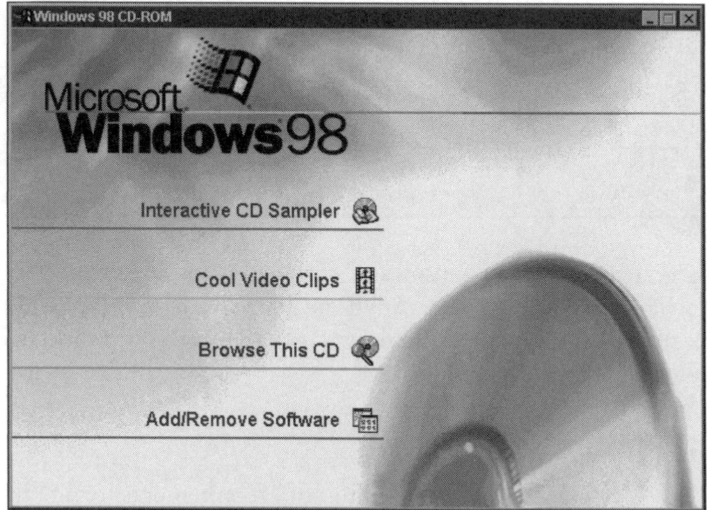

Figure 4-4 The opening screen of the Windows 98 CD provides links you can use to navigate the CD

4

A+ OS 2.1

Important folders on the CD and their contents include the following:

- *CD sample* contains subfolders that provide a catalog of and demos of Microsoft products.
- *Drivers* lists hardware drivers by category.
- *Oldmsdos* contains old DOS tools that can be useful in setup and troubleshooting.
- *Sysrec* contains system recovery tools.

Table 4-3 lists some important files on the Windows 9x CD.

Table 4-3 Important files on the Windows 9x CD

File	Function
Autorun.inf	Launches the interactive interface for the CD. (This is the interface shown in Figure 4-4.)
Readme.txt	Explains the layout of the CD and gives the locations of other readme files.
Setup.exe	Begins installation of the OS.
Batch.exe	Creates files that can be used for automated Windows 9x installations.
Checklinks.exe	Contains the Link Check Wizard, which can help you find and fix broken links and program shortcuts.
Netmon.386	Contains the Network Monitor, which enables you to monitor network performance remotely for Windows 9x computers.
Regserv.exe	The Microsoft Remote Registry, which provides a means to remotely view and edit the Windows 9x registry.
Textview.exe	Launches a text viewer that can quickly display text files without having to go through opening and operating a more complex word processing application.
Where.exe	Gives you a tool that you can use from the command line to locate a specific file on your hard drive.

This list does not give a comprehensive inventory of the contents of the installation CD but is an overview of what you will find there. Any time after you have installed Windows 9x, you can refer back to the CD to access utilities and tutorials on how to use the operating system and the tools that are included with it.

Preparing for Installation

A+ OS 2.1

Before installing Windows 9x, verify that the minimum requirements for the hardware are met. In order for Windows 9x to perform satisfactorily, the PC should meet the recommended requirements. Minimum and recommended requirements for Windows 95 and Windows 98 are listed below:

Minimum and recommended requirements for Windows 95:

- 486DX, 25 MHz or higher processor
- 4 MB of RAM (8 MB is recommended)
- 40 to 45 MB of hard disk storage, depending on the installation

A+ OS 2.1

Minimum and recommended requirements for Windows 98:

- 486DX, 66 MHz or higher processor
- 24 MB of RAM (32 MB is recommended)
- From 140 to 315 MB of hard disk storage, depending on the installation

Windows 9x is most likely to be installed as an upgrade from DOS with Windows 3.x, as an upgrade from Windows 95 to Windows 98, or on a clean hard drive. If you have been having problems with your current operating system and applications, consider doing a clean install rather than an upgrade. A **clean install** ignores any settings in the currently installed OS, including information about installed hardware or software. Therefore, after the clean install, you must reinstall all hardware and application. Therefore, before deciding to do a clean install, verify that you have all the application software installation CDs or floppy disks and then back up all data on the drive. Also take the time to verify that the backup of data is good, and verify that you have all device driver software.

You do not need to format the hard drive, although you should delete all folders on the hard drive used for the OS or applications, including the \Windows folder, files, and subfolders before you begin the installation. This will force Setup to perform a clean install and make certain no corrupted system files or applications remain. If you like, you can also format the hard drive. Do this if you suspect that a virus is present. If you suspect a boot sector virus is present, use the Fdisk/MBR command (discussed in Chapter 3) to rewrite the master boot sector program. Then do the clean install.

After Windows 9x is installed, reinstall all the application software and then, if you formatted the hard drive, restore the data from backups. This method takes longer than an upgrade, but you get the advantage of a fresh start, and any problems with corrupted applications or system settings will not follow you into the new installation.

An **upgrade install** carries forward as much information as it can about what the current OS knows concerning installed hardware and software, user preferences, and other settings. An upgrade is faster than a clean install because you don't need to reinstall software and hardware. However, problems with an old installation sometimes carry forward into the upgrade.

You can perform either an upgrade or a clean install with either the Windows 9x for a New PC or the Windows 9x Upgrade CD. If you are doing an upgrade, the old operating system must be in good enough shape to boot up because you must begin an upgrade from within the currently installed OS.

Installing Windows 9x as a Clean Installation

A+ OS 2.1

Recall from the case project at the end of Chapter 2 that you can change CMOS settings to specify the order in which system BIOS looks for an OS on the drives on your PC. You might need to change the boot order in CMOS, depending on how you plan to load the OS. Older PCs could only boot from a hard drive or floppy disk. This meant that to use a CD-ROM drive, you had to first boot these PCs from floppy disks and then install the CD-ROM drivers. There are more choices with newer PCs, some of which can boot from

A+ OS 2.1 a hard drive, floppy drive, Zip drive, CD-ROM drive, or other type of drive. These newer PCs have drivers for drive types other than hard drives and floppy drives written into their BIOS, allowing you to boot from a different medium.

If the PC is on a network, it is possible to install the OS from another computer on the network. However, if you want to do an upgrade, you must begin the upgrade from within the current OS. Therefore, if you are performing an installation across a network, you are forced to do a clean install.

Windows 9x comes on a set of floppy disks or on a CD. If you are installing the OS from floppy disks, you can boot from the hard drive or floppy disk. To boot from the floppy disk, insert the Windows 9x Disk 1, which is bootable, and boot the PC. At the A prompt, enter the command *Setup.exe*. You can also boot from a hard drive, go to a C prompt, and insert the Windows 9x Disk 1 in the floppy disk drive. Enter the command *A:\Setup* to execute the Setup program on the floppy disk. Either way, the Windows 9x setup screen appears. Follow the directions on the screen.

Your CD-ROM drive might be configured to automatically run a CD when it is first inserted. This Autoplay feature will cause the Setup opening menu to appear without your entering the Setup command. To disable the feature, hold down the Shift key while inserting the CD.

If you are installing the OS from a CD (if your PC can boot from a CD-ROM drive) insert the CD in the drive and reboot. If your PC cannot boot from a CD, boot from a floppy disk or hard drive, then insert the CD in the CD-ROM drive and enter the command *D:\Setup.exe*, substituting the drive letter of your CD-ROM drive for *D* if necessary.

To speed up the installation, you can copy the files and folders on the Windows 98 CD to a folder on your hard drive and run the Setup program from that folder. Also, having the Windows 98 CD files on your hard drive makes it easier to access the files later when adding Windows components or updating drivers.

Installing 9x as an Upgrade

A+ OS 2.1 If you are doing an upgrade, before you begin the installation, prepare your hard drive by doing these things:

- Verify that you have enough space on the hard drive. Delete files in the Recycle Bin and temporary directories.
- Run ScanDisk to check and repair errors on the hard drive. From Windows 95, click Start, Programs, Accessories, System Tools, ScanDisk and scan each logical drive in the system. From a Windows startup disk or from DOS, enter the command *Scandisk* at the command prompt. You will learn more about ScanDisk in the next chapter.

A+ OS 2.1

- Run a current version of antivirus software to check for viruses.
- If you are upgrading from Windows 3.x, save configuration files so that you can backtrack to it if necessary. Save Autoexec.bat and Config.sys, found in the root directory, and all files with .ini or .grp file extensions in the \Windows directory to a disk. In Windows 3.x, files with the .grp file extension are **group files**, which contain information about a program group displayed in Program Manager.
- Check Config.sys and Autoexec.bat for potential problems. Verify that any hardware devices using device drivers loaded from these files are working under the old OS so you know your starting point when troubleshooting problems under the new OS.

The Windows 9x upgrade process will move commands in Autoexec.bat used to load TSRs required for 16-bit Windows programs to Winstart.bat. Look for the Winstart.bat file in the root directory after the installation is done. If setup did not find any TSRs to put in the file, it will not be created.

- If there are TSRs such as QEMM386 (a memory manager by Quarterdeck) loaded from Config.sys or Autoexec.bat, and problems arise because they are running during the installation, disable them by converting these lines to remarks or comments by typing *REM* at the beginning of the command lines. Later, after the installation, you can activate them again by removing the REMs at the beginning of lines.
- If you are connected to a network, verify that the connection is working. If it is, Windows setup should be able to reestablish the connection correctly at the end of the installation.
- If you are upgrading from Windows 95 to Windows 98, create a Windows 95 rescue disk for use in the event that the installation fails.
- Decide if you want to use FAT16 or FAT32 for your file system. If you choose FAT16, you can later convert to FAT32 using the Windows Drive Converter. After Windows 98 is installed, to access the Converter, click Start, Programs, Accessories, System Tools, Drive Converter (FAT32). As an alternative, you can use the Run dialog box: For the 16-bit version, enter *cvt.exe*, and for the 32-bit version, enter *cvt1.exe*, and then click OK. The Drive Converter Wizard steps you through the process. Figure 4-5 shows you the first screen of the Drive Converter Wizard.

A+ OS 2.1

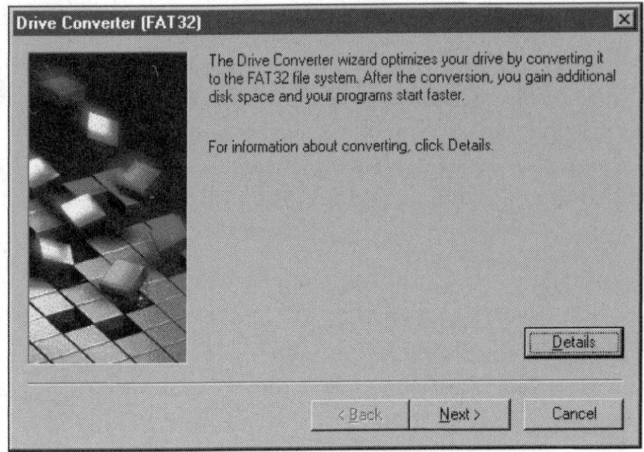

Figure 4-5 Use the Drive Converter Wizard to convert your hard drive to the FAT 32 file system

- If you are installing Windows on a compressed drive, be aware that the registry can reside on any compressed drive, but the swap file can reside on a compressed drive only if it is compressed using protected-mode software such as DriveSpace. (Compressed drives, discussed in more detail in Chapter 11, are hard drives that have a portion of their data compressed in order to save space on the drive.) DriveSpace marks the area for the swap file as uncompressible. If your drive is compressed with real-mode compression software, such as DoubleSpace, then know that you cannot put the swap file on this compressed drive. Best practice is to back up the data and then uncompress the drive. You can later compress it using Windows 98 DriveSpace.

If you used DOS DoubleSpace (available with DOS 6 and 6.2) to compress the drive, type DBLSPACE at the DOS prompt. If you used DriveSpace (available with DOS 6.22), type DRVSPACE. These utilities will give you statistics about the compressed drive and also allow you to change the size of the uncompressed part of the drive, called the host drive.

Once you have prepared your hard drive for an upgrade installation, do the following to get to the setup screen:

1. Start the PC, loading the current operating system.
2. Close all open applications, including any antivirus software that is running.
3. Insert the CD in the CD-ROM drive or the floppy disk in the floppy drive. When upgrading from Windows 95 to Windows 98, open the Run dialog box and enter the command **D:\Setup.exe**, substituting the drive letter for the CD-ROM drive or floppy drive in the command line. Click **OK**.
4. Follow the instructions on the setup screen. When you are given the opportunity to select the folder to install Windows, select the folder that the current OS is installed in; most likely that is \Windows. If you use the same folder, Setup will use whatever settings it finds there.

Installation Process from the Setup Screen

A+ OS 2.1

Once you get to the setup screen, the installation process is the same, no matter whether you are doing an upgrade or a clean install. When installing Windows 9x, you are given the option of creating the Startup disk as discussed in the previous chapter. Be sure to do that to help prepare for emergencies. During the installation, you will also be asked to choose from four setup options:

- *Typical.* This option installs all of the components that are usually installed with Windows 9x. Most often, this is the option to choose.
- *Portable.* Use this option when installing Windows 9x on a notebook computer.
- *Compact.* Use this option if you are short on hard drive space and want the smallest possible installation. No optional components are installed during the installation. After the installation, if you need a component, you can install it by double-clicking the Add/Remove Programs applet in the Control Panel.
- *Custom.* Use this option if you know you will need components that are not normally installed under the Typical installation. You are given the opportunity to select any group of components to be included in the installation.

Windows 9x Setup begins installation in real mode and then switches to protected mode. During real mode, it runs ScanDisk, checks for existing Windows software, performs several system checks, loads the extended memory driver, looks for existing TSRs, and starts Windows, if it is not already started. The Windows logo screen is the first thing the user normally sees during the installation. Setup then switches to protected mode.

Setup creates the registry, getting it ready to contain the hardware information, and then searches for hardware. It loads its own drivers for the detected hardware, or, if it cannot detect the hardware, requests the drivers from the user. Setup then copies the drivers to the hard drive from the installation source or from a floppy disk, CD or other source provided by the user.

Up to this point, if Setup fails and you reboot the PC, you boot into the old OS. At this point, Setup alters the boot records on the hard drive to point to the Windows 9x file, Io.sys, rather than to the old OS system files. After this point, if Setup fails and you reboot, you reboot into Windows 9x.

During a normal installation, the PC reboots and Windows 9x is loaded. Some initial startup programs are run to set the time zone and to change existing application programs to Windows 9x. Depending on the hardware present, the PC may reboot again to load new drivers.

A+ OS 2.1

During the installation, Setup records information in log files. The primary log file is Setuplog.txt, a text file that is used by Windows to determine how far it got into the installation when it is recovering from a crash. Figure 4-6 shows a portion of Setuplog.txt in which the system ran a virus check on CMOS and began checking drives. The Detection Log (Detlog.txt) keeps a record of hardware detected, as shown in Figure 4-7.

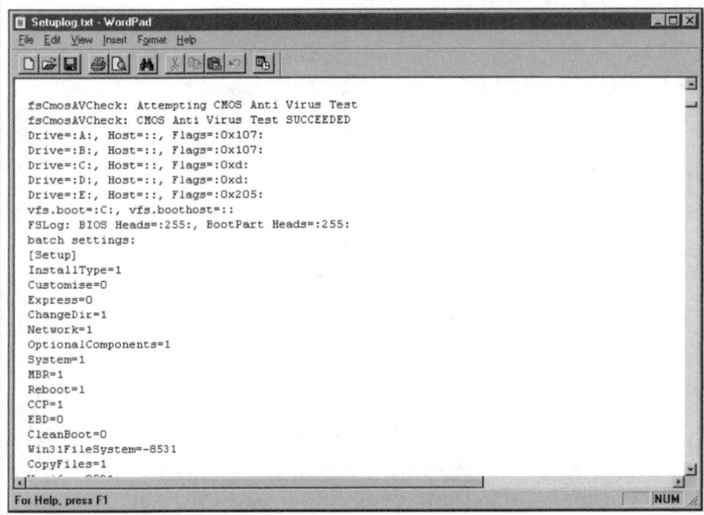

Figure 4-6 Windows records information about the setup process in Setuplog.txt

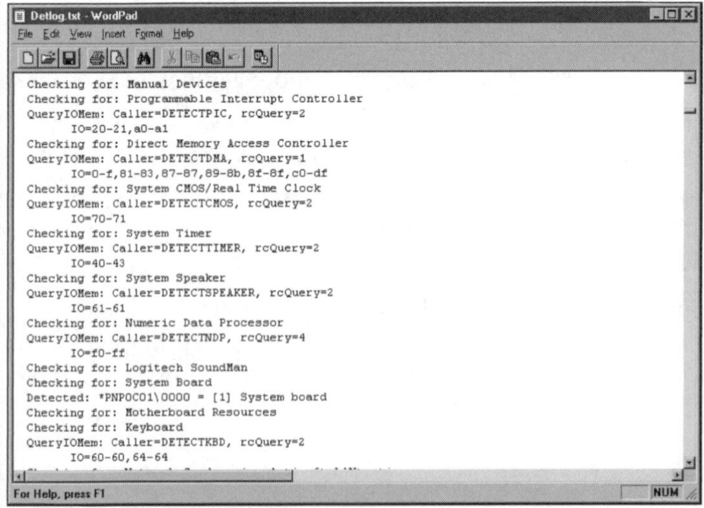

Figure 4-7 The Detlog.txt file shows what hardware has been detected

A+ OS 2.1 If the system fails to respond during the hardware detection phase, an entry is recorded in Detcrash.log, a binary file used by Windows to help recover from a crash caused by a problem with hardware. Windows does not use the contents of Detlog.txt; it is created only for the benefit of the user.

For example, if Setup suspects that a network card is present, because it sees a network driver installed in Config.sys, it records in Setuplog.txt and Detlog.txt that it is about to look for the card. If it successfully finds the card, it records the success in Detlog.txt. However, if an error occurs while Setup is searching for the card, an entry is made in the Detcrash.log file.

4

If the system crashes while trying to detect the network card and Setup is then restarted, it looks at Detcrash.log and Setuplog.txt to determine what it was trying to do at the time of the crash. It skips that step and goes on to the next step, so that it doesn't make the same mistake twice.

Even though Setup might crash several times during the installation process, progress is still being made. By reading the content of the log files, Setup is able to skip steps that cause a problem and move forward.

Be careful not to delete the log files during the installation process, especially if you've just experienced a crash. Also, restart by using the power on/power off method so that the ISA bus is fully initialized, which does not always happen during a warm boot.

In certain situations you might want to force Setup to begin installation at the beginning instead of looking to Setuplog.txt for the entry point, for example when you think you might have resolved a problem with hardware and want Setup to attempt to find the hardware again. To do that, delete Setuplog.txt to force a full restart.

Customizing Setup

Windows and other software store information about an installation on the setup CD or floppy disks in information files. These **information (.inf) files** are text files with an .inf file extension. One .inf file is Msbatch.inf. Information about your installation can be stored in this file, which can then be used to do an automatic, hands-free installation. All the questions that a user must answer during an installation can be answered by entries in this file so that a user has little to do but begin the installation. For more information about hands-free installations, see the *Microsoft Windows 95 Resource Kit* or the *Windows 98 Resource Kit* by Microsoft Press.

You can add several switches to the Setup.exe command that starts the setup process. Some of these switches and what they do are listed in Table 4-4.

Table 4-4 Switches for the Setup command

Switch	Description
Setup /?	Display help for each command-line switch.
Setup /D	Don't use the existing version of Windows to begin Setup. Use this option if you suspect corrupted Windows system files when upgrading Windows.
Setup /IC	Perform a clean boot. Use this option if you suspect drivers loaded from Autoexec.bat or Config.sys are causing a problem with the installation.
Setup /IH	Run ScanDisk in the foreground so that you can view results. Use this option if setup failed earlier and you want to check for hard drive corruption.
Setup /IL	Load the driver for a Logitech mouse. Use this option if you are using a Logitech Series C mouse.
Setup /IN	Do not set up the network.
Setup /IS	Do not run ScanDisk.
Setup /PI	Keep hardware settings that are not default settings. Use this option if a previous try of the installation caused a legacy hardware device to fail.

Table 4-5 lists some problems that might occur while installing Windows 9x and what to do about them.

Table 4-5 Some problems and solutions when installing Windows 9x

Symptom	Description and Solution
An error message about BIOS appears during installation	This is most likely caused by BIOS not allowing changes to the boot sector to protect it from viruses. Disable the feature in CMOS setup.
Windows 9x stalls during the first restart after installation	This is probably caused by legacy hardware not configured correctly. Try the following: ■ Remark (REM) out all entries in Config.sys and Autoexec.bat. ■ Disable the ISA enumerator by commenting out this line in System.ini: Device=ISAPNP.386.
During the first restart after installation, an error message appears with information about a bad or missing file.	Probably caused by an error in Config.sys or Autoexec.bat. Try renaming both files so they are not executed. If this solves the problem, then comment out each line in the file, one at a time, until you know which line caused the problem.
During the first restart after the installation, you get an error message about a missing or damaged VxD file.	Run Windows setup again and select the option to Verify or replace the missing VxD (virtual device driver).
After upgrading from Windows 95 to Windows 98, the startup screen still says Windows 95	This can be caused by one of two problems. The Io.sys file might not have been updated. Use the Sys C: command to replace it. The file Logo.sys is in the root directory, which overrides the logo screen embedded in Io.sys. Delete or rename the file.

Table 4-5 Some problems and solutions when installing Windows 9x (continued)

Symptom	Description and Solution
"Invalid system disk" error appears during setup.	■ Suspect a boot sector virus. Run a current version of antivirus software. ■ If this error occurs while installing Windows when disk management software such as DiskPro is running, Windows might have damaged the hard drive MBR. To recover from this problem, see the documentation for the disk management software.

4

For specific error messages that occur during installation and what to do about them, go to the Microsoft Web site *support.microsoft.com* and search on the error message.

A+ OS 2.1

Configuring the Windows 9x Startup with Msdos.sys

In Windows 9x, the file Msdos.sys is a text file containing several parameters that affect how the OS boots. You can change some of the entries in this file to customize the boot process. The file is a hidden, read-only, system file, so before you can edit it, you must first use the Attrib command at the command prompt or menus from Explorer to make the file available for editing. Also, make a backup copy of the file in case you want to revert to the form it was in before the changes were made.

From a command prompt, follow these steps to change the options in Msdos.sys:

1. Go to an OS command prompt.
2. Go to the root directory of your hard drive by entering:

   ```
   CD\
   ```

3. Make the file available for editing by entering:

   ```
   ATTRIB -R -H -S MSDOS.SYS
   ```

4. Make a backup copy of the file by entering:

   ```
   COPY MSDOS.SYS MSDOS.BK
   ```

5. Use Edit.com to edit the file by entering:

   ```
   EDIT MSDOS.SYS
   ```

6. Save the file and return it to a hidden, read-only, system file by entering:

   ```
   ATTRIB +R +H +S MSDOS.SYS
   ```

Table 4-6 lists each entry in the Msdos.sys file and its purpose. You can refer to this table as you read about the different options available when installing and configuring Windows 9x.

Table 4-6 Contents of the Msdos.sys file options section

Command Line Variable Name	Purpose of the Values Assigned to the Variable
AutoScan	0 = Computer does not scan hard drive. 1 = (Default) Prompts the user before running ScanDisk. on the hard drive when booting up after the computer is not shut down properly. 2 = Automatically scans without prompting the user.
BootMulti	0 = (Default) Boot only to Windows 9x. 1= Allows for a dual boot.
BootWin	1 = (Default) Boot to Windows 9x. 0 = Boot to previous version of DOS.
BootGUI	1 = (Default) Boot to Windows 9x with the graphic user interface. 0 = Boot only to the command prompt for DOS 7.0 (the DOS core of Windows 95) or 7.1 (the DOS core of Windows 98). Autoexec.bat and Config.sys will be executed, and you will be in real-mode DOS.
BootMenu	0 = (Default) Don't display the Startup Menu. 1= Display the Startup Menu.
BootMenuDefault	1 through 8 = The value selected from the Startup Menu by Default (Normally this value should be 1).
BootMenuDelay	n = Number of seconds delay before the default value in the Startup Menu is automatically selected.
BootKeys	1= (Default) The function keys work during the boot process (F4, F5, F6, F8, Shift+F5, Ctrl+F5, Shift+F8). 0 = Disable the function keys during the boot process. (This option can be used to help secure a workstation.)
BootDelay	n = Number of seconds the boot process waits (when it displays the message "Starting Windows 95" or "Starting Windows 98") for the user to press F8 to get the Startup Menu (default is 2 seconds).
Logo	1= (Default) Display the Windows 9x logo screen. 0 = Leave the screen in text mode.
Drvspace	1= (Default) Load Drvspace.bin, used for disk compression, if it is present. 0 = Don't load Drvspace.bin.
DoubleBuffer	1= (Default) When you have a SCSI drive, enables double buffering for the drive (see the drive documentation). 0 = Don't use double buffering for the SCSI drive.
Network	1= If network components are installed, include the option, "Safe mode with network support" in the Startup Menu. 0 = Don't include the option on the Startup Menu. (This will normally be set to 0 if the PC has no network components installed. The Startup Menu will be renumbered from this point forward in the menu.)

Table 4-6 Contents of the Msdos.sys file options section (continued)

Command Line Variable Name	Purpose of the Values Assigned to the Variable
BootFailSafe	1= (Default) Include Safe mode in the Startup Menu. 0 = Don't include Safe mode in the Startup Menu.
BootWarn	1= (Default) Display the warning message when Windows 9x boots into Safe mode. 0 = Don't display the warning message.
LoadTop	1= (Default) Load Command.com at the top of conventional memory. 0 = Don't load Command.com at the top of conventional memory. (Use this option when there is a memory conflict with this area of memory.)

Figure 4-8 shows a sample Msdos.sys file. The lines containing x's at the bottom of the file are used to ensure that the file size is compatible with other programs.

```
[Paths]
WinDir=C:\WIN95
WinBootDir=C:\WIN95
HostWinBootDrv=C

[Options]
BootMulti=1
BootGUI=1
BootMenu=1
Network=0
;
;The following lines are required for compatibility with other programs.
;Do not remove them (MSDOS.SYS needs to be >1024 bytes).
;xxxxxxxxxxxxxxxxxxxxxxxxxxxxxxxxxxxxxxxxxxxxxxxxxxxxxxxxxxxxxxxxxxxxa
;xxxxxxxxxxxxxxxxxxxxxxxxxxxxxxxxxxxxxxxxxxxxxxxxxxxxxxxxxxxxxxxxxxxxb
;xxxxxxxxxxxxxxxxxxxxxxxxxxxxxxxxxxxxxxxxxxxxxxxxxxxxxxxxxxxxxxxxxxxxc
;xxxxxxxxxxxxxxxxxxxxxxxxxxxxxxxxxxxxxxxxxxxxxxxxxxxxxxxxxxxxxxxxxxxxd
;xxxxxxxxxxxxxxxxxxxxxxxxxxxxxxxxxxxxxxxxxxxxxxxxxxxxxxxxxxxxxxxxxxxxe
;xxxxxxxxxxxxxxxxxxxxxxxxxxxxxxxxxxxxxxxxxxxxxxxxxxxxxxxxxxxxxxxxxxxxf
;xxxxxxxxxxxxxxxxxxxxxxxxxxxxxxxxxxxxxxxxxxxxxxxxxxxxxxxxxxxxxxxxxxxxg
;xxxxxxxxxxxxxxxxxxxxxxxxxxxxxxxxxxxxxxxxxxxxxxxxxxxxxxxxxxxxxxxxxxxxh
;xxxxxxxxxxxxxxxxxxxxxxxxxxxxxxxxxxxxxxxxxxxxxxxxxxxxxxxxxxxxxxxxxxxxi
;xxxxxxxxxxxxxxxxxxxxxxxxxxxxxxxxxxxxxxxxxxxxxxxxxxxxxxxxxxxxxxxxxxxxj
;xxxxxxxxxxxxxxxxxxxxxxxxxxxxxxxxxxxxxxxxxxxxxxxxxxxxxxxxxxxxxxxxxxxxk
;xxxxxxxxxxxxxxxxxxxxxxxxxxxxxxxxxxxxxxxxxxxxxxxxxxxxxxxxxxxxxxxxxxxxl
;xxxxxxxxxxxxxxxxxxxxxxxxxxxxxxxxxxxxxxxxxxxxxxxxxxxxxxxxxxxxxxxxxxxxm
;xxxxxxxxxxxxxxxxxxxxxxxxxxxxxxxxxxxxxxxxxxxxxxxxxxxxxxxxxxxxxxxxxxxxn
;xxxxxxxxxxxxxxxxxxxxxxxxxxxxxxxxxxxxxxxxxxxxxxxxxxxxxxxxxxxxxxxxxxxxo
;xxxxxxxxxxxxxxxxxxxxxxxxxxxxxxxxxxxxxxxxxxxxxxxxxxxxxxxxxxxxxxxxxxxxp
;xxxxxxxxxxxxxxxxxxxxxxxxxxxxxxxxxxxxxxxxxxxxxxxxxxxxxxxxxxxxxxxxxxxxq
;xxxxxxxxxxxxxxxxxxxxxxxxxxxxxxxxxxxxxxxxxxxxxxxxxxxxxxxxxxxxxxxxxxxxr
;xxxxxxxxxxxxxxxxxxxxxxxxxxxxxxxxxxxxxxxxxxxxxxxxxxxxxxxxxxxxxxxxxxxxs
```

Figure 4-8 A sample Msdos.sys file

Instructions for Specific Upgrades

You have just learned the basic installation process for Windows 9x. Although most actual installations will follow this general outline, depending on exactly what version and features you are installing, each type of upgrade has its own issues. This section discusses things to consider when upgrading to Windows 95, 98, and Me from earlier operating system versions.

Installing Windows 9x over DOS and Windows 3.x

If DOS and Windows 3.x reside on the PC prior to installing Windows 9x, you can perform an upgrade or a clean install. If you choose an upgrade, this is what happens:

- Windows 9x Setup copies information about existing application programs from the .ini files of Windows 3.x into the Windows 9x registry, eliminating the need for you to install the existing programs into Windows 9x.
- These programs are added to the Start menu of Windows 9x.
- Existing programs can find their .dlls in the same Windows\System folder as they did with Windows 3.x. (DLLs, or dynamic link libraries, contain programming routines for common tasks and will be covered in detail in the next chapter.)

It is possible to install Windows 9x on the same hard drive as another operating system. This is called a dual boot and is covered in Chapter 6. However, there is usually little need to leave DOS or Windows 3.x on the drive. When upgrading from Windows 3.x to Windows 9x, first start Windows 3.x and enter the Setup command using File Manager.

A+ OS 2.2

Upgrading from Windows 95 to Windows 98

Upgrading from Windows 95 to Windows 98 is relatively easy, because the two OSs are similar. This upgrade is not as complex as upgrading from DOS with Windows 3.x. Follow these guidelines when upgrading from Windows 95 to Windows 98:

- As with any OS installation, you need to check whether your hardware is compatible with the OS you are planning to install. In this case, most hardware that will work with Windows 95 will work with Windows 98.
- Use up-to-date virus software and virus definitions to scan for viruses on your hard drive.
- You also need to check software packages and programs for compatibility. You can do this by checking the documentation or the manufacturer's Web site for each program. If you are planning an OS upgrade, a software manufacturer will often provide a downloadable **patch**, also called a **service pack**, to make the software compatible with the new OS. The search utility at *www.microsoft.com/windows/compatible/* provides a quick way to determine whether a particular product has been tested for compatibility with Windows.
- Make sure you have at least one full backup of your system as it was under Windows 95. If the upgrade to Windows 98 fails for any reason, you can use your Windows 95 backup to restore the system to the point where you were before you attempted the upgrade. How to perform a backup is covered in Chapter 11.

A+ OS 2.2 Once you have backed up your system and made sure its hardware and software are compatible with Windows 98, use the following procedure to perform the upgrade:

1. If your system BIOS runs a program to protect the boot sector of your hard drive from viruses, enter CMOS setup and disable the program because it might interfere with the installation. After the installation you can turn the program back on.
2. Start Windows 95 and close any open applications. If you have antivirus software running in the background, close the software. Close any icons open in the System Tray.
3. Insert the upgrade CD in the CD-ROM drive. Click **Start**, **Run** and enter **D:\Setup** in the Run dialog box (where D is the drive letter of the CD-ROM drive), then click **OK**.
4. When the Setup program opens, it will provide a series of windows to guide you through the setup process. All you have to do is follow the prompts and provide any requested information. Always create the emergency startup disk when you are prompted to do so.
5. After Setup is complete, open and test some of the applications you already had installed under Windows 95. Any problem you have with a particular application may be solved by uninstalling and then reinstalling it, or installing any necessary patches to make it work with Windows 98.
6. Once the upgrade from Windows 95 to Windows 98 is complete and you have verified that your system is working, it is a good idea to back up your system again.

Upgrading from Windows 98 to Windows Me

If you are upgrading from Windows 98 to Windows Me, use the same pre-upgrade checklist that is given for the Windows 95 to Windows 98 upgrade in the previous section. Remember to check the compatibility of hardware and software and to back up your system before you begin. To check whether a particular hardware product has been tested for use with Windows Me, go to *www.microsoft.com/windowsme/upgrade/compat/default.asp*.

In addition to the guidelines in the previous section, do the following before upgrading to Windows Me:

- Uncompress any portions of your hard drive that are compressed. If you are not sure whether your hard drive is compressed, run ScanDisk, which will tell you. Windows Me will not install on a compressed hard drive.
- Uninstall power management tools and disk management tools.
- Read the readme.txt file and any other setup information provided on the Windows Me disk.

The steps to upgrade Windows Me are the same as for Windows 98.

Downloading and Installing Updates for Windows 9x

A+ OS 2.2

Between releases of OS versions, manufacturers often produce OS updates in the form of patches or service packs that add features, fix bugs, or address security issues. The Microsoft Web site *windowsupdate.microsoft.com/*, provides you with a list of updates available for your OS. In Windows 98 and Windows Me, you can access this page by clicking Windows Update on the Start menu. The update process will examine your system and recommend available updates for you to select, download, and install following directions on the screen.

USING WINDOWS 9X

Now that you have learned how to install and upgrade Windows 9x, let's look at some things you need to know about using it. As a PC technician, you will need to be familiar with keyboard shortcuts for Windows as well as how to manage the desktop and use Windows Explorer.

Keystroke Shortcuts in Windows

A+ OS 1.1

Table 4-7 lists a few handy keystrokes to use when working with Windows, including the function keys you can use during startup. You can also use the mouse to accomplish some of these tasks, but keystrokes are faster for experienced typists. Also, sometimes in troubleshooting situations, the mouse is not usable. At those times, knowing the keystrokes is very valuable.

Table 4-7 Keystrokes to help make it easier to work with Windows

General Action	Keystrokes	Description
While loading Windows	F4	Load previous version of DOS.
	F5	Start in safe mode.
	F8 or Ctrl	Display Startup menu.
	Shift + F8	Step-by-step confirmation.
Working with text anywhere in Windows	Ctrl + C Ctrl + Ins	Shortcut for Copy.
	Ctrl + A	Shortcut for selecting all text.
	Ctrl + X	Shortcut for Cut.
	Ctrl + V Shift + Ins	Shortcut for Paste.
	Shift + arrow keys	Hold down the Shift key and use the arrow keys to select text, character by character.
Managing programs	Alt + Tab	While holding down the Alt key, press Tab to move from one loaded application to another.
	Ctrl + Esc	Display the Start menu.

A+ OS 1.1

Table 4-7 Keystrokes to help make it easier to work with Windows (continued)

General Action	Keystrokes	Description
	Alt + F4	Close a program window, or, if no window is open, shut down Windows.
	Double-click	Double-click an icon or program name to execute the program.
	Ctrl + Alt + Del	Display the Task List, which you can use to switch to another application, end a task, or shut down Windows.
Managing files, folders, icons and shortcuts	Ctrl + Shift while dragging a file	Create a shortcut.
	Ctrl while dragging a file	Copy a file.
	Shift + Delete	Delete a file without placing it in the Recycle Bin.
	F2	Rename an item.
	Alt + Enter	Display an item's Properties window.
Selecting items	Shift + click	To select multiple entries in a list (such as filenames in Explorer), click the first item and then hold down the Shift key and click the last item you want to select in the list. All items between the first and last are selected.
	Ctrl + click	To select several items in a list that are not listed sequentially, click the first item to select it. Hold down the Ctrl key as you click other items anywhere in the list. All items you have clicked on are selected.
Using menus	Alt	Press the Alt key to activate the menu bar.
	Alt, letter	After the menu bar is activated, press a letter to select a menu option. The letter must be underlined in the menu.
	Alt, arrow keys	After the menu bar is activated, use the arrow keys to move over the menu tree.
	Alt, arrow keys, Enter	After the menu bar is activated and the correct option is highlighted, press Enter to select the option.
	Esc	Press Escape to exit a menu without making a selection.
Managing the desktop	Print Screen	Copy the desktop into the Clipboard.
	Ctrl + Esc	Display the Start menu and move the focus to the menu. (Use the arrow keys to move over the menu.)
	Alt + M	After the focus is on the Start menu, minimizes all windows and moves the focus to the desktop

A+ OS 1.1

Table 4-7 Keystrokes to help make it easier to work with Windows (continued)

General Action	Keystrokes	Description
Working with windows	Ctrl + Tab and Ctrl + Shift + Tab	Move through tabbed pages in a dialog box.
	Shift + Close (X) button on a window	Close current folder and its parent folders.
	F5	Refresh the contents of a window.
Using the Windows key (Key is labeled with the Windows flag icon)	Win	Display the Start menu.
	Win + E	Start Windows Explorer.
	Win + M	Minimize all windows.
	Win + Tab	Move through items on task bar.
	Win + R	Display the Run dialog box.
	Win + Break	Display the System Properties window.
Using the Applications key (key is labeled with a box and arrow icon)	Application key	When an item is selected, display its shortcut menu.

Managing the Windows 9x Desktop

A+ OS 1.1

From the Windows 9x desktop you can make applications automatically load at startup, create shortcuts to files and applications, and make the environment more user-friendly. In this section, you will learn some ways to manage the Windows 9x desktop.

To control display settings, right-click anywhere on the desktop and select Properties from the shortcut menu. The Display Properties window appears as shown in Figure 4-9. Some of the more common things you can do from each tab on the window are:

- *Background*. Select desktop wallpaper or pattern.
- *Screensaver*. Select screensaver and change its settings; change power settings for monitor.
- *Appearance*. Pick and customize a color scheme for the desktop.
- *Effects*. Specify icon settings.
- *Web*. Set Active Desktop properties.
- *Settings*. Change color range and display size.

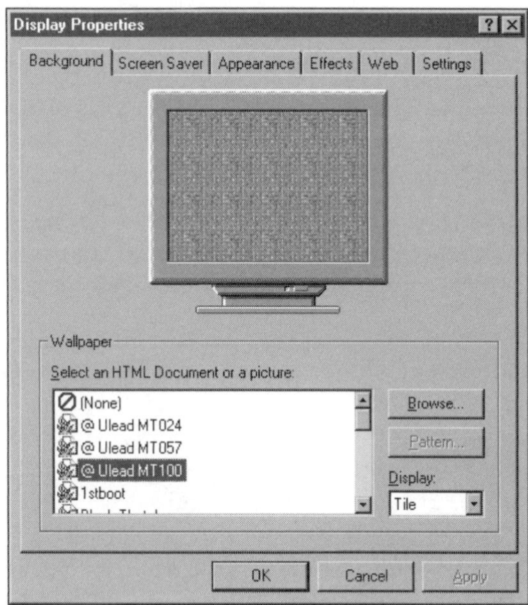

Figure 4-9 The Display Properties window lets you change settings for your desktop

A+ OS 1.1

You can also hide and unhide the taskbar at the bottom of the desktop. To do that, click Start, Settings, Taskbar and Start Menu. The Taskbar Properties window appears. (You can also reach this window by right-clicking on the Taskbar and selecting Properties from the shortcut menu.) Then click the Taskbar Options tab and select Auto hide (see Figure 4-10).

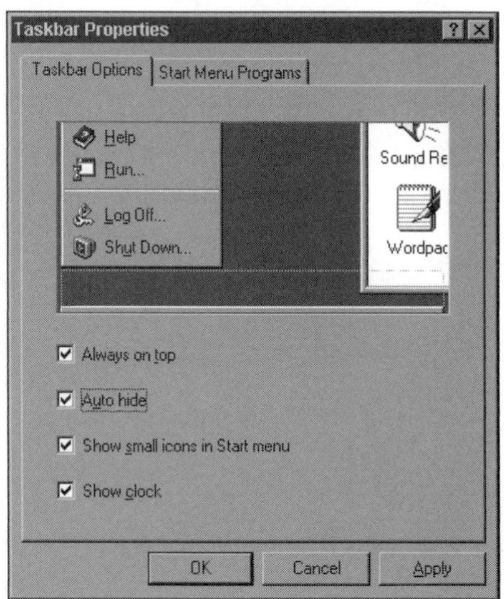

Figure 4-10 Use the Taskbar Properties window to change taskbar settings

A+ OS 1.1

Working with Shortcuts

A **shortcut** on the desktop is an icon that points to a program that can be executed or to a file or folder. The user double-clicks the icon to load the software. A shortcut can be created in several ways. One way is through the Start Menu Programs tab on the Taskbar Properties window you saw in Figure 4-10.

From here, click the Add button. The Create Shortcut Wizard appears, as shown in Figure 4-11. Enter the name of the program you want to create a shortcut to, or browse for the file on your computer. In this example, we will be creating a desktop shortcut to the Notepad application.

Once you have entered or selected the name of the program for which you want to create a shortcut, click Next. You will then be given the option to select where to place the shortcut. Select Desktop at the top of the folder list to create a desktop shortcut, and then click Next. Follow the directions in the wizard to complete the process. Remember that you can create a shortcut for a program or a data file, name it, and select where to place it (either on the desktop or in the Start menu). If you want a program to load whenever Windows 9x starts, create a shortcut and put the shortcut in the StartUp folder of the Start menu. All items in the StartUp folder are automatically executed when Windows 9x starts.

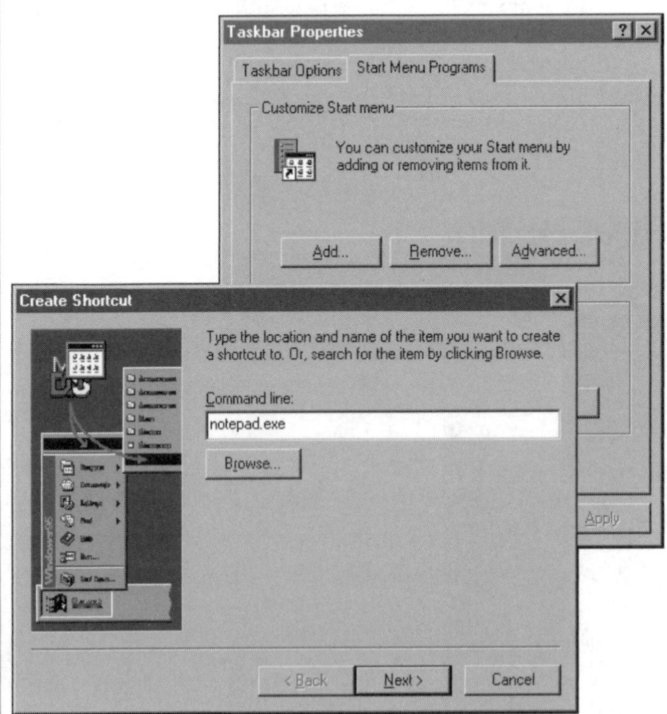

Figure 4-11 Select the item you want to point the shortcut to

A+ OS 1.1

To edit a shortcut, right-click the shortcut and select *Properties* from the menu. To delete a shortcut, select *Delete* from this same menu.

Managing Icons

An icon on the desktop can be a shortcut to an application or it can represent a file that belongs to an application. The telltale sign of the difference is the small bent-arrow shortcut symbol on the icon, as seen in Figure 4-12. The icon on the right represents the document file MyLetter1.doc, stored in the \Windows\Desktop folder, and the icon on the left is a shortcut to the file MyLetter2.doc, which can be stored anywhere on the drive. Also shown in Figure 4-12 are the contents of the \Windows\Desktop folder as seen by Explorer. You can add an icon to the desktop by putting a file in this folder. One way to delete an icon on the desktop is to delete the corresponding file in this folder; however, as you will see, this method can cause problems for the user.

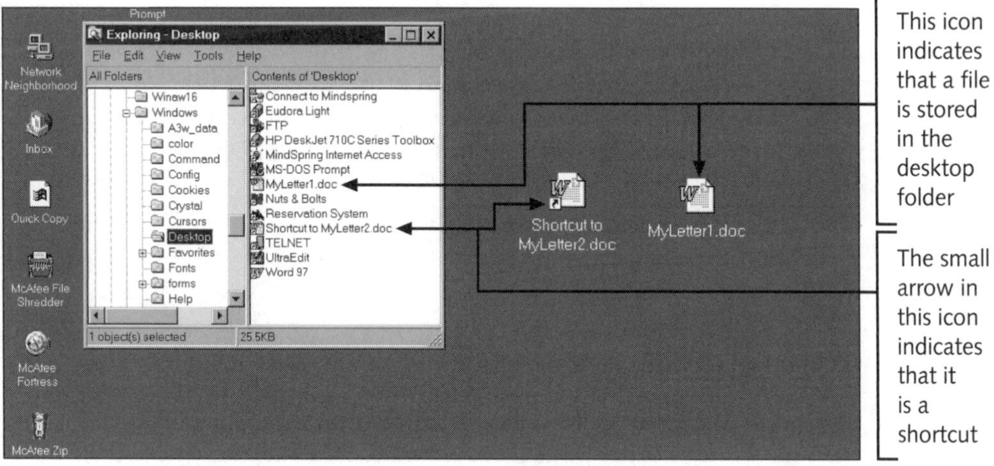

Figure 4-12 One icon is a shortcut, and the other icon represents a file stored in the Desktop folder

If you delete a shortcut icon from the desktop or the \Windows\Desktop folder, such as Shortcut to MyLetter2.doc, the shortcut is gone, but the actual file that the shortcut points to is not deleted. If you delete a document icon, such as MyLetter1.doc, the document itself will be deleted.

An error can occur if the actual document file, MyLetter2.doc, is deleted, but the shortcut to the deleted document remains on the desktop. Figure 4-13 shows a sample error message that occurs when this shortcut is used.

A+ OS 1.1

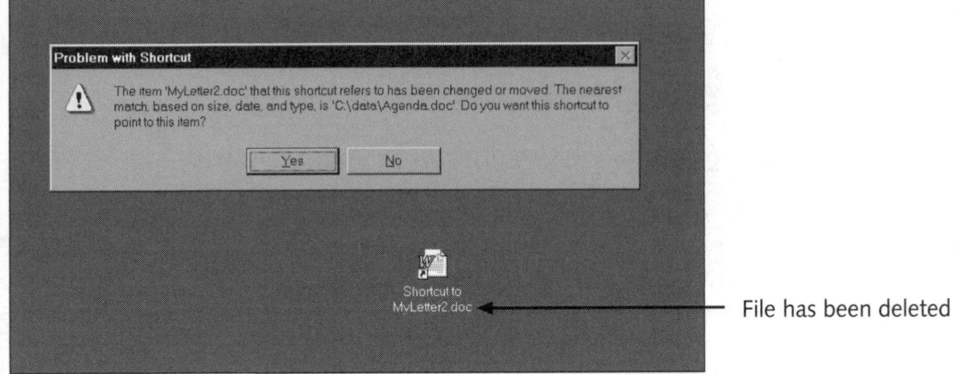

Figure 4-13 The file that the shortcut points to has been deleted, which causes an error when the shortcut is used

Using Windows Explorer to Manage Floppy Disks and Hard Drives

A+ OS 1.1 1.5

In the last chapter you learned how to use the command prompt of Windows 9x to manage a floppy drive and a hard drive. In this section, you will learn how to use Windows Explorer to manage floppy disks and hard drives in Windows 9x. Windows 9x Explorer is the primary tool for managing the files and folders on your hard drive and disks. Open Explorer in Windows 9x (click Start, Programs, Windows Explorer, or right-click My Computer and select Explore from the menu) and follow the directions below to manage files and folders. Figure 4-14 shows computer resources in the My Computer folder as seen when using Windows Explorer. (You can also access My Computer by double-clicking on the icon on the desktop.)

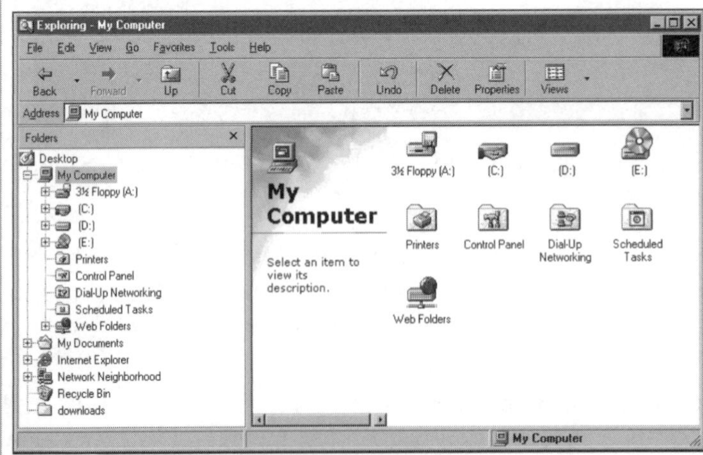

Figure 4-14 The My Computer view in Windows Explorer

A+ OS 1.1 1.5

Shortcut Menu Options

The easiest way to manage drives, disks, folders, and files in Windows Explorer is to use the shortcut menus. To access the shortcut menu, right-click the icon representing the item you want to work with. The shortcut menu for the floppy drive is shown in Figure 4-15 as an example.

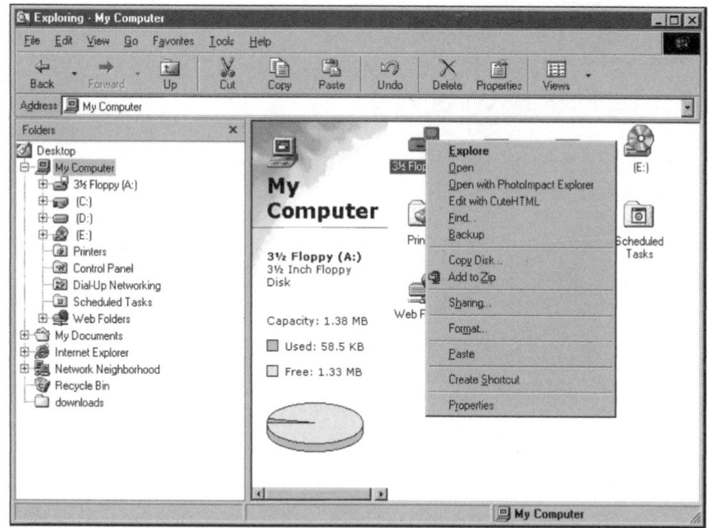

Figure 4-15 Use the shortcut menu to manage items in Explorer

Some of the tasks you can perform from a shortcut menu are listed below.

- If you select Explore, the contents of the selected disk or folder in the floppy drive will be shown in the current Explorer window. If you select Open, the contents of the disk or folder will be shown in a separate window.
- The Create Shortcut option will create a shortcut icon for the selected item. (You learned about creating shortcuts earlier in this chapter.)
- Selecting the Properties option brings up a dialog box showing information about the selected item and allows you to change settings for the item. You first learned about viewing Properties in Chapter 3.
- If you have selected a disk or drive, the shortcut menu will contain a Format option. Recall that you can use Explorer to format a floppy disk, as you learned in the previous chapter, by selecting Format from the shortcut menu.
- The Backup option enables you to make a backup of a disk, and the Sharing option enables you to share a drive, folders, or files with other users on your network. Backup and Sharing are covered in later chapters.
- For floppy drives, if you select Copy Disk, a dialog box opens as shown in Figure 4-16, where the disk listed under "Copy from" is the source disk, and the disk listed under "Copy to" is the target disk. Click Start to copy the disk.
- The shortcut menu of a folder allows you to create a new file. The menu lists applications you can use to create the file.

A+ OS 1.1 1.4 1.5

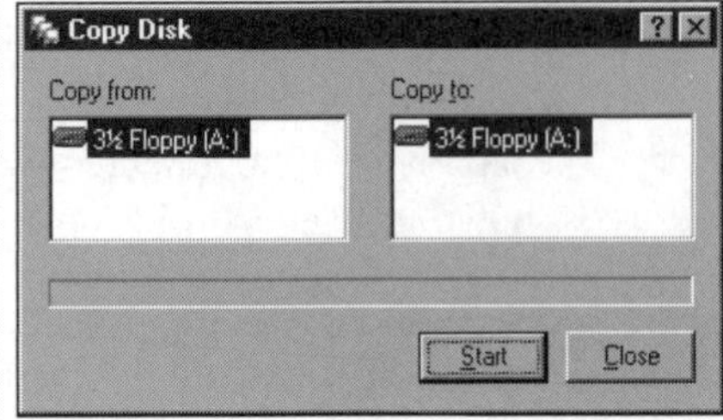

Figure 4-16 Copying a disk using Windows 9x

- The shortcut menu for files gives you additional options such as printing and e-mailing the file.

As you can see, some of the options on shortcut menus are the same for files, folders, drives, and disks, and others are specific to the particular item you are looking at. The additional shortcut menu options may be different, depending on what programs you have installed to work with a particular item.

Now let's look in more detail at ways to use Windows 9x Explorer to work with files and folders on your hard drive.

Create a New Folder

To create a folder (equivalent to using the MD command from the command line, which you learned in the last chapter), do the following. Select the folder you want to be the parent folder by clicking the folder name. For example, to create a folder named Chess under the folder named Games, first click the Games folder. Then click the File menu. Select New from the menu. Then select Folder from the submenu that is displayed. The new folder will be created under Games, but its name will be New Folder. Click the folder name once to open the text box and highlight the current folder name, New Folder. Type Chess to change the folder name to Chess, as in Figure 4-17. The maximum depth of folders under folders depends on the length of the folder names.

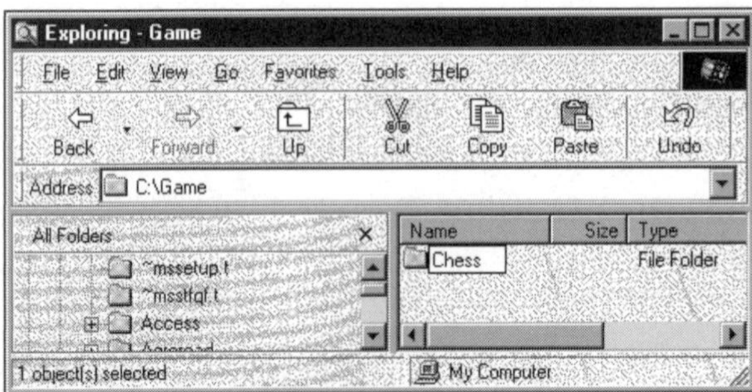

Figure 4-17 Edit the new folder's name

Delete a Folder

To delete a folder (similiar to using the RD command from the command line) from Explorer, right-click the folder and select Delete from the shortcut menu. A confirmation

A+ OS 1.1 1.4 1.5

dialog box asks you if you are sure you want to delete the folder. If you click Yes, the folder and all of its contents, including subfolders, will be sent to the Recycle Bin. Empty the Recycle Bin to free your disk space. Files and folders sent to the Recycle Bin are not deleted until you empty it.

File Attributes

Using Explorer, you can view and change the file attributes (similar to using the command-line Attrib command). From Explorer, right-click a file and select Properties from the shortcut menu. The Properties window appears, as shown in Figure 4-18. From the Properties window, you can change the read-only, hidden, and archive attributes of the file.

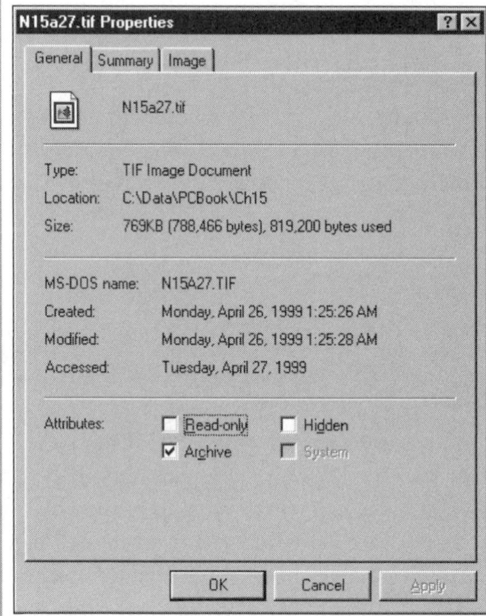

Figure 4-18 Properties of a file in Windows 98

Folder Properties

You can also view and change the properties assigned to folders. Select the folder and from the Explorer menu, click View, Folder Options, and then click the View tab. From this window you can change how and when files are displayed in the folder.

Windows 98 identifies file type primarily by the file extension. In Windows Explorer, by default, Windows 9x hides the file extensions of those files for which it knows which application to use to open or execute the file. For example, just after installation, it hides .exe, .com, .sys, and .txt file extensions but will not hide .doc, .ppt, or .xls files until the software to open these files has been installed. To display all file extensions, in the Folder Options windows, uncheck Hide file extensions for known file types.

INSTALLING HARDWARE WITH WINDOWS 9X

A+ OS 1.1 2.4

In this section, you will learn how to add new hardware to Windows 9x systems and install 16-bit and 32-bit device drivers, using a CD-ROM drive as an example. You will also learn about Plug and Play support in Windows 9x.

Adding New Hardware

A+ OS 1.1 2.4

After a device is physically installed in a system, the next step is to install the software necessary to interface with it. This software, called a device driver, is written to interface with the specific device and the specific operating system. Knowing how to install and troubleshoot device drivers is an essential skill of a PC support technician.

Installing and Using Device Drivers Under Windows 9x

For Windows 9x or Windows 2000/XP, when a new device is installed and you power up the PC, Windows recognizes it and immediately launches the Add New Hardware Wizard. If the wizard does not automatically launch, you can manually start it. Go to Control Panel and double-click the Add New Hardware icon, which launches the wizard.

The Control Panel contains several applets, or small programs, that are used to manage Windows. You can view these applets in a list or as icons. Use the View menu in Control Panel to change the way they are displayed.

One step in the wizard is to select the hardware device from a list of devices. If you click OK, Windows will use a Windows driver for the device, or you can click Have Disk to use your own drivers (see Figure 4-19). If you have a driver on a floppy disk or CD or have downloaded a driver from the Internet to a folder on your hard drive, click Have Disk and point the wizard to the disk, CD, or folder on the hard drive that contains the driver. Sometimes you must select a folder on the disk or CD for the operating system to use such as \Win98 to locate the drivers to install under Windows 98 (or \Win2k for Windows 2000, which you will learn more about in later chapters).

A+ OS 1.1 2.4

4

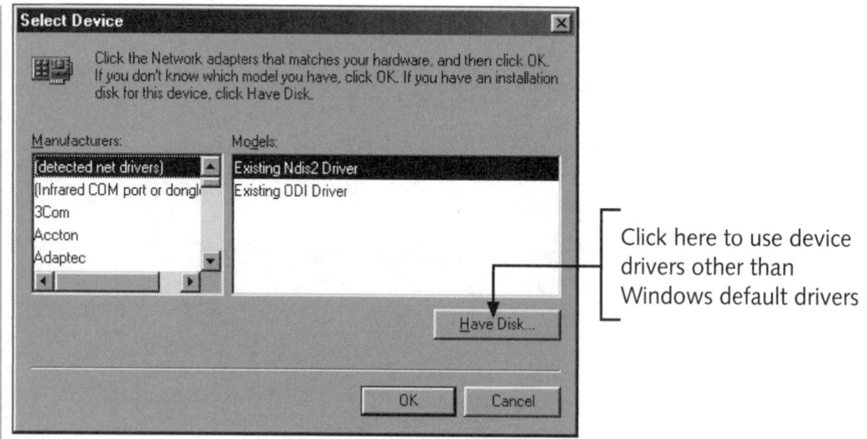

Figure 4-19 To use device drivers supplied by the device manufacturer, click Have Disk

Viewing and Changing Current Device Drivers

You can view and change current device drivers from the Control Panel. For example, in Windows 98, to view the current video driver, click Start, Settings, Control Panel, and then double-click Display. Click the Settings tab to view the currently installed display driver, as shown in Figure 4-20.

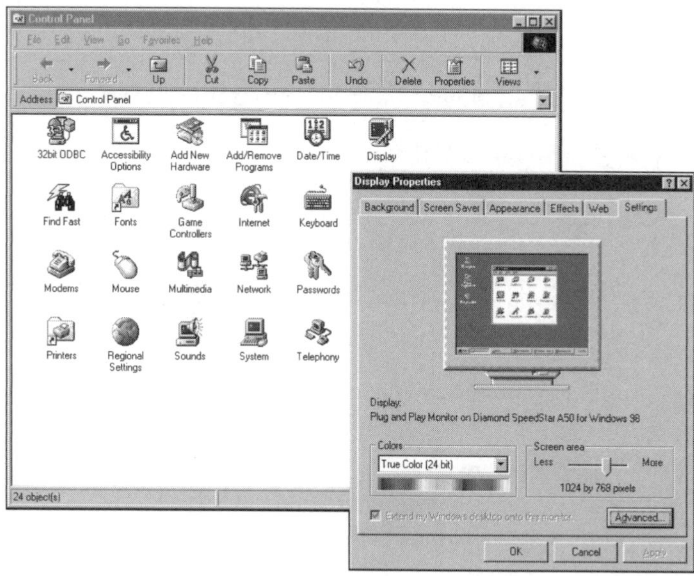

Figure 4-20 Use the Settings tab of Display Properties to view the currently installed display driver

To change the video card driver, click Advanced, click the Adapter tab, and then click the Change button. You see the Windows 98 Update Device Driver Wizard. Click Next to see the dialog box in Figure 4-21, which includes options to let Windows 98 search for a new driver from its list of Windows drivers or to display a list of all the drivers in a specific

A+ OS 1.1 2.4

location, so you can select the driver you want. To provide your own driver, click the second option and then click Next. Then, click Have Disk to provide the new driver from a floppy disk, a CD, or a file downloaded from the Internet.

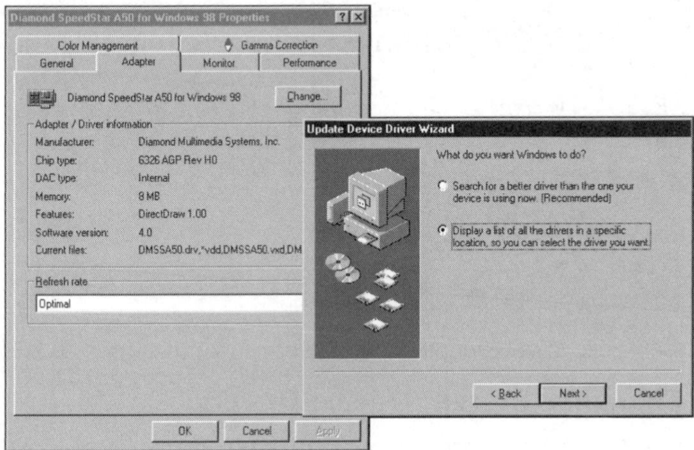

Figure 4-21 The Windows 98 Update Device Driver Wizard enables you to install a new device driver for a previously installed device

If the new driver fails, try uninstalling the device and then reinstalling it. To uninstall a device, access Device Manager (click Start, Settings, Control Panel, double-click System, then click Device Manager), select the device and then click Remove (see Figure 4-22). Then reboot the PC and allow the Found New Hardware Wizard to launch.

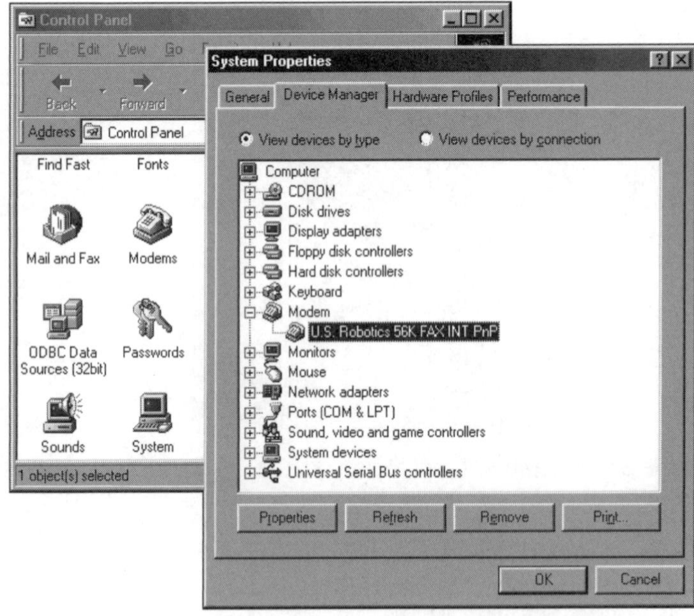

Figure 4-22 Use Device Manager to uninstall a device

A+ OS 2.4

Installing a CD-ROM Drive with Windows 9x

Now that you have an overview of the process of adding new hardware and device drivers in Windows 9x, let's look at installing a CD-ROM drive as an example and consider how and when you would use 16-bit and 32-bit drivers.

To use the 32-bit Windows driver for your CD-ROM drive, click Start, Settings, Control Panel, and then double-click Add New Hardware. Click Next when you are prompted to begin installing the software for the new device. Complete the installation by following the directions on the Add New Hardware window.

When Windows 9x starts up after you've installed the CD-ROM drive, it assigns the next available drive letter to the drive. To dictate what the drive letter should be, use Device Manager. Click Start, Settings, Control Panel, and then double-click System. Click the Device Manager tab. Select the CD-ROM drive and click Properties, then click the Settings tab (see Figure 4-23), where the drive is designated E:. Select a range of letters to be used by the drive and click OK.

When you update or install additional features on application software, some software expects the same drive letter for the CD-ROM drive that was used when it was first installed. Permanently setting the CD-ROM drive letter satisfies the requirements of this software.

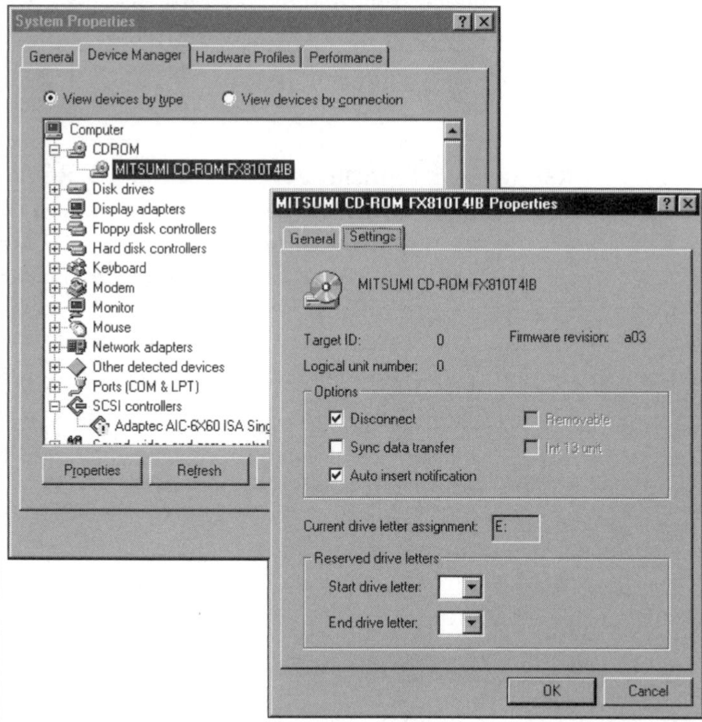

Figure 4-23 You can specify the drive letter to be assigned to the CD-ROM drive from the Properties box for the drive

A+ OS 2.4 Windows 9x supports a wide variety of CD-ROM drives, so most manufacturers assume that Windows will provide 32-bit drivers, and ship the accompanying floppy disk only with 16-bit drivers. You would use these drivers in a situation where your hard drive has failed and you are booting from the rescue disk. Windows 98 automatically puts its own 16-bit drivers on that rescue disk; later in this section, you will learn how to add them to a Windows 95 startup disk that does not include support for CD-ROM drives. These 16-bit drivers supplied by Windows 9x may not work with your CD-ROM drive. If they do not, you would use the 16-bit drivers provided by the manufacturer.

Testing the Drive

The drive is now ready to use. Press the eject button to open the drive shelf, and place a CD in the drive. Since data on CDs is written only on the bottom, be careful to protect it. Damage to either side of the disk can make it unreadable, but the bottom of the disk is the more sensitive side. Now access the CD using Explorer (use the assigned drive letter). If you have a problem reading the CD, verify that the CD is placed in the tray label-side-up and that the format is compatible with your drive. If one CD doesn't work, try another; the first CD may be defective or scratched.

A CD-ROM drive can be set so that when you insert a CD, software on the CD automatically executes through, a feature called Autorun or Autoplay. To turn the feature on, from Device Manager, right-click on the CD-ROM drive and select Properties. From the Properties window, select the Settings tab and then select Auto insert notification. To prevent a CD from automatically playing when the feature is enabled, hold down the Shift key when inserting the CD.

A+ OS 2.4 3.2 **Update Your Windows 95 Rescue Disk to Include Access to the CD-ROM Drive** In Chapter 3 you created a Windows emergency startup disk to start a system in the event of a hard drive failure. This rescue disk needs to include tools to access the CD-ROM drive, because Windows 9x is normally loaded from a CD-ROM. When you are recovering from a failed hard drive, you will not have access to the 32-bit Windows drivers on the hard drive. Windows 98 automatically adds the real-mode CD-ROM device drivers to the rescue disk, but Windows 95 does not. This section explains how to add this functionality to a Windows 95 rescue disk.

The CD-ROM drive you learned how to install in Chapter 2 came with a disk that includes the following files:

- *Install.exe.* The CD-ROM installation program
- *Cdtech.sys.* CD-ROM device driver
- Instruction files and documentation

Two files are required to access a CD-ROM drive while in real mode: the 16-bit device driver provided by the manufacturer of the CD-ROM drive (or a generic real-mode driver that works with the drive), which in this case is Cdtech.sys, and the 16-bit real-mode OS interface to the driver, Mscdex.exe. The device driver is loaded from Config.sys, and Mscdex.exe is loaded from Autoexec.bat.

A+ OS 2.4 3.2 If you have run the installation program that came with the CD-ROM drive (Install.exe), then your Autoexec.bat and Config.sys files on your hard drive should already have the correct entries in them. You can add these lines to these same files on your rescue disk, correcting paths to the two files as needed. Copy the two files to your rescue disk so you can access the CD-ROM drive when you boot from this disk, even when the hard drive is not accessible. For example, on a rescue or boot disk designed to access the CD-ROM drive without depending on any files or commands on the hard drive, the Config.sys file might contain this command (the parameters in the command lines are explained below):

```
DEVICE = A:\CDTECH.SYS /D:MSCD001
```

The Autoexec.bat file might contain this command line:

```
MSCDEX.EXE /D:MSCD001 /L:E /M:10
```

The explanations of these command lines are as follows:

- Two files needed to manage the drive are Mscdex.exe and Cdtech.sys, which must be copied to this disk into the root directory.
- When the program Mscdex.exe executes, it uses the MSCD001 entry as a tag back to the Config.sys file to learn which device driver is being used to interface with the drive, which in this case is Cdtech.sys.
- To Mscdex.exe, the drive is named MSCD001 and is being managed by the driver Cdtech.sys.
- Mscdex.exe will use Cdtech.sys as its "go-between" to access the drive.
- Mscdex.exe also assigns a drive letter to the drive. If you want to specify a certain drive letter, use the /L: option in the command line. In our example, the CD-ROM drive will be drive E. If you don't use the /L: option, then the next available drive letter is used.
- The /M: option controls the number of memory buffers.
- If the files referenced in these two commands are stored on the floppy disk in a different directory from the root directory, then include the path to the file in front of the filename.

If your hard drive fails and you start up from your rescue disk, once the CD-ROM drivers are loaded and the CD-ROM drive is recognized, you can copy files needed to troubleshoot the system from the Windows 9x CD, which will be in drive E. If you decide to reinstall Windows, you can type E:\Setup at the command prompt.

If you have installed 16-bit device drivers from your Config.sys and Autoexec.bat files, when Windows 9x is installed, it will often ignore existing Config.sys and Autoexec.bat lines. It turns these lines into comment lines by adding REM to the beginning of the line and handles the CD-ROM drive through its own protected-mode drivers.

A+ OS 2.4

Optimizing CD-ROM Cache

Recall from Chapter 3 that a cache is a location in memory or the hard drive used to store frequently used data. For CD-ROM drives, a memory cache contains data that was recently read from the CD. Recall that Mscdex.exe is the 16-bit OS utility that manages a CD-ROM drive. The 32-bit CD-ROM utility is CDFS (CD file system), which is automatically loaded by Windows 9x if it detects a CD-ROM drive. CDFS has a caching function similar to hard drive caching done by Vcache. It uses a memory cache to speed up reading from a CD. CDFS decides how much memory to use when caching data, based on the speed of the CD-ROM drive and how much memory is installed in the system. You can affect this decision by using the Performance tab in System Properties. Click Start, Settings, Control Panel, and then double-click System. In the Properties dialog box, click the Performance tab and then click File System. Click CD-ROM on the File System Properties box, as seen in Figure 4-24. By changing the CD-ROM speed in this box, you are changing the amount of memory allotted to the cache. The amount is displayed in the last sentence on this box.

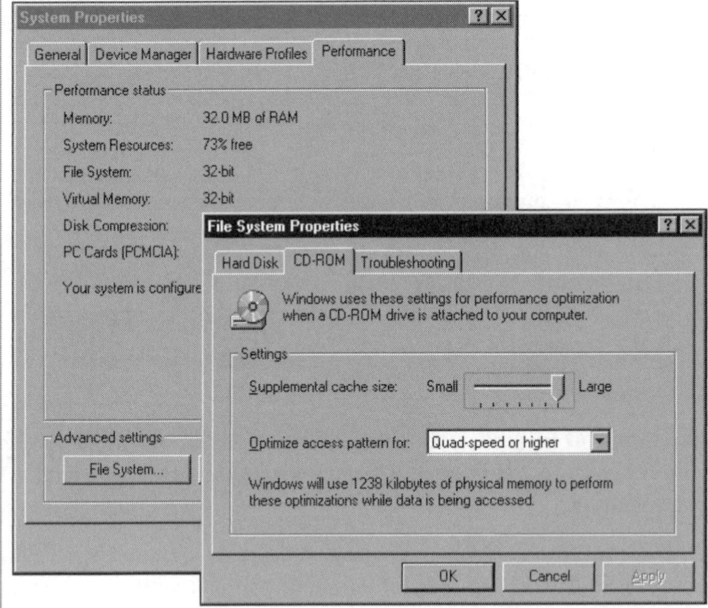

Figure 4-24 By changing the CD-ROM speed in the File System Properties box, you can change the amount of memory VCACHE uses

Plug and Play and Hardware Installations

A+ OS 2.4

Plug and Play (PnP) is a set of design specifications for both hardware and software that works toward effortless hardware installations. For a system to be truly Plug and Play, it must meet these criteria:

- The system BIOS must be PnP.

A+ OS 2.4 3.2

- All hardware devices and expansion cards must be PnP-compliant.
- The OS must be Windows 9x or another OS that supports PnP.
- A 32-bit device driver (VxD) must be available (provided by the device manufacturer or Windows). VxDs are covered later in the chapter.

If all these things are true, hardware installation should be just a matter of installing the new hardware device, turning on the PC, and perhaps providing the 32-bit driver, if it is not included with Windows 9x. During the boot process, Windows 9x surveys the devices and their needs for resources and allocates resources to each device. Windows 9x is free to assign these resources to the devices and avoids assigning the same resource to two devices. For PnP to work, each device in the system must be able to use whatever resources the OS assigns to it.

Components of Plug and Play

A Plug and Play OS such as Windows 9x provides two main services: resource management and run-time configuration. **Resource management** occurs at startup as system resources are allocated to devices. **Run-time configuration** is an ongoing process that monitors any changes in system devices, such as the removal of a PC Card on a notebook computer or docking and undocking a notebook computer to and from a docking station. The BIOS must be able to recognize these changes during OS run time (any time the OS is running) and communicate them to the OS.

Windows 9x uses four components in implementing PnP architecture:

- The Configuration Manager controls the configuration process of all devices and communicates these configurations to the devices.
- The **hardware tree** is a database built each time Windows 9x starts up that contains a list of installed components and the resources they use.
- The **bus enumerator** locates all devices on a particular bus and inventories the resource requirements for these devices.
- The **resource arbitrator** decides which resources are assigned to which devices.

Plug and Play BIOS

As discussed in Chapter 3, BIOS that is PnP-compliant gathers resource configuration information prior to loading Windows 9x, presenting to Windows 9x details it can use to complete the process. Motherboards manufactured after 1994 most likely contain PnP BIOS. PnP BIOS can also be ESCD (extended system configuration data) BIOS. ESCD BIOS creates a list of configuration changes that you have made manually when installing legacy devices and stores that list on the BIOS chip. Even if the hard drive crashes or you must reload Windows 9x, the configuration changes are still available from the BIOS when it goes through the boot process, and it presents the information to Windows 9x at startup.

To discover if your BIOS is PnP, look for a message about the BIOS type on the startup screen. Information about the BIOS might also be displayed on the CMOS setup screen or written on the BIOS chip (see Figure 4-25). You can also use MSD, a 16-bit command-line

A+ OS 2.4 3.2 diagnostic utility, and choose Computer from the menu to get information about your BIOS. The documentation for the motherboard should also say whether the BIOS is PnP.

If the BIOS is not Plug and Play, you can still use Plug and Play Windows 9x software for hardware devices that are Plug and Play. However, you might need to manually configure the hardware, or, in some cases, disable the Plug and Play features of the interface card.

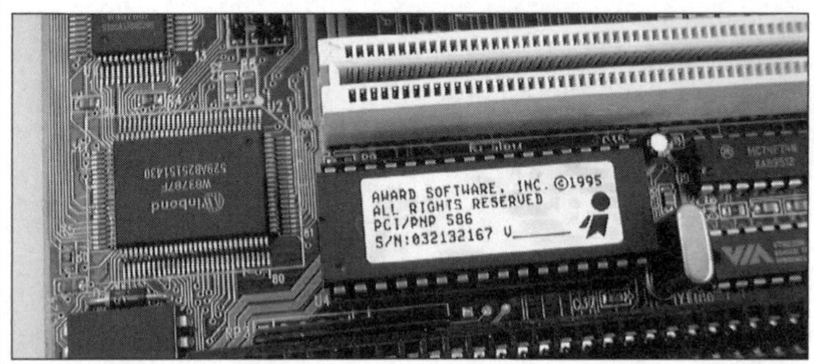

Figure 4-25 Plug and Play BIOS is found on most motherboards built after 1994

INSTALLING APPLICATIONS IN WINDOWS 9X

A+ OS 2.4 As the bridge between earlier and later versions of Windows, Windows 9x can use both 16-bit and 32-bit software. This section shows you how to install both. Troubleshooting and uninstalling Windows 9x applications are covered in the next chapter.

Preparing for Software Installation

A+ OS 2.4 As with installing hardware, there are several things you can do before installing software on Windows 9x to prepare your system and to increase the likelihood that the installation will be successful:

- *Check available resources.* Check your computer resources to make sure you have (1) enough space on your hard drive, (2) the minimum requirements for memory, and (3) the proper CPU and video monitor. Read the documentation for the software you are installing and make sure you can fulfill any other requirements of the particular software program. The minimum requirements for the software should be listed in the installation manual. Remember that you should not completely fill your hard drive with software and data, because the operating system needs extra space for temporary files and for the swap file, which changes in size depending on how much space is needed. Additionally, recall what you learned about fragmented files in Chapter 3. If your hard drive is too full and you add a new file, the file cannot be written all in one place and will be split up into pieces (fragmented) and stored wherever there is available space on the hard drive. The system will then have to look in several different places on the hard drive to find the whole file, slowing down performance. You will learn more about these performance issues in Windows 9x in the next chapter.

A+ OS 2.4

For best performance with Windows 9x, allow a minimum of 100 MB of unused hard drive space for working temporary files used by applications.

- *Protect the original software.* For floppy disks, write-protect the original disks before you begin the installation (set the notch on the disk to open). After the installation is complete, put the original disks or CD-ROM from which you installed the software in a safe place. If you have the original software handy, it will be easier for you to reinstall should something go wrong with the installed software.
- *Back up the registry and system configuration files.* Many older software packages will want to edit Config.sys, Autoexec.bat, Win.ini, and/or System.ini files during the installation. Newer software might add its own entries to the Windows registry. Before you begin the installation, make backup copies of all of these files so that you can backtrack if you want to. (You will learn more about backing up the registry in the next chapter.)

4

Performing Software Installations

A+ OS 2.4

To install software designed for Windows 9x, access the Control Panel and double-click the Add/Remove Programs icon. Insert the software CD in the CD-ROM drive or the floppy disk in the floppy disk drive and then click the Install button. Follow directions on the setup screen. If the CD-ROM drive is set to Autorun, a setup screen might automatically appear as soon as you insert the software installation CD in the drive. For older software, click Start and Run, which displays the Run dialog box. Enter the drive and name of the installation program, for example, *A:Install* or *D:Setup*. Either way, the installation program loads and begins executing. If the installation program asks you a question you cannot answer, you can always abandon the installation and try again later.

Most software will ask you for a serial number unique to your copy of the software, which will probably be written on the CD-ROM or on the first floppy disk, or it might be stamped on the documentation. Write the serial number on the floppy disk or on the CD case, so that you will have it if you lose the documentation later. Copyright agreements often allow you to install the software on only one computer at a time. This serial number identifies the copy of the software that you have installed on this machine.

After the installation is complete and the software is working, update your backup copies of Autoexec.bat, Config.sys, System.ini, Win.ini, and the registry so that they, too, reflect the changes that the application software made to these configuration files.

Troubleshooting Software Installations

If you are having difficulty with the installation of software in Windows 9x, try the following:

- If an application locks up when you first open it, try deleting all files and folders under \Windows\Temp. A software installation sometimes leaves files and folders in the Windows temporary directories. To conserve space on the hard drive, delete all files and folders under \Windows\Temp.

- Look at the Readme.htm hypertext file in the \Windows directory, which will point you to the Programs.txt file, also in the \Windows directory. If there is a problem with the software that was known when Windows was shipped, information about the problem and what to do about it might be in these text files. You can also check the Web site of the software manufacturer or the Microsoft Web site for additional insight.

A **hypertext** file is a text file that contains hypertext tags to format the file and create hyperlinks to different points in the file or to other files. Hypertext files are used on the World Wide Web and are read and displayed using a Web browser such as Microsoft Internet Explorer or Netscape Navigator. To read a hypertext file using Windows Explorer, double-click the filename, and your default browser will open the file.

Supporting DOS Applications Under Windows 9x

A+ OS 1.1 2.4

Windows 3.x used **PIF (program information file)** files to manage the virtual machine environment for DOS applications and provided a PIF editor to alter these files. Each application had its own PIF file that was used to specify the DOS environment that Windows 3.x created for it. If an application had no PIF file, Windows 3.x used the settings in the _Default.pif file in the \Windows\System folder.

Windows 9x manages the environment for DOS applications in a similar, but slightly different, fashion. The Apps.inf file contains a section named [PIF95] that contains a master list of settings to be used for all DOS applications listed in the file.

If you want to customize the settings for a DOS application, use the Properties feature of the DOS program file, which will create an individual PIF for the program file and serves as the PIF editor. Right-click the program filename and select Properties from the menu that is displayed. Windows searches for the program's PIF file and, if none is found, creates one using default values. If Windows 9x was installed over Windows 3.x, then _Default.pif still exists in the \Windows\System directory and default values are read from it. Regardless of where the default values come from, any changes made are stored in the PIF for the application. To make the changes, using Explorer, right-click the program filename and select Properties from the shortcut menu. Click the Program tab. (*Note*: the Program tab will not be present for Windows applications.) See Figure 4-26.

If you select Use current MS-DOS configuration, Windows executes the contents of Dosstart.bat, stored in the Windows folder. **Dosstart.bat** is a type of Autoexec.bat file that is executed in two situations: when you select Restart the computer in MS-DOS mode from the shutdown menu, or when you run a program in MS-DOS mode. This file can be used to load real-mode device drivers, but Set commands are not executed.

If you select Specify a new MS-DOS configuration, you can make changes to Autoexec.bat and Config.sys files used for this MS-DOS mode only. For example, if the application runs slowly in DOS mode and does a lot of disk accessing, you can add entries

A+ OS 1.1 2.4

to run real-mode SmartDrive here. SmartDrive normally is not run under Windows 9x, having been replaced by the faster 32-bit Vcache. In this situation, since Windows 9x does not manage disk access in MS-DOS mode, loading SmartDrive from this window is appropriate, since Vcache will not be running.

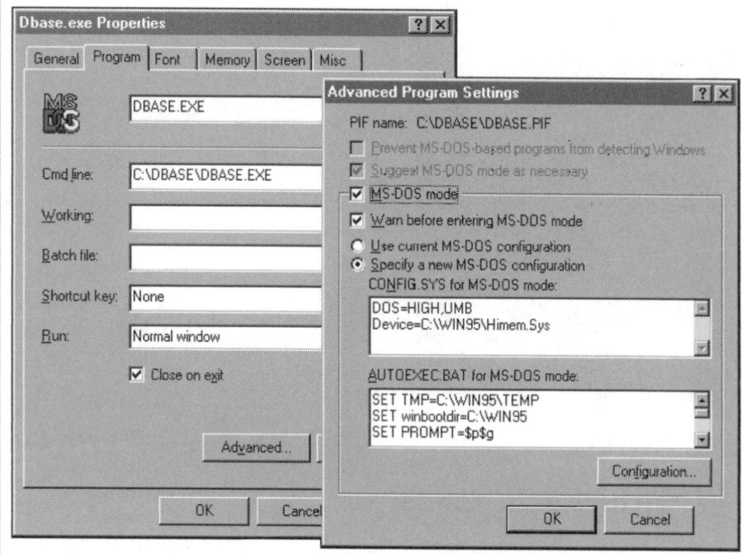

Figure 4-26 Properties sheets for a DOS application affect the way Windows 9x provides an environment for the application

Memory Management with DOS Applications in Windows 9x

When running DOS applications under Windows 9x, a DOS-like environment must be provided to the application. For example, to provide a DOS environment for the DOS program Edit.com on a PC running Windows 9x, go to Explorer and find the file Edit.com in the \Windows\Command directory. Right-click on the filename and select Properties from the drop-down menu that appears. The entries on this Properties Window make up the PIF for this application, which describes the environment that the DOS program uses.

Click the Memory tab, and the screen shown in Figure 4-27 appears, listing the memory options available. From the Memory tab, you can specify how much conventional and extended memory will be made available to the application, or leave the settings at Auto, which allows the application to use whatever is available. The last entry on the tab is MS-DOS protected-mode (DPMI) memory. This entry assigns the amount of protected-mode memory allowed the application. If you check Protected in the Conventional memory frame, the OS will protect memory used by the OS from the application.

Many DOS applications run with no problems using the default Auto settings. However, sometimes a DOS application has a problem with being given too much memory. Limit the amount of memory given the application by using the Properties sheet shown in Figure 4-27.

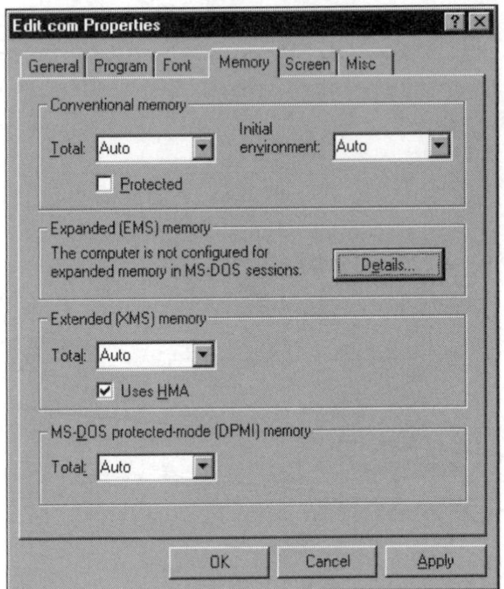

Figure 4-27 Setting up memory for a DOS application running under Windows 9x

A+ OS 1.1

Real Mode vs. Virtual Real Mode

An OS that supports protected mode can allow a 16-bit program that is written to work in real mode to run in virtual real mode (sometimes referred to as virtual DOS mode). Figure 4-28 shows the difference between real mode and virtual real mode. In virtual real mode, the program "thinks" it is really working in a real-mode environment. It "thinks" that:

- It is the only program running.
- It has all memory available to it, all 1024K of memory addresses that directly point to RAM.
- It accesses data using a 16-bit data path.

Underneath this environment, the OS is managing memory for the application. It receives the data in a 16-bit path, but is free to use a 32-bit data path to access memory and is also free to use virtual memory for the data.

A+ OS 1.1

4

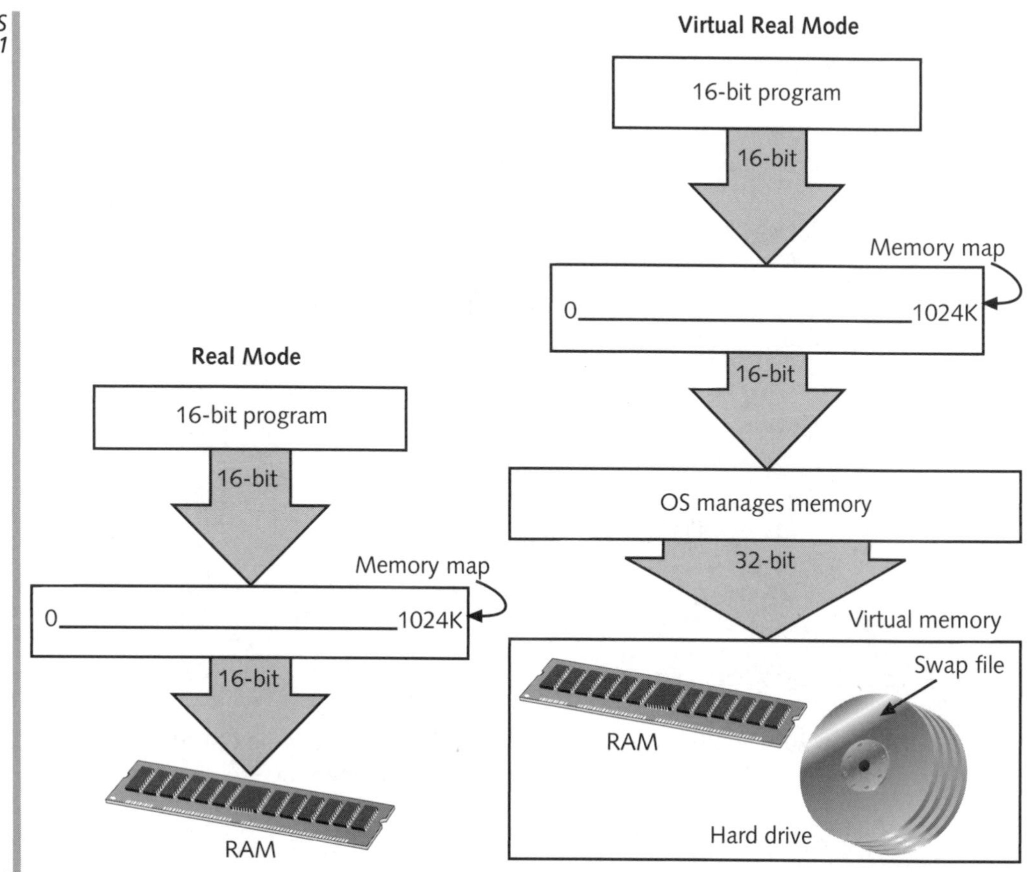

Figure 4-28 Virtual real mode provides "DOS in a box" to a 16-bit application that was written to run in real mode

Recall that there are two types of 16-bit applications: those written for DOS and those written for Windows 3.x. DOS 16-bit applications expect to run in real mode with no other applications running with them. A Windows 3.x 16-bit application expects to allow Windows to manage memory for it and expects that other applications might also be running in a cooperative multitasking environment.

When Windows 9x runs a 16-bit DOS application, ordinarily it is run in virtual DOS mode in a **virtual DOS machine (VDM)**, sometimes called a **DOS box**, rather than in real mode. In a VDM, the application "thinks" it is running in real mode, but the OS is managing hardware resources using 32-bit drivers and providing virtual memory to the application. If you want a DOS application to have a "real" real mode rather than a virtual real mode, access the Properties box for the application. For example, once again using Edit.com as our example of a 16-bit application, right-click the program filename in Explorer (or you can right-click on the shortcut icon to the program) and select Properties. Click the Program tab and click Advanced. The Advanced Program Settings box is displayed as in Figure 4-29. Click MS-DOS mode to run the application in real mode. You can then choose to give the program its own private set of Config.sys and Autoexec.bat settings to be executed before the program runs. This information is stored in the PIF created for the shortcut. When you execute the shortcut or program, Windows 9x will shut down and reboot in real mode before executing the program.

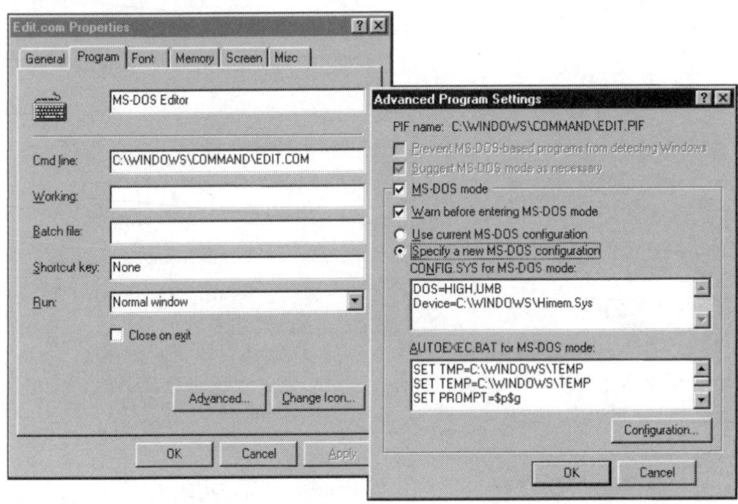

Figure 4-29 Use the Advanced Program Settings dialog box to run a 16-bit application in a real-mode environment in Windows 9x

To access real mode in Windows 9x, select Start and Shutdown. When the Shut Down Windows dialog box appears, select Restart in MS-DOS mode.

MANAGING MEMORY WITH WINDOWS 9X

Memory management did not change fundamentally from DOS to Windows 9x; with Windows 9x memory is still organized as conventional, upper, and extended as it was under DOS. However, Windows 9x has made some improvements in the allocation of this memory and in the automation of the process that make it easier to manage memory. In effect, Windows 9x, which is mostly a 32-bit OS, "lives" in extended memory together with its device drivers and applications and only uses base and upper memory for 16-bit components. This section covers some of the other ways memory is managed in Windows 9x.

Memory Management with Device Drivers in Windows 9x

A+ OS 1.1

One of the major improvements in memory management in Windows 9x is the new level of 32-bit protected mode drivers. These 32-bit drivers are automatically loaded into extended memory (not conventional or upper memory) when Windows 9x loads, thus eliminating the

A+ OS 1.1

need to use the older and slower 16-bit drivers loaded from DEVICE= entries in Config.sys.

Windows 9x offers many 32-bit drivers that can replace older 16-bit drivers written for DOS in real mode. These 32-bit drivers are sometimes called **virtual device drivers** or **VxD drivers**; they have .vxd or .386 file extensions and operate in protected mode.

Another memory management improvement in Windows 9x is that it frees up more of conventional and upper memory, because it no longer uses Smartdrv.exe or Share.exe, two TSRs that required a lot of memory below 1 MB. Smartdrv.exe, a 16-bit driver used to manage disk caching, was replaced by Vcache, 32-bit disk caching that is built into Windows 9x. The 16-bit Share.exe was replaced by the 32-bit Vshare.386, a part of Vmm32.exe that is automatically loaded when Windows 9x starts.

4

If you are using all 32-bit drivers and applications in a Windows 9x environment, memory management requires no work on your part. Just let Windows 9x automate the process for you.

Managing Memory for 16-bit Drivers

If you are using older 16-bit drivers under Windows 9x, search for 32-bit drivers to replace them. Look on the device manufacturer's Web site or the Microsoft Web site. If you can't find replacements, you might need to provide some of the same memory management aids needed by DOS.

In Chapter 3, you learned about Himem.sys and Emm386.exe, the two files that Windows uses to manage memory above 640K. Windows 9x uses Himem.sys to manage extended memory just as DOS does, but, instead of being loaded from Config.sys, it's automatically loaded by Io.sys without requiring an entry in Config.sys. When using this automatic method, Io.sys does not load Himem.sys until after the commands in Config.sys have been executed. If you are using Config.sys to load Emm386.exe, then you must include Himem.sys in Config.sys along with Emm386.exe because Emm386.exe must find Himem.sys already loaded before it can load.

If you need to load a 16-bit device driver into a UMB (upper memory block), then you must have a Config.sys file with these lines in it:

```
DEVICE=Himem.sys
DEVICE=Emm386.exe NOEMS
DOS=HIGH,UMB
```

The DEVICEHIGH command to load the driver into a UMB must appear after these three lines in the Config.sys file. However, if you are using all 32-bit drivers, you don't even need the Config.sys file.

To know whether a driver is 16-bit or 32-bit, look at how Windows loads it. If the driver is a 32-bit driver written for Windows 9x, it is loaded from the registry. System.ini can contain both 16-bit and 32-bit drivers. If the driver is loaded from Autoexec.bat or Config.sys, it is a 16-bit driver written for DOS.

During the Windows 9x installation, Windows 9x setup tries to substitute 32-bit drivers for all 16-bit drivers it finds in use, and, if it can, to eliminate the Autoexec.bat and Config.sys files altogether. However, if it can't substitute a 32-bit driver for an older 16-bit driver, it puts (or keeps) the proper lines in the Config.sys file and sets itself up to use the older driver.

Windows 9x Swap File

A+ OS 1.1 2.5 Windows 9x automates the managing of virtual memory for you, and Microsoft recommends you allow that. To see what virtual memory options Windows 9x offers, click Start, point to Settings, click Control Panel, then select System and select the Performance tab. Click Virtual Memory, and the dialog box in Figure 4-30 is displayed. These settings are used to tell Windows how to manage the swap file. Unless you have a good reason to do otherwise, check Let Windows manage my virtual memory settings.

One reason you might want to manage virtual memory yourself is to make the size of the file permanent in order to prevent Windows from resizing the file, which can slow down performance. To improve performance, first defragment the hard drive so there is plenty of unfragmented space for the file. Then set the maximum and minimum size of the file to the same value, which forces the size to not change. If you have the available hard drive space, set the size to about 2.5 times the amount of RAM.

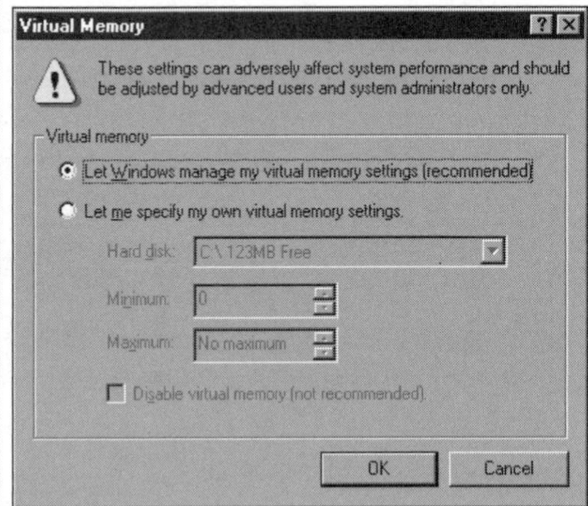

Figure 4-30 Options for managing virtual memory in Windows 9x

Notice in Figure 4-30 that you can specify the location of the swap file. The name of the swap file in Windows 9x is **Win386.swp**, and its default location is C:\Windows. You can choose to put the swap file on a compressed drive, but Windows does not compress the swap file itself, in order to better ensure the safety of the file.

Virtual Machine Manager

A+ OS 1.1 2.5

How does Windows 9x provide virtual memory addresses to DOS and 16-bit Windows application programs? By **memory paging**, which involves swapping blocks of memory stored in RAM to the hard drive. Memory paging is managed by the Virtual Machine Manager (VMM).

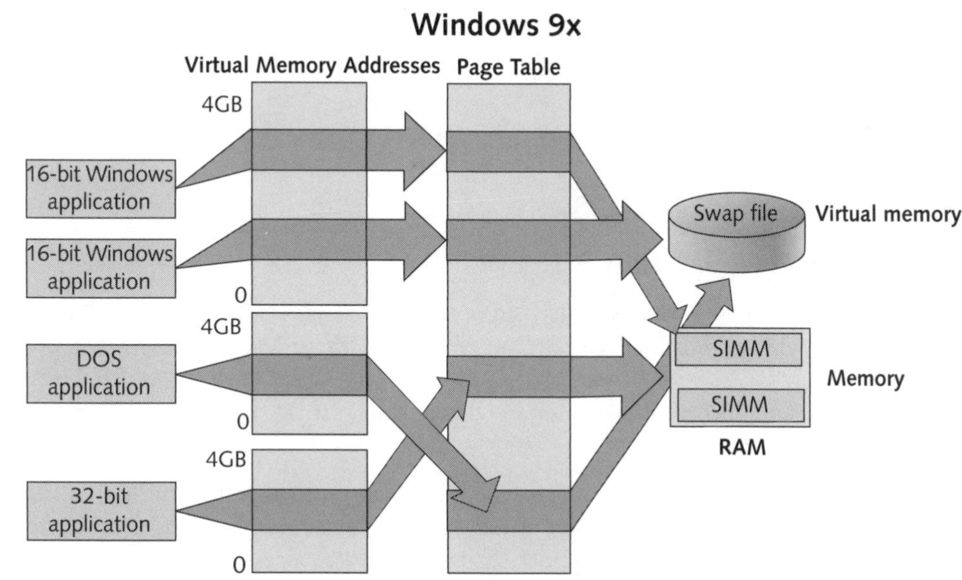

Figure 4-31 How Windows 9x manages memory

As you can see in the Figure 4-31, Windows 9x has virtual memory stored in a swap file and provides virtual memory addresses to application programs. In Figure 4-31, you see three sets of virtual memory addresses. Each set can contain up to 4 GB of addresses, depending on the amount of virtual memory available. The top set is being used by two 16-bit applications. The second set of virtual addresses is being used by a single DOS application, and a third set of addresses is being used by a 32-bit application. Each virtual machine for DOS has a set of virtual memory addresses. The 16-bit Windows programs share a single set of virtual memory addresses, and each 32-bit program has its own individual set of addresses.

In Figure 4-31, all these virtual addresses map onto the page table, which in turn maps onto either physical memory (RAM) or virtual memory on the hard drive (the swap file). Not all virtual memory addresses in Windows 9x have physical or virtual memory assigned to them. These virtual addresses remain unassigned until an application program uses them.

In Windows 9x, the VMM controls the page table, moving 4K pages in and out of physical RAM. If a program requests memory that the memory manager knows is stored in the swap file, the manager generates a **page fault**, which causes the manager to go to the drive to return the data from the swap file to RAM. This action is called a **page-in**. If RAM is full, the manager takes a page and moves it to the swap file, which is called a **page-out**.

A+ OS 1.1 2.5

If RAM is full much of the time, the VMM might spend excessive time moving pages in and out of RAM, which can cause excessive hard drive use and a decrease in overall system performance and can even cause the system to lock up or applications to fail. This situation is sometimes called **disk thrashing** and can cause premature hard drive failure. Symptoms of excessive memory paging are:

- Very high CPU use
- Very slow system response
- Constant hard drive use

To avoid excessive memory paging, leave fewer application programs open at the same time or install more RAM.

GETTING HELP FROM MICROSOFT

Microsoft offers some excellent support for its products. For those serious about learning to provide professional support for Windows 95 or Windows 98, two good books are *Microsoft Windows 95 Resource Kit* and *Microsoft Windows 98 Resource Kit*, both by Microsoft Press. These books expand on many of the concepts you have learned in this chapter about installing and using Windows 9x.

Another valuable source of information, including software utilities, enhancements, and troubleshooting guidelines for Windows 3.x and Windows 9x is the Microsoft Web site. For Microsoft Technical Support Knowledge Base, access *support.microsoft.com/search*.

Figure 4-32 shows the beginning query screen for this Web site. Follow the steps given there to research specific or general topics for Microsoft products. For example, if you want to learn more about how to optimize Windows 95, under My Search is about:, choose *Windows 95*, and enter *optimize* as the key word to search for. Click GO. A list of related articles is displayed. Click the article to display it.

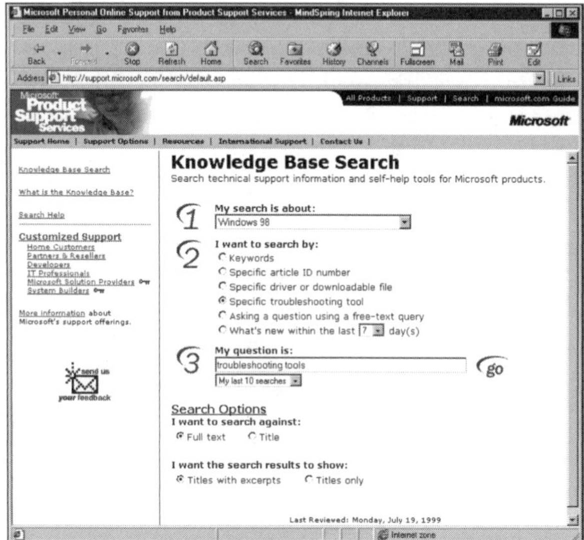

Figure 4-32 Microsoft Technical Support Web site

The Microsoft Web site (*www.microsoft.com*) contains many links on hardware and software compatibility, such as the ones you saw earlier in this chapter in the sections on installing hardware and software. These and other Microsoft support links will be useful when you troubleshoot Windows 9x, which you will learn how to do in the next chapter.

Chapter Summary

- The Windows 9x core consists of the kernel, the user, and the GDI and relates to users, software, and hardware by way of the following modules: the VMM, the IFS manager, the Configuration Manager, and the WDM driver manager.
- Virtual memory uses hard drive space as memory in order to increase the total amount of memory available. In Windows, virtual memory is stored in the swap file.
- The Windows 9x swap file is Win386.exe, and its default location is C:\Windows.
- Although Windows 9x supports 16-bit drivers, it is best to use 32-bit drivers whenever possible because they are faster, can be stored in extended memory, and can be dynamically loaded.
- Virtual machines are multiple logical machines within one physical machine. If an application crashes or produces another type of error within a virtual machine, only that virtual machine is affected, instead of the entire system.
- Since DOS applications do not account for sharing of resources, Windows can give each DOS application its own virtual machine and therefore its own resources.
- Windows 95 requires a 486DX, 25 MHz or higher processor; 4 MB of RAM, with 8 MB recommended; and 40 to 45 MB of hard disk storage. Windows 98 requires a 486 DX, 66 MHz or higher processor; 24 MB of RAM, with 32 MB recommended; and 140 to 315 MB of hard disk storage, depending on the installation.

- When you are installing Windows 9x as a clean install, you may need to change the boot order in CMOS, depending on what type of drive you plan to load the OS from.
- Before installing 9x as an upgrade, verify that you have enough hard drive space, run ScanDisk or Chkdsk, run antivirus software, back up critical system files, disable TSRs that might cause problems if they are running during installation, verify that any network connections are working, make sure that the swap file is put on a drive compressed with protected-mode software, and decide whether you want to use FAT16 or FAT32.
- Once you reach the setup screen, if Windows is already installed and you want to do a clean install, install the new OS in a different folder than the one used by the currently installed OS, which is probably \Windows.
- During setup, you can choose from Typical, Portable, Compact, or Custom installations.
- Windows 9x setup begins installation in real mode and later switches to protected mode.
- Setuplog.txt and Detlog.tst are two files in which Windows records information about the setup process. Windows uses Setuplog.txt to determine how far it got into an installation when recovering from a crash. Detlog.txt keeps a record of hardware detected. Detcrash.log is a binary file used by Windows to help recover from a crash caused by a problem with hardware.
- Information about your Windows installation can be stored in information files, which are text files with an .inf extension, and then used to do a hands-free installation.
- Msdos.sys contains several parameters that affect how the OS boots. To edit Msdos.sys, you must first change the file attributes.
- If you are installing Windows 9x as an upgrade to DOS and Windows 3.x, you will generally overwrite DOS and Windows 3.x.
- Upgrading from Windows 95 to Windows 98 is relatively easy because of the similarity of the two OSs. Before performing the upgrade, check hardware and software compatibility, run antivirus software, and back up your system. The Setup Wizard on the Windows 98 CD will guide you through the setup process. Once setup is complete, test installed applications and back up your system again.
- To upgrade to Windows Me, make the same preparations as for other upgrades. In addition, uncompress your hard drive, uninstall power and disk management tools, close open applications, and read the readme.txt file and other setup information before performing the upgrade.
- On the Microsoft Web site, you can find a list of available updates for whatever version of Windows you have installed.
- Keystroke shortcuts in Windows are useful for experienced typists who may find them faster than the mouse; they are also useful in troubleshooting situations when the mouse does not work.
- From the Windows 9x desktop, you can make applications automatically load at startup, create shortcuts to files and applications, and make the environment more user-friendly.
- In the Display Properties window, you can change the background, screensaver, appearance, icon effects, Active Desktop settings, color range, and display size for the desktop.
- You can create a desktop shortcut, which is an icon pointing to a program, file, or folder, using the Start Menu Programs tab on the Taskbar Properties window. An icon that represents a file itself rather than a shortcut will not have the small arrow that is a part of shortcut icons.

- When adding new hardware to Windows 9x, use the Add New Hardware Wizard. Select the hardware from a list of devices to use a Windows driver, or click Have Disk to use your own drivers (from a manufacturer's disk or from the Internet, downloaded to a folder on your hard drive).
- You can view and change current device drivers from the Control Panel. Windows provides an Update Device Driver Wizard to help you with this process.
- If you have problems with a hardware device or a software program, uninstalling and then reinstalling it might solve the problem.
- Some manufacturers of hardware devices include a disk with 16-bit drivers to be used when Windows 32-bit drivers cannot be accessed, such as when you are booting from a rescue disk.
- When you create a rescue disk in Windows 98, it automatically includes 16-bit CD-ROM drivers on the disk. Windows 95 does not automatically include 16-bit drivers when you create a rescue disk, but you can add them to the disk.
- A cache is a location in memory used to store frequently used data. A CD-ROM cache contains data that was recently read from the disk. CDFS is the disk-caching software for Windows 9x.
- For a Windows 9x system to be truly Plug and Play, the system BIOS must be PnP, all hardware devices and expansion cards must be PnP compliant, and a 32-bit device driver must be available for any installed hardware device.
- For Plug and Play systems, system resources are allocated to devices at startup in the resource management process, and the ongoing run-time configuration process monitors changes in system devices and the corresponding need for resources, and communicates this information to the OS.
- The four components that Windows uses in implementing PnP architecture are the configuration manager, the hardware tree, the bus enumerator, and the resource arbitrator.
- To learn if your BIOS is PnP, look for a message about the BIOS type on the startup screen.
- Windows Explorer is the primary tool for managing the files and folders on your hard drive and disks. Use the shortcut menus within Explorer by right-clicking the item you want to work with and choosing from the options on the menu that appears.
- Create a new folder by selecting the parent folder and then clicking File, New, and Folder. Change the name from New Folder to the desired folder name. To delete a folder, right-click the folder and select Delete from the shortcut menu. All folder contents and subfolders will be deleted.
- By default, Windows 9x Explorer hides file extensions of the files for which it knows which application to use to open or execute the file. By clicking View, Folder Options and the View tab and unselecting Hide file extensions for known file types, you can make Explorer display all file extensions.
- Windows 9x can run both 16-bit and 32-bit software. Use the Add/Remove Programs icon in the Control Panel to install 32-bit software designed for Windows 9x. For older 16-bit software, use the Run dialog box.
- Before installing software with Windows 9x, verify that you have the required system resources, read the documentation, make sure you have a copy of the original software that you keep in a safe place, and back up the registry and system configuration files.

- If you have a problem with a software installation, check the Readme.htm file and the Programs.txt file in the \Windows directory. These files will contain information about software issues known when Windows was shipped. You can also check the Microsoft Web site for information.
- If you are having a problem with a software installation, try deleting the files and folders in the \Windows\Temp folder.
- Windows 9x manages DOS applications differently than Windows 3.x. To customize the settings for a DOS application, use the Properties feature of the DOS program file, which will create an individual PIF for the program file and serve as the PIF editor.
- Dosstart.bat is a type of Autoexec.bat file that is executed when you select Restart the computer in MS-DOS mode or when you run a program in MS-DOS mode.
- An OS that supports protected mode can create a virtual real mode for a 16-bit application so that the application thinks it is the only program running, has all memory available to it, and accesses data using a 16-bit data path. When Windows 9x runs a 16-bit DOS application, it is ordinarily run in a virtual DOS machine.
- Windows 9x still organizes memory as conventional, upper, and extended but has made improvements in memory allocation and automation, such as automatically loading 32-bit drivers into extended memory, and freeing up conventional and upper memory by discontinuing use of the TSRs Smartdrv.exe and Share.exe.
- Windows 9x automates the management of virtual memory through the Virtual Machine Manger and memory paging.
- For detailed information on and support for Windows 9x and other Microsoft products, consult the Microsoft Resource Kits and the Microsoft Web site.

Key Terms

application program interface (API) call
bus enumerator
clean install
Configuration Manager
disk thrashing
DOS box
Dosstart.bat
GDI (Graphics Device Interface)
group files
hardware tree
hypertext
information (.inf) file
Installable File System (IFS)
memory paging
page fault
page-in
page-ou
patch
PIF (program information file)
resource arbitrator
resource management
run-time configuration
service pack
shortcut
System File Protection
System Restore
upgrade install
user component
virtual device driver (VxD)
virtual DOS machine
virtual machine
Virtual Machine Manager (VMM)
virtual memory
VxD
WDM (Win32 Driver Model)
Win386.swp

Review Questions

1. Name one Windows 9x release that does not support USB.
2. What are the three core components of Windows 9x?
3. ________________ uses hard drive space so that it acts like memory.
4. Give three reasons why it is preferable to use 32-bit drivers over older 16-bit drivers.
5. What is a virtual machine? How does Windows 9x use virtual machines differently from Windows 3.x to handle DOS applications and 16-bit Windows applications?
6. What is the function of the Autorun.inf file included on the Windows 9x installation CD? the Setup.exe file? The Readme.txt file?
7. What are the processor, RAM, and hard disk space requirements for Windows 95? For Windows 98?
8. List at least five things you need to do to prepare your hard drive for an upgrade install of Windows 9x.
9. What are the four types of installations that you can choose during setup of Windows 9x?
10. Windows 9x installation begins in ________________ mode and then switches to ________________ mode.
11. What are the log files Setuplog.txt, Detlog.txt, and Detcrash.log used for?
12. List the five basic tasks that Setup performs for you during a Windows 95 to Windows 98 upgrade.
13. What type of disk should you always create when prompted to do so during Windows 9x setup? Why is this such an important step?
14. Name two things you should do after completing a Windows 9x upgrade.
15. Windows Me (will/will not) run on a compressed hard drive.
16. Give two different situations in which Windows keyboard shortcuts might be useful.
17. What is the Windows keyboard shortcut used to display the startup menu while Windows is loading? To go through step-by-step confirmation of startup? To move from one loaded application to another?
18. How do you access the Display Properties window? What are two settings you can change from this window?
19. How is a shortcut icon different from an icon that points directly to a file or program? What happens if you delete a shortcut icon? A file or program icon?
20. When adding hardware to Windows 9x, how do you indicate that you want to use a Windows driver? A manufacturer-provided or downloaded driver?
21. Explain when and why you would use 16-bit and 32-bit drivers when installing a CD-ROM drive with Windows 9x.
22. What Windows component manages the interface to a CD-ROM drive including the CD-ROM cache?
23. Windows ________________ automatically puts its own 16-bit drivers on the rescue disk when you create the disk; Windows ________________ does not, though you can add them to the disk later.

24. What are the four components that Windows 9x uses to implement Plug and Play architecture?
25. How can you determine whether your BIOS is Plug and Play compatible?
26. ________________ is the primary tool for managing files, folders, and disks in Windows 9x.
27. Name three file extensions that Windows Explorer hides by default and three that it does not. How does it decide which file extensions to hide?
28. Use the ________________ applet in Control Panel when installing 32-bit software designed for Windows 9x. Use the ________________ option on the Start menu when installing older 16-bit software.
29. List three things you should do to prepare your system before installing new software.
30. What is virtual real mode? Do you have to use it to handle DOS applications within Windows 9x, or can you run them in "real" real mode?
31. How is memory management in Windows 9x similar to memory management under DOS? How is it different?
32. What is a page fault? A page-in? A page-out?
33. Define memory paging. What problem can excessive memory paging cause? What are some symptoms of this problem?

HANDS-ON PROJECTS

Practicing Keystrokes

Disconnect your mouse and reboot your PC. Practice using the keyboard to do the following in order to prepare for a situation where you must troubleshoot a system when the mouse is not working.

1. Open Explorer and select the file Io.sys in the root directory of the hard drive. The file will be hidden so you must unhide the file. To do that, from the View menu, select Folder Options, click the View tab, and then select Show all files. List the keys you needed to do this step.
2. What is the exact size of the file in bytes and the date and time the file was last modified?
3. Which key do you press to move down through the logical drives listed in Explorer?
4. Which key do you press to move down through files listed in a folder in Explorer?

Backing Up Critical Windows 9x Files

Keep a copy of critical Windows 9x files in a separate directory. Each time you install or uninstall hardware or software, redo the backup.

1. Using Windows 9x Explorer, create a new folder called Win-bak.ini.
2. In the C:\Windows folder highlight the **System.ini** and **Win.ini** files. Copy them by pressing **Ctrl+C**.
3. Click the **Win-bak.ini** directory, then paste the copied .ini files into the Win-bak.ini file by pressing **Ctrl+V**.

4. Using Explorer, set View, Options to **Show all files**.
5. Copy C:\Windows\System.dat to C:\ Win-bak.ini (do not drag!).
6. Copy C:\Windows\User.dat to C:\ Win-bak.ini (do not drag!).
7. Copy C:\Autoexec.bat to C:\Win-bak.ini (do not drag!).
8. Copy C:\Config.sys to C:\Win-bak.ini (do not drag!).

Note that your PC might not have Autoexec.bat or Config.sys. Also, the files System.dat and User.dat hold the registry. You will learn more about these files in the next chapter.

Installing a Windows Component

Under the Control Panel, Add/Remove Programs applet, look for Windows components that are not installed and install one. You will need access to the Windows 98 CD or the files on the CD copied to the hard drive or a network drive.

Using Shortcuts

Create a shortcut on your desktop to Notepad (Notepad.exe), a text editor. Using a second method for creating shortcuts, add a shortcut to the Windows command prompt (Command.com). First, locate the two program files on your hard drive by clicking Start, Find and using the Find dialog box. Then create the shortcuts. List the steps you took to create each shortcut.

Create a DOS Box Shortcut to Run Commands in Real Mode

Create a shortcut on your desktop to the Windows command window, a DOS box that you can use to enter MS-DOS commands. Then change the properties of the shortcut so that the program providing the DOS box, Command.com, runs in real mode. Describe what happens when you execute the shortcut. List the steps you took to return to the Windows desktop from the command prompt.

Case Project

Install Windows 9x

This project will erase everything on your hard drive. Do not do it if you have important data on the hard drive.

Prepare your hard drive for a clean install of Windows 9x by formatting the hard drive. Follow the instructions in the chapter to install Windows 9x using a Typical installation. Create the rescue disk when prompted to do so. Write down each decision you had to make as you performed the installation. If you get any error messages during the installation, write them down and also list the steps you took to recover from the error. How long did the installation take?

CHAPTER

5

SUPPORTING AND TROUBLESHOOTING WINDOWS 9X

In this chapter, you will learn:

- How the boot process works in Windows 9x, and how to troubleshoot it
- About the Windows 9x registry
- About tools used to monitor, control, and troubleshoot Windows 9x
- How to troubleshoot hardware and applications in Windows 9x
- How to troubleshoot Windows 9x performance

In the previous chapter, you learned how to install and use Windows 9x. You learned about some important configuration files and utilities that are a part of Windows 9x, as well as about some problems that may occur in the process of installing or using it. In this chapter, you will learn more about the boot process for Windows 9x, how to troubleshoot software and hardware, and how to use important utilities and system files in the troubleshooting process. This chapter also covers Windows 9x security, Windows 9x performance, and the Windows 9x registry.

BOOTING WINDOWS 9X

In Chapter 3, you learned how to boot to a command prompt. In this section, you will learn about the startup process in Windows 9x, including the differences between booting Windows 95 and booting Windows 98/Me. Finally, you will learn how to cause an application to load at startup. First, though, you'll learn more about important files that Windows 9x uses when booting up.

Files Used to Customize the Startup Process

A+ OS 1.1 1.2 1.5

There are several files that Windows 9x uses to control the startup process. Recall that DOS requires Io.sys, Msdos.sys, and Command.com in the root directory of the boot device in order to load. In addition, Autoexec.bat and Config.sys are text files that can contain settings for environmental variables and commands to load drivers and TSRs. Windows 9x supports Autoexec.bat and Config.sys for backward compatibility with DOS.

If Autoexec.bat or Config.sys files are present in the root directory, the command lines in them are executed during the boot. They are used to customize the loading process. Just as DOS uses text files to contain information about what is loaded, Windows 3.x also uses text files to hold custom settings that help control the loading process. These files are called initialization files, and some of the entries in these files are read and used by Windows 9x. However, most of Windows 9x settings are stored in the Windows registry rather than in text files.

These text files can be edited with the Edit.com program from the command prompt or any text editor from within Windows. The Windows System Configuration Editor **(Sysedit)** is a handy Windows text editor designed to be used with these files. To use Sysedit, type *sysedit* in the Run dialog box. These files are automatically displayed for editing: Autoexec.bat, Config.sys, **Win.ini**, **System.ini**, and **Protocol.ini** (see Figure 5-1).

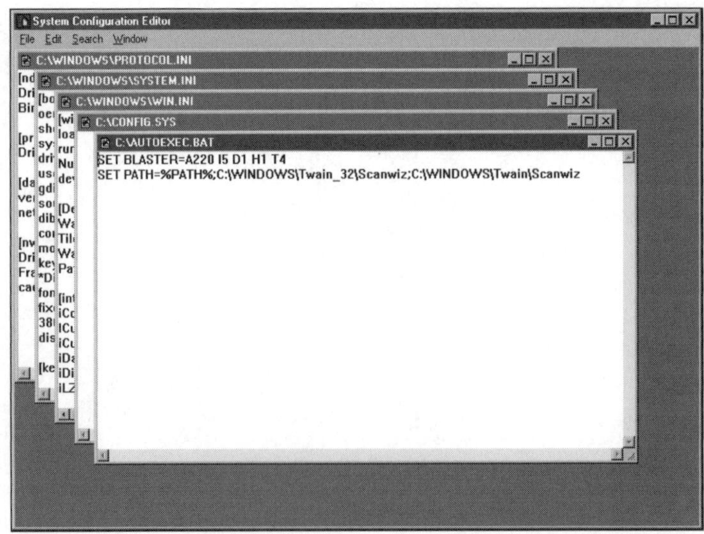

Figure 5-1 Sysedit can be used to edit Windows system files

A+ OS 1.1 1.2 1.5

Recall that an initialization file, which has an .ini file extension, is a file used by Windows or application software to store configuration information needed when Windows or an application is first loaded. An application can have its own .ini files and registry and can also store its information in the Windows .ini files and the Windows registry. Table 5-1 shows Windows .ini files, which Windows 9x supports for backward-compatibility with Windows 3.x.

Table 5-1 Windows .ini files

Windows Initialization File	General Purpose of the File
System.ini	Contains hardware settings and multitasking options for Windows. The [386Enh] section loads protected mode (32-bit) drivers for older applications, which may cause problems in more recent operating systems.
Progman.ini	Contains information about Program Manager groups.
Win.ini	Contains information about user settings, including printer, fonts, file associations, and settings made by applications.
Control.ini	Contains information about the user's desktop, including color selections, wallpaper, and screen saver options.
Mouse.ini	Contains settings for the mouse.
Protocol.ini	Contains information about the configuration of the network.

The contents of files with an .ini extension are organized into sections, which are each given a name. Within a section, values are assigned to variables using this format:

```
[SECTION NAME]
KEY NAME=value
```

Any value to the right of the key name becomes available to Windows or an application software program reading the file; in other words, the key name acts much like the Set command in Autoexec.bat, which assigns a value to a system variable.

System.ini and Win.ini are used by both Windows 3.x and Windows 9x. A sample Windows 9x System.ini file is shown in Figure 5-2. The two sections required for the boot process are [boot] and [386Enh]. Windows 3.x kept many more entries in these sections than does Windows 9x, which really only uses these files for backward compatibility with older applications.

Initialization files are only read when Windows or an application using .ini files starts up. If you change the .ini file for an application, you must restart the software for the change to take effect. If you want the application to ignore a line in the .ini file, you can turn the line into a **comment** line by putting a semicolon or the letters REM at the beginning of the line.

The maximum file size of .ini files is 64K, although files greater than 32K can cause some application software problems. Most applications have a setup program in their program group that is used to make changes to their .ini files.

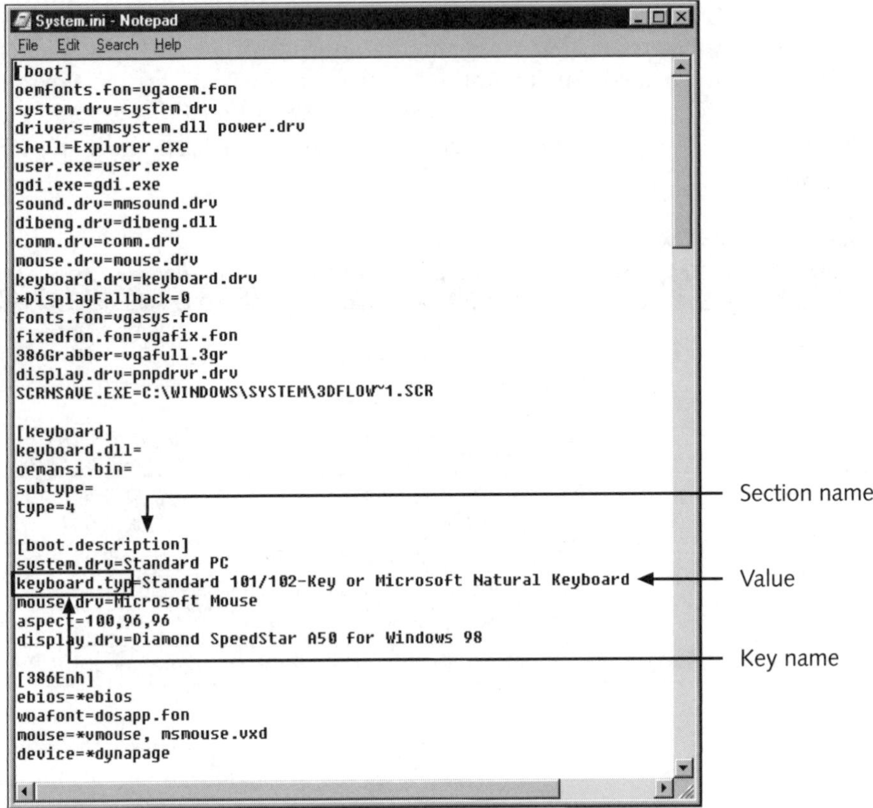

Figure 5-2 A sample Windows 98 System.ini file

Sometimes it is necessary to manually edit an .ini file that belongs to an application, but you should normally not edit System.ini or other Windows 9x initialization files. Incorrect changes to these files might result in Windows not running correctly, and Windows sometimes overwrites these files when changes are made to Windows through the Control Panel.

We now turn our attention to studying the Windows 9x startup process, in which these and other files are used.

The Windows 9x Startup Process

A+ OS 2.3

Windows 9x first loads in real mode and then switches to protected mode. With DOS, the two core real-mode system files responsible for starting up the OS, Io.sys and Msdos.sys, remain in memory, running even after the OS is loaded. With Windows 9x, Io.sys is responsible for only the initial startup process performed in real mode. Then, control is turned over to Vmm32.vxd, which works in protected mode, and Io.sys is terminated.

A+ OS 2.3 Windows 9x includes a file named Msdos.sys, but it is only a text file that contains some parameters and switches that can be set to affect the way the OS boots.

Startup in Windows 9x is a five-phase process, as shown in Figure 5-3. We will look at each phase in turn.

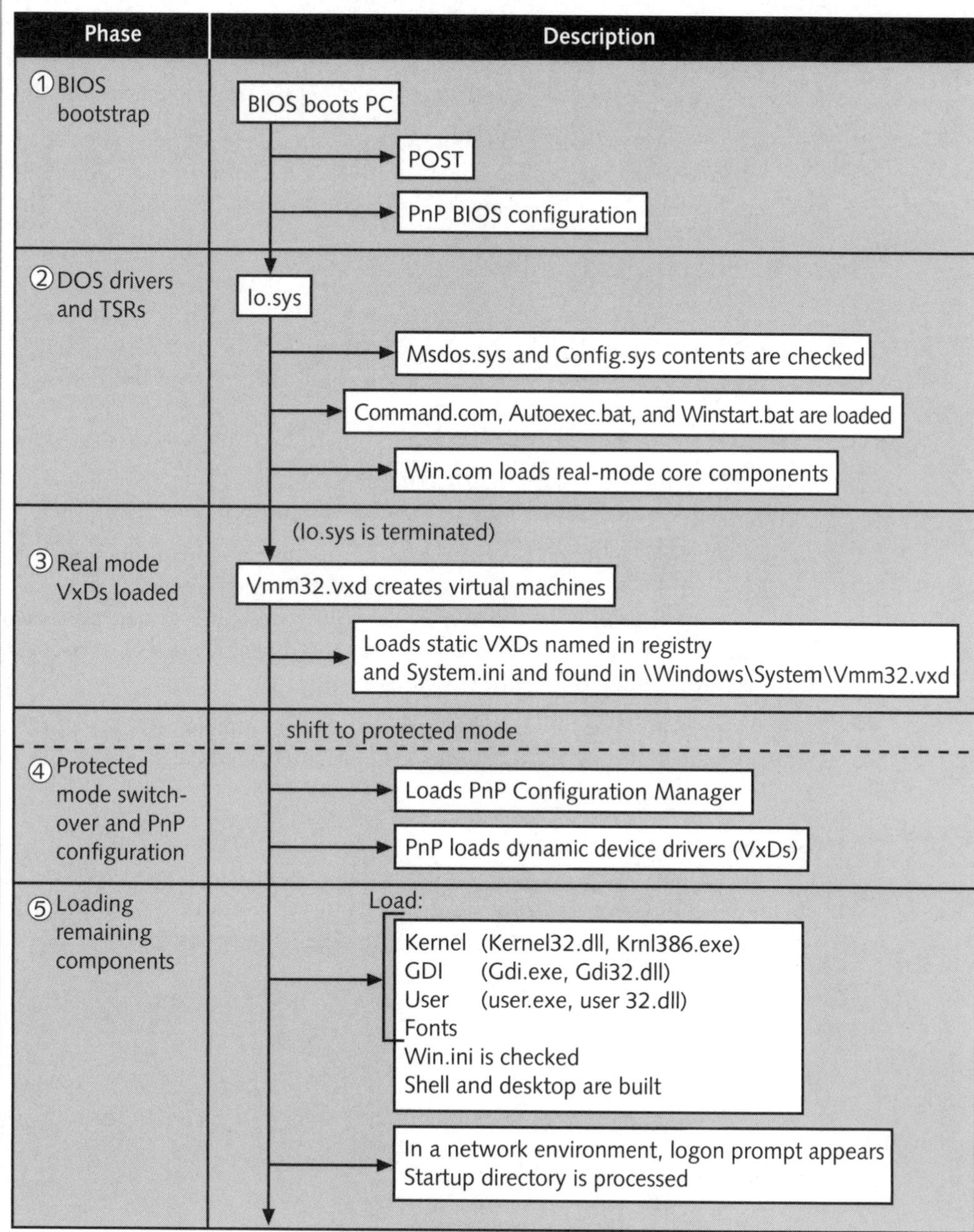

Figure 5-3 Windows 9x core components and the loading process

A+ OS 2.3

Phase 1: BIOS POST and Bootstrap

Startup BIOS begins the process. If the BIOS is a **Plug and Play (PnP) BIOS**, it examines the devices on the system and determines which ones are Plug and Play compliant. BIOS first enables the devices that are not Plug and Play and then tries to make the Plug and Play devices use the leftover resources. It also looks to permanent RAM for information about hardware and uses that information to help in configuring PnP devices that have their configuration information recorded there. It performs POST and saves information that Windows Configuration Manager later uses to complete the hardware configuration.

BIOS looks for a device (hard drive, floppy disk, CD-ROM drive, and so forth) containing the OS and loads Windows 9x. The Master Boot Record on the boot device executes the bootstrap loader, which looks for the initial hidden file of Windows 9x (Io.sys).

Phase 2: The OS is Loaded

In Phase 2, BIOS turns control over to Io.sys, which creates a real-mode operating system environment. Next, Io.sys checks the text file Msdos.sys for boot parameters. Then Io.sys automatically loads the following drivers if they are present: Himem.sys, Ifshlp.sys, Setver.exe, and Drvspace.bin (or Dblspace.bin).

- Himem.sys provides access to extended memory.
- 16-bit programs use Ifshlp.sys to access the file system.
- Setver.exe is included for backward-compatibility with DOS applications that expect all DOS components to be from the same version. Setver.exe "asks" the DOS application what version of DOS it expects to use and presents DOS components to that application as if they were all from that version, even if they are actually from different versions.
- Drvspace.bin and Dblspace.bin provide disk compression. One of these two files is loaded only if Io.sys finds Dlbspace.ini or Drvspace.ini in the root directory of the boot drive.

Io.sys also sets several environmental variables to default settings. Entries in Io.sys cannot be edited, but an entry in Config.sys overrides the default entry in Io.sys. Therefore, if you want to use settings different from the default, put the command in Config.sys, which is executed at this point in the load. Here are the default Io.sys entries:

- Files=60
- Lastdrive=z
- Buffers=30
- Stacks=9,256
- Shell=Command.com
- Fcbs=4

A+ OS 2.3

Next, Io.sys loads Command.com and follows instructions stored in Autoexec.bat and Winstart.bat. The default assignments made to environmental variables that were stored in Autoexec.bat in DOS are listed below:

- Tmp=c:\windows\temp
- Temp=c:\windows\temp
- Prompt=pg
- Path=c:\windows;c:\windows\command

The Tmp and Temp variables are used by some software to locate where to put their temporary files. You can change any of these by making an entry in Autoexec.bat. Next, Io.sys loads Win.com. Then Win.com loads other real-mode core components.

5

Phase 3: Static VxDs

In Phase 3, Io.sys relinquishes control to the virtual machine manager (VMM) component housed in Vmm32.vxd along with some VxDs. Recall that a VxD is a virtual device driver that works with a virtual machine to provide access to hardware for software running in the VM. Under Windows 3.x, these VxDs were loaded from System.ini and had a .386 file extension. Under Windows 9x, if stored in individual files, they have a .vxd file extension. They are called **static VxDs** because once they are loaded into memory, they remain there. (Conversely, **dynamic VxDs** are loaded into and unloaded from memory as needed.)

Vmm32.vxd is built specifically for a particular computer when Windows 9x is installed and contains some VxDs critical for a successful boot; each installation of Windows will have a different build of this file. (The VxD drivers that are now included in Vmm32.vxd were listed in the [386enh] section of System.ini under Windows 3.x.) Vmm32.vxd terminates Io.sys and, while still in real mode, loads static VxD device drivers as identified in four different locations. They can be embedded in Vmm32.vxd, named in the registry or System.ini, or stored in the .vxd files in the \Windows\System\Vmm32 directory.

If you suspect a problem with a VxD that is part of the Vmm32.vxd file, then store a new version of the .vxd file in the \Windows\System\Vmm32 directory. If Windows finds a VxD driver there, it uses that driver instead of the one embedded in Vmm32.vxd. Also, VxD drivers are listed in the registry and in System.ini. Normally, the entries are the same, and entries in System.ini are only listed there for backward-compatibility. However, if an entry in System.ini differs from an entry in the registry, the value in System.ini is used.

Phase 4: Protected-Mode Switchover and PnP Configuration

At the beginning of Phase 4, Vmm32.vxd switches to protected mode and loads Configuration Manager. Configuration Manager is responsible for configuring legacy and PnP devices. It will use any information that PnP BIOS might have left for it and loads the 32-bit VxDs for the PnP devices.

A+ OS 2.3

Phase 5: Loading-Remaining Components

In Phase 5, with Vmm32.vxd still in control, the three core components are loaded, and fonts and other associated resources are loaded. Win.ini is checked, and commands stored there are executed to allow for backward-compatibility. The shell and user desktop are loaded. If the computer is working in a networked environment, a logon dialog box is displayed, and the user can log on to Windows 9x and the network. Finally, any processes stored in the Startup directory are performed.

Differences Between the Windows 95 and Windows 98/Me Boot Process

Windows 98 made some minor changes in what happens during startup to speed up the boot process. For instance, Windows 95 waits two seconds while "Starting Windows 95" is displayed so that you can press a key to alter the boot process. Windows 98 eliminated this two-second wait and, in its place, allows you to press and hold the Ctrl key as it loads. If you do that, you see the startup menu that is also available with Windows 95.

Loading an Application at Startup

A+ OS 2.3

If you want an application to automatically load at startup, you can:

- Place a shortcut in the C:\\Windows\All Users\Startup Menu\Programs\StartUp folder. (You learned how to create shortcuts in Chapter 4.)
- Put the name of the program file in the Load= or Run= line in Win.ini.
- Manually edit the registry key HKEY_LOCAL_MACHINE\SOFTWARE\Microsoft\Windows\CurrentVersion\Run (modifying the registry is covered later in this chapter).

Troubleshooting the Windows 9x Boot Process

A+ OS 2.3 3.1

In the previous section, you learned about the steps in the Windows 9x boot process and the files used in the process. When the boot process does not complete correctly, here are the basic steps you go through to troubleshoot it:

1. Check and address any error messages that occur during a normal boot.
2. If you cannot boot to a normal desktop, boot in safe mode and begin troubleshooting there.
3. If you cannot boot using safe mode, the GUI portion of the OS is not functioning. Boot to the command prompt using the startup menu. Use commands at the C prompt for troubleshooting.
4. If the startup menu is not accessible, the MS-DOS core of the OS is not functioning. Boot from an emergency startup disk and try to access drive C.
5. If you cannot access drive C, then the hard drive is not accessible.

Error Messages Received While Loading Windows 9x

A+ OS 2.3 3.1

Error messages are your first indications that something is going wrong with the Windows 9x boot process. You can use these messages to figure out how to solve some Windows 9x boot problems. Table 5-2 shows error messages that Windows 9x might produce, along with what to do when you see them. Specific errors are covered later in this section.

Table 5-2 Error messages received while loading Windows 9x

Error Message or Problem	What to Do
"MS-DOS compatibility mode"	■ Windows is using real-mode drivers to access the hard drive rather than the preferred 32-bit drivers. After backing up the Config.sys and System.ini files, remove any references to real-mode drivers for the hard drive in these files. ■ The problem might be due to an outdated motherboard BIOS. Consider updating the BIOS.
"Bad or missing file" "Real mode driver missing or damaged" "Error in config.sys line xx"	■ Verify that Config.sys, Autoexec.bat, (root directory of the hard drive) and System.ini (Windows folder) are present and in the right location. ■ Check Config.sys and Autoexec.bat for errors using the step-by-step confirmation option from the Windows 9x startup menu. To check System.ini, rename the file so that it will not be used and boot with a bare bones version of the file. ■ Look in the Win.ini file for applications that are attempting to load at startup but that have been deleted or uninstalled. Check the Load= or Run= lines.
Cannot open file *.inf	■ This error is caused by insufficient memory. Disable any TSRs running in Autoexec.bat. ■ Close any applications that are running or remove them from the Start folder.
Insufficient disk space	Run ScanDisk and Defragmenter. Check free space on the hard drive.
"Invalid system disk" "Bad or missing command.com"	■ Suspect a boot sector virus. Run a current version of antivirus software. ■ Io.sys could be missing or corrupted. Restore the file from a backup or an emergency startup disk. To restore all real-mode files needed to begin loading Windows 9x, do the following: (1) boot from a Windows 9x emergency startup disk, (2) to restore Io.sys, Msdos.sys, Drvspace.bin, and Command.com, execute the command SYS C:, (3) remove the floppy disk and reboot.
Invalid VxD dynamic link call from IFSMGR	This error is caused by a missing or corrupted Msdos.sys file. Restore the file from a backup or from an emergency startup disk.
Missing system files	Run the SYS C: command.
System Registry file missing	Either System.dat or User.dat is corrupted or missing. For Windows 95, restore them by using either System.da0 or User.da0. For Windows 98/Me, run ScanReg.

5

A+ OS 2.3 3.1

Table 5-2 Error messages received while loading Windows 9x (continued)

Error Message or Problem	What to Do
VxD error returns to command prompt	A VxD file is missing or corrupted. Run Windows Setup from the Windows 9x CD and choose Verify installed components.
Error containing the text "Kernel32.dll"	An error that contains this text probably indicates a corrupted kernel. Try restoring system files. If that doesn't work, reinstall Windows. *Note*: this error may appear at other times, not just during the boot process.

Windows has several tools you can use to help troubleshoot problems with booting. These utilities listed below are discussed later in the chapter.

- Use System Configuration Utility (Msconfig) to limit what loads during the boot in order to attain the cleanest possible boot.
- Use Device Manager to disable a device that you think is causing a problem.
- Use Automatic Skip Driver Agent (ASDA) to keep Windows from installing a driver that might be corrupted, including built-in Windows drivers.
- The Windows 9x startup menu includes safe mode, the command prompt, and other troubleshooting options.

Microsoft Windows 9x Startup Menu

A+ OS 2.3 3.1

Normally, when you load Windows, the message *Starting Windows* displays and then the OS loads. However, you can force the menu to appear rather than the *Starting Windows* message by tapping the F8 key or holding down the Ctrl key during the boot.

Startup Menu Options

The Microsoft Windows 9x startup menu options are:

1. Normal
2. Logged (\BOOTLOG.TXT)
3. Safe Mode
4. Safe Mode with network support
5. Step-by-step confirmation
6. Command prompt only
7. Safe Mode command prompt only
8. Previous version of MS-DOS

A+ OS 2.3 3.1

What to expect when you select each option on the menu is described next. Option 4 is displayed if the OS is configured for a network, and Option 8 is displayed if a previous version of DOS was retained during the Windows 9x installation.

Normal In Msdos.sys, if BootGUI=1, then this option starts Windows 9x. If BootGUI=0, then this option will boot to the DOS 7.0 or DOS 7.1 prompt (the DOS core of Windows 9x). Either way, the commands in Autoexec.bat and Config.sys will be executed.

5

If a problem appears when you boot in normal mode, but does not appear when you boot in safe mode, then suspect that Config.sys, Autoexec.bat, System.ini, and Win.ini are the source of your problem. To eliminate Config.sys or Autoexec.bat as the source of the problem, boot using the step-by-step confirmation option on the startup menu. To eliminate Win.ini or System.ini as the source of the problem, use the following procedure:

1. Change the name of the System.ini file in the Windows folder to System.sav.
2. Find the System.cb file in the Windows folder and make a copy of it. Rename the copy System.ini. Do not rename the original System.cb file because you may need it at another time.
3. In the [boot] section of the System.ini file, add this line and then save the file:

   ```
   drivers=mmsystem.dll
   ```

4. Change the name of the Win.ini file in the Windows folder to Win.sav.
5. Restart your computer.

If this works, the problem was in the Win.ini or System.ini files, and you can reexamine these files in detail to determine the exact source of the problem.

If your mouse stops working when you copy the System.cb file and rename it to System.ini, add the following lines in the specified sections of the new System.ini file:

```
[boot]
mouse.drv=mouse.drv
[386Enh]
mouse=*vmouse, msmouse.vxd
```

Logged (\BOOTLOG.TXT) This option is the same as Normal, except that Windows 9x tracks the load and startup activities and logs them to the Bootlog.txt file. A portion of a sample Bootlog.txt file is shown in Figure 5-4. Notice that this file contains information about which components were loaded successfully and which ones were not. This file can be a helpful tool when troubleshooting.

A+ OS 2.3 3.1 3.2

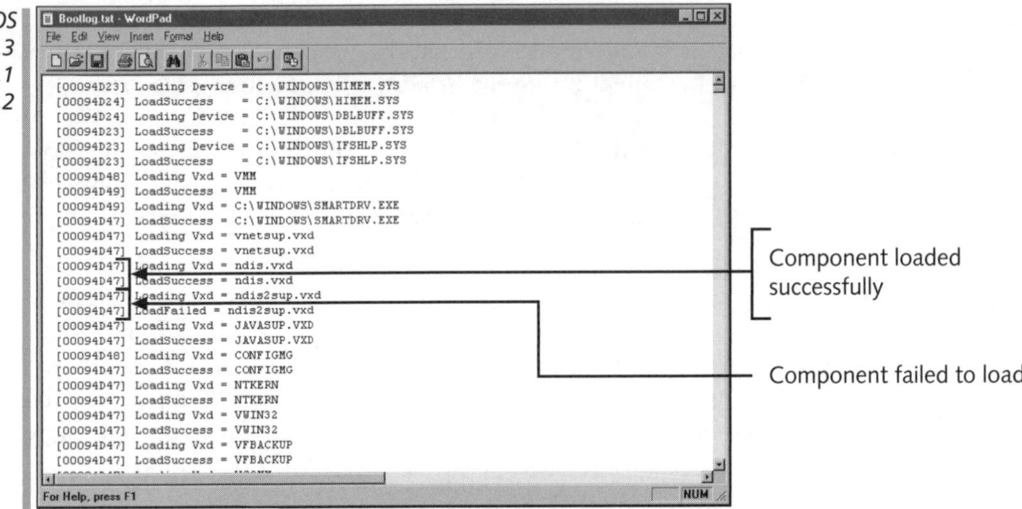

Figure 5-4 The Bootlog.txt file contains information about successful and unsuccessful boot activities

Safe Mode When you are having problems with the Windows 9x boot process but no error message appears during the boot, you can use safe mode to troubleshoot the problems. You can reach safe mode either from the startup menu or by pressing F5 while Windows is loading. Figure 5-5 shows Windows 98 booted into safe mode. Safe mode does not execute entries in the registry, Config.sys, Autoexec.bat, and the [Boot] and [386Enh] sections of System.ini. Also, when you enter safe mode, Windows 98/Me includes support for networks, but Windows 95 does not.

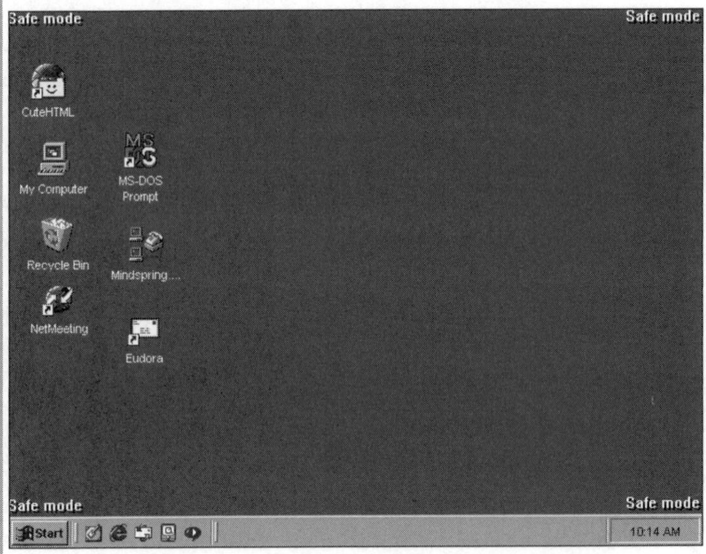

Figure 5-5 Windows 98 safe mode

A+ OS 2.3 3.1 3.2

Safe mode starts Windows 9x with a minimum default configuration to give you an opportunity to correct an error in the configuration. For example, if you selected a video driver that is incompatible with your system, when Windows 9x starts, it detects the problem and enters safe mode with a standard VGA driver selected. You can then go to Device Manager, select the correct driver, and restart Windows.

From the startup menu, you can choose to enter safe mode yourself if you know of a problem you want to correct. For example, if you have previously selected a group of background and foreground colors that makes it impossible to read the screens, you can reboot and choose safe mode. Safe mode gives you the standard color scheme along with the VGA mode. Go to Display Properties, make the necessary corrections, and reboot.

Sometimes you will use safe mode for troubleshooting when you don't know exactly what the problem is. In that situation, once you are in safe mode, use the following checklist:

- Use a current version of antivirus software to scan for a virus.
- Sometimes loading in safe mode is all that is needed. Try to reboot the PC in normal mode.
- If the Safe Recovery dialog box appears, select the option of Use Safe Recovery. Windows 9x will then attempt to recover from previous boot problems. Try to boot again.
- If you were having problems with a device installation before the Windows failure, disable or remove the device in Device Manager. Reboot after disabling each device that you suspect to be a problem.
- If you have just made configuration changes, undo the changes and reboot.
- Look for real-mode drivers or TSRs (programs loaded in Config.sys, Autoexec.bat, or System.ini) that might be causing a problem and disable them by inserting a semicolon or a REM at the beginning of the command line.
- Try to boot again. If the problem is still not solved, restore the registry. For Windows 95, overwrite System.dat with System.da0 and User.dat with User.da0 after making backups of these files. For Windows 98/Me, use ScanReg to restore the registry from backups. (How to do this covered later in the chapter.)
- Run ScanDisk to repair errors on the hard drive and optimize the drive. While in safe mode, select Start, Programs, Accessories, System Tools, ScanDisk. Under Type of Test, select Thorough. (See Figure 5-6.)
- Run the Defragmenter utility to optimize the drive. (You will learn more about this later in the chapter.)
- For Windows 98/Me, run System File Checker to verify system files.
- For Windows 98/Me, run Automatic Skip Driver Agent (covered later in the chapter) to skip loading any driver that is causing a problem. Reboot and examine the Asd.log file for recorded errors.

A+ OS 1.5 2.3 3.1 3.2

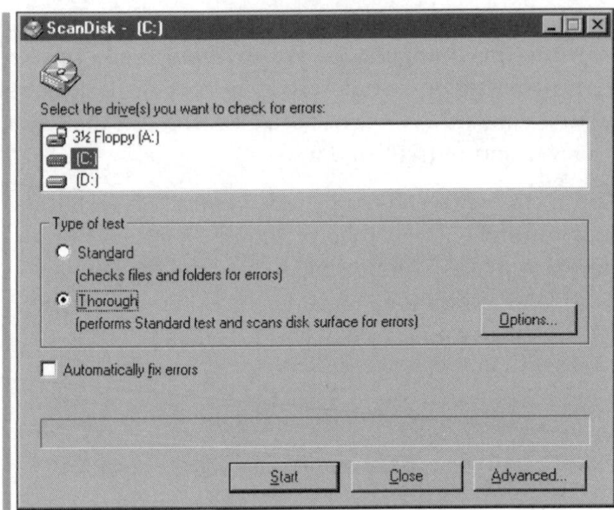

Figure 5-6 Use ScanDisk to check the hard drive for errors

- For Windows 98/Me, use the System Configuration Utility to further reduce the system to essentials and reboot. If the problem goes away, restore one item at a time until the problem returns so as to identify the item that is the source of the problem.
- Using Explorer, search for files in system folders that have changed recently. To sort file and folder names by date last modified using Explorer, click Modified. To reverse the sort order, hold down the Ctrl key while clicking Modified. If software or drivers have been installed recently, suspect that they might be the source of the problem.

Safe Mode with Network Support This option allows you access to the network when booting into safe mode. It is useful if Windows 95 is stored on a network server and you need to download changes to your PC in safe mode. This option is not available on the startup menu in Windows 98/Me, which automatically includes network support.

To eliminate the network connection as a source of a boot problem you are troubleshooting, first boot in safe mode without network support and then boot in safe mode with network support. If the boot without network support is successful but the boot with network support gives errors, then suspect that the network drivers might be the source of the problem. For Windows 98/Me, disable the network card in Device Manager to eliminate the network drivers as the source of the problem.

Step-by-Step Confirmation This option asks for confirmation before executing each command in Io.sys, Config.sys, and Autoexec.bat. You can accomplish the same thing by pressing Shift+F8 when the message *Starting Windows 95/98* appears.

A+ OS 1.1 1.2 2.3 3.1 3.2

Command Prompt Only This option executes the contents of Autoexec.bat and Config.sys but doesn't start Windows 9x. You will be given a DOS prompt. Type WIN to load Windows 9x. This command executes the file Win.com. There are several switches you can use with the WIN command when troubleshooting the OS. Table 5-3 shows these switches.

Table 5-3 Switches Used with the WIN command

Command/Switch	Purpose
WIN /D:M	Starts Windows in safe mode.
WIN /D:F	Turns off 32-bit disk access; use this option if there appears to be a problem with hard drive access
WIN /D:S	Instructs Windows not to use memory address F000:0, which is used by BIOS
WIN /D:V	Instructs Windows that the system BIOS should be used to access the hard drive rather than the OS
WIN /D:X	Excludes all upper memory addresses from real mode drivers

In a troubleshooting situation, try each switch until you get one that works. You can then identify the source of the problem and can sometimes put entries in the System.ini file to make the switch a permanent part of the load.

A+ OS 2.3 3.1 3.2

Safe Mode Command Prompt Only This option does not execute the commands in Autoexec.bat or Config.sys. You will be given a DOS prompt.

Previous Version of MS-DOS This option loads a previous version of DOS if one is present. You can get the same results by pressing F4 when the message *Starting Windows 95/98* appears. This option is not available in Windows 98 SE or Windows Me.

Troubleshooting with the Startup Menu

If you are have tried using the previous tools, but have not yet identified the source of the problem, use the following checklist to troubleshoot using the startup menu:

- Try a hard boot. A soft boot might not do the trick, because TSRs are not always "kicked out" of RAM with a soft boot.
- If you have not already done so, try safe mode next.
- Try the option Step-by-step confirmation next. Look for error messages caused by a missing or corrupted driver file. Try not allowing real-mode drivers to load. Once the problem command within Autoexec.bat or Config.sys is identified, you can eliminate the command or troubleshoot it. Specific commands in these files and their purposes were covered in Chapter 3.
- Use the Logged option next and examine the Bootlog.txt file that is created to see if it identifies the problem.

A+ OS 2.3 3.1 3.2

- Try booting using the Command prompt only option. From the command prompt, run the real-mode version of ScanDisk, which you will find in the \Windows\Command folder, to scan the hard drive for errors. From a command prompt, enter this command: C:\Windows\Command\Scandisk. If the Scandisk.exe program on the hard drive is corrupted, use the one on the emergency startup disk.
- For Windows 98/Me, from the command prompt, type Scanreg/Fix and try to reboot.
- For Windows 98/Me, from the command prompt, next type Scanreg/Restore and select the latest known good backup of the Windows 9x registry. Try to reboot.
- From the command prompt, you can use the WIN command with the switches that you saw in Table 5-3. If one of these commands solves the problem, look for real-mode drivers that might be in conflict, eliminating those that you can. Examine Bootlog.txt for errors and try booting from safe mode again.
- Try booting with Safe Mode command prompt only. Remember that when you are in safe mode, the registry is not executed. If you suspect a corrupted registry, restore it to its last saved version as you learned to do earlier. Then try the WIN command, with or without the switches as necessary.

Using the Startup Disk for Troubleshooting

A+ OS 2.3 3.1 3.2

If you cannot solve the boot problems you are experiencing by using the troubleshooting utilities within Windows or on the startup menu, use an emergency startup disk to recover from the failed boot. If you do not have an emergency startup disk, create one on another computer and use it to work with the computer that is having the problem. Before using the startup disk, it is a good idea to check it for viruses on a working computer by scanning it with antivirus software. If you find a virus on the emergency startup disk, destroy the disk and use a working computer to create a new one.

To use the emergency startup disk, place it in the floppy disk drive and turn on the PC. It will boot to a startup menu or to an A prompt, depending on the version of Windows 9x you are using. Figure 5-7 shows the Startup Menu.

If you are using a version for which the startup disk boots to a menu, select the first option, which is to start the PC with CD-ROM support. The OS will then examine the system for problems and then provide an A prompt where you can enter commands.

If the system has failed to boot from the hard drive, the first step in troubleshooting at this point is to see if you can access the hard drive. To do that, enter DIR C: at the A prompt. If this step works, then the problem lies in the software that is used on the hard drive to boot, including the OS boot record, OS hidden files, and command interface files. If you cannot access the hard drive, the problem is with the partition table, the Master Boot Record, hard drive, its cabling, or its power source. In this case, you need to examine the hard drive for errors.

A+ OS 2.3 3.1 3.2

```
Microsoft Windows 98 Startup Menu
________________________________________________
________________________________________________

1. Start Computer With CD-ROM Support.
2. Start Computer Without CD-ROM Support.
3. View the Help File.

   Enter A Choice:              Time Remaining: 30




F5=Safe Mode Shift+F5=Command Prompt Shift+F8=Step Configuration[N]
```

Figure 5-7 Windows 98 rescue disk startup menu

Use Fdisk to examine the partition table. If the table is corrupted, most likely you have lost everything on your hard drive. Try using the Fdisk /MBR command to restore the Master Boot Record on the drive. If this does not work, try creating new partitions on the drive and formatting the drive. All data and software on the drive will be lost. If you cannot use Fdisk on the drive, treat the problem as a hardware problem. Hardware troubleshooting is not covered in this book. (Refer to the *A+ Guide to Managing and Maintaining PC Hardware*, Course Technology 2002, ISBN 0-619-12002-9.)

After you have completed troubleshooting the hard drive, eliminating physical problems with the hard drive subsystem, CMOS, and the partition table, the next step is to run the Windows 9x Setup program. When given the opportunity, select Verify installed components. Setup will then restore damaged or missing system files.

5

The Windows 9x Registry

A+ OS 1.1

In supporting and troubleshooting Windows 9x, you need to understand the role of the registry and .ini files. The registry is a database of configuration information and settings for users, hardware, applications and the OS. Starting with Windows 9x, the registry takes over the essential functions of .ini files. However, Windows 9x still supports .ini files for compatibility with Windows 3.x and legacy software and hardware devices. Entries that 16-bit Windows applications make in Win.ini and System.ini are not added to the registry because these applications cannot access the registry. Entries made in .ini files by applications that can access the registry are copied into the registry. In this section, you will examine how the registry is organized, what kinds of information are in the registry, how and why you might edit the registry, and how to recover from a corrupted registry.

How the Registry Is Organized

A+ OS 1.1 1.2

The registry organizes information in a hierarchical database with a treelike, top-to-bottom design. The Windows 9x System.ini file contains setup parameters. Refer back to Figure 5-2, which shows a portion of the System.ini file. Notice that section names appear in square brackets, key names to the left of the equal signs, and values assigned to these key names to the right of the equal signs. The Windows 9x registry takes on a similar design but enhances it by allowing for keys to cascade to several levels on the tree. Figure 5-8 shows a portion of a Windows 9x registry. Consider names on the left of the window as similar to section names in System.ini; these names are called **keys** by Windows 9x. On the right of the window are value names, such as ScreenSaveTime, and to the right of each name is the **value data** assigned to that name, such as "60." The value names, called values by Windows 9x, are similar to the key names in System.ini, and the value data are similar to the values assigned to key names in System.ini.

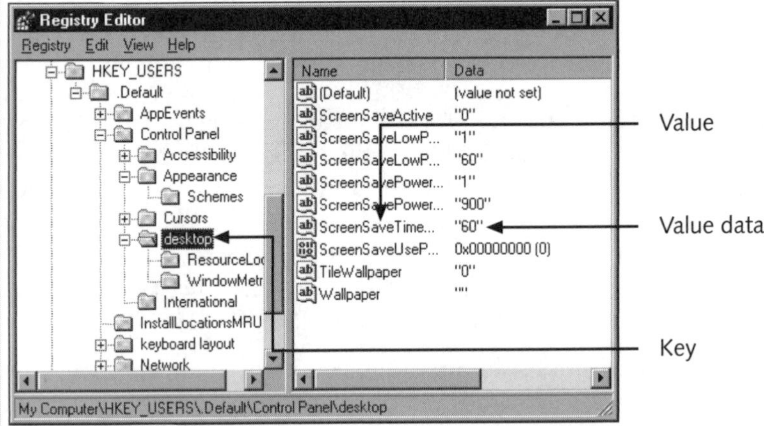

Figure 5-8 Structure of the Windows 9x registry

The registry is organized into six major keys, or branches, which are listed in Table 5-4. The registry is contained in two files, System.dat and User.dat, located in the Windows directory as hidden, read-only, system files, although the information forms only a single database.

Table 5-4 Six major branches, or keys, of the Windows 9x registry

Key	Description
HKEY_CLASSES_ROOT	Contains information about file associations and OLE data (this branch of the tree is a mirror of HKEY_LOCAL_MACHINE\Software\Classes).
HKEY_USERS	Includes user preferences, including desktop configuration and network connections.

A+ OS 1.1

Table 5-4 Six major branches, or keys, of the Windows 9x registry (continued)

Key	Description
HKEY_CURRENT_USER	If there is only one user of the system, this is a duplicate of HKEY_USERS, but for a multiuser system, this key contains information about the current user preferences.
HKEY_LOCAL_MACHINE	Contains information about hardware and installed software.
HKEY_CURRENT_CONFIG	Contains the same information in HKEY_LOCAL_MACHINE\Config and has information about printers and display fonts.
HKEY_DYN_DATA	Keeps information about Windows performance and Plug-and-Play information.

Recovering from a Corrupted Registry

A+ OS 3.1

Windows 95 has a way to recover from a corrupted registry that is different from the method used by Windows 98/Me. These methods are discussed next.

Windows 95 Backup of the Registry

Windows 95 maintains a backup copy of the two registry files called System.da0 and User.da0. Each time Windows 95 boots successfully, it makes a backup copy of these two files. If Windows 95 has trouble loading and must start in safe mode, it does not back up the registry.

If Windows 95 does not find a System.dat file when it starts, it automatically replaces it with the backup System.da0. If both System.dat and User.dat are missing, or if the WinDir= command is missing in Msdos.sys, Windows 9x tells you that the registry files are missing and starts in safe mode. It then displays the Registry Problem dialog box. Click the Restore From Backup and Restart buttons. The registry files are restored from System.da0 and User.da0. If these files are also missing, the registry cannot easily be restored. You can either restore the files from your own backups or run Windows 9x Setup. There is another option. Look for the file System.1st in the root directory of the hard drive. This is the System.dat file created when Windows 9x was first installed. In an emergency, you can revert to this file.

A+ OS 1.5 3.1

Windows 98/Me Registry Checker

Windows 98/Me offers a utility called the Registry Checker, which is not available with Windows 95. It automatically backs up the registry each day, and by default, it keeps the last five days of backups. In an emergency, you can recover the registry from one of these backups. You can also tell Registry Checker to make an additional backup on demand, such as when you have just made changes to the registry and want to back up these changes before you make new changes.

To access Registry Checker, select Start, point to Programs, Accessories, System Tools, and then click System Information. The Microsoft System Information window opens (see Figure 5-9). From the menu bar, select Tools and then Registry Checker. Registry

A+ OS 1.5 3.1

Checker tells you if the registry is corrupted and will fix it, if allowed. You can also create a new backup at this time.

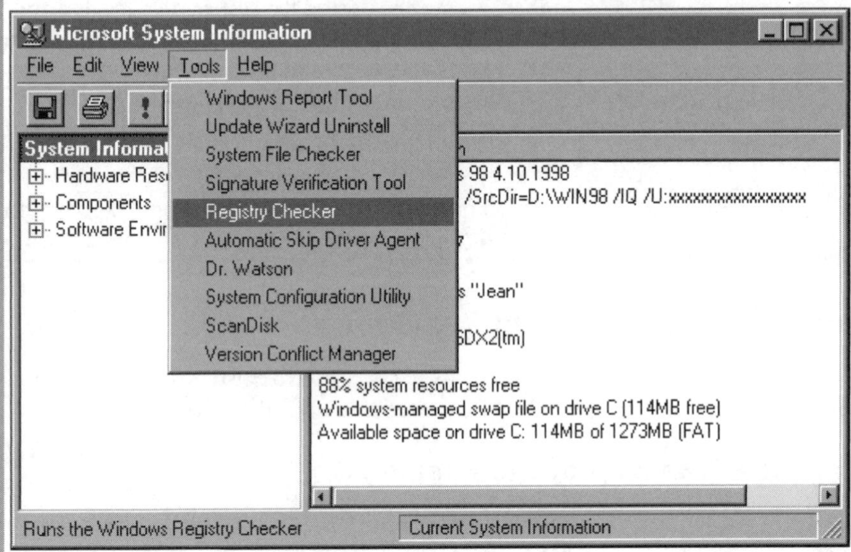

Figure 5-9 The Registry Checker is available under Programs, Accessories, System Tools, System Information Tool; it is used to back up, restore, and repair the Windows 98 registry

Backups are kept in cabinet files in the \Windows\Sysbckup folder as rb001.cab, rb002.cab, and so on. To revert to one of these backups, you must first be in MS-DOS mode. For Windows Me, boot from a bootable disk. For Windows 98, boot from a bootable disk or boot to a MS-DOS prompt from the Windows 98 startup menu (Windows Me does not have this option on the startup menu). From the MS-DOS prompt (not a DOS box within a Windows session), use the commands in Table 5-5 to repair or recover the registry.

Table 5-5 Commands used to repair or recover the registry

Command	Purpose
Scanreg /Restore	Restores the registry from a previous backup. A screen is displayed asking you which backup to use.
Scanreg /Fix	Repairs the corrupted registry. If the problem is inherent to the registry itself, this might work. If the problem is that you want to undo a successful change to the registry, then use the Restore option instead.
Scanreg /Backup	Creates a new backup of the registry at the DOS prompt. Don't do this if the registry is giving you problems.
Scanreg /Opt	Optimizes the registry. ScanReg will look for and delete information in the registry that is no longer used. This reduces the size of the registry, which might speed up booting.
Scanreg /?	Help feature of ScanReg.

Modifying the Registry

When you make a change in Control Panel or Device Manager or many other places in Windows 9x, such as when you install software, the registry is modified automatically. For most users, this is the only way they will ever change the registry. However, there are rare occasions when you might need to edit the registry manually. One example would be if you accidentally deleted the device driver for a hardware device but Device Manager says that the device is still installed. Another example would be if the wrong software starts when Windows 9x is loaded and you cannot correct the problem by changing the Startup folder. Both these problems can be corrected by manually editing the registry.

The first step in editing the registry is to back up the two files System.dat and User.dat. Sometimes the files are small enough to fit on floppy disks and can be copied using Explorer. If the files are too large to copy to floppy disk, copy them to a different folder on the hard drive or use compression software such as PKZIP to copy them to floppy disks. For Windows 98/Me, use Registry Checker to back up the registry. Third-party utility software such as Norton Utilities (*www.symantec.com*) has a registry editor that allows for backing up the registry before entering the editor. The following directions use the Windows 9x Regedit utility to edit the registry.

After backing up the registry files, the next step is to use Regedit.exe, located in the Windows folder. You can use Explorer to locate the file, then double-click it, or you can click Start, and then Run, and type Regedit in the Run dialog box. When you do, the window in Figure 5-10 opens. Open one branch of the tree by clicking on the + sign to the left of the key, and close the branch by clicking on the – sign.

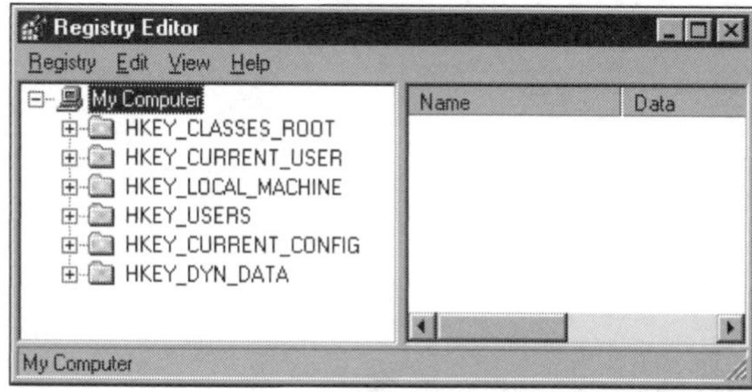

Figure 5-10 The six major keys, or branches, of the registry seen in the Registry Editor

To search for an entry in the registry, click Edit, and then click Find. The Find dialog box is displayed, as in the screen in Figure 5-11, which is ready to find the text "software" in the registry. Enter the key, the value, or the value data, and then click Find Next. You can choose to search keys, values, and/or value data by clicking on the check boxes in the dialog box.

A+ OS 1.1

For example, suppose that the wrong programs start when you load Windows 9x. First try to correct the problem without editing the registry. Using Explorer, open the C:\\Windows\All Users\Start Menu\Programs\StartUp folder. Delete any items that you don't want to start when you load Windows. If this does not correct the problem, the problem might be caused by a wrong entry recorded in the registry. Try editing the registry.

A+ OS 1.1

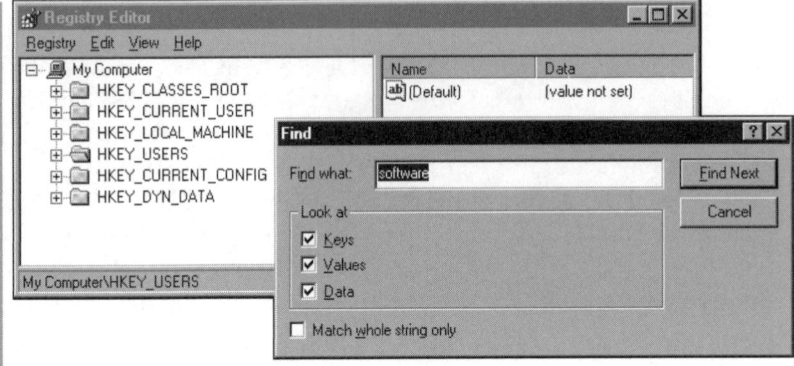

Figure 5-11 Searching for entries in the registry

First locate Shell Folders, which will be in the following branch: HKEY_CURRENT_USER\Software\Microsoft\Windows\CurrentVersion\Explorer\Shell Folders. Search for these keys and subkeys one at a time. (Search for HKEY_CURRENT_USER. After you have located it, search for Software, and continue through the list until you come to Shell Folders.)

The value name Startup= in the Shell Folders subkey should be "C:\Windows\Start Menu\Programs\Startup." If the data is incorrect, right-click Startup and select Modify from the shortcut menu. Figure 5-12 shows the Edit String dialog box that is displayed. Change the value data and then click OK.

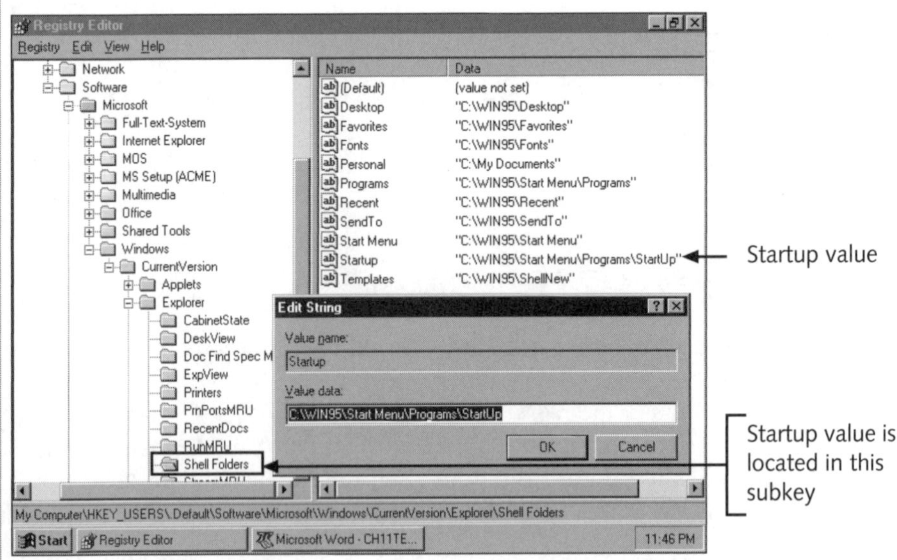

Figure 5-12 Editing an entry in the registry using Regedit.exe

TOOLS USED TO MONITOR, CONTROL, AND TROUBLESHOOT WINDOWS 9X

A+ OS 1.5

Windows 9x offers several tools, some of which are listed in Table 5-6, to monitor and improve system performance, control the OS, and to help with troubleshooting. Several of the major tools are covered in this section.

Table 5-6 Windows 9x system performance and troubleshooting tools

Tool	Win 95	Win 98/Me	Description
Automatic Skip Driver Agent File name: Asd.exe Location: \Windows		X	Automatically skips drivers that prevent Windows from loading and records problems encountered in the log file Asd.log. To run, select Automatic Skip Driver Agent from the Tools menu of the System Information window.
Microsoft System Information File name: MSInfo32.exe Location: \Program Files\Common files\Microsoft shared\Msinfo	X	X	Displays system information, including installed hardware and device drivers. To run, click Start, Programs, Accessories, System Tools, System Information or type Msinfo32.exe in the Run dialog box.
Hardware Diagnostic tool (Hwinfo.exe)		X	Displays the same information as System Information, but in text form. Enter hwinfo /ui in the Run dialog box.
Registry Checker File name: Scanreg.exe Location: \Windows\Command		X	Backs up, verifies, and recovers the Registry. To run, select Registry Checker from the Tools menu of the System Information window.
Windows Update File name: Iexplore.exe Location: *www.microsoft.com/windowsupdate*	X	X	Download service packs (fixes) for Windows from the Microsoft Web site.
System options in Control Panel	X	X	Several applets in Control Panel can be used in monitoring and tweaking system performance.
System Configuration Utility Filename: MsConfig Location: \Windows\System		X	Allows you to temporarily modify the system configuration to help with troubleshooting. To run, select System Configuration Utility from the menu Tools of the System Information window or type Msconfig in the Run dialog box.
System File Checker File name: Sfc.exe Location: \Windows\System		X	Verifies system files. This tool scans for changed, deleted, or corrupted system files and restores them from the originals on the Windows CD-ROM. To run, select System File Checker from the Tools menu of the System Information window.

A+ OS 1.5 3.1 3.2

Table 5-6 Windows 9x system performance and troubleshooting tools (continued)

Tool	Win 95	Win 98/Me	Description
System Monitor File name: Sysmon.exe Location: \Windows		X	System Monitor tracks the performance of some important system components. To run, click Start, Programs, Accessories, System Tools, System Monitor.
Microsoft Backup (\Program Files\Accessories\Backup\Msbackup.exe)	X	X	Backs up files and folders to prevent loss when your hard drive fails. To run, click Start, Programs, Accessories, System Tools, Backup. The utility is covered in Chapter 11.
System Recovery File name: pcrestor.bat Location: On the Windows 98/Me CD in \Tools\Sysrec		X	Uses a full system backup created by Microsoft Backup to reinstall Windows and restore the system to its state as of the last backup.
Dr. Watson File name: Drwatson.exe Location: \Windows		X	Traps errors in log files created by applications and takes a snapshot of the system to use for troubleshooting.
Scheduled Task Wizard File name: Mstask.exe Location: \Windows\System	X	X	Schedule tasks such as MS Backup to run at predetermined times.
Version Conflict Manager File name: Vcmui.exe Location: \Windows		X	Installs Windows files over a newer file that might be in the \Windows folder and subfolders.
System Configuration Editor File name: Sysedit.exe Location: \Windows\System	X	X	Text editor to edit files that configure how Windows loads. To run it, enter Sysedit.exe in the Run dialog box. Sysedit automatically opens Protocol.ini, System.ini, Win.ini, Config.sys and Autoexec.bat for editing.
Task Manager File name: Taskman.exe Location: \Windows	X	X	Run, switch and end applications, and access the Shutdown menu. To run it, type Taskman in the Run dialog box.
Signature Verification Tool File name: sigverif.exe Location: \Windows		X	Checks system drivers for digital signatures given them by Microsoft, which ensures they have been tested by Microsoft. To run it, use the System Information window.
Digital Signature Check		X	Identifies drivers that have been digitally signed by Microsoft to verify their integrity. To use it, enabled this key in the registry: HKEY_LOCAL_MACHINE\Software\Microsoft\Driver Signing.

As Table 5-6 shows, some tools are only available with Windows 98/Me. Many of these tools are accessed from the Microsoft System Information window. To access this window, click Start, point to Programs, Accessories, System Tools, and then click System Information. The dialog box illustrated in Figure 5-13 opens. The System Information utility is available under Windows 95 but does not include the tools listed in Table 5-6.

A+ OS 1.5

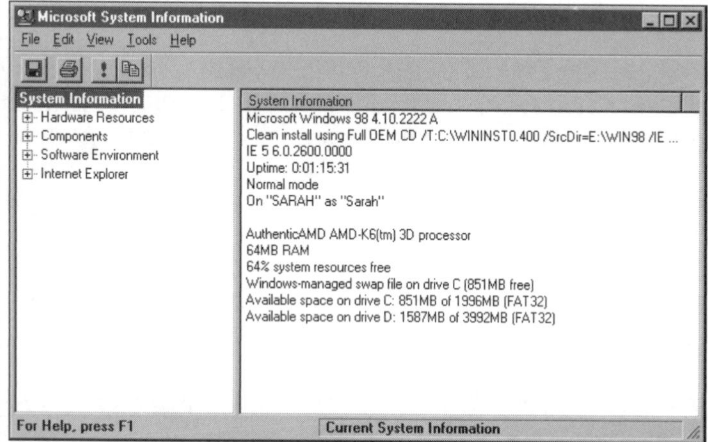

Figure 5-13 Some performance and troubleshooting tools can be accessed through the System Information window

One tool that is available from the System Information window is the System File Checker, which is illustrated in Figure 5-14. To use the utility to restore damaged Windows system files, click Tools on the System Information window and then select System File Checker.

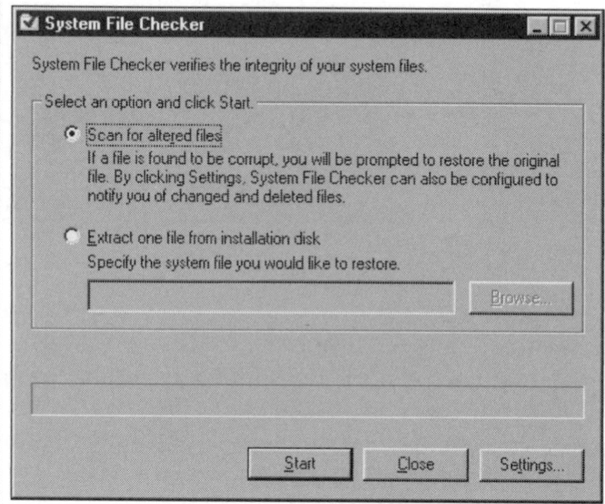

Figure 5-14 The Windows 98 File Checker verifies system files

The same information displayed by the System Information tool can be displayed in text format using the Hardware Diagnostic tool (Hwinfo.exe). To use the tool, type *hwinfo /ui* in the Windows Run dialog box. The Hardware Info window reports information about hardware devices, including drivers used, keys from the registry and how they are used, configuration information, and error and warning information. You can sort and filter the report so that only information about devices with problems is listed.

System Applet in Control Panel

A+ OS 1.5

To access the System applet in Control Panel, click the System icon. The applet offers several tools for performance monitoring and troubleshooting. For example, the Performance tab in Figure 5-15 shows a performance report from two computers, one in need of performance tuning and one running at optimal performance. Key messages to look for on this screen (see Figure 5-15a) are "Some drives are using MS-DOS compatibility" under File System, and "MS-DOS compatibility mode" under Virtual Memory. These messages mean that real-mode drivers are being used, which can slow down performance, especially when used with hard drive access. Figure 5-15b indicates that both these components are using 32-bit protected-mode drivers.

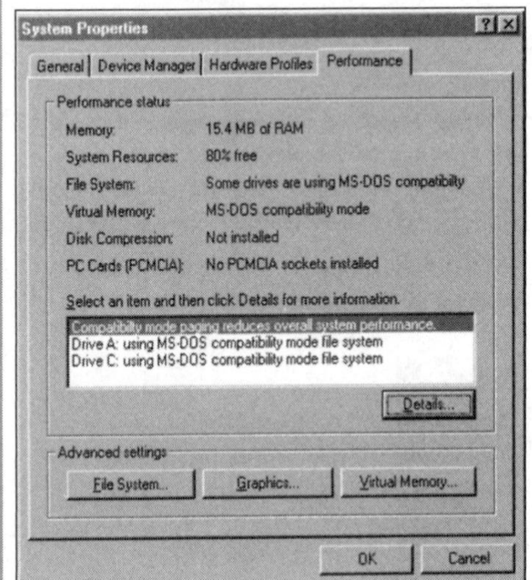

a. Adjustments are needed in order to use 32-bit protected-mode resource

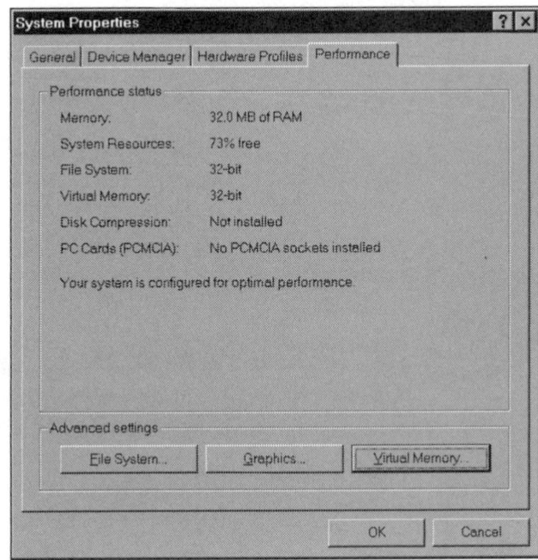

b. System running at optimal performance

Figure 5-15 The Performance tab under System Properties in Control Panel can tell you if your file system and virtual memory are running at optimal performance

Whenever you see MS-DOS mode (real mode) drivers being used, make the effort to do whatever you can to see that these drivers are replaced with 32-bit protected-mode drivers. One important tool to use for this process is the file Ios.ini, a text file that contains the Windows 9x Safe Driver List. Windows 9x uses this list to determine if it can safely substitute a protected-mode driver for a real-mode one. Also, if it attempts to make the substitution but fails, it often records the problem in another file, Ios.log. Check this file for information about the problem.

If a real-mode driver is being used, and you believe that a protected-mode driver should be used in its place, first check Ios.log for any error messages. If you don't find an error message, add the real-mode driver name to the safe driver list in the Ios.ini file. Anything following the semicolon on the line is a comment. You can also use REM to comment out a line.

A+ OS 1.5

Sample lines in the Ios.ini file are:

```
[SafeList]
386max.sys   ;  Qualitas
extrados.pro;  Qualitas Memory Manager
extrados.max;  Qualitas Memory Manager
4dos.com     ;  4DOS shell program
ad-dos.com   ;  Afterdark
ad-wrap.com ;  Afterdark
adi2.com     ;  Afterdark
aspi3x70.sys;  DTC SCSI driver
```


If you are using third-party disk compression software, such as Stacker, make sure to use a 32-bit version of the software. (You will learn more about disk compression in Chapter 11.) When converting from Windows 3.x to Windows 9x, also upgrade Stacker. If you are still using a 16-bit version of the software, most often an error message about the problem can be found in Ios.log.

System Monitor

A+ OS 1.5

System Monitor allows you to monitor how system resources are being used by applications. It can monitor the file system, memory, the kernel, printer sharing services, and network performance data. System Monitor is not automatically installed in a typical installation. To install it, go to Control Panel, Add/Remove Programs. Click Windows Setup, and then select Accessories. To run System Monitor, click Start, point to Programs, Accessories, System Tools, and then click System Monitor.

Figure 5-16 shows System Monitor tracking the kernel and disk cache hits and misses. Under the File menu, you can add and delete items the monitor is tracking. Use System Monitor to help determine if an application is using an inordinate amount of resources or has a memory leak. A memory leak occurs when you exit software and it unloads from memory, but it does not release the memory addresses that it was using for its data back to the OS. Memory leaks can occur when software is corrupted, poorly written, or plagued with a virus. You notice memory leaks when your system gets sluggish after you have launched and exited an application several times before rebooting the system. A reboot releases all memory addresses.

System Configuration Utility

A+ OS 1.5

Like loading Windows in safe mode, the System Configuration Utility (mswnconfig.exe) reduces the startup process to its essentials. If starting Windows in this condition eliminates the problem you are troubleshooting, you can use this utility to add items back one at a time until the problem occurs; the source of the problem is related to the last item you added. To use the utility, do the following:

1. To access the utility, click **Start**, point to **Programs**, **Accessories**, **System Tools**, and then click **System Information**. The Microsoft System Information window opens (see Figure 5-9).

A+ OS 1.5

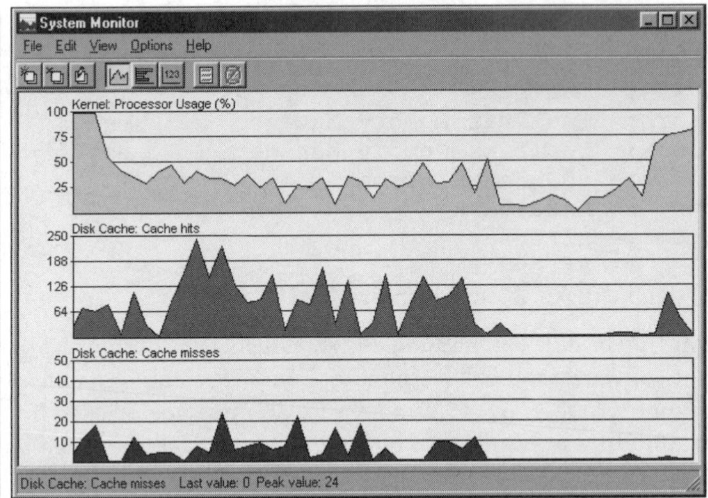

Figure 5-16 System Monitor can track the performance of several system resources

2. From the **Tools** menu, select **System Configuration Utility**. The System Configuration Utility dialog box opens, as in Figure 5-17. Another way to access the window is to type Msconfig in the Run dialog box.
3. To diagnose a problem, select **Diagnostic startup – interactively load device drivers and software**, and then click **OK** to restart your computer.

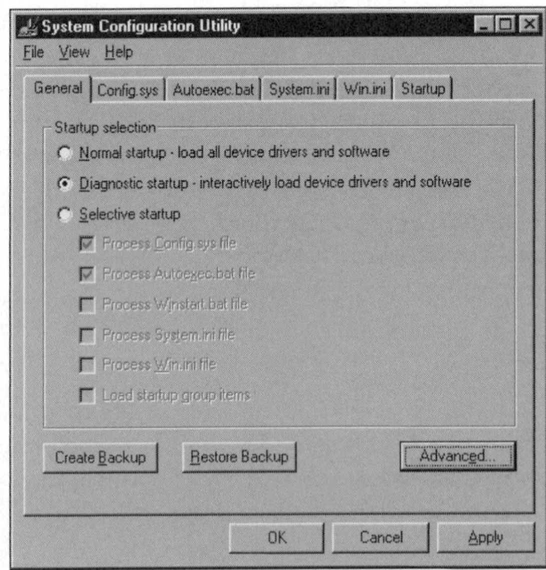

Figure 5-17 The Windows 98 System Configuration Utility helps troubleshoot Windows configuration problems

A+ OS 1.5

4. If this solves the problem, then the clean start was successful. Next, select **Selective startup** from the screen shown in Figure 5-17 and methodically select first one item and then another to restore, until the problem reappears. Begin by restoring all entries in Autoexec.bat and Config.sys, to determine if real-mode drivers and programs loaded from these files are the source of the problem.
5. If the problem still occurs, even with the clean boot, then try these things:
   - If you have not already done so, scan for a virus, using a current version of antivirus software.
   - Use Registry Checker to check for corrupted system files.
   - Use System File Checker to check for corrupted system files.
   - Check the CMOS setup screen for wrong settings.

5

Tools to Manage Security

There are several tools and methods in Windows 9x to create, update, and use passwords and user profiles. These tools can be used to avoid or address problems caused by unauthorized access to certain machines or computer features. How to secure files and folders that are shared on a network is covered in Chapter 12.

A+ OS 4.1

User Profiles

Windows 9x (as well as Windows NT/2000/XP) offers **user profiles** that allow the system to restore user preferences each time a user logs on to the system. A user profile can include software and hardware settings such as how the desktop is displayed, what shortcuts are on the desktop, and what printers or other hardware devices are available for a user. When several users use the same computer, user profiles can be a handy way for each user to keep individual settings. Also, on a network, a roaming profile follows the user from computer to computer on the network. User profiles can be collected into a **group profile** so that changes to the group profile affect all users assigned to that group.

There are many security advantages to having a different profile for each user. When you set a user profile, you also set a logon password that a user must type in when booting up the computer. Each user profile has a different logon password, and the settings of the profile can limit what files, folders, applications, and hardware devices the user has access to. In this way, you can limit what users can do on the PC and on the network. To create user profiles, open the Users applet in the Control Panel. The Multi-user Wizard will step you through the process.

In a network environment, Windows 9x can use policy files to define user, network, and computer settings. A policy file has a .pol file extension; examples are Policy.pol and Config.pol. Using the System Policy Editor, a network administrator can create a policy file that affects the entire network, a group of users, or a single user on the network. The policy file can reside on the network server and is read when Windows 9x first boots. Entries in the policy file override entries in the Windows 9x registry, including those placed there by the User applet.

Screen Saver Passwords

Sometimes a user will leave his or her computer idle for a period of time, allowing the screen saver to activate. Setting a screen saver password prevents unauthorized users from accessing the computer logged in under an authorized user's profile while the authorized user is away. Once the screen saver password is set and the screen saver activates, you must enter the correct password to close the screensaver and return to the desktop and any open files and applications. A screen saver password does not protect files on the system. Any user can reboot and access the hard drive without knowing a screen saver password.

To create a screen saver password, click the Screen Saver tab in the Display Properties window. Select a screen saver and check Password protected. To set the password, click the Change button and then enter and confirm a password (see Figure 5-18). Click OK to save your password and then click OK to exit the Display Properties window.

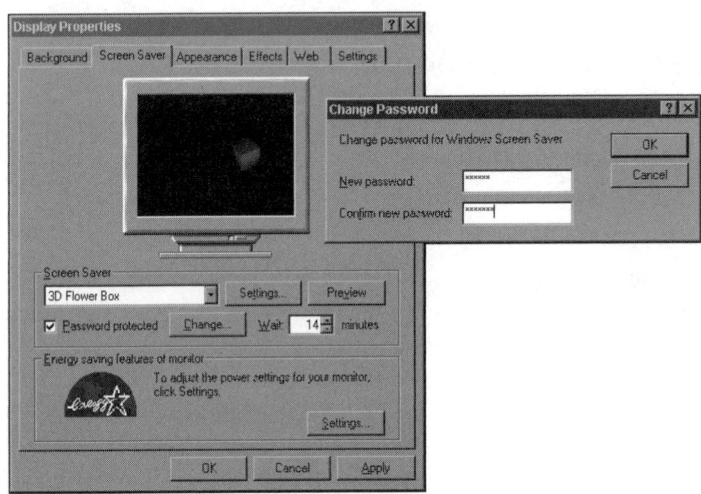

Figure 5-18 You must confirm a screen saver password to set it

Managing a Hard Drive

A+ OS 1.5 2.5

Earlier in the chapter, you saw the tools ScanDisk and Defrag, both of which check and repair problems with a hard drive, listed as tools to use when troubleshooting the boot process. In the last chapter, you saw how they are used to prepare a hard drive before upgrading Windows. You can also use these utilities when troubleshooting hard drive problems or even software problems that could be caused by an improperly running hard drive. Even when you are not having problems with your hard drive, it is a good idea to run these utilities occasionally to check the health of the drive and possibly avert future problems.

Defrag

Fragmentation is the undesirable placement of a single file in several cluster locations that are not right next to each other, so that data access time is increased. When a hard drive is new and freshly formatted, the OS writes files to the drive beginning with cluster 2, placing

A+ OS 1.5 2.5

the data in consecutive clusters. Each new file begins with the next available cluster. Later, after a file has been deleted, the OS writes a new file to the drive, beginning with the first available cluster in the FAT. If the OS encounters used clusters as it is writing the file, it simply skips these clusters and uses the next available one. In this way, after many files have been deleted and added to the drive, files become fragmented. Fragmentation occurs when files are written to a drive in more than one group of contiguous clusters. The clusters that make up a file are together called a **chain**. For a well-used hard drive, it is possible to have a file stored in clusters at 20, 30, 40, or more locations. Fragmentation is undesirable because (1) when the OS has to access many different locations on the drive to read a file, access time slows down, and (2) if the file should become corrupted, recovering a fragmented file is more complicated than recovering a file in one continuous chain.

5

For these reasons, one routine maintenance task is to periodically **defragment** the hard drive. Windows 9x includes a real-mode version of the utility called the Defrag command, and there is a defragmentation utility available from the Windows desktop that has a graphical interface. You can also use third-party software such as Norton Utilities. Regardless of the method used, you should defragment your hard drive every six months or so as part of a good maintenance plan.

To graphically see how badly a drive is fragmented, use Norton Utilities, Windows Disk Defragmenter, or another disk utility to view your FAT. Norton highlights the clusters for each file in a different color so you can easily identify all the clusters that belong to a single file. By moving your cursor over the FAT, you can easily see whether your hard drive is badly fragmented.

To use Windows 9x Disk Defragmenter, choose Start, then Programs, then Accessories, and then System Tools. The menu in Figure 5-19 is displayed. (Two of the other menu items, ScanDisk and DriveSpace, will be discussed next.) Click Disk Defragmenter and select the drive from the dialog box that is displayed. Click OK. When the operation is complete, the message in Figure 5-20 appears; click Yes to exit.

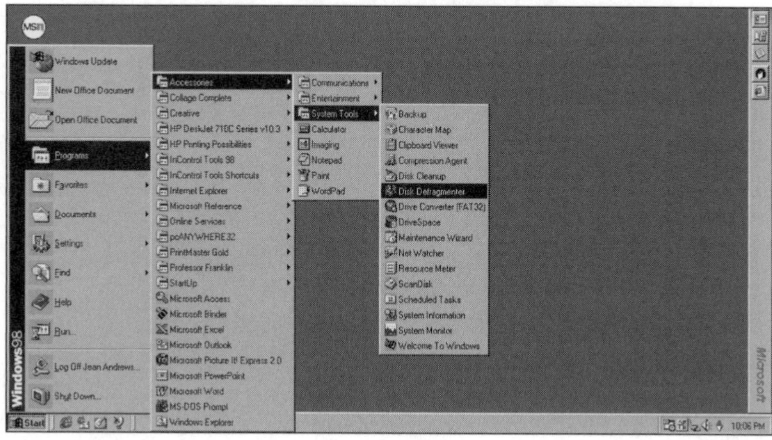

Figure 5-19 Windows 98 utilities

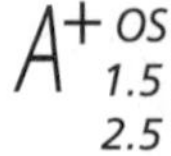

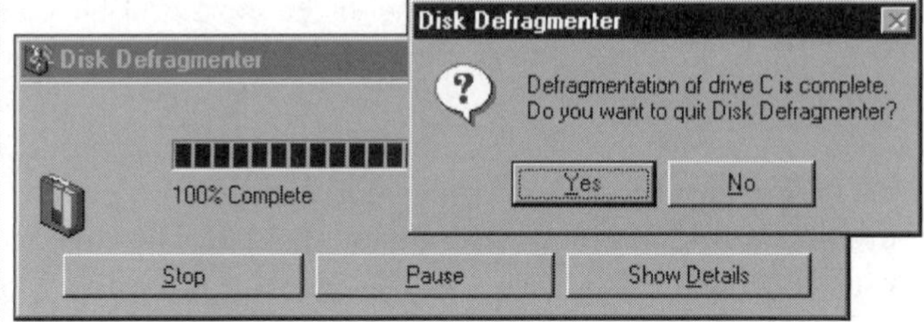

Figure 5-20 Disk Defragmenter results

Defragmenting a large hard drive may take a long time, so plan for this before you begin. If you want to watch the progress as it moves through the FAT, click Show Details on the Disk Defragmenter dialog box.

ScanDisk

As you learned in Chapter 3, a directory on either a floppy disk or hard drive is a table holding information about files in that directory or folder. The directory contains the number of the first cluster in the file. The FAT holds the map to all the other clusters in the file. Occasionally, the mapping in the FAT becomes corrupted, resulting either in lost clusters or in cross-linked clusters, as shown in Figure 5-21. Here File 3 has lost direction and is pointing to a cluster chain that belongs to File 4. Clusters 29–31 are called **cross-linked clusters** because more than one file points to them, and clusters 15–17 and 28 are called **lost clusters**, or **lost allocation units**, because no file in the FAT points to them.

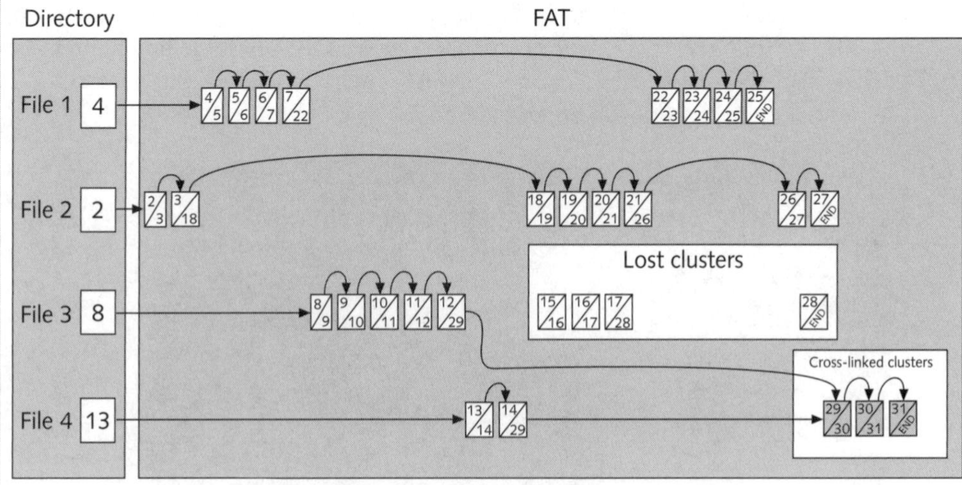

Figure 5-21 Lost and cross-linked clusters

To repair cross-linked and lost clusters, use the ScanDisk utility in either MS-DOS mode or from the Windows 9x desktop. For example, in real mode, at the command prompt,

A+ OS 1.5

enter the command *Scandisk*. The screen in Figure 5-22 is displayed. When the program finishes scanning the disk, it returns you to a command prompt.

From the Windows desktop, click Start, then Programs, then Accessories, then System Tools, and then ScanDisk, as shown in Figure 5-19. The ScanDisk utility first asks which drive you want to scan and gives you the choice between a standard and thorough scan. The standard scan checks files and folders for errors. The thorough scan does all that the standard scan does plus checks the disk surface. Click Start to begin the scan. Errors are reported as they occur, and final results are displayed as in Figure 5-23.

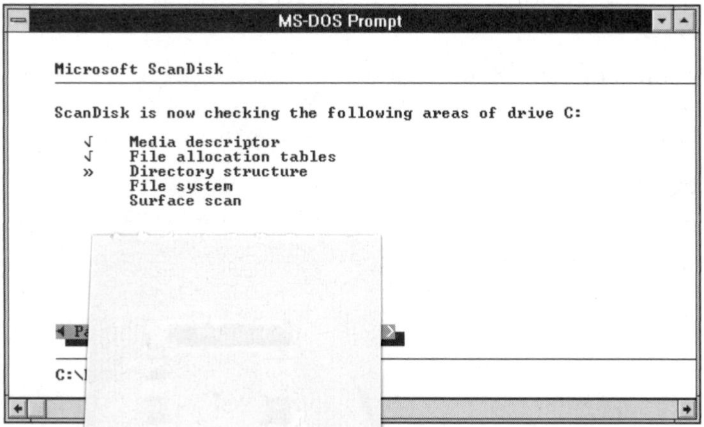

Figure … S mode

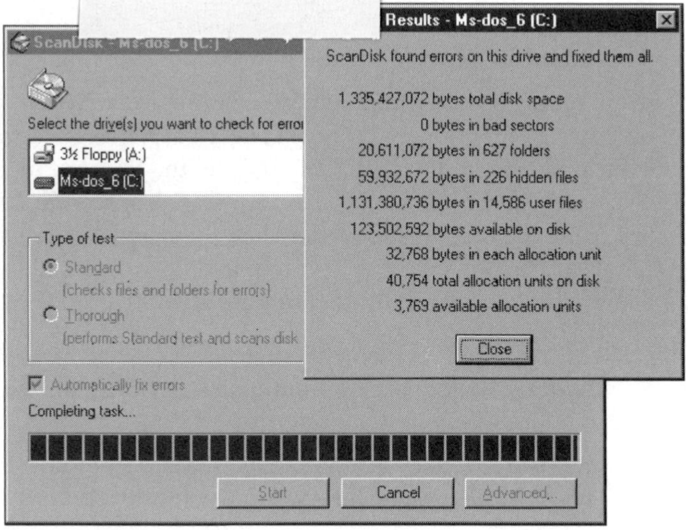

Figure 5-23 ScanDisk results

Using DOS Commands Under Windows 9x

A word of caution: using some DOS commands on a hard drive that uses Windows 9x as the OS may cause damage to a hard drive's file structure. With a Windows 9x upgrade, some of these dangerous commands are erased from the \DOS directory on the hard drive. However, you will find DOS commands that come with Windows 9x stored in the \Windows\Command directory, and some of these should not be used. Here are the ones to avoid:

- Don't use disk utility software that does not know about VFAT, long filenames or FAT32, including older versions of Norton Utilities and Central Point PC Tools.
- Don't use Fdisk, Format C:, Sys C:, or Chkdsk while in a DOS session within Windows 9x.
- Don't optimize or defragment your hard drive using software that does not know about long filenames; look for the Windows 9x compatibility message on the package.
- Don't run hard drive cache programs unless they are written especially for Windows 9x. Remember that Windows 9x has its own built-in caching software.
- Don't use the older DOS backup programs such as Backup or Msbackup, because the long filename information might not be saved during the backup.

Device Manager

A+ OS 1.5 3.2

Device Manager gives a graphical view of hardware devices configured under Windows and the resources and drivers they use. Using Device Manager, you can make changes, update drivers, and uninstall device drivers. You can also use Device Manager to print a report of system configuration. When a device driver is being installed, Windows 9x might inform you that there is a resource conflict, or the device might simply not work. Use Device Manager as a useful fact-finding tool for the resolution of the problem.

Device Manager is one tab on the System Properties window. To access System Properties, right-click the My Computer icon on the desktop and select Properties from the shortcut menu, or double-click the System icon in Control Panel. From the System Properties window, click the Device Manager tab. The list of devices is displayed, as seen in Figure 5-24. A "+" beside the device name indicates that you can click the device for a list of manufacturers and models installed. The open diamond symbol indicates a SCSI device, and the three-forked symbol is used for USB. Symbols that indicate a device's status are:

- A red X through the device name indicates a disabled device.
- A exclamation point on a yellow background indicates a problem with the device (the device might still be functioning).
- A blue I on a white field indicates that automatic settings were not used and resources have been manually assigned. It does not indicate a problem with the device.
- For Windows Me, a green question mark indicates a compatible driver is installed, (not the driver designed for the device), which means the device might not be fully functioning.

A+ OS 1.5 3.2

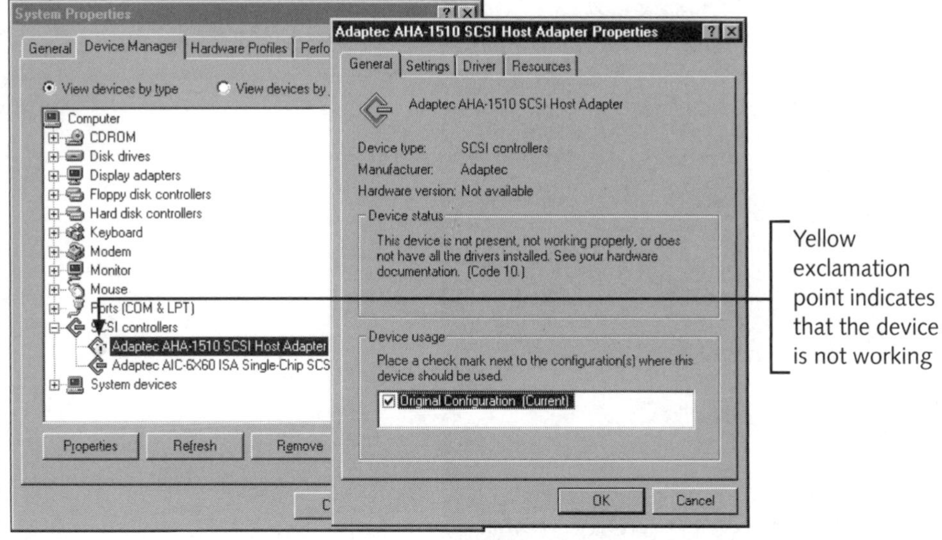

Figure 5-24 The Properties box of an installed device that is not working

To see a better explanation of a problem, click the device and select Properties. The Device Properties dialog box opens, which can give you helpful information about solving problems including I/O addresses, DMA channels, and IRQs used by the device as well as the names of devices that are also attempting to use the same resources.

In fact, before you start hardware installation, you might want to use Device Manager to print a summary of all hardware installed on the PC and resources being used. This printout can be a record of your starting point before the installation as well as a tool to help resolve conflicts during the installation. To print this summary, access Device Manager and click Print. From the Print dialog box, select All Devices and System Summary for a complete listing.

If you have a problem with an installed device, use Device Manager to uninstall the device. Select the device and click the Uninstall button. Then reboot and reinstall the device looking for problems during the installation that point to the source of the problem. Sometimes reinstalling a device is all that is needed to solve the problem.

Dr. Watson

A+ OS 3.1 3.2

A troubleshooting tool you can use when you are having problems running an application is Dr. Watson. **Dr. Watson** is a Windows utility that can record detailed information about the system, errors that occur, and the programs that caused them in a log file named \Windows\Drwatson\WatsonXX.wlg, where XX is an incrementing number. Start Dr. Watson (see Figure 5-25) and then reproduce the application error.

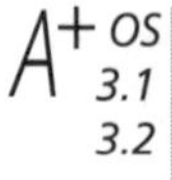

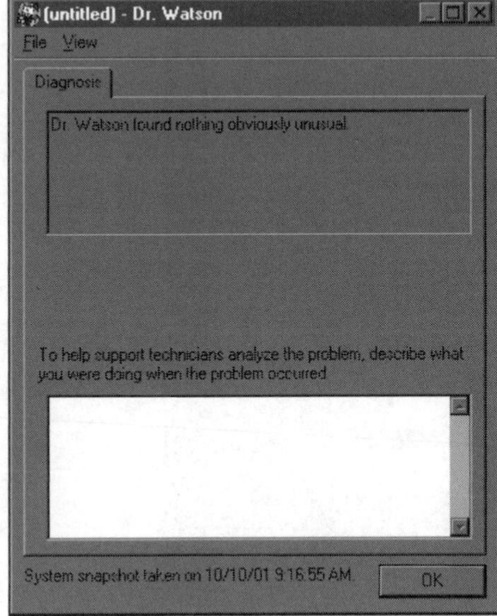

Figure 5-25 The Dr. Watson opening window

Then look at the events logged in the Dr. Watson window under the Diagnosis tab. Use this information to check the Microsoft Web site, *support.microsoft.com*, for the problem and solution. For errors that you cannot reproduce at will, you can load Dr. Watson each time Windows starts by creating a shortcut to Drwatson.exe in the Startup folder.

Windows Help and the Microsoft Web Site

Windows Help might provide useful information when trying to resolve a problem. To access the Troubleshooting tool of Windows Help, click Start, click Help, and then click Troubleshooting. The Help information includes suggestions that can lead you to a solution. For example, in Figure 5-26, the Hardware Troubleshooter suggests that you check to see that the device is not listed twice in Device Manager. If this were the case, you should remove the second occurrence of the device.

Also, the Microsoft Web site, *support.microsoft.com*, has lots of information on troubleshooting. Search on the device, an error message, a Windows utility, a symptom, a software application, an update version number, or key words that lead you to articles about the problem and solutions.

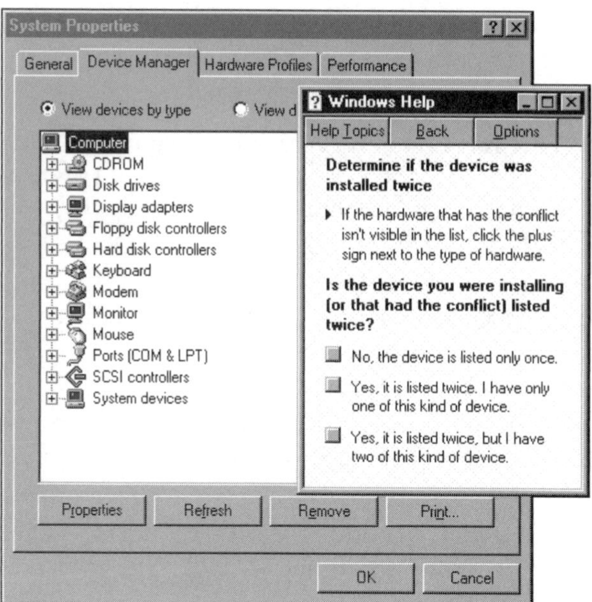

Figure 5-26 Troubleshooter making a suggestion to resolve a hardware conflict

TROUBLESHOOTING HARDWARE IN WINDOWS 9X

A+ OS 3.2

Now that you know about some of the tools used for troubleshooting, you will now learn about the general approaches you should take to troubleshooting problems.

Troubleshooting a PC problem begins with isolating it into one of two categories: problems that prevent the PC from booting and problems that occur after a successful boot. Begin by asking the user questions like these to learn as much as you can:

- When did the problem start?
- Were there any error messages or unusual displays on the screen?
- What programs or software were you using?
- Did you move your computer system recently?
- Has there been a recent thunderstorm or electrical problem?
- Have you made any hardware, software, or configuration changes?
- Has someone else been using your computer recently?
- Can you show me exactly what you did when this problem occurred? (Have the user reproduce the problem and watch each step.)
- Next, ask yourself, "Does the PC boot properly?" If not, then begin troubleshooting the failed boot.

A+ OS 3.2

Here are some general tips for troubleshooting hardware devices:

- Try rebooting your computer. The problem with the device may disappear when Windows redetects it.
- Frequent system lockups might indicate corrupted memory modules. Try using memory testing software to check for intermittent memory errors, which indicate the module needs replacing. An example of memory testing software is DocMemory by CST, Inc. (*www.docmemory.com*).
- For external devices such as monitors, printers, and scanners, try turning on the device before turning on the computer. If you have your computer on and you are rebooting, leave the device on and online.
- If a device doesn't work with one application, try it with another. If the problem only occurs with one application, the problem is probably not with the hardware device but with that application.
- Check Device Manager for errors it reports about the device. If it reports errors, use the Hardware Troubleshooter in Device Manager to help resolve the problem or go to the Microsoft Web site and search on the error message.
- The driver might be corrupted or need updating. Look on the Web for updated device drivers. Search the device manufacturer's Web site or the Microsoft Web site for information about problems with the device and solutions.
- Use Device Manager to uninstall the device and then reinstall it. If you uninstall the device and then reboot, Windows should recognize an uninstalled device and automatically launch the Found New Hardware Wizard. If it doesn't launch, then chances are the device is not working or is not PnP. Special considerations for legacy devices are covered in the next section.
- For PnP devices on expansion cards such as sound cards, modems, and network cards, if you uninstall the device in Device Manager and Windows does not recognize the device when you reboot, the device might not be working. The expansion card needs to be reseated or moved to a different expansion slot. If that doesn't work, the card needs replacing.
- If none of these things work, ask yourself what has changed since the device last worked. For example, maybe you have added another hardware device that is conflicting with the one you are using, or maybe you have added software that conflicts with the software that the problem device is using. Try disabling other devices or try uninstalling software that you suspect is causing the problem. Use Automatic Skip Driver Agent to eliminate other devices that might prevent this one from working.
- The problem might be caused by a lack of resources. If your system is running low on memory or has too many applications open, it might not be able to support a device. A corrupted Windows system file or registry can also cause problems with hardware devices. Try verifying system files or restoring the registry from backup.

- If you still have not resolved the problem, consider it a hardware problem. How to resolve hardware problems is not covered in this book.

Troubleshooting Legacy Devices and Drivers

A+ OS 2.4

A device or expansion card that is not PnP is a legacy device. Legacy devices are not able to have their resources assigned to them by PnP, and legacy drivers are older 16-bit drivers that cannot be loaded into extended memory.

Legacy 16-bit drivers are loaded from entries in Autoexec.bat, Config.sys, or System.ini files. These entries are created by an install or setup program that comes with the device drivers and is executed when you install the device. If you are having a problem with a legacy device, do the following:

- Make every effort to find a protected-mode driver for the device. Check the Microsoft Web site and the Web site of the device manufacturer.
- If you cannot find a protected-mode driver, check the entries in Autoexec.bat, Config.sys, and System.ini for errors. Try running the install program again.
- If you are attempting to load the drive high and the MEM report says it's not loaded high, check for errors in these command lines: Device=HIMEM.SYS, Device=EMM386.EXE, and DOS=UMB in the Config.sys file. Then look for either the Devicehigh= command in Config.sys or the Loadhigh command in Autoexec.bat. See Chapter 3 for more information about using upper memory.
- Two legacy devices might be in conflict. Use the System Configuration Utility to disable one device or the other to verify the conflict. Also, Device Manager sometimes is aware of a legacy conflict and suggests a substitution for system resources. A hardware technician uses DIP switches or jumpers on a legacy device to configure it to use a different set of system resources.

Conflicts with Upper Memory Addresses

A device might be attempting to use upper memory addresses that the OS is using for a UMB. When the OS creates a UMB, it assigns memory addresses that it "thinks" are not being used by devices. However, some devices don't tell the OS what memory addresses they are using until the device is activated after booting. This delay causes the OS to think that the memory addresses assigned to a device are available, and the OS creates and loads a TSR into the UMB. If this conflict happens, the system might hang, the TSR might not work properly, and/or the device might not work properly. Try the following approach:

1. Read the documentation that came with the device to find out which memory addresses it is using. Also, try using MSD to display how memory is being used. Once you know the memory addresses being used, you can change the Emm386.exe command line so that this range of addresses is not used.

A+ OS 2.4

2. Use the Exclude option for the Emm386.exe command line to exclude certain memory addresses. Do not use the last numeral in the hex address in the command line. For example, suppose you read from the documentation that came with the device that it uses addresses CC000 to CFFFF. To exclude these addresses from the addresses used by UMBs, use this command line:

```
DEVICE=EMM386.EXE NOEMS X = CC00 - CFFF
```

Notice in the command line that the last digit of an upper memory address is omitted in the exclude entry. Reboot your computer to activate the change. The memory conflict problem should then be solved.

When reading the documentation, you will find that most addresses are given in hex rather than decimal form. (See Appendix C for an explanation of the hex number system.) Sometimes the memory addresses are written without the last hexadecimal numeral. For example, if the documentation says that the device uses C800 through CFFF, interpret this to mean that the upper memory address range is C8000 through CFFFF. Once you have discovered that the two devices use the same memory addresses, find out if one can use alternate addresses. If so, your problem is solved.

TROUBLESHOOTING APPLICATIONS IN WINDOWS 9X

A+ OS 3.3

Remember that Windows 9x supports 16-bit DOS applications, 16-bit Windows 3.x applications, and newer 32-bit applications. This section looks at problems that can occur with all three types of applications and what to do about them. Problems can be caused by viruses, the application itself, by other applications, by the OS, or by hardware.

Here is the general process to use when troubleshooting problems with applications:

- Address any error messages that appear when using the software.
- If you don't understand the error message, write it down or print it and look it up on the Microsoft support Web site or the Web site of the product manufacturer. Follow the directions given on the Web sites to resolve the problem.
- Read the documentation that came with the application and documents on the manufacturer Web site. Perhaps you are using a function incorrectly.
- A virus might be the source of the problem. Run current antivirus software.
- Consider that data files might be corrupted. Try creating new data files used by the software.
- Consider that the hardware the software is using might have a problem. For the hard drive, run ScanDisk and Defrag and check for free disk space. Delete files in the \Windows\Temp folder. For a device other than the hard drive, try using another application to access the device.
- Try uninstalling and reinstalling the software. Back up the data first.

A+ OS 3.3

- Perhaps the problem is caused by a conflict with other software. Software conflicts are addressed later in this section.
- Launch Dr. Watson and then try to reproduce the error with the application. Look in the Dr. Watson log files for clues and search the Microsoft Web site.
- Perhaps OS files are corrupted that the application depends on. Try restoring Windows system files. Check the Microsoft Web site for Windows 9x service packs that might resolve the problem. Install all Windows service packs. You might have to reinstall Windows.

Problems with a Software Program Itself

A+ OS 3.3

Suppose the computer boots with no errors, and all but one software package on this computer works correctly. When you try to load the problem software package, however, you get an error message and the software terminates. In this situation, you can probably conclude that the software caused the error. Here are some questions you can ask to troubleshoot the problem:

- *Has this software ever worked?* If it has not, then try installing it again. Maybe wrong information was given during the installation. Be sure you check the requirements for the software. Maybe you don't have enough memory or space on your hard drive to create the necessary working files.
- *When was the last time the software worked?* What happened differently then? Did you get an error message that seemed insignificant at the time? What has happened to your computer since the software last worked? Have you added more software or changed the hardware configuration?
- *Could a virus be causing the problem?* Run a current version of antivirus software.

Consider reinstalling the software even if it has worked in the past. Maybe a program file has become corrupted. Before you reinstall it, however, consider whether reinstallation will erase any data that this software has placed on your hard drive. If you're not sure, back up the data. Maybe you can just copy the data to another directory while you reinstall the program. If the installation does erase the data in the original directory, you can copy one file and then another back to the original directory. If you load the program without the data and it works, but the problem recurs when you put the data back in the original directory, then you've found the corrupted data file that caused the problem.

Software often uses configuration files and scripting files that are specific to a particular PC or user. If you reinstall the software, most likely you will lose the configuration information. Either save the configuration files before you begin or print the contents of the files. See the software documentation for the names and location of the configuration files (file extensions of .ini, inf, and .cfg are common). Consider that the problem with the software might be a corrupted configuration file.

A+ OS 3.3

If an application locks up, press Ctrl+Alt+Del and select the program in the Close Program dialog box. Click End Task.

Uninstalling Software

Uninstalling software is clean and easy if the software comes with a well-written uninstall program. Use the Add/Remove Program utility in Control Panel to uninstall it. However, some uninstall programs are not all that great, and sometimes a user will simply delete the folders that contain the software, leaving behind DLL files in the \Windows\System directory, entries in the registry, shortcuts on the desktop, and so on for you, the PC technician, to clean up. Even worse, the user or an uninstall program might delete a DLL file needed by another application or make a wrong deletion in the registry. A **DLL (dynamic-link library)** file is a file with a .dll extension that contains a library of programming routines (or mini programs) to perform common tasks.

When software is installed, it can do these things:

- Create new folders that belong to the application only and store files there
- Store files used only by the application in folders also used by other software. An example is an application's .ini file stored in the \Windows folder.
- Create or overwrite files used by other software. An example is \Windows\system\CTL3D.DLL, a file used by several applications that might be updated by a software installation.
- Make changes to the Windows registry
- Make changes to .ini files that belong to Windows

When software is uninstalled, deleting folders and their contents that belong only to the application is safe. Deleting entire sections in Windows .ini files that are named after the software or a branch in the registry tree that contains the application's name is also safe. But problems might occur when a change is made to a registry entry that other software depends on or when files are deleted that are used by other software.

Figure 5-27 shows the results of such an error. The problem, in this case, can be resolved by reinstalling the OCR software.

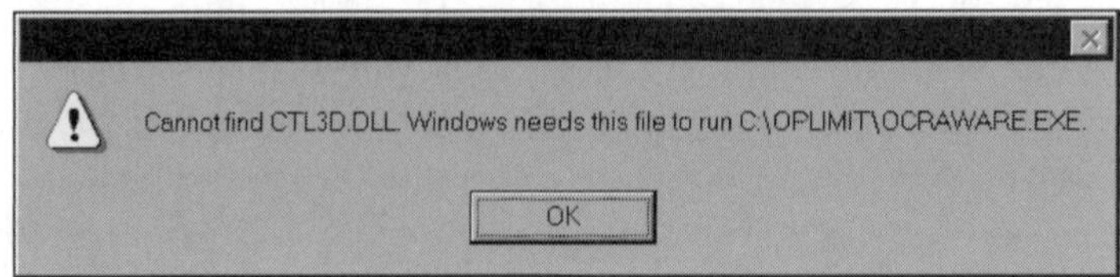

Figure 5-27 The results of an uninstall program deleting a file needed by another application

Sometimes an application is set to automatically launch at startup. After the program is uninstalled, if errors occur when Windows is loaded, look for entries in these places that were not removed by the uninstall program:

- Check the Win.ini file for entries in the Load= and Run= command lines.
- Check the Windows Startup folder for shortcuts.
- Check the registry key HKEY_LOCAL_MACHINE\SOFTWARE\Microsoft\Windows\CurrentVersion\Run.

TROUBLESHOOTING PROBLEMS WITH WINDOWS PERFORMANCE

A+ OS 1.1

If you have just installed Windows and it is performing slowly, check that the minimum hardware requirements have been met. Perhaps you need to upgrade memory or install an additional hard drive. If Windows was once working fine, but is now generally sluggish, applications are slow to load and run, or the system locks up at unexplained times, do the following:

- Check the hard drive. Run ScanDisk and Defrag. Delete unneeded files and empty the Recycle Bin. Generally clean up the hard drive making plenty of room for the swap file and temporary files used by applications.
- Suspect a virus. Run a current version of antivirus software. Clean or delete all files that contain viruses. Restore system files.
- Check for applications loaded at startup that are using up system resources. Close applications not currently in use.
- Look for icons in the **System Tray**, the small area on the right side of the taskbar at the bottom of the screen. These icons represent small applets that are loaded at startup and take up system resources. Keep these icons to a minimum.
- Clean up the registry using the Scanreg /opt command.
- Monitor the system using System Monitor, looking for applications that use an unusual percentage of system resources. Update these applications with the latest versions.
- Remove extraneous software such as fancy screen savers and desktop wallpaper and photos.

CHAPTER SUMMARY

- Windows 9x does not need Autoexec.bat or Config.sys to boot but includes them for backward-compatibility with DOS. If they are present in the root directory, their commands are executed during the boot process, overriding the corresponding settings stored in Io.sys and the registry.
- Initialization files, which have the .ini file extension, are used by Windows or application software to store configuration information needed when Windows or an application is first loaded.

- The five phases of the Windows 9x boot process are BIOS POST and bootstrap, the loading of the OS, the loading of real mode VxDs, protected-mode switchover and PnP configuration, and loading remaining components.
- Applications are loaded at startup by a shortcut in the Startup folder, the name of the program file in the Load= or Run= line in Win.ini, or an entry in the registry.
- When troubleshooting Windows 9x boot problems, first check error messages, then boot in safe mode, then boot to the command prompt using the startup menu, and finally try booting from an emergency startup disk.
- Using some DOS commands on a hard drive that uses Windows 9x as the OS may cause damage to a hard drive's file structure
- To force Windows 9x startup menu to appear, hold down either the Ctrl key or the F8 key during the boot.
- To eliminate Win.ini as the cause of a boot problem, rename it Win.sav and reboot. To eliminate System.ini as the cause of a boot problem, rename it System.sav, make a copy of the System.cb file, and rename that copy System.ini.
- In Logged mode, Windows tracks startup activities and logs them to the Bootlog.txt file.
- You can reach safe mode either from the Windows startup menu or by pressing F5 while Windows is loading.
- When you enter safe mode, Windows 98/Me automatically includes support for networks, but Windows 95 does not.
- Safe mode starts Windows 9x with a minimum default configuration to give you an opportunity to correct an error in the configuration.
- Choosing Command Prompt Only from the startup menu executes the contents of Autoexec.bat and Config.sys but does not start Windows and instead brings you to a DOS prompt. Use the WIN command to load Windows 9x.
- Use the startup disk to recover from a failed boot when you cannot solve the problem using the startup menu, or when you cannot boot from the hard drive. If you do not have a startup disk or if the one you have is corrupted with a virus, use a working computer to create a new one.
- Starting with Windows 9x, the Windows registry takes over the essential functions of .ini files. However, Windows 9x still supports System.ini and Win.ini for backward-compatibility with legacy hardware devices and legacy software applications.
- The registry is contained in two files, System.dat and User.dat. Windows 95 maintains backups of these files, called System.da0 and User.da0, that you can use when troubleshooting. Windows 98/Me keeps compressed backup files of the registry and system files in cabinet files named Ra000.cab, Ra001.cab and so forth.
- Changes in Control Panel, Device Manager, and other locations in Windows 9x can make changes to the registry automatically. The Regedit utility is used to edit the registry manually.
- User profiles allow the system to restore user preferences each time a user logs on to the system. User profiles include hardware and software settings as well as access permissions.
- Logon passwords and screen saver passwords help prevent unauthorized access to a computer.

- The Registry Checker (Scanreg.exe) backs up, verifies, and recovers the registry. It automatically backs up the registry every day and keeps the last five days of backups.
- The System Configuration Utility (Msconfig) allows you to temporarily modify the system configuration to help with troubleshooting. It reduces the startup process to its essentials.
- The Dr. Watson utility (Drwatson.exe) helps you troubleshoot applications by trapping errors in log files and taking a snapshot of the system.
- The System Configuration Editor (Sysedit.exe) is a text editor that is used to edit system files. When you run Sysedit, it automatically opens Protocol.ini, System.ini, Win.ini, Config.sys, and Autoexec.bat.
- The Ios.ini file contains the Windows 9x Safe Driver List. Windows 9x uses this file to determine whether it can safely substitute a protected mode driver for a real-mode one.
- System Monitor allows you to monitor how system resources are being used by applications.
- When troubleshooting hardware devices, try checking whether a problem device works with one application or not another or reversing changes made since the device last worked.
- Use the tools ScanDisk (which checks for physical errors on the drive) and Defrag (which reverses the effects of fragmentation and makes sure files are stored in contiguous clusters) to maintain and troubleshoot your hard drive.
- Clusters to which more than one file points in the FAT are called cross-linked clusters, and clusters to which no file points are called lost clusters. Both can be repaired with ScanDisk.
- Dr. Watson is a Windows utility that can record detailed information about the system, errors that occur, and the programs that caused them.
- Device Manager lists hardware devices installed on a system. For more information about a specific device in Device Manager, click the device and select Properties.
- Legacy devices demand specific resources and cannot have resources assigned by Plug and Play. Windows 9x sometimes has problems with the drivers, memory, and system resources needed for legacy devices.
- Some software problems can be solved by uninstalling and reinstalling the software. Before uninstalling software, save data and configuration files connected to the application. Be very careful when manually uninstalling software not to delete DLL files that are shared with other applications. Problems with DLL files can also be caused when new software is installed and conflicts with existing files.
- To improve performance, close applications you are not currently using and reduce the number of icons in the system tray.

5

Key Terms

chain
comment
cross-linked clusters
defragment
Dr. Watson
DLL (dynamic-link library)
dynamic VxD
fragmentation
group profile
keys
lost allocation units
lost clusters
memory leak
Plug and Play BIOS
Protocol.ini
Static VxD
Sysedit
System.ini
System Tray
user profile
value data
Win.ini

Review Questions

1. Name three security measures used in Windows 9x.
2. What is a comment line? How is a comment line noted within a file?
3. Explain the purpose of the System Configuration Utility. How would you use it in troubleshooting?
4. The Windows registry takes over the functions of ________________ files.
5. Name four configuration files that Windows 9x includes for backward-compatibility with legacy software and hardware.
6. The Windows registry is contained in two files, ________________ and ________________. The Windows 95 backups of these files are called ________________ and ________________.
7. Which version of Windows includes the Registry Checker? How often does this utility back up the registry?
8. Explain the difference between the Regedit and Scanreg utilities.
9. Name the files that Sysedit automatically displays for editing. Give a short description of each.
10. What is the maximum size of .ini files? Can all applications use .ini files of this size?
11. List the five phases of the Windows 9x boot process and give a short description of each.
12. Explain how the file Setver.exe is used in Windows 9x.
13. How is a 16-bit driver loaded into a UMB in Windows 9x?
14. What Msdos.sys entry can be used to backtrack from a Windows 9x installation to the underlying version of DOS? What happens when this entry is set to =0? To =1?
15. How is the boot process for Windows 98 different from the boot process for Windows 95?
16. Give three ways you can cause an application to load at startup. Explain how to keep an application from loading at startup if you don't want it to.

17. Place these tools in the order in which you would use them when troubleshooting the Windows 9x boot process: emergency startup disk, safe mode, error messages, and the command prompt.
18. List the options on the Windows 9x startup menu and give a short description of each. Which option appears for Windows 95 but not for Windows 98, and why? Which option appears for Windows 95/98, but not for Windows Me?
19. Which startup menu options execute Autoexec.bat and Config.sys? Which do not?
20. Explain how to eliminate the following files as the source of a boot problem: Win.ini, System.ini, Config.sys, and Autoexec.bat.
21. Define fragmentation. What problems can it cause? What utility is used to fix it?
22. What is the difference between cross-linked clusters and lost clusters? What utility is used to repair them?
23. Give at least four problems that can occur with legacy hardware installations and explain how they can be solved.
24. What command in Config.sys is used to instruct the OS to load a device driver high? When might it not work, and how would you solve that problem?
25. You have a network card installed on your computer, and it is working properly. When you install a new scanner card, neither the scanner card nor the network card works. What could cause this problem, and how would you fix it?
26. What Windows utility allows you to control which drivers are loaded during Windows startup?
27. Explain the function of DLL files, including what happens if they are deleted or overwritten.
28. ________________ is a Windows utility that can record detailed information about the system, errors that occur, and the programs that caused them in a log file.
29. Which registry key keeps information about Windows performance and Plug and Play?
30. Under what circumstances does Windows read initialization files?
31. Should you ever edit .ini files or the Windows registry? If so, when? If not, why not?
32. What parts of the Windows load does safe mode not execute?
33. Name two ways to end an application that is hung without rebooting the PC.

HANDS-ON PROJECTS

Examining Your PC

1. List all of the .ini files stored in your home or lab computer's Windows directory.
2. Print out your home or lab computer's System.ini file and identify each hardware component that is referenced.
3. On a Windows 9x system, click the **Start** button, then click **Run**: and enter **Edit C:\Msdos.sys**. Then, select **File**, **Print** and print the contents of this file.

4. Follow these steps to list Windows troubleshooting tools:
   a. Click the Windows 9x **Start** button.
   b. Choose the **Settings** option.
   c. Select **Control Panel**.
   d. List at least six Control Panel utilities that can be used to configure hardware and resolve hardware problems.

Using the Windows 9x Startup Menu

As soon as your computer displays the message "Starting Windows 95/98" during the boot process, press the **F8** function key. Select **Logged(\Bootlog.txt)**. After the boot is complete, open the file named **Bootlog.txt** and print out its contents. Shut down Windows, reboot the computer, and then press **F8** again. Select the **Safe Mode** option and note the differences in the screen's appearance. Shut down Windows, reboot the computer, and then press **F8** again. This time choose the **Step-by-step confirmation** option. Write down each command that executes.

Examining the Windows 95 Registry

Examine the Windows 95 registry to determine if your version of Windows 95 includes support for USB devices. The USB support update module is an add-on module for Windows 95 OSR 2.0. For a PC with Windows 95 to have this support, OSR 2 would have been installed and then the USB update added. To determine the installed version of the OS, look in the registry for these two values:

- HKEY_LOCAL_MACHINE\SOFTWARE\Microsoft\Windows\CurrentVersion\Version
- HKEY_LOCAL_MACHINE\SOFTWARE\Microsoft\Windows\CurrentVersion\VersionNumber

OSR2.0 with the USB update has the version and version number:

- Version "Windows 95" and Version Number "4.03.1212" or "4.03.1214."

Print your screen showing the values for your PC. Do you have USB support installed?

Using Windows Utilities and Files

1. Place a shortcut to Task Manager on your desktop. Print a screen shot of the Properties window of the shortcut. Test the shortcut.
2. Cause Sysedit to automatically launch at startup. Print the screen showing how you did this.
3. Edit Msdos.sys so that it automatically displays the startup menu when loading Windows. Print the contents of the file.

Troubleshooting a Boot Problem

Edit the Config.sys file on your PC. If you are using an installation of Windows 9x that does not use a Config.sys file, then create one. Enter a command line in the file that you know will cause an error. Boot the PC. Press **F8** during the boot and walk through the boot process to demonstrate how this procedure can be used to diagnose a problem with startup files.

Correct the command line in Config.sys and boot again, walking through each command in the boot process.

Using the Help Feature in Windows 9x

Research the Help feature in Windows 9x by doing the following:

1. From the **Start** button, choose **Help**, and then select the **Index** tab. Type the first few letters of the words "trails, mouse pointer," and then click the index entry you want. Click **Display**. Print the instructions to change the trails of your mouse pointer.
2. Print the list of steps in Windows Help for making a backup of the \Windows\System folder to disk. List the steps to restore the \Windows\System folder from disk.
3. Print the list of problems that the Windows 98 Display Troubleshooter addresses.

Tools for Troubleshooting a Device Driver

Using Automatic Skip Driver Agent (ASDA), disable one or more devices at startup. Print a screen shot of ASDA showing the devices disabled. Reboot and verify that the devices are not available. Using ASDA, enable the devices, reboot, and verify that the devices are working.

Be sure you have the drivers for the devices available on the hard drive, floppy disk, or CD. Using Device Manager, uninstall a device. Print a screen shot of Device Manager showing that the device is not installed. Reinstall the device and verify that it is working.

CHAPTER

6

UNDERSTANDING AND SUPPORTING WINDOWS NT

In this chapter, you will learn:

- About the new Windows architecture introduced with Windows NT
- How to install and customize Windows NT
- How to use and support Windows NT
- About the Windows NT boot process
- How to troubleshoot Windows NT

This chapter introduces you to Windows NT Workstation, including basic architecture, installation, maintenance, and troubleshooting. There are two versions of Windows NT: Windows NT Workstation and Windows NT Server. You can use Windows NT Workstation on a standalone PC or as the operating system on a workstation connected to a network. Windows NT Server, which is not covered in this book, can be used the same way and can also provide a domain environment on a network. There have been several upgrades of Windows NT; the last is version 4, which is the subject of this chapter.

A Break with the Past: A New Windows Architecture

Recall from Chapter 1 that Windows NT was designed with a different architecture than Windows 9x and provided the Windows OS family's first break with DOS. Windows 2000 and Windows XP, which you will learn about in the next chapters, also use the Windows NT architecture.

Windows NT was designed to be architecturally more like the Unix OS than like Windows 9x and is intended to port to several non-Intel-based platforms; to provide a high level of security, performance, and reliability; and to offer strong networking features. Windows NT also supports **POSIX (Portable OS Interface)**, a set of standards based on Unix and adopted by the United States federal government to better ensure that operating systems and software can port more easily from one platform to another.

To "port" a program or OS means to move it from one computer to another computer.

Windows NT was also designed with a strong emphasis on room for improvements and expandability, primarily accomplished by its modular approach to dealing with applications and hardware. We will begin this section by looking at that approach and then move to a discussion of user and kernel modes in Windows NT.

The Modular Concept of Windows NT

Here's an analogy to help you understand the modular concept of Windows NT. The idea is to isolate one process from another so that a change in one process has the least possible effect on the other processes. Consider the self-serve restaurant in Figure 6-1. In the process illustrated in Figure 6-1, customers arrive for breakfast, walk to the back of the restaurant, tell the cook what they want, wait for him to cook it, take it back to a table, and eat. Customers are responsible for getting their own drinks, silverware, and so forth. If someone in the kitchen moves the silverware or installs a new and different drink-dispensing machine, every customer must learn a new process so the system can continue to work. This process is nonmodular and clearly does not minimize the effect that a change in one part of the process has on other parts of the process.

Now consider Figure 6-2. A counter has been added, and customers are not allowed behind this counter. They come to the counter and tell others in the kitchen what they want to eat, and someone in the kitchen brings the food, drink, and silverware to them at the counter. Things work a little better now. When processes change in the kitchen, only employees who work in the kitchen must be retrained. However, there is still a flaw in the efficiency of this design. Every kitchen worker must know how to cook and make drinks and where the silverware is located. This model introduces some benefits of a modular design but still has flaws.

Figure 6-1 In a nonmodular restaurant model, every customer is responsible for many of the steps in the process

Figure 6-2 In a partially modular restaurant model, customers are isolated from some processes

Figure 6-3 further refines the process, and our restaurant is now a full-service, highly modular affair. Employees are divided into four groups, each with a different function. The first and second groups of employees, the hosts and hostesses, waiters, and waitresses, interact with the customers, greeting them at the door, showing them their seats, taking orders, and serving food. The second group (the waiters and waitresses) also serves as an interface between customers and counter workers. The third group (the counter workers) stands between the kitchen counter and the customer counter, where the drink machines and the silverware are located. The waiters and waitresses pass food requests to the counter workers, who pass the requests to the fourth group, the kitchen workers, who now only prepare the food. When the food is passed back to the counter workers, these workers gather up drinks, silverware, and food and pass them on to the waiters and waitresses, who serve the customers. This model uses a more modular arrangement that provides the benefits of separating processes from each other, even though the overhead (the additional resources needed to implement the new model) is higher than in the other models.

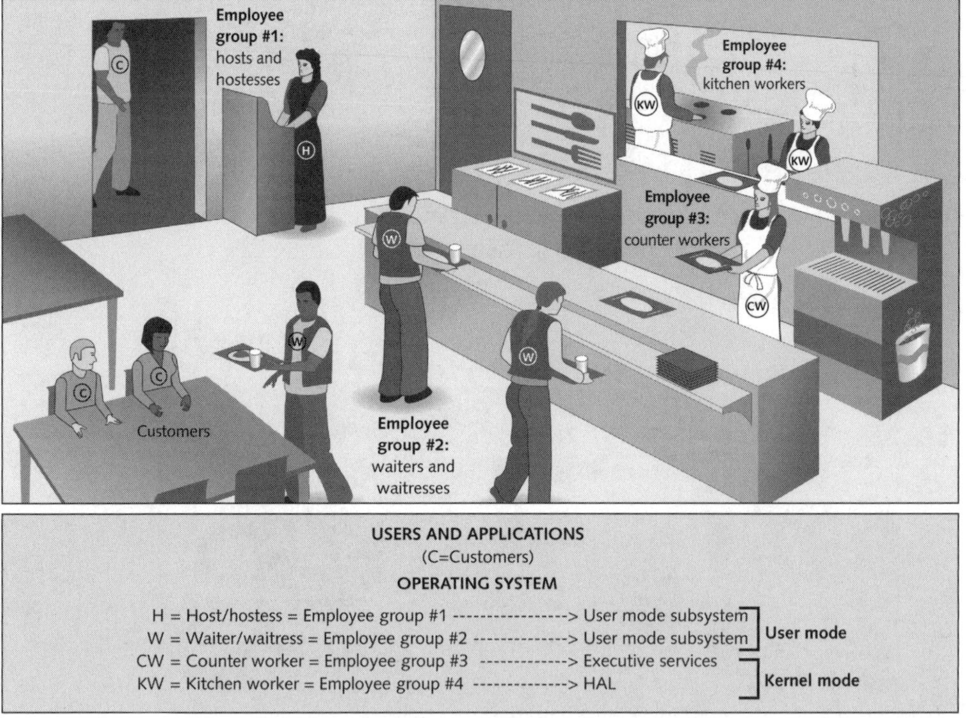

Figure 6-3 In a highly modular restaurant model, employees are grouped by function, and customers interact only with one group of employees; employee groups are analogous to different parts of the Windows NT operating system

In this model, if the drink machine is upgraded, only the counter workers must be retrained. If the oven or stove in the kitchen is replaced with an altogether new electronic unit, only the kitchen workers change their methods. The counter workers are unaffected. The waiters and waitresses don't need to know how to communicate with the cook, but can focus on customer service. The customer is isolated from the entire process. In comparing Figures 6-1 and 6-3, on first appearance it looks as though the process has been complicated. There are more workers, and customers now have to wait to be seated. In fact, a new layer of complexity has been added, and two counters are required. However, it turns out that the advantages of the new system outweigh its disadvantages and overhead. Not only can equipment be easily upgraded without having to retrain so many people or reorient customers to the new procedures, but the integrity of the operation is enhanced: because the processes have been separated from each other, they can now be more easily controlled. Standards and procedures can be more easily applied to each segment of the process because fewer people are involved at each step in the operation, which reduces confusion and improves the overall efficiency of the operation. In summary, the three main reasons to use the highly modular model rather than the nonmodular model are:

- To make upgrades of equipment easier (some employees and all customers are unaffected)
- To increase the overall efficiency of the operation (each part of the process involves fewer people than in the other models)
- To better ensure the integrity of processes (standards are more easily enforced)

The process of running the restaurant can be viewed as analogous to the way operating systems run a computer: the modular approach is analogous to the Windows NT OS, and the nonmodular approaches are analogous to earlier OSs. Customers can be viewed as a combination of users and applications software; employees can be viewed as the OS; the stove, drink machine, silverware stand, and so on, can be viewed as the hardware; and the cook can be viewed as those parts of the OS that relate directly to hardware, system BIOS, and device drivers. The process illustrated in Figure 6-1 is most analogous to DOS, in which applications were allowed "behind the counter" to interact directly with BIOS and device drivers, and even to perform some of their own operations with hardware, rather than necessarily turning to the OS to perform hardware operations. For example, in DOS, an application program written to address specific hardware configurations might depend on video BIOS always being found at certain memory addresses, and the program could access that BIOS directly.

The process illustrated in Figure 6-2 is most analogous to a model of the Windows 9x OS, because the customers (the applications) are isolated from some of the interaction with the equipment (hardware), but not all. Notice, for instance, that the silverware stand is still available for customer use; similarly, in Windows 9x, a 16-bit program can interact directly with video memory and other resources.

The process illustrated in Figure 6-3 is most analogous to the Windows NT OS, which includes an additional layer between the applications (customers) and hardware (the restaurant equipment); applications (customers) are almost completely isolated from interaction with hardware (restaurant equipment). The access that programs have to system resources is controlled through the two Windows NT modes: user mode and kernel mode.

Windows NT Modes

Windows NT operates in two modes, user mode and kernel mode, which each take advantage of different CPU functions and abilities (see Figure 6-4). **User mode** is a non-privileged processor mode in which programs have only limited access to system information and can access hardware only through other OS services. Several **subsystems** or OS modules described in more detail below use it. **Kernel mode** is a privileged processor mode in which programs have extensive access to system information and hardware. Kernel mode is used by two main components: the HAL (hardware abstraction layer), which was introduced in Chapter 1, and a group of components collectively called **executive services**, which interfaces between the subsystems in user mode and the HAL. Executive services components manage hardware resources by way of the HAL and device drivers. Applications in user mode have no access to hardware resources. In kernel mode, executive services have limited access to hardware resources, but the HAL primarily interacts with hardware.

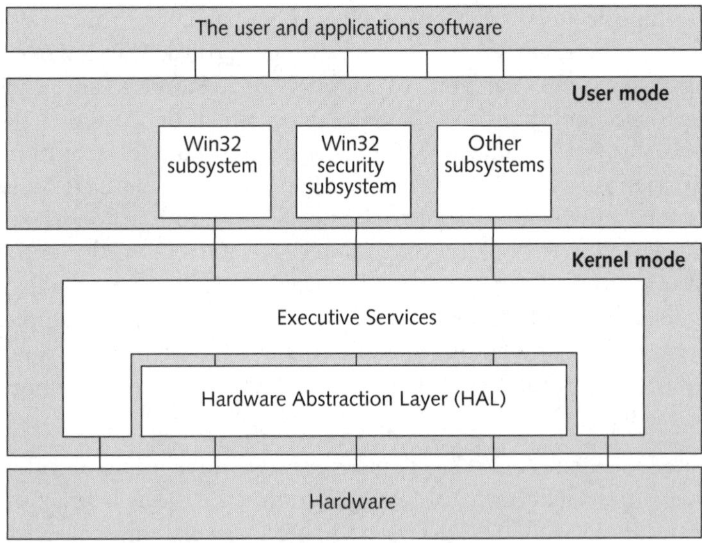

Figure 6-4 User mode and kernel mode in Windows NT and how they relate to users, application software, and hardware

Memory management is an excellent example of how the user mode subsystems, executive services, and the HAL cooperate in Windows NT. Windows NT provides memory addresses to an application by way of the Win32 user mode subsystem. When an application requests this subsystem to write data to some of these assigned addresses, the subsystem turns to executive services. The component within executive services that manages memory, the virtual memory manager, is responsible for coordinating the interface between the user subsystem and the HAL. The virtual memory manager presents the request to the HAL, which is responsible for the actual writing of the data to memory and responds to the memory manager when finished. The memory manager then reports back to the user subsystem, which, in turn, reports back to the application. You will learn more about memory management under Windows NT later in the chapter.

Windows NT was designed to easily port to different hardware platforms. Because only the components operating in kernel mode actually interact with hardware, they are the only parts that need to be changed when Windows NT moves from one hardware platform to another. For instance, if a major piece of hardware changes, the HAL must change. Minor hardware changes might cause changes in one or more executive services components. When hardware changes are made, the subsystems in user mode require little or no change. When hardware improves, making new resources available to software, the software applications are not responsible for knowing how to interface with the hardware resources.

Limiting access to hardware mainly to the HAL increases OS integrity because more control is possible. With this isolation, an application cannot cause a system to hang by making illegal demands on hardware. Overall performance is increased because the HAL and executive services can operate independently of the slower, less efficient applications using them.

On the other hand, Windows NT requires much more robust hardware and can support more powerful applications than Windows 9x or DOS. The increased overhead of this OS only benefits you when hardware and applications software are hefty enough to take advantage of the more powerful OS.

User Mode

The purpose of the subsystems in user mode is to interface with the user and with applications; the tools you view when running Windows NT are primarily running in user mode. In Figure 6-4, note the Win32 subsystem, which is probably the most important user mode subsystem because it manages all 32-bit programs and provides an environment for these programs, including the user interface (such as the one for Explorer). (Remember from earlier chapters that 32-bit programs are programs written for protected mode using 32-bit code.) The Win32 security subsystem provides logon to the system and other security functions, including privileges for file access. Other subsystems might or might not be running while the Win32 subsystem and security subsystem are running.

All applications relate to Windows NT by way of the Win32 subsystem, either directly or indirectly. Figure 6-5 shows how various programs that run under Windows NT interact with subsystems. For instance, each DOS application resides in its own NTVDM. An **NTVDM (NT virtual DOS machine)** is a carefully controlled environment that Windows NT provides in which a DOS application can only interface with one subsystem and cannot relate to anything outside the system. All the 16-bit Windows 3.x applications reside in a **Win16 on Win32 (WOW)** environment. Within the WOW, these 16-bit applications can communicate with one another, and they can communicate with the WOW, but that's as far as their world goes. Figure 6-5 shows three 16-bit Windows 3.x applications residing in a WOW that resides in one NTVDM. Because each DOS application expects to run as the only application on a PC, each has its own NTVDM.

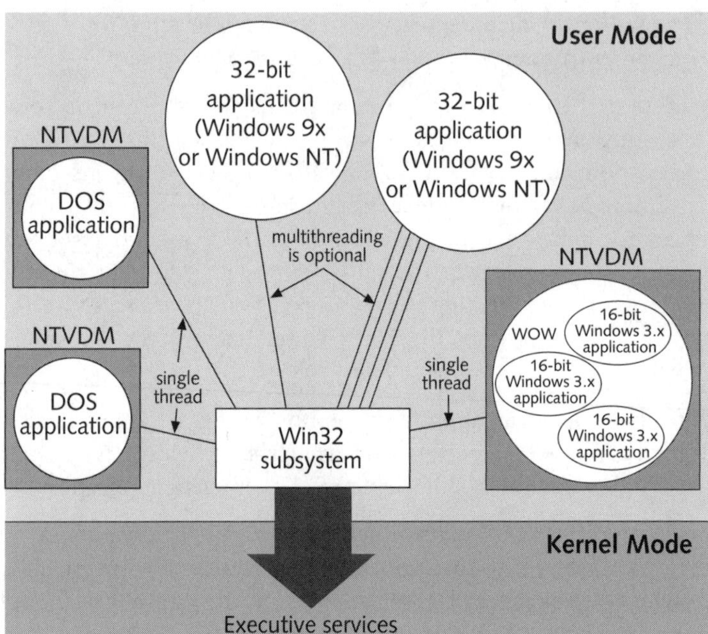

Figure 6-5 Environment subsystems in Windows NT user mode include NTVDMs for DOS and Windows 3.x applications and optional multithreading for 32-bit applications

You can see in Figure 6-5 that 32-bit applications do not require an NTVDM and can relate to the Win32 subsystem directly, because they are written to run in protected mode. The figure shows that 32-bit applications can also use a single line of communication (called single-threading) with the Win32 subsystem or can use multiple lines for interfacing (called **multithreading**) with the Win32 subsystem, depending upon what the process requests. A **thread** is a single task that the process requests from the kernel, such as the task of printing a file. A **process** is a program or group of programs that is running, together with the system resources assigned to it, such as memory addresses, environmental variables, and other resources. Sometimes a process is called an instance, such as when you say, "Open two instances of Internet Explorer." Technically, you are saying to open two Internet Explorer processes. An example of multithreading is Microsoft Word requesting that the subsystem read a large file from the hard drive while performing a print job at the same time. Single-threading happens when the application does not expect both processes to be performed at the same time but simply passes one request followed by another.

Kernel Mode

Remember that the kernel mode of Windows NT is the mode used by executive services and the HAL, which interface more directly with the hardware than do the subsystems operating in user mode. Figure 6-6 expands the information from Figure 6-4 to show several of executive services components operating in kernel mode. Most interaction with the hardware is done by executive services passing the request to the HAL. However, from the diagram, you see that executive services include device drivers, which have direct access to the hardware.

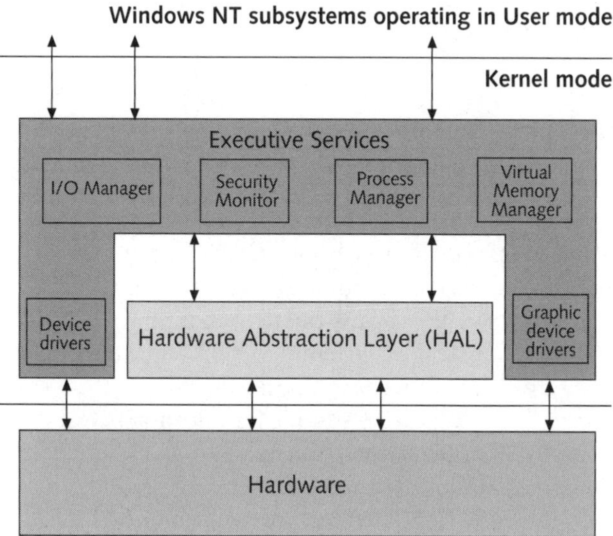

Figure 6-6 Components in the Windows NT kernel mode relate to subsystems in user mode and relate to hardware

Only kernel mode components can access hardware. However, in DOS, applications can access hardware resources directly, or they can use an API call to ask DOS to perform the task. In Windows NT, if a DOS application tried to directly access the printer port LPT1, Windows NT would shut down the DOS application. But if the DOS application tried to access the printer by passing a DOS API call to the Windows NT NTVDM, it would be allowed to proceed.

INSTALLING WINDOWS NT

Because Windows NT differs so fundamentally from Windows 9x, there is no automatic upgrade path from Windows 9x to Windows NT. When you change a PC from Windows 9x to Windows NT, you can install Windows NT in a different folder. No system settings in Windows 9x will be transferred to Windows NT. After Windows NT is installed, you must reinstall each application on the PC under Windows NT. Windows NT can be present as the only OS on a PC, or it can be installed on the same PC as Windows 9x. (How to set up this "dual boot" is coming up.)

The main reason that Windows 9x cannot be easily upgraded to Windows NT is that their registries are not compatible, which makes it difficult to transfer information from one to the other. (Remember that a registry is a database containing all configuration information for the OS. The Windows NT registry is not covered in detail in this chapter; you will learn more about it in Chapter 8.) Again, realize that Windows NT is not the next stepping stone beyond Windows 9x but is instead a new road altogether.

Before covering the installation process in detail, we'll look at two issues you need to consider before installing Windows NT: how to partition your hard drive and which file system to use.

Hard Drive Partitions

A+ OS 1.4 2.1

Windows NT assigns two different functions to hard drive partitions holding the OS (see Figure 6-7). The **system partition**, normally drive C, is the active partition of the hard drive. This is the partition that contains the OS boot record. Remember that the MBR looks to this OS boot record for the boot program as the first step in turning the PC over to an OS. The other partition, called the **boot partition**, is the partition where the Windows NT operating system is stored. The system partition and the boot partition can be the same partition, or they can be separate partitions. Windows NT is designed to use two partitions in this way so that the Windows system files do not have to be stored on the same partition that is used to boot the OS. Both partitions can be formatted with either FAT16 or NTFS. However, Windows 9x and DOS cannot read files formatted with NTFS. If you want these OSs to access this partition, you must use the FAT16 file system.

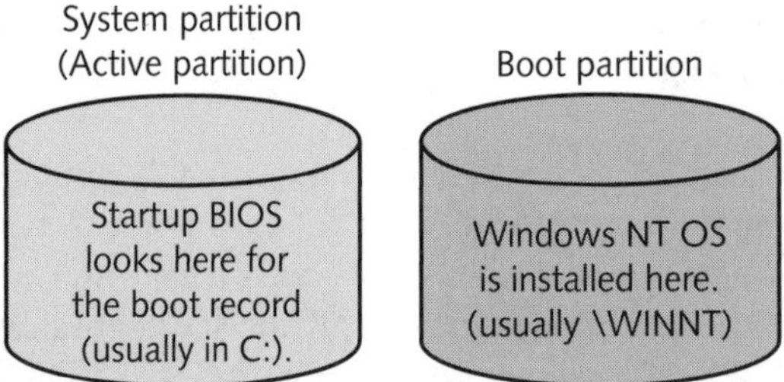

Figure 6-7 Two types of Windows NT/2000/XP hard drive partitions

Don't be confused by the terminology here. It is really true that, according to Windows NT terminology, the Windows NT OS is on the boot partition, and the boot record is on the system partition, even though that might sound backward. The PC boots from the system partition and loads the Windows NT operating system from the boot partition.

Recall that Windows 9x, using Fdisk, can create two partitions, a primary partition and an extended partition. The primary partition contains drive C, and the extended partition can contain several volumes or logical drives. Also recall that each FAT16 volume can be no larger than 2 GB. Using Windows NT, you can have up to four partitions. The first partition must be a primary partition and, if it is the boot device, can have only a single drive C. There can be up to four primary partitions on the drive, each containing a single logical drive. However, one of the four partitions can be an extended partition, which means it can have several volumes or logical drives. Because of the way Windows NT uses the FAT, each FAT16 volume can be up to 4 GB.

A Choice of File Systems

A+ OS 1.4 2.1

Windows NT can work with two types of file systems: the FAT16 file system, which is used by Windows 9x and its predecessors, and the Windows NT file system (NTFS), which does not work with Windows 9x or DOS. Windows NT does not support FAT32. (Recall that FAT32 was introduced by Windows 95 OSR2 and uses 32 bits for each FAT entry.) Windows NT also does not support the High Performance File System (HPFS) used by OS/2. If a hard drive is using HPFS, use the Windows NT Convert.exe utility to convert an HPFS partition to an NTFS partition. This program can also convert a FAT16 partition to NTFS.

Even though Windows NT 4.0 does not support FAT32, you can use third-party utility software packages, such as FAT32 for Windows NT 4.0 by Winternals (*www.winternals.com*) to manage the interface, making it possible for Windows NT to read from and write to FAT32.

The FAT16 file system uses three components to manage data on a logical drive: the FAT, directories, and data files. In contrast, the NTFS file system uses a database called the **master file table (MFT)** as its core component. The MFT tracks the contents of a logical drive using one or more rows in the table for each file or directory on the drive. As shown in Figure 6-8, the MFT contains in one record, or row, information about each file, including header information (abbreviated H in Microsoft documentation), standard information (SI) about the file (including date and time), filename (FN), security information about the file, called the security descriptor (SD), and data about the location of the file. Entries in the MFT are ordered alphabetically by filename to speed up a search for a file listed in the table. When a drive is formatted for NTFS, each cluster on the hard drive can range from 512 bytes on smaller disks to 4K on larger disks. Clusters are numbered sequentially by logical cluster numbers (LCN) from the beginning to the end of the disk.

Referring again to Figure 6-8, note that the data area in the MFT record is 2K for small hard drives but can be larger for larger hard drives. For small files, if the data can fit into the 2K area, the file, including its data, is fully contained within the MFT. For small files, all the cluster information for a file can fit into this one data area, including all the cluster numbers for the file. Each cluster number is stored in a 64-bit entry, compared to either 16 bits for FAT16 or 32 bits for FAT32.

If the file is moderately large and the data does not fit into the MFT, the data area in the MFT becomes an extended attribute (EA) of the file, which points to the location of the data. The data itself is moved outside the table to clusters called runs. The record in the MFT for this moderately large file contains pointers to these runs. Each data run, or cluster, assigned to the file is assigned a 64-bit virtual cluster number (VCN). The MFT maps the VCNs for the file onto the LCNs for the drive. This mapping is stored in the area of the MFT record that would have contained the data if the file had been small enough. If the file is so large that the pointers to all the VCNs cannot be contained in one MFT record, then additional MFT records are used. The first MFT record is called the base file record and holds the location of the other MFT records for this file.

A+ OS 1.4 2.1

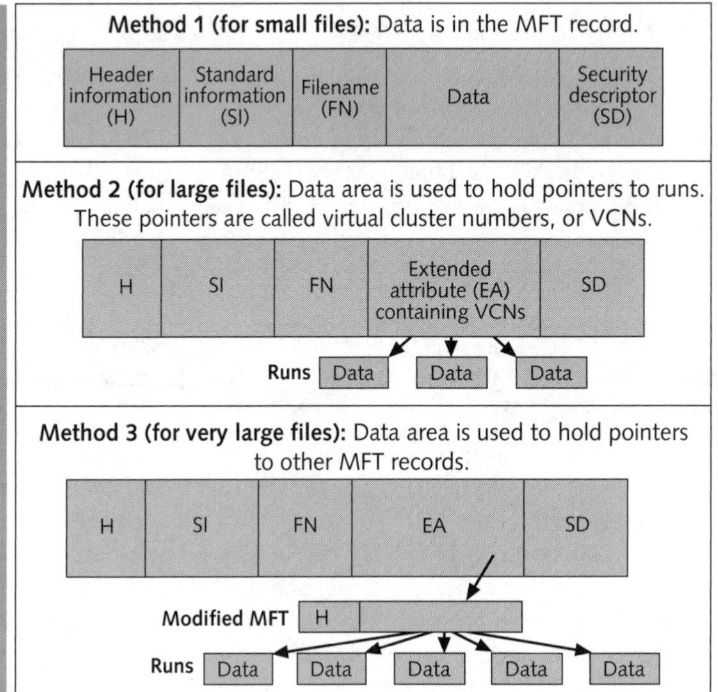

Figure 6-8 The Windows NT file system Master File Table uses three methods to store files, depending on the file size

Advantages of NTFS and FAT16

When choosing between the NTFS file system and the FAT16 file system, consider the advantages that NTFS offers over the FAT:

- NTFS is a recoverable file system. NTFS retains copies of its critical file system data and automatically recovers a failed file system, using this information the first time the disk is accessed after a file system failure.
- NTFS offers increased security over the FAT file system. Security is provided for each file, and auditing information about access to files is more complete.
- NTFS provides added security in the event you boot from floppy disks:
  - If the file system for the active partition of a PC is FAT, you can boot from a DOS or Windows 9x boot disk and bypass the Windows NT security logon. When you use NTFS, you can boot from a DOS or Windows 9x boot disk to an A:\> prompt, but you cannot access the hard drive. You can still boot the PC from Windows NT boot disks, but the Windows NT logon is required.
  - If you boot a PC using a DOS or Windows 9x boot disk, you will be able to access the hard drive of a Windows NT system that is using the FAT file system, but you cannot access an NTFS file system.

A+ OS 1.4 2.1

- If you boot a PC using the three Windows NT startup disks, you will only be able to access the NTFS file system if you provide an administrator account and password. Every Windows NT workstation has an **administrator account** by default. An administrator has rights and permissions to all computer software and hardware resources and is responsible for setting up other user accounts and assigning privileges to them.

- NTFS supports mirroring drives, meaning that two copies of data can be kept on two different drives to protect against permanent data loss in case of a hard drive crash. This feature makes the NTFS an important alternative for file servers.
- NTFS uses smaller cluster sizes than does FAT16, making more efficient use of hard drive space when small files are stored.
- NTFS supports large-volume drives. NTFS uses 64-bit cluster numbers, whereas FAT16 uses 16-bit cluster numbers. Because the number of bits assigned to hold each cluster number is so large, the cluster number itself can be a large number, and the table can accommodate very large drives with many clusters. Overall, NTFS is a more effective file system for drives over 1 GB and offers more robust drive compression, allowing compression of individual folders and files.

The advantages of the FAT file system over NTFS include:

- The FAT16 file system has less overhead than the NTFS file system and, therefore, works best for hard drives that are less than 500 MB.
- The FAT file system is compatible with Windows 9x and DOS operating systems. If you plan to use either DOS or Windows 9x on the same hard drive as Windows NT, use the FAT file system so that DOS and Windows 9x can access files used by Windows NT.
- In the event of a serious problem with Windows NT, if you are using FAT16 on the active partition of the drive, you can boot the PC from a DOS or Windows 9x startup disk, and gain access to the drive.

You can choose to have Windows NT use NTFS by directing it to convert the hard drive from FAT16 to NTFS or by having Windows NT partition a drive so that one partition of the drive uses the FAT format and the other uses the NTFS format. Windows NT allows you to format logical drives with either FAT16 or NTFS on the same extended partition.

Preparing to Install Windows NT

A+ OS 1.4 2.1

Before beginning the installation of Windows NT or upgrading from DOS or Windows 9x to Windows NT, you need to prepare for the installation. To determine if your hardware can support Windows NT, begin by searching the HCL. If a device on your system is not on the HCL, contact the manufacturer for a Windows NT driver. If no driver exists, you cannot use the device with Windows NT.

Be sure you have enough hard drive space. Windows NT requires about 120 MB of drive space to install itself, and more if the cluster size is large. In addition, a floppy drive and CD-ROM drive are required. For computers without a CD-ROM drive, Windows NT can be installed from a server over a network.

A+ OS 2.1

If you are using an Intel-based computer, you can use the **NT Hardware Qualifier (NTHQ)** program found on the Windows NT installation CD-ROM to determine if your system can handle Windows NT. To use Qualifier, boot from a disk onto which you have copied the program, and the utility will examine your system to determine if all hardware present qualifies for NT. Use the following directions to create and use the NT Hardware Qualifier:

Create the NTHQ bootable disk using any computer that has DOS or Windows 9x installed:

1. Insert a bootable disk in drive A.
2. To have Windows NT create the Hardware Qualifier disk, from a DOS prompt or from the Run dialog box of Windows 9x, enter this command substituting the drive letter of your CD-ROM drive:

   D:\Support\Hqtool\MakeDisk.bat

3. Using the computer that you want to install Windows NT, boot from the newly created disk. The following message will be displayed on your screen:

   `Preparing NTHQ`

   You can watch as NT tells you it is creating a RAM drive and copying files to it. Next a screen appears informing you that the log file the utility generates will take several minutes and will be written to the disk and saved as Nthq.txt.

4. Print the log file.

Figure 6-9 contains a portion of a sample report from the NTHQ. Note that the two devices listed at the top were not found in the NTHQ. To determine if these devices will work with Windows NT, check the latest HCL on the Microsoft Web site (*www.microsoft.com/hwtest*) or contact the manufacturer of each device.

```
Adapter Description: CIRRUS LOGIN PnP V34 MODEM
Adapter Device ID: CIR1000
Listed in Hardware Compatibility List: Not found-check the latest HCL

Adapter Description: OPL3-SAX Sound Board
Adapter Device ID: YMH0024
Listed in Hardware Compatibility List: Not found-check the latest HCL

Adapter Description: S3 Inc. 801/928/964
Listed in Hardware Compatibility List: Yes

Adapter Description: Adaptec AHA-1522
Listed in Hardware Compatibility List: Yes

Adapter Description: Sound Blaster Adapter or compatibles
Listed in Hardware Compatibility List: Yes

Adapter Description: Joystick/game port
Listed in Hardware Compatibility List: Yes
```

Figure 6-9 Sample log file from the NT Hardware Qualifier

A+ OS 2.1 The next sections give step-by-step instructions to install Windows NT as the only OS on a system, and as the second OS on a system that already has Windows 9x, creating a dual boot.

Installing Windows NT as the Only OS

A+ OS 2.1 Windows NT comes with three disks that contain a simplified version of Windows NT, enough to boot a PC. If the hard drive does not contain an OS, the installation begins by booting from these three disks. After Windows NT has loaded these three disks, it can access the CD-ROM drive, and installation continues from the CD. The program on the CD executed at that point is Winnt.exe, which is a 16-bit program. A faster version of Winnt.exe on the CD-ROM named Winnt32.exe, a 32-bit program, can, in certain situations, be used instead of Winnt.exe. Winnt32.exe can be run only after Windows NT has already been installed the first time; it is used to upgrade from an older version of NT to a new version or to reinstall a corrupted version and must be executed from within Windows.

The three startup disks can later be used to boot the PC if files on the hard drive become corrupted. You can also create a new set of bootable disks.

Follow these steps to install Windows NT as the only OS:

1. Insert the Windows NT CD in the CD-ROM drive, insert setup disk 1 into the floppy drive, and boot the PC. You will be asked to insert disk 2.
2. You see a *Welcome to Setup* message. You will be asked to insert disk 3. Press **Enter** to continue. Setup lists the mass storage devices it detected. Press **Enter** to continue.
3. The licensing agreement appears. Scroll to the bottom of the document and press **F8** to indicate your agreement and continue.
4. Setup lists hardware and software components it detected. Press **Enter** to continue.
5. Setup lists existing partitions and space available for creating new partitions. For example, if part of the drive has previously been formatted as drive C with 2047 MB of storage and the other part is still unpartitioned, the following information appears:

   ```
   2442 MB Disk 0 at Id 0 on bus 0 on atapi

   C: FAT 2047 MB

   Unpartitioned space 394 MB
   ```

   Setup is listing the spaces on the hard drive where it can install the OS, and asking you to make the choice. For this example, highlight **Unpartitioned Space**, and then press **C** to create a new partition.
6. Setup asks you for the size of the partition, creates it, informs you it will next format the partition, and prompts you to select a file system for the partition. It then lists the following file systems:

   ```
   Format the partition using the FAT file system
   Format the partition using the NTFS file system
   ```

   Select a file system and press **Enter**.

A+ OS 2.1

7. After the formatting is completed, Setup asks for this information:

```
Setup installs Windows NT files onto your hard disk.
Choose the location where you want those files to be
installed: \WINNT
```

The default choice is to install Windows NT in the \Winnt directory. Accept the default by pressing **Enter**.

8. Setup now asks for permission to examine the hard drive for corruption. You can either allow it by pressing **Enter** or skip this examination by pressing **Esc**.

9. Setup tells you that it is copying files to the hard drive. After the copying is complete, the following message appears:

```
Press ENTER to restart your computer.
```

When your computer restarts, Setup will continue.

10. Up to this point in the installation, all screens appeared to be DOS-like with little graphic user interface and no use of the mouse. When the PC reboots, you are using a true Windows GUI. The opening screen lists the three steps that Windows NT performs to complete the installation:

    1) Gathering information about your computer

    2) Installing Windows NT networking

    3) Finishing Setup

    The first item in the list is highlighted. Using the mouse, click **Next** to continue the installation.

11. Setup offers four options: Typical, Portable, Compact, and Custom. Select **Typical** and then click **Next** to continue.

12. Setup requests a name and the name of your organization. Provide them.

13. You are then asked to enter the CD key that identifies the copy of Windows NT being installed. Provide that.

14. Setup then requests a computer name. You are told that the name must be 15 characters or less and must be unique for your network. This computer name will later be used to identify this computer on a network. Enter the name, and then click **Next**.

15. Setup asks for the password for the administrator account. Administrators have full privileges on the workstation. Users have fewer privileges, depending on what the administrator assigns them. If other users who will not have administrator privileges will be using this workstation, or if you are concerned about security at this PC, enter a password, then enter it again to confirm it. If you are the sole user of this PC and security is not an issue, you do not need to enter a password. Just press **Enter**.

A+ OS 2.1

16. Setup gives you the option to create an Emergency Repair Disk (ERD, discussed later in the chapter). Select **Yes** to create the Emergency Repair Disk, and then click **Next** to continue.
17. Setup gives you the option to choose what components to install. Since you can later easily install components not installed during the installation, choose **Install the most common components**.
18. Setup returns to the opening Windows NT setup screen (see Step 11) and continues with Installing Windows NT networking. Click **Next** to continue.
19. The choices presented are:

    Do not connect this computer to a network at this time
    This computer will participate on a network:
      Wired to the network:
        Your computer is connected to the network by an ISDN Adapter or Network Adapter.
      Remote access to the network:
        Your computer uses a modem to remotely connect to the network.

    For this example, choose **Do not connect the computer to a network at this time**, and then click **Next** to continue.
20. Setup returns to the opening screen (see Step 11). Click **Finish** to finish Setup. You are asked to select the date and time from the Date/Time Properties sheet. Click **Close**.
21. Setup automatically detects the correct display adapter. You can change any options on the Display Properties sheet and then click **OK**.
22. Setup requests that you insert a blank disk labeled Emergency Repair Disk. Insert a blank disk, and then click **OK**. Setup creates the repair disk.
23. You are instructed to remove the CD and disk from the drives and restart the PC. The installation is done.

If you are having problems with Windows NT detecting your hard drive, the problem might be out-of-date system BIOS. Try flashing BIOS and then attempting the Windows NT installation again.

Installing Windows NT as the Second OS on the Hard Drive

A+ OS 2.1

Installing Windows NT on a hard drive to create a dual boot begins differently, but is otherwise the same as installing Windows NT as the only OS. The Windows NT installation files are stored in the \I386 directory on the CD-ROM drive. If hard drive space is plentiful, you can copy the contents of the \I386 directory and its subdirectories to the hard drive and perform the installation from there, which is faster because access to the hard drive is faster than access to the CD-ROM drive. If the computer is connected to a

A+ OS 2.1

network, the contents of the \I386 directory can be copied to a network server, and the Winnt.exe program can be executed from the server to install Windows NT on the PC, if certain conditions exist. (Installations from servers are not covered in this chapter.)

Remember that Windows NT can coexist on the same PC with either Windows 9x or DOS. The ability to boot from either Windows NT or another OS, such as Windows 9x or DOS, is called a **dual boot**. In a dual boot arrangement, the system partition must be FAT rather than NTFS, so that the non-NT OS (Windows 9x or DOS) can read it. When Windows 9x is used for a dual boot, the Windows 9x Msdos.sys file has the multiboot configuration entry, BootMulti=1. The main reason for having a dual boot is to accommodate legacy hardware or software that will not work under Windows NT.

Remember that Windows NT cannot access a FAT32 drive without third-party software. If you are using Windows 98 with FAT32 and want to create a dual boot with Windows NT, first convert to FAT16 or use third-party software to manage the Windows NT and FAT32 interface. Otherwise, Windows NT will not be able to access data on the FAT32 volume. To convert from FAT32 to FAT16, use a third-party utility such as Partition Magic.

Windows NT resides on the boot partition, which can also be formatted for the FAT16 file system and can share the same partition with the other OS or reside on a second partition, such as drive D. You can format this second partition with either FAT or NTFS. If drive D is NTFS, Windows 9x cannot read any data stored on that drive. If drive D is a FAT16 partition, either OS can read data from either drive.

After both operating systems are installed, a **boot loader menu** appears, asking which OS to boot. The disadvantages of a dual boot are that application software cannot be shared between the two OSs; you must install applications in each OS. Also, you must reboot the PC to move from one OS to the other.

To install Windows NT with Windows 9x loaded, insert the Windows NT installation CD in the drive. If the PC autodetects the CD, you see the Windows NT opening screen. Click Windows NT Setup. If the PC does not autodetect the CD, click Start, Run and enter this command in the Run dialog box substituting the drive letter of your CD-ROM drive for D: D:\I386\Winnt.exe. If you want a dual boot, do not choose to store Windows NT in the C:\Windows folder because this will overwrite Windows 9x.

After the installation is complete, when the PC reboots, it detects two OSs, and shows a startup menu (called the boot loader menu), giving you the choice between Windows NT Workstation Version 4.0 and Microsoft Windows (Windows 95 or 98). Select Windows NT Workstation version 4.0, which then loads.

After a Windows NT installation is done, access the Internet and download and install any updates, service packs, and patches from the Microsoft Web site.

Supporting Windows NT

Recall that Windows NT manages devices, programs, and system resources more efficiently than Windows 9x in many cases and that Windows NT was designed to work with networks and to provide greater security. This section discusses supporting Windows NT, including information on its architecture, how to install hardware and software, and how to handle networking with Windows NT. You will also learn about supporting legacy applications and constructing user profiles for security.

Memory in Windows NT

A+ OS 1.1 2.5

As you learned in Chapter 3, managing memory under DOS and Windows 9x can be complicated because of having to deal with conventional, upper, and extended memory for backward-compatibility. Windows NT eliminates that complexity, because memory is simply memory; in other words, memory addresses are all used the same way. It also loses some backward-compatibility.

The Windows NT memory management model is illustrated in Figure 6-10, which shows the object-oriented approach to memory management. The application or device driver only says, "I want memory." It can not say to Windows NT which physical memory or which memory addresses it wants, or even the range of addresses that it wants to fall within. Windows NT uses its virtual memory manager to interface between the application or driver and the physical and virtual memory that it controls. Memory is allocated in 4K segments called **pages**. Applications and devices that are written for Windows NT only know how many pages they have. The virtual memory manager takes care of the rest. It is free to store these pages in RAM or on the hard drive in the swap file named **Pagefile.sys** (see Figure 6-10).

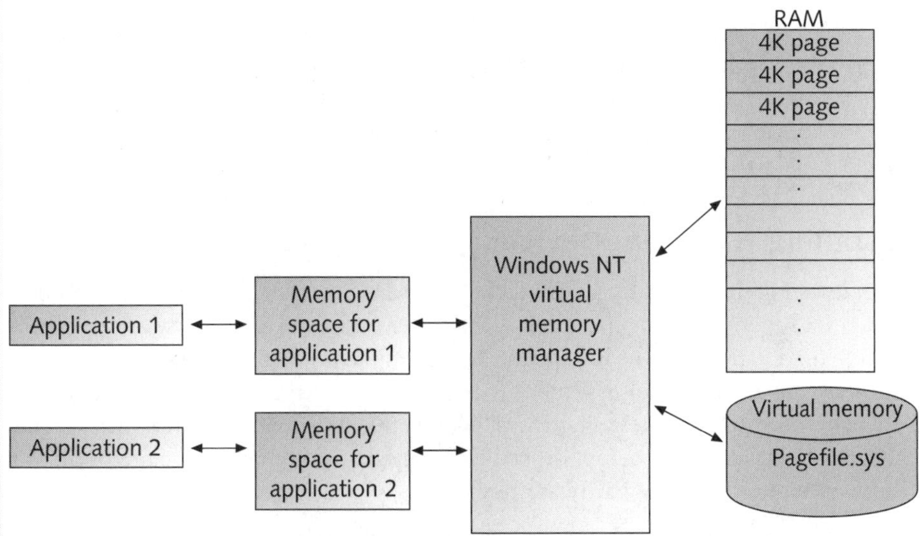

Figure 6-10 Windows NT memory management

Installing Hardware and Software

A+ OS 2.4 3.2

Hardware and software are installed using the Windows NT Control Panel (see Figure 6-11), which looks like, and works in a similar way to, that of Windows 9x (which you saw in earlier chapters). With both hardware and software installations, changes are made to the registry. We next look at examples of each, including how to manage legacy software.

Figure 6-11 The Windows NT Control Panel

Windows NT does not have a Device Manager. When installing and troubleshooting hardware, look for individual icons in the Control Panel to manage hardware devices. For a detailed report of the system configuration, use the WinMSD command. At a command prompt enter `WinMSD/a/f`. The command creates the report in the current directory.

Installing Hardware Devices

Windows NT builds its list of available hardware devices each time it is booted. This list is not permanently kept in the registry. However, when a new hardware device is installed, device driver information is kept in the registry. New hardware devices are installed from the Control Panel because Windows NT does not support Plug and Play and therefore does not have an Add New Hardware Wizard that automatically launches at startup as does Windows 9x. The steps below describe the installation of a sound card, because this installation is typical of many hardware devices.

1. To install a sound card, access the **Control Panel** and double-click the **Multimedia** icon. The Multimedia Properties dialog box is displayed.
2. Click the **Devices** tab to see a list of multimedia devices.

A+ OS 2.4

3. Select **Audio Devices**, and then click the **Add** button. The Add dialog box opens. You can either select a device driver from the list or click Unlisted or Updated Driver to install your own device driver from disk or CD-ROM.

4. If you choose to install your own driver, click **Unlisted or Updated Driver**, and then click **OK**. The Install Driver dialog box is displayed, asking for the location of the driver. As the example shown in Figure 6-12 shows, the vendor-provided driver is selected. Several versions of the driver (for each of the OSs supported) are located in directories on the CD-ROM that comes with the sound card.

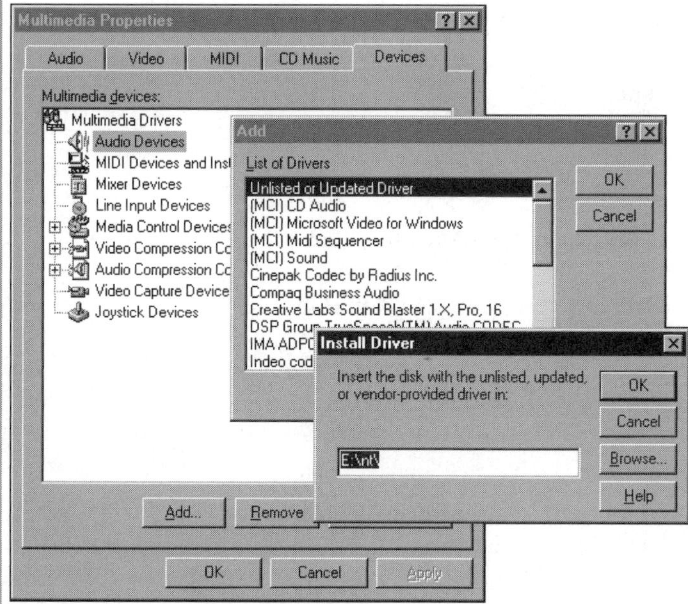

Figure 6-12 When installing a device driver, you can use a driver provided by Windows NT or one from the device vendor

5. In the example CD, the location for the driver is E:\nt\. Enter the path, and then click **OK** to continue the installation. If Windows NT already has the driver you are installing, the OS gives you the choice to use the driver provided by the vendor or the Windows NT driver.

6. The driver is copied to the hard drive, then the hardware setup dialog box is displayed, as seen in Figure 6-13. The suggested I/O address, IRQ, and DMA channel are selected, but you can change these values if you are aware of a conflict. Otherwise, leave the values as suggested and click **OK** to complete the installation.

7. The Windows NT registry is then updated, and you are asked to restart the PC so the changes to the registry can take effect.

A+ OS 2.4

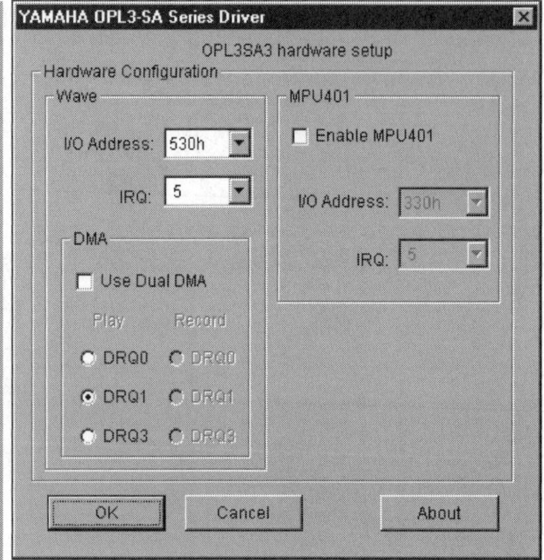

Figure 6-13 Windows NT suggests a hardware setup for the new device

8. Install the CD Player component of Windows NT to use the new sound card. As with many devices, software is necessary to use the sound card. The next step is to double-click the Add/Remove Programs icon of the Control Panel and install the CD Player component of Windows NT in order to use the sound card to play audio CDs. This installation window works just as with Windows 9x.

This example is typical of many hardware installations. The Control Panel was used to install the device driver, and you saw how Windows NT suggests the hardware setup resources to use. Next time the PC boots, the registry tells the **Ntldr (NT Loader)** program to load the sound card device driver. (The Ntldr file is the initially executed Windows NT OS file and is similar to Io.sys in DOS and Windows 9x.) As the driver loads, it looks to the registry for the list of resources that it will use.

The software to use the CD player is also installed from the Control Panel. This information is now kept in the registry to be used each time the OS loads. The OS uses this registry information to provide the CD Player option under Start, Accessories, Multimedia.

Installing Software

Software is installed from the Control Panel using the Add/Remove Programs icon. Installation works very much the same way as under Windows 9x. Access the Control Panel by clicking Start, pointing to Settings, and clicking Control Panel. From the Control Panel, double-click the Add/Remove Programs icon. The Add/Remove Programs Properties dialog box opens. Any software that installs with a Setup.exe or Install.exe program can be installed using this dialog box. Click Install, and the dialog box requests the location of the setup program.

To add new components to Windows NT that were not installed when Windows NT was originally installed, click the Windows NT Setup tab of the Add/Remove Programs Properties dialog box. You see a list of all of the Windows NT components. From this list, you can choose to install new components or to uninstall components that are already installed.

Even though it would be convenient if all software running under Windows NT were written in the newer 32-bit code used by Windows 9x and Windows NT, this doesn't always happen. As explained earlier, Windows NT makes provisions for running DOS applications by creating a separate NTVDM for each application, so that each program can run in its native environment. Windows 16-bit applications can run in individual NTVDMs, or several 16-bit Windows applications can run in the same NTVDM so they can share resources. How to do this is discussed next.

Windows NT Networking

One of the main reasons Windows NT is chosen as an OS is its strong networking features. Remember that there are two versions of Windows NT: Windows NT Workstation and Windows NT Server. In a general PC environment, a workstation is a desktop PC that both accesses a network and works as a standalone PC. In the most general sense, a server is a computer that contains data, software, and security validation files that are shared simultaneously by workstations on the network. A server on the network is generally not also a workstation. Even though it may have a keyboard and monitor connected to it, these are generally only used by a network administrator to administer and monitor the network; the server is solely dedicated to serving the network.

All the functionality offered by Windows NT Workstation is available with Windows NT Server. The primary difference between the two is that Windows NT Server offers the additional functionality of administering and monitoring the network from this centralized location. However, either OS can be configured to work as one node in a workgroup or as one node on a domain. A **workgroup** is a logical group of computers and users that share resources (Figure 6-14), where the control of administration, resources, and security is distributed throughout the network. A Windows NT **domain** is a group of networked computers that share a centralized directory database of user account information and security for the entire set of computers (Figure 6-15). A workgroup uses a peer-to-peer networking model, and a domain uses a client/server networking model.

When a group of computers is connected to share resources, you can configure these computers as a network using the workgroup model (the network is administered from individual PCs in a workgroup), or use the domain model (the network is administered from a centralized location in the domain). Resources including data, software, and printers can be shared using either model.

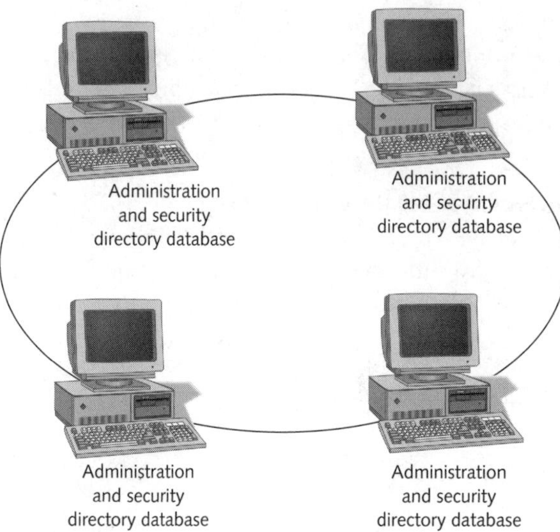

Figure 6-14 A Windows NT workgroup

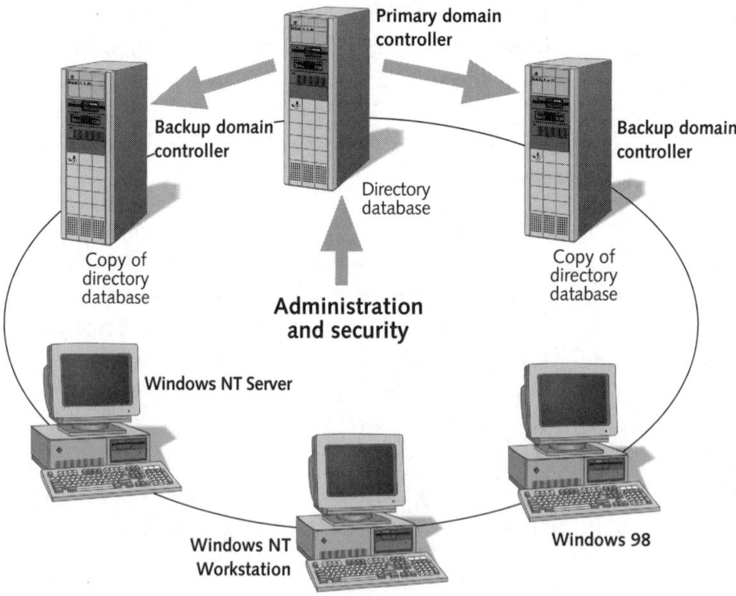

Figure 6-15 A Windows NT domain

Also, as you learn about workgroups and domains, remember that in either case, the group of computers is a logical group, not a geographical group. A workgroup of computers can be in a single building, or it can include PCs in other cities. Distance makes no difference, as long as there is networked connectivity either over phone lines or by other means. PCs are grouped together to share resources. For example, a sales staff member might need to share a marketing database, and the accounting staff of a company might need to share a journals database. People in both groups are spread over several cities. Members of the sales staff make up the sales workgroup, and members of the accounting staff make up the accounting workgroup, so each user can access shared resources within the appropriate group.

When you implement Windows NT Workstation, it is often necessary to set users up in a workgroup with other PCs using Windows NT or Windows 9x and to configure the PCs to be members of a domain controlled by a Windows NT server. Understanding the concepts of workgroups and domains and how they are managed is the first step in learning how to support them.

Using Workgroups and Domains

In a workgroup, every computer has its own directory database of user accounts and security policies. Each computer in a workgroup manages the accounts on that computer for other users and computers that want to access information on it. If you are a member of a workgroup and want to allow another user on another PC to access files on your PC, you must establish an account for that user. The information about that account is kept only on your PC.

A workgroup can be made up of computers that use either Windows NT Workstation or Windows NT Server. However, PCs that have Windows NT Server installed must be configured as standalone units. A workgroup does not require a Windows NT server to be present. Workgroups have no centralized account management or security. Workgroups are generally used for a small group of workstations, and the PC support person usually manages each user account on each PC in the workgroup. A domain is used for a large number of workstations, and security for the domain shifts to a business-wide or enterprise function of a network administrator controlling security from a single console.

In a Windows NT domain, a network administrator manages access to the network through a centralized database. In Figure 6-15, you see the possible different components of a Windows NT domain. Every domain has a **primary domain controller (PDC)**, which stores and controls a database of (1) user accounts, (2) group accounts, and (3) computer accounts. This database is called the directory database or the **security accounts manager (SAM)** database.

An administrator logged on to any workstation or server on the domain can update the directory database by accessing the PDC, but the domain can have only one PDC. One or more read-only backup copies of the directory database can be kept on other computers. Each computer with a backup of the directory database is called a **backup domain controller (BDC)**. A system can be set up so that whenever the database on the PDC is updated, copies are written to each BDC; this is called replication or automated duplication. In Figure 6-15, there are two BDCs, each keeping a copy of the directory database. BDCs use their copy of the SAM database to authenticate users as they log on, thereby relieving the PDC of the burden of authentication functions. This sharing of functions improves performance in domains with many (more than 1000) workstations.

Workstations on the domain are in the lower part of Figure 6-15. A Windows NT network can contain these OSs functioning in these ways:

- Windows NT Server functioning as a PDC, a BDC, or as a standalone server (a server on the network that has no domain controller functions)
- Windows NT Workstation functioning as a workstation or as a standalone server
- Windows 9x, Windows 2000 Professional, or Windows XP Professional acting as clients on the network.

UNDERSTANDING THE WINDOWS NT BOOT PROCESS

A+ OS 1.2 2.3

Understanding the boot process and making changes to it are critical when supporting Windows NT. (Windows 2000 and Windows XP use this same boot process.) In this section you will learn what happens during the boot and in the next section you will learn how to solve boot problems.

The following is a look behind the scenes with a description of each step in the boot process. As you read, refer to Table 6-1 for an outline of the boot sequence for Intel-based computers.

1. *BIOS executes POST.* First, startup BIOS performs POST, which happens just as it would regardless of the OS present. After POST, BIOS turns to the hard drive to load an OS. Remember from earlier chapters that BIOS looks for the partition information at the beginning of the hard drive.
2. *BIOS executes the MBR program.* The first thing in the partition information that BIOS needs is the MBR (Master Boot Record) containing the master boot program. Remember from earlier chapters that the master boot program is the very first thing written in the first sector of a hard drive. The master boot program is followed by the partition table itself, and both are stored in the master boot sector. BIOS executes this master boot program, which examines the partition table, looking for the location of the active partition on the drive, and then turns to the first sector of the active partition to find and load the program in the boot sector of that active partition. So far in the boot process, nothing is different between Windows NT and other OSs.

Table 6-1 Steps in the Intel-based CPU boot process

Description	Step
POST (power-on self test) is executed.	1. Performed by startup BIOS
MBR (Master Boot Record) is loaded, and the master boot program within the MBR is run. (The master boot program is at the very beginning of the hard drive, as part of the partition table information. The program searches for and loads the OS boot record of the active partition.)	2. Performed by startup BIOS

A+ OS 1.2 2.3

Table 6-1 Steps in the Intel-based CPU boot process (continued)

Description	Step
The boot sector from active partition is loaded, and program in this boot sector is run.	3. Performed by MBR program
Ntldr (NT Loader) file is loaded and run.	4. Performed by boot sector program
The processor is changed from real mode to flat memory mode, in which 32-bit code can be executed.	5. Performed by Windows NT loader
Minifile system drivers (described below) are started so files can be read.	6. Performed by Windows NT loader
Read Boot.ini file and build the boot loader menu described in the file. (This menu is discussed later in the chapter.)	7. Performed by Windows NT loader
If the user chooses Windows NT, then run Ntdetect.com to detect hardware present; otherwise, run Bootsect.dos.	8. Performed by Windows NT loader
Ntldr reads information from the Registry about device drivers and loads them. Also loads the Hal.dll and Ntoskrml.exe.	9. Performed by Windows NT loader
Ntldr passes control to Ntoskrml.exe; load is complete.	10. Last step performed by the loader

6

3. *The MBR program executes the OS boot program.* Remember that when DOS or Windows 9x boots, the OS boot sector contains the name of the initial OS load program, Io.sys. When Windows NT is installed, it edits this boot sector of the active partition, instructing it to load the Windows NT program Ntldr at startup, instead of Io.sys. (It does this even when the PC is configured for a dual boot.)

4. *The boot program executes Ntldr.* With the execution of Ntldr, Windows NT then starts its boot sequence. This program is responsible for loading Windows NT and performing several chores to complete the loading process. It then passes off control to the OS.

5. *Ntldr changes the processor mode and loads a file system.* Up to this point, the CPU has been processing in real mode; every program had complete access to system resources. Windows NT does not process in real mode. Ntldr is a 32-bit program and begins by changing the CPU mode from real mode to a 32-bit mode called **32-bit flat memory mode**, in order to run its 32-bit code. Next a temporary, simplified file system called the **minifile system** is started so that Ntldr can read files from either a FAT or an NTFS file system.

6. *Ntldr reads and loads the boot loader menu.* Ntldr then is able to read the Boot.ini file, a hidden text file that contains information needed to build the boot loader menu discussed earlier. The menu is displayed, and the user can make a selection or, after the preset time expires, the default selection is used.

7. *Ntldr uses Ntdetect.com.* If Ntldr is to load Windows NT as the OS, Ntldr runs the program Ntdetect.com, which checks the hardware devices present and passes the information back to Ntldr. This information will later be used to update the Windows NT registry concerning the last-known good hardware profile used.

A+ OS 1.2 2.3

8. *Ntldr loads the OS and device drivers.* Ntldr then loads Ntoskrnl.exe, Hal.dll, and the System hive. The System hive is a portion of the Windows NT registry that includes hardware information that is now used to load the proper device drivers for the hardware present. You will learn more about this System hive in Chapter 8.
9. *Ntldr passes control to Ntoskrnl.exe.* Ntldr then passes control to Ntoskrnl.exe, and the boot sequence is complete.
10. *An operating system other than Windows NT is chosen.* If a selection was made from the boot loader menu to load an OS other than Windows NT, such as DOS or Windows 9x, Ntldr does not load Ntdetect.com or complete the remaining chores to load Windows NT. Instead, Ntldr loads and passes control to the program Bootsect.dos, which is responsible for loading the other OS.

When repairing a corrupted hard drive, a support person often copies files from one PC to another. However, the Bootsect.dos file contains information from the partition table for a particular hard drive and cannot be copied from another PC.

The files needed to successfully boot Windows NT are listed in Table 6-2. (In the table, references to *winnt_root* follow Microsoft documentation conventions and mean the name of the directory where Windows NT is stored, which is \Winnt by default.)

Table 6-2 Files needed to successfully boot Windows NT

File	Location
Ntldr	Root directory of the system partition (usually C:\)
Boot.ini	Root directory of the system partition (usually C:\)
Bootsect.dos	Root directory of the system partition (usually C:\)
Ntdetect.com	Root directory of the system partition (usually C:\)
Ntbootdd.sys*	Root directory of the system partition (usually C:\)
Ntoskrnl.exe	*winnt_root*\system32 directory of the boot partition
Hal.dll	*winnt_root*\system32 directory of the boot partition
System	*winnt_root*\system32\config of the boot partition
Device drivers	*winnt_root*\system32\drivers of the boot partition

*Ntbootdd.sys is only used with a SCSI boot device.

Troubleshooting Windows NT

In this section, you will learn about troubleshooting Windows NT, including the boot process and some diagnostic tools that you can use for maintenance and troubleshooting. Many of the general troubleshooting tips you learned in earlier chapters apply to Windows NT as well. Since you have just learned about the Windows NT boot process, we will begin this section with a discussion of troubleshooting that process.

Troubleshooting the Windows NT Boot Process

A+ OS 2.3 3.1

Listed below are the things you can do and the order in which you should do them to troubleshoot a failed Windows NT boot. You will learn more about these tools and processes in this section. Remember that Windows NT does not have a safe mode as does Windows 9x and several of the useful troubleshooting utilities of Windows 9x that you learned about in the last chapter are missing from Windows NT.

To recover from a failed Windows NT boot, do the following:

- If the Windows NT startup menu appears (it will if it thinks there is a problem you need to know about), use the Last Known Good configuration to return to the last registry values that allowed for a successful boot. Any configuration changes since the last good boot will be lost.
- If you cannot boot from the hard drive, boot using the three boot disks that came with the OS. If you don't have these three disks, you can create them on another PC that is working. Check for corrupted boot and system files that you can replace.
- Boot from the three disks and select the option "To repair a damaged Windows NT version 4.0 installation."
- Try reinstalling Windows NT into the same folder it currently uses. Tell the Setup program this is an upgrade.
- As a last resort, if you are using the NTFS file system and you must recover data on the hard drive, move the hard drive to another system that is running Windows NT and install the drive as a secondary drive. You might then be able to recover the data.

6

Last Known Good Configuration

Each time Windows NT boots and the first logon is made with no errors, the OS saves a copy of the hardware configuration from the registry, which is called the Last Known Good configuration. (All hardware configuration sets stored in the registry, including the Last Known Good are called control sets.) The next time the PC boots, if an error occurs, it can use the Last Known Good configuration.

The key in the registry that contains the Last Known Good configuration is:

```
HKEY_LOCAL_MACHINE\HARDWARE
```

If Windows NT detects the possibility of a problem, it adds the Last Known Good option to the Windows NT startup menu. You can select this Last Known Good option to revert back to the control set that was used for the last good boot. For example, if you install a new device driver, restart Windows NT, and find that the system hangs, you can use the Last Known Good option to revert back to the previous configuration.

Because the configuration information is not saved to the Last Known Good control set until after the logon, if you are having trouble with the boot, don't attempt to log on. Doing so will cause the Last Known Good to be replaced by the current control set, which might have errors.

A+ OS 2.3 3.1 3.2

For example, if you have installed a new video driver and you restart Windows, but the screen is very difficult to read, don't log on. Instead, press the reset button to reboot the PC. When given the choice, select Last Known Good from the startup menu.

To prevent hard drive corruption, if you are having problems booting Windows NT, wait for all disk activity to stop before pressing the reset button or turning off the PC, especially if you are using the FAT file system.

If you accidentally disable a critical device, Windows NT decides to revert to the Last Known Good for you. You are not provided with a menu choice.

Reverting to the Last Known Good causes the loss of any changes made to the hardware configuration since the Last Known Good was saved. Therefore, it is wise to make one change at a time to the hardware configuration and reboot after each change. That way, if problems during booting are encountered, only the most recent change is lost. When installing several hardware devices, install them one at a time, rebooting each time.

If you are having problems booting in Windows NT, don't log on, because if you do, you will overwrite your previous Last Known Good.

Windows NT Boot Disks

With Windows 9x and DOS, any single disk could be formatted as a boot disk or system disk. Windows NT is different. It requires three disks to hold enough of Windows NT to boot. However, formatting a single disk just to hold data or software can be done using Explorer.

When a disk is formatted by Windows NT, the boot sector is written to boot the Ntldr program instead of Io.sys as in DOS and Windows 9x. To format a disk, use Windows NT Explorer. Right-click the *3½ Floppy (A:)* line in Explorer and choose Format from the shortcut menu. Figure 6-16 is displayed.

The only file system available for a floppy disk is FAT. Note in the figure that there is no option to make the disk a system disk or boot disk. If you try to boot from a disk that has been formatted by Windows NT, this error message appears:

```
BOOT: Couldn't find NTLDR
Please insert another disk
```

Windows NT comes with a set of three disks that are initially used to boot the machine before the installation continues from the CD-ROM. After the OS is installed, you can use these disks in an emergency to boot the OS. These three disks come with Windows NT, but you can make extra sets. The set of boot disks is the same no matter what PC you are using. The disks contain no special information about your system.

A+ OS 2.3 3.1 3.2

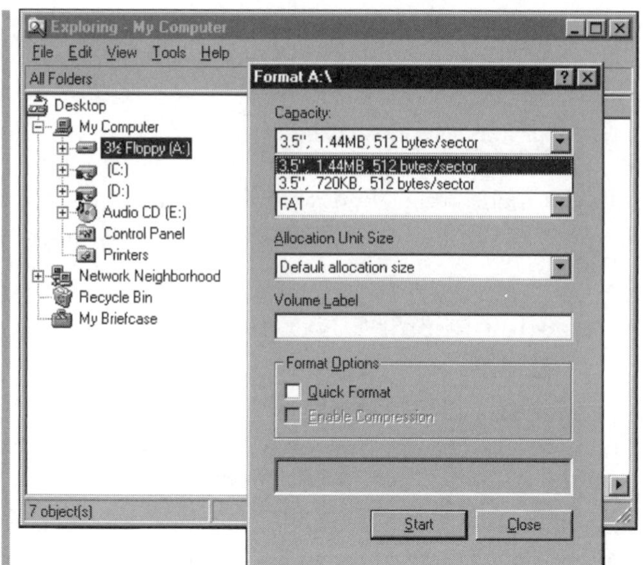

Figure 6-16 Windows NT dialog box used to format a disk

If the original three disks to boot Windows NT become corrupted or are lost, you can make extra copies using Winnt32.exe if you are running Windows NT, or using Winnt.exe if you are running another OS, such as DOS or Windows 9x. You do not have to be working on the PC where you intend to use the disks in order to make them, since the disks don't contain unique information for a specific PC.

Creating Windows NT Boot Disks Proceed as follows to create boot disks using Windows NT:

1. Click **Start**, **Run** and then enter the path and name of the program with the /OX parameters. These parameters say to only create the set of three disks, without performing a complete installation. Note the E:\I386\winnt32.exe/ox entry in the Run dialog box of Figure 6-17. This is the command line from within Windows NT used to create the disks when drive E contains the Windows NT installation CD.

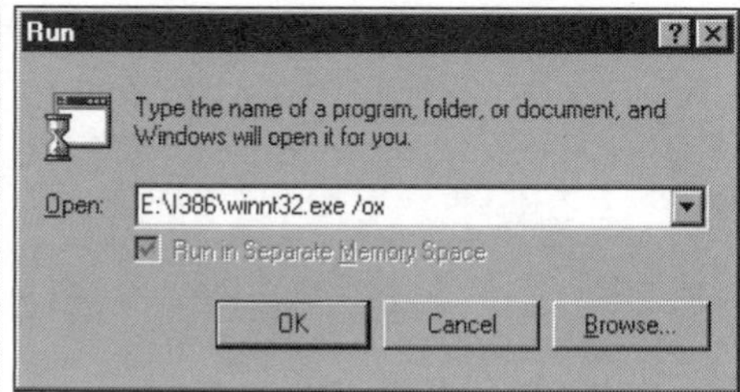

Figure 6-17 Using Winnt32.exe to create a set of boot disks

6

A+ OS 2.3 3.1 3.2

2. The program asks for the location of the installation files. In this example, you would enter E:\I386. You are then prompted to insert three disks. The program creates the disks beginning with disk 3, then 2, then 1.

Windows NT does not have a safe mode as does Windows 9x, so if the PC later cannot boot Windows NT from the hard drive, these three disks can be used to load Windows NT, which loads using a generic VGA mode. After Windows NT is loaded, use the Emergency Repair Disk to restore critical system files to their state at the time the last update was made to the Emergency Repair Disk.

The Windows NT Emergency Repair Disk

A fourth important disk is the **Emergency Repair Disk (ERD)**, which does contain information unique to your OS and hard drive. You are given the opportunity to create the disk during installation. Always create this disk, because it is your record of critical information about your system that can be used to fix a problem with the OS.

The ERD enables restoration of the Windows registry on your hard drive, which contains all the configuration information for Windows. In addition, information that is used to build a command window to run DOS-like commands is also included on the disk. The files on the ERD are listed in Table 6-3. Files stored on the ERD are also written to the hard drive during the installation process. Using Explorer, you can see the files listed in the \winnt_root\repair folder.

Table 6-3 Files on the Windows NT Emergency Repair Disk

File	Description
Setup.log	A read-only, hidden system file that is used to verify the files installed on a system
System._	A compressed file containing part of the registry
Sam._	A compressed file containing some of the security part of the registry
Security._	A compressed file containing some of the security part of the registry
Software._	A compressed file containing software information in the registry
Default._	A compressed file containing part of the registry
Config.nt	The Windows NT version of Config.sys used in creating a command window
Autoexec.nt	The Windows NT version of Autoexec.bat
Ntuser.da_	A compressed file containing information about authorized users of the system

After the installation, you can create a new ERD or update the current one by using the Rdisk.exe utility in the \winnt_root\system32 folder. You should update the disk any time you make any major changes to the system, for example, you install hardware or software. To use the Rdisk.exe utility, click Start, Run, and then either click Browse or enter the path to the utility. Add the /S option so that the utility also updates the registry.

If Windows NT is stored on drive D, the command line is:

D:\WINNT\System32\rdisk.exe /s

A+ OS 2.3 3.1 3.2

First, files are updated in the *winnt_root*\repair directory, then you are given the opportunity to create a new ERD.

Using the Boot Disks and the ERD to Recover from a Failed Boot

In the case of problems with the OS, there are several things you can do to attempt to load Windows NT from the hard drive, which are beyond the scope of this book. However, in the case of a hard drive failure, you can boot from the set of three boot disks that come with the Windows NT CD or that you made using either Winnt.exe or Winnt32.exe. The Windows NT programs on these disks may also request that you provide the ERD. Insert the first boot disk and reboot. You will be prompted to insert disk 2, followed by disk 3. The Setup menu in Figure 6-18 is then displayed. Select the option to repair a damaged installation by pressing R and follow directions on screen.


```
Windows NT Workstation Setup

Welcome to Setup.
The Setup program for the Microsoft(R) Windows NT(TM) OS version 4.0
prepares Windows NT to run on your computer.

      *To learn more about Windows NT Setup before continuing, press F1
      *To set up Windows NT now, press ENTER
      *To repair a damaged Windows NT version 4.0 installation, press R
      *To quit Setup without installing Windows NT, press F3
```

Figure 6-18 Windows NT Workstation Setup menu

Chapter Summary

- Windows NT comes in two versions, Windows NT Workstation and Windows NT Server. Both versions can operate on standalone PCs or on a network, but Windows NT Server can also operate as a controller in a network domain.
- Windows NT can operate using two different file systems: FAT16 and NTFS. NTFS offers more security and power than does FAT16, but FAT16 is backward-compatible with older OSs.
- A PC can be configured to dual boot between Windows NT and another OS such as DOS or Windows 9x.
- Windows NT works on different platforms and with different software because of its modular approach to interfacing with both.
- The two architectural modes of Windows NT are user mode and kernel mode. Kernel mode is further divided into two components: executive services and the hardware abstraction layer (HAL).
- A process is a unique instance of a program running together with the program resources and other programs it may use.
- An NTVDM provides a DOS-like environment for DOS and Windows 3.x applications.

- Windows 3.x 16-bit applications run in a WOW.
- A workgroup is a group of computers and users sharing resources. Each computer maintains a list of users and their rights on that particular PC.
- A domain is a group of computers and users that is managed by a centralized controlling database on a computer called the primary domain controller (PDC).
- The NT Hardware Qualifier is on the Windows NT CD-ROM and can be used to survey the hardware devices on a PC to determine if they qualify to run under the Windows NT OS.
- Four disks are important in recovering from a failed Windows NT boot. Three disks are required to boot Windows NT, and an Emergency Repair Disk (ERD) can be prepared to recover critical system files on the hard drive.

Key Terms

32-bit flat memory mode
administrator account
backup domain controller (BDC)
boot loader menu
boot partition
domain
dual boot
Emergency Repair Disk (ERD)
executive services
kernel mode
master file table (MFT)
minifile system
multithreading
NTHQ (NT Hardware Qualifier)
Ntldr (NT Loader)
NTVDM (NT virtual DOS machine)
Pagefile.sys
pages
POSIX (Portable Operating System Interface)
primary domain controller (PDC)
process
security accounts manager (SAM)
subsystems
system partition
thread
user mode
VDD (virtual device driver)
workgroup
WOW (Win16 on Win32)

Review Questions

1. What are the two versions of Windows NT 4.0?
2. Why can't a 16-bit device driver work under Windows NT?
3. What layer of Windows NT is most responsible for interacting with hardware?
4. What is one reason that interaction with hardware is limited to only one or two components of the OS?
5. Can an application or device driver specify which physical memory or memory addresses it wants in Windows NT? Why or why not?
6. Before you install Windows NT, how can you determine if the OS supports all the hardware on your PC?
7. What is one reason not to upgrade from Windows 98 to Windows NT?
8. What is one reason to upgrade from Windows 98 to Windows NT?

9. What two file systems does Windows NT support?
10. If you have Windows 98 installed on a PC using FAT32 and you are creating a dual boot with Windows NT, what must you do first so that Windows NT can access the entire hard drive?
11. If you are upgrading a PC from Windows 98 with FAT32 to Windows NT, how will having FAT32 on the hard drive change the results of the upgrade, as opposed to an installation that begins with FAT16?
12. How many bits are used to store a cluster number in the Windows NT NTFS file system?
13. What is the file system that is common to DOS, Windows 9x, and Windows NT?
14. What file system cannot be read by DOS or Windows 9x, but can be used by Windows NT?
15. Windows NT is installed using a system partition and a boot partition. Which of these partitions must be the active partition of the hard drive?
16. Which part of the Windows NT architecture makes it possible for Windows NT to port to more than one platform?
17. What are the two modes of the Windows NT architecture?
18. Which of these two modes contains the NTVDM?
19. Why do 32-bit applications not need to reside in an NTVDM?
20. What is one function of a backup domain controller in a Windows NT domain?
21. In a Windows NT workgroup, where is access to an individual workstation on the network controlled?
22. In a Windows NT domain, where is access to an individual workstation on the network controlled?
23. What is the term for the 4K segments in which Windows NT allocates memory?
24. What is the first Windows NT program that is loaded and run when Windows NT is booted?
25. How many floppy disks are needed in order to boot Windows NT from disk?
26. In what two places can the Windows NT virtual memory manager store memory pages?
27. A software developer comes to you with a problem. She has been asked to convert software that she has written for Windows 9x to Windows NT. The software consists of two 16-bit programs that work equally well under Windows 3.x and Windows 9x. She was able to convert one of the programs to a 32-bit version, but had to leave the other program in 16-bit code. Both programs run at the same time and share data in memory. However, when she runs the two programs under Windows NT, the 32-bit program cannot read data written to memory by the 16-bit program. Why not? What should she do so that the two programs can work under Windows NT?

HANDS-ON PROJECTS

Using the Control Panel

1. Shut down and restart Windows NT and observe the number of seconds that the boot loader program waits until Windows NT is loaded. Change the number of seconds to wait so that the number of seconds is doubled. Verify that the change has been made, by rebooting. When you have verified the change, return the number of seconds to the original value.
2. Check under the Accessories and Games sections of Windows NT and install a new game or accessory. Verify that the program is installed.
3. Change the colors in the Display Properties box and verify the changes.
4. Restore the PC to default display settings.

Using the Internet for Problem Solving

Access the *support.microsoft.com* Web site for Windows NT Workstation support. Print one example of an article from the Knowledge Base that addresses a problem with booting Windows NT.

Running a 16-bit Application

Try running a DOS utility such as MSD (from Chapter 2) under Windows NT. What error message do you get? Why?

Using the Internet for Research

You want to install Windows NT on a PC using a dual boot with Windows 98. The Windows 98 logical drive is using FAT32, and you want Windows NT to be able to access the data files on this logical drive. Using the Internet, look for third-party software that will allow Windows NT to read from and write to FAT32 volumes. Answer these questions:

1. What software allows Windows NT to read FAT32 volumes? How much does it cost? What URL did you use to answer the question?
2. What software allows Windows NT to read from and write to FAT32 volumes? How much does it cost? What URL did you use to answer the question?

CASE PROJECT

Install Windows NT

To do this project, you will need a computer that has a Pentium-compatible processor or higher, 16 MB of RAM (32 MB is better), and 125 MB of free hard disk space. Following instructions given in the chapter, install Windows NT as a second OS on a system that already has Windows 9x installed, or, if you don't have Windows 9x available, then install Windows NT as the only OS on the hard drive. If you are creating a dual boot, install Windows NT on a different logical drive than the other OS. Use the NTFS file system for Windows NT. Write down each decision you had to make during the installation and each answer you had to provide the setup process.

CHAPTER

7

INSTALLING AND USING WINDOWS 2000 PROFESSIONAL

In this chapter, you will learn:

- About the architecture of Windows 2000
- How to install Windows 2000
- How to use Windows 2000
- How to install hardware and software under Windows 2000

Windows 2000 is the culmination of the evolution of Microsoft operating systems from the 16-bit DOS operating system to a true 32-bit, module-oriented operating system, complete with desktop functionality, user-friendly Plug and Play installations, and other easy-to-use features. Windows 2000 comes in several versions, some designed for the desktop and others designed for high-end servers. Windows 2000 Server, Advanced Server, and Datacenter Server are network server OSs, upgrades from Windows NT Server. Windows 2000 Professional is the next generation of Windows NT Workstation, and has become popular as a corporate desktop OS. This chapter focuses on Windows 2000 Professional. While taking advantage of the user-friendly features of Windows 98, Windows 2000 is founded on the technology of Windows NT and is committed to leaving behind the compromises that Windows 9x made with legacy hardware and application software. In addition, Windows 2000 introduces many new features, including a new approach to managing hard drive storage, called dynamic storage. In this chapter, you will learn about the architecture of Windows 2000, how to install the OS as well as hardware and applications with it, and how to use it.

WINDOWS 2000 ARCHITECTURE

In Chapter 6, you learned about the architecture of Windows NT, which Windows 2000 uses as well. You can also refer back to the survey of operating systems in Chapter 1, which described some of the differences between Windows NT and Windows 2000. This section looks at these differences in more detail.

As you learned in the last chapter, Windows NT does not support Plug and Play or the FAT32 file system and does not have a safe mode or Device Manager. Windows 2000 supports all of these.

New Features

A feature new to Windows 2000 is **Active Directory**, a directory database service that allows for a single point of administration for all shared resources on a network. Active Directory can track the location of files; peripheral devices, including printers, scanners, and other hardware; databases; Web sites; users; services; and so forth. It uses a locating method similar to that used by the Internet. Windows 2000 Server versions provide Active Directory, and Windows 2000 Professional acts as an Active Directory client, or user of the directory.

Recall from Chapter 6 that a Windows NT client/server network has one primary domain controller and may have one or more backup domain controllers. A Windows NT network can have no more than one primary domain controller, which maintains the only copy of the directory database that can be edited. When the directory database is changed, such as when a new user is added to the network, only the directory database on the primary domain controller is updated. The primary domain controller updates the directory databases on the backup domain controllers. With Windows 2000, a network can have any number of domain controllers, each keeping a copy of the directory that can be edited (see Figure 7-1). An administrator can update the directory on any one of these domain controllers, which will then communicate the change to the other domain controllers.

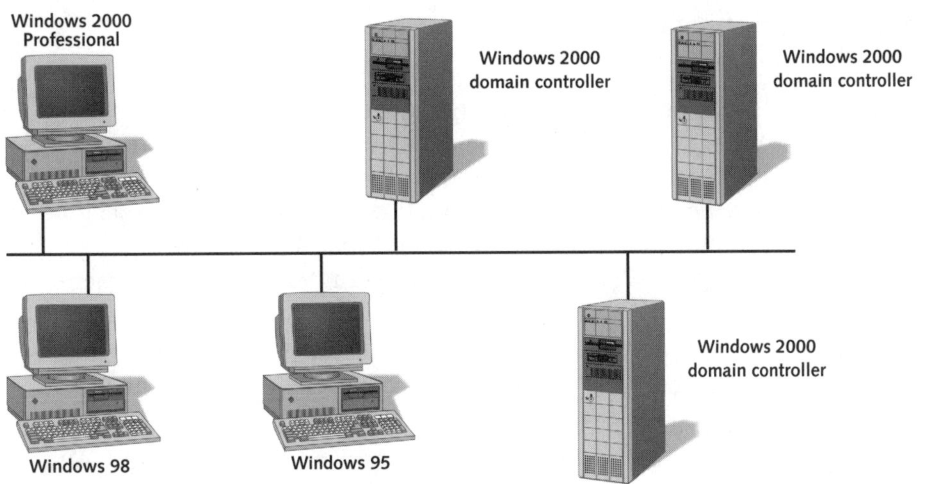

Figure 7-1 Windows 2000 allows for multiple domain controllers, each keeping a read/write copy of the domain database

When both Windows NT and Windows 2000 domain controllers are on the same network, conflicts can result because of the differences in the way the domain controllers work in each OS. For this reason, Windows 2000 runs in two modes: mixed mode and native mode. **Native mode** is used when no Windows NT domain controllers are present, and **mixed mode** is used when there is at least one Windows NT domain controller on the network. Mixed mode is necessary in a situation where a large network is being upgraded from Windows NT to Windows 2000 and some servers have received the upgrade but others have not. When installing Windows 2000 Server, the installer can choose mixed mode during the installation process and later migrate to native mode by using the Microsoft Management Console (MMC), which you will learn about in the next chapter. Once you have changed a domain to native mode, you cannot change it back to mixed mode.

Windows 2000 includes several new diagnostic and recovery tools, including Recovery Console, safe mode (similar to Windows 98 safe mode), and File Protection (which prevents system files from being corrupted or erased). For backups, Windows NT provides a backup utility to tape only, but Windows 2000 allows backups to tape, Zip drives, recordable CD-ROMs, and external hard drives. Windows 2000 supports the Internet Printing Protocol (IPP) so that users can print directly to a printer's URL anywhere on the Internet. In addition, several other features new to Windows 2000 are designed to support and improve Internet services for users.

Basic Disks and Dynamic Disks

Windows 2000 offers two ways to configure a hard drive: as a basic disk or a dynamic disk. A **basic disk** is the same as the configuration used with DOS, Windows 9x, and Windows NT. By default, Windows 2000 uses basic disk configuration. With basic disk, you generally create partitions of a set size and then do not change them. If you want to change the size of a partition, you either have to reinstall Windows (if Windows is installed on that partition) or use special third-party software that allows you to change the size of a partition without losing your data. Within partitions, you create logical drives (sometimes called basic volumes) of set size.

Dynamic disks, which are new to Windows 2000, don't use partitions or logical drives; instead, they use **dynamic volumes**, which are called dynamic because you can change the size. Data to configure the disk is stored in a disk management database that resides in the last 1 MB of storage space at the end of a hard drive. DOS, Windows 9x, and Windows NT cannot read dynamic disks. Dynamic disks are compatible only with Windows 2000 and Windows XP.

A dynamic volume is contained within a dynamic disk and is a logical volume similar to a logical drive in a basic disk. There are three types of dynamic volumes:

- A **simple volume** corresponds to a primary partition on a basic disk and consists of disk space located on a single physical disk.
- A **spanned volume** appears as a simple volume but can use space from two or more physical disks. It fills up the space allotted on one physical disk before moving onto the next. This increases the amount of disk space available for a volume. However, if one physical disk on which data that is part of a spanned volume fails, all the data in the volume is lost.
- A **striped volume** also can use space from two or more physical disks and increases the disk space available for a simple volume. The difference between a spanned volume and a striped volume is that a striped volume writes to the physical disks evenly rather than filling up allotted space on one and then moving on to the next. This increases disk performance as compared to access time with a spanned volume.

Figure 7-2 illustrates the difference between basic disk and dynamic disk organization. A basic disk or a dynamic disk can use any file system supported by Windows 2000 (FAT16, FAT32, and NTFS). Once Windows 2000 is installed, you can use the Windows 2000 Disk Management utility to switch from basic to dynamic or dynamic to basic and change the file system on either type disk. You will learn more about Disk Management in Chapter 8 and how to use different volume types to protect your data in Chapter 11.

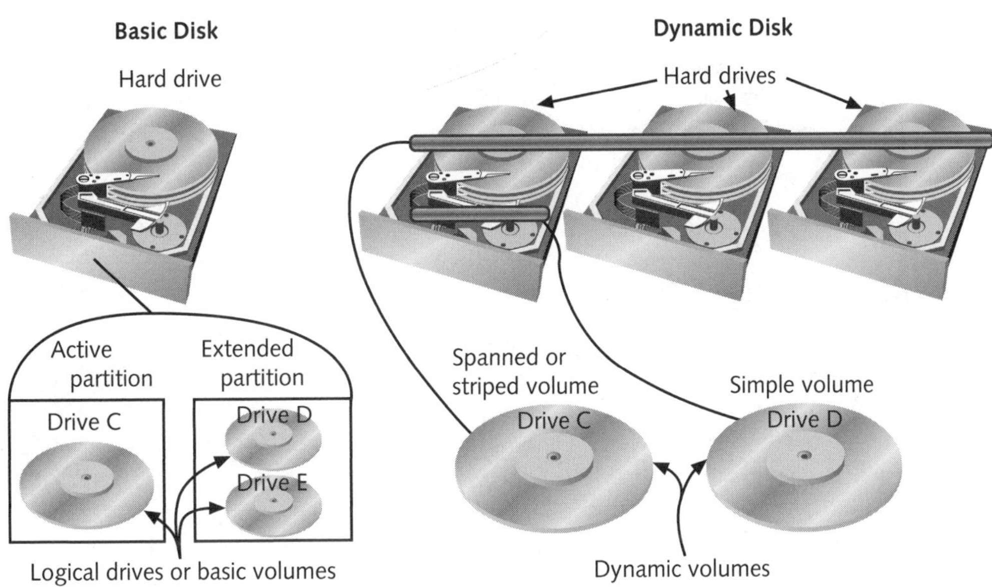

Figure 7-2 Basic disks use partitions and logical drives to organize a hard drive, and dynamic disks use dynamic volumes to organize multiple hard drives

7

INSTALLING WINDOWS 2000 PROFESSIONAL

A+ OS 2.1

This section looks at installing Windows 2000 on a system with a newly installed hard drive, called a clean install, and also installing Windows 2000 as an upgrade from Windows 9x or Windows NT, called an upgrade installation. Just as with Windows NT, Windows 2000 can be installed to be dual-booted with another OS. Before any type of installation, verify that your system meets the minimum requirements for Windows 2000. You must have at least 650 MB of free space on your hard drive, at least 64 MB of RAM and a 133 MHz Pentium-compatible CPU or higher. As you read the following instructions, notice how the installation process is similar to that of Windows NT Workstation discussed in Chapter 6.

Plan the Installation

A+ OS 2.1

Windows 2000 has its roots in Windows NT. Just as with Windows NT, it does not use system BIOS to interface with hardware devices. For that reason, a hardware device must be designed to specifically interact with Windows 2000. Use the hardware compatibility list (HCL) to determine if all the hardware devices in your system qualify for Windows 2000. A version of the HCL is on the Windows 2000 CD in the \Support folder. However, to see the latest version of the list, check the Microsoft Web site at *www.microsoft.com/hcl*. Don't assume that because a device is compatible with Windows NT, it will work with Windows 2000. There are some instances in which this is not the case, so check the HCL for Windows 2000 to be sure.

Microsoft sometimes puts last-minute documentation in a Release Notes file in the root directory of an installation CD. Check the directory for Readme.htm and search it for information that might be important for the installation.

A+ OS 2.1

Software applications must also qualify for Windows 2000. To verify that all the applications you intend to use on the Windows 2000 PC are certified to work with Windows 2000, search the list of compatible software applications list at *www.microsoft.com/windows2000/professional/howtobuy/upgrading/compat*. If an application is not on the list, it might still work with Windows 2000. You can verify that by checking with the application manufacturer's Web site or technical support, or you can just install the application under Windows 2000 and test it yourself.

Support for ACPI

Recall from Chapter 2 that the Advanced Configuration and Power Interface (ACPI) standards developed by Intel, Microsoft, and Toshiba apply to system BIOS, the OS, and certain hardware devices and software to control when a device goes into an inactive state in order to conserve power. To take full advantage of Windows 2000 power management abilities, your system BIOS must be ACPI-compliant. If you have a BIOS that is not ACPI-compliant and you install Windows, Windows will not install ACPI support and will install an older HAL that does not support ACPI. If you later flash your BIOS to make it ACPI-compliant, you will have to reinstall Windows to include ACPI support.

Some BIOS manufacturers offer a BIOS upgrade to make older systems compliant. Most system BIOSs made after January, 1999 are compliant. To learn if your BIOS is compliant, when you are upgrading from Windows 98 to Windows 2000, you can check for the ACPI feature under the Windows 98 Device Manager. Look for ACPI, Advanced Configuration and Power Management Interface in the Device Manager list of devices. Because Windows 95 and Windows NT do not support ACPI, it is not listed under these OS installations. You can also check the Web site of the BIOS manufacturer or the Microsoft Web site.

Microsoft calls a BIOS that is ACPI-compliant a "good BIOS" and puts it on the Good BIOS list. The Microsoft site allows you to search for ACPI-compatible computers. When you search by model and manufacturer, the Microsoft Web site tells you if the system is compatible with Windows 2000 and sometimes provides a link to the BIOS Web site where you can download an upgrade to the BIOS. If you are upgrading BIOS, do that before you begin the Windows 2000 installation. If the system is not ACPI-compliant, you can still install Windows 2000 but you cannot use some power management features.

For Microsoft links to hardware and software, and BIOS compatibility checks, see this URL: *www.microsoft.com/windows2000/professional/howtobuy/upgrading/compat/default.asp.*

Selecting a File System

When selecting a file system for an upgrade or replacing Windows 2000 with an existing OS, plan the installation by assuming that you have a basic disk. Later, after Windows 2000 is installed, you can switch to dynamic disk if you like. Plan which partition on the hard drive will hold Windows 2000 and what file system you will use on that partition. Windows 2000 supports the FAT16, FAT32, and NTFS file systems. For compatibility with Windows 98, use

A+ OS 2.1 the FAT32 file system. For compatibility with DOS or Windows 95, use FAT16, and for the most security, use NTFS. If the hard drive is not yet partitioned or formatted, Windows 2000 does that for you during the installation. As an alternative, you can also use Fdisk to create a partition before you begin the installation. Create only a single partition, and then, after the installation, you can use Disk Management to create other partitions.

The NTFS file system supports encryption (encoding files so they can't be deciphered by others), compression (reducing the size of files and folders), and disk quotas (limiting the hard drive space available to a user). If you want to use any of these features, use NTFS because they are not supported by FAT file systems. (Windows 9x supports compression of an entire logical drive, but not of individual files or folders.)

Table 7-1 summarizes which file systems are supported by which operating systems. You will need this information when planning your Windows 2000 installation. Windows versions not discussed in this chapter are included for comparison.

Table 7-1 Operating system support for file systems

	DOS	Windows 95	Windows 98	Windows NT	Windows 2000	Windows XP
FAT16	X	X	X	X	X	X
FAT32		X (for OSR2)	X		X	X
NTFS				X	X	X

Installing Windows 2000 on Networked Computers

If you are installing Windows 2000 on a networked PC, consider where the Windows 2000 installation files are stored. You can install the OS from a CD in the computer's CD-ROM drive, or you can store the files on a file server on the network and perform the installation from the file server. If you will be doing multiple installations on the network, consider using a file server. Copy all the files from the \i386 folder on the Windows 2000 CD to a folder on the file server and then share that folder on the network. Later, during the installation, when you are ready for the CD, point the setup program to the file server folder instead.

Windows 2000 offers a number of options for installation that can be automated without requiring someone to sit at the computer responding to the questions that setup asks during the installation process. One method is called an **unattended installation** and is performed by storing the answers to installation questions in a text file or script that Windows 2000 calls an **answer file**. A sample answer file is stored on the Windows 2000 CD. If you must perform many installations on computers that have the same Windows 2000 setup, it might be worth your time to develop an answer file to perform unattended installations. How to set up unattended installations is beyond the scope of this chapter. Another option is drive imaging. After the installation, use the sysprep.exe utility to remove configuration settings such as the computer name that uniquely identifies this PC. Then clone the entire hard drive to a new PC using third-party drive-imaging software.

A+ OS 2.1

To learn how to create an unattended installation of Windows 2000, go to the Microsoft Support Web site (*support.microsoft.com*) and search on the Microsoft Knowledge Base article Q216258. You can also search the Web site for other articles on this subject.

When installing Windows 2000 on a network, just as with other operating systems, you need to know how to configure the computer to access the network. You should know these things before you begin the installation:

- The computer name and workgroup name for a peer-to-peer network
- The username, user password, computer name, and domain name for a domain network
- For TCP/IP networks, how the IP address is assigned, either dynamically (gets its IP address from a DHCP server when it first connects to the network) or statically (IP address is permanently assigned to the workstation). If the IP address is statically assigned, then have the IP address to assign the workstation. (DHCP servers, which are used to assign IP addresses when a computer connects to a network, are covered in Chapter 12.)

Upgrade or Clean Install?

If you are installing Windows 2000 on a new hard drive, then you are doing a clean install, but if Windows 9x or Windows NT is already installed on the hard drive, then you have three choices:

- You can perform a clean install, overwriting the existing operating system and applications.
- You can perform an upgrade installation.
- You can install Windows 2000 in a second partition on the hard drive and create a dual-boot situation.

There are advantages and disadvantages to each of these options.

Clean Install, Erasing Existing Installations If the hard drive does not have a lot of important data on it or if the data can be backed up, a clean install that overwrites the existing installation has some advantages. One advantage is that you get a fresh start. With an upgrade, problems with applications or the OS might follow you into the Windows 2000 load. If you erase everything (format the hard drive), then you are assured that the registry as well as all applications are as clean as possible. The disadvantage is that, after Windows 2000 is installed, you must reinstall application software on the hard drive and restore the data from backups. If you do a clean install, you can choose to format the hard drive first, or simply do a clean install on top of the existing installation. If you don't format the drive, the data will still be on the drive, but the previous operating system settings and applications will be lost.

A+ OS 2.1

If you decide to do a clean install, verify that you have all the application software CDs or floppy disks and software documentation. Back up all the data and verify that the backups are good. Then, and only then, format the hard drive or begin the clean install without formatting the drive. If you don't format the hard drive, be sure to run a current version of antivirus software before you begin the installation.

Upgrade the Existing Operating System All versions of Windows 9x and Windows NT Workstation 3.51 and higher can be upgraded to Windows 2000. The advantages of upgrading are that all applications and data are carried forward into the new Windows 2000 environment, most OS settings carry forward, and the installation is faster. If you perform an upgrade, you must begin the installation while you are in the current OS. If you are working from a remote location on the network, you cannot do an upgrade.

You cannot upgrade a compressed Windows 9x drive. You must first uncompress it before you can upgrade to Windows 2000 Professional.

Create a Dual Boot Don't create a dual boot unless you need two operating systems, such as when you need to verify that applications and hardware will work under Windows 2000 before you delete the old OS. Windows 2000 does not support a second operating system on the same partition, so you must have at least two partitions on the hard drive. All applications must be installed on each partition to be used by each OS.

Recall that Windows NT/2000/XP can support up to four partitions on a hard drive. All four can be primary partitions (which can have only one logical drive) or one of the partitions can be an extended partition (which can have several logical drives). For the first primary partition, the active partition, that drive is drive C. For a dual boot with Windows 2000, one OS is installed in the active partition on drive C, and the other OS is installed on another partition's logical drive.

You must decide what file system to use for the Windows 2000 partition: FAT16, FAT32, or NTFS. If you choose to use a dual boot with DOS, use FAT16 for the Windows 2000 partition so that DOS can read the partition. For Windows 9x, use either the FAT16 or FAT32 file system, not NTFS, so that Windows 9x can read the Windows 2000 partition.

Windows 2000 uses the latest version of NTFS that was first introduced by Windows NT Server 4.0, NTFS Version 5.0 (NTFS5). NTFS4 is used by Windows NT Workstation 4.0. The NTFS5 version includes numerous enhancements over previous versions, but cannot be read by Windows NT Workstation 4.0 unless Windows NT 4.0 Service Pack 4 is applied. For this reason, if you create a dual boot between Windows 2000 and Windows NT using NTFS for both operating systems, you can encounter the following problems:

- The file system data structures might not be the same.
- Disk utilities, such as Chkdsk under Windows NT, might not work on the drive.

A+ OS 2.1

- Windows NT will not be able to read encrypted files and folders.
- You cannot use Windows 2000 to repair a damaged Windows NT 4.0 NTFS partition. Windows NT 4.0 only allows access to an NTFS drive from within Windows NT 4.0 and not from any other OS.

For these reasons, using a dual boot between Windows 2000 and Windows NT is not recommended.

Features new to NTFS under Windows 2000 include file and folder encryption (protects from unauthorized access), disk quotas (controls user disk space), and mount points (adds a remote volume to a system without using a drive letter). These features were not included in Windows NT and might cause conflicts if you set up Windows 2000 and Windows NT as a dual boot.

Planning an Upgrade from Windows 9x to Windows 2000

So far in this chapter, you have learned that there are many similarities in structure between Windows 2000 and Windows NT. When you are upgrading from Windows 9x to Windows 2000, the Windows 2000 registry is not compatible with the Windows 9x registry; therefore, during an upgrade, Windows 2000 cannot easily import settings from the Windows 9x registry, even though it attempts to do so. Because of the difference in structure in the Windows 9x registry and the Windows 2000 registry, transfer of information from one to the other will not be as complete as with an upgrade from Windows NT. Until you have performed the upgrade, you will not know exactly what Windows 2000 was able to import from Windows 9x, though Setup might inform you or ask for additional help in some cases.

To test your system and be alerted to potential problems, it is a good idea to run the Check Upgrade Only mode of Windows 2000 Setup, which does not actually install Windows 2000 but instead just checks for compatibility and reports any upgrade issues with hardware or software. Run the utility to produce the report, Upgrade.txt, which is stored in the C:\Windows directory.

Hardware Compatibility One issue to consider in upgrading from Windows 9x to Windows 2000 is that Windows 2000 does not import drivers from Windows 9x, because they are generally not compatible. As you learned earlier, a hardware device must be designed to be compatible with Windows 2000. If you want to install a device for which there is no device driver included in Windows 2000, you might have to download a driver from either the Microsoft site or the manufacturer's Web site. Check for compatibility and make sure you have all the required device drivers before you begin your Windows 9x-to-Windows 2000 upgrade. Windows 2000 attempts to carry over installed hardware devices that are compatible with Windows 2000, asking for new drivers where necessary; it ignores and does not install incompatible devices. If Setup cannot find a critical driver such as the driver to control a hard drive, it will cancel the upgrade.

Another thing you need to know is that Windows 2000 deletes all the Windows 9x system files and replaces them with Windows 2000 system files in the same directory.

A+ OS 2.1

Software Compatibility Basically, the main advantage in performing an upgrade from Windows 9x to Windows 2000 rather than doing a clean install of Windows 2000 is that you do not have to reinstall software that is compatible with Windows 2000. If an application was written for Windows 9x, it might or might not be compatible with Windows 2000. Windows 9x applications store registry data differently from Windows 2000 applications and may rely on APIs specific to Windows 9x. If an application doesn't work after you upgrade to Windows 2000, try reinstalling it. If that doesn't work, check the software manufacturer's Web site for a patch or upgrade.

Planning an Upgrade from Windows NT to Windows 2000

Upgrading to Windows 2000 from Windows NT is much easier than upgrading from Windows 9x. However, here are some considerations you need to be aware of before performing the upgrade:

- You must install networking on Windows NT 3.51 machines before upgrading, or you will not be able to log on to Windows 2000.
- If you are upgrading from Windows NT using NTFS, Setup automatically upgrades to the Windows 2000 version of NTFS.
- If you are upgrading from Windows NT using FAT16 or Windows NT with third-party software installed that allows it to use FAT32, Setup will ask you whether you want to upgrade to NTFS.

Hardware Compatibility Generally, most hardware devices and their corresponding drivers that worked under Windows NT will work under Windows 2000 as well, although some third-party drivers might need to be updated for Windows 2000. As always, it is a good idea to check the HCL on the Microsoft Web site or run the Check Upgrade Only mode of Windows 2000 Setup.

Software Compatibility Nearly all applications that run with Windows NT Workstation 3.51 and later will run with Windows 2000 without modification. Here are some exceptions:

- Antivirus software and third-party network software, both of which must be removed before upgrading to Windows 2000
- Some disk management tools
- Custom tools for power management, which are replaced in Windows 2000 by ACPI. Windows 2000 also provides minimal support for APM (Advanced Power Management) which also must be removed before the upgrade. Windows 2000 considers APM a legacy tool, uses it only on notebook computers, and uses only enough APM features to support the battery on a notebook computer. With ACPI-compliant BIOS, the BIOS senses information about the system and turns that information over to the OS to make decisions and manage the power management functions of the system.

A+ OS 2.1

- Custom solutions that are workarounds for Windows NT not supporting Plug and Play, which are unnecessary in Windows 2000 because it provides complete support for Plug and Play
- Software to monitor and control a UPS (uninterruptible power supply)

Now that you have learned about advantages and disadvantages to installing Windows 2000 as a clean install and as an upgrade, including issues to consider with specific upgrades, let's look at step-by-step procedures for how to do both.

When installing Windows from across the network to a remote PC, you can only do a clean install. In this situation, run the Winnt.exe setup program. When working at the local computer, to perform a clean install, you can boot from the Windows CD or run Winnt32.exe from a command prompt. If you want to perform an upgrade, you must execute the Winnt32.exe program from within Windows. In any case, the program executed is called Setup in Windows documentation.

Clean Installation

A+ OS 2.1

The Windows 2000 package comes with documentation and a CD. For United States distributions, the package includes a floppy disk to provide 128-bit data encryption. (This disk is not included in distributions to other countries because of laws that prohibit 128-bit data encryption software from leaving the United States.)

If your PC is capable of booting from a CD, then insert the CD and turn on the PC. The Welcome to the Windows 2000 Setup Wizard screen appears. See Figure 7-3. Select Install a new copy of Windows 2000, and then click Next and proceed to Step 6 below. However, if your PC does not boot from a CD and you have a clean, empty hard drive, first create a set of Windows 2000 setup disks to boot the PC and to begin the installation process. The remaining installation will be done from the CD.

To make the four setup disks, follow these directions:

1. Using a working PC, format four floppy disks.
2. Place the Windows 2000 CD in the CD-ROM drive and a formatted floppy disk in the floppy disk drive. For Windows 9x, click **Start**, **Run** and enter this command in the Run dialog box: **D:\bootdisk\makeboot.exe A:** , substituting the drive letter of the CD-ROM drive for D: and the letter of the floppy drive for A:.
3. Insert new disks in the drive as requested. Label the disks Windows 2000 Setup Disks 1, 2, 3, and 4.
4. Now begin the Windows 2000 installation. Boot the PC from the first setup disk created above. You will be asked to insert each of the four disks in turn and then asked to insert the Windows 2000 CD.
5. The Windows 2000 license agreement appears. Accept the agreement and the Welcome screen appears, as shown in Figure 7-3. The setup process is now identical to that of booting directly from the CD. Save the four setup floppy disks in case you have future problems with Windows 2000.

A+ OS 2.1

Figure 7-3 Using the Setup Wizard, you can do an upgrade, do a clean install, or create a dual boot

7

6. Windows 2000 searches the hard drive for partitions and asks which partition to use. If the partitions are not created, it creates them for you. You are asked to decide which file system to use. If the hard drive has already been formatted with the FAT16 or FAT32 file system, you are asked if you want to upgrade to the NTFS file system. Be aware that if you convert the file system to NTFS, you cannot revert to FAT16 or FAT32. You can also convert from FAT16 or FAT32 to NTFS after the installation is complete. If the hard drive is already partitioned and contains a partition larger than 2 GB and if you select the FAT file system, then Windows 2000 automatically formats the drive using the FAT32 file system. It puts the entire partition into one logical FAT32 drive.
7. During the installation, you are given the opportunity to change your keyboard settings for different languages, enter your name and company name, and enter the product key found on the CD case. You are also given the opportunity to enter date and time settings and an administrator password. Be sure to remember the password. It is required when you log on to the system later to set up new users and perform other administrative tasks. If you forget it and no one else has administrator privileges, you might have to reinstall Windows 2000.
8. If Setup recognizes that you are connected to a network, it provides the Networking Settings window to configure the computer to access the network. If you select Typical settings, then Setup automatically configures the OS for your network. After the installation, if the configuration is not correct, you can make changes.
9. At this point in the installation, you are asked to remove the Windows 2000 CD and click **Finish**. The computer then restarts. After Windows 2000 loads, it

A+ OS 2.1

completes the process of connecting to the network. You are asked questions about the type of network (for example, does the network use a domain or workgroup?). When the configuration is complete, verify that you have access to the network if there is one.

Clean Install When the Hard Drive Has an Operating System Installed

A+ OS 2.1

Using Windows 9x, if your PC automatically detects a CD in the CD-ROM drive, follow these directions to do a clean install when another OS is already installed:

1. Using antivirus software, scan memory and your hard drive for viruses.
2. Insert the Windows 2000 CD in the CD-ROM drive. If your PC detects the CD, a window opens with the message "This CD-ROM contains a newer version of Windows that the one you are presently using. Would you like to upgrade to Windows 2000?" Answer **No**. The Install Windows 2000 window appears (see Figure 7-4).

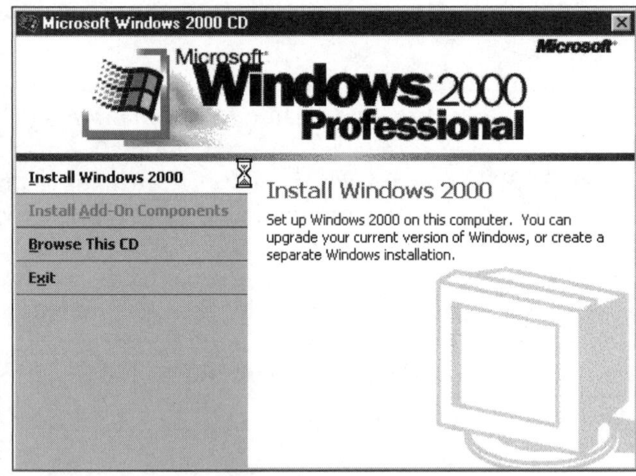

Figure 7-4 Windows 2000 Setup window

3. Click **Install Windows 2000**. The Windows Setup Wizard opens, as in Figure 7-3. Select **Install a new copy of Windows 2000 (Clean Install)**. You will be asked to accept the license agreement, which is displayed; enter the product key from the back of the CD case, and you will be given the opportunity to select special options. After a reboot, the installation process continues as described above.

A+ OS 2.1

If your PC does not automatically recognize a CD, then insert the CD in the CD-ROM drive and do the following:

1. Click **Start**, **Run**. In the Run dialog box, enter the command: **D:\i386\winnt32.exe**. Substitute the drive letter of the CD-ROM drive for D:.
2. The Windows 2000 Setup Wizard appears, as in Figure 7-3. Select **Install a new copy of Windows 2000 (Clean Install)**. The installation process continues as described above.

Upgrade Installation

A+ OS 2.1

To upgrade your operating system from Windows 9x or Windows NT using the Windows 2000 CD, first prepare for the installation by doing the following:

1. Verify that all devices and applications are Windows 2000-compatible. Download and install any patches or upgrades from hardware or software manufacturers.
2. Using antivirus software, scan memory and your hard drive for viruses.
3. Back up all critical system files and data files. Back up the registry in case you need to backtrack to the current installation. If you have important data on your hard drive, back up the data.
4. Close all applications and disable any virus-scanning software. If the hard drive is compressed, decompress the drive.

7

You are now ready to perform the upgrade. Do the following:

1. Insert the Windows 2000 CD in the CD-ROM drive. If your system is set to automatically detect the CD, it runs the setup program and shows a message asking if you want to upgrade your computer to Windows 2000. Answer **Yes**, and the installation process begins. If Windows does not detect the CD, then click **Start**, **Run**, enter **D:\i386\winnt32.exe** in the Run dialog box, and then click **OK**. Substitute the drive letter of the CD-ROM drive for D:. On the Welcome to Windows 2000 Setup Wizard Screen, select **Upgrade to Windows 2000 (Recommended)**. Follow the directions on the screen.
2. Windows 2000 Setup performs the upgrade in two major stages: the Report phase and the Setup phase. During the Report phase, Windows 2000 Setup scans the hardware, device drivers, current operating system, and applications for compatibility. Also, in the Report phase, you are given the opportunity to provide third-party DLL files that make a device driver or application Windows 2000-compatible, if Setup recognizes that the device driver or application will not work without the fix. Next, Setup generates a report of its findings. If findings indicate that an unsuccessful installation is likely to happen, you can abandon the installation and perhaps check with hardware and software manufacturers for fixes. In the Report phase, Setup also creates an answer file that it will use during the Setup phase, installs the Windows 2000 boot loader, and copies Windows 2000 installation files to the hard drive.

A+ OS 2.1

3. The PC reboots and the Setup phase begins, which has two parts: the Text mode and the GUI mode. In the Text mode, Setup installs a Windows 2000 base in the same folder that the old OS is in, usually C:\Windows for Windows 9x and C:\WINNT for Windows NT. This target folder cannot be changed at this point. Setup then moves the Windows registry and profile information to %windir%\setup\temp, where %windir% is the path to the Windows folder, which most likely is C:\Windows\setup\temp.
4. The PC reboots again, and the GUI mode of Setup begins. Setup reads information that it saved about the old Windows system and makes appropriate changes to the Windows 2000 registry. It then migrates application DLLs to Windows 2000 and reboots for the last time. The upgrade is now done.

During installation, Windows 2000 records information about the installation to a file called Setuplog.txt. This file is useful when troubleshooting any problems that occur during installation.

After the Installation: Backing Up the System State

A+ OS 1.1 1.5

After you have completed installing Windows 2000, do the following:

1. Access the Internet and download and install all OS service pack, updates and patches.
2. Verify that all hardware is working and install additional devices, such as printers, as needed.
3. Create user accounts for Windows 2000. (How to do this is covered later in the chapter.) You can also install any additional Windows components at this time.
4. Verify that the system is functioning properly and back up the system state. This backup of the system can later be used to help you recover the OS in the event of system failure. (You will learn more about recovering from system failure in Chapter 8.)

Windows 2000 calls the files critical to a successful operating system load the **system state data**. This includes all files necessary to boot the OS, the Windows 2000 registry, and all system files in the %SystemRoot% folder, the folder in which Windows 2000 is installed. For an upgrade, the folder will most likely be C:\Windows, the original Windows folder before the upgrade. For a clean install the default folder is C:\WINNT. When you perform a backup of the system state data, you cannot select which of these files you want to back up because Windows 2000 will always back up all of them. Here is the process:

1. Click **Start**, point to **Programs**, **Accessories**, **System Tools**, and then click **Backup**. The Backup dialog box opens. Click the **Backup** tab. See Figure 7-5.

A+ OS 1.5

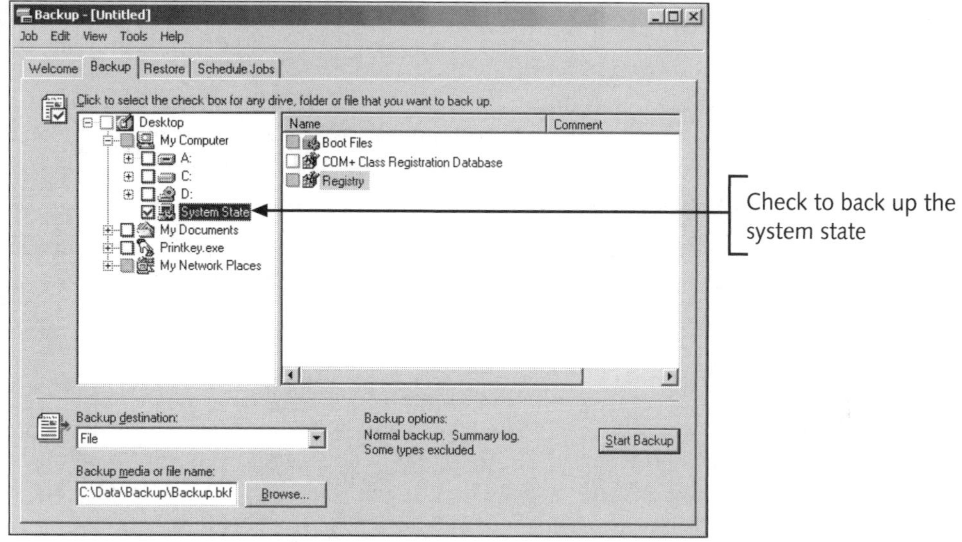

Figure 7-5 Back up the Windows 2000 registry and all critical system files

2. Check the **System State** box in the list of items you can back up. Notice in Figure 7-5 that the system state includes the boot files and the registry. It also includes the COM+ (Component Object Model) Registration Database, which contains information about applications and includes files in the Windows folders.
3. Select the destination for the backup. You can back up to any media, including a folder on the hard drive, Zip drive, tape drive, or network drive. Click **Start Backup** to begin the process.

Later, if you have problems with a corrupted Windows 2000 installation, you can click the Restore tab in the Backup window illustrated in Figure 7-5 to restore the system to its state at the last backup.

When you back up the system state, the registry is also backed up to the folder %SystemRoot%\repair\RegBack. If you later have a corrupted registry, you can copy files from this folder to the registry folder, which is %SystemRoot%\System32\Config.

USING WINDOWS 2000

A+ OS 2.2

In Chapter 4, you learned how keyboard shortcuts and Windows Explorer help you in using Windows 9x. Much of the information you learned about using Windows 9x applies to Windows 2000 as well. However, there are important differences and improvements that you need to know about, including how to manage the desktop and how to increase security of files and resources. As with any version of Windows, additional Windows components can be installed using the Add/Remove Programs applet in Control Panel.

7

Managing the Desktop

There are two basic ways to set up your desktop. One is the classic Windows style, used in Windows 95 and later versions, in which you single-click to select an item and double click to open it, and all your desktop content is offline and localized to your computer. The second is to use Active Desktop, which allows you to set your desktop to behave like a Web page and include Web content.

To activate Active desktop, right click anywhere on the desktop and select Show Web Content from the shortcut menu. Because Active Desktop uses considerable system resources, it is not recommended for most situations.

Managing Shortcuts

In Chapter 4 you learned how to create and manage desktop shortcuts and icons in Windows 9x and about keystroke shortcuts when using Windows 9x. You can use that same information with Windows 2000. As a reminder, here are three different ways to create a shortcut in Windows 2000:

- Select (single-click) the file, folder, or program in Explorer or in a My Computer window. From the File menu, select Create Shortcut.
- In Explorer, on the File menu, click New and then click Shortcut.
- Right-click on the file, folder, or program to which you want to create a shortcut and select Create Shortcut from the menu.

Once the shortcut is created in the same folder as the file it pertains to, drag the shortcut to the desktop.

A+ OS 1.1

Managing the Start Menu

As you know from earlier chapters and probably also from your own experience, the Start menu in Windows shows frequently used files and programs. This enables you to access these items quickly rather than having to search for them in Windows Explorer or with the Find command.

There are many ways you can customize the Start menu. For example, you can set the Program menu to only display recently used applications and show an arrow at the bottom by which you can expand the menu and access programs that were not initially shown. To make this change:

1. Click **Start**, **Settings**, and **Taskbar and Start Menu**.
2. The Taskbar and Start Menu Properties window opens. Click to place a check next to **Use Personalized Menus** (Figure 7-6).
3. Click **Apply** to execute the change, and then click **OK** to close the window.
4. Click **Start** and point to **Programs**. Only recently used programs are shown. (See Figure 7-7.)

A+ OS 1.1

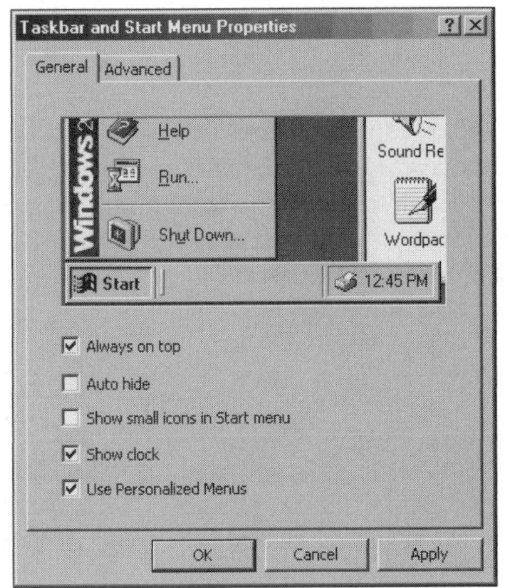

Figure 7-6 Change Start menu and taskbar options

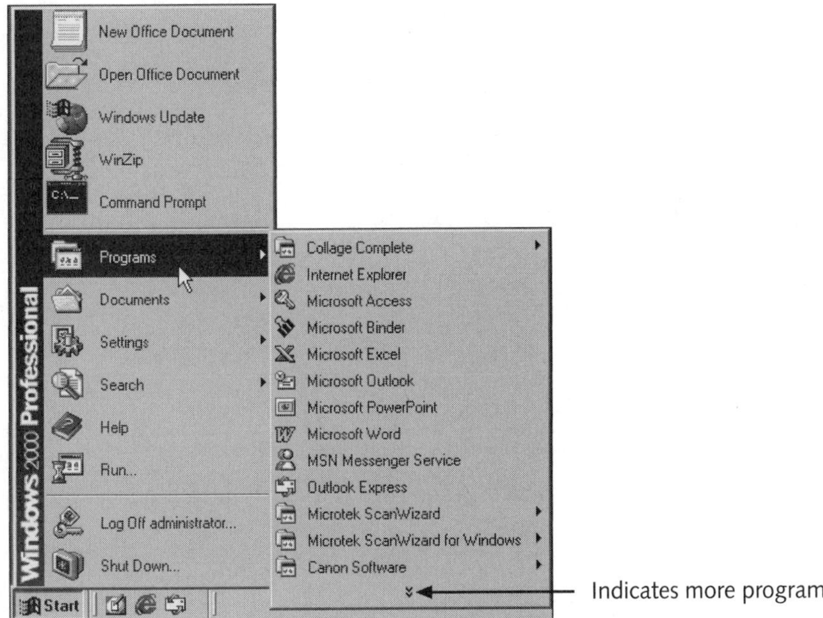

Figure 7-7 A personalized menu shows only recently accessed programs

5. Notice in Figure 7-7 that there is a small double arrow at the bottom of the personalized menu. To access programs not shown on the personalized menu, click the arrow. The complete menu appears with the programs that were not shown on the personalized menu shaded in a lighter color.

7

A+ OS 1.1 Notice in Figure 7-6 that you selected the personalized menus option from the General tab of the Taskbar and Start Menu Properties window. The Advanced tab offers additional options for customizing the Start menu (Figure 7-8). From this window, you can add, remove, and sort Start menu items as well as add commands or tools that are not usually shown on the Start menu. As an alternative to using personalized menus, you can even choose to display the Programs menu as a scrolling list. The scrolling list under Start Menu Settings offers a variety of options. To activate an option, scroll through the list and check the items that you want, and then click Apply and OK.

Managing the Taskbar

As with the Start menu, the taskbar in Windows 2000 offers more options for customization than were available with earlier versions of Windows. (One option that was available with Windows 9x, auto-hiding the taskbar, was covered in Chapter 4 and works the same way with Windows 2000.) The taskbar can show status information, provide quick links to common programs and files, and include an address bar in which to type paths and URLs to go to.

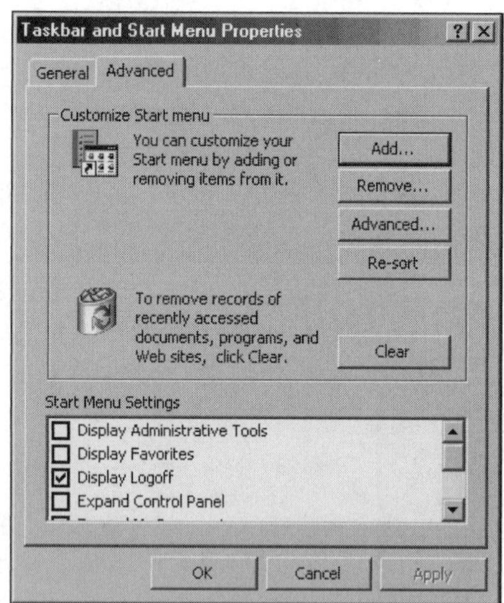

Figure 7-8 The Advanced tab offers many ways to customize the Start menu

The General tab of the Taskbar and Start Menu Properties window, which you saw in Figure 7-6, offers options to auto-hide the taskbar or to set it to be always on top of whatever windows are open. You can reach additional options for customizing the taskbar by right-clicking it and selecting options from the shortcut menu. For example, to add toolbars to the taskbar, right-click it, point to Toolbars, and then select the desired toolbar from the menu that appears (see Figure 7-9). Figure 7-10 shows the taskbar with toolbars added. Notice the system tray (systray) on the right side of the taskbar that contains icons indicating the status of several currently running services such as the sound controls.

A+ OS 1.1

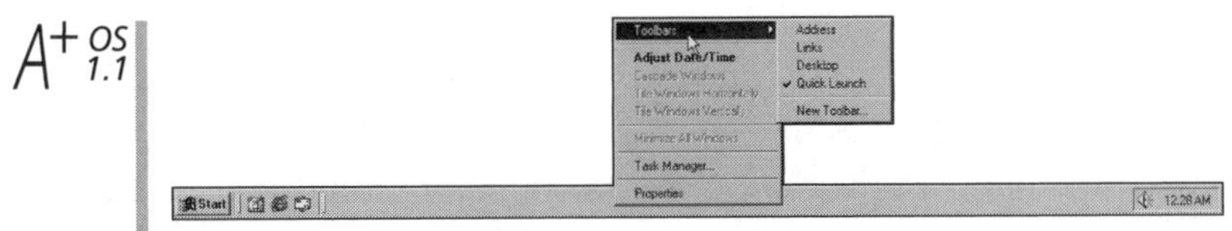

Figure 7-9 Use this shortcut menu to add toolbars to the taskbar

Figure 7-10 Adding toolbars to the taskbar gives you quick access to common programs, tools, and locations

7

INSTALLING HARDWARE AND APPLICATIONS

A+ OS 2.4

This section discusses how to install hardware and software and includes special considerations for legacy hardware and software. As with Windows 98, Windows 2000 has an Add New Hardware wizard that automatically launched when new hardware is detected, and software is best installed from the Add/Remove Programs icon of Control Panel.

Installing Hardware

A+ OS 2.4

Windows 2000 can automatically detect and install Plug and Play devices, as long as you also have Plug and Play BIOS and drivers and devices that are Plug and Play compliant. If a device is Plug and Play, Windows 2000 automatically does the following:

- Identifies the device you are installing
- Determines what system resources the device needs and assigns them so that there are no conflicts with other devices
- Configures the device as necessary
- Loads any device drivers that are needed to run the device
- Informs the system of any changes in configuration

For PnP devices, the Add New Hardware Wizard automatically launches at startup. Any user can complete the installation if the following are true: installing the device drivers can be done without user input, all files necessary for a complete installation are present, the drivers have been digitally signed (digital signatures are covered next), and there are no errors during installation. If any of these conditions don't exist, the installation is abandoned until someone with administrator privileges logs on.

Most devices that are designed to work with Windows 2000 are Plug and Play compatible. If a device is not Plug and Play, you can use the Add/Remove Hardware applet in Control Panel to install the device if you are logged on with administrator privileges.

A+ OS 2.4

If you are using the Add/Remove Hardware Wizard, you will have to provide information such as where the driver for the device is located. Some devices that don't work with Windows 2000 may be completely incompatible and will not work at all. After a device is installed, if you have a problem with the device, you can attempt to update the device driver as follows:

1. In the Control Panel, double-click the **System** icon.
2. The System Properties window opens. Select the **Hardware** tab. See Figure 7-11.
3. Click the **Device Manager** button. The Device Manager opens, as shown in Figure 7-11. Expand the device class tree by clicking the plus sign, and locate the device for which you want to update a driver. For this example, we are using the floppy disk drive.

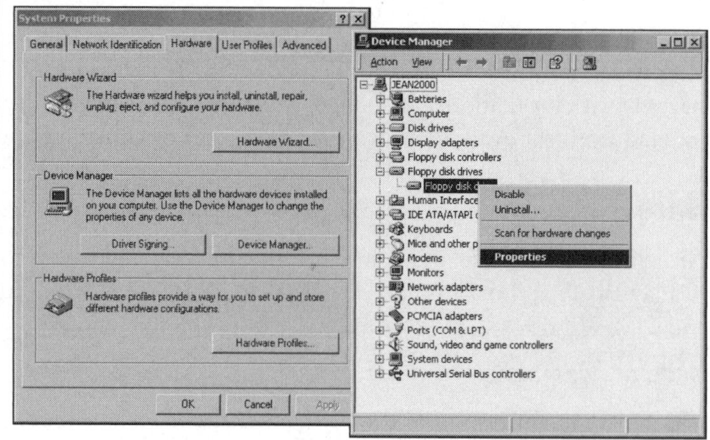

Figure 7-11 Use Device Manager to access a device's properties

4. Right-click the floppy drive and select **Properties** from the shortcut menu (Figure 7-11).
5. The Floppy disk drive Properties window opens (see Figure 7-12).On the **Driver** tab, click **Update Driver**. The Update Device Driver Wizard is displayed. Follow directions on screen to update the driver, if an update exists.

You must be logged on with administrator privileges to make changes from the Device Manager.

A+ OS 2.4

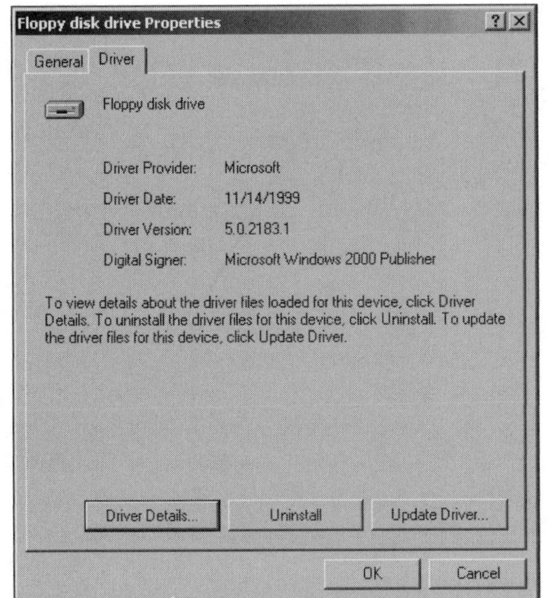

Figure 7-12 A device's Properties window provides a way to update its drivers

Installing Applications

The process of installing applications in Windows 2000 is not much different than in earlier versions of Windows. If you are familiar with the installation wizards and setup programs that were used with Windows 9x, you should recognize all but a few minor details of these same components in Windows 2000.

The Windows 2000 Add/Remove Programs utility looks significantly different than in Windows 9x, and it provides more options. From the Windows 2000 Add/Remove Programs window, you can change or remove presently installed programs (Figure 7-13); add new programs from a CD-ROM, a floppy disk, or from Microsoft over the Internet, and add or remove Windows components. Note that, in Figure 7-13, the drop-down menu in the upper-right corner is expanded for you, showing how you can sort the view of presently installed programs.

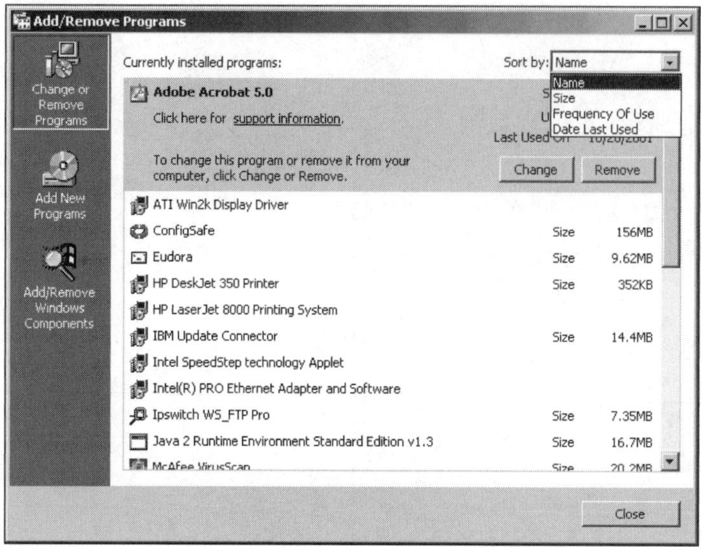

Figure 7-13 Making changes to currently installed programs

CHAPTER SUMMARY

- Windows 2000 makes use of ACPI-compliant system BIOS in order to fully enable power management features.
- If a system does not have ACPI BIOS, upgrade the BIOS before you do the installation, if the BIOS manufacturer offers the upgrade.
- Windows 2000 Active Directory is a new feature of Windows 2000 that provides a centralized point of administration for all shared resources on a network.
- Windows 2000 can have more than one domain controller, whereas Windows NT can have only a single primary domain controller.
- Windows 2000 allows for printing to a URL so that you can send a print job to anywhere on the Internet.
- Windows 2000 offers a clean install and an upgrade installation. A clean install overwrites all information from previous operating system installations on the hard drive.
- Both hardware and software must be compatible with Windows 2000. Check the HCL and the Compatible Software Applications list on the Microsoft Web site before beginning an installation.
- Windows 2000 supports the FAT16, FAT32, and NTFS file systems.
- Windows 2000 supports a dual boot, but each operating system must be installed in its own partition, and an application must be installed twice, once for each OS.
- A Windows 2000 upgrade installation is done in two phases, the Report phase and the Setup phase.

- Windows 2000 can run in native mode and mixed mode. Native mode is used when all domain servers are Windows 2000 servers. Mixed mode is used when a domain has both Windows 2000 and Windows NT servers controlling the domain.
- Windows 2000 supports basic disks and dynamic disks. Both types can use the FAT16, FAT32, and NTFS file systems. Dynamic disks are compatible only with Windows 2000 and Windows XP.
- Backing up the system state helps to ensure that you can recover from a failed OS, restoring the OS to its state at the time of the last backup.
- Windows 2000 Active Desktop allows you to view online content from the desktop.
- Windows 2000 supports Plug and Play and will automatically launch the Add New Hardware Wizard when it senses a new device has been installed on the system.
- Windows 2000 has a Device Manager to view, uninstall, and update devices.
- Applications can be installed using the Add/Remove Programs applet in Control Panel.

Key Terms

Active Directory
answer file
basic disk
dynamic disk
dynamic volume
encryption
mixed mode
native mode
simple volume
spanned volume
standard user
striped volume
system state data
unattended installation

Review Questions

1. What is required before Windows 2000 can provide full power management functionality?
2. Name three manufacturers responsible for the initial development of ACPI?
3. What three file systems does Windows 2000 support?
4. Explain the difference between Windows 2000 native mode and mixed mode.
5. When you print to a printer URL on the Internet, what protocol are you using?
6. If you are installing Windows 2000 on a new hard drive and your system cannot boot from a CD, how do you begin the installation?
7. If you want to access a hard drive using either DOS or Windows 2000, what file system must you use?
8. If you install Windows 2000 on an 8-GB hard drive, use a single partition for the drive, and choose not to use the NTFS file system, what file system will Windows 2000 automatically use?
9. What is the command to create a set of Windows 2000 boot disks?

10. What file must you create before you can do an unattended installation of Windows 2000?
11. If your BIOS is not ACPI-compliant, what should you do before you install Windows 2000?
12. List the operating systems that qualify for a Windows 2000 upgrade.
13. Basic disks divide a hard drive into _________________, but dynamic disks divide hard drives into _________________.
14. Explain the difference between a spanned volume and a striped volume.
15. What Windows 2000 tool can be used to switch between a basic disk or dynamic disk organization for a hard drive?
16. What was the first Windows OS to support FAT32?
17. Which Windows OS does not support FAT32?
18. If an administrator is concerned about security on a system, which file system is appropriate?
19. How do you access System Properties in Windows 2000?
20. Can you perform an upgrade of Windows 2000 from a remote computer on the network? Explain your answer.
21. List the steps necessary to access the Windows 2000 Backup utility.
22. For a person to be able to install hardware, what privileges or permissions must be assigned to his or her user account?
23. Explain how you would use My Computer to create a desktop shortcut.
24. Explain how you would uninstall a device in Windows 2000.
25. When backing up the system state, where does Windows 2000 store a copy of the registry?

Hands-on Projects

Preparing for Windows 2000

Use the Microsoft Web site to research whether your home or lab PC qualifies for Windows 2000. Fill in the following table and print the Web pages showing whether each hardware device and application installed on your PC qualifies for Windows 2000.

Hardware Device or Application	Specific Device Name or Application Name and Version	Does It Qualify for Windows 2000?
System board BIOS		
Video card		
Modem card (if present)		
Sound card (if present)		
Printer (if present)		
Network card (if present)		
CD-ROM drive (if present)		
DVD drive (if present)		
SCSI hard drive (if present)		
Other device		
Application 1		
Application 2		
Application 3		

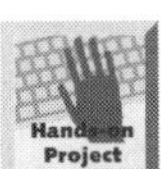

List Windows Components

After installing Windows 2000, list the Windows components included under Add/Remove Programs applet in Control Panel that Windows 2000 Setup did not install on your PC.

Back Up the System State

Back up the Windows 2000 system state to a folder named C:\MyBackup. You will use this backup in the next chapter in a recovery process. Print a screen shot of Explorer showing the size of the backup file in the MyBackup folder.

Case Project

Installing Windows 2000 Professional

Install Windows 2000 Professional. If you have Windows 98 already installed, then install Windows 2000 as a dual boot with Windows 98. If you don't have Windows 98 installed, then perform a clean installation. Use the NTFS file system. Write down every decision you made during the installation and every value that you entered. How long did the installation take?

CHAPTER

8

MANAGING AND TROUBLESHOOTING WINDOWS 2000

In this chapter, you will learn:

- About the boot process for Windows 2000
- How to troubleshoot the Windows 2000 boot process
- How to use tools for maintenance, troubleshooting, and performance monitoring in Windows

In the last chapter, you learned how Windows 2000 is structured, how it is different from other versions of Windows, and how to install and work with it. This chapter covers managing, supporting, and troubleshooting Windows in more detail, including problems you might have with the boot process or with system errors and performance after the system is running. You will learn about many useful tools and sources of information to use when working with Windows 2000.

UNDERSTANDING THE BOOT PROCESS

The Windows 2000 boot process works just like the Windows NT process. You can review these steps in Chapter 6. In this section, we look at some of the troubleshooting tools provided by Windows 2000 to solve boot problems, but first let's turn our attention to customizing the boot process.

Customizing the Boot Process

A+ OS 2.3

The Boot.ini file contains information about how the Windows 2000 boot is configured and can be used to customize the boot process. As you learned in Chapter 6, Ntldr reads this file and uses it to see what operating systems are available and how to set up the boot. Figure 8-1 shows an example of a Boot.ini file.

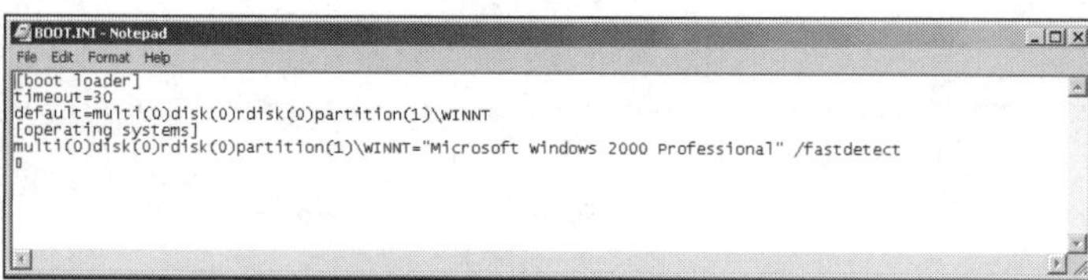


```
[boot loader]
timeout=30
default=multi(0)disk(0)rdisk(0)partition(1)\WINNT
[operating systems]
multi(0)disk(0)rdisk(0)partition(1)\WINNT="Microsoft Windows 2000 Professional" /fastdetect
```

Figure 8-1 A sample Boot.ini file

There are two main sections in Boot.ini: the [boot loader] section and the [operating systems] section. The [boot loader] section contains the number of seconds the system gives the user to select an operating system before it loads the default operating system; this is called a timeout. In Figure 8-1, the timeout is set to 30 seconds. If the system is set for a dual boot, the path to the default operating system is also listed in the [boot loader] section.

The [operating systems] section of the Boot.ini file provides a list of operating systems that can be loaded, including the path to the boot partition of each operating system. Here is the meaning of each entry in Figure 8-1 that points to the location of the OS:

- *Multi (0)*. Use the first hard drive controller
- *Disk (0)*. Only used when booting from a SCSI hard drive
- *Rdisk (0)*. Use the first hard drive
- *Partition (1)*. Use the first partition on the drive

Recall from earlier chapters that you can use the Advanced Options menu when troubleshooting the boot process. You can set the OS to use many of the options found on the Advanced Options menu by adding certain switches to the end of entries in the [operating systems] section in the Boot.ini file. Some of those switches are shown in Table 8-1.

A+ OS 2.3

Table 8-1 Switches for entries in the Boot.ini [operating systems] section

Switch	Purpose
/basevideo	Boots using the standard VGA video driver. This switch is generally used when another video driver is malfunctioning.
/bootlog	Writes information about the boot to the file Ntbtlog.txt, which is located in the C:\WINNT folder.
/debug	Loads the kernel debugger and allows a host debugger to access the system
/fastdetect=COM2	Specifies a COM port that you do not want the OS to inspect for the presence of a peripheral device.
/maxmem:*n*	Used when memory chips are suspected to be corrupted. The *n* is the amount of memory that the operating system is to use. It ignores the rest.
/noguiboot	Boots the operating system without displaying boot status graphically. This parameter does not affect whether the system boots to a command prompt or to the Windows GUI.
/safeboot:*parameter*	Starts the computer in safe mode, with these parameters: ■ *Minimal* boots the computer in safe mode with minimal drivers and without network support. ■ *Network* boots into Safe Mode with network support.
/sos	Used to determine whether a corrupted device driver is causing startup problems. This switch displays the names of device drivers as they are loaded.

In Figure 8-1, the only switch used in this Boot.ini file is /fastdetect with no COM port following, which means that peripherals connected to any COM port are not inspected at startup.

The recommended way to change Boot.ini settings, which is also easier and safer than manually editing the file, is through the System Properties window:

1. On the Start menu, point to **Settings**, and then click **Control Panel**.
2. Double-click the **System** icon.
3. The System Properties window opens. Click the **Advanced** tab (see Figure 8-2).
4. Click the **Startup and Recovery** button.
5. The Startup and Recovery window opens (see Figure 8-3). Change settings as desired, and then click **OK** to save them (or Cancel if you do not want to save them).

A+ OS 2.3

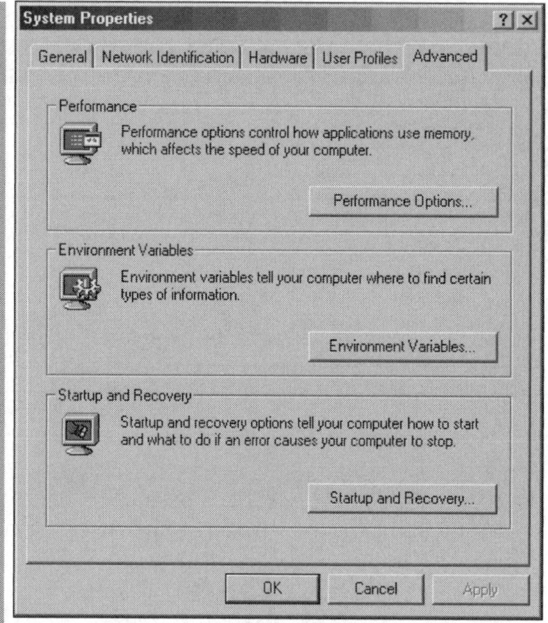

Figure 8-2 You can access startup and recovery options from the System Properties window

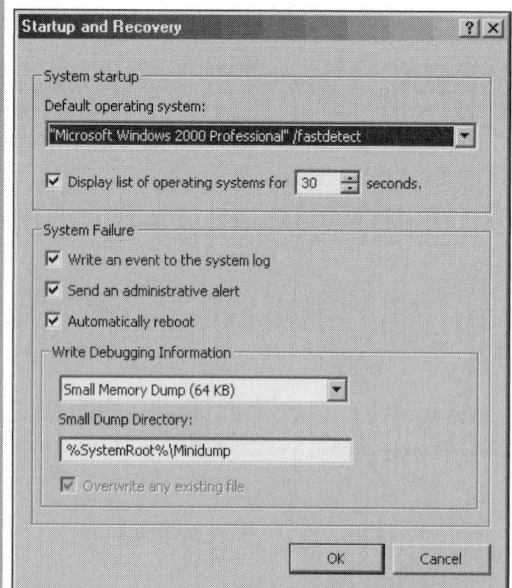

Figure 8-3 Changing the default operating system and timeout value in the Startup and Recovery window changes the Boot.ini settings

A+ OS 2.3 From the Startup and Recovery window, you can designate the default operating system and set the timeout value in the System startup pane. The default is 30 seconds, and you can change that value to reflect how long you want the system to wait before starting the default operating system. If you set the value to 0, the system will start the default operating system automatically and will not give the user a choice.

If you cannot get to the System Properties window, you can also edit the Boot.ini file using Notepad, as shown in Figure 8-1. The file is a hidden system file; therefore, in order to view it, you must first change the folder options to display these type files. In Windows Explorer, select the root directory, click Tools, Folder Options, and then select the View tab (see Figure 8-4). Uncheck the option to *Hide protected operating system files*.

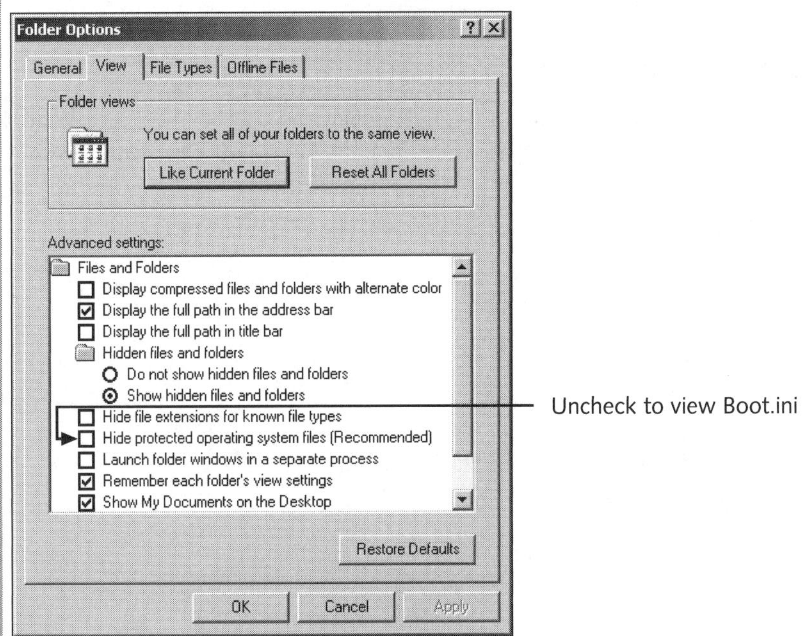

8

Figure 8-4 Change the folder options so that protected operating system files are not hidden

From a text editor such as Notepad, you can set the timeout value to –1, which will cause the system to wait for a selection indefinitely. You cannot set the timeout to –1 from the Startup and Recovery window.

TROUBLESHOOTING THE BOOT PROCESS

A+ OS 2.3 3.1 When problems arise with booting, as with all PC problems, try the simple things first. Turn off the power and restart the system. Check for loose cables, switches that are not on, stuck keys on the keyboard, a wall outlet switch turned off, and similar easy-to-solve problems. The

A+ OS 2.3 3.1 3.2

next step is to determine at what point in the boot process the system fails. Ask what has happened since the last successful boot. Has new hardware or software been installed? Has there been a power surge or electrical storm? Has a user tinkered with the system? If you cannot pinpoint the source of the problem, then you have several tools to help you troubleshoot the boot process. Windows 2000 offers an Advanced Options menu, which includes starting the computer in safe mode. Use this option to prevent many device drivers and system services that normally load during the boot process from loading. You can then fix or disable these devices or services once the OS loads. The second utility, called the Recovery Console, is new to Windows 2000. It provides a command-line interface that allows you to perform maintenance and repairs to the hard drive. Another tool is the emergency startup disk, which is used to recover from problems with corrupted or missing operating system files or a corrupted hard drive boot sector. These three tools are discussed next.

Advanced Options Menu

As a PC boots, when the message *Starting Windows* appears at the bottom of the screen, press the F8 key to display the Windows 2000 **Advanced Options menu**, shown in Figure 8-5. As with the Windows 9x startup menu, this menu can be used to diagnose and fix problems when booting Windows 2000. The purpose of each option on the menu is outlined in the following sections.

Windows 2000 Advanced Options Menu
Please select an option:

Safe Mode
Safe Mode with Networking
Safe Mode with Command Prompt

Enable Boot Logging
Enable VGA Mode
Last Known Good Configuration
Directory Services Restore Mode (Windows 2000 domain controllers only)
Debugging Mode

Boot Normally

Use ↑ and ↓ to move the highlight to your choice.
Press Enter to choose.

Figure 8-5 Press the F8 key at startup to display the Windows 2000 Advanced Options menu

Safe Mode Safe mode boots the OS with a minimum configuration and can be used to solve problems when a new hardware installation is causing problems or a user has made settings that are causing problems. Safe mode boots with the mouse, monitor with basic video, keyboard, and mass storage drivers loaded. It uses the default system services (it does not load any extra services) and does not provide access to a network. When you boot in safe mode, you see "Safe Mode" in all four corners of your screen. You have a GUI interface in safe mode. Once the OS loads in safe mode, you can disable

A+ OS 2.3 3.2

the problem device, scan for viruses, run diagnostic software, or take other appropriate action to diagnose and solve problems. When you load Windows 2000 in safe mode, all files used for the load are recorded in the Ntbtlog.txt file.

Safe Mode with Networking Use this option when you are solving a problem with booting and need access to the network to solve the problem. For example, if you have just attempted to install a printer, which is causing the OS to hang when it boots, and the printer drivers are downloaded from the network, boot into safe mode with networking. Uninstall the printer and then install it again from the network. Also use this mode when the Windows 2000 installation files are not loaded from CD, but from the network, and you need to access these files.

Safe Mode with Command Prompt This safe mode option does not automatically load a GUI desktop. Use it to get a command prompt. If safe mode does not load the OS, then try this option.

8

Enable Boot Logging When you boot with this option, Windows 2000 loads normally and you access the regular desktop as usual. However, all the files used during the load process are recorded in a file, Ntbtlog.txt. Use this option to see what did and did not load during the boot process. If you are having a problem getting a device to work, check Ntbtlog.txt for its driver files. Boot logging is much more effective if you have a copy of the file that was made when everything was working as it should, and then you can compare the good load to the bad load, looking for differences.

Enable VGA Mode Use this option when the video setting is such that you can't see well enough to fix a bad setting. This can happen because of a corrupted video driver or when a user has created a desktop with black fonts on a black background, or something similar. Booting in this mode gives you a very plain VGA video. Go to the Display settings, correct the problem, and reboot normally.

Last Known Good Configuration Just as with Windows NT, Windows 2000 keeps the Last Known Good configuration in the registry. Use this option if you suspect the system was configured incorrectly. Windows 2000 will be restored to the settings of the last successful boot and all system setting changes made after this last successful boot are lost.

Each time the system boots completely and the user logs on, the Last Known Good is saved. If you have booted several times since a problem started, the Last Known Good will not help you recover from the problem, since all saved versions of the Last Known Good reflect the problem.

Directory Services Restore Mode (Windows 2000 Domain Controllers Only) This option applies only to domain controllers and is used as one step in the process of recovering from a corrupted Active Directory. Recall that the Active Directory is the domain database managed by the domain controller that tracks users and resources on the domain. The details of how all this works are beyond the scope of this chapter.

A+ OS 2.3 3.1

Debugging Mode This mode gives you the opportunity to move system boot logs from the failing computer to another computer for evaluation. Connect another computer to the failing computer by way of the serial port. In this mode, Windows 2000 sends all the boot information to the serial port. The details of how to do this can be found in the *Windows 2000 Professional Resource Kit* (Microsoft Press).

Recovery Console

The Advanced Options menu can be of help if the problem is a faulty device driver or system service. However, if the problem goes deeper than that, the next tool to use is the **Recovery Console**. Use it when the operating system does not start properly or hangs during the load. The Recovery Console does not use a GUI, and with it you can access the FAT16, FAT32, and NTFS file systems.

The purpose of the Recovery Console is to allow you to repair a damaged registry, system files, or file system on the hard drive. You must enter the Administrator password in order to use the Console and access an NTFS volume. If the registry is so corrupted that the Recovery Console cannot read the password in order to validate it, you are not asked for the password, but you are limited in what you can do at the Console. You are not allowed into all folders, and you cannot copy files from the hard drive to a floppy disk without setting certain parameters.

The Recovery Console software is located on the Windows 2000 CD and also on the four Windows 2000 setup disks. If you have not already created the setup disks, you can go to a working Windows 2000 PC and create the disks by following the directions given in Chapter 7. Follow these steps to load Windows 2000 from the disks and access the Recovery Console:

1. Insert the first of the four setup disks and restart the PC. You are directed to insert each of the four disks in turn, and then the Setup screen appears as shown in Figure 8-6.

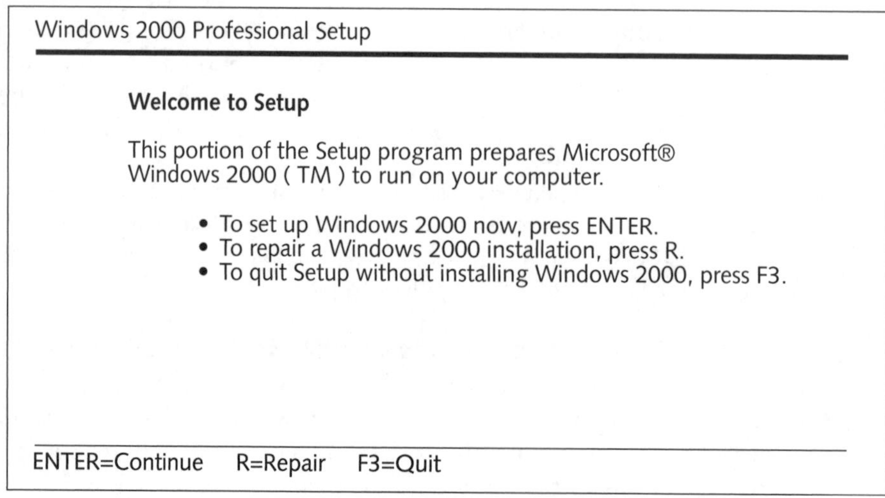

Figure 8-6 Use this Windows Setup screen to access the Recovery Console

A+ OS 2.3 3.1

2. Type **R** to select the To repair a Windows 2000 installation option. The Windows 2000 Repair Options window opens. See Figure 8-7. Type **C** to select the Recovery Console.

3. The Windows 2000 Recovery Console window opens. See Figure 8-8. The Recovery Console looked at the hard drive and determined that there was only a single Windows 2000 installation on the drive installed in the C:\WINNT folder. (The WINNT folder might be on a different drive on your machine.) Press **1**, and then press **Enter** to select that installation.

```
Windows 2000 Professional Setup

    Windows 2000 Repair Options:

        • To repair a Windows 2000 installation by using
          the recovery console, press C.

        • To repair a Windows 2000 installation by using
          the emergency repair process, press R.

    If the repair options do not successfully repair your system,
    run Windows 2000 Setup again.

C=Console   R=Repair   F3=Quit
```

Figure 8-7 Windows 2000 offers two repair options

```
Microsoft Windows 2000 ( TM ) Recovery Console.

The Recovery Console provides system repair and recovery functionality.

Type EXIT to quit the Recovery Console and restart the computer.

1: C:\WINNT

Which Windows 2000 installation would you like to log onto
(To cancel, press ENTER)? 1
Type the Administrator password:
C:\WINNT>
```

Figure 8-8 The Windows 2000 Recovery Console command prompt

4. Enter the Administrator password and press **Enter**. If you don't know the password, you cannot use the console.

A+ OS 2.3 3.1

You now have a command prompt. You can use a limited group of DOS-like commands at this point to recover a failed system. These commands are listed and described in Table 8-2. To leave the Recovery Console and start Windows 2000, type **Exit** at the command prompt.

At the command prompt, to retrieve the last command, press F3. To retrieve the command one character at a time, press the F1 key.

Table 8-2 Commands available from the Recovery Console

Command	Description
Attrib	Changes the attributes of a file or folder (works the same as the DOS version, as in the following example): `Attrib -r -h -s filename` This command removes the read, hidden, and system attributes from the file.
Batch	Carries out commands stored in a batch file: `Batch file1 file2` The commands stored in file1 are executed, and the results written to file2. If no file2 is specified, results are written to the screen.
Cd	Displays or changes the current directory.
Chkdsk	Checks a disk and repairs or recovers the data.
Cls	Clears the screen.
Copy	Copies a single uncompressed file, for example: `Copy A:\File1 C:\WINNT\File2` Copies the file on the floppy disk named File1 to the hard drive, WINNT folder, naming the file File2. Use the command to replace corrupted files. No wildcard characters are allowed.
Del	Deletes a file: `Del File1`
Dir	Lists files and folders.
Disable	Used when a service or driver starts and prevents the system from booting properly: `Disable servicename` This command disables a Windows 2000 system service or driver, restarts the computer without it, and helps you determine the problem.
Diskpart	Creates and deletes partitions on the hard drive. Enter the command with no arguments to display a user interface.
Enable	Enables a Windows 2000 system service or driver: `Enable servicename`
Exit	Quits the Recovery Console and restarts the computer.
Expand	Expands a compressed file and copies it from a floppy disk or a CD to the destination folder. For example: `Expand A:\File1 C:\WINNT` Expands the file on the floppy disk, copying it to the hard drive.

A+ OS 2.3 3.1

Table 8-2 Commands available from the Recovery Console (continued)

Command	Description
Fixboot	Rewrites the OS boot sector on the hard drive. If a drive letter is not specified, the system drive is assumed. `Fixboot C:` Use this command when the boot sector is damaged.
Fixmbr	Rewrites the Master Boot Record boot program. This command is the same as Fdisk/MBR. Use this command when the Master Boot Record is damaged.
Format	Formats a logical drive. If no file system is specified, NTFS is assumed: `Format C:/fs:FAT32` Uses FAT32 file system `Format C:/fs:FAT` Uses FAT16 file system
Help	Help utility appears for the given command:`Help Fixboot`
Listsvc	Lists all available services.
Logon	Allows you to log on to an installation with the Administrator password.
Map	Lists all drive letters and file system types.
Md or Mkdir	Creates a directory: `MD C:\TEMP`
More or Type	Displays a text file on screen: `TYPE filename.ext`
Rd or Rmdir	Deletes a directory: `RD C:\TEMP`
Rename or Ren	Renames a file: `Rename File1.txt File2.txt`
Set	Displays or sets Recovery Console environmental variables.
Systemroot	Sets the current directory to the directory where Windows 2000 is installed.
Type	Displays contents of a text file: `Type File1.txt`

Using the Recovery Console to Restore the Registry If you suspect that the registry is damaged, you can use the Recovery Console commands to restore the registry from the last backup that you have created. The registry consists of five files, Default, Sam, Security, Software, and System, which are stored in the %SystemRoot%\System32\Config folder. A backup of the registry is stored in the %SystemRoot%\Repair\RegBack folder every time you back up the system state (see Figure 8-9).

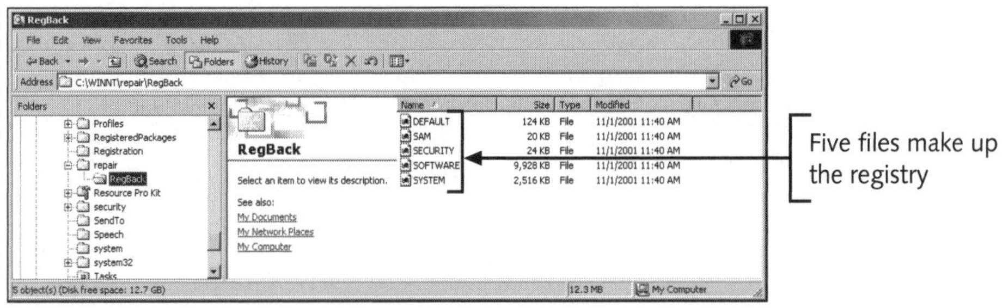

Figure 8-9 Windows puts a backup of the registry in the C:\WINNT\repair\RegBack folder

8

A+ OS 2.3 3.1 3.2

In Microsoft documentation, %SystemRoot% means the Windows 2000 folder on the boot partition. In most cases, that folder is C:\WINNT.

To restore the registry from this backup using the Recovery Console, first rename the registry files so that you can backtrack if necessary. From the Recovery Console command prompt, perform the steps outlined in Table 8-3. These actions will restore the registry to its state at the time of the last backup.

Table 8-3 Steps to restore the registry

Command	Description
1. Systemroot	Makes the Windows folder the current folder.
2. CD System32\Config	Makes the Windows registry folder the current folder.
3. Ren Default Default.save Ren Sam Sam.save Ren Security Security.save Ren Software Software.save Ren System System.save	Renames the five registry files.
4. Systemroot	Returns to the Windows folder.
5. CD repair\RegBack	Makes the registry backup folder the current folder.
6. Copy default C:\WINNT\system32\config Copy Sam C:\WINNT\system32\config Copy Security C:\WINNT\system32\config Copy Software C:\WINNT\system32\config Copy System C:\WINNT\system32\config	Copies the five registry files from the backup folder to the registry folder.

Installing the Recovery Console Although the Recovery Console is often launched from the Windows CD to recover from system failure, you can also install it on your working system so it appears on the Start menu. Use it to address less drastic problems that occur, when you can access the menu. To install the Recovery Console:

1. Open a command window in Windows 2000.
2. Change from the current directory to the \I386 folder on the Windows 2000 CD.
3. Enter the command **winnt32 /cmdcons**. The Recovery Console is installed.
4. Restart your computer. Recovery Console should now be shown with the list of available operating systems on the Start menu.

Emergency Repair Process

If options on the Advanced Options menu fail to recover the system and the Recovery Console fails to do so, your next option is the **Emergency Repair Process**. Use this option only as a last resort because it restores the system to the state it was in immediately

A+ OS 2.3 3.1 3.2

after the Windows 2000 installation. All changes since the installation will be lost. The process uses an Emergency Repair Disk (ERD), but the disk does not contain the same information as does the Windows NT ERD (Windows NT Emergency Repair Disk).

Recall that the Windows NT ERD contains a copy of the registry, and that you should update the disk any time you make significant changes to the registry. You can then use the disk to repair a corrupted registry, restoring it to its state when you last updated the ERD.

The Windows 2000 ERD contains information about your current installation, but does not contain a copy of the registry because it is too large to fit on a single floppy disk. The Windows 2000 ERD points to a folder on the hard drive where the registry was backed up when Windows 2000 was installed. This folder is %SystemRoot%\repair, which most likely is C:\WINNT\repair.

A+ OS 1.1 2.3 3.1 3.2

Using the Windows 2000 ERD to recover from a corrupted registry returns you to the installation version of the registry, and you lose all changes to the registry since that time. Because of the way the ERD works, you do not need to update the disk once you've created it. Before a problem occurs, follow these directions to create the disk:

1. Click **Start**, point to **Programs**, **Accessories**, and **System Tools**, and then click **Backup**. The Backup window appears with the Welcome tab selected. See Figure 8-10. Select **Emergency Repair Disk**.
2. The Backup tab and the Emergency Repair Diskette dialog box open. If you check the box shown in Figure 8-11, the system backs up your registry to a folder under the Repair folder, %SystemRoot%\repair\RegBack.
3. Click **OK** to create the disk. Label the disk Windows 2000 Emergency Repair Disk, and keep it in a safe place.

A+ OS 2.3 3.1 3.2

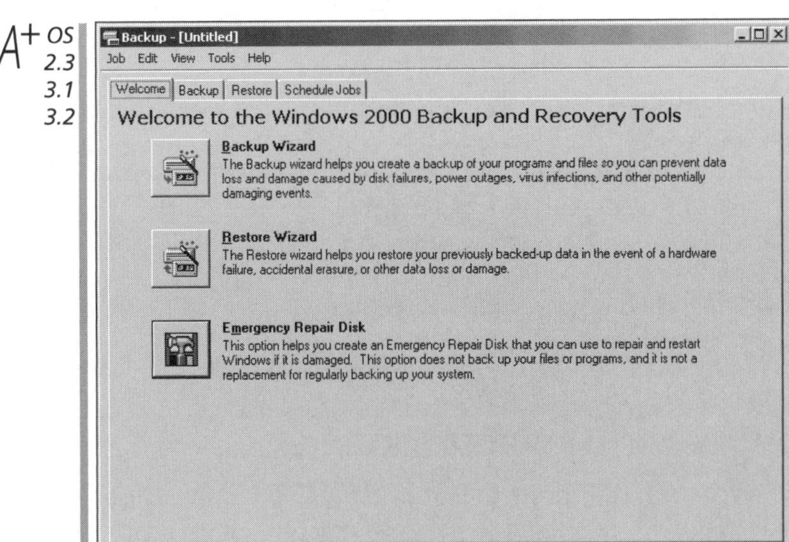

Figure 8-10 Use the Backup window to back up the registry and create an emergency repair disk

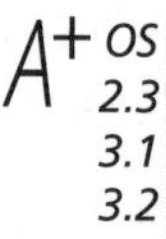
OS 2.3 3.1 3.2

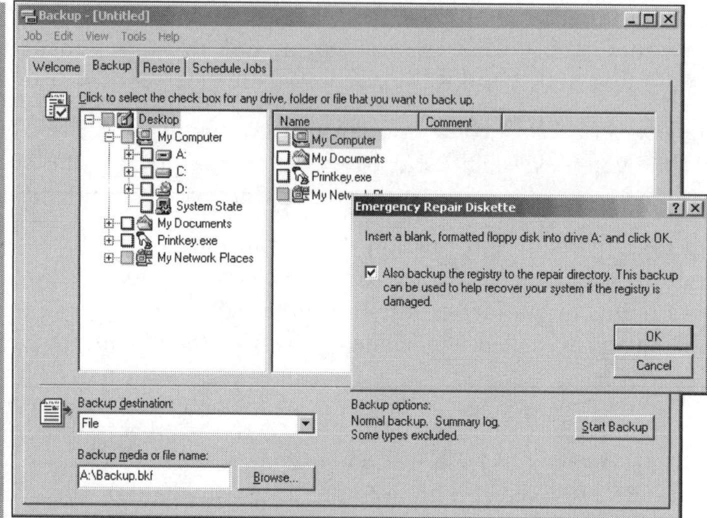

Figure 8-11 Create an ERD and back up the registry to the hard drive

If your hard drive fails, you can use the ERD to restore the system, including system files, boot files, and the registry, to its state at the end of the Windows 2000 installation. To do that follow these steps:

1. Boot the PC from the four Windows 2000 setup disks. The Setup menu appears (refer back to Figure 8-6). Select option **R**.
2. When the Windows 2000 Repair Options window opens (refer back to Figure 8-7), select option **R**.
3. You are instructed to insert the Emergency Repair Disk. Follow the instructions on the screen to repair the installation.

If this process does not work, then your next option is to reinstall Windows 2000. Be sure to use ScanDisk to scan the hard disk surface for errors before you do the installation. If you suspect that a virus has damaged the file system, also use the Fixmbr command or the Fdisk /MBR command discussed in earlier chapters to replace the master boot program in case it has been corrupted by the virus. Windows 2000 also offers a utility called InoculateIT Antivirus AVBoot, which is a command-line tool that can scan memory, the MBR sector, and OS boot sectors for viruses. You will learn to use the utility in a project at the end of the chapter.

Tools for Maintenance and Troubleshooting

In this section, you will learn about many tools you can use for maintenance and troubleshooting in Windows. You learned about some tools earlier in this chapter, as well as in previous chapters on other versions of Windows. This section covers some additional tools. You will learn how use these tools to manage hard disks, applications, system processes, and other components of Windows.

Using the Backup Tool to Restore the System State

A+ OS 1.1

In Chapter 7, you learned how to back up the system state after installing Windows 2000 and verifying that the system is working. To use the backup (Ntbackup.exe) to restore the system state after a system failure or the registry becoming corrupted, begin the same way you did to make the backup by clicking Start, pointing to Programs, Accessories, and System Tools and then clicking Backup. The dialog box opens with the Backup tab showing. Click the Restore tab, which is shown in Figure 8-12.

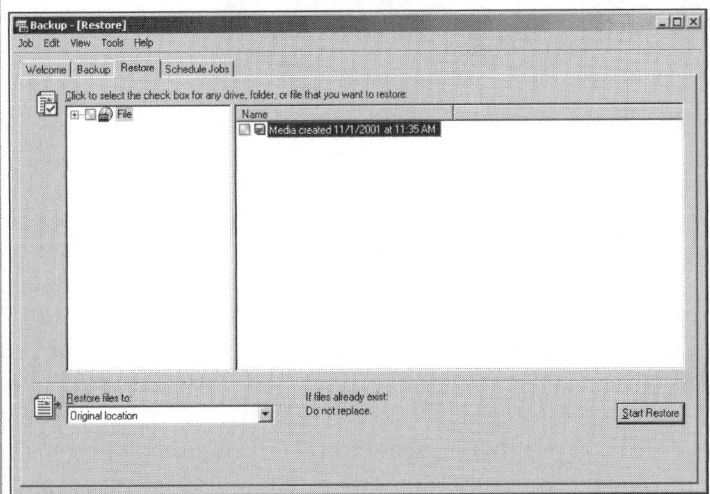

Figure 8-12 Restore the system state from the Restore tab of the Backup window

From the Restore tab, you select the backup you want to restore and, in the drop-down menu in the bottom-left corner, the location to which it is to be restored. Click the Start Restore button in the bottom-right corner to start the process. Remember that you can restore the system state as a way of restoring the registry.

8

Windows 2000 Support Tools

A+ OS 3.3

Windows 2000 offers several support tools that you can install. They are located in the \Support\Tools folder of the Windows 2000 CD. To install them, run the Setup program in that folder. Enter this command in the Run dialog box: D:\Support\Tools\Setup.exe. Substitute the drive letter of the CD-ROM drive for D in the command line. The list of tools installed is shown in Figure 8-13.

In addition to the support tools described here, third-party diagnostic software can be of help. For example, ConfigSafe by imagineLAN, Inc. (*www.imaginelan.com*) is a utility that tracks configuration changes to Windows 9x or Windows NT/2000/XP and can restore the system to a previously saved configuration.

A+ OS 3.3

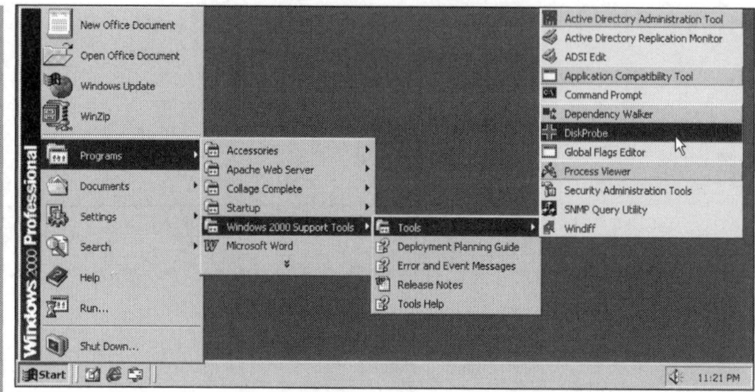

Figure 8-13 Windows 2000 support tools

One of these utilities is Dependency Walker, which lists all the files used by an application. It can be useful when troubleshooting a failed application installation if you have a report of files used by the application on a computer where the installation is good. Compare the reports, looking for DLL files that are missing on the bad installation or are not the correct size or are incorrectly date stamped. Software applications often use DLL files for added functionality and to relate to the operating system. To use the utility, click Start, point to Programs, Windows 2000 Support Tools, and Tools, and then click Dependency Walker. Figure 8-14 shows the resulting Dependency Walker window. Click File, Open, and select the main executable file for an application. In the figure, Apache.exe is selected. Apache is a popular Web server application. The window lists all supporting files that Apache.exe uses and how they are dependent on one another.

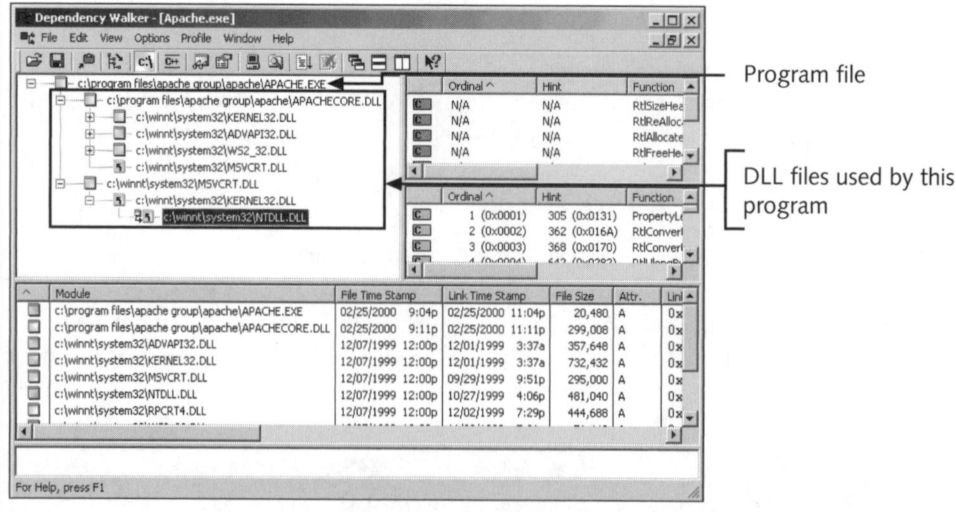

Figure 8-14 You can use Dependency Walker to solve problems with applications

Windows File Protection

Windows 2000 provides a feature called **WFP (Windows File Protection)** to protect system files such as .sys, .dll, or .exe files from modification. Earlier versions of Windows would sometimes allow these files to be overwritten by unsigned, non-Microsoft versions during program installations. Changes to shared system files can cause errors within a program, incompatibility between two or more programs, mismatches between file versions, or even system instability.

WFP prevents these problems and protects files from modification through two tools. One is a background process that notifies WFP when a protected file is modified. WFP then checks the file signature to see whether it is the correct Microsoft version of the file. If the file version is not correct, WFP looks in the Dllcache folder, which contains cached copies of system files, or asks for the Windows 2000 CD to be inserted so that it can find the file and restore it from there. Replacing incorrect system files with correct ones from the Windows 2000 CD requires administrative permissions. If a non-administrator user is logged on when WFP activates, WFP will not prompt that user for insertion of the Windows 2000 CD and will wait until an administrator logs on to request the CD and replace the file.

If a file has been modified, is correctly signed as a Microsoft-approved version, and is not present in the Dllcache folder, WFP adds it to that folder to be used as the correct version on future scans.

When WFP restores a file, it shows the following message by default, replacing *file_name* with the name of the system file it restored:

```
A file replacement was attempted on the protected system
file file_name. To maintain system stability, the file has
been restored to the correct Microsoft version. If
problems occur with your application, please contact the
application vendor for support.
```

If you see this message, carefully note what application was working at the time and what had just happened before the message. In addition to software installations, viruses, and software applications, errors can cause attempted modifications to system files, and it is important for you to have as much information as possible in order to figure out which applications might need to be scanned for viruses or replaced altogether.

The other tool that WFP provides is the **SFC (System File Checker)**. There are several situations in which the system or an administrator might use this tool. If the administrator set the system to perform an unattended installation, after Setup is completed, the SFC checks all protected system files to see whether they were modified by programs added during the installation, as well as the catalog files that contain the file signatures. If any incorrect modifications have been made or if any important system files are found to be unsigned, WFP retrieves a copy of the file from the Dllcache folder or requests it from the Windows 2000 CD.

An administrator can also activate the SFC manually from a command prompt and use it to verify that the system is using correct versions of all protected system files, either as a preventative maintenance measure or when it is suspected that system files have become corrupted or deleted. To use System File Checker, from the command prompt, the administrator types *Sfc.exe* with one of the switches shown in Table 8-4. You can also access the Run dialog box from the Start menu and type *C:\WINNT\system32\sfc.exe /scannow* (or another switch).

Table 8-4 Switches for the Sfc.exe utility

Switch	Function
/cachesize=x	Sets, in megabytes, the size of the file cache.
/cancel	Discontinues scans of protected system files.
/enable	Enables normal operation of WFP.
/purgecache	Empties the file cache and immediately scans all protected system files, populating the Dllcache folder with confirmed correct versions of system files (may require insertion of the Windows 2000 CD as source for correct versions).
/quiet	Replaces incorrect versions of system files with correct ones without prompting the user.
/scanboot	Performs a scan of protected system files every time the system boots.
/scannow	Performs an immediate scan of protected system files.
/scanonce	Performs a scan of protected system files the next time the system boots.
/?	Displays a list of available switches for the sfc command.

Command Window

A+ OS With Windows 2000, executing **CMD.exe** or Command.com from the Run dialog box
1.1 opens a command interpreter window where you can use DOS-like commands at a com-
1.3 mand prompt. The Cmd.exe is the 32-bit version of the older 16-bit Command.com used
1.5 with DOS. A command window is also available under Start, Programs, Accessories, Command Prompt. (In Windows 9x, it was listed as MS-DOS Prompt under Start, Programs.) Type Exit to close the window. You can also execute single commands from the Run dialog box without having to open the command window.

To add a command prompt icon to your desktop for easy access, locate the icon in Windows Explorer under Start, Programs, Accessories, Command Prompt and, while holding down the Ctrl key, drag the icon to your desktop.

Disk Properties Window

A+ OS 1.4

The Disk Properties window provides a way for you to perform routine maintenance on a drive. It is not new to Windows 2000, but is included here to make the list of maintenance tools more complete. To access the window, using Windows Explorer, right-click the icon for the drive that you want to work with and select Properties from the shortcut menu. The Properties window for the selected drive opens, as shown in Figure 8-15. The General tab, which appears in front when you first open the window, provides information about the name, type, and file system of the selected drive, as well as the amount of free and used space.

Notice that the drive in Figure 8-15 is using the FAT32 file system. Compare this window for a FAT32 disk to the window shown in Figure 8-16 for an NTFS disk. One difference in the two windows is the Disk Properties window for an NTFS disk includes the option for drive compression at the bottom of the window. For an NTFS disk, check Compress drive to save disk space, and then click Apply to compress the volume. Later, if you decide to not use compression, clear the check box.

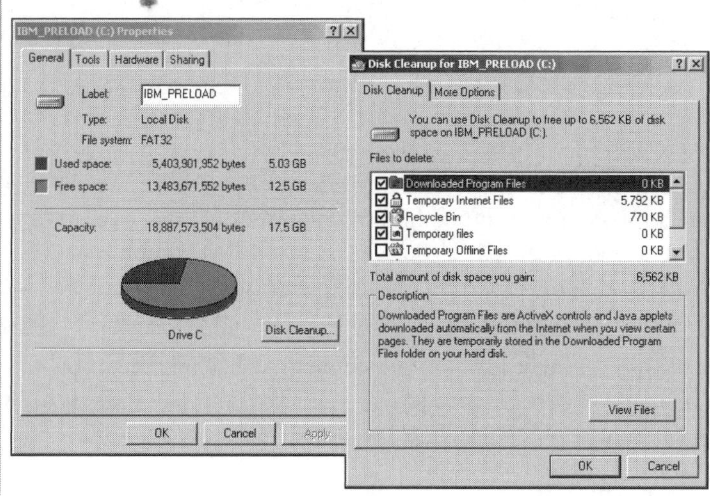

Figure 8-15 The Disk Properties window provides a shortcut to disk management tools

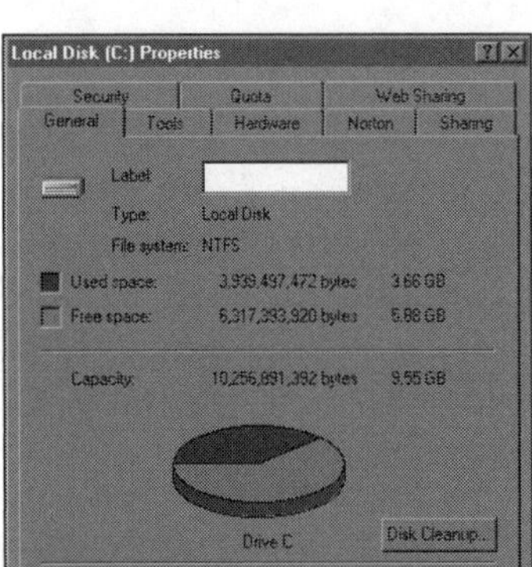

Figure 8-16 Disk Properties window for an NTFS disk

A+ OS 1.4

If you are using NTFS, you can also compress a single folder or file from the General tab of its Properties window.

A+ OS 1.5 2.5

If you click the Disk Cleanup… button to the right of the drive space graphic, the Disk Cleanup window opens with the Disk Cleanup tab showing, as shown in Figure 8-19. From this view, you can select nonessential files to delete in order to save drive space. Disk Cleanup tells you how much total space you can save and how much space each type of removable file is taking up; it also provides a description of each type of file. Included in the list are temporary files created by applications that the applications no longer need.

Going back to the Properties window for the drive, if you click the Tools tab, you can access three drive management tools that you are already familiar with: ScanDisk (listed as Error checking), Backup, and Defrag. The Properties window for a drive just provides another way for you to access these tools.

Computer Management

A+ OS 1.5 2.5

Computer Management is a window that consolidates several tools that you can use to manage the local PC or other computers on the network. Computer Management combines several Windows 2000 administrative tools. To use most of these tools, you must be logged on as an administrator, although you can view certain settings and configurations in Computer Management if you are logged in with lesser privileges. To access Computer Management, from the Control Panel, open the Administrative Tools window and then double-click the Computer Management icon. The Computer Management window appears. See Figure 8-17. Some of the tasks you can perform from this window include monitoring problems with hardware, software, and security. You can share folders, view device configurations, add new device drivers, start and stop services, and manage server applications.

A+ OS 1.5

By default, the Administrative Tools group is located in the Control Panel. In addition, you can add the Administrative Tools group to the Start menu under Start, Programs, Administrative Tools. To do that, right-click the taskbar and select Properties. On the Taskbar and Start Menu Properties window, select the Advanced tab. Check Display Administrative Tools, and click OK.

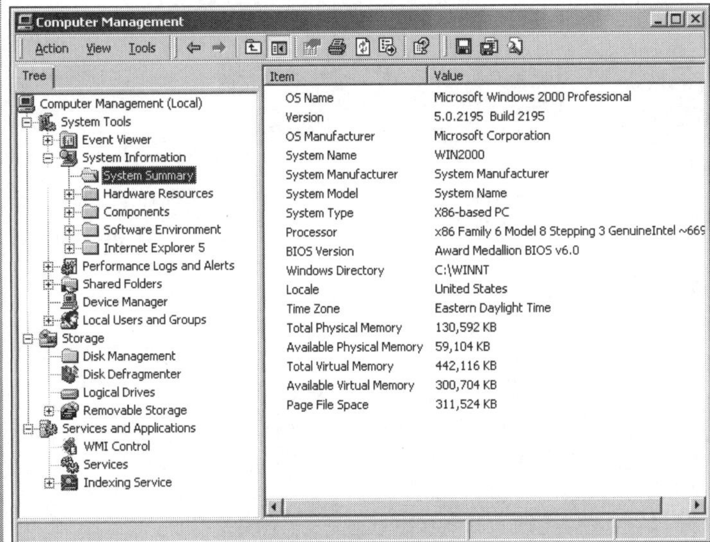

Figure 8-17 Computer Management combines several administrative tools into a single easy-to-access window

Disk Management

The Computer Management console contains a tool called **Disk Management** that you can use to create partitions on basic disks or volumes on dynamic disks and to convert a basic disk to a dynamic disk. This graphical, user-friendly utility replaces the Fdisk utility of earlier Windows OSs. To access the utility, in the Computer Management console, select Disk Management.

When Disk Management first loads, it examines the drive configuration for the system and displays all drives laid out in a graphical format so you can see how each drive is allocated.

The Disk Management window shown in Figure 8-18 has three drives displayed: Disk 0 is a basic hard drive using the NTFS file system. Disk 1 is a dynamic hard drive that has not yet been allocated into volumes, and there is also a CD-ROM drive shown that has a CD in the drive.

After you install a new second hard drive in the system, when you first access Disk Management, it will ask you if you want to create a basic disk or dynamic disk using the new drive. (Basic and dynamic disks were discussed in Chapter 7.) Then Disk Management

A+ OS 1.5

displays the new disk with unallocated space, as shown in Figure 8-18. This second hard drive has been designated as a dynamic disk.

To create a volume on this dynamic disk, do the following:

1. Right-click on an unallocated area of the drive and select **Create Volume** from the shortcut menu (see Figure 8-18).
2. The Create Volume Wizard launches. Click **Next** to continue.

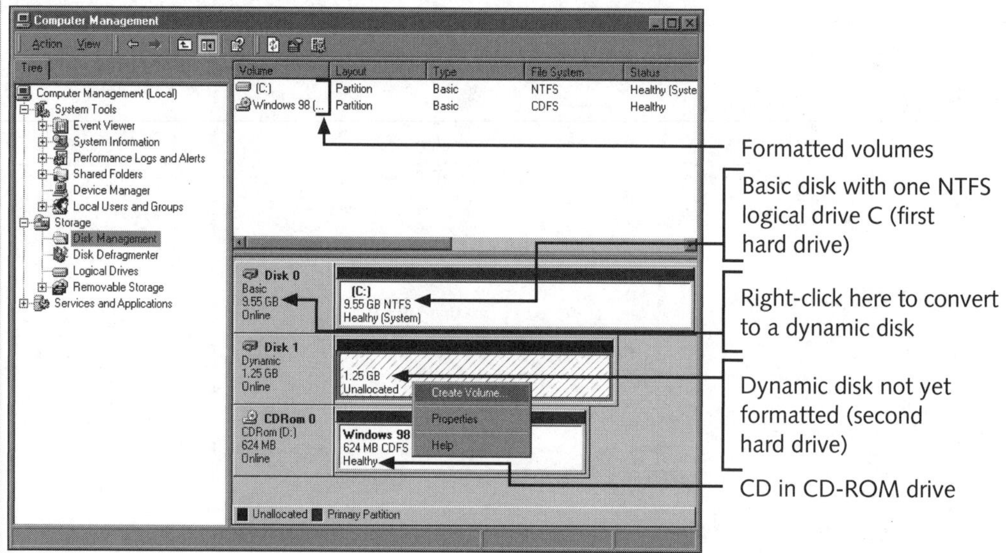

Figure 8-18 Create a volume on an unallocated dynamic disk

3. On the next screen (see Figure 8-19), you would select a volume type, either Simple volume, Spanned volume, or Striped volume. In our example, Simple volume is the only one available, because we are working with only one dynamic drive. You would have to have more than one dynamic drive to specify a volume as striped or spanned. Click **Next** to continue.
4. Follow the wizard through the process of specifying the volume size, a drive letter, file system (NTFS, FAT or FAT32), and allocation unit size (default is 512 bytes). The wizard then creates the dynamic volume.

The process for creating a partition on a basic disk is similar, with the main difference being that the wizard is called the Create Partition Wizard. Access it by right-clicking the unallocated portion of the basic disk, selecting Create Partition, and following the directions in the wizard.

A+ OS 1.5

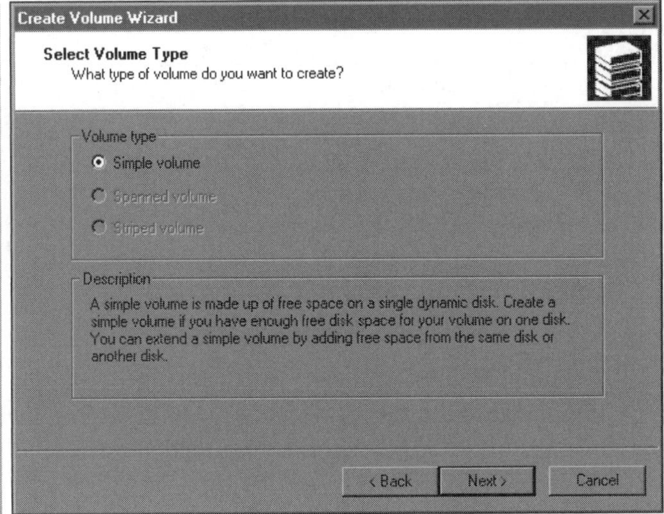

Figure 8-19 Disk Management provides the Create Volume Wizard to help you create volumes

8

Converting from a Basic Disk to a Dynamic Disk When you are creating partitions on a basic disk, you should always leave at least 1 MB of space unallocated. If you later decide to convert this basic disk to a dynamic disk, the conversion will require 1 MB of free space to store a database of configuration information for all dynamic disks on the computer. The Disk Management tool can be used to accomplish this conversion by right-clicking on the small frame (see Figure 8-18) at the basic drive you want to upgrade and selecting Upgrade to Dynamic disk from the shortcut menu. This process also converts the partitions on the basic disk to volumes on the new dynamic disk. Table 8-5 shows how parts of a basic disk change when it is converted.

Table 8-5 Conversion of space from basic to dynamic

Type of basic disk space before upgrade	Type of dynamic disk space after upgrade
System partition	Simple volume
Boot partition	Simple volume
Primary partition	Simple volume
Extended partition	Simple volume
Logical drive	Simple volume
Free space	Unallocated space

The only way to make a dynamic disk into a basic disk is to delete everything on the dynamic disk, including all data and all volumes, and recreate a basic disk in the resulting unallocated space. Obviously, all the data on the disk will be lost, so be sure to first back up your data.

To change a dynamic disk to a basic disk, delete everything on the dynamic disk, open Disk Management, right-click the dynamic disk that you want to change back to a basic disk, and select Revert to Basic Disk.

Microsoft Management Console

A+ OS 1.1

When Windows combines several administrative tools into a single window, the window is called a **console**. Individual tools within the console are called **snap-ins**. An example of a console is Computer Management. Event Viewer and System Information are two snap-ins in that console. Another example of a console is Recovery Console, which was introduced earlier in the chapter. Windows offers a way for you to create your own customized consoles using the console-building utility **Microsoft Management Console (MMC)**. Table 8-6 lists some available snap-ins for MMC.

Table 8-6 Some available MMC snap-ins

Snap-in	Description
Active X Control	Enables you to add Active X controls to your system.
Certificates	Provides certificate management at the user, service, or computer level.
Component Services	Links to the Component Services management tool, which is located on the Control Panel.
Computer Management	Links to the Computer Management tools on the Control Panel.
Device Manager	Lets you see what hardware devices you have on your system and configure device properties.
Disk Defragmenter	Links to the Disk Defragmenter utility.
Disk Management	Links to the Disk Management tool.
Event Viewer	Links to the Event Viewer tool, which displays event logs for the system.
Fax Service Management	Enables you to manage fax settings and devices.
Folder	Enables you to add a folder to manage from MMC.
Group Policy	Provides a tool to manage group policy settings.
Indexing Service	Searches files and folders using specified parameters.
IP Security Policy Management	Manages Internet communication security.
Link to Web Address	Enables you to link to a specified Web site.

A+ OS 1.1

Table 8-6 Some available MMC snap-ins (continued)

Snap-in	Description
Local Users and Groups	Provides a tool to manage settings for local users and groups.
Performance Logs and Alerts	Gives you an interface from which to set up and manage logs of performance information and alerts about system performance.
Removable Storage Management	Enables you to manage settings and configuration information for removable storage devices such as Zip drives and tape backup drives.
Security Configuration and Analysis	Enables you to manage configuration of security settings for computers that use security template files.
Services	Provides a centralized interface for starting, stopping, and configuring system services.
Shared Folders	Provides information about shared folders, files that are open, and current sessions.
System Information	Contains information about the system that you can use when troubleshooting.

Creating a Customized Console

As with the Computer Management console, you must have administrative privileges to perform most tasks from the MMC. You can use MMC to create your own customized consoles. You can also save the console to a file, which is assigned a .msc file extension. Store the file in the C:\Documents and Settings*user*\Start Menu\Programs\Administrative Tools folder to make it appear as a program when you click Start, and point to Programs, Administrative Tools. In the path, substitute the name of the user. For example, for the Administrator, the path to the .msc file is C:\Documents and Settings\Administrator\Start Menu\Programs\Administrative Tools.

Once you create a console, you can copy the .msc file to any computer or place a shortcut to it on the desktop.

Follow these directions to open MMC and create a console that contains some popular utility tools:

1. Click **Start**, **Run**, enter **MMC** in the Run dialog box, and then click **OK**. An empty console window appears, as shown in Figure 8-20.

A+ OS 1.1

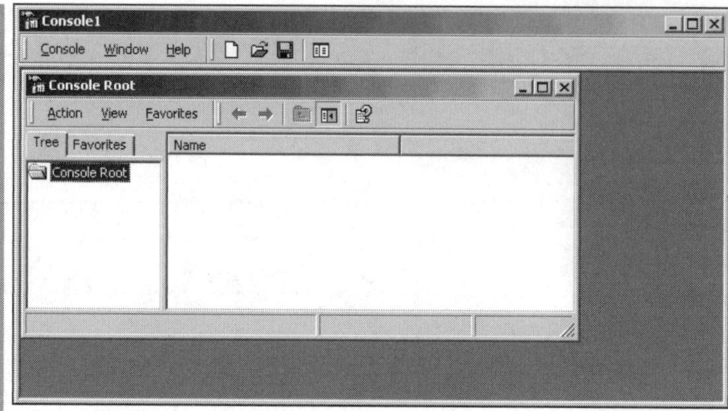

Figure 8-20 An empty console

2. Click **Console** on the menu bar, and then click **Add/Remove Snap-in**. The Add/Remove Snap-in window opens. The window illustrated in Figure 8-21 is empty because no snap-ins have been added to the console.
3. Click **Add**. You see a list of snap-ins that can be added to a console, as shown in Figure 8-21. Select a snap-in, and then click **Add**.
4. A dialog box opens that allows you to set the parameters for the snap-in. The dialog box offers different selections, depending on the snap-in being added. When you have made your selections, click **Finish**. The new snap-in appears in the Add/Remove Snap-in window.
5. Repeat Steps 3 and 4 until you have added all the snap-ins that you want to the console. When you are finished, from the Add Standalone Snap-in window illustrated in Figure 8-22, click **Close**, then click **OK**.
6. Figure 8-22 shows a console with four snap-ins added. To save the console, click **Console** on the menu bar, and then click **Save As**. The Save As dialog box opens.

A+ OS 1.1

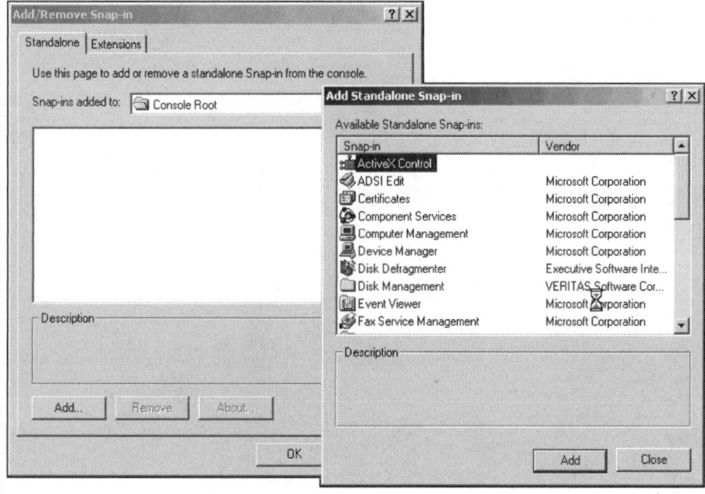

Figure 8-21 List of snap-ins available to be added to a console

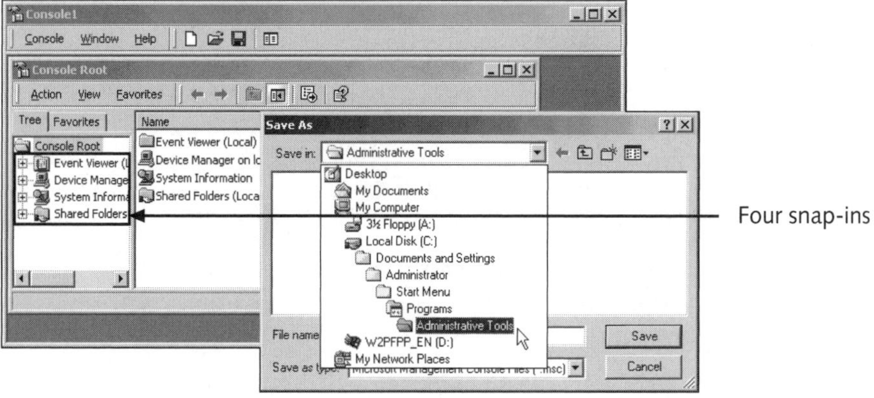

Figure 8-22 Saving a console with four snap-ins

7. The default location for the console file is shown in Figure 8-22—this is the location that ensures the console appears as an option under Administrative Tools on the Start menu. Select this location for the file, name the file, and click **Save**.

8. Close the console window by clicking **Console**, **Exit**.

To use the console, click Start, Programs, Administrative Tools, and select the console.

A+ OS 1.5 3.1 3.2 3.3

Event Viewer

In the list of MMC snap-ins, you saw that there is one that connects to the Event Viewer tool, which displays logs about significant system events that occur in Windows NT/2000/XP or in applications running under these OSs, such as a hardware or network failure, OS error messages, or a device or service has failed to start. There are three different logs shown in Event Viewer, which are displayed in Figure 8-23:

A+ OS 1.5 3.1 3.2 3.3

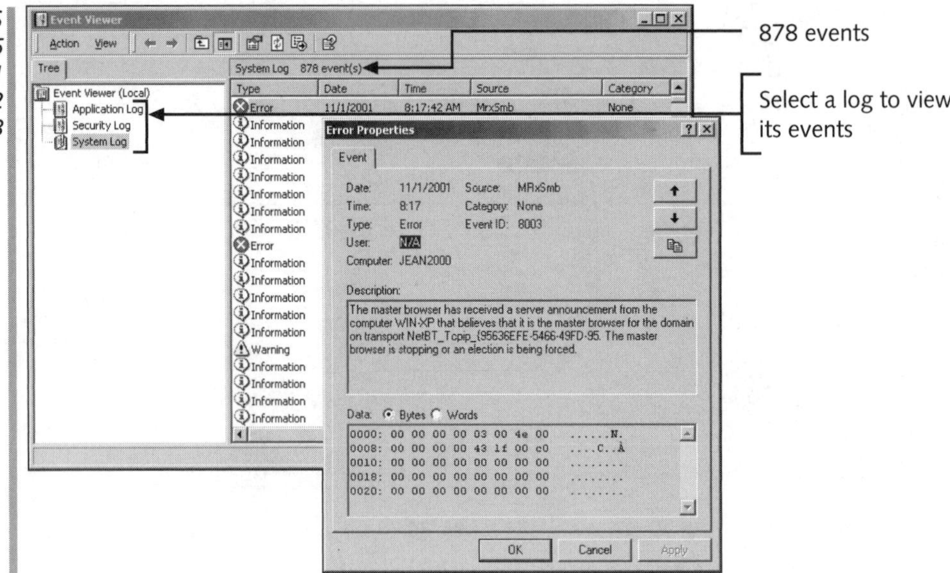

Figure 8-23 Use Event Viewer to see information about security audits in the security log and error, warning, or information events for the system and application logs

- *The application log* records application events that the developer of the program sets to trigger a log entry. One type of event recorded in this log is an error recorded by the Dr. Watson utility, which you will learn about later in the chapter.
- *The security log* records events based on audit policies, which an administrator sets to monitor user activity such as successful or unsuccessful attempts to access a file or log on to the system. Only an administrator can view this log.
- *The system log* records events triggered by components of Windows 2000, such as a device driver failing to load during the boot process. Windows 2000 sets which events are recorded in this log. All users can access this log file.

There are three types of events recorded in the system and application logs:

- *Information* events are recorded when a driver, service, or application functions successfully.
- *Warning* events are recorded when something happens that may indicate a future problem but does not necessarily indicate that something is presently wrong with the system. For example, low disk space might trigger a warning event.
- *Error* events are recorded when something goes wrong with the system, such as a necessary component failing to load, data getting lost or becoming corrupted, or a system or application function ceasing to operate.

You can open Event Viewer from the Computer Management Console, or you can locate it by double-clicking the Administrative Tools icon in the Control Panel. To view a log

A+ OS 1.5 3.1 3.2 3.3

within Event Viewer, in the left pane click the log that you want to view. This will cause a summary of events to be shown in the right pane. Double-click a specific event to show details about it. (See Figure 8-23.)

Notice in the figure that 878 events are listed in the system log. You may only want to view certain events, without reading through the entire list to find what you're looking for. To filter events, right-click on a log in the left pane and select Filter from the shortcut menu. There are several criteria you can use to filter events, which are listed in Table 8-7.

Table 8-7 Log properties that can be used to filter events

Property	Description
Category	The category that the event falls under, such as an attempt to log on to the system or access a program.
Computer	The name of a computer on the system.
Event ID	A number that identifies the event, making it easier for support personnel to track events.
Event source	The application, driver, or service that triggered the event.
Event type	The type of event, such as information, error, or warning.
From: To:	The range of events that you want to view. You can view the events from first to last event, or you can view all events that occurred in a specific date and time range.
User	The logon name for a user.

Another way you can avoid a ballooning log file is to set a size limit and specify what is to happen when the log reaches this limit. If you right-click a log, select Properties from the shortcut menu, and click the General tab, you can set the maximum size of the log in megabytes (as well as view general information about the log). You can set it so that the log overwrites events as needed, overwrites events that are more than a specified number of days old, or does not overwrite events at all. Select this last option when system security is high and you do not want to lose any event information. If you select this option, the system will simply stop recording events when the log file reaches the maximum size. (See Figure 8-24.)

To allow the system to record events in the log after a log reaches maximum size, you will have to review the events and clear the log manually by clicking the Clear Log button from the Properties window or selecting Clear All Events from the Action menu. Before the log is cleared, Event Viewer will give you a chance to save it.

A+ OS 1.5 3.1 3.2 3.3

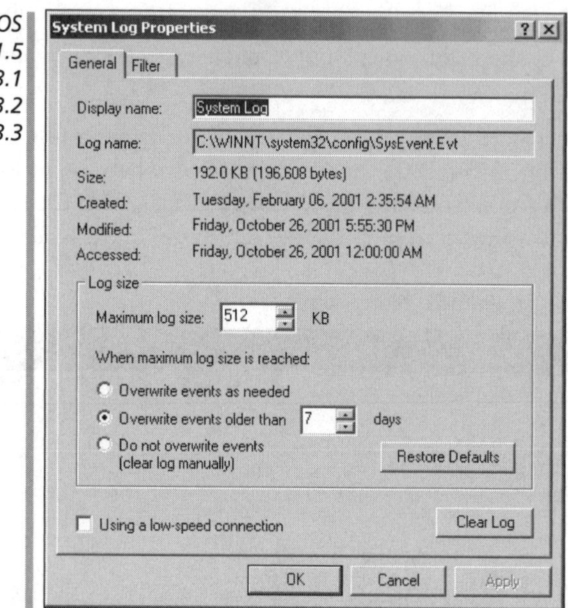

Figure 8-24 View information about a log, including maximum size of the log file, in the Log Properties window

Performance Monitoring and Optimization

Maintaining optimal performance, or addressing performance problems when they develop, involves a three-part process in which you analyze data provided by monitoring tools such as Task Manager and System Monitor, determine areas in which performance is below the baseline, and identify and take the steps necessary to correct the problem.

Principles for Optimizing Performance

Here are some principles to remember when trying to optimize performance on your system:

- One of the most important things you can do is establish a **baseline** of acceptable performance for your system, defining what you will consider normal performance under a typical workload. Figure out what resources the system uses when you are running all required programs and services, which will help you decide whether you need to add additional resources (such as more RAM) to the system. Heavily used Windows 2000 computers may benefit from having as much as 512 MB of RAM, whereas machines on which usage is more moderate may only need 128 MB of RAM.
- If you add RAM, remember that you will need to increase the size of the paging file. You might also increase paging file size if the peak usage of the paging file is too close to the limit.

- Replacing one component may not help that much if other components have not been upgraded. For example, if you install a faster CPU, you need to look at the amount of RAM and the size of the hard drive as well.
- Applications are assigned a priority level, which determines its position in the queue for CPU resources. This priority level can be changed for applications that are already loaded by using Task Manager. If an application is performing slowly, increase its priority. You should only do this with very important applications, because giving an application higher priority than certain background system processes can sometimes interfere with the operating system.
- In general, upgrading an existing PC is recommended as long as the cost of the upgrade stays below half the cost of buying a new machine. Even if you just keep the case, power supply, and an expansion card or two, buying a new motherboard and hard drive can be almost like having a whole new system at a lower cost.

8

The rest of this section discusses two tools that you can use to monitor system performance: Task Manager and System Monitor.

A+ OS 1.5 3.2

Task Manager

Task Manager (Taskman.exe) allows you to view applications and processes that are running on your computer as well as performance information for the processor and the memory. There are three ways that you can access Task Manager:

- Press the Ctrl, Alt, and Delete keys simultaneously. The Windows Security window will open. Click the Task Manager button.
- Right-click a blank area on the taskbar and select Task Manager from the shortcut menu.
- Press the Ctrl, Shift, and Esc keys simultaneously.

Task Manager has three tabs: Applications, Processes, and Performance. Under the Applications tab (see Figure 8-25), each application that is loaded can have one of two statuses: Running or Not Responding. If an application is listed as Not Responding, you can end it by selecting it and clicking the End Task button at the bottom of the window. You will lose any unsaved information in the application.

The Processes tab lists system services and other processes associated with applications together with how much CPU time and memory the process is using. This information can help you determine which applications are slowing your system down. The Performance tab, seen in Figure 8-26, shows more detail about how a program is using system resources. You can use these views to identify which applications and processes are using the most CPU time.

A+ OS 1.5 3.2

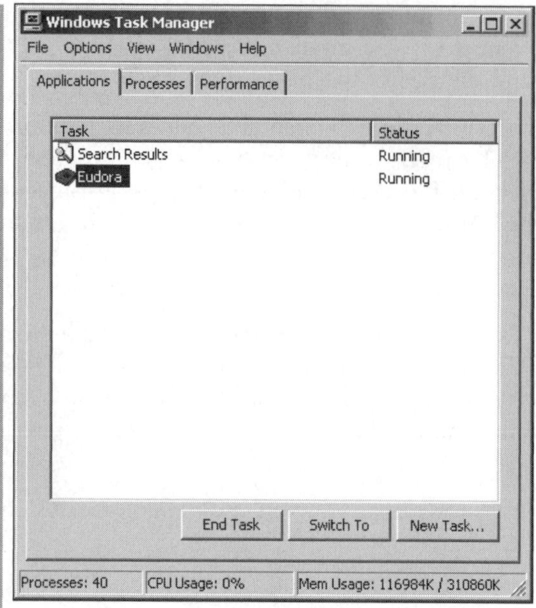

Figure 8-25 The Applications tab in Task Manager shows the status of active applications

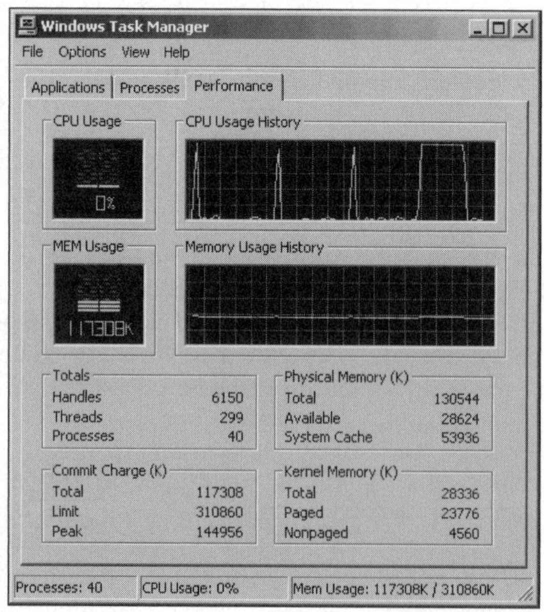

Figure 8-26 The Performance tab shows more detail about how system resources are being used

A+ OS 1.5 3.2

On the Performance tab in Figure 8-26 note the four frames at the bottom of the window. These frames give the following information:

- The *Totals* frame indicates how much the system is currently being used by counting handles (indicates a device or file is being accessed), threads (unit of activity within a process), and processes (programs running). Use these entries to know how heavily the system is used.
- The *Physical Memory* frame lists Total (amount of RAM), Available (RAM not used), and System Cache (RAM in use). Use these entries to know if you must upgrade RAM.
- The *Commit Charge* frame lists Total (current size of virtual memory, also called the page file or swap file), Limit (how much of the page file can be allocated to applications before the size of the page file must be increased), and Peak (maximum amount of virtual memory used in this session). Use these entries to learn if you must increase the size of the page file.
- The *Kernel Memory* frame indicates how much RAM and virtual memory is used by the OS. This frame lists Total (sum of RAM and virtual memory), Paged (how much of the page file is used by the OS), and Nonpaged (how much RAM is used by the OS). Use this frame to how much memory the OS is using. If this is high, look for OS processes you can eliminate.

By reading the information in the frames in Figure 8-30, you can see that the OS is using about 28 MB of memory. The system contains about 130 MB of RAM, and the paging file maximum size is set to about 311 MB. How to change the maximum and initial size of the page file is covered later in the chapter.

A+ OS 1.5

System Monitor

In most cases, you can get what information you need from Task Manager to determine if the system is in need of performance tuning or upgrading. If this information is not detailed enough, use System Monitor, which provides more detail than Task Manager on system performance. There are three components of System Monitor: objects, instances, and counters. Objects are hardware or software system components, and instances are multiples of objects. For example, Microsoft Word is an object, but if you have Word open in two separate windows on the desktop, then there are two instances of this one object running. Counters show information on specific characteristics of an object and constantly gather the data and update the counter display. You can specify which counters to show for an object.

Important objects to monitor using System Monitor include Memory, Paging File, Processor, and Physical Disk (the hard drive). In the following example, we will access System Monitor and then add and view counters for the Memory object.

1. In the Control Panel, double-click the **Administrative Tools** icon.
2. From the Administrative Tools window, double-click the **Performance** icon.

8

A+ OS 1.5

3. The Performance window opens. See Figure 8-31. System Monitor is highlighted and the System Monitor details pane shows on the right. The pane is blank because no objects are presently being monitored. Right-click in that pane and select **Add Counters** from the shortcut menu (see Figure 8-27).

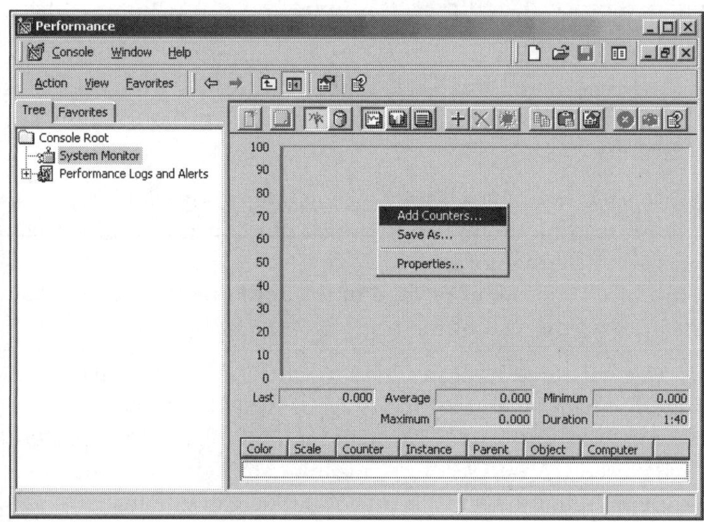

Figure 8-27 Access System Monitor through the Performance window

4. The Add Counters window opens (Figure 8-28). From the Performance object drop-down list, select the **Memory** object.

5. You have the option to view all counters, but that makes for a messy display that is hard to read. By default, the radio button is selected beside the option Select counters from list. Locate and click the **Available Bytes** counter, which will tell you how much physical memory remains. Click **Add**.

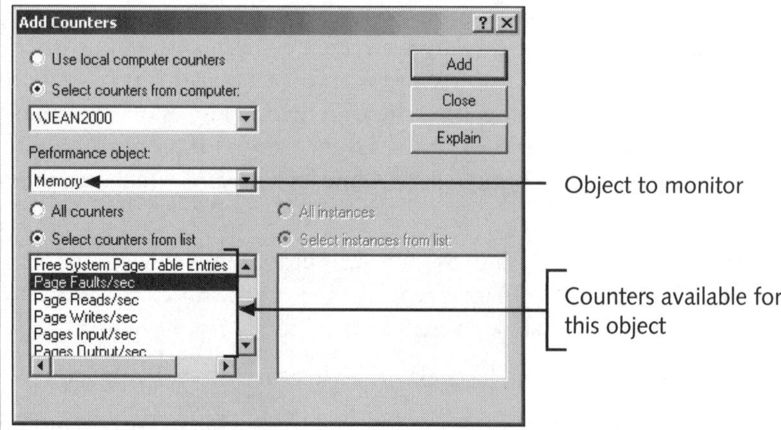

Figure 8-28 In the Add Counters window, select a performance object and counters to monitor

A+ OS 1.5

6. Scroll down in the list until you see the **Page Faults/sec** counter. This will tell you how many pages were requested but were not immediately available in memory. Click **Add**.
7. Click **Close** to close the Add Counters window.

Figure 8-29 shows System Monitor in the process of monitoring the two counters you selected. The lines tracking the counters are color-coded to match the counters listed at the bottom of the graph. Look at the left side of the graph. The line representing Page Faults/sec begins at 0 and spikes when an application is opened. The line representing Available Bytes begins at 30 and dips lower, meaning fewer bytes are available, when applications are active. The vertical line on the right moves to the right as monitoring continues.

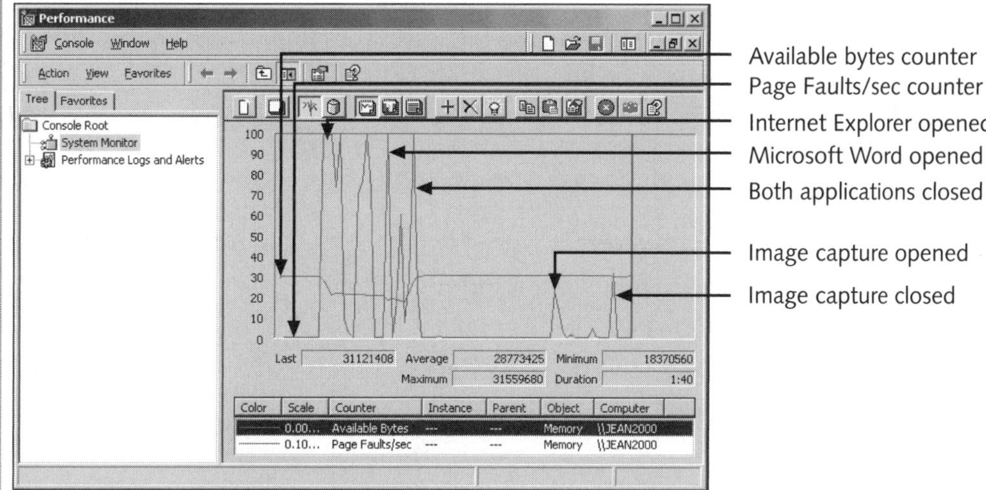

Figure 8-29 System Monitor shows how changes in system activity affect the selected object and counters

8

Managing Virtual Memory

A+ OS 2.5

Under Windows 2000, the default size of the paging file is set to 1.5 times the amount of RAM installed. You might need to make changes to the paging file in order to improve system performance. Here are some guidelines to remember in managing paging files:

- Set the initial and maximum sizes of the file to the same value. This will prevent disk fragmentation that might result from setting them to two different values. Windows 2000 does not normally need to change the size of the paging file during processing.
- To calculate the appropriate size of a paging file, multiply the counter Paging File object, % Usage Peak counter, which shows how much of the paging file the system is using, by the size of Pagefile.sys.

A+ OS 2.5

- Two situations in which you might want to change the size of the paging file are when 70% of the paging file is being used or when the Memory object, % Committed Bytes In Use counter, reaches 85%.
- When changing the size of a paging file, remember that you need to balance the size of the file with disk space usage and that Windows 2000 requires at least 5 MB of free space on a disk. In other words, don't make the file too large, especially when the disk it is stored on is active or has limited space. Test performance as you change paging file size, and make changes gradually.
- Moving the paging file to another volume besides the boot volume can help conserve disk space on the boot volume and optimize performance, especially when a system has multiple hard disks.
- In deciding where to put the paging file, know that memory dumps (covered in the next section) cannot be captured if the paging file is on a different physical disk from the operating system.

To change virtual memory settings and paging file size in Windows 2000, do the following:

1. Open the **Control Panel**.
2. Double-click the **System** icon.
3. The System Properties window opens. Click the **Advanced** tab.
4. Click the **Performance Options** button.
5. The Performance Options window opens. Click the **Change...** button.
6. The Virtual Memory window opens. In this window, you can change the size of the paging file and view information about the paging file and the registry. Figure 8-30 shows all three windows.

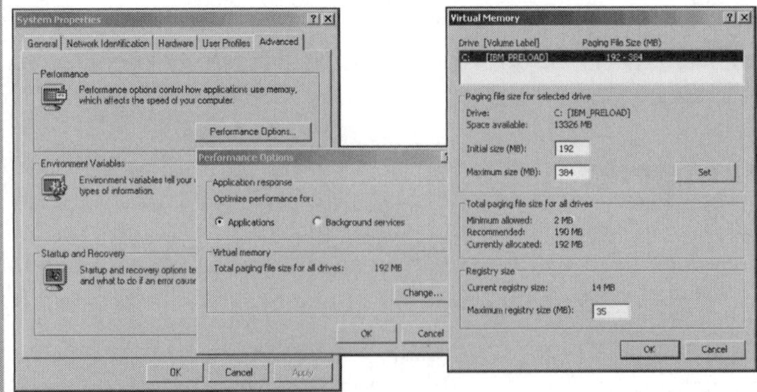

Figure 8-30 Use the System Properties window to change paging file settings

Dr. Watson and Memory Dumps

A+ OS 3.1 3.2 3.3

Two tools that can produce text output useful in diagnosing problems with the OS and applications are Dr. Watson and memory dumps. Recall from Chapter 5 that Dr. Watson is used to debug errors in applications by recording error events to a log file when illegal operations occur. It can help solve problems such as when an application fails to install or load, when the

A+ OS 3.1 3.2 3.3

system locks up, or when error messages appear. In Windows 2000, these events are recorded in the Drwtsn32.log file. Dr. Watson automatically launches when an application error occurs or you can manually launch it by entering Drwtsn32.exe in the Run dialog box or at a command prompt. The log file is written to the\Documents and Settings*user*\Documents\DrWatson folder.

Another tool that is helping in understanding what happened when an error occurred is a **memory dump**, which saves the contents of memory at the time an error halted the system to a file called a **dump file**. The dump file is created in the event of a stop error. A **stop error** is an error severe enough that the operating system stops all processes. How to capture and interpret memory dumps is beyond the scope of this book.

Windows Update

A+ OS 2.2 3.2

In the process of maintaining and troubleshooting Windows 2000, remember that the Microsoft site offers patches, fixes, and updates for known problems and has an extensive knowledge base documenting known problems and their solutions. Recall that you learned how to download a critical update package in Chapter 4; the process is basically the same for Windows 2000 as it was for Windows 9x. You can access Windows Update by going to the Microsoft site and locating it from there, or you can click Windows Update on your Start Menu, which will take you directly to the site. If you think you might later want to uninstall a critical update or service pack, when given the opportunity, select the *Save uninstall information* option.

Later, to uninstall the fix, again execute the downloaded file. When given the option, select *Uninstall a previously installed service pack*.

In addition to critical updates and service packs that Microsoft creates to address known problems with Windows, the Windows Update tool will also use ActiveX controls to scan your system, find your device drivers and system files, and compare these files to the ones on the Windows Update server. If you do not already have Active Setup and the Active X controls installed on your computer, a prompt to install them will pop up when you access the site. Once Windows Update has scanned your system and located update packages and new versions of drivers and system files, it will offer you the option of selecting files for download.

Because of the open access that ActiveX controls have to the Windows operating system, there is some risk of an ActiveX control causing damage to data or software on your computer. Some system administrators require that ActiveX controls be disabled when they are not specifically needed for tasks such as Windows Update downloads.

In addition to the information in this chapter, other important sources of information about Windows 2000 are the Microsoft Web site at *support.microsoft.com* and the *Windows 2000 Professional Resource Kit* by Microsoft Press. The *Resource Kit* includes a CD that contains additional Windows 2000 utilities. These resources can further help you understand Windows 2000 and solve problems with the OS. Also, remember that user manuals are an excellent source of information as well as the Web, training manuals, and product installation documentation.

CHAPTER SUMMARY

- The Windows 2000 boot process works like the Windows NT process.
- The boot process can be customized with entries in Boot.ini. The Boot.ini file can be edited with a text editor, but it is best to change the file using the System Properties window.
- Tools to use to troubleshoot problems loading Windows 2000 are the Advanced Options menu, the Recovery Console, and the Emergency Repair Process.
- Press F8 when starting Windows 2000 to access the Advanced Options menu.
- The Advanced Options menu includes safe mode, safe mode with networking, safe mode with command prompt, enable boot logging, enable VGA mode, Last Known Good configuration, directory services restore mode, and debugging mode.
- The Recovery Console is a command interface with a limited number of commands available to troubleshoot a failing Windows 2000 load. The console requires that you enter the Administrator password.
- Access the Recovery Console by first booting from the Windows 2000 CD or from the four setup disks, or the console can be installed under the startup menu and accessed from there.
- Using the Recovery Console, you can restore the registry to the state it was in at the time of the last backup of the registry.
- The Emergency Repair Process lets you restore the system to its state at the end of the Windows 2000 installation. Don't use it unless all other methods fail because you will loose all changes made to the system since the installation. It requires the emergency startup disk.
- Back up the Windows 2000 system state on a regular basis using the Backup utility. This backup includes system files, files to load the OS, and the registry. Back up the system state before editing the registry.
- Windows 2000 Support Tools can be installed from the Windows 2000 CD and include several utilities to support hardware and applications.
- Windows File Protection (WFP) protects the system files against an application, virus, or user changing or deleting them. System File Checker is part of the WFP system.
- A command window (called a DOS box in Windows 9x) is provided by Command.com or CMD.exe. The command prompt is sometimes called a DOS prompt.
- The Disk Properties window gives information about a disk and can be used to clean up a disk, defragment the disk, and check and repair errors on the disk using ScanDisk.
- Disk Management is a tool found in the Computer Management console. Disk Management replaces Fdisk in older Windows OSs and is used to partition and format a hard drive, and convert a basic disk to a dynamic disk.
- Microsoft Management Console (MMC) can be used to create customized consoles to manage the OS.
- Event Viewer is used to view system, application, and security events
- When monitoring performance, begin by establishing a baseline that helps determine what performance should be expected of a system.

- Task Manager is used to measure performance, giving information about the processor, memory, the hard drive, and virtual memory.
- System Monitor gives more detail than does Task Manager and can be used to monitor performance over time of objects and instances by using counters that you select for the monitoring.
- Virtual memory is managed from the System applet of Control Panel, Advanced tab.
- Information about application errors and stop errors can be recorded by Dr. Watson and memory dumps.
- Windows Update uses the Microsoft Web site to download patches and fixes to Microsoft OSs and applications.
- Sources of support for Windows 2000 include the Microsoft support Web site at *support.microsoft.com* and the *Windows 2000 Professional Resource Kit* by Microsoft.

KEY TERMS

Advanced Options menu
baseline
Cmd.exe
console
Disk Management
dump file
Emergency Repair Process
hardware profile
Microsoft Management Console (MMC)
memory dump
Recovery Console
SFC (System File Checker)
snap-ins
stop error
WFP (Windows File Protection)

REVIEW QUESTIONS

1. What does *%SystemRoot%* mean?
2. List the steps to restore the Windows 2000 system state from the backup made with the Backup utility.
3. In what folder does Windows 2000 store a backup of the registry when backing up the system state?
4. Under what circumstances would you use the Enable VGA Mode option on the Advanced Option menu?
5. What key do you press to display the Advanced Option menu during startup?
6. What is the purpose of safe mode with networking under the Advanced Options menu?
7. What is the name of the log file that Windows 2000 uses when booting in safe mode?
8. List the steps to load the Recovery Console when using the four Windows 2000 rescue disks.
9. Why is the Administrator password required in order to use the Recovery Console?
10. In Question 9 above, under what circumstances is the password not required?
11. What is the purpose of the Systemroot command under the Recovery Console?

12. Under the Recovery Console, what is the command that gives the same results as Fdisk/MBR?
13. What is the command to install the Recovery Console on the startup menu?
14. Under the Recovery Console, what is the name of the command used to create and delete partitions?
15. Before you can perform the Windows 2000 Emergency Repair Process, what disk must you have? What is contained on the disk?
16. When would you use System File Checker? What is the command to execute it?
17. What is the command to install the Windows 2000 Support Tools?
18. What is the name of the log file created by Dr. Watson?
19. What is the 32-bit program that provides a command window? What is the 16-bit program that provides a command window?
20. Name two Windows utilities that can be used to monitor the OS performance.
21. What tool can you use to create a console containing Device Manager and Event Viewer? What is the file extension assigned to the console file?
22. When you partition a basic disk, why is it important to leave 1 MB of space free on the hard drive?
23. Name one snap-in contained in the Computer Management console.
24. What is the program filename for System File Checker?
25. Give one reason why you should make the paging file maximum size the same as the paging file initial size.
26. List the steps to change the size of the paging file.
27. List three ways to access the Task Manager.
28. List the steps used to end an application when the application refuses to respond to keystrokes or the mouse action.
29. What are the three logs kept by Event Viewer?
30. In what folder do you put a console file that you want displayed when you click Start, Programs, Administrative Tools when you are logged on as an administrator?

HANDS-ON PROJECTS

Using the Microsoft Knowledge Base

Using the Microsoft support Web site (*support.microsoft.com*), print information about the following:

1. Troubleshooting IEEE 1394 devices running under Windows 2000 Professional.
2. How to set up Windows 2000 to support multiple CPUs.
3. Information on how to set up and troubleshoot multiple monitors with Windows 2000 Professional.

Using DiskProbe to Back Up the MBR

DiskProbe edits individual sectors on a hard drive and can edit the MBR, boot sectors, the FATs and NTFS file system tables as well as data files. Research DiskProbe and find the directions that show you how to back up the MBR, which contains the partition table. Follow these directions and answer these questions:

1. Find the document Dskprtrb.doc in the C:\ProgramFiles\Support Tools folder, which describes how to use DiskProbe. Print the page from the document that describes how to save the MBR record to a floppy disk.
2. If the Windows 2000 Support Tools are not installed, install them now.
3. Execute DiskProbe (click **Start**, point to **Programs**, **Windows 2000 Support Tools**, and **Tools**, and then click **DiskProbe**).
4. Follow the directions to save the MBR, including the partition table, to a floppy disk.
5. How many bytes of data are included in the MBR? What is the size of the file?
6. What is the disadvantage of using DiskProbe to restore the MBR in the event it becomes corrupted?

Creating a Windows 2000 Antivirus Boot Disk

Windows 2000 offers an antivirus program that can scan memory, the MBR sector, and OS boot sectors for viruses. Follow these directions to create the boot disk and scan your system for viruses. Use the disk when you suspect that a virus has attacked your Windows 2000 hard drive.

1. Insert the Windows 2000 CD in the CD-ROM drive and insert an empty floppy disk in the floppy disk drive.
2. Click **Start**, **Run**. From the Run dialog box, enter this command; substituting the drive letter for your CD-ROM drive for D:

   D:\VALUEADD\3RDPARTY\CA_ANTIV\Makedisk.bat
3. Label the disk Windows 2000 AVBoot.
4. Boot from the floppy disk. When the scan is completed, Windows 2000 will automatically load.

Note: If your PC is not set to boot from a floppy disk before booting from the hard drive, change the boot sequence in CMOS setup.

Using Dependency Walker

Follow these steps to use Dependency Walker to list the files used by Internet Explorer:

1. If the Windows 2000 Support Tools are not installed, install them now.
2. Execute Dependency Walker (click **Start**, point to **Programs**, **Windows 2000 Support Tools**, and **Tools**, and then click **Dependency Walker**).
3. Set Dependency Walker to show all the supporting files used by Internet Explorer.
4. List the files or print the screen showing them.

Creating Baselines for Your System

In the chapter, you learned about several tools you can use to establish baselines for a system before a problem occurs. Baselines can be created (1) when the OS is first installed, (2) when major changes are made, and (3) on a periodic basis such as once a month. One tool to help establish a baseline is the boot log. Using the Windows 2000 Advanced Options menu, boot with Enable Boot Logging. Print the Ntbtlog.txt file created. Then boot with safe mode. Again print the Ntbtlog.txt file. Compare the two files and mark the differences. Keep these two reports in case you ever have problems booting this system since they can provide a picture of what a normal boot should be.

Finding Windows 2000 Utilities

The table below lists, on the left side, some important Windows utilities that were covered in this chapter. Fill in the right side of the table with the filename and path of each utility. *Hint*: You can use Explorer or Search to locate files.

Utility	Path and File Name
System File Checker	
Disk Defragmenter	
Command window	
Chkdsk	
Dependency Walker	
Task Manager	

CHAPTER

9

Installing and Using Windows XP Professional

In this chapter, you will learn:

- About the features and architecture of Windows XP
- How to install Windows XP
- How to use Windows XP
- How to install hardware and applications with Windows XP

Windows XP is the latest generation of Microsoft operating systems. Windows XP currently comes as Windows XP Home Edition, Windows XP Professional, and Windows XP 64-bit Edition, although Windows .NET, an edition for the advanced server market, will likely be available by the time this book is published. This chapter focuses on Windows XP Professional, which is the upgrade from Windows 2000 Professional. Features of Windows XP that you already learned about in chapters on earlier versions of Windows are not covered in detail, where they have not changed in Windows XP; the discussion focuses on new features or changes to existing ones. This chapter builds the foundation you will need to manage and provide technical support for Windows XP, which is the focus of the next chapter.

Features and Architecture of Windows XP

Windows XP integrates features of Windows 9x and 2000, while providing added support for multimedia and networking technologies. The look and feel of Windows XP is slightly different from its predecessors, and utilities and functions are organized differently under menus and windows. You'll see many of these differences in this chapter.

Windows XP is replacing all previous versions of Windows in the home market and for the corporate desktop. If your hardware and applications qualify, select Windows XP Home Edition for a home PC over Windows 98/Me. For a corporate environment, use Windows XP Professional over Windows NT/2000. The only exception to this is compatibility issues with older hardware and software.

Windows XP Features

Windows XP Home and Windows XP Professional have these features, among others:

- A new user interface, shown in Figure 9-1. Notice how different it looks from the desktops for earlier Windows versions such as Windows 98 and Windows 2000.

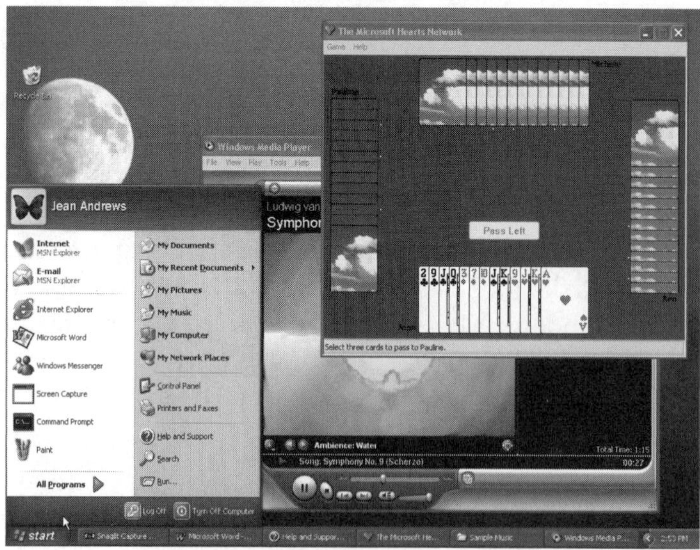

Figure 9-1 The Windows XP desktop and Start menu

- The ability for two users to be logged on simultaneously. Each user has a separate profile, and Windows XP can switch between users, keeping a separate set of applications open for each user.
- Windows Media Player for Windows XP, a centralized application for working with digital media
- Windows Messenger for instant messaging, conferencing, and application sharing

- An expanded Help feature
- Advanced security features

In addition to these features of Windows XP Home edition, Windows XP Professional offers:

- A way for someone to remotely control your computer called Remote Desktop
- A way for an administrator to manage user profiles from a server (roaming profiles)
  - Additional security features
  - Multilingual capabilities
  - Support for new higher-performance processors

There is also Windows XP 64-bit Edition, designed to be used with a high-end 64-bit CPU such as the Intel Itanium. This version of Windows XP is designed mostly for servers or heavily technical workstations that need greater amounts of memory and higher performance than standard desktop PCs, such as for scientific and engineering applications. For example, an aircraft designer who uses software to simulate how various conditions affect aircraft materials might use Windows XP 64-bit Edition on a system that supports resource-intensive simulation and animation applications.

Windows Internet Explorer, Windows Media Player, a firewall, and other Microsoft products are tightly integrated with the Windows XP operating system. Some users see this as a disadvantage and others see it as an advantage. Tight integration allows applications to easily interact with other applications and the OS, but, on the other hand, makes it more difficult for third-party software to compete with Microsoft applications.

Windows XP provides several enhancements over Windows 2000 and other earlier versions. Table 9-1 summarizes the advantages and disadvantages of Windows XP.

Table 9-1 Advantages and disadvantages of Windows XP

Advantages	Disadvantages
Provides better integration of Windows 9x and NT than did Windows 2000.	Requires nearly a gigabyte of hard drive space for the operating system itself, and at least a 233 MHz processor with 64 MB of RAM.
Offers significant GUI enhancements over earlier versions of Windows.	Programs used with Windows XP may need more than the minimum system system specifications for the operating system.
Adds features but uses only slightly more total memory for the OS than does Windows 2000.	Nearly eliminates support for device drivers not approved by Microsoft.
Adds advanced file sorting options, such as sorting pictures by resolution or sound files by artist.	Security concerns with centralized storage of online information in Microsoft Passport, a repository of the user IDs and passwords you use on the Internet.
Includes built-in support for compressed files.	
Has improved troubleshooting tools and is generally more stable than previous Windows OSs.	

Windows XP Architecture

Windows XP uses the same kernel architecture as Windows NT and Windows 2000, with components operating in either user mode or kernel mode. Figure 9-2 shows how the different OS components relate. Notice in the figure that some low-level device drivers such as those that access the hard drive have direct access to hardware, just as they do with Windows NT and Windows 2000. All 16-bit and 32-bit applications relate to the kernel by way of the Win32 subsystem operating in user mode. As you will see in the next chapter, the boot process is also the same, and the files needed for a successful boot are the same as those for Windows NT/2000.

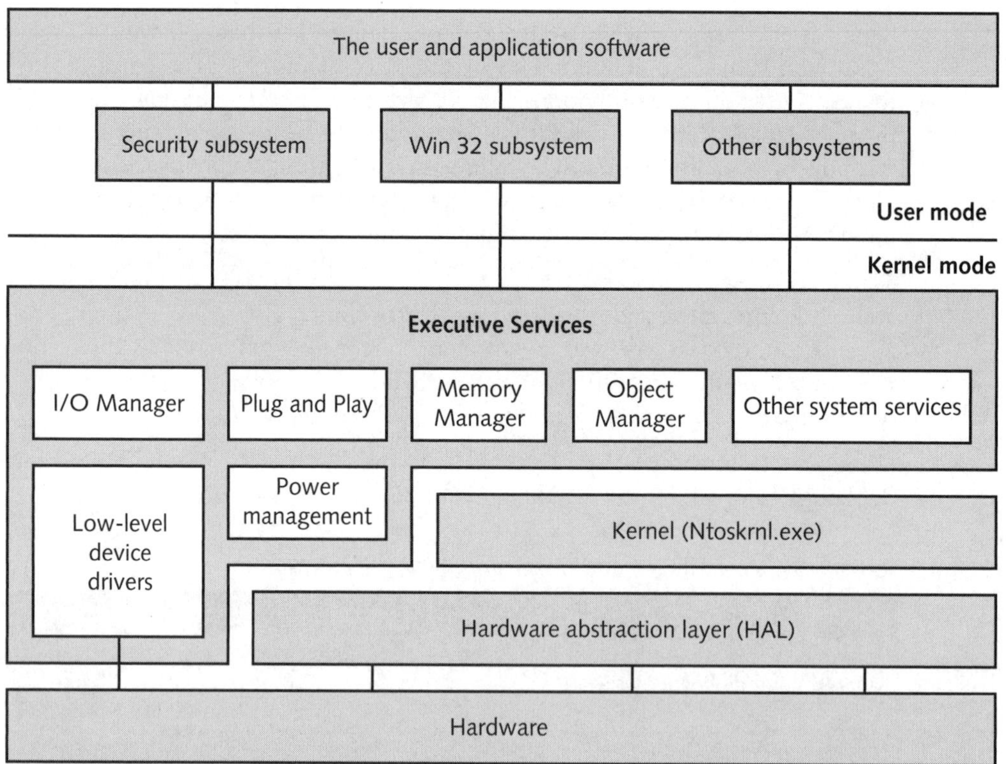

Figure 9-2 The Windows XP architecture uses the same basic structure and components as Windows NT and Windows 2000

Windows XP is generally more stable than Windows NT and Windows 2000. It was designed to avoid situations which caused drivers and applications to bring down the Windows NT/2000 systems. Installing Windows XP should also be easier than installing Windows NT or Windows 2000. In addition, Windows XP has increased security, including a built-in Internet firewall designed to protect a home PC connected directly to the Internet by way of an always-on connection such as cable modem or DSL. Firewalls, cable modems, and DSLs are covered in Chapters 11 and 12.

INSTALLING WINDOWS XP

A+ OS 2.1

Installing Windows XP involves many of the same considerations and decisions that you learned about when installing Windows 2000. In this section, you learn how to install Windows XP as a clean install and as an upgrade, including how to set up a dual boot.

Planning the Installation

A+ OS 2.1

Before installing Windows XP, do the following:

- Verify that the system meets the minimum and recommended requirements shown in Table 9-2.
- Check the hardware compatibility list (HCL) to verify that all installed hardware components are compatible with Windows XP.
- Decide how you will partition your hard drive and what file system you will use.
- For a PC on a network, decide whether the PC will be configured as a workstation in a workgroup or as part of a domain. (Workgroups and domains were covered in Chapter 6.)
- Make a final checklist and verify that you have done all of the above and are ready to begin the installation.

Table 9-2 Minimum and recommended requirements for Windows XP Professional

Component or Device	Minimum Requirement	Recommended Requirement
One or two CPUs	Pentium II 233 MHz or better	Pentium II 300 MHz or better
RAM	64 MB	128 MB up to 4 GB
Hard drive partition	2 GB	2 GB or more
Free space on the hard drive partition	640 MB (bare bones)	2 GB or more
CD-ROM drive	12x	12x or faster
Accessories	Keyboard and mouse or other pointing device	Keyboard and mouse or other pointing device

Remember that the requirements of an OS will vary depending on which version you have installed and what applications and hardware you have installed with it.

Minimum Requirements and Hardware Compatibility

Recall from earlier chapters that you can use the My Computer icon on the Windows desktop to determine the current CPU and available RAM. To see how much hard drive space is available, using Windows Explorer, right-click on the drive letter and select Properties from the shortcut menu. Part of the installation process for an upgrade is to clean up the hard drive, which might free up some hard drive space. Even though Windows XP

A+ OS 2.1

requires only 640 MB to install, you cannot achieve acceptable results unless you have at least 1.5 GB of free hard drive space on the volume that holds Windows XP.

There are several ways you can verify that software and hardware qualify for Windows XP. One way is to run the Readiness Analyzer. Use this command from the Windows XP CD, substituting the drive letter for your CD-ROM drive for D in the command line:

```
D:\I386\Winnt32 /checkupgradeonly
```

Depending on the release of Windows XP, your path might be different. The process takes about 10 minutes to run and displays a report that can be saved and later printed. The default name and path of the report is C:\Windows\compat.txt. The report is important if you have software you are not sure will work under Windows XP. If the analyzer reports that your software will not work under Windows XP, you might choose to upgrade the software or set up a dual boot with your old OS and Windows XP (dual-boot setup is covered later in the chapter).

Readiness Analyzer also checks hardware compatibility. Another way to verify your hardware is to go to the Microsoft Web site at *www.microsoft.com/hwdq/hcl*. Search on each hardware device by type (see Figure 9-3). There might be a copy of the Windows XP Professional HCL in the hcl.txt file on the Windows XP CD in the support folder. But for the most up-to-date information, use the Microsoft Web site.

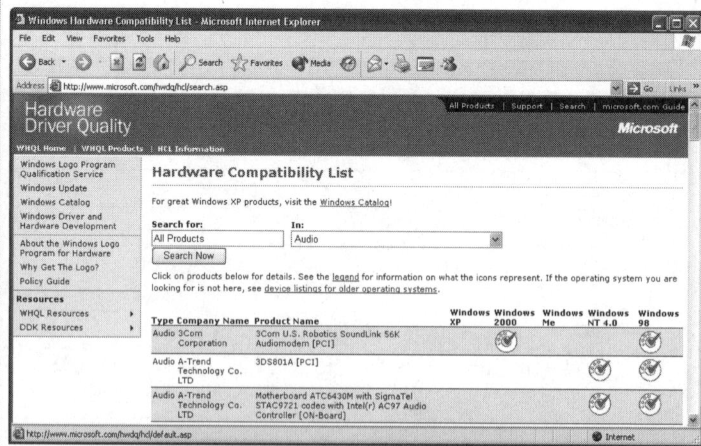

Figure 9-3 Search for each hardware component by type to determine if it qualifies for Windows XP

If your hardware does not qualify for Windows XP, check the hardware manufacturer's Web site for an upgrade and download the upgrade drivers before you begin the installation. If you plan to erase the hard drive as part of the installation, store these drivers on a floppy disk or on a network drive until you're ready to install them under Windows XP. If you can't find an upgrade, sometimes a device will work if you substitute a Windows driver written for a similar device. Check the documentation for your device, looking for information about other devices it will emulate. It is especially important to know that

A+ OS 2.1

your network card or modem card qualifies for Windows XP before you install the OS because you will need the card to access the Internet to get upgrades. If you are not sure an important hardware component qualifies, then install Windows XP as a dual boot with your current OS. Later, when you get the component working under Windows XP, you can uninstall the other OS.

Hard Drive Partitions and File Systems

Windows XP needs at least a 2-GB partition for the installation and should have about 1.5 GB of free space on that partition. You can install Windows XP on the same partition as another OS, but Windows XP will overwrite the existing OS on that partition. If you do not have a free 2-GB partition for the installation, you must delete smaller partitions and repartition the drive. Deleting a partition erases all data on that partition, so be sure to create backups first. Follow these general directions to ensure that partitions on the hard drive are adequate to install Windows XP:

- For Windows 9x, use Fdisk at the command prompt, and, for Windows 2000, use Disk Management to determine what partitions are on the drive, how large they are, what logical drives are assigned to them, and how much free space is on the drive that is not yet partitioned.
- If existing partitions are too small, look at the free space on the drive. If there is enough free space that is not yet partitioned, use that free space to create a new partition that is at least 2 GB.
- If you cannot create a 2-GB or larger partition, back up your data, delete the smaller partitions, and create a 2-GB active partition on the drive.
- If you have free space on the drive for other partitions, don't partition them at this time. First, install Windows XP and then use Disk Management under Windows XP to partition the remaining free space on the drive.

The same concerns about selecting a file system for Windows 2000 apply to Windows XP. The file systems supported by Windows XP are the same as those supported by Windows 2000: FAT16, FAT32, and NTFS. Recall that the NTFS file system used by Windows 2000 was incompatible with the Windows NT NTFS file system, making for a potential problem when installing Windows 2000 and Windows NT on the same PC as a dual boot. Because the Windows XP NTFS file system is the same as that of the Windows 2000 NTFS file system, a dual boot between these two OSs should not be a problem. Here are the general directions for selecting a file system:

- Use the NTFS file system if you are interested in file and folder security, file compression, control over how much disk space a user is allowed, or file encryption.
- Use the FAT16 or FAT32 file system if you are setting up a dual boot with Windows 9x, and each OS must access all partitions.
- Use the FAT16 file system if you are setting up a dual boot with MS-DOS or Windows NT, and each OS must access all partitions.

A+ OS 2.1

Joining a Workgroup or a Domain

If you are installing Windows XP on a network, you must make decisions about how you will access the network. If you have less than 10 computers networked together, Microsoft recommends that you join these computers in a workgroup where each computer controls its own resources. In this case, each user account is set up on the local computer, independently from user accounts on other PCs. There is no centralized control of resources. For more than 10 computers, Microsoft recommends that you use a domain controller running a network operating system such as Windows 2000 Server to control resources on the network. (Windows XP Professional installed on a workstation can then be a client on this Windows network. Also, it is expected that Microsoft will soon release Windows .NET, a server OS.) You will also want to use a domain controller if you want to administer and secure the network from a centralized location or if there are several centralized resources on the network that are shared by many users. How to manage workgroups is covered in Chapter 11, but managing a domain controller is beyond the scope of this book.

Upgrade or Clean Install?

If you plan to set up a dual boot, then you will perform a clean install for Windows XP. If you already have an OS installed and you do not plan a dual boot, then you have a choice between an upgrade and a clean install. Things to consider when making this decision are:

- You can use the less expensive upgrade version of Windows XP Professional to upgrade from Windows 98, Windows Me, Windows NT 4.0, and Windows 2000 to Windows XP Professional.
- You can use the less expensive upgrade version of Windows XP Home Edition to upgrade from Windows 98 or Windows Me to Windows XP Home Edition.
- When using FAT16, so that the partition will be compatible with Windows 9x, make it no larger than 2 GB.
- If you currently have Windows 95 installed, you must do a clean install using the more expensive For a New PC version of Windows XP Professional or Windows XP Home Edition.
- Regardless of whether you have an OS currently installed, you can still choose to do a clean install if you want a fresh start. Unless you erase your hard drive, reformat it, or delete partitions before the upgrade, data on the hard drive is not erased even if you convert to a new file system during the installation. However, OS settings and installed software will not carry forward into the new installation.

Final Checklist

Before you begin the installation, complete the final checklist shown in Table 9-3 to verify that you are ready to begin.

A+ OS 2.1

Table 9-3 Checklist for use before installing Windows XP

Things to Do	Further Information
Does the PC meet the minimum or recommended hardware requirement?	CPU: RAM: Hard drive size: Free space on the hard drive:
Have you run the Readiness Analyzer or checked the Microsoft Web site to verify that all your hardware and software qualify?	List hardware and software that need to be upgraded:
Do you have the product key available?	Product key:
Have you decided how you will join a network?	Workgroup name: Domain name: Computer name:
Will you do an upgrade or clean install?	Current operating system: Does the old OS qualify for an upgrade?
Verify that your hard drive is ready.	Size of the hard drive partition: Free space on the partition: File system you plan to use:
For a clean install, will you set up a dual boot?	List reasons for a dual boot: For a dual boot Size of the second partition: Free space on the second partition: File system you plan to use:
Have you backed up important data on your hard drive?	Location of backup:

Installation Process

Follow these general directions to perform a clean install of Windows XP on a PC that does not already have an OS installed:

1. Boot from the Windows XP CD, which displays the menu in Figure 9-4. Select the first option and press **Enter**. This menu might change slightly from one Windows XP build to another. If your PC does not boot from a CD, go to a command prompt and enter the command D:\i386\Winnt.exe, substituting the drive letter for your CD-ROM drive for D. (The path might vary depending on the release of Windows XP.) The End-User License agreement appears. Accept the agreement.

9

A+ OS 2.1

Windows XP Professional Setup
===================== =

Welcome to Setup.

This portion of the Setup program prepares Microsoft (R) Windows (R) XP to run on your computer.

- To set up Windows XP now, press ENTER.
- To repair a Windows XP installation using Recovery Console, press R.
- To quit Setup without installing Windows XP, press F3.

ENTER=Continue R=RepairF3=Quit

Figure 9-4 Windows XP Professional Setup opening menu

2. Setup lists all partitions that it finds on the hard drive, the file system of each partition, and the size of the partition. It also lists any free space on the drive that is not partitioned. From this screen, you can create and delete partitions and select the partition on which you want to install Windows XP. If you plan to have more than one partition on the drive, create only one partition at this time. The partition must be at least 2 GB in size and have 1.5 GB free. After the installation is done, you can use Disk Management to create the other partitions. Figure 9-5 shows an example of the list provided by Setup when the entire hard drive has not yet been partitioned.
3. If you created a new partition in Step 2, Setup asks you which file system you want to use to format the partition, NTFS or FAT. If the partition is at least 2 GB in size, the FAT file system will be FAT32. Select a file system for the partition. The Setup program formats the drive, completes the text-based portion of setup and loads the graphical interface for the rest of the installation. The PC then restarts.
4. Select your geographical location from the list provided. Windows XP will use it to decide how to display dates, times, numbers, and currency. Select your keyboard layout. Different keyboards can be used to accommodate special characters for other languages.

A+ OS 2.1

Windows XP Professional Setup
====================== =

The following list shows the existing partitions and unpartitioned space on this computer.

Use the UP and DOWN ARROW keys to select an item in the list.

- To set up Windows XP on the selected item, press ENTER.
- To create a partition in the unpartitioned space, press C.
- To delete the selected partition, press D.

28663 MB Disk 0 at Id 0 on bus 0 on atapi [MBR]

Unpartitioned space 28663 MB

ENTER=Install C=Create Partition F3=Quit

Figure 9-5 During Setup, you can create and delete partitions and select a partition on which to install Windows XP

5. Enter your name, the name of your organization, and your product key.
6. Enter the computer name and the password for the Administrator account. This password is stored in the security database on this PC. If you are joining a domain, the computer name is the name assigned to this computer by the network administrator managing the domain controller.

It is *very* important that you not forget the Administrator password. You will not be able to log onto the system without it.

7. Select the date, time, and time zone. The PC might reboot.
8. If you are connected to a network, you will be asked to choose how to configure your network settings, Typical or Custom. The Typical setting installs Client for

A+ OS 2.1

Microsoft Networks, File and Printer Sharing, and TCP/IP using dynamically assigned IP addresses. The Custom setting allows you to configure the network differently. If you are not sure which to use, use the Typical settings. You can change them later. How networks are configured is covered in Chapter 11.

9. Enter a workgroup or domain name. If you are joining a domain, the network administrator will have given you specific directions on how to configure user accounts on the domain.

For a clean install on a PC that already has an OS installed, follow these general directions:

1. Close any open applications. Close any boot management software or antivirus software that might be running in the background.
2. Insert the Windows XP CD in the CD-ROM drive. Autorun launches the opening window shown in Figure 9-6.

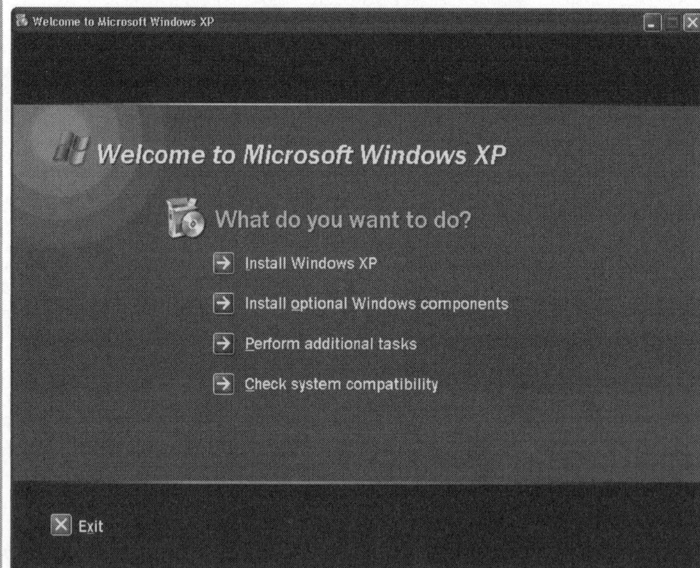

Figure 9-6 Windows XP Setup menu

3. Select the option to **Install Windows XP**. On the next screen, under Installation Type, select **New Installation**. Read and accept the licensing agreement. The installation process works the same as described above, picking up with Step 3.

When performing an upgrade to Windows XP, follow these general directions:

1. Before you begin the installation, do the following to prepare the system:
   - Clean up the hard drive: erase unneeded or temporary files, empty the Recycle Bin, run Disk Defragmenter, and do a ScanDisk of the drive.
   - If you have determined that you must upgrade hardware or software and that these upgrades are compatible with your old OS, perform the upgrades and verify that the hardware or software is working.

A+ OS 2.1

- If you do not have the latest BIOS for your motherboard, flash your BIOS.
- Back up important files.
- Scan the hard drive for viruses using a current version of antivirus software.
- If you have a compressed hard drive, uncompress the drive. The only exception to this is that if you are using Windows NT file compression on an NTFS drive, you do not need to uncompress it.
- Uninstall any hardware or software that you know will not be compatible with Windows XP and for which you do not have an upgrade available.

2. Insert the Windows XP Upgrade CD in the CD-ROM drive. The Autorun feature should launch the Setup program, with the menu shown in Figure 9-6.
3. If the Setup menu does not appear, you can enter the Setup command in the Run dialog box. Select the option to **Install Windows XP**.
4. On the next screen, under Installation Type, select **Upgrade**. The following menu gives you two options:
   - *Express Upgrade.* This upgrade uses existing Windows folders and uses all existing settings it can.
   - *Custom Upgrade.* This upgrade allows you to change the installation folder and the language options. Using this option, you can also change the file system to NTFS.
5. Select the type of upgrade and accept the licensing agreement.
6. Select the partition on which to install Windows XP. If the drive is configured as FAT and you want to convert to NTFS, you specify that now. Note that Windows XP has an uninstall utility that allows you to revert back to Windows 98 if necessary. This uninstall tool will not work if you convert FAT to NTFS.
7. Setup performs an analysis of the system and reports any problems with compatibility. Stop the installation if the problems indicate that you will not be able to operate the system after the installation.
8. For an upgrade from Windows 98 or Windows Me to Windows XP, the Setup program converts whatever information in the registry it can to Windows XP. At the end of the installation process, you are given the opportunity to join a domain. For Windows NT and Windows 2000 upgrades, almost all registry entries are carried forward into the new OS, and the information about a domain is not requested because it is copied from the old OS into Windows XP.

Upgrading from Windows NT or Windows 2000 to Windows XP is the easiest type of upgrade because these operating systems all have similar registries and support applications and devices in the same way. Nearly all applications that run on Windows NT or Windows 2000 will run on Windows XP. When upgrading from Windows NT to Windows XP, the NTFS file system is automatically converted to the Windows XP version.

A+ OS 2.1

Antivirus software designed to be used the Windows NT NTFS file system might not run under the Windows XP NTFS file system because of the way some antivirus programs filter software as it accesses the file system. You might have to upgrade your antivirus software once Windows XP is installed.

Setting Up a Dual Boot

You can configure Windows XP to set up a dual boot with another operating system. Start the installation as you would for a clean install on a PC with another operating system already installed. When given the opportunity, choose to install Windows XP on a different partition than the other OS. Windows XP recognizes that another OS is installed and sets up the Startup menu to offer it as an option for booting. After the installation, when you boot with a dual boot, the Startup menu automatically appears, asking you to select an operating system, as shown in Figure 9-7.

```
Please select the operating system to start:

    Microsoft Windows XP Professional
    Microsoft Windows 98

Use the up and down arrow keys to move the highlight to your choice.
Seconds until highlighted choice will be starting automatically: xx
Press ENTER to choose.

For troubleshooting and advanced startup options for Windows, press F8.
```

Figure 9-7 Menu displayed for a dual boot

The first active partition (drive C) must be set up with a file system that both operating systems understand. For example, for a dual boot with Windows 98, use the FAT32 or FAT16 file system. For a dual boot with Windows 2000, use either the FAT or the NTFS file system. The other operating system should be installed first, and then you can install Windows XP in a different partition. When you install Windows XP on another active partition or an extended partition, it will place only the files necessary to boot in the first active partition, which it calls the system partition. This causes Windows XP to initiate the boot rather than the other OS. The rest of Windows XP is installed on a second partition, which Windows XP calls the boot partition. This is the same way that Windows NT and Windows 2000 manage a dual boot with an older OS.

A+ OS 2.1

When setting up a dual boot, always install the older operating system first.

Earlier Windows operating systems were not aware of applications installed under the other OS in a dual boot, but Windows XP is. For example, if you set up a dual boot with Windows XP and Windows 98, an application installed under Windows 98 can be executed from Windows XP. This application might be listed under the Start menu of Windows XP. If it is not, you can use Windows XP Explorer to locate the program file. Double-click the application to run it from Windows XP. This makes it easier to implement a dual boot because you don't have to install an application under both OSs.

After the Installation

Immediately after you have installed Windows XP, there are several things to do to activate the OS, prepare the OS for use, and to back up the hard drive in preparation for a disaster. These steps are discussed in this section.

Product Activation

Product activation is a method used by Microsoft to prevent unlicensed use of its software, so you must purchase a Windows XP license for each installation of Windows XP. The method was introduced with Microsoft Office XP, and Microsoft has said it will continue using it for all future Microsoft products. The first time you log on to the system after the installation is complete, the Activate Windows dialog box appears giving these three options (see Figure 9-8):

- Yes, let's activate Windows over the Internet now
- Yes, I want to telephone a customer service representative to activate Windows
- No, remind me to activate Windows every few days

If you choose to activate Windows over the Internet and are connected to the Internet, the process is almost instant. Windows XP sends a numeric identifier to a Microsoft server, which sends a certificate activating the product on your PC. You have up to 60 days after installation to activate Windows XP, after which time the system will refuse to boot. If you install Windows XP from the same CD on a different computer and you attempt to activate Windows from the new PC, a dialog box appears telling you of the suspected violation of the license agreement. You can call a Microsoft operator and explain what caused the discrepancy. If your explanation is reasonable (for example, you uninstalled Windows XP from one PC and installed it on another), the operator can issue you a valid certificate. You can then type the certificate value into a dialog box to complete the boot process.

Now access the Internet and download any service packs, updates, or patches for the OS from the Microsoft Web site. You can also install any additional Windows components at this time.

A+ OS 2.1

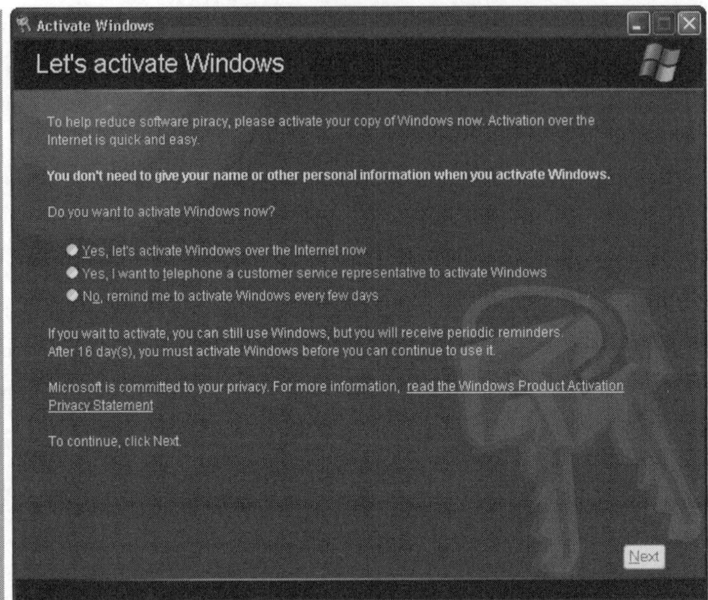

Figure 9-8 Product activation is a strategy used by Microsoft to prevent software piracy

Transferring User Files and Preferences to a New PC

Windows XP offers a utility that helps you transfer user files and preferences from one computer to another that has just had Windows XP installed. The **User State Migration Tool (USMT)** transfers user files and folders, display properties, taskbar options, and browser and e-mail settings from a Windows 9x or Windows NT/2000/XP computer. This utility can help make a smooth transition for a user moving from one PC to another; copying files and reconfiguring OS settings is not necessary. The process involves three steps:

1. Use a Windows XP computer to create a disk that contains the Files and Settings Transfer Wizard. This PC need not be the same PC that will later receive the transfer.
2. Use the disk on the source computer (the user's old computer) to run the Wizard and copy the user state to a server hard drive or removable media such as a Zip drive.
3. On the destination computer (the user's new computer), use the Wizard to transfer the user state to this computer.

To begin the process, use the Files and Settings Transfer Wizard to create the disk. To access the Wizard, click Start, All Programs, Accessories, System Tools, Files and Settings Transfer Wizard. The Wizard launches and the Welcome to the Files and Settings Transfer Wizard window opens. Click Next and the Wizard asks you if this is the New computer or Old computer. Select New computer, and then click Next. Figure 9-9 shows the next screen,

A+ OS 2.1

on which you can choose to create the disk or declare that you are ready to put the information on the new computer. On the screen, note that you can also use the Windows XP CD to launch the Wizard on the old computer rather than creating the disk.

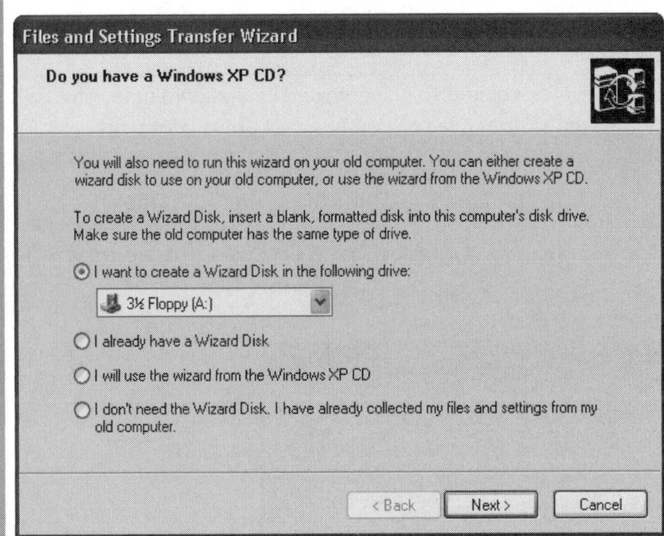

Figure 9-9 The first step in using the Files and Settings Transfer Wizard is to create the Wizard Disk

After you have created the disk or chosen to use the Windows XP CD, go to the old computer, launch the Wizard, and retrieve the files and settings. Then, return to this screen on the new computer and choose to put the information on the new computer.

Instead of using the Wizard, you can also use two commands at the command prompt. Scanstate copies the information to a server or removable media, and Loadstate copies the information to the destination computer. These utilities can be included in batch files and executed automatically when implementing Windows XP over a large number of computers in an enterprise. For details on how to use the command lines in a batch file, see the *Windows XP Resource Kit* by Microsoft Press.

A+ OS 3.2

Preparing for Later Problems with the OS

Once the installation is completed, hardware and software are installed, and user preferences are set, it is a good idea to guard against later problems with the OS by creating a backup of the hard drive. Windows XP offers a utility called the **Automated System Recovery (ASR)** process that allows you to restore an entire hard drive volume or logical drive to its state at the time the backup of the volume was made. This process creates the backup and also creates an ASR floppy disk that allows you to use the backup to recover the system later. You will learn how to recover a failed system using a backup in the next chapter. In this section, you learn how to create the backup.

9

A+ OS 3.2

The backup file created will be just as large as the contents of the hard drive volume, so you will need a massive backup medium such as another partition on this or another local hard drive or file server, a tape drive, or a writeable CD-R or CD-RW drive.

Do not back up the logical drive or volume to a folder on the same volume. The ASR backup process allows you to do this, but restoring later from this backup will not work.

Follow these directions to create the backup and the ASR floppy disk:

1. Click **Start**, **All Programs**, **Accessories**, **System Tools**, **Backup**. The Backup and Restore window appears (see Figure 9-10).

Figure 9-10 Use the Backup or Restore Wizard to back up the hard drive partition once the Windows XP installation is completed

2. Click the **Advanced Mode** link. The Backup Utility window appears. Click **Automated System Recovery Wizard**. On the following screen, click **Next**.
3. The Backup Destination window appears. Select the location of the medium to receive the backup and insert a disk into the floppy disk drive. This disk will become the ASR disk. Click **Next**.
4. Click **Finish**. The backup process shows its progress as seen in Figure 9-11.

A+ OS 3.2

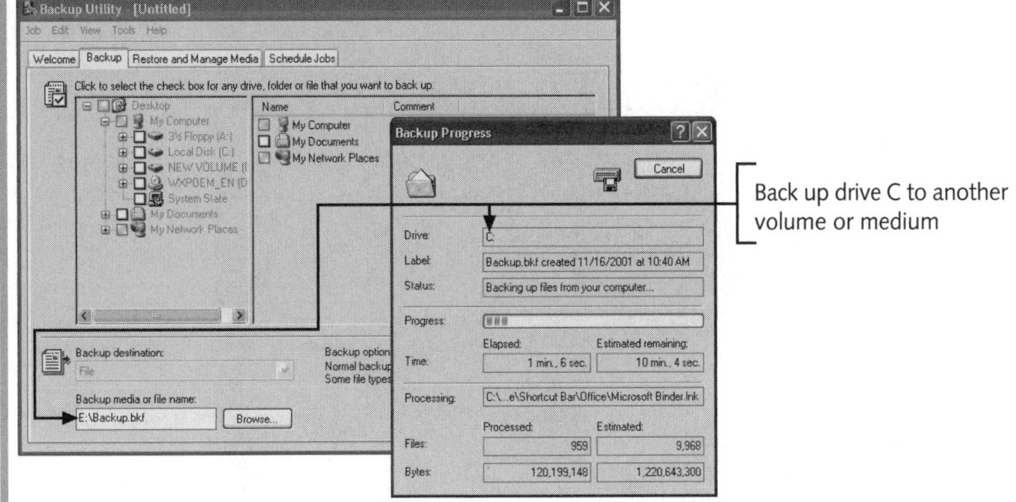

Figure 9-11 The Backup utility can create a backup of drive C and an ASR disk to be used later for the Automated System Recover Utility

5. When the backup is finished, label the ASR disk with the name of the disk, the date it was created, and the computer's name, and put it in a safe place.

Just as with Windows 2000, you can back up the system state as discussed in Chapter 7. If you back up the system state when you complete an installation, and a failure occurs in the future, you can restore the system state without overwriting user data on the hard drive. This is less drastic than the Automated System Recovery process that restores the entire volume.

Using Windows XP

Now that you have learned how to successfully install Windows XP and guard the system against a potential failure, let's take a closer look at how it works and what it can do. When you use Windows XP for the first time, one difference you will note immediately is the desktop, seen in Figure 9-12. When the OS is first installed, the Recycle Bin is the only shortcut on the desktop. The Start menu also is organized with a more graphical look. Notice in Figure 9-12 that the username for the person currently logged on shows at the top of the Start menu. Applications at the top of the Start menu are said to be "pinned" to the Start menu and are permanently listed there until you change them in a Start menu setting. Applications that are used often are listed below the pinned applications and can change from time to time. The programs in the white column of the Start menu on the left side are user oriented, and the programs in the dark column on the right side of the menu are OS oriented.

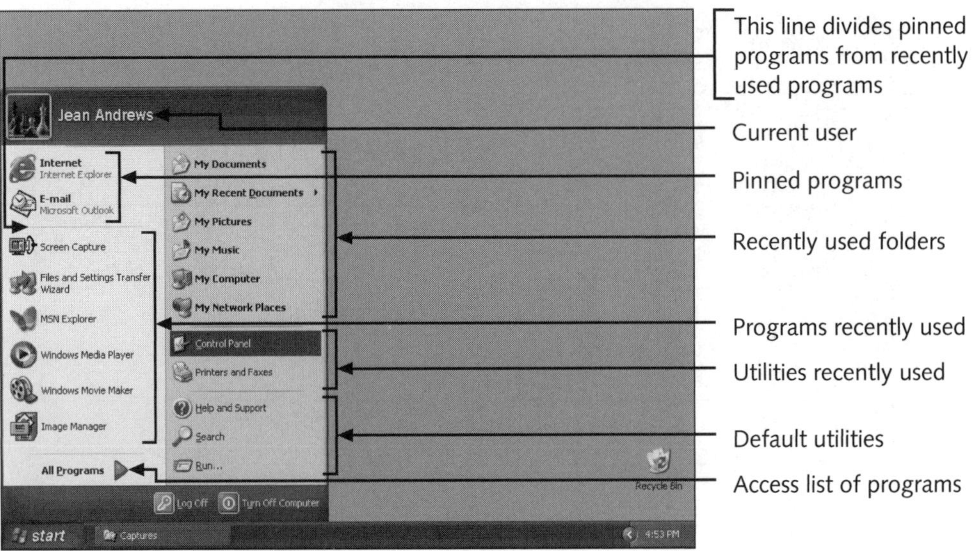

Figure 9-12 The Windows XP desktop and Start menu

When you click All Programs, the list of currently installed software appears. Figure 9-13 shows the default entries under Accessories, System Tools. You have already seen two of these, Backup and Files and Settings Transfer Wizard. Also, after Windows is installed, you can use the Activate Windows option on this menu to activate Windows XP. You will learn about some of the other options on this menu later in this chapter and in the next chapter.

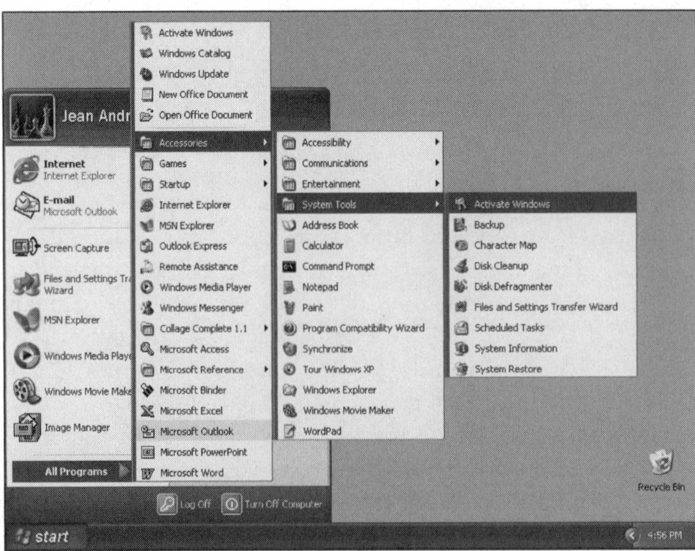

Figure 9-13 Click Start, All Programs to view the list of currently installed software

When you drill down to windows and menus on these windows, you will notice you have more control over how and where things are displayed. Overall, if you are familiar with earlier versions of Windows, learning to use Windows XP is easy and intuitive. One example of how you can change the way a window appears is through the Control Panel. To access the Control Panel, click Start, All Programs, and Control Panel. Figure 9-14 shows the Control Panel in Category View. Select a category in order to see the applets in that category, or click Switch to Classic View to see the applets when you first open the Control Panel as you did with earlier versions of Windows.

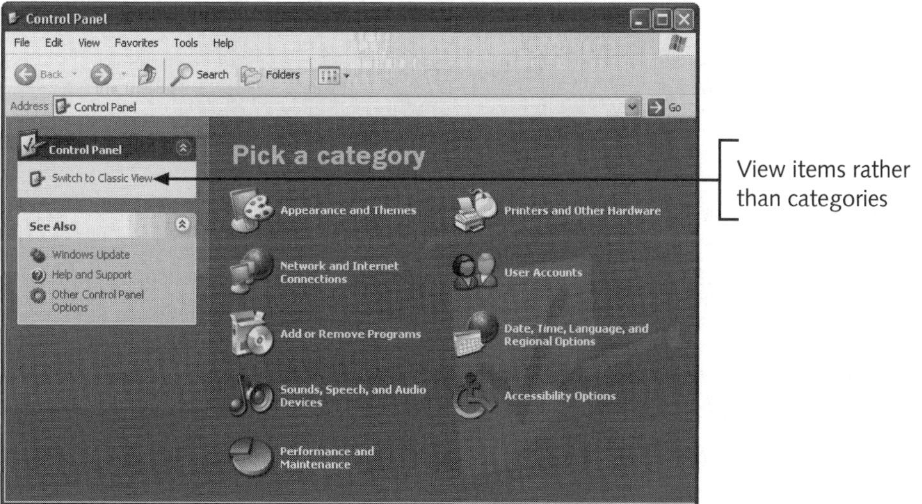

Figure 9-14 The Control Panel is organized by category, although you can easily switch to Classic View

Customizing the Windows XP Desktop

There are several things you can do to customize the Windows XP desktop. For example, you can change the background on the desktop (called the wallpaper), create shortcuts, and control what goes in the system tray. This section looks at each of these ways to make the desktop look and work the way you want it to.

Each user account has a different desktop configuration, so if you want to create a customized desktop for a user, you must first log on to the system under that user account.

Managing Shortcuts

When you first install Windows XP, by default only the Recycle Bin shows on the desktop. To add other shortcuts that normally were on the Windows 2000 desktop, right-click anywhere on the desktop and select Properties from the shortcut menu. (You can also select the Display icon in Control Panel.) The Display Properties window appears (see Figure 9-15). Click the Desktop tab.

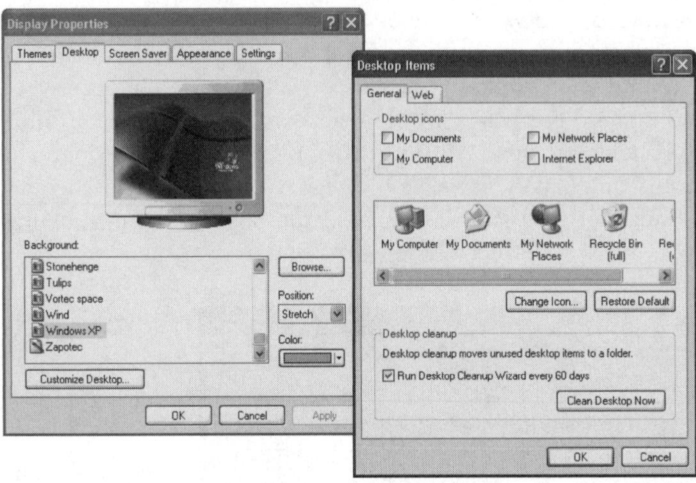

Figure 9-15 Managing the Windows XP desktop

Click Customize Desktop to display the Desktop Items window, also shown in Figure 9-15. You can check My Documents, My Computer, My Network Places, and Internet Explorer to add these icons to the desktop. Also notice on this window the option to have Windows clean up your desktop by moving any shortcuts that you have not used in the last 60 days to a separate folder.

You can add a program shortcut to the desktop by right-clicking a program name in the Start, All Programs list and then selecting Copy from the shortcut menu. Then right-click anywhere on the desktop and select Paste from the shortcut menu. A shortcut is created and placed on the desktop. You can also use Windows Explorer to create a shortcut. From Explorer, right-click a program filename or the filename of a document or data file, and then select Create Shortcut from the shortcut menu (see Figure 9-16). Then drag the created shortcut to the desktop.

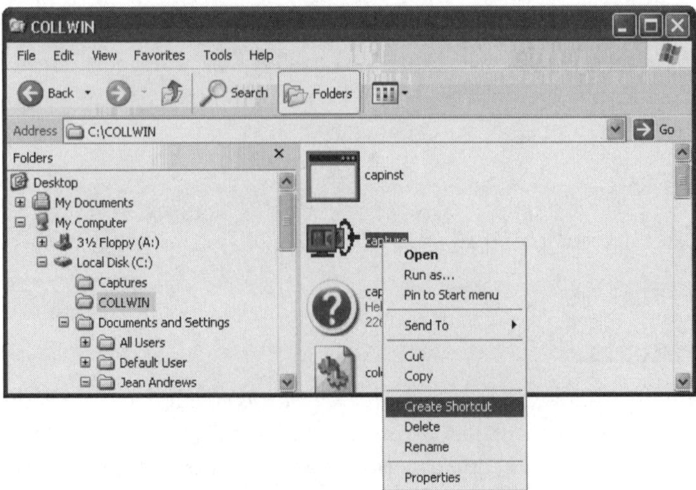

Figure 9-16 Create a shortcut to a file using the file's shortcut menu in Explorer

A+ OS 1.1

Windows XP Taskbar and System Tray

The taskbar can be controlled from the Taskbar and Start Menu windows. Access these windows by using the Taskbar and Start menu icon in Control Panel or by right-clicking the taskbar and selecting Properties. Either way, the window in Figure 9-17 appears. From it you can add items to and remove items from the Start Menu, control how the taskbar manages items in the system tray, and specify how the taskbar is displayed.

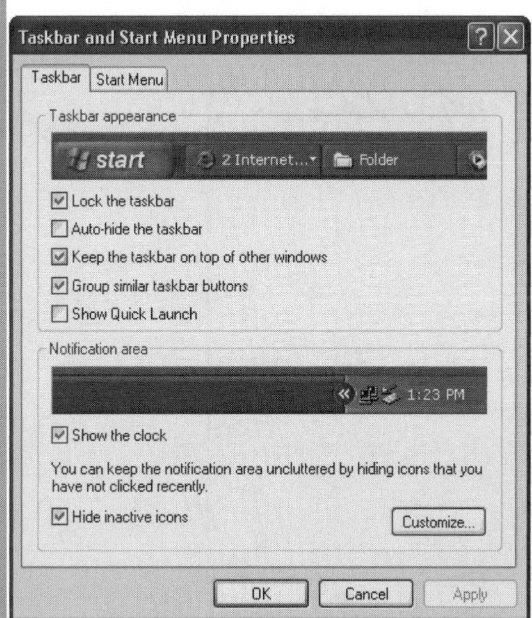

Figure 9-17 Use the Taskbar and Start Menu Properties window to control what is displayed in the Start menu and taskbar

You might want to display frequently used programs as icons in the taskbar. To do that, right-click the taskbar, select Toolbars, and then click Quick Launch. Also, the system tray sometimes gets cluttered with several icons for running services such as the volume control and network connectivity. Windows XP automatically hides these icons. When they are hidden, to unhide them, click the left arrow on the right side of the taskbar. In addition, by using the options available on the taskbar shortcut menu, you can add programs to the Quick Launch toolbar, customize the taskbar properties, and add new toolbars to the taskbar.

Windows Messenger

By default, when Windows XP first starts, it loads Windows Messenger, which takes up system resources even if you are not using it. To stop Windows Messenger from loading at startup, on the Windows Messenger menu, click Tools and then click Options. The Options window opens as shown in Figure 9-18. Click the Preferences tab and uncheck Run this program when Windows starts. Click OK.

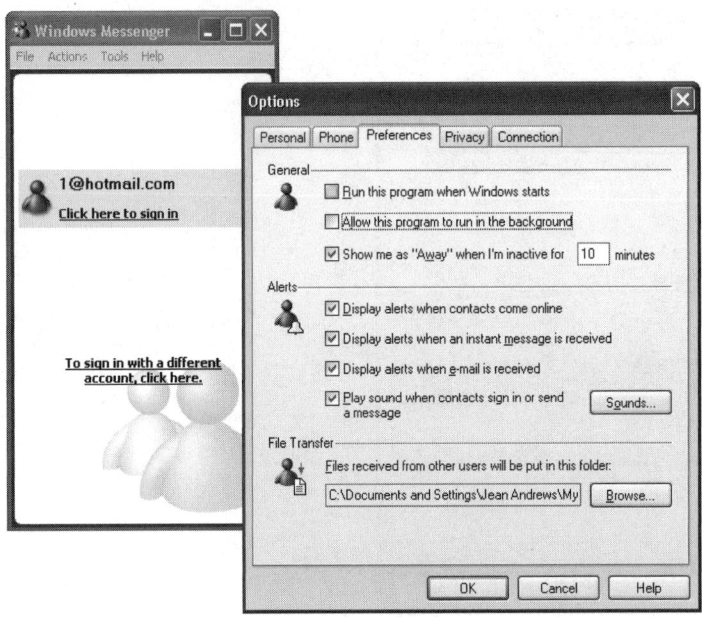

Figure 9-18 Disable Windows Messenger at startup

Managing Audio and Video

Windows XP has several built-in features to manage audio and video, including support for inputting images from digital cameras and scanners, a Windows Movie Maker for editing video, and Windows Media Player, Version 8. (Windows Me has Media Player, Version 7.) With Media Player you can play DVDs, CDs, and Internet radio. There's a jukebox for organizing audio files, including MP3 files used on music CDs. You can also burn your own music CDs using Media Player with a CD-R or CD-RW drive. To access the Media Player, click Start, All Programs, Windows Media Player. Figure 9-19 shows the Media Player window.

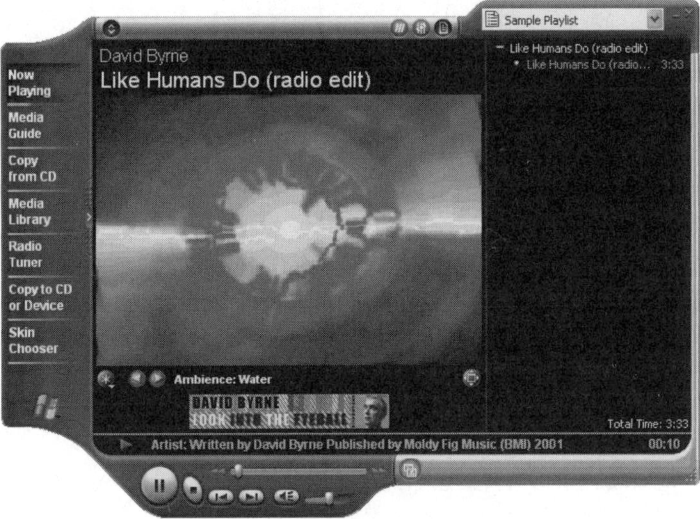

Figure 9-19 Windows Media Player

Just as with older versions of Windows, you can record and manage sound from the Entertainment group of Windows and manage sounds for Windows events from the sounds applet in Control Panel. To record sound, if you have a microphone connected to a sound card, click Start, All Programs, Accessories, Entertainment, and Sound Recorder. The Sound Recorder appears, as shown in Figure 9-20. Click the Record button (red dot in lower-right corner) to record a sound, such as your own voice, into a sound file. There are several types of sound files, including MP3 files (with the .mp3 file extension), which can be used on audio CDs, and Wave files (with the .wav file extension). Windows uses .wav files to record sound. Later, you can substitute this .wav file for one of the Windows sounds that is played when you open or close applications, shut down Windows, or perform many other Windows activities that can be accompanied by sound. To change the sounds for various Windows events, from Control Panel, open the Sounds and Audio Devices applet, and select the Sounds tab.

Figure 9-20 Record sounds using Windows Sound Recorder

Media Player has its own volume control, but there is another way to adjust sound. From the Control Panel, open the Sounds and Audio Devices applet and select the Volume tab. If you check Place volume icon in the taskbar, you can easily adjust the sound from the taskbar.

Two ways to control sound volume are to use the Windows controls or use the manual controls on an amplifier or speaker.

Multiple Logins and Remote Assistance

Windows XP allows more than one user to be logged in at the same time. To switch from one account to another, click Start, Log OFF. The Log Off Windows dialog box opens, giving you two choices: Switch User and Log Off. Click Switch User, and then select a new account from the list of user accounts. After you enter a password, the screen will go blank and then the desktop configured for the new user appears. Each user can have his or her own set of applications open at the same time. When users switch back and forth, Windows keeps separate instances of applications open for each user.

Windows XP also offers a new feature called **Remote Assistance**. Using this utility, a user sitting at the PC can give a support technician at a remote location full access to the desktop so the technician can use the desktop just as she would if sitting in front of the PC. This is useful when the user is inexperienced and is having trouble following the technician's directions as the technician is investigating and troubleshooting problems with Windows XP.

INSTALLING HARDWARE AND APPLICATIONS

A+ OS 2.4

In this section, you will learn how to install hardware and applications under Windows XP, and you will also learn several ways to solve problems with both. Later in this chapter and the next chapter, you will learn about more tools and procedures you can use to troubleshoot a failed system, program, or hardware device. We will first look at how to install hardware.

Installing Hardware

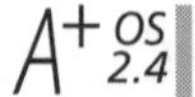

Since Windows XP is relatively new to the market, a device might not come with a Windows XP-compatible driver. To see if a hardware device has a driver that is known to be compatible with Windows XP, see the Microsoft Web site *www.microsoft.com/technet* and search on the driver or device. Download the latest driver from the Microsoft Web site or the Web site of the device manufacturer. Windows XP offers three processes that can help solve problems with devices:

- Verifying that the driver is certified by Microsoft
- Providing a way to automatically find an update for a driver
- Rolling back a driver in case an updated driver fails

A+ OS 2.4 3.2

Just as with earlier Windows operating systems, when Windows XP is first started, if it senses a new device is present, it automatically launches the Found New Hardware Wizard, which gives you two options:

- Install the software automatically (Recommended)
- Install from a list or specific location (Advanced)

Select the option to Install the Software automatically, and then click Next. During the installation process, you are given the opportunity to click Have Disk to provide a driver supplied by the manufacturer, rather than selecting the device from a list, which results in using a Windows driver. First, attempt to use the Windows XP driver. If it causes problems, search both the Microsoft Web site and the manufacturer's Web site for the latest updated driver. If the Wizard does not automatically launch when you start Windows, you can start it using the Add Hardware icon in Control Panel.

Using Device Manager

9

After a device is installed, you can use Device Manager to verify that Windows XP sees no problems with the device. There is more than one way to access Device Manager. One way is to click Start, right-click My Computer, and then select Manage from the shortcut menu. The Computer Management window appears (see Figure 9-21). This powerful tool offers several important utilities to support Windows XP, some of which you learned about in earlier chapters, that function the same as they did with Windows 2000 (such as Event Viewer), and some of which you will learn about in this chapter. Under System Tools, click Device Manager to view it. With Device Manager selected, use the View menu to control how you view devices and resources in Device Manager, similarly to previous versions of Windows. Another way to access Device Manager is to open the System applet in Control Panel, select the Hardware tab, and click Device Manager.

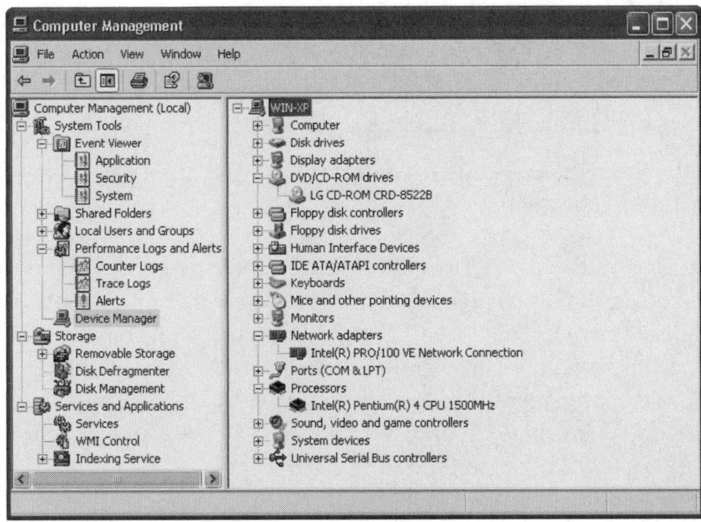

Figure 9-21 Device Manager is one tool available in the Computer Management window

A+ OS 2.4 3.2

Using Device Manager, you can verify that there are no resource conflicts with the device and that it is working properly as viewed by Windows XP. From Device Manager, Windows XP offers a way to update a driver using the Update Device Driver Wizard. Right-click a device and select Properties from the shortcut menu. The Properties window for that device appears (see Figure 9-22). Select the Driver tab and click Update Driver... to launch the Wizard and follow directions on the screen. The Wizard goes to the Microsoft Web site, searches for updates to the driver, informs you if there is an update, and asks permission to install the update. Windows XP will only suggest an update if the hardware ID of the device is an exact match to the hardware ID of the update. A hardware ID is a number assigned to a device by the manufacturer that uniquely identifies the product.

If you do not have an always-on connection to the Internet, connect to the Internet before you launch the Update Device Driver Wizard.

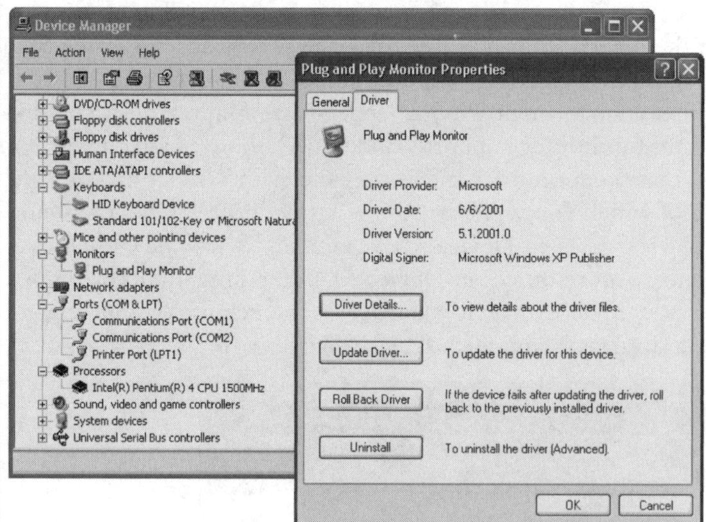

Figure 9-22 Use the Properties window for a device to obtain an updated driver from the Microsoft Web site

If you update a driver and the new driver does not perform as expected, you can revert to the old driver by using the Driver Rollback feature. To revert to a previous driver, from the Properties window for the device (see Figure 9-22), click Roll Back Driver. If a previous driver is available, it will be installed. In many cases, when a driver is updated, Windows saves the old driver in case you want to revert to it. Note that Windows does not save printer drivers when they are updated and also does not save any drivers if they are not functioning properly at the time of an update.

You can also copy an older driver from another PC or a backup medium to this PC for a rollback. Two files are needed: a .sys file and an .inf file. The .sys file is the actual driver,

A+ OS 2.4 3.2 and the .inf file contains information about the driver. Put these files in the %systemroot%\system32\reinstallbackups\ folder, and then perform the rollback.

By default, Device Manager does not show legacy devices that are not Plug and Play. To view legacy devices that are installed, on the View menu of Device Manager, check Show hidden devices (see Figure 9-23).

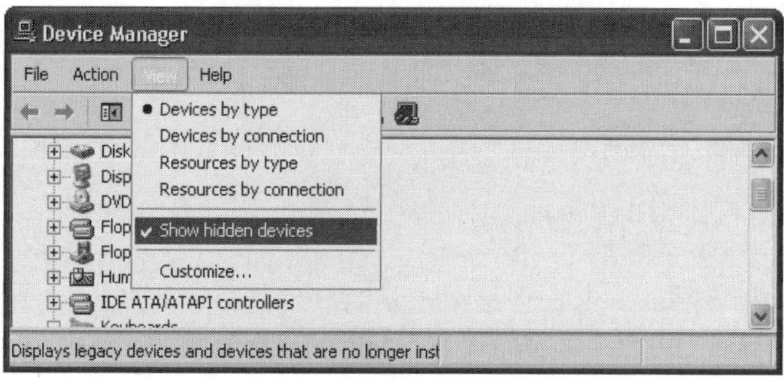

Figure 9-23 By default, Windows XP does not display legacy devices in Device Manager. Show these hidden devices by using the View menu.

Windows 2000 and Windows XP support the verification of digital signatures assigned to device drivers. If you suspect a problem with a driver, run **Sigverif.exe** to scan for drivers that are not digitally signed. To use the utility, enter the command in the Run dialog box. Also, during an installation, you can control how Windows handles a driver not digitally signed by using the Hardware tab of the System Properties window.

Installing Applications

Applications are installed under Windows XP as they are under other Windows OSs. You can use the Add or Remove Programs icon in Control Panel, or you can run the application's setup program from the Run dialog box. You can install software only if you have Administrator privileges. An installed program is normally made available to every user when they log on. If a program is not available to all users, try installing the program files in the Documents and Settings\All Users folder.

You can cause a program to automatically launch each time you start Windows by putting a shortcut to the program in the Startup menu folder for the user. For each user, this folder is Documents and Settings*Username*\Start Menu\Programs\Startup. If you want the software to automatically start up for all users, put the shortcut in this folder: Documents and Settings\All Users\Start Menu\Programs\Startup.

Software is uninstalled using the Add and Remove Programs applet in Control Panel. Open the applet and select the software to uninstall (see Figure 9-24). Then click the

Change/Remove icon. If other users are logged on to the system, the Warning message in Figure 9-24 appears. Log everyone off, and then uninstall the software.

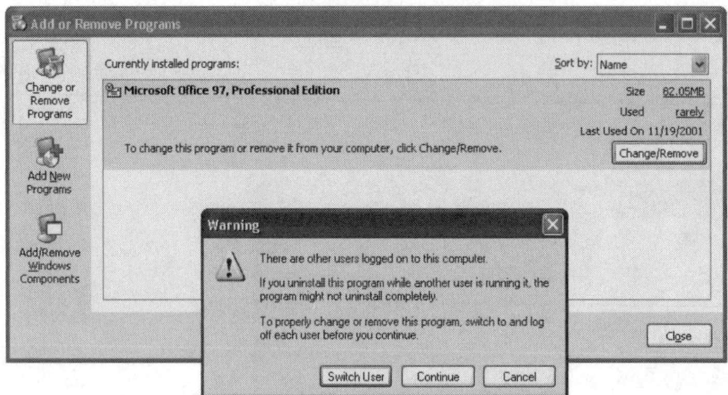

Figure 9-24 To uninstall software using the Add or Remove Programs applet, only one user should be logged on to the system

Installing Legacy Software

DOS and Windows 9x applications that do not work under Windows NT and Windows 2000 are more likely to work under Windows XP. Some legacy applications that you should not attempt to run under Windows XP are older versions of antivirus software, and maintenance and cleanup utilities. In these cases, it is best to upgrade your software to versions that are designed to work under Windows XP.

If a legacy application does not start up and run successfully after you have installed it, try the following:

- Check the Microsoft Web site for updates to Windows XP or the Microsoft application (*windowsupdate.microsoft.com*). How to perform Windows XP updates is covered in the next chapter.
- Check the software manufacturer's Web site for updates or suggestions on how to run the software under Windows XP.
- Consider upgrading the software to a later version.
- Use the Windows XP Compatibility Mode utility.

The **Compatibility Mode utility** provides an application with the environment it expects from the operating system for which it was designed, including Windows 95, Windows 98, Windows Me, Windows NT, and Windows 2000. (Compatibility mode does not apply to DOS applications.) There is more than one way to use the utility, but the easiest way is to create a shortcut on the desktop to an installed application and then set the properties of the shortcut to use compatibility mode. After you have created the shortcut to the application, right-click it and select Properties from the shortcut menu. The Properties window is displayed (see Figure 9-25). Select the Compatibility tab. Check *Run this program in compatibility mode for*, and then select the operating system that you want Windows XP to emulate. Click Apply to apply the change. Run the software to find out whether the problem is solved.

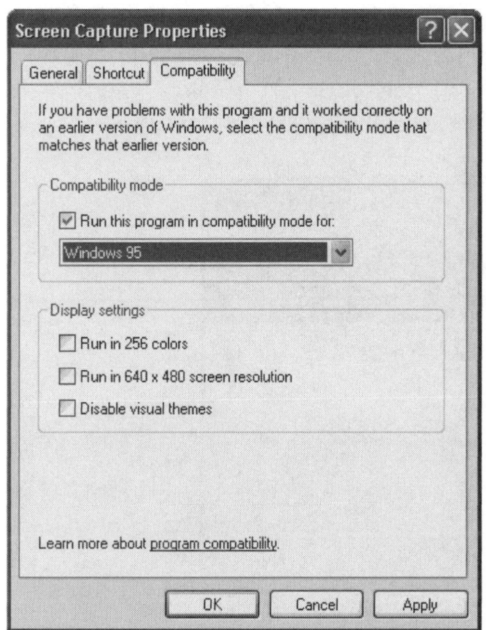

Figure 9-25 Setting Windows XP to run a legacy program in compatibility mode

If it is not solved, if you like, you can provide Microsoft with information that might help it fix the problem in some future Windows XP update. To provide the information, run the Program Compatibility Wizard. Click Start, All Programs, Accessories, Program Compatibility Wizard. Follow directions on the Wizard screen to locate the program file. After you locate the program file, you are asked to test the application and then respond to the questions show in Figure 9-26.

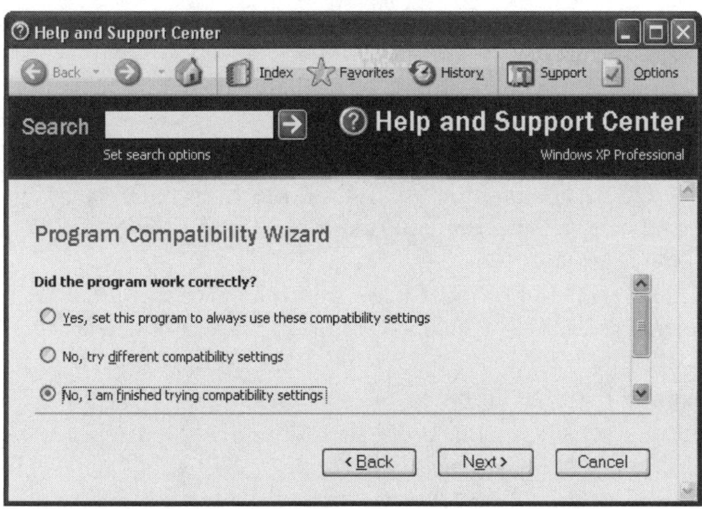

Figure 9-26 Using the Program Compatibility Wizard

If you answer, "No, I am finished trying compatibility settings," then the screen in Figure 9-27 appears. If you respond Yes to the question, "Would you like to send this information to Microsoft?", then the information needed to help Microsoft solve problems with the application is transmitted to the Microsoft Web site over the Internet.

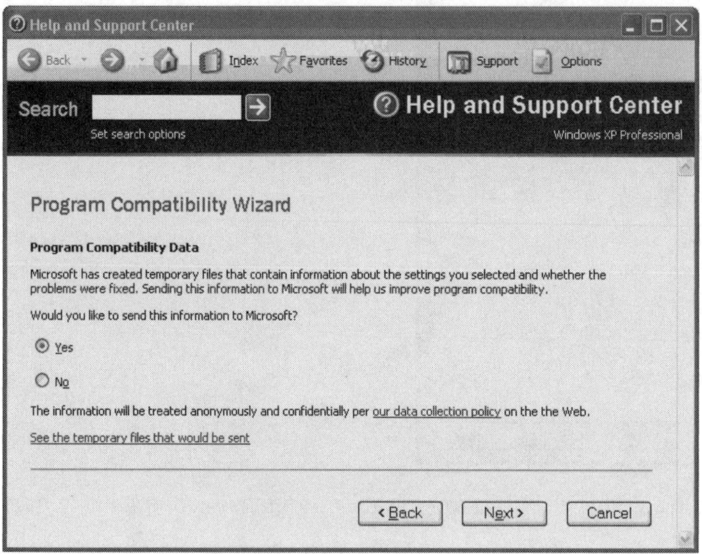

Figure 9-27 If running a legacy program in compatibility mode does not solve the problem, you can send helpful information to Microsoft

CHAPTER SUMMARY

- There are presently three versions of Windows XP: Windows XP Home Edition, Windows XP Professional, and Windows XP 64-bit Edition. Windows .NET is expected to be released soon.
- Windows XP integrates features of Windows 9x and 2000, while providing added support for multimedia and networking technologies.
- Though the Windows XP interface looks different from that of earlier versions of Windows and the OS organizes some utilities and functions differently, Windows XP is built on the same basic architecture as Windows NT and Windows 2000 and has the same basic kernel structure.
- Windows XP requires only 640 MB of free hard drive space for installation; however, acceptable performance cannot be achieved without 1.5 GB of free space on the Windows XP partition.
- Windows XP supports the same file systems as Windows 2000: FAT16, FAT32, and NTFS.
- You can install Windows XP as a dual boot with Windows 2000, because they both use the same version of NTFS. To dual boot Windows XP with Windows 9x or Windows NT, you must use FAT32. Always install the other OS first, and install Windows XP on a different partition than another OS.

- A clean install is required if you plan to dual boot Windows XP with another OS. Perform an upgrade if you have another version of Windows installed and you do not plan to dual boot.
- Before upgrading to Windows XP, clean up the hard drive by deleting unnecessary files and running Disk Defragmenter and ScanDisk, uncompress the drive, and delete known incompatible software.
- An Express Upgrade uses existing folders and settings as much as possible. A Custom Upgrade allows you to changes folders, language, and the file system.
- Unlike earlier versions of Windows, Windows XP is aware of applications installed under another OS when it is installed as a dual boot.
- Microsoft uses product activation to prevent the use of its software products, including Windows XP, on more than one computer.
- The User State Migration Tool (USMT) enables a user to make a smooth transition from one computer to another by transferring user files and settings. The Scanstate and Loadstate commands accomplish the same thing from the command prompt.
- Differences in the Windows XP desktop from earlier versions include the absence (by default) of any shortcuts other than the Recycle Bin and more graphical organization of the Start menu.
- In the Windows XP Control Panel, you can view applications in Category View or Classic View, which is the way it looked in earlier versions of Windows.
- Windows XP allows more than one user to be logged on at the same time, each with his own instances of open applications.
- Windows XP offers processes to help in finding updates for a driver, rolling back a driver if an update fails, and verifying that a driver is certified by Microsoft.
- The Computer Management, Disk Management, and Device Manager tools work much the same way in Windows XP as they did in Windows 2000.
- Windows XP Device Manager hides legacy devices (non-Plug and Play devices) by default.
- You can only install software in Windows XP if you have administrator privileges.
- DOS applications and older Windows applications that did not work under earlier versions of Windows are more likely to work under Windows XP.
- Compatibility mode in Windows XP provides an application written for Windows 9x or later with the environment for which it was designed.

Key Terms

Automated System Recovery (ASR)
Compatibility Mode utility
product activation
Remote Assistance
Sigverif.exe
User State Migration Tool (USMT)

Review Questions

1. Name the three main versions of Windows XP.
2. What are at least three similarities between Windows XP and Windows 2000? At least three differences?
3. How much free space on a partition does Windows XP require for installation? How much does it require for acceptable operation?
4. How much memory is required to install Windows XP? How much is recommended to run applications under Windows XP?
5. When you are trying to determine if your computer can support Windows XP, list the steps to find out how much RAM is currently installed.
6. Which version of Windows XP must be installed on a system that is using the Intel Itanium processor? Why?
7. How many processors in a system can Windows XP support?
8. List two different ways to check hardware and software compatibility for Windows XP.
9. If you find out that one of your applications is not supported by Windows XP and you still want to use XP, how can you solve this incompatibility problem?
10. What file system do you use if you are installing Windows XP as a dual boot with Windows 9x? Windows NT? Windows 2000?
11. Name at least four things you should do before performing an upgrade to Windows XP.
12. What are the two upgrade options for Windows XP? Explain how they differ.
13. How long do you have to activate Windows XP? What happens if you don't?
14. What is the first Microsoft product to use product activation?
15. Explain the purpose of the USMT utility and list the three steps needed to use it.
16. What two commands can you use from the command prompt to perform the same functions as the Files and Settings Transfer Wizard?
17. How are the Windows XP desktop and Start menu different from those in Windows 2000?
18. Give two different ways to create shortcuts in Windows XP.
19. What are two ways you can access the Windows XP Device Manager?
20. Name the two files that are needed to copy an older driver from another PC or a backup medium to your Windows XP PC for a device driver rollback.
21. What is the path for the report file created when you run Readiness Analyzer?
22. Which OS are DOS applications more likely to work under: Windows 2000 or Windows XP?

23. List at least three things you can do if a legacy application does not start up and run correctly after you install it under Windows XP.
24. What legacy applications should you not attempt to run under Windows XP?
25. Where should you place a shortcut if you want the associated application to start automatically on startup for all users? Give the entire path.

HANDS-ON PROJECTS

Using Shortcuts

Create a shortcut on your desktop to Notepad (Notepad.exe), a text editor. Using a second method for creating shortcuts, add a shortcut to the Windows command prompt (Cmd.exe). First, locate the two program files on your hard drive by clicking Start, Search and using the Search dialog box. Then create the shortcuts. List the steps you took to create each shortcut.

Prepare for an Upgrade

On a PC with Windows 2000 or an earlier version of Windows installed, run the Readiness Analyzer from the Windows XP CD to determine whether the PC is ready for Windows XP installation. Make a list of any hardware or software components that are found to be incompatible with Windows XP, and draw up a plan for getting the system ready for an XP upgrade.

Update Windows

On a Windows XP system that is connected to the Internet, click Start, All Programs, Windows Update. This takes you to the Microsoft Web site where the site will search your system and recommend Windows XP updates. Print the Web page showing a list of recommended updates. For a lab PC, don't perform the updates unless you have the permission of your instructor.

Install Windows XP

This project will erase everything on your hard drive. Do not do it if you have important data on the hard drive.

Prepare your hard drive for a clean installation of Windows XP by formatting the hard drive. Follow the instructions in the chapter to install Windows XP. Put Windows XP in a partition that is 2 GB in size. Write down each decision you had to make as you performed the installation. If you get any error messages during the installation, write them down and also list the steps you took to recover from the error. How long did the installation take?

Once you have installed Windows XP, use Disk Management to partition and format the remainder of the hard drive. Print a screen shot of Disk Management showing the two partitions. Create an ASR backup of the system partition in the second partition. Print a screen shot showing the files on the ASR floppy disk, using Windows Explorer to view the files.

CHAPTER

10

MANAGING AND SUPPORTING WINDOWS XP

In this chapter, you will learn:

- How to use Windows XP features to secure the PC and protect users and their data
- About the Windows NT/2000/XP registry
- About tools for troubleshooting and maintaining Windows XP
- How to troubleshoot the Windows XP boot process

You were introduced to Windows XP in the last chapter and learned how to install and use it. This chapter takes you further in learning to support this OS. You will learn about security features that protect the Windows XP system, its users, and their data. You'll also learn how the Windows NT/2000/XP registry is organized and how to edit it, and about many troubleshooting tools available under Windows XP. Finally, you will learn how to troubleshoot the Windows XP boot process. In later chapters, you will learn more about how Windows XP is used on networks and about additional security features it has when networked.

SECURITY USING WINDOWS NT/2000/XP

A+ OS 1.4

Security under Windows NT/2000/XP has two goals: to secure the system resources, including hardware and software, from improper use; and to secure users' data from improper access. In this section you will learn about some of the features of Windows NT/2000/XP that support these goals. At the heart of Windows NT/2000/XP security is the concept of user accounts.

User Accounts and Profiles

A+ OS 1.4

A **user account** defines a user to Windows and records information about the user, including the user name, password used to access the account, groups that the account belongs to, and the rights and permissions assigned to the account. There are three types of user accounts in Windows NT/2000/XP:

- **Global user accounts**, sometimes called domain user accounts, are used at the domain level, are created by an administrator, and stored in the SAM (security accounts manager) database on a domain controller. A user can log on to any computer on the networked domain using a global user account; the information about a global user account's rights and permissions apply to each workstation in the domain. The centralized SAM database is part of Active Directory, which is a repository of information used to manage a Windows network and is itself managed by Windows 2000 Server or soon-to-come Windows .NET.
- A **local user account** is created on a local computer and allows a user access to only that one computer. An administrator creates a local user account, assigns a user name and password to the account, and gives it rights and permissions. As a general rule, a user account should not be given more rights than necessary for a user to do his or her job. For example, an administrator who is responsible for setting up and maintaining user accounts in an office workgroup can set the permissions on a user account to deny the user the right to install a printer, install software, or do anything else that changes the PC software or hardware environment.
- **Built-in user accounts**. Every Windows XP workstation has two built-in user accounts that are set up when the OS is first installed: an administrator account and a guest account. An administrator has rights and permissions to all computer software, data, and hardware resources. Under Windows NT/2000/XP, the administrator has the ability to create other user accounts and assign corresponding rights and permissions to individual accounts, to groups of selected accounts, or to all accounts that use the computer. A guest account has very limited privileges and allows access to a computer by someone who does not have a user account. The guest account is useful in a business environment where many people use a computer for limited purposes, yet it is not practical for them to have a unique user account.

How user accounts are set up depends on whether the computer is a standalone workstation (not networked), belongs to a workgroup, or belongs to a domain. Recall from Chapter 6 that in a workgroup, each computer manages the security for its own resources. Each local user account is set up on the local computer independent of other accounts on other PCs,

A+ OS 1.4

and there is no centralized control of resources. If a user on one computer needs access to resources on another computer in the workgroup, the other computer must have the same user account and password set up as is on the first computer. This chapter focuses on setting up security for standalone workstations and for workstations in a workgroup. Managing user accounts at the domain level is not covered.

After an administrator creates a local user account and the user logs on for the first time, the system creates a **user profile** for that user. When the user changes settings to customize his or her computer and then logs off, the user profile is updated so that settings can be restored the next time the user logs on.

If the computer is networked to other computers in a Windows workgroup, the administrator must create a user account on each computer in the workgroup that this user needs to access. When the user logs on to each computer in the workgroup, he or she would have to reestablish the user profile at each computer, and re-create desktop settings and application settings for each computer unless the administrator implements a feature called roaming user profiles. With **roaming user profiles**, settings established by a user at one computer are stored in a file on a file server on the network and shared with all computers in the workgroup. When a user moves from one computer to another computer in the workgroup, the roaming profile follows the user so that he or she does not have to redo settings at each computer.

Another type of profile used with workgroups is a **mandatory user profile**. This profile is a roaming user profile that applies to all users in a user group; individual users cannot change the profile. It is used in situations where users are limited to performing only specific job-related tasks. A profile that applies to a group of users is called a **group profile**. An administrator creates roaming and mandatory profiles using the Computer Management console under the Administrative Tools applet in the Control Panel.

You can view all the profiles stored on a Windows XP computer using the System Properties window. Click Start and right-click My Computer. Select Properties and then click the Advanced tab. Under User Profiles, click the Settings button (see Figure 10-1). Next, we turn our attention to how to create and manage local user accounts.

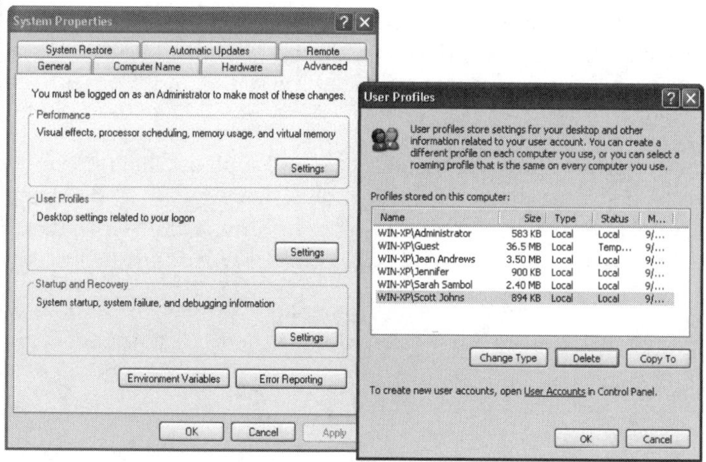

Figure 10-1 View all user profiles stored on this PC using the System Properties window

A+ OS 1.4

Administering Local User Accounts

When setting up accounts for users where security is a concern, here are a few guidelines about passwords for users and administrators:

- Usernames for Windows NT/2000/XP logon can consist of up to 15 characters.
- Passwords can be up to 127 characters.
- Do not use a password that is easy to guess, such as one consisting of real words, your telephone number, or the names of pets.
- The most secure type of password uses a combination of letters, numbers, and even non-alphanumeric characters.
- User accounts can be set up with or without passwords. Passwords provide greater security. Where security is a concern, always set a password for the Administrator account.
- Passwords can be controlled by the administrator but, generally, users should be allowed to change their own passwords.

An administrator can create a user account using the Computer Management console or the User Accounts applet in Control Panel. If the account is created in Computer Management it will have Limited privileges. If it is created using the Control Panel, it will have Administrator privileges. To create a local user account using Computer Management, follow these steps:

1. Log on to the computer as the administrator.
2. Click **Start** and right-click **My Computer**. Select **Manage** from the shortcut menu. The Computer Management console window opens. (Note that you can also access Computer Management by way of the Control Panel, Administrative Tools applet.)
3. Expand **Local Users and Groups** by clicking the plus sign to its left. Right-click **Users** and select **New User** from the shortcut menu. The New User window opens (see Figure 10-2). Enter the User name, enter the password twice, and check the boxes to decide how and when the password can be changed. You can also enter values for the Full name and Description to help identify the user. Click **Create**.
4. The account is created with the default type of Limited, which means the account cannot create, delete or change other accounts, make system-wide changes, or install software. If you want to give the account Administrative privileges, then open the **Control Panel** and double-click the **User Accounts** applet.
5. The User Accounts window opens, listing all accounts. To make changes to an account, click **Change an account**, and then click the account you want to change.

A+ OS 1.4

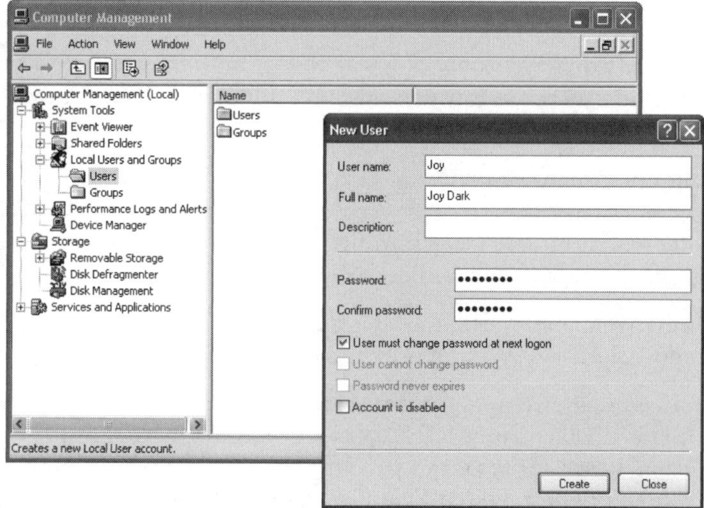

Figure 10-2 Create a user account using either Computer Management or the User Account applet in Control Panel

6. In the next window, you can choose to change the name of the account, change the password, remove a password, change the picture icon associated with the account, change the account type, or delete the account. Click **Change the account type**.
7. In the next window, select **Computer administrator** and click **Change Account Type**. Click **Back** twice on the menu bar to return to the opening window.

Sometimes a user forgets his or her password or the password is compromised. If this happens, and you have Administrator privileges, you can access the account by way of Control Panel or the Computer Management Console and provide the user with a new password from there. This action is called resetting the password. However, resetting a password under Windows XP causes the OS to lock out the user from using encrypted e-mail or files or using Internet passwords stored on the computer.

For this reason, all new users should create a **forgotten password floppy disk** that can be used if the user forgets their password. To create the disk, open the User Accounts applet in Control Panel, click your account, and select Prevent a forgotten password under Related Tasks in the left pane of this window. Follow the Wizard to create the disk. If a user enters a wrong password at logon, he or she is given the opportunity to use the forgotten password floppy disk to log on.

The forgotten password floppy disk should be kept in a protected place so that others cannot use it to gain unauthorized access to the computer.

A+ OS 2.4

Controlling How a User Logs On

With Windows NT/2000, there was only one way to log on to the system: by pressing the Ctrl-Alt-Del keys to bring up the logon window. In a Windows XP workgroup, you have some log-on options:

- The default option is a Welcome screen that appears when the PC is first booted or comes back from a sleep state. All users are listed on the Welcome screen along with a picture (which can be the user's photograph); a user clicks his or her user name and enters the password.
- Instead of the Welcome screen, the user must press Ctrl-Alt-Del to get to a logon window similar to Windows NT/2000.
- Fast User Switching enables more than one user to be logged on to the system. If this option is disabled, only one user is logged on at a time. If the option is enabled, when a user clicks Start, Log Off, then the Log Off Windows dialog box offers three options: Switch User, Log Off, and Cancel. When Fast User Switching is disabled, the Switch User option is not displayed. Disable Fast User Switching when you want to conserve resources because performance suffers when several users leave applications open.

To change the way a user logs on, from Control Panel, open the User Accounts applet. Click Change the way users log on or off (see Figure 10-3). Make your selections and click Apply Options to close the dialog box.

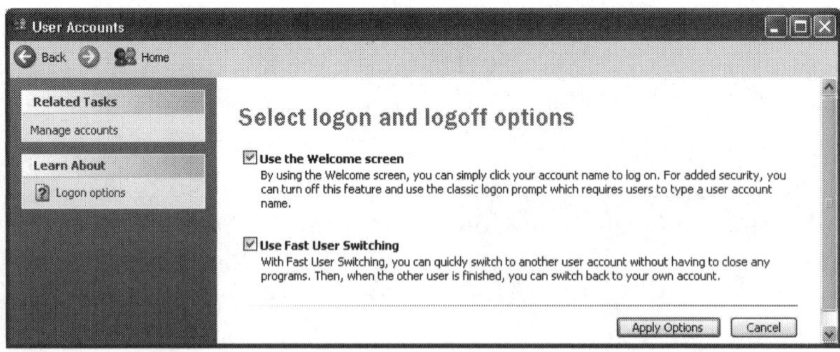

Figure 10-3 Options to change the way users log on or off

User Groups

User groups are an efficient way for an administrator to manage multiple user accounts that require the same privileges and similar profiles. When installed, Windows XP sets up several user groups including:

- **Administrators**, who have access to all parts of the system, can install or uninstall devices and applications, and perform all administrative tasks
- **Backup Operators** can back up and restore any files on the system regardless of their access privileges to these files.

A+ OS 2.4

- **Power Users** can read from and write to parts of the system other than their own local drive, install applications, and perform limited administrative tasks.
- **Limited Users** (known as Users in Windows NT/2000) have read-write access only on their own folders, read-only access to most system folders, and no access to other users' data. They cannot install applications or carry out any administrative responsibilities.
- **Guests** use a workstation once or only occasionally and have limited access to files and resources. A guest account has permission to shut down a computer.

Creating a New User Group

You can also create your own user group and customize the permissions and profiles for this group of users. To create a new group:

1. Click **Start**, right-click **My Computer** and select **Manage** from the menu.
2. The Computer Management console opens. Expand **Local Users and Groups** by clicking the plus sign.
3. To create a new group, right-click the **Groups** folder and select **New Group**... from the shortcut menu.
4. The New Group window opens, as shown in Figure 10-4. In this window, enter a name and description for the new group and click the **Add** button to find and select users to be added to this group. When finished, click **Create** to finish creating the group.

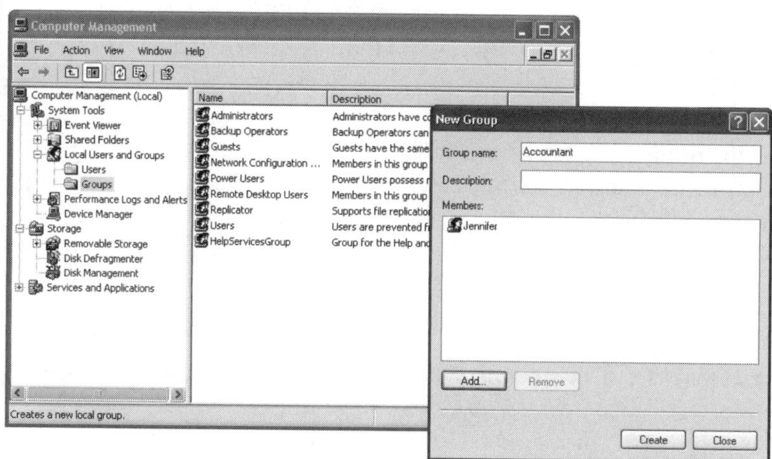

Figure 10-4 Create a new user group

You can also change the profile settings that are assigned users in a group. For example, to control what a user or a user group can do, including the ability to change the system date and time, go to the Control Panel and access the Administrative Tools applet. Double-click the Local Security Policy icon. The Local Security Settings window appears (see Figure 10-5). Under Local Policies, the User Rights Assignment group lists several activities, which can

A+ OS 2.4 be managed by changing the user groups that have the right to do these activities. Right-click Change the system time, and then select Properties from the shortcut menu. The Change the system time Properties window appears, as shown in Figure 10-5. From this window you can add and remove the user groups that have the right to change the system time.

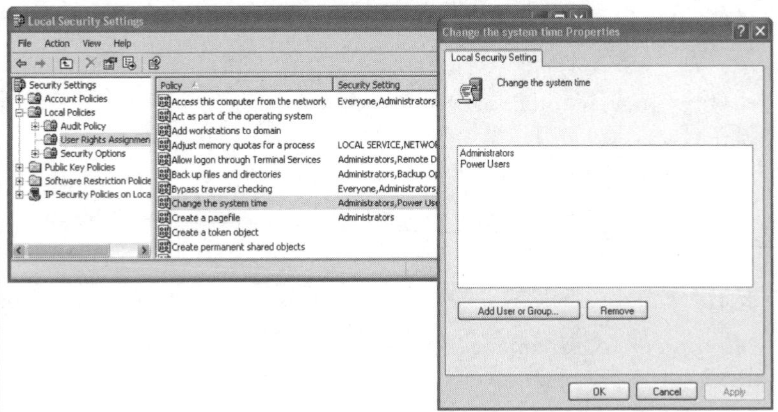

Figure 10-5 Local policies can be assigned to a user group, affecting all users in the group

Group Policy

Another way to control how the system can be used is by applying settings called a **Group Policy** to your computer. Group Policy is normally intended to be used on a domain, although you can use it on a standalone computer or a computer in a workgroup. Group Policy can be applied to your computer, regardless of the currently logged-on user (called Computer Configuration), or can be applied to each user who logs on (called User Configuration). The Group Policy console is a Microsoft Management Console (MMC) snap-in that can be accessed by typing gpedit.msc in the Run dialog box. From the console you can control things such as how Media Player, Internet Explorer, and NetMeeting work, as well as many Windows settings and components. For a standalone computer or a computer in a workgroup, use Computer Configuration instead of User Configuration to implement Group Policy settings.

Disk Quotas

An administrator can set **disk quotas**, which limit how much disk space a user has access to. This is important when two or more users are using a single computer and need to share its storage capacity. A disk quota does not specify where a user's files must be located; it just specifies how much total space the user can take up on a volume. The disk quota set applies to all users. You can set disk quotas only if you are using NTFS.

To set disk quotas:

1. Log on as an administrator and open **My Computer**.
2. Find the partition on which you want to set a disk quota. Right-click it and select **Properties** from the shortcut menu.

3. Click the **Quota** tab and the **Enable quota management** check box. See Figure 10-6.

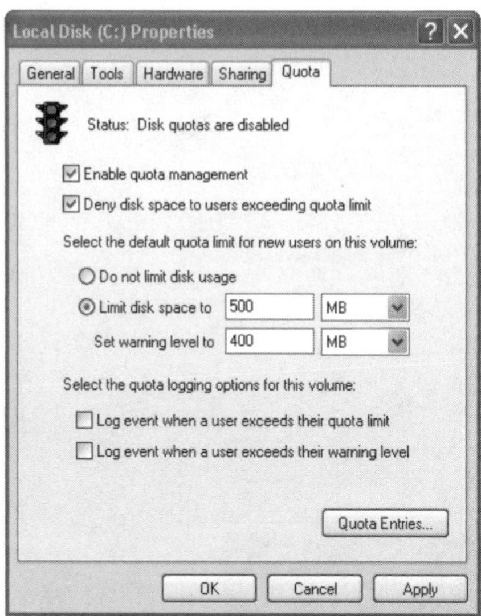

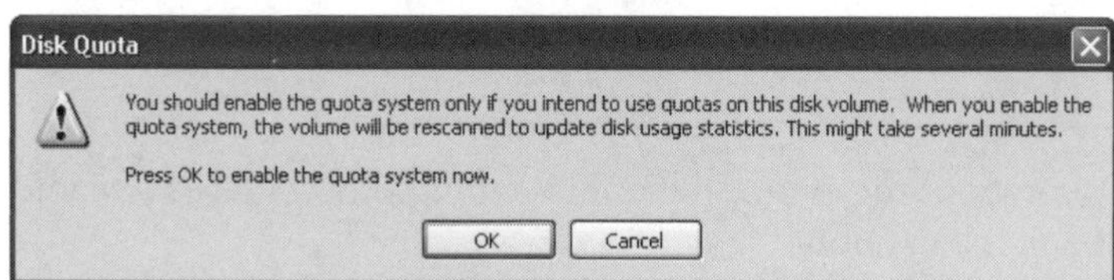

Figure 10-6 Setting disk quotas

4. In this view, you can specify that users have unlimited access to disk space, you can specify the amount of space for users, and you can set a level of disk space used that will trigger a warning message to a user. For this example, all users are restricted to 500 MB of storage space and warned at 400 MB.
5. Click the **Limit disk space to** radio button, enter **500** in the box next to it, and select **MB** from the drop-down menu to the right of the box.
6. In the box next to Set warning level to, enter **400**, and select **MB** from the drop-down menu. This will warn users when they have used 400 MB of their allotted 500 MB of storage space.
7. Click **Deny disk space to users exceeding quota limit** so that no user can use more than the specified amount of disk space.
8. Click **OK**. You will be prompted to enable disk quotas. Click **OK** on the prompt. (See Figure 10-7.)

10

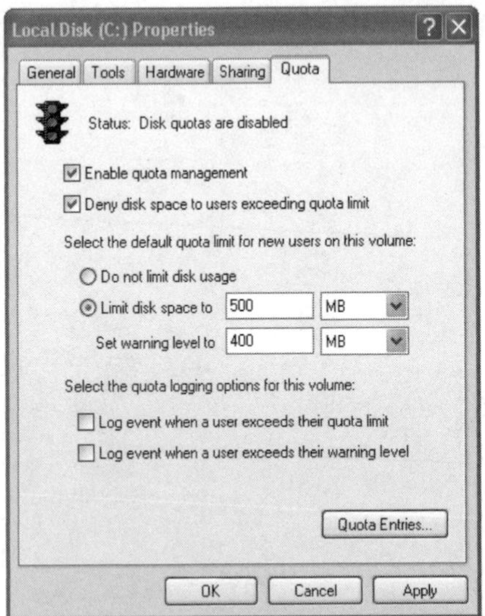

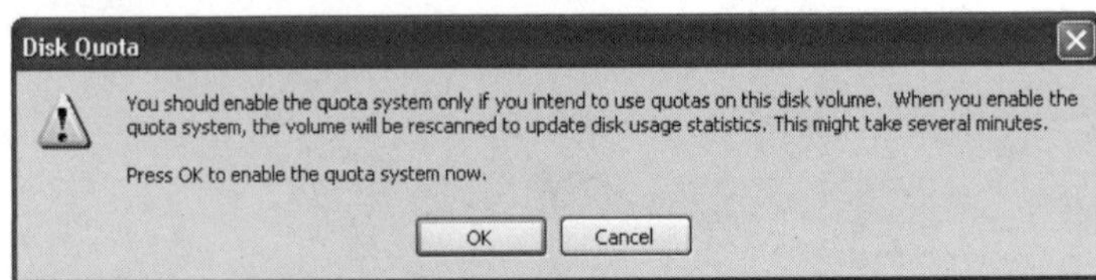

Figure 10-7 The prompt at the end of the quota-setting process gives you information about enabling quotas

EFS (Encrypted File System)

A+ OS 1.4

Another Windows 2000/XP security feature is the **Encrypted File System (EFS)**. EFS applies only to the Windows 2000/XP NTFS file system. In the past, it was possible to bypass an existing operating system's security measures by installing a new operating system or booting from a startup disk. In Windows 98, a password could be put on a file using a FAT file system, but you could boot from a startup disk, get to the file at a command prompt, copy it to a floppy disk, and access the file without using the password. That method does not work with EFS, which protects encrypted data even when someone who is not authorized to view those files or folders has full access to a computer's data storage. When an unauthorized user attempts to access an EFS-encrypted file, he or she receives the error "Access Denied."

Encryption is the process of putting readable data into code that must be translated before it can be accessed. This is usually done by using a **key** to encrypt the data and also provides a way to "unlock" the code and translate it back into readable data.

Do not confuse the term "key" as it is used in encryption with the term "registry key," which applies to information placed in the registry.

A+ OS 1.4

To ensure that a file can be accessed if a user is not available or has forgotten the password to log on to the system, an administrator for the OS can decrypt a file. In this case, the administrator is called a data recovery agent (DRA).

How to Use Encryption

A user does not have to go through a complex process of encryption to use EFS; from a user's perspective, it's just a matter of placing a file in a folder marked for encryption. Encryption can be implemented at either the folder or file level. At the folder level, if the folder is marked for encryption, every file created in the folder or copied to the folder will be encrypted. At the file level, each file must be encrypted individually. Encrypting with EFS at the folder level is encouraged and considered a "best practice strategy" because it provides greater security, since any file placed in an encrypted folder is automatically encrypted without the user having to remember to encrypt it. An encrypted file remains encrypted if you move it from an encrypted folder to an unencrypted folder on the same logical drive.

In the following example, you will encrypt the My Documents folder for an existing user named User2, create a file in that folder that will automatically become encrypted because the folder is encrypted, and decrypt the folder so that others can access it.

1. In Windows Explorer, locate the My Documents folder for User2. In this example, the correct path is C:\Documents and Settings\User2\My Documents.
2. Right-click the **My Documents** folder and choose **Properties** from the shortcut menu. The My Documents Properties window appears (see Figure 10-8).

10

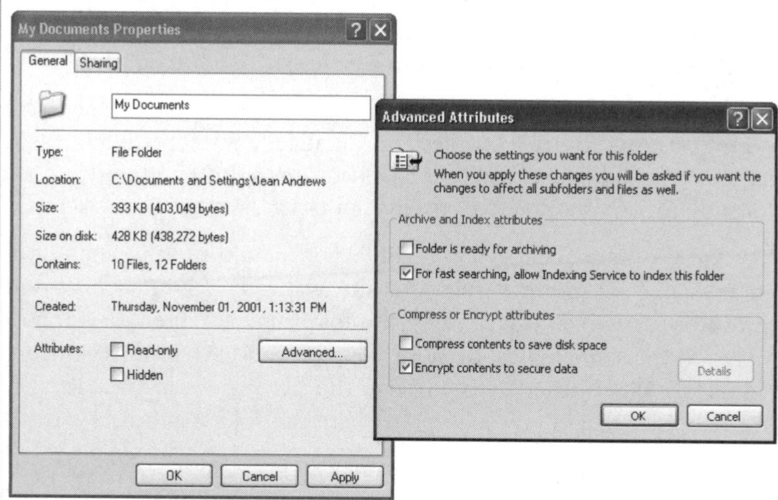

Figure 10-8 Encrypt folder contents

3. If necessary, click the **General** tab. Click the **Advanced** button. The Advanced Attributes window appears.
4. Check the box labeled **Encrypt contents to secure data** and click **OK** (Figure 10-8).

A+ OS 1.4

5. Click **Apply**. This causes the Confirm Attribute Changes window to open if any files or folders exist in the selected folder (see Figure 10-9).

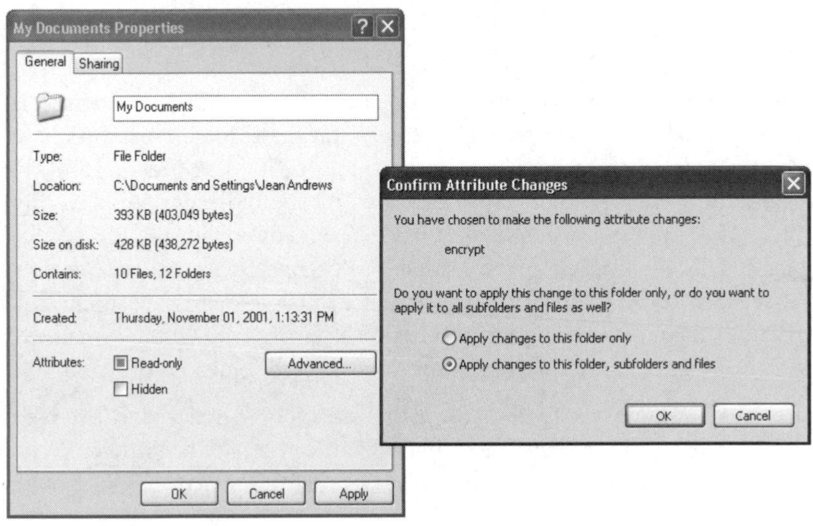

Figure 10-9 Apply changes to all folder contents

6. In this example, the subfolder My Pictures exists within the My Documents folder. If necessary click the radio button next to the option **Apply changes to this folder, subfolder, and files** to encrypt any existing objects in this folder and subfolders. (If you do not want to apply the changes to all subfolders and files, you select Apply changes to this folder only.) Click **OK**.
7. Open Microsoft Word, type some text into a file, and save the file to User2's **My Documents** folder. This file is automatically encrypted, because the My Documents folder is encrypted. If an unauthorized user attempts to access the encrypted document, they will receive an error message.

To allow others on the network to view this file, you would move or copy it to a folder that is not encrypted. Encryption is removed automatically when a file is sent over the network or moved off a logical drive where the folder is encrypted. If you move the file to another folder on the same logical drive or volume, you have to decrypt it manually. In this next example, to allow other users to view the file stored on your local hard drive, move the file to a folder that is not encrypted, share the folder, and decrypt the file.

To decrypt a file, from the file's Properties window, click the Advanced button. On the Advanced Attributes window, uncheck Encrypt contents to secure data, and then click OK.

The Cipher Command

If you are encrypting a large number of files or folders from a command prompt or using a batch file, you can use the Cipher command:

```
CIPHER [/E, /D] [/S:dir] [pathname[...]]
```

A+ OS 1.4

- `/E` encrypts the specified files or folders.
- `/D` decrypts the specified files or folders.
- `/S:dir` applies the action to the specified folder (directory) and all its subfolders.
- `Pathname` is the name of the file or folder and its path that is to be encrypted or decrypted.

For example, at the command prompt, to decrypt all the files in the C:\Public folder, use this command:

```
Cipher /D C:\Public\*.*
```

Internet Connection Firewall

A+ OS 4.2

Windows 2000/XP offers several security features that protect the system from unauthorized access over a network or over the Internet, which you will learn about in later chapters. One feature new to Windows XP is Internet Connection Firewall. A **firewall** is hardware or software that acts to protect a computer or network from unauthorized access. **Internet Connection Firewall (ICF)** is Windows XP software that is designed to protect a PC from unauthorized access from the Internet when the PC is connected directly to the Internet.

10

You should not use ICF on a PC that gets its Internet access from a LAN (local area network) because it can prevent others on the LAN from accessing resources on the PC.

ICF works by examining every communication that comes to the PC to determine if the communication has been initiated by the PC or is being initiated by an outside device or computer. If the communication is initiated by some other source than the PC, it is refused. With ICF, you can browse the Web, but those on the Web cannot initiate a communication with your PC in order to gain unauthorized access to data stored there.

To enable ICF, open the Network Connections applet in Control Panel and right-click on the network connection icon that you use to connect to the Internet and select Properties from the shortcut menu. This might be a connection to the Internet by way of a dial-up modem, a cable modem, or a DSL connection. (All these type connections are covered in later chapters.) The connection Properties box opens as shown in Figure 10-10 for a modem connection. Click the Advanced tab and select Protect my computer and network by limiting or preventing access to this computer from the Internet. If you would like the firewall to record in a log file packets that it drops, click Log dropped packets. Click OK. Remember, don't do this for a regular network connection if you want others on the network to have access to resources on your PC.

We now turn our attention to several of the utilities that allow you to customize and troubleshoot Windows XP. We begin with looking at the Windows NT/2000/XP registry and how to edit it.

A+ OS 4.2

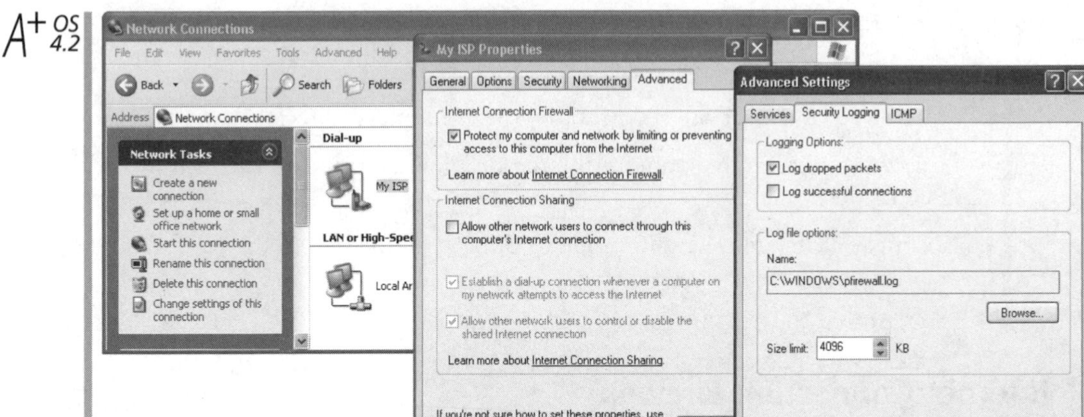

Figure 10-10 Enable Internet Connection Firewall and log dropped packets

THE WINDOWS NT/2000/XP REGISTRY

A+ OS 1.1 1.2

The Windows NT/2000/XP registry is a hierarchical database containing information about all the hardware, software, device drivers, network protocols, and user configuration needed by the OS and applications. Many components depend on this information, and the registry provides a secure and stable location for it. Table 10-1 lists ways in which some components use the registry.

In the next section, you will look at how the registry is organized, how to view the contents of the registry, how to back up and recover the registry, and how Windows makes changes to the registry.

How the Registry Is Organized

A+ OS 1.1 1.2

When studying how the registry is organized, keep in mind that there are two ways to look at this organization, the physical organization and the logical organization.

Logical Organization of the Registry

Logically, the organization of the registry looks like an upside-down tree with five branches, called keys or subtrees (see Figure 10-11), which are categories of information stored in the registry. Each key is made up of several subkeys that may also have subkeys under them, and subkeys hold, or contain, values. Each value has a name and data assigned to it. Data in the registry is always stored in values, the lowest level of the tree.

A+ OS 1.1 1.2

Table 10-1 Components that use the Windows NT/2000/XP registry

Component	Description
Setup programs for devices and applications	Setup programs can record configuration information in the registry and query the registry for information needed to install drivers and applications.
User profiles that are maintained and used by the OS	Windows maintains a profile for each user that determines the user's environment. User profiles are kept in files, but when a user logs on, the profile information is written to the registry, where changes are recorded and then later written back to the user profile file. The OS uses this profile to control user settings and other configuration information specific to this user.
Files active when Ntldr is loading the OS	During the boot process, NTDetect.com surveys the hardware devices present and records that information in the registry. Ntldr loads and initializes device drivers using information from the registry, including the order in which to load them.
Device drivers	Device drivers read and write configuration information from and to the registry each time they load. The drivers write hardware configuration information to the registry and read it to determine the proper way to load.
Hardware profiles	Windows can maintain more than one set of hardware configuration information (called a **hardware profile**) for one PC. The data is kept in the registry. An example of a computer that has more than one hardware profile is a notebook that has a docking station. Two hardware profiles describe the notebook, one docked and the other undocked. This information is kept in the registry.
Application programs	Many application programs read the registry for information about the location of files the program uses and various other parameters that were stored in .ini files under Windows 9x.

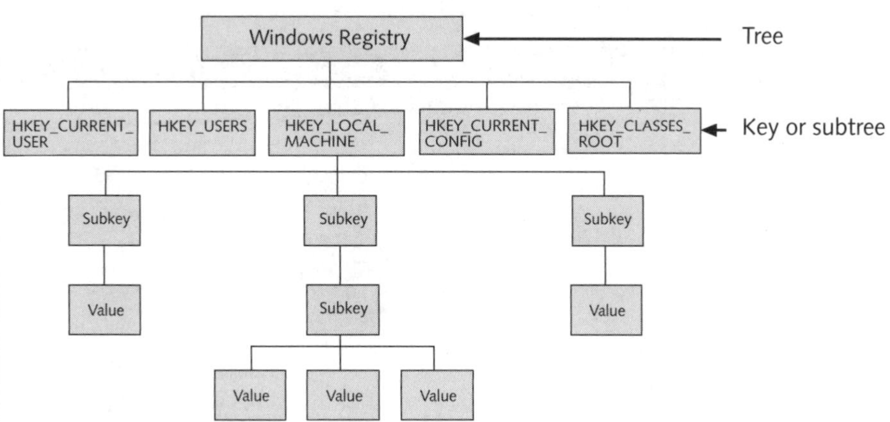

Figure 10-11 The Windows NT/2000/XP registry is logically organized in an upside-down tree structure of keys, subkeys, and values

10

A+ OS 1.1 1.2 Figure 10-12 shows the Windows Registry Editor, the window you see when you first open the editor: there are five high levels, one for each key or subtree. Notice in the figure that the HKEY_CURRENT_USER subtree has been opened to show subkeys under it, several of which have their own subkeys. If you click on a subkey that has a value assigned to it, that value appears in the right side of the window. Later in this section, you will see how to edit values in the registry.

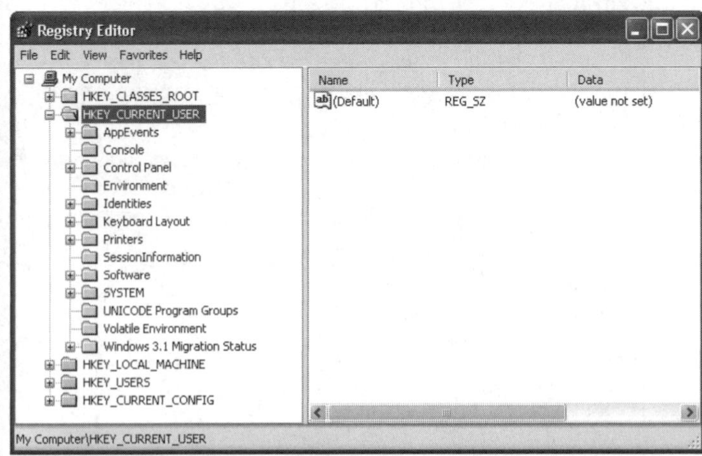

Figure 10-12 Windows Registry Editor shows the five high-level subtrees in the Windows NT/2000/XP registry

The five subtrees of the registry, displayed in Figure 10-12, are listed in Table 10-2 together with their primary functions. As you can notice from the table, the HKEY_LOCAL_MACHINE subtree is the mainstay key of the registry.

Table 10-2 The five subtrees of the Windows NT/2000/XP registry

Subtree (Main Keys)	Primary Function
HKEY_CURRENT_USER	Contains information about the currently logged-on user.
HKEY_CLASSES_ROOT	Contains information about software and the way software is configured. This key points to data stored in HKEY_LOCAL_MACHINE.
HKEY_CURRENT_CONFIG	Contains information about the active hardware configuration, which is extracted from the data stored in the HKEY_LOCAL_MACHINE subkeys called SOFTWARE and SYSTEM.
HKEY_USERS	Contains information used to build the logon screen and the ID of the currently logged-on user.
HKEY_LOCAL_MACHINE	This key contains all configuration data about the computer, including information about device drivers and devices used at startup. The information in this key does not change when different users are logged on.

A+ OS 1.1 1.2

Physical Organization of the Registry

The physical organization of the registry is quite different from the logical organization. Physically, the registry is stored in five files called **hives**. There is not a one-to-one relationship between the subtrees and these five files, even though there are five of each. Figure 10-13 shows the way the subtrees are stored in hives, as follows:

- HKEY_LOCAL_MACHINE consists of four hives, the SAM hive, the Security hive, the Software hive, and the System hive.
- HKEY_CURRENT_CONFIG data is kept in portions of two hives: the Software hive and the System hive.
- HKEY_CLASSES_ROOT data is kept in a portion of the Software hive.
- HKEY_USERS data is kept in the Default hive.
- HKEY_CURRENT_USER data is kept in a portion of the Default hive.

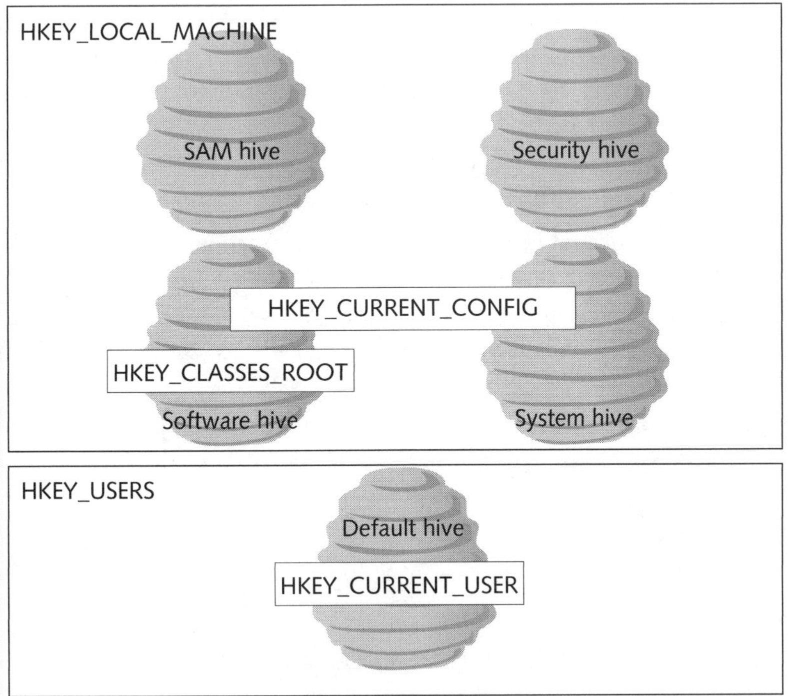

Figure 10-13 The relationship between registry subtrees (keys) and hives

From Figure 10-13, you can also see that some subtrees use data that is contained in other subtrees. For instance, the HKEY_CURRENT_USER data is a subset of the data in the HKEY_USERS subtree. HKEY_CURRENT_CONFIG and HKEY_CLASSES_ROOT subtrees use data that is contained in the HKEY_LOCAL_MACHINE subtree. However, don't let this physical relationship cloud your view of the logical relationship among these

10

A+ OS 1.1 1.2 subtrees. Even though data is shared among the different subtrees, logically speaking, none of the five subtrees is considered subordinate to any other.

The registry hives are stored in the \%SystemRoot%\system32\config folder as a group of files. In a physical sense, each hive is a file. Each hive is backed up with a log file and a backup file, which are also stored in the \%SystemRoot%\system32\config folder.

Editing the Registry

A+ OS 1.5 When you make a change in Control Panel, Device Manager, or many other places in Windows NT/2000/XP, the registry is modified automatically. For most users, this is the only way they will ever change the registry. However, there are rare occasions when you might need to edit the registry manually, such as when you are following the directions of Microsoft technical support staff to delete references in the registry to viruses or worms. Changes to the registry take effect immediately and are permanent.

Before you edit the registry, you should back it up so that you can restore it if something goes wrong. Backing up the system state, which you learned how to do in Chapter 7, is one way to back up the registry. In Chapter 7, you backed up the system state after a Windows 2000 installation, but you can also back up the system state at any time. When the system state is backed up, the Backup utility also puts a copy of the registry files in the %SystemRoot%\repair folder.

Windows NT/2000 offers two registry editors, each with a slightly different look and feel, although they both accomplish the same thing. They are:

- Regedt32.exe, located in the \%SystemRoot%\system32 folder, which shows each key in a separate window. Use it to edit the registry.
- Regedit.exe, located in the \%SystemRoot% folder, which shows all keys in the same window and has a look and feel similar to Explorer. Use it to search and view the registry.

To access a registry editor, type the program name in the Run dialog box. With Windows XP, if you type either Regedt32 or Regedit in the Run dialog box, the Regedit.exe program is launched.

In the example below, we use Regedit.exe under Windows XP to view the registry and take a look at registry values. To access Regedit.exe, double-click the filename in Explorer or enter the filename in the Run dialog box. Figure 10-14 shows a detailed view of the registry.

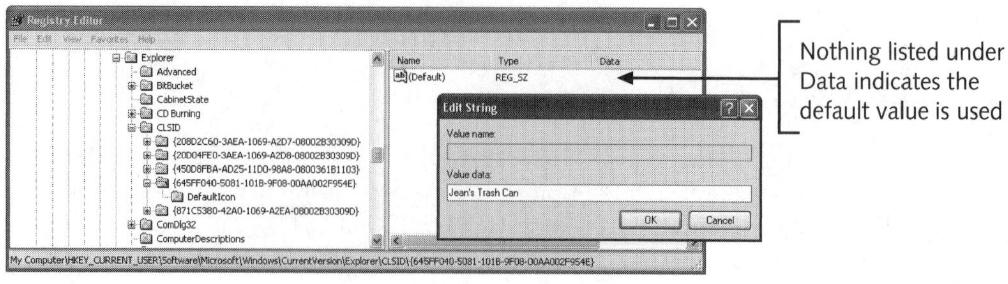

Figure 10-14 Editing a registry subkey value

A+ OS 1.5

Let's look at one example of editing the registry. Follow these directions to first back up the system state before editing the registry:

1. Click **Start**, **All Programs**, **Accessories**, **System Tools**, **Backup**. The Backup or Restore Wizard appears.
2. Click **Advanced Mode**. The Backup Utility window appears. Click the **Backup** tab.
3. Check the **System State** box and under **Backup media or file name:**, select the location to store the backup.
4. Click **Start Backup**. The Backup Job Information dialog box appears. Click **Start Backup**. After the backup is done, click **Close** to close the Backup utility.

To change the name of the Recycle Bin on the Windows XP desktop for the currently logged on user, do the following:

1. To open Registry Editor, click **Start**, **Run** and type **Regedit** in the Run dialog box. Click **OK**. The Registry Editor window appears.
2. Locate the following subkey, which is the name of the Recycle Bin on the Windows desktop, by double-clicking on the yellow folder icon of each subkey, moving down through the tree to the lowest subkey value. As you move down the tree, if the currently selected subkey has a value, that value displays in the right pane of the window.

   HKEY_CURRENT_USER\Software\Microsoft\Windows\CurrentVersion\Explorer\CLSID\645FF040-5081-101B-9F08-00AA002F954E
3. Figure 10-14 shows the subkey displayed. The right pane shows nothing listed under Data, which results in the default value used, which is Recycle Bin. Position the window on the screen so that you can see the Recycle Bin icon.
4. Double-click the name of the value in the right pane. The Edit String dialog box appears. The Value data should be empty in the dialog box. If a value is present, you have selected the wrong value. Check your work and try again.
5. Enter a new name for the Recycle Bin. For example, in Figure 10-14, the new name is "Jean's Trash Can". Click **OK**.
6. To see your change, right-click somewhere on the desktop and select **Refresh** from the shortcut menu. The name of the Recycle Bin changes.
7. To restore the name to the default value, on the Registry Editor window, again double-click the name of the value. The Edit String dialog box appears. Delete your entry and click **OK**.
8. To verify the change is made, right-click on the screen and select **Refresh** from the shortcut menu. The Recycle Bin name should return to its default value.

From these directions, you can see that changes made to the registry take effect immediately. Therefore, take extra care when editing the registry. If you make a mistake and don't know how to correct a problem you have created, then you can restore the system state to recover.

Other Maintenance and Troubleshooting Tools

A+ OS 3.1

This section discusses other commonly used tools that Windows XP provides for maintenance and troubleshooting. Some tools are new or changed in Windows XP, and some operate the same way as they did under Windows 2000. Table 10-3 lists several tools and their functions. Some tools are executed from a command line (have an .exe file extension), others are Microsoft Management Console snap-ins (have a .msc file extension), and others are graphical tools built into Windows XP (such as Device Manager). MMC was discussed in Chapter 8. MMC snap-ins are executed from the Run dialog box or can sometimes be accessed using Windows menus. Some command-line programs can be executed from the Run dialog box and all of them can be executed from a command prompt window.

Several of the tools listed in the table are discussed later in the chapter. For more extensive information about any of these tools, search Help and Support on your Windows XP computer, search the Microsoft Knowledge Base at *support.microsoft.com*, or see the book, *Microsoft Windows XP Professional Resource Kit Documentation* by Microsoft Press. In addition, to get help about a command-line tool, from a command prompt, enter the tool name followed by /?. For example, to get help about Defrag, enter Defrag /?.

Table 10-3 Windows XP maintenance and troubleshooting tools

Tool	Description
Add or Remove Programs in Control Panel	Uninstall software that is causing a problem
Automated System Recovery (ASR)	Drastically recovers a failed system. Only use this as a last resort, because the logical drive on which Windows is installed is formatted and restored from the most recent backup. All data and applications written to the drive since the last backup are lost.
Backup (Ntbackup.exe)	Backs up and restores data and software
Boot logging	An option on the Advanced Options startup menu to log events to the Ntbtlog.txt file.
Bootcfg (Bootcfg.exe)	Views and edits the contents of the Boot.ini file used to hold startup settings.
Cacls.exe	Changes access control lists (ACL) assigned to a file or group of files to control what users have access to a file and the type of access they have (read, write, change, or full). For more information on CACLS, type Help Cacls at a command prompt.
Chkdsk (Chkdsk.exe)	Checks and repairs errors on a logical drive
Cipher.exe	Displays and changes the encryptions applied to files and folders using the NTFS file system.
Compact.exe	Displays and changes the compressions applied to files and folders using the NTFS file system.
Computer Management (Compmgmt.msc)	Console provides access to several snap-ins used to manage and troubleshoot a system
Convert.exe	Converts a FAT16 or a FAT32 logical drive to NTFS.

A+ OS 3.1 3.2

Table 10-3 Windows XP maintenance and troubleshooting tools (continued)

Tool	Description
Defrag.exe	A command-line tool to defragment a logical drive or floppy disk, it is similar to the graphic tool, Disk Defragmenter.
Dependency Walker (Depends.exe)	Provides a list of files needed for an application to load.
Device Driver Roll Back	Replaces a driver with the previous one that worked before the current driver was installed.
Device Manager	Displays and changes device drivers and other hardware settings.
DirectX Diagnostic Tool (Dxdiag.exe)(API)	Used to troubleshoot problems with the DirectX application programming interface used by Microsoft.
Disk Cleanup (Cleanmgr.exe)	Deletes unused files to make more disk space available.
Disk Defragmenter (Dfrg.msc)	Defragments a logical drive or floppy disk.
Disk Management (Diskmgmt.msc)	Displays and changes partitions on hard drives and formats drives.
DiskPart (Diskpart.exe)	A command-line tool to manage partitions and volumes of a hard drive similar to the graphic tool, Disk Management. Use DiskPart to write scripts to automate disk management tasks.
Dr. Watson (Drwtsn32.exe)	Records errors and information about those errors when applications fail. Errors are recorded in a log file named **Drwatson.log**. Note this is a different name than the log file in Windows 2000 which is Drwtsn32.log.
Driver Signing and Digital Signatures (Sigverifi.exe)	Verifies that drivers, software, and system files have been approved by Microsoft.
Error Reporting	Produces an error report and sends it to Microsoft when the error occurs and the PC is connected to the Internet.
Event Viewer (Eventvwr.msc)	Records and displays system problems.
Expand.exe	Extracts a file from a cabinet file or compressed file.
Fsutil (Fsutil.exe)	Displays information about drives and file systems and does advanced management tasks on those drives.
Group Policy (Gpedit.msc)	Displays and changes policies controlling users and the computer.
Help and Support	Provides helpful information, connects to Windows newsgroups, enables Remote Assistance, and steps you though many other troubleshooting tasks.
Last Known Good Configuration	A startup option used when normal or safe mode do not work. Using this tool, you can revert the system back to before a driver or application was installed that is giving problems.
Performance Monitor (Perfmon.msc)	Reports information about performance problems.
Program Compatibility Wizard	Looks at legacy software and attempts to resolve issues that prevent the software from working in Windows XP.

A+ OS 3.1 3.2

Table 10-3 Windows XP maintenance and troubleshooting tools (continued)

Tool	Description
Recovery Console	Provides a command line to perform troubleshooting tasks when the desktop will not load.
Registry Editor (Regedit.exe)	Displays and changes entries in the registry.
Remote Assistance	Allows a user to share his computer with a support technician at a remote location so that the technician can control the computer
Remote Desktop	Allows a support technician to control a Windows XP computer remotely.
Runas.exe	Runs a program using different permissions than those assigned to the currently logged-on user.
Safe Mode	Loads the Windows desktop with a minimum configuration and then is used to troubleshoot problems with device drivers, display settings, and other startup options that are causing problems.
SC (Sc.exe)	Communicates commands to the Service Controller, which starts, stops, and manages programs that run in the background such as device drivers or Internet Connection Firewall.
Services (Services.msc)	Graphical version of SC.
System Configuration Utility (Msconfig.exe)	Controls settings used to troubleshoot a failing system.
System File Checker (Sfc.exe)	Verifies the version of all system files when Windows loads.
System Information (Msinfo32.exe)	Displays information about hardware, applications, and Windows that is useful when troubleshooting. Figure 10-15 shows a view of the System Information window.
System Information (Systeminfo.exe)	A version of System Information to be used from a command-prompt window. Information is listed onscreen as text only. To direct that information to a file, use the command Systeminfo.exe >Myfile.txt. Later the file can be printed and used to document information about the system.
System Restore	Used to restore the system to a previously working condition, it restores the registry, some system files, and some application files.
Task Killing Utility (Tskill.exe)	Stops a process or program currently running. Useful when managing background services such as an e-mail server or Web server.
Task Lister (Tasklist.exe)	Lists currently running processes similar to the list provided by Task Manager.
Task Manager (Taskman.exe)	Lists and stops currently running processes. Use Task Manager to stop an application that is locked up.
Uninstall Windows XP Professional	Used to uninstall Windows XP and revert back to a previously installed OS.
Windows File Protection	Protects system files and restores overwritten system files as needed.
Windows Update (Wupdmgr.exe)	Updates Windows by examining the system, comparing it to available updates on the Microsoft Web site, and recommending appropriate updates.

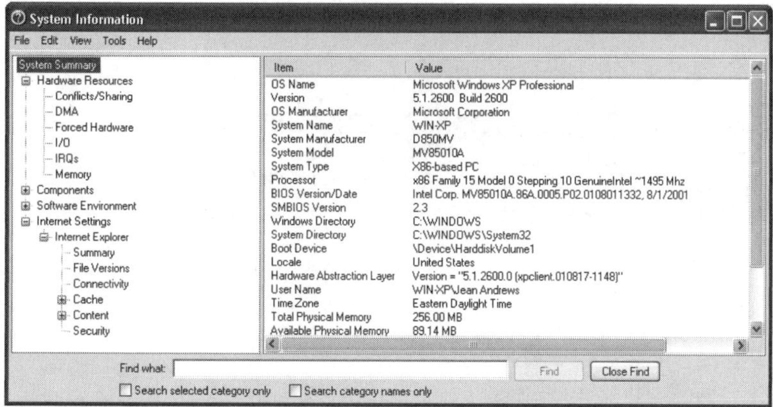

Figure 10-15 The System Information window displays important information about the system's hardware, software, and environment

Help on the Web

Microsoft offers help and updates on the Web. In earlier chapters, you learned to use the Microsoft Knowledge Base at *support.microsoft.com*. This section shows you how to access the Windows Update feature and Windows XP newsgroups.

A+ OS 2.2

Windows Update

Windows XP has an automated way to update the OS, applications, and device drivers made available on the Microsoft Web site. If no user interaction is required, anyone can perform the update, but if decisions must be made during the update, only someone with administrator privileges can perform the update. To do an update, including updating the OS, software and drivers, click Start, All Programs, and Windows Update. The Update Wizard takes you to the Microsoft Windows Update Web site (see Figure 10-16). Click Scan for updates and follow the directions onscreen. This update process includes updating drivers, a process that can also be started from Device Manager, as you learned in the last chapter.

A+ OS 2.2

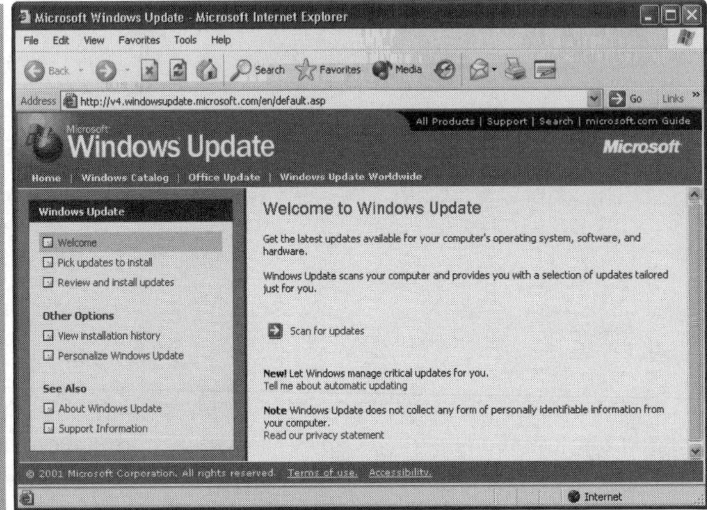

Figure 10-16 The Windows Update utility manages the process of downloading updates from the Microsoft Web site

If there is an update available for your computer, a screen similar to that shown in Figure 10-17 appears. Note in the figure that the update process found one critical update, nine updates to Windows XP that are not considered critical, and no updates for drivers. To view information about these updates, click them. In this example, the Critical Update was designed to solve a problem with security, and the nine noncritical updates were about running Java applets, connecting to a UPS (uninterruptible power supply) service, using a CD burner, running legacy applications using compatibility mode, problems with the Files and Settings Transfer Wizard, problems using Remote Assistance across a firewall, and problems with Windows Messenger and Movie Maker. By default, only the critical update is selected for installation. To install noncritical updates, select the updates you want and then click Add. After you have selected what to update, click *Review and install updates* and follow the directions on the screen.

A+ OS 2.2

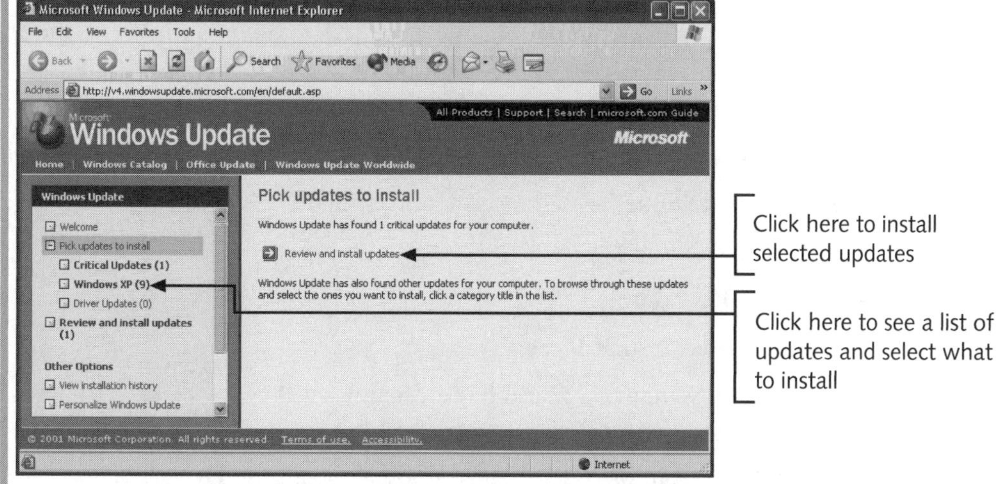

Figure 10-17 Windows Update process found updates appropriate to this computer

Windows XP does not ship with support for USB 2.0 (USB Hi-Speed). If you have a USB 2.0 port on your PC, the Update Wizard will recommend that you update the USB driver to support USB 2.0, unless you have already installed a third-party USB 2.0 driver. If you want to download the Microsoft USB 2.0 driver, first uninstall the third-party driver and then perform Windows Update.

10

Windows Newsgroups

If you have exhausted your sources of information and still have not resolved a problem, sometimes you can get help from a Windows newsgroup. To access a newsgroup, click Start, Help and Support. On the Help and Support window, click Get support, or find information in Windows XP newsgroups. Then click Go to a Windows Web site forum. Click Go to Windows Newsgroup. On the forum, you can post a question or read questions and answers posted by other users. Microsoft does not support this forum, so be careful about following the advice of users posting answers to questions on the forum.

In addition to newsgroups and the Microsoft Web site, many good Windows support Web sites exist. To get a very long list of these sites, go to a search engine on the Web such as *www.google.com* and enter Windows Help in the search box.

Troubleshooting the Boot Process

A+ OS 2.3 3.1 3.2

The Windows XP boot process works the same way as the Windows NT and Windows 2000 boot process. Refer to Chapter 6 for a review of the process and the files that are required for a successful boot. Many of the tools you learned about in Chapter 8 to recover from a failed Windows 2000 boot also work under Windows XP. They are briefly mentioned in this section to make the troubleshooting process complete. In addition, Windows XP has

A+ OS 2.3 3.1 3.2 added two tools for solving problems with the boot process: System Restore and Automated System Recovery. The tools to use when troubleshooting a failed boot are listed below in the order you should use them. Each tool discussed is more drastic than the one before it, affecting more of the system, installed hardware and software, and user data.

- Last Known Good Configuration and, in certain situations, Driver Rollback
- Safe mode from the Advanced Options menu
- System Restore
- Recovery Console
- Automated System Recovery
- Reinstall Windows XP using the Windows XP CD

You learned how to use the Last Known Good Configuration in Chapter 6, under Windows NT and Windows 2000. In addition, you can use Driver Rollback discussed in Chapter 9 if you suspect that a single device driver is the source of the problem. The Windows XP Advanced Options menu, shown in Figure 10-18, is also similar to that of Windows 2000. Refer to Chapter 8 for a discussion of each of the options on the menu and how to use them. Try Safe Mode with Networking first. If that doesn't work, try Safe Mode.

To access the Advanced Options menu, press F8 while Windows is loading.

```
Windows Advanced Options Menu
Please select an option:

    Safe Mode
    Safe Mode with Networking
    Safe Mode with Command Prompt

    Enable Boot Logging
    Enable VGA Mode
    Last Known Good Configuration (your most recent settings that worked)
    Directory Services Restore Mode (Windows domain controllers only)
    Debugging Mode

    Start Windows Normally
    Reboot
    Return to OS Choices Menu

Use the up and down arrow keys to move the highlight to your choice.
```

Figure 10-18 Windows XP Advanced Options menu

A+ OS 2.3 3.1 3.2

The next tool to use if these don't work is System Restore, a tool new to Windows XP, which is discussed next. If that doesn't work, then try the Recovery Console. Commands for the Recovery Console for Windows XP are the same as for Windows 2000 and were covered in Chapter 8. If the Recovery Console fails, then use the Automated System Recovery process to restore the hard drive to its state as of the last ASR backup. If you don't have an ASR backup, then your only recourse is to reinstall Windows XP following directions given earlier in the chapter. Be sure to scan for viruses before you reinstall.

System Restore

A+ OS 2.3 3.1

The **System Restore** utility is new to Windows XP. It is similar to ScanReg used on previous versions of Windows. ScanReg is not included in Windows XP. However, System Restore cannot be executed from a command prompt. If you can load Windows XP, then you can use System Restore to restore the system state to its condition at the time a snapshot was taken of the system settings and configuration. The restore process does not affect user data on the hard drive but can affect installed software and hardware, user settings, and OS configuration settings. The restoration is taken from a snapshot of the system state that was created earlier called a **restore point**. The system automatically creates a restore point before you install new software or hardware or make other changes to the system. You can also manually create a restore point at any time. To create a restore point, do the following:

1. Click **Start**, **All Programs**, **Accessories**, **System Tools**, and **System Restore**. The System Restore window appears.
2. The System Restore window gives you two choices: Restore my computer to an earlier time and Create a restore point. Select **Create a restore point** and then click **Next**.
3. Type a description of the restore point, such as "Just before I updated the video driver." The system automatically assigns the current date and time to the restore point.
4. Click **Create** and then **Close**. The restore point is saved.

Before using System Restore to undo a change, if the change was made to a hardware device, first try Driver Rollback so that as few changes as possible to the system are lost. If Driver Rollback does not work or is not appropriate, do the following to revert the system back to the restore point:

1. Click **Start**, **All Programs**, **Accessories**, **System Tools**, and **System Restore**.
2. If necessary, click **Restore my computer to an earlier time**, and then click **Next**. A window appears as shown in Figure 10-19. Notice in the figure that there are two restore points, one created by the system and one created manually.
3. Select the date and time and the specific restore point. Click **Next** twice.

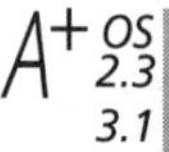

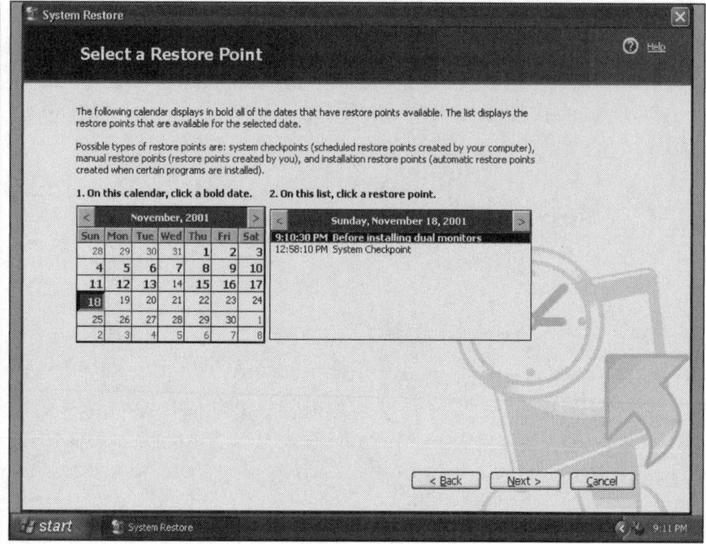

Figure 10-19 Restore points are automatically created daily and every time software or hardware is installed

Windows XP will reboot and restore the system state to the settings saved in the restore point. Changes to user data will not be affected but any installation or configuration changes made after the restore point are lost.

When selecting a restore point, select a point as close to the present as you can so that as few changes to the system as possible are lost. If System Restore does not work, try booting into safe mode and using it there. When you select Safe Mode from the Advanced Options menu, Windows XP asks if you want to go directly to System Restore rather than to safe mode. If safe mode does not work, then try going directly to System Restore.

The main difference between System Restore and Automated System Recovery is that System Restore does not affect user data on the hard drive, but Automated System Recovery does. In order to make it possible to recover a failed system without destroying data, make it a habit to always create a restore point every time you make a change to the system.

Windows XP Startup Disk

A+ OS 2.3 3.1 3.2

Using Windows Explorer, you can create an MS-DOS startup disk that can be used to boot into MS-DOS mode giving you an A prompt. If the hard drive is not using the NTFS file system, then you can access the drive and recover data files. You cannot launch Windows XP using the startup disk or use it to recover from a failed installation. To create a startup disk, using Windows Explorer, right-click on drive A and select Format from the shortcut menu. The Format window opens, as shown in Figure 10-20. Check Create an MS-DOS startup disk, and then click Start. The unhidden files put on the startup disk are

A+ OS 2.3 3.1 3.2 shown in the Explorer window in Figure 10-21. In addition to these files, Autoexec.bat, Config.sys, and the Windows 98 versions of Io.sys and Msdos.sys are also placed on the disk as hidden files.

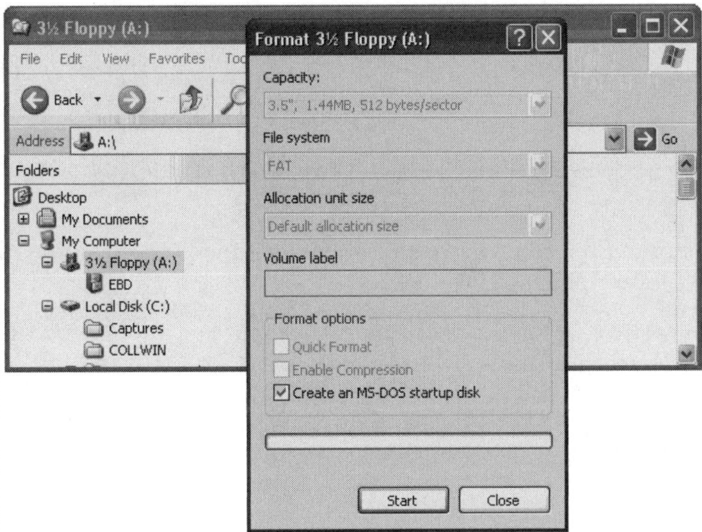

Figure 10-20 Windows XP gives you the ability to create an MS-DOS startup disk

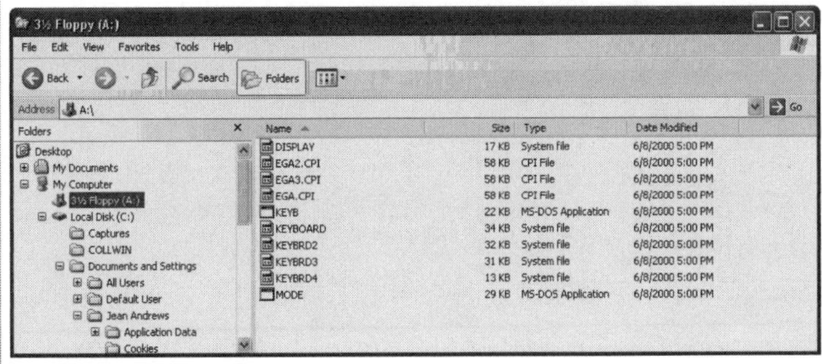

Figure 10-21 Files on the MS-DOS startup disk created by Windows XP

Automated System Recovery

A+ OS 2.3 3.1 3.2 After you finished the Windows XP installation, if you created the Automated System Recovery disk set of the installation, you can use this or a later set of the recovery disks to restore the system partition to its state when the backup was made. You will lose any changes made to the volume or logical drive holding Windows XP since the backup. Everything on the volume since making the ASR backup and disk is lost, including software and device drivers installed, user data, and any changes to the system configuration. For this reason, it's a good idea to periodically make fresh copies of the ASR disk set. You learned how to make this backup and disk in the previous chapter.

A+ OS 2.3 3.1

If you use the Automated System Recovery process, be aware that you will lose all data stored on the Windows XP volume since the last backup was made.

To revert the hard drive to its state when the last ASR disk set was made, do the following:

1. Insert the Windows XP CD in the CD-ROM drive and hard boot the PC.
2. A message says "Press any key to boot from CD." Press any key.
3. A blue screen appears with the message, "Press F6 to load RAID or SCSI drivers." If your system uses RAID or SCSI, press **F6**.
4. At the bottom of the blue screen, a message says, "Press F2 to run the Automated System Recovery process." Press **F2**.
5. The screen shown in Figure 10-22 appears, instructing you to insert the ASR floppy disk. Insert the disk, and then press **Enter**.

```
Windows Setup
===========

        Please insert the disk labeled:

Windows Automated System Recovery Disk

            Into the floppy drive.

         Press any key when ready.
```

Figure 10-22 Automatic System Recovery process must have the ASR floppy disk

6. Windows XP Setup does the following:
   - Loads files it needs to run
   - Repartitions and reformats the drive
   - Installs Windows from the Windows XP CD
   - Launches the Automatic System Recovery Wizard to restore the Windows system state, applications, and data as they were when the last ASR backup was made

The ASR recovery process erases everything on the volume being restored. Figure 10-23 shows one of the above steps in the recovery process, in which you reformat the logical drive just before the Windows XP installation process begins.

A+ OS 2.3 3.1

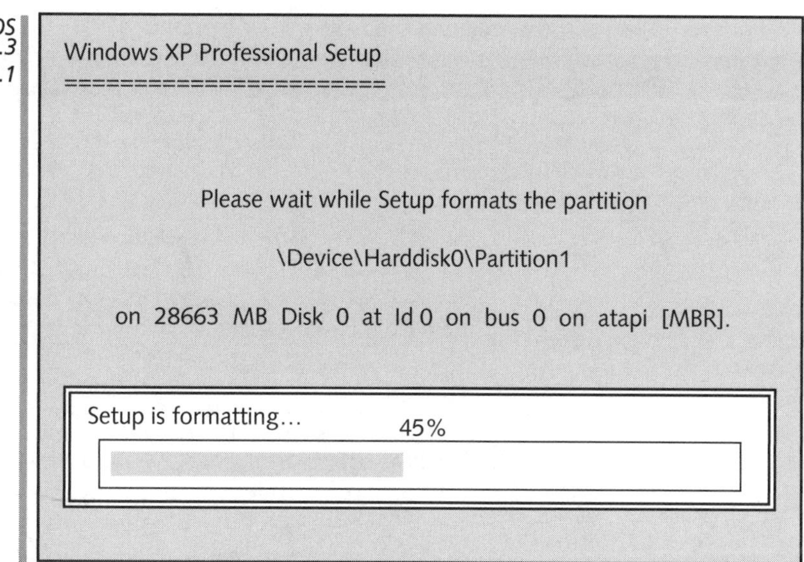

Figure 10-23 As part of the Automatic System Recovery process, Windows XP Setup repartitions and reformats the volume holding Windows XP

Error Messages and Their Meanings

A+ OS 2.3 3.1 3.3

Table 10-4 lists some Windows XP error messages and what they mean. Most of these errors occur when booting.

Table 10-4 Windows XP error messages and their meanings

Error Message	What It Means and What to Do About It
Invalid partition table Error loading operating system Missing operating system	These messages are displayed by the program in the MBR when it cannot find the active partition on the hard drive or the boot sector on that partition. Use Fdisk or Diskpart from a command prompt to check the hard drive partition table for errors. Sometimes Fdisk/mbr might solve the problem. Third-party recovery software such as PartitionMagic might help. If a setup program such as Data Lifeguard from Western Digital or MaxBlast from Maxtor came bundled with the hard drive, use the program to examine the drive. Check the hard drive manufacturer's Web site for other diagnostic software.
A disk read error occurred NTLDR is missing NTLDR is compressed	A disk is probably in the floppy disk drive. Remove the disk and reboot. When booting from the hard drive, these errors occur: if Ntldr has been moved, renamed, or deleted, or is corrupt, if the boot sector on the active partition is corrupt, or if you have just tried to install an older version of Windows, such as Windows 98, on the hard drive. First try replacing Ntldr. Then check Boot.ini settings.

A+ OS 2.3 3.1 3.3

Table 10-4 Windows XP error messages and their meanings (continued)

Error Message	What It Means and What to Do About It
An error is displayed in text against a blue screen and then the system halts. These Windows NT/2000/XP errors are called **stop errors** or **blue screens** (BSOD).	Stop errors are usually caused by viruses, errors in the file system, a corrupt hard drive, or a hardware problem.
Stop 0x00000024 or NTFS_File_System	The NTFS file system is corrupt. Immediately boot into the Recovery Console. Copy important data files that have not been backed up to other media before attempting to recover the system.
Stop 0x00000050 or Page_Fault_in_Nonpaged_Area	Most likely RAM is defective.
Stop 0x00000077 or Kernel_Stack_Inpage_Error	There are bad sectors on the hard drive, there is a hard drive hardware problem, or RAM is defective. Try running Chkdsk or Scandisk.
Stop 0x0000007A or Kernel_Data_Inpage_Error	There is a bad sector on the hard drive where the paging file is stored; there is a virus or defective RAM. Try running Chkdsk or Scandisk.
Stop 0x0000007B or Inaccessible_Boot_Device	There is a boot sector virus or failing hardware. Try Fdisk/mbr or fixmbr.

CHAPTER SUMMARY

- Windows NT/2000/XP requires a valid user account before you can use Windows. The user account identifies the user to Windows. Permissions assigned to a user account control what the user can and cannot do and access under Windows.
- Local user accounts apply to a single standalone computer or a single computer in a workgroup; global user accounts are managed from a domain controller and apply to every computer in the domain.
- When using Windows in a domain, global user account information is stored in the SAM, which is part of Active Directory in Windows 2000 Server and Windows .NET.
- When a user makes changes to the system, the changes are often recorded in the user profile so the next time the user logs on, these changes automatically take effect.
- Methods that administrators can use to manage and secure multiple computers and users include roaming user profiles, mandatory user profiles, and group profiles.
- Passwords on user accounts are needed to secure computers and their resources. Passwords should not be easy to guess and should be a combination of letters, numbers, and non-alphanumeric characters.
- An administrator can create a user account using the Computer Management console or the User Accounts applet in Control Panel.

- Resetting a password under Windows XP causes the OS to lock out the user from using encrypted e-mail or files or using Internet passwords stored on the computer. For that reason, it is a good idea for a user to create a Windows XP forgotten password floppy disk.
- Windows XP user groups include Administrators, Backup Operators, Power Users, Limited Users, and Guests. In this list, each group has fewer permissions and rights than the previous group.
- Using disk quotas, an administrator can limit the amount of hard drive space a user can use.
- File and folder encryption in Windows 2000/XP require using the NTFS file system.
- Internet Connection Firewall (ICF) prevents communication from the Internet to access the system if the communication has not been initiated by the local computer.
- The Windows NT/2000/XP registry is logically organized into five subtrees or keys and physically organized into five files called hives. There is no one-to-one correspondence between the subtrees and the hives.
- The registry is edited using a registry editor which is accessed by entering Regedit in the Run dialog box. Changes to the registry are immediate, so always make a backup of the system state before editing the registry.
- Windows XP offers many troubleshooting and maintenance tools. Some are available from the command line. Others are Microsoft Management Console (MMC) snap-ins and others are built into Windows XP.
- You can get help on the Web for Windows XP. Microsoft offers Windows Update and Microsoft Knowledge Base. There are also Windows newsgroups and other Web sites where you can get help.
- Two recovery tools new to Windows XP are Automated System Recovery and System Restore.
- The Automated System Recovery (ASR) process creates a backup and an ASR floppy disk that can be used to restore the backup of the volume or logical drive holding Windows XP.
- The Windows XP System Restore utility is similar to ScanReg in earlier versions of Windows but cannot be executed at a command prompt. System Restore restores the system state using restore points, which are snapshots of the system state.

Key Terms

Backup Operator
blue screen
built-in user account
disk quota
Drwatson.log
Encrypted File System (EFS)
encryption
firewall
forgotten password floppy disk
global user account
group profile
Guest user
hardware profile
hive
Internet Connection Firewall (ICF)
key
Limited user
local user account
mandatory user profile
Power User
restore point
roaming user profile
stop error
System Restore
user account
user profile

Review Questions

1. Which operating system has the most security: Windows 9x or Windows XP?
2. What is the difference between joining a workgroup and joining a domain?
3. Where is user account information stored on a Windows 2000 domain?
4. When is the local user profile created?
5. How are a roaming profile and a mandatory profile the same? How are they different?
6. What is the difference between the tools ASR and System Restore?
7. What are two important criteria that make for a good password?
8. What can a user do to keep from having the administrator reset a forgotten password?
9. Which user group has more rights, Power Users or Administrators?
10. When using Group Policy on a computer in a workgroup, which type of configuration do you use?
11. What do you implement to control how much disk space a user can take up?
12. Suppose a user has encrypted important data files and now is no longer working for your company. How do you decrypt these files so they can be read?
13. What is the easiest way to give others access to a file that you have encrypted?
14. What command can you use at the command prompt to encrypt a file?
15. If your computer at home is connected to the Internet by way of your spouse's computer, which is connected to the Internet using cable modem, which computer should have Internet Connection Firewall enabled?
16. Which applet in Control Panel is used to enable and disable Internet Connection Firewall?
17. Which Windows registry subtree contains information about the currently logged-on user?

18. Which Windows registry subtree gets all its information from the HKEY_LOCAL_MACHINE subtree?
19. In Windows NT/2000/XP, a file that contains part of the Windows registry is called a(n) ________________.
20. What is the Windows XP command to access the registry editor?
21. How do Dr. Watson and the registry editor differ in Windows XP from how they were in Windows 2000?
22. What is the name of the snap-in file for Disk Defragmenter?
23. Looking at a program filename and file extension, how can you tell if the program is an MMC snap-in or a command-line program?
24. What is the name of the log file created when boot logging is enabled from the Advanced Options startup menu?
25. Place these tools in the order in which you should try them when troubleshooting the boot process: Recovery Console, Advanced Options Menu, System Restore.
26. What is a restore point, and what is it used for?
27. ScanReg has been replaced by System Restore in Windows XP. What main advantage does ScanReg have over System Restore?
28. Can you use an MS-DOS startup disk to launch Windows XP? To recover data files? To recover from a failed installation of Windows XP?
29. When trying to restore a failed system, what should you do next if Recovery Console does not work?
30. What are two recovery tools new to Windows XP that are used to recover from a failed boot?

HANDS-ON PROJECTS

Problem Solving Using the Microsoft Knowledge Base

Your hard drive has been attacked by a malicious virus and you have decided to restore it from the last backup made by the ASR backup process. However, you cannot find the ASR floppy disk required for the restore process. Search the Microsoft Knowledge Base for the steps to re-create the ASR floppy disk when the ASR backup is available. Print the Knowledge Base article.

Microsoft Management Console

Microsoft Management Console under Windows XP works the same way it does under Windows 2000. Follow the step-by-step directions in Chapter 8 to create a customized console in Windows XP. Put two snap-ins in the console: Device Manager and Event Viewer.

Using System Restore

Create a restore point. Make a change to the display settings. Restore the system using System Restore. Are the changes still in effect? Why, or why not?

Using the ASR Process

Create an ASR backup following directions in the chapter. Add a few data files to the hard drive. Restore the system using the ASR process. Do the data files still exist on the hard drive? Why, or why not?

Internet Connection Firewall

Using the Windows XP Help and Support Center, answer these questions about Internet Connection Firewall:

1. List the steps to view the contents of the log file that ICF uses to record dropped packets.
2. What is the filename of this log file?
3. What applet in Control Panel can you use to change the location of this file?
4. Which version of Windows XP does not include ICF? Why do you think this is so?
5. Explain how you could use ICF to record when others on your local network access your Windows XP computer.

CHAPTER

11

SUPPORTING HARD DRIVES

In this chapter, you will learn:

- About supporting hard drives and making backups
- About viruses and other computer infestations, and how to protect against them

So far in this book we have focused on specific operating systems, which is where your focus will be as a software technician. Many functions are common to all Windows operating systems, and this chapter is a consolidation of several of these common functions. You will learn about supporting hard drives, including how to protect against viruses. This chapter covers disk compression and caching for hard drives, as well as several ways to create hard drive backups. In addition, it discusses different types of viruses that can infect your hard drive as well as how to remove and prevent them.

SUPPORTING HARD DRIVES

The most important secondary storage device in your computer is the hard drive. In this section, you will learn about disk compression, disk caching, and how to make backups.

Disk Compression

A+ OS 1.1 **Disk compression** software can help meet the ever-increasing demand for more space on hard drives to hold improved software. Software packages requiring 200 to 250 MB of hard drive space were unheard of three or four years ago but are now common. The sizes of hard drives have increased proportionately. Even so, we often seek ways to cram more onto nearly full hard drives.

Software to manage disk compression works by (1) storing data on your hard drive in one big file and managing the writing of data and programs to that file, and (2) rewriting data in files in a mathematically coded format that uses less space. Most disk compression programs combine these two methods. This section covers disk compression methods under several versions of Windows.

Disk compression does save hard drive space, but you need to carefully consider the risks involved as well as performance issues such as longer disk access time. If you do choose to use disk compression, keep good backups of both the data and the software. If the data and software on your drive are especially valuable, you may want to invest in a larger hard drive instead of using compression.

Disk Compression in Windows 9x

A **compressed drive** is not a drive at all; it's a file. Figure 11-1 shows the two parts of a compressed drive. The **host drive**, in this case drive H, is not compressed and is usually a very small partition on the drive, generally under 2 MB. The host drive contains a special file called a **CVF (compressed volume file)**. The CVF holds everything on drive C, compressed into just one file.

Although there are several disk compression utilities on the market, Windows 9x offers its own, called **DriveSpace**. DriveSpace does the following things to compress a drive:

- Assigns a different drive letter to the hard drive, such as H
- Compresses the entire contents of the hard drive into a single file on drive H
- Sets up the drive so that Windows 9x and other applications view this compressed file as drive C
- Configures Windows 9x so that each time it boots, the DriveSpace driver will load and manage the compressed drive

A+ OS 1.1

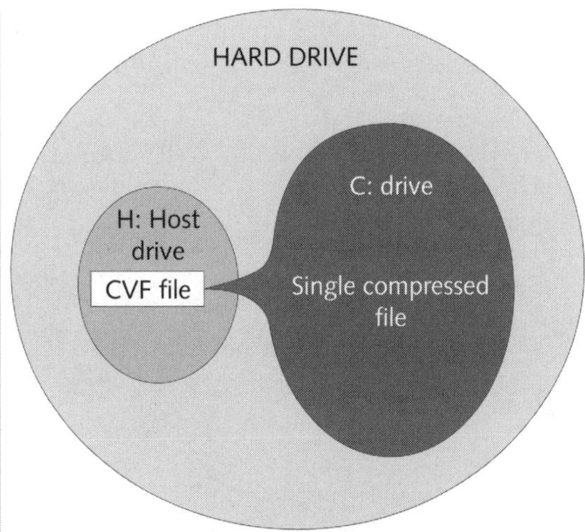

Figure 11-1 A compressed drive

DriveSpace does not work with FAT32 under Windows 98.

11

Follow these steps to compress a drive in Windows 98 using DriveSpace:

1. Click **Start**, then **Programs**, then **Accessories**, then **System Tools**.
2. Click **DriveSpace** to display the dialog box in Figure 11-2. Drive A is used as the example here, but drive C gives similar results.

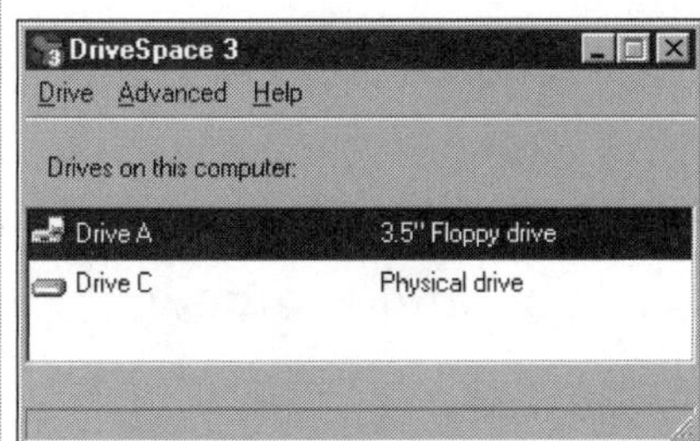

Figure 11-2 Selecting a drive using DriveSpace for Windows 98

3. Select drive A by clicking on it, and then choose **Compress** from the Drive menu. A dialog box is displayed, showing how much space would be created by compressing the drive. To get the most resources out of compression, begin with a relatively free hard drive.

A+ OS 1.1

4. Click **Options**, and the Compression Options box in Figure 11-3 appears. Note that you can allow extra space on drive H that will not be compressed. Click **OK**.
5. Click **Start** to begin compression. Dialog boxes appear, informing you that compressed drives will not be accessible to other OSs and suggesting that you make backups before compressing the drive.

If a Windows 9x utility such as DriveSpace is missing from a menu list, the component might not have been installed when Windows was installed. To install a Windows component after Windows is installed, go to Control Panel, select Add/Remove Programs, and click the Windows Setup tab.

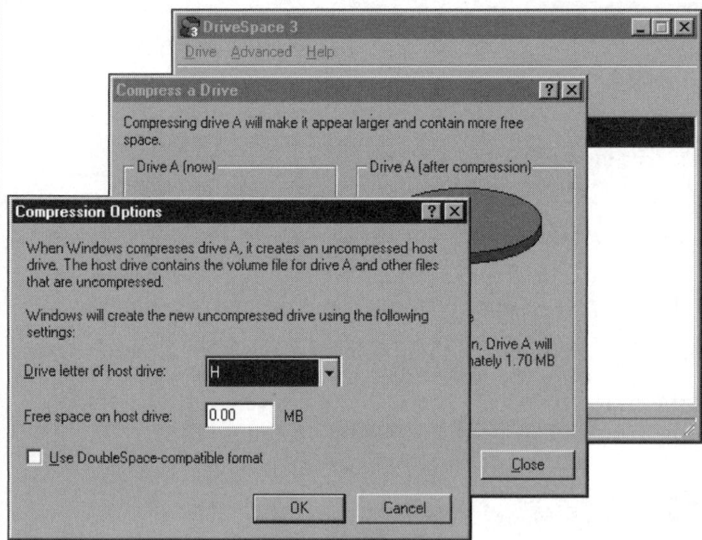

Figure 11-3 Drive compression options

A+ OS 1.2

Disk Compression Under Windows 2000 and Windows XP

In Chapter 8, you learned about file and folder compression under Windows 2000; this section covers compression of an entire volume. Disk and file compression work the same under Windows 2000 and Windows XP. Windows 2000 will be used in this section.

You can compress an entire volume under Windows 2000 as long as the volume is using NTFS. When you place a file or folder on a compressed volume, it will automatically be compressed. When you read a compressed file from a compressed volume, it will be decompressed automatically and will then be recompressed when it is saved back to the compressed volume.

A+ OS 1.2

To compress an NTFS volume:

1. Open Windows Explorer.
2. Locate and right-click the root folder for the volume you want to compress. You will find it in the left pane of Windows Explorer.
3. Select **Properties** from the shortcut menu. The Properties box appears.
4. If necessary, click the **General** tab (see Figure 11-4). Click the check box labeled **Compress drive to save disk space**. Click **OK**.
5. The Confirm Attribute Changes dialog box appears. Indicate whether you want to compress only the root folder or the entire volume, and then click **OK** to begin compression.

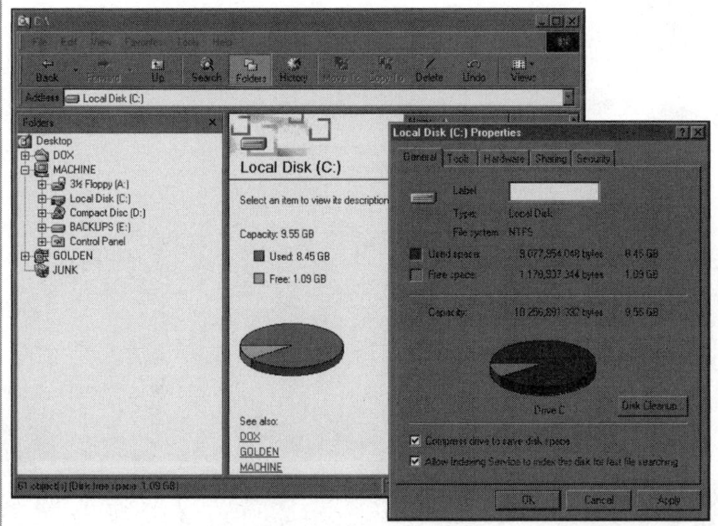

Figure 11-4 Compressing a NTFS volume

Disk Caching

A+ OS 2.5

A **disk cache** is a temporary storage area in RAM for data being read from or written to a hard drive, and is used to speed up access time to the drive. The process of disk caching works like this:

1. The CPU asks for data from a hard drive.
2. The hard drive controller sends instructions to the drive to read the data and then sends the data to the CPU.
3. The CPU requests more data, quite often data that immediately follows the previously read data on the hard drive.
4. The controller reads the requested data from the drive and sends it to the CPU. Without a cache, each CPU request requires that data be read from the hard drive, as indicated in the top part of Figure 11-5.

A+ OS 2.5

With a hard drive cache, the cache software handles the requests for data, as seen in the lower part of Figure 11-5. The cache program reads ahead of the CPU requests by guessing what data the CPU will request next. Since most data that the CPU requests is in consecutive areas on the drive, the cache program guesses correctly most of the time. The program stores the read-ahead data in memory (RAM). When the CPU requests the next set of data, if the cache program guessed right, the program can send that data to the CPU from memory without having to go back to the hard drive. Some cache software caches entire tracks at a time; other software caches groups of sectors.

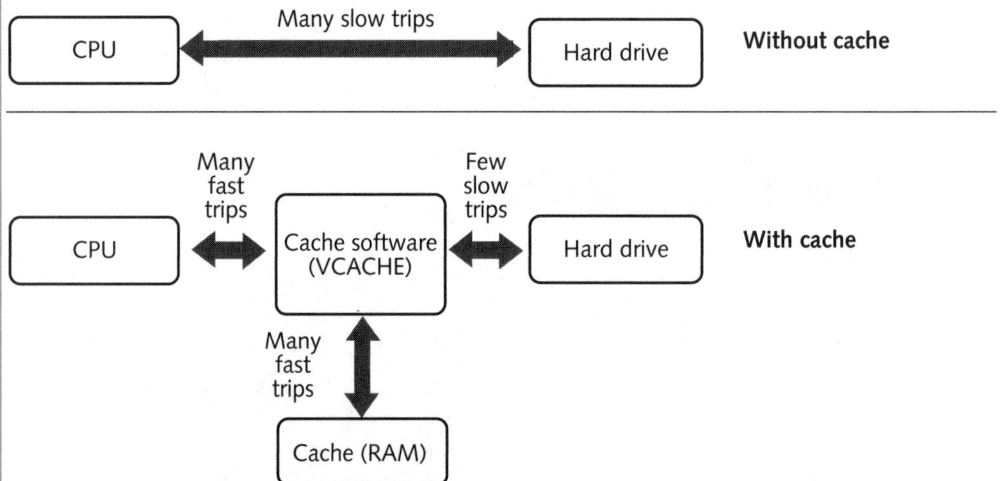

Figure 11-5 A CPU asking a hard drive for data without cache (upper part) and with cache (lower part)

Hardware Cache or Software Cache

There are two kinds of hard drive caches: hardware and software. Some hard drive controllers have a **hardware cache** built right into the controller circuit board. The BIOS on the controller contains the cache program, and RAM chips on the controller hold the cache.

A **software cache** is a cache program that is stored on the hard drive like other software and is loaded into memory usually when a computer is booted. The software cache program uses system RAM to hold the cache.

There are advantages and disadvantages to both kinds of hard drive cache. A hardware cache does not use RAM on the system board, but a software cache uses RAM for both the cache program itself and the data being cached. Therefore, a disadvantage of a software cache is that RAM is used that might otherwise be used for applications software and its data.

On the other hand, a software cache is faster because of where the data is stored. Since data is stored in RAM, when the CPU is ready for the data, the data only needs to travel from RAM to the CPU on the system bus, the fastest bus on the motherboard. Since the hardware cache is on the controller board, when the CPU is ready for data stored in this cache, the data must travel from the controller board over one or more buses to the CPU.

A+ OS 2.5

Another disadvantage of a hardware cache is that it is a permanent part of the hard drive controller, and today's hard drives have the controller built into the drive housing. Exchanging hard drives to upgrade to a faster hardware cache is impractical, whereas upgrading to a faster software cache is a viable option.

When buying a new hard drive, check whether it includes hardware caches as an option. A controller with its own hardware cache is slightly more expensive than one without a cache.

How Disk Caching Methods Have Changed

As operating system technologies have changed, so have software disk caching methods. The following is a summary of how different OSs have accomplished disk caching.

- *DOS.* Before disk caching came along, DOS used buffers to speed up disk access. A **buffer** is an area in memory where data waiting to be read or written is temporarily stored. Disk caches do a better job of speeding up disk access than buffers, so the only reason to use buffers today is to satisfy the requirements of older software that uses them. Buffers are implemented by putting the Buffers=[*number*] command in Config.sys. This command specifies how many buffers DOS is to make available for use while data is being read.
- *DOS with Windows 3.x.*DOS with Windows 3.x used **SMARTDrive**, a 16-bit real mode software cache utility that came with DOS and Windows 3.x. SMARTDrive caches data both being read from and written to the hard drive and caches data being read from floppy disks.
- *Windows 9x.* Windows 9x has a built-in 32-bit, protected-mode software cache called **VCACHE**, which is automatically loaded by Windows 9x without entries in Config.sys or Autoexec.bat. VCACHE doesn't take up conventional memory or upper memory space the way SMARTDrive does, and it does a much better job of caching.
- *Windows NT/2000/XP.* Versions of Windows after 9x use automated disk caching as an inherited Windows component. When working with caching under these versions of Windows, remember that you can monitor physical disk performance using the counters discussed in Chapter 8.

Troubleshooting Hard Drives

If a hard drive is not functioning and data is not accessible, setting priorities helps focus your work. For most users, the data is the first priority unless they have a recent backup. The software can also be a priority if it is not backed up. Reloading software from the original installation disks or CD-ROM can be time-consuming, especially if the configuration is complex or you have written software macros or scripts that are not backed up.

If you have good backups of both the data and software, the hardware might be your priority. It could be expensive to replace, and downtime can be costly. The point is, when trouble arises, determine your main priority and start by focusing on that.

Be aware of what resources are available to help you resolve a problem:

- Documentation often lists error messages and their meanings.
- The Internet can also help you diagnose hardware and software problems. Go to the Web site of the manufacturer of the product and search for FAQs (frequently asked questions) list or bulletin board. It's likely that others have encountered the same problem and have posted the question and answer. If you search and can't find your answer, then you can post a new question.
- Technical support from the ROM BIOS, hardware, and software manufacturers can help you interpret an error message, or it can provide general support in diagnosing a problem. Most technical support is available during working hours by telephone. Check your documentation for telephone numbers. An experienced computer troubleshooter once said, "The people who solve computer problems do it by trying something and making phone calls, trying something else and making more phone calls, and so on, until the problem is solved." There is a lot of truth in that statement.

Remember one last thing. After making a reasonable and diligent effort to resolve a problem, getting the problem fixed could become more important than resolving it yourself. There comes a time when you might need to turn the problem over to a more experienced technician.

Troubleshooting Hard Drives with Third-Party Software

To troubleshoot hard drive problems, you might need to know how to use third-party utility software. Three popular utility software programs are Norton Utilities, SpinRite, and PartitionMagic. The following descriptions tell you what to expect from the software when you have a hard drive failure. Note that these are *not* complete listings of all the utility software functions, or of all available software packages. See specific software documentation for more detail.

- *Norton Utilities* (*www.symantec.com*) offers several easy-to-use tools to prevent damage to a hard drive, recover data from a damaged hard drive, and improve system performance. Many of the functions of these tools have been taken over and improved by utilities included with recent versions of Windows. The most commonly used Norton Utilities tools now are the recovery tools. Two examples are Norton Disk Doctor, which automatically repairs many hard drive and floppy disk problems without your intervention, and UnErase Wizard, which allows you to retrieve files that you deleted accidentally. When using Norton Utilities, be certain you are using the version of the software for the operating system you have installed. Using Norton with the wrong OS can do damage.

- *PartitionMagic* by PowerQuest Corporation (*www.powerquest.com*) lets you manage partitions on a hard drive more quickly and easily than with Fdisk for Windows 9x or Disk Management for Windows NT/2000/XP. You can create new partitions, change the size of partitions, and move partitions without losing data or moving the data to another hard drive while you work. You can switch between FAT16 and FAT32 without disturbing your data, and you can hide and show partitions to secure your data.
- *SpinRite* by Gibson Research (*www.grc.com*) is hard drive utility software that has been around for years. Today, SpinRite is still a DOS application without a sophisticated GUI interface, but it has been updated to adjust to new drive technologies. It supports FAT32, SCSI, Zip drives, and Jaz drives. You can boot your PC from a floppy disk and run SpinRite from a floppy, which means that it doesn't require much system overhead. Because it is written in a language closer to the binary code that the computer understands, it is more likely to detect underlying hard drive problems than software that uses Windows, which can stand as a masking layer between the software and the hard drive. SpinRite analyzes the entire hard drive surface, performing data recovery of corrupted files and file system information. Sometimes, SpinRite can recover data from a failing hard drive when other software fails.

Always check compatibility between utility software and the operating system with which you plan to use it. One place you can check is the service and support section of the software manufacturer's Web site.

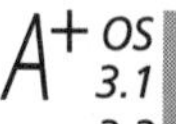

Software Problems with Hard Drives

Problems with hard drives can be caused by either hardware or software. Problems can also be categorized as those that prevent the hard drive from booting and those that prevent data from being accessed. Here are some general software causes of hard drive problems. The root cause of many of these causes is a virus:

- Corrupted OS files
- Corrupted partition table, boot record, or root directory, making all data on the hard drive inaccessible
- Corruption of the area of the FAT that points to the data, the data's directory table, or the sector markings where the data is located
- Corruption of the data itself

Resolving Hard Drive and Data Access Problems The software problems listed earlier can all prevent data or programs on the hard drive from being accessible. For a hard drive and its data to be accessible by DOS or Windows, these items, listed in the order they are accessed, must be intact for a FAT file system: the partition table, the boot record, the FAT, the root directory, the system files, and data and program files.

A+ OS 3.1 3.2

- *Partition table.* When the partition table is damaged, BIOS will try to load the OS, first reading the master boot program at the beginning of the partition table information on the hard drive. If the partition table is damaged, this error message appears:

  ```
  Invalid drive or drive specification
  ```

  In this case, you should still be able to boot from a floppy disk. When you get to the A prompt and try to access the hard drive by entering C:, you will get the same error. To restore the boot program in the partition table (the MBR, or Master Boot Record), which is at the very beginning of the partition table information, for Windows 9x or Windows NT, use this command:

  ```
  A> Fdisk /Mbr
  ```

  For Windows 2000/XP, from the Recovery Console, use this command:

  ```
  Fixmbr
  ```

  Oftentimes, these commands solve the problem of a damaged partition table.

- *Boot record.* If the OS boot record on a hard drive is damaged, you cannot boot from the hard drive. After you boot from a floppy disk and try to access the hard drive, you might get one of these error messages:

  ```
  Invalid media type
  Non-DOS disk
  Unable to read from Drive C
  ```

  If the OS boot record is damaged, the best solution is to recover it from the backup copy you made when you first became responsible for the PC. (Norton Utilities can be used to make the backup.) If you don't have a backup, try to repair it using Norton Disk Doctor or SpinRite.

- *FAT and root directory.* The partition table and the boot record are easily backed up to disk; they will not change unless the drive is repartitioned or reformatted. Always back them up as soon as you can after you buy a new computer or become responsible for a working one. Unlike the partition table and the boot record, the FAT and the root directory change often and are more difficult to back up. The success of Windows or third-party utilities in repairing a damaged FAT or root directory depends on the degree of damage to the tables. If these tables are damaged, you may receive this error message:

  ```
  Sector not found reading drive C, Abort, Retry, Ignore,
  Fail?
  ```

  Try copying important files on the drive to another medium. If you encounter the error above, type *I* to ignore the bad sector and continue copying. Norton Disk Doctor might be able to repair the FAT or root directory.

A+ OS 3.1 3.2

- *System files.* If the two OS hidden files (Io.sys and Msdos.sys) are missing or corrupted, you should see one of these error messages:

  ```
  Non system disk or disk error…
  ```

  ```
  Invalid system disk…
  ```

  Use the following command to copy the two hidden files and the Command.com file from a rescue disk to the hard drive:

  ```
  A:\> Sys C:
  ```

- *Data and program files.* Data and program files can become corrupted for many reasons, ranging from power spikes to user error. If the corrupted file is a program file, the simplest solution might be to reinstall the software or recover the file from a previous backup. How to restore a data file that is not backed up is covered in the next section, along with problems that can cause data and program file corruption.

Data and Program File Corruption To restore a data file that is not backed up, you have three options:

- Use operating system tools and commands to recover the file.
- Use third-party software such as Norton Utilities or SpinRite to recover the file.
- If neither of these approaches works, you can turn to a professional data recovery service. These services can be expensive, but, depending on how valuable the data is, the cost might be justified.

When a data file or program file is damaged, portions of the file may still be intact. The basic approach to recovering data in this situation is to create a new file on another disk or on the hard drive, containing all the sectors from the original file that can be read from the damaged disk or hard drive. Use the Copy command and when you get an error message, try to move on to the next sector. Some of the file might be copied to the new media. Then edit the newly created file to replace the missing data.

How successfully an OS recovers data depends on how badly damaged the file is. A few examples of how data commonly becomes damaged and what can be done to recover it are discussed below. If a file has been accidentally erased, or the disk or hard drive is otherwise damaged, remember these two things:

- Don't write anything to the disk or hard drive, because you might overwrite data that you could otherwise recover.
- If you are recovering data from a disk, use Diskcopy in DOS or, for Windows 9x, use Copy Disk in Explorer to make a copy of the disk before you do anything else. If Copy Disk or Diskcopy doesn't work, try copying the disk with a third-party program such as Norton Utilities.

A+ OS 3.1 3.2

Here are some problems you may experience with files and the file system:

- *Corrupted file header.* If an application cannot open or read one of its data files, the file header might be corrupted. Many applications place header information (called the file header) at the beginning of the file. This data follows a different format from the rest of the file. The application uses it to identify the file and its contents. If the file header is lost or corrupted and an application needs that header to read the file, you can sometimes recover the contents by treating the file as an ASCII text file.

Most applications let you import a text file, and then convert it to the application's format. Read your application's documentation to learn how to import a text file.

- *Lost clusters.* A disk can develop lost clusters (also called lost allocation units) if a program cannot properly close a file it has opened. For example, if you boot your computer while an application is running (not a good thing to do for this very reason), the application will not have the opportunity to close a file and may lose clusters. Another way clusters can be lost is if you remove a floppy disk from a drive while the drive light is still on (also not a good thing to do). Some older applications, such as early versions of MS Access, might not complete writing a file to a floppy disk until the application is closed or another data file is opened. In this case, you must close the application or open a new file before it is safe to remove the floppy disk.

  Lost clusters are clusters that are not incorporated into a file. The Chkdsk and Scandisk commands turn the clusters into a file with the name File0000.chk or a similar filename with a higher number, and store the file in the root directory. To use this utility at a command prompt to access lost clusters, use the command with the /F option, like this:

  ```
  C:\> Chkdsk A:/F
  ```

  Often the file created can be used by the application that it belongs to, although you might have to change the file extension so the application will recognize the file. You can also use the ScanDisk utility described in Chapter 5 to accomplish the same results.

  If the drive is compressed, try booting to a command prompt and using ScanDisk to recover the compressed data. Include the name of the compressed volume file on the host drive, like this:

  ```
  Scandisk drvspace.nnn
  ```

  or

  ```
  Scandisk dblspace.nnn
  ```

  Substitute the file extension for the compressed volume file on the host drive (for example, Drvspace.001 or Dblspace.001).

A+ OS 3.1 3.2

- *Erased file.* If a file has been deleted, it can sometimes be recovered. First look for the file in the Recycle Bin. If it's not there, at a command prompt try the Unerase or Undelete command, which recovers some erased files.

Viruses cause many file system problems. When you have a problem with a corrupted system file, program file or data file, run a current version of antivirus software. The software will probably not help in recovering the file, but might prevent other files from becoming infected.

Making Backups

A+ OS 1.2

Losing data due to system failure, a virus, file corruption, or some other problem can really make you appreciate the importance of having backups. This section covers the hardware and software needed to make backups of data and software from a hard drive. Windows 9x and Windows NT/2000/XP offer backup tools, which are also covered in this section.

With data and software, here's a good rule of thumb: if you can't get along without it, back it up.

You can use sophisticated methods to create backups in which the backup process is selective, only backing up what's changed, what has not been recently backed up, and so forth. Traditionally, these methods all involve backing up to tapes, because a tape is most likely to be large enough to contain an entire backup of a hard drive. In the discussions below of specific backup methods, we use tapes as our medium. These backup methods are designed to reuse tapes and to make the backup process more efficient. On a network, often the backup media is a device such as another hard drive or a tape drive on a computer somewhere on the network. Full, incremental, and differential backup methods speed up the backup process, and scheduled backups minimize the inconvenience to users. Selective backups only back up data that changes often on the hard drive. By selecting only certain critical folders on the drive to back up, the backup routine goes much faster, and recovery of lost data is much easier.

The Child, Parent, Grandparent Method

Before you perform routine hard drive backups, devise a backup plan or procedure. One common plan, called the **child, parent, grandparent backup method**, makes it easy to reuse tapes. This method is explained in Table 10-1. Put the plan in writing and keep a log of backups performed.

A+ OS 1.2

Table 11-1 The child, parent, grandparent backup method

Name of Backup	How Often Performed	Storage Location	Description
Child backup	Daily	On-site	Keep four daily backup tapes and rotate them each week. Label the four tapes Monday, Tuesday, Wednesday, and Thursday. A Friday daily (child) backup is not made, because on Friday you'll make the parent backup.
Parent backup	Weekly	Off-site	Perform the weekly backup on Friday. Keep five weekly backup tapes, one for each Friday of the month, and rotate them each month. Label the tapes Friday 1, Friday 2, Friday 3, Friday 4, and Friday 5.
Grandparent backup	Monthly	Off-site, in a fireproof vault	Perform the monthly backup on the last Friday of the month. Keep 12 tapes, one for each month. Rotate them each year. Label the tapes January, February, and so on.

Full, Incremental, and Differential Backups

Some backup methods are more efficient because they do not always create a complete backup of all data. A **full backup** backs up all data from the hard drive or an area of the hard drive. An **incremental backup** backs up only files that have changed or that have been created since the last backup, whether that backup is itself an incremental or full backup. **Differential backups** back up files that have changed or been created since the last full backup.

Begin by performing a full backup. The next time you back up, choose the incremental method to back up only files that have changed or been created since the full backup. The second time you perform an incremental backup, you back up only the files that have changed or been created since the last incremental backup.

For example, using the child, parent, grandparent method, you can perform a full backup each Friday. Monday through Thursday, you perform incremental backups. The advantage of this method is that incremental backups are faster and require less tape space than full backups. The disadvantage is that, to recover data, you must begin with the last full backup and work your way forward through each incremental backup until the time that the data was lost. This process can be time-consuming. Plan to make a full backup after at least every sixth or seventh incremental backup. The Windows 9x and Windows NT/2000/XP backup utilities support incremental backups.

If you create differential backups with the child, parent, grandparent method, create a full backup on Fridays. On Monday, do a differential backup to back up all files that have changed since Friday. On Tuesday, a differential backup also backs up all files that have changed since Friday (the full backup). Differential backups don't consider whether other differential backups have been performed. Instead, they compare data only to the last full

A+ OS 1.2

backup, which is how differential backups and incremental backups differ. Another difference is that incremental backups mark files as having been backed up, but differential backups do not. The advantage of differential backups over incremental ones is that if you need to recover data, you only need to recover from the last full backup and the last differential backup. Differential backups are not supported by Windows 95 but are supported by Windows 98 and Windows NT/2000/XP.

Scheduling Backups

Backups can be performed manually by a user sitting at the computer or can be scheduled to run automatically without user interaction. A scheduled backup is automatically performed by software when the computer is commonly not in use, such as during the middle of the night. Windows 98 and Windows NT/2000/XP support scheduling any program (including backup tasks) to execute at designated dates and times without user intervention.

Using Windows 98, do the following to create a program called Batch.bat to run a backup and schedule it to run at 11:59 p.m. every Monday night:

1. Using Notepad or WordPad, type this command line, where the tape drive is E and the /S parameter tells the OS to include subdirectories when copying (hidden files will not be copied, but data is not usually hidden):

   ```
   Xcopy C:\Data\*.* E: /S
   ```

2. Save the file as **\Data\Batch.bat**, and exit the text editor.
3. Double-click **My Computer** on the desktop, and then double-click **Scheduled Tasks** to open the Scheduled Tasks window (see Figure 11-6).

11

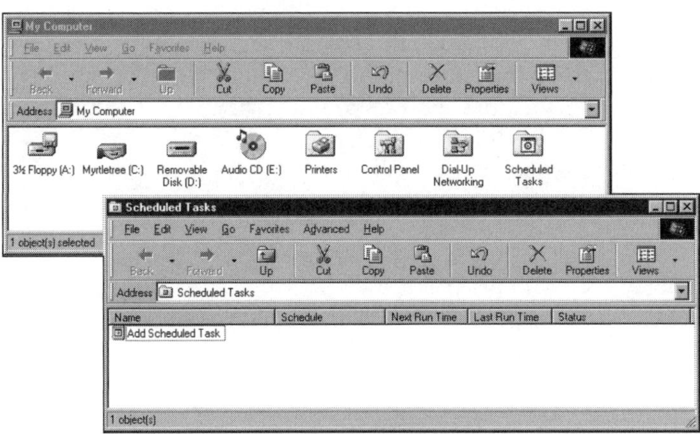

Figure 11-6 Add a scheduled task under Windows 98

4. Double-click **Add Scheduled Task**. The Scheduled Task Wizard appears. Select the program to schedule: Click **Browse**, find and click the **Batch.bat** file in the \Data folder, and then click **Open**.

5. Enter a name for the scheduled task, select how often to perform the task, and then click **Next** (see Figure 11-7).
6. Enter the start time and select the day of the week for the task to execute. For example, enter **11:59 PM every Monday**. Click **Next**.
7. The wizard reports the scheduled task parameters. Click **Finish**.

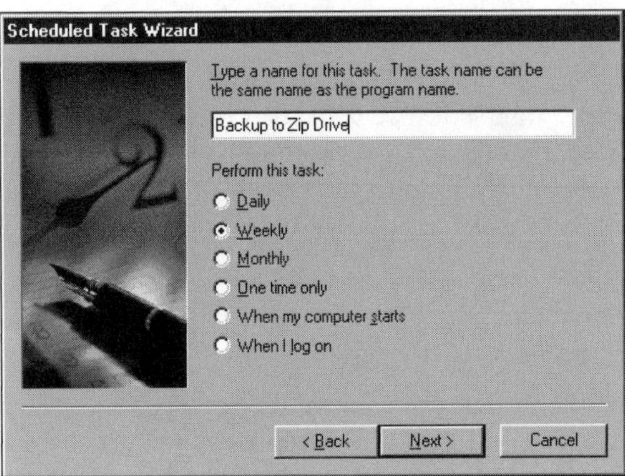

Figure 11-7 Name the scheduled task and select how often it runs

8. To change the settings for a scheduled task, double-click **My Computer**, double-click **Scheduled Tasks**, and then right-click the task in the Scheduled Task window. Select **Properties** from the shortcut menu. The task Properties dialog box opens (see Figure 11-8).
9. Click the **Settings** tab to change the task settings. Notice at the bottom of the Settings sheet that you can direct the scheduler to wake the computer to perform the task. This feature requires a motherboard that supports the option for software to power up the PC. To learn if your motherboard supports the feature, see CMOS setup or the motherboard documentation. If not, then the PC must be turned on for the scheduler to work.

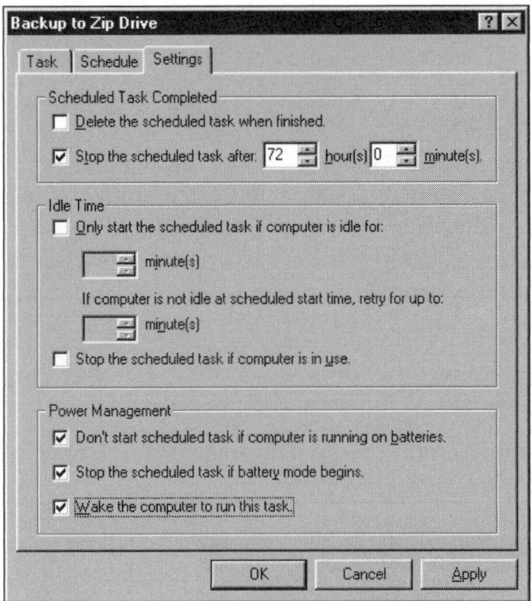

Figure 11-8 With some computers, the task scheduler can power up the computer to run the task

A+ OS 1.2 You have just learned how to use a batch file to execute a scheduled backup. Windows offers a more powerful and sophisticated utility called Windows Scripting Host (WSH), which uses Windows commands to execute scripts that programmers have written using a scripting language such as VBScript or JScript. This utility is good for making backups also. The script is stored in a file that can be placed as an icon on the desktop. To run the script, type *wscript.exe filename* in the Run dialog box, substituting filename with the name of the script file, or double-click on the desktop icon. You can also make a script file run as a scheduled task.

A+ OS 1.5

Backup Software

Most tape drives come with some backup software. You can also purchase third-party backup software or use Windows 9x or Windows NT/2000/XP for backing up your hard drive. Because the software only backs up files that are not currently in use, close all files before performing a backup.

Windows 9x Backup Utility Windows 9x offers a backup utility that can back up to removable disks and tape drives. Windows 98 supports many popular backup devices that Windows 95 did not, including those using parallel ports, IDE/ATAPI devices, and SCSI devices. To use drives and tapes not supported by Windows 9x, use third-party backup software.

If the Windows 9x Backup component is not installed under Windows 9x, use the Control Panel, Add/Remove Programs applet to install it. You will need the Windows 9x CD or

A+ OS 1.5

other access to the installation files. To use the Windows 98 Microsoft Backup utility (msbackup.exe), do the following:

1. Click **Start**, point to **Programs**, **Accessories**, **System Tools**, and then click **Backup**. The Backup Wizard first searches for backup devices such as Zip or tape drives. If it finds none, it asks if you want to install one. Otherwise, it displays a window asking if you want to create a new backup job or open an existing job. The Backup utility keeps information about backup jobs under a name that you give it, so you can use the same job many times. Select **Create a new backup job**, and then click **OK** to continue.
2. The Backup Wizard asks you questions about what type of backup you want (for example, back up all files or only those files that have changed since the last backup). Make your selections, and then click **Next**.
3. The Microsoft Backup utility opens the Backup window, as shown in Figure 11-9.

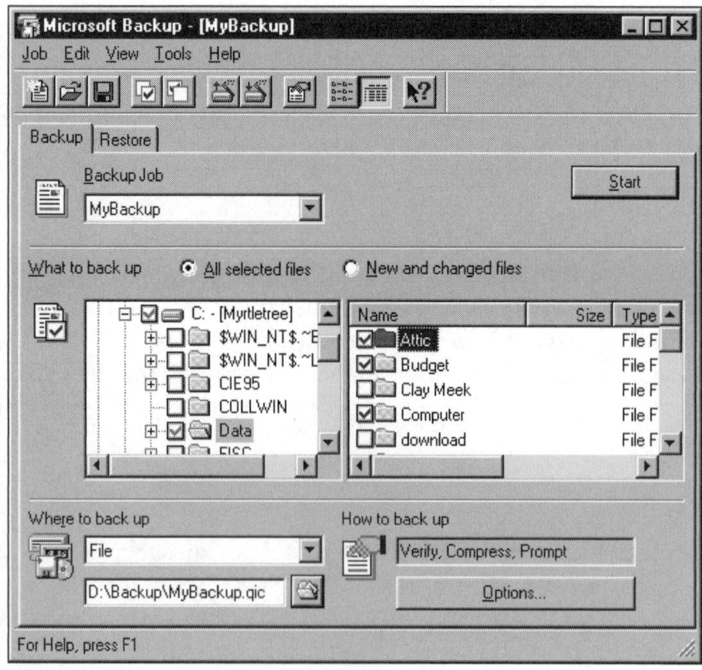

Figure 11-9 Windows 98 Microsoft Backup allows you to select files and folders to back up

4. To back up only certain folders, files, or logical drives, check the boxes to the left of their names. To display a list of all subfolders under a folder, click the box with the + sign in it. Backup indicates that only parts of a folder or drive are selected for backup by placing a gray check in the box.

A+ OS 1.5

5. In the **Where to back up** list box of the Backup window shown in Figure 11-9, select the medium and directory to use. In the figure, the medium is drive D, a Zip drive. The backup file will go into a folder named \Backup.
6. Click **Start** to begin the backup.

To recover files, folders, or the entire hard drive from backup using the Windows 98 Backup utility, follow these directions:

1. On the Backup utility window, shown in Figure 11-9, click the Restore tab. Select the backup job to use for the restore process. The Backup utility displays the folders and files that were backed up with this job. You can select the ones that you want to restore.
2. Click **Start** to restore the files.

Windows 2000/XP Backup Utility

To perform a backup for Windows 2000/XP (using Ntbackup.exe), follow these steps:

1. For Windows 2000, on the Start menu, click **Programs**, **Accessories**, **System Tools**, **Backup**. For Windows XP, click **Start**, point to **All Programs**, **Accessories**, **System Tools**, and click **Backup**. The Backup or Restore Wizard appears. Click **Advanced Mode**.
2. The Backup utility opens. Click the **Backup** tab (see Figure 11-10). If you want to perform a backup immediately, check the drive and subfolders to back up. Note the box labeled **Backup media or file name** in the lower-left corner, which says where to back up to. Click the **Start Backup** button in the lower-right corner to perform the backup.

11

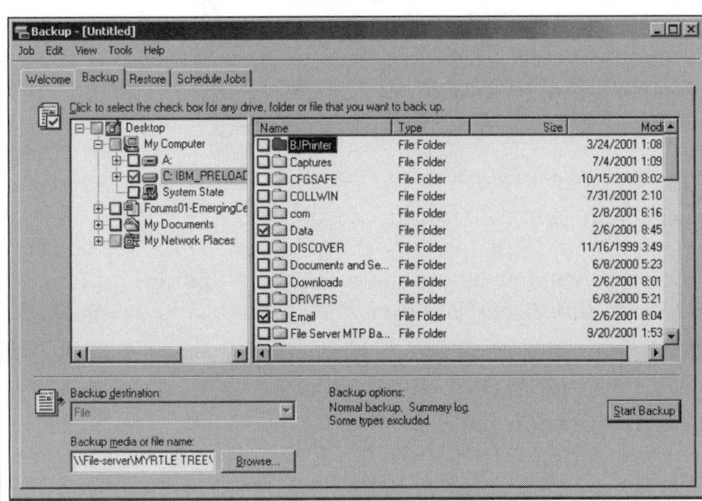

Figure 11-10 You can perform an immediate backup from the Backup tab

A+ OS 1.5

3. To perform a scheduled backup, begin by clicking the **Schedule Jobs** tab. Select a date on which you want to schedule a backup, and then click the **Add Job** button.

4. The Backup Wizard opens. On the first screen, click **Next**. Select **Backup selected files, drives, or network data** and click **Next**.

5. On the next screen, the Backup Wizard allows you to select what you want to back up. Select what you want to back up, and then click **Next**.

6. Follow the steps through the wizard to select the type of backup (Normal, Copy, Incremental, Differential, or Daily) and how to verify the data after the backup, control access to the backed-up data, and label the backed-up data. When asked if you want to perform the backup now or later, select **Later** and click **Next**.

7. The When to Back Up window appears (see Figure 11-11) for you to specify when to perform the backup and give it a name. Note that you can perform an immediate backup from the wizard instead of using the method you learned in step 1. After specifying a name and date for the job, click the **Set Schedule** button.

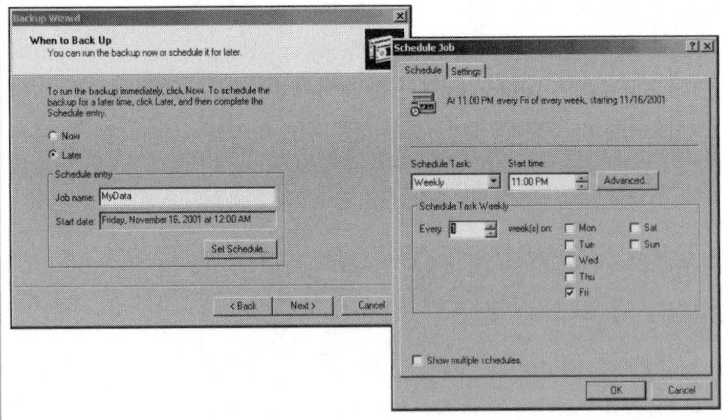

Figure 11-11 Select a name and date for the backup job

8. The Schedule Job window appears, also shown in Figure 11-11. Schedule how often the backup is to occur, and then click **OK**.

9. Click **Next** in the wizard and follow the remaining instructions to complete the backup. At the end of the process, the wizard gives you an on-screen report summarizing information about the backup.

Disk Cloning Software

For Windows 9x, you can back up a hard drive so that you can replicate the drive to a new computer or to another drive on the same computer, such as when you deploy a new operating system with application software on multiple computers in a corporate or educational lab. This process is called **disk cloning** or **disk imaging** and is best done with software designed for that purpose. Examples of disk imaging software are Drive Image by PowerQuest (*www.powerquest.com*), ImageCast by Innovative Software (*www.imagecast.com*), and Norton Ghost by Symantec Corp (*www.symantec.com*).

Planning for Disaster Recovery

The time to prepare for a disaster is before it occurs. If you have not prepared, the damage from a disaster will most likely be greater than if you had made and followed disaster plans. Suppose the hard drive on your PC stopped working and you lost all its data. What would be the impact? Are you prepared for this event? Backups are important, but you should also know how to use them to recover lost data. Also know when the backup was made and what to do to recover information entered since the last backup. Here's where careful recordkeeping can pay off.

When you perform a backup for the first time or set up a scheduled backup, verify that you can use the backup tape or disks to successfully recover the data. This is a very important step in preparing to recover lost data. After you have created a backup tape, erase a file on the hard drive, and use the recovery procedures to verify that you can recreate the file from the backup. This verifies that the tape or floppy disk works, that the recovery software is effective, and that you know how to use it. After you are convinced that the recovery works, document how to perform the recovery.

Verify that your recovery plan will work by practicing it before a disaster occurs.

Always record your regular backups in a table with the following information:

- The folders or drives backed up
- The date of the backup
- The type of backup
- The name of the tape used

Refer to this table to recover data that was lost days or weeks before you discovered that it should be recovered. Keep the records in a notebook. You can also store the records in a log file (a file where events are logged or recorded) each time you back up.

Volume Types and Fault Tolerance

A+ OS 2.1 2.2

Some methods of hard drive partitioning are more fault tolerant than others. **Fault tolerance** is the ability of a computer to respond to a fault or catastrophic event, such as a hardware failure or power outage, in such a way that data is not lost. One data duplication method is **RAID (redundant array of inexpensive disks)**, which involves writing data to multiple hard drives to provide better performance and data recovery. The different types of volumes and types of RAID are listed and described in Table 11-2.

Table 11-2 Types of volumes and RAID levels

Volume Type or RAID Level	Intended Purpose	Description
Simple	Uses only a single hard drive	Simple volumes on dynamic disks are equivalent to the basic drive.
Spanned	Increases system performance and volume capacity	Data fills up one drive before moving on to the next. The set of drives is treated as a single volume (a single virtual drive). Reading from more than one disk can improve performance.
RAID 0: Disk striping without parity	Increases system performance and volume capacity	With disk striping, data is alternately written to two or more hard drives, creating a single logical drive on one or more physical drives. Because more than one drive is doing the work, performance improves.
RAID 1: Disk mirroring or disk duplexing	Provides fault tolerance	Data is written twice, once to each of two drives. Disk mirroring uses only a single HDD controller. Disk duplexing uses two controllers, one for each drive.
RAID 5: Disk striping with parity	Increases performance and volume capacity and provides fault tolerance	Data is written to three or more drives, and parity information is distributed across these drives, so that if one drive fails, the other drives can re-create the data stored on the failed drive.

Windows 9x does not support fault-tolerant methods. Windows NT uses a slightly different terminology to describe fault-tolerant volumes than does Windows 2000/XP. Table 11-3 summarizes which methods are used by the various OSs. The table uses the prevalent terms that are used in each OS documentation to describe the methods supported.

A+ OS 2.1 2.2

Table 11-3 Types of volumes and RAID used in different versions of Windows

Windows Version	Volume Types Supported
Windows 9x	---
Windows NT	RAID-0 (striped), RAID-1 (mirrored), RAID-5
Windows 2000	Simple, spanned, striped (RAID-0), mirrored (RAID-1), RAID-5
Windows XP	Simple, spanned, striped (RAID-0), mirrored (RAID-1), RAID-5

Windows 2000 Professional and Windows XP support RAID 0 and call it a striped volume. In addition to spanned volumes and striped volumes, Windows 2000 Server and Windows XP support RAID 1, which they call a mirrored volume, and RAID 5, which they call a RAID-5 volume.

To create any type of RAID volume under Windows 2000 or Windows XP, you must use dynamic drives. However, if you are upgrading from Windows NT and already have a RAID system set up, Windows 2000 and Windows XP support the setup using basic drives. The primary advantage of using dynamic drives over basic drives is that the 1-MB database not only contains information about the volumes on its hard drive, but also contains information about all volumes on all hard drives in the system. This database is automatically replicated on all drives. If one database fails, it is quickly and automatically restored using a copy of the database on another drive. Dynamic drives have little advantage for a system with only a single hard drive, especially considering that only Windows 2000 and Windows XP can read dynamic drives.

11

VIRUSES AND OTHER COMPUTER INFESTATIONS

A+ OS 3.3

A computer support person needs to know how to protect computers against computer infestations (including viruses), how to recognize them, and how to get rid of them. Understanding what infestations are, how they work, and where they hide helps technicians deal with them successfully. A computer **infestation** is any unwanted program that is transmitted to a computer without the knowledge of the user or owner, and is designed to do varying degrees of damage to data and software. Computer infestations do not damage PC hardware, although, when boot sector information is destroyed on a hard drive, it can appear as though the hard drive is physically damaged. What most people refer to as viruses really fall into four categories of computer infestations: viruses, Trojan horses, worms, and logic bombs. The four types of infestations differ in the way they spread, what damage they do, and how they hide.

Because viruses are by far the most common of the four kinds of computer infestations, one of the most important defenses against computer infestations is **antivirus (AV) software** that is designed to discover and remove a virus. This section looks at several AV programs and how to use them effectively.

Understanding Computer Infestations

A+ OS 3.3

A **virus** is a program that can replicate by attaching itself to other programs. The infected program must be executed for a virus to run. The virus might then simply replicate, or also do damage by immediately performing some harmful action. A virus might be programmed to perform a negative action in the future, such as on a particular date (for instance, Friday the 13th), or when some logic within the host program is activated.

A virus is different from a **worm**, a program that spreads copies of itself throughout a network without a host program. A worm is seldom seen except on a network, where it creates problems by overloading the network as it replicates. Worms do damage by their presence rather than by performing a specific damaging act, as a virus does. A worm overloads memory or hard drive space by replicating repeatedly.

A **Trojan horse** is a third type of computer infestation that, like a worm, does not need a host program to work; rather it substitutes itself for a legitimate program. Trojan horses cannot replicate themselves. (This last statement has some exceptions. One Trojan horse program was disguised as an automatic backup utility downloadable from the Internet. When used, it created backups and replicated itself to the backups. It was programmed to damage several systems on Friday the 13th. In this case, the Trojan horse program is also considered a virus because of its ability to replicate.) Because Trojan horse infestations cannot replicate and require human intervention to move from one location to another, they are not as common as viruses.

A **logic bomb** is dormant code added to software and is triggered by a predetermined time or event. For example, an employee might put code into a program to destroy important files if his or her name is ever removed from the payroll file. Also, viruses, Trojan horses, logic bombs, and worms can occur in combination such as when a virus gains access to a network by way of a Trojan horse. The virus plants a logic bomb within application software on the network that sets off a worm when it executes.

Where Viruses Hide

A program is called a virus because (1) it has an incubation period (does not do damage immediately), (2) it is contagious (can replicate itself), and (3) it is destructive. There are several types of viruses and methods that viruses use to avoid detection by antivirus software.

Boot Sector Virus A boot sector virus hides in a boot sector program. It can hide on a hard drive either in the program code of the Master Boot Record or in the boot record program that loads the OS on the active partition of the hard drive. On a floppy disk, a boot sector virus hides in the boot program of the boot sector. One of the most common ways a virus spreads is from a floppy disk used to boot a PC. When the boot program is loaded into memory, so is the virus, which can then spread to other programs.

A+ OS 3.3

Many CMOS setups have an option that prevents writing to the boot sector of the hard drive, which can protect against some boot sector viruses. This feature must be turned off before installing Windows 9x, or Windows NT/2000/XP, which must write to the boot sector during installation. Windows 9x does not tell you that you must turn the feature off and start the installation over until about halfway through the installation.

File Viruses A **file virus** hides in an executable (.exe or .com) program or in a word-processing document that contains a macro. A **macro** is a small program contained in a document and can be automatically executed when the document is first loaded, or later by pressing a key combination. For example, a word-processing macro might automatically read the system date and copy it into a document when you open the document. Viruses that hide in macros of document files are called macro viruses. **Macro viruses** are the most common viruses spread by e-mail, hiding in macros of attached document files.

One well-known example of a macro virus is Melissa, first introduced on Friday, March 26, 1999, in a Word 97 macro. The virus immediately spread around the world within one working day. The e-mail that initially spread Melissa looked like this:

```
From: (name of infected user)
Subject: Important Message From (name of infected user)
To: (50 names from alias list)
Here is that document you asked for ... don't show  anyone
else ;-)
Attachment: LIST.DOC
```

11

When the recipient opened the document, a macro executed and immediately e-mailed the List.doc to 50 e-mail addresses listed in the user's address book. The virus infected other Word documents, which, when e-mailed, also spread the virus.

Melissa drops its payload, or activates, when a document is opened when the minutes of the hour match the day of the month (for example, at 09:18 on the 18th day of a month). It then inserts a phrase from the Simpsons TV show into the current document.

One type of file virus searches a hard drive for files with .exe file extensions and then creates another file with the same filename with a .com file extension, and stores itself there. When the user launches a program, the OS first looks for the program name with the .com file extension. It then finds and executes the virus. The virus is loaded into memory and loads the program with the .exe extension. The user appears to have launched the desired program. The virus is then free to do damage or spread itself to other programs.

Multipartite Viruses A **multipartite virus** is a combination of a boot sector virus and a file virus. It can hide in either type of program.

Cloaking Techniques

A virus is programmed to attempt to hide from antivirus (AV) software. AV software can only detect viruses that are identical or similar to ones it has been programmed to search out and recognize. AV software detects a known virus by looking for distinguishing characteristics called the **virus signature**, which is why it is important to update your AV software.

A+ OS 3.3

Antivirus software cannot detect a virus it does not know to look for. Therefore, upgrade your AV software regularly, to keep your protection current as new viruses are discovered.

A virus attempts to hide from AV software in two ways: by changing its distinguishing characteristics (its signature) and by attempting to mask its presence. Three types of viruses that are categorized according to their cloaking techniques are polymorphic, encrypting, and stealth viruses, which are discussed next.

Polymorphic Viruses A **polymorphic virus** changes its distinguishing characteristics as it replicates. Mutating in this way makes it more difficult for AV software to recognize the presence of the virus.

Encrypting Viruses One key symptom AV software looks for is a program that can replicate itself. An **encrypting virus** can transform itself into a nonreplicating program to avoid detection. However, it must revert to a replicating program to spread or replicate and can then be detected by AV software.

Stealth Viruses A **stealth virus** actively conceals itself, using one or more of the following techniques:

- Because AV software can detect a virus by noting the difference between a program's file size before the virus has infected it and after the virus is present, the virus alters OS information to mask the size of the file it is hiding in.
- The virus monitors when files are opened or closed. When it sees that the file it is hiding in is about to be opened, it temporarily removes itself or substitutes a copy of the file that does not include the virus. The virus keeps a copy of this uninfected file on the hard drive just for this purpose.

The Damage an Infestation Can Cause

Viruses, worms, and Trojan horses have not been known to physically damage a hard drive or other hardware device. The damage they do ranges from minor, such as displaying bugs crawling around on a screen, to major, such as erasing everything written on a hard drive. Infestation damage is called the payload and can be accomplished in a variety of ways. A virus can be programmed to drop its payload only in response to a triggering event such as a date, opening a certain file, or pressing a certain key. Figure 11-12 shows the results of a harmless virus that simply displays garbage on the screen.

How Infestations Spread

Understanding how infestations spread is essential to understanding how to protect your computer against them. Some computers are more vulnerable than others, depending on user habits. Below is a list of user activities that make a computer susceptible to infestations.

- Trading floppy disks containing program files
- Connecting the computer to an unprotected network

A+ OS 3.3

- Buying software from unreliable sources
- Downloading programs from the Internet
- Using floppy disks from unknown sources
- Using shared network programs
- Using used, preformatted floppy disks
- Reading e-mail that automatically executes a word processor to read attached files
- Executing attachments to e-mail messages without first scanning them for viruses
- Not write-protecting original program disks

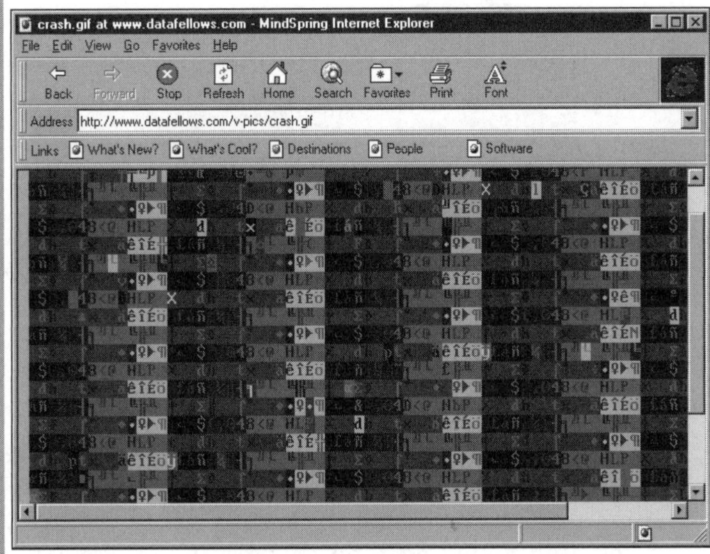

Figure 11-12 The crash virus appears to be destructive, making the screen show only garbage, but does no damage to the hard drive data

How a Virus Replicates Once a program containing a virus is copied to your PC, the virus can spread only when the infected program is executed. The process is shown in Figure 11-13. Recall from earlier chapters that the first step in executing a program, whether it is stored in a program file or in a boot sector, is to load the program into memory. Viruses hidden in a program can then be executed from memory. A virus can either be a **memory-resident virus** and stay in memory, still working, even after the host program is terminated, or a **non-memory-resident virus**, which means that it is terminated when the host program is closed.

After a virus is loaded into memory, it looks for other programs that are loaded into memory. When it finds one, it copies itself there and into that same program file on disk. From Figure 11-13, you can see that a virus becomes more dangerous the longer it stays loaded into memory and the more programs that are opened while it is there. For this reason, if you want to use a computer that has been used by other people, such as in a computer lab,

A+ OS 3.3

always reboot before you begin work to clear memory of programs. Use a hard boot, not just a soft boot, to erase all memory-resident programs (including a memory-resident virus) from memory.

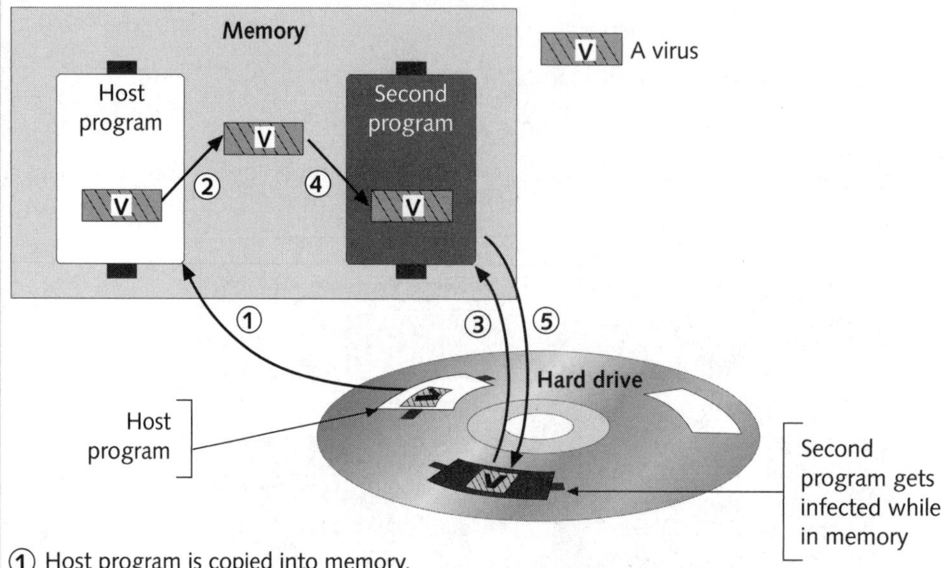

① Host program is copied into memory.
② The virus may or may not move itself to a new location in memory.
③ A second program is opened and copied into memory.
④ The virus copies itself to the second program in memory.
⑤ The newly infected second program is written back to the hard drive.

Figure 11-13 How a virus replicates

How a Trojan Horse Gets into Your Computer A Trojan horse is an infestation that masquerades as a legitimate program. One interesting example of a Trojan horse is the AOL4FREE program. Originally this was an illegal program that could provide unauthorized access to America Online. After the program's usefulness was blocked by AOL, a new program emerged, also called AOL4FREE, which was not an online access program, but a destructive Trojan horse. People passed the program around, thinking that it would provide illegal access to AOL; however, if executed, it actually erased files on their hard drives.

A+ OS 3.3

Virus Hoaxes

A virus hoax is a letter or e-mail warning about a nonexistent virus. The warning is itself a pest because it overloads network traffic. Here's an example of a virus hoax e-mail message I received:

```
There is a new virus going around in the last couple of
days!! DO NOT open or even look at any mail that you get that
says: "Returned or Unable to Deliver." The virus will erase
your whole hard drive and attach itself to your computer
components and render them useless. Immediately delete any
mail items that say this. AOL has indicated this is a very
dangerous virus, and there is NO remedy for it at this time.
Please be careful and forward to all your online friends ASAP.
This is a new email virus and not a lot of people know about
it; just let everyone know, so they won't be a victim. Please
forward this email to your friends!!!
```

Viruses are getting more powerful every day, but it is unlikely that this message is accurate. It is unlikely that a virus can render computer components useless. No virus has been known to actually do physical damage to hardware, although viruses can cause a PC to be useless by destroying programs or data, and a few viruses have been able to attack system BIOS code on the motherboard. However, some can hide in word-processing documents containing macros that are attached to an e-mail message, and a few viruses are able to hide in Web pages that are transmitted as e-mail messages and interpreted by e-mail software when you first open the message. But most importantly, don't be gullible and take the bait by forwarding the message to someone else. The potential damage a hoax like this can do is to overload an e-mail system with useless traffic, which is the real intent of the hoax. When I received this e-mail, there were over a hundred names on the distribution list.

11

Before forwarding a virus warning, you can check the Web sites of virus software manufacturers such as the ones listed later in this section. In addition, here are some Web sites that specialize in debunking virus hoaxes:

- *hoaxbusters.ciac.org* by Computer Incident Advisory Capability
- *www.hoaxinfo.com* by Jeff Richards
- *www.hoaxkill.com* by Oxcart Software
- *www.viruslist.com* by Kaspersky Lab
- *www.vmyths.com* by Rhode Island Soft Systems, Inc

These are many sources for checking for virus hoaxes. Using a search engine, type "virus hoax," a similar phrase, or the name of the virus or virus warning, and you'll find a wealth of information. Always check before sending!

Protecting Against Computer Infestations

A+ OS 3.3

You can do a lot to protect your computer against viruses and other infestations. Your first line of defense is to regularly make backups and use antivirus software. After that, use wisdom when managing programs. Here are some general guidelines:

- Buy antivirus software and set your computer to automatically run the AV program at startup.
- Keep your AV software current by periodically downloading upgrades from the Internet. Many antivirus programs now offer an update feature that does this automatically.
- Set a virus scan program to automatically scan word-processing documents and other e-mail attachments as they are opened. Some Web-based e-mail clients, such as Yahoo! Mail, offer the option to scan attachments before downloading them.
- Establish and faithfully execute a plan to make scheduled backups of your hard drive to protect against potential infestation damage.
- Only buy software from reputable vendors.
- Don't trade program files on floppy disks.
- Don't use floppy disks from unknown sources, and always scan floppy disks for viruses, no matter where they came from.
- Download software from the Internet sparingly, and then always scan program files for viruses before executing them.
- Never use pirated software.
- Format floppy disks before first use.
- Write-protect original program floppy disks or use CDs to install programs.
- In a business environment, adopt strict company policies against using unauthorized software.
- Before using a running computer that others have already used, hard-boot the computer.
- Set your computer CMOS settings to boot from drive C, then drive A.
- Turn on antivirus protection for your MBR in the CMOS settings, if available.

Virus Symptoms

Here are some warnings that suggest a virus is at work:

- A message appears that a downloaded document contains macros, or an application asks whether it should run macros in a document. (It is best to disable macros if you cannot verify that they are from a trusted source and that they are free of viruses or worms.)

A+ OS 3.3

- A program takes longer than normal to load.
- The number and length of disk accesses seem excessive for simple tasks.
- Unusual error messages occur regularly.
- Less memory than usual is available.
- Files mysteriously disappear or appear.
- Strange graphics appear on your computer monitor, or the computer makes strange noises.
- There is a noticeable reduction in disk space.
- The system cannot recognize the hard drive when you have booted from a floppy disk.
- The system cannot recognize the CD-ROM drive, although it has worked earlier.
- Executable files have changed size.
- Executable files that once worked no longer work and give unexpected error messages.
- The access lights on the hard drive and floppy drive turn on when there should not be any activity on that device. (However, sometimes an OS will perform routine maintenance on the drive when the system has been inactive for a while.)
- Files constantly become corrupted.
- Strange or bizarre error messages appear.
- DOS or Windows error messages about the FAT or partition table are displayed.
- The hard drive boots but hangs up before getting a DOS prompt or Windows desktop.
- File extensions or file attributes change without reason.
- A message is displayed from the virus scanner software.
- The number of bad sectors on the hard drive continues to increase.
- The MEM command reveals unfamiliar TSRs loaded into memory.

What to Do When You Suspect a Virus Infestation

If you suspect a virus, run a virus scan program to detect and delete the virus. If the antivirus software is not already installed, you can still use it. Consult the documentation for instructions on how to proceed. In many cases, the installation process detects the virus and eliminates it before continuing the installation. However, if the AV software does not recognize the virus, or if the virus successfully hides, the AV program cannot detect the virus. If the AV software found nothing, but you still suspect a virus, get the latest upgrade

A+ OS 3.3

of your AV software and try it or another AV program. Also download recent virus definitions; these are usually part of automatic AV software updates. If you know the name of the virus, check the Web site of the antivirus software for information about the virus and how to remove it.

Table 11-4 lists some popular antivirus software and Web sites that provide information about viruses.

Table 11-4 Antivirus software and information

Antivirus Software	Web Site
Norton AntiVirus by Symantec, Inc.	*www.symantec.com*
Dr. Solomon's Software	*www.drsolomon.com*
McAfee VirusScan by McAfee Associates, Inc.	*www.mcafee.com*
ESafe by Aladdin Knowledge Systems, Ltd.	*www.esafe.com*
F-Prot by Frisk Software International	*www.f-prot.com*
Command AntiVirus by Command Software	*www.commandcom.com*
PC-cillin by Trend Micro (for home use)	*www.antivirus.com*
NeaTSuite by Trend Micro (for networks)	*www.antivirus.com*

When selecting antivirus software, look for the ability to do the following:

- Download new software upgrades and virus definitions from the Internet so that your software knows about new viruses
- Automatically execute at startup
- Detect macros in a word-processing document as it is loaded by the word processor
- Automatically monitor files being downloaded from the Internet, including e-mail attachments and attachments sent during a chat session such as when using AOL Instant Messenger.
- The ability to both automatically and manually scan for viruses

Using Antivirus Software

Antivirus software can work at different times to scan your hard drive or a floppy disk for viruses. Most AV software can be configured to scan memory and the boot sector of your hard drive for viruses each time your PC is booted. Often it's not practical to have it scan the entire hard drive each time you boot, because that takes too much time. Consider scheduling the AV software to run at the same time every day, such as during the lunch hour.

Some AV software can run continuously in the background and scan all programs that are executed. However, the software can cause problems with other software, especially during installations. If you are having a problem installing a new application, try terminating your AV software first.

A+ OS 3.3 Make sure your AV software can scan files as they are downloaded from the Internet or a network, and that it can scan documents for macro viruses each time a document is opened by a word processor. Make sure the AV software can scan both files and boot sectors of hard drives and disks.

CHAPTER SUMMARY

- Disk compression works by storing data on a drive in one big file and managing how data and programs are written to that file, and by rewriting data files in a mathematically coded format that uses less space. Most compression software combines these two methods.
- Volumes can be compressed under Windows 2000 as long as they are using NTFS.
- Disk caching uses temporary storage to speed up access to hard drive data and can be controlled either by hardware or software.
- DOS used buffers rather than disk caching. Windows 3.x and 9x used built-in caching programs. Windows NT/2000/XP use automated caching.
- Three third-party utility software programs used to work with hard drives are Norton Utilities, SpinRite, and PartitionMagic.
- Hard drive problems can be caused by corruption in OS files, the partition table, the boot record, the root directory, the FAT, sector markings, or data itself.
- For DOS or Windows to be able to access a hard drive using the FAT file system, the following items must be intact, listed in the order in which they are accessed: the partition table, the boot record, the FAT, the root directory, the system files, and data and program files.
- The child, parent, grandparent backup method involves reusing tapes by making daily, weekly, and monthly backups.
- A full backup backs up all data from a hard drive. A differential backup backs up files that have changed or been created since the last full backup. An incremental backup backs up only files that have changed or been created since the last backup, whether or not it was a full backup.
- You can create backups using utilities included with tape drives or with Windows, or you can purchase third-party software.
- Disk cloning replicates a hard drive to a new computer.
- It is important to create and test a plan for disaster recovery, including keeping records of backups and recovery procedures.
- To create a RAID volume using Windows 2000 or Windows XP, you must use a dynamic drive.
- Viruses, which replicate by attaching themselves to other programs, are the most common type of computer infestation. Other types include Trojan horses, worms, and logic bombs.
- Viruses can hide in the boot sector, files, macros within files, or in both the boot sector and a file.
- Types of viruses that attempt to hide from antivirus software are polymorphic viruses, encrypting viruses, and stealth viruses.

- Damage from viruses ranges from an altered monitor display to the erasure of files, or even an entire hard drive.
- Use antivirus software both to clean out known viruses and to scan regularly for undetected and unmanifested ones.

Key Terms

antivirus (AV) software
buffer
child, parent, grandparent backup method
compressed drive
CVF (compressed volume file)
differential backup
disk cache
disk cloning
disk compression
disk imaging
DriveSpace
encrypting virus
fault tolerance
file virus
full backup
hardware cache
host drive
incremental backup
infestation
logic bomb
macro
macro virus
memory-resident virus
multipartite virus
non-memory-resident virus
polymorphic virus
RAID (redundant array of inexpensive disks or **redundant array of independent disks)**
SMARTDrive
software cache
stealth virus
Trojan horse
VCACHE
virus
virus signature
worm

Review Questions

1. Explain two disadvantages of data compression.
2. Give the most common drive letter and the filename for a host drive used for data compression.
3. Explain how DriveSpace compresses a drive.
4. What file system is it necessary for a volume to be using if it is to be compressed under Windows 2000?
5. How is a hardware cache different from a software cache?
6. Name and define the method DOS used to speed up disk access.
7. How is disk caching accomplished in Windows 2000? Windows 9x? Windows 3.x with DOS?
8. List three third-party utility programs used to support hard drives.
9. List the name and function of two common Norton Utilities programs.
10. List at least four causes of hard drive problems.
11. What items must be intact in order for DOS or Windows to be able to access a hard drive using the FAT file system? List them in the order in which they are accessed.
12. What error message might appear if the partition table is damaged? The boot record? The FAT? The system files?

13. If a file header is lost or corrupted and an application needs that header to read the file, how can you recover the contents of the file?
14. Explain how lost clusters are caused and what you can do to recover from them.
15. If an erased file is not found in the Recycle Bin, what command can you use at a command prompt to attempt to recover the file?
16. Explain the child, parent, grandparent method of making backups.
17. What is the difference between an incremental backup and a differential backup?
18. What versions of Windows support incremental backups? Differential backups?
19. What is the Windows Scripting Host utility used for, and what is the command line to execute it?
20. What process is used to replicate a hard drive to a new computer? When might you use this process, and what are some examples of software designed to perform it?
21. Why should you create a disaster recovery plan? What type of information would you include in it?
22. Which method of fault tolerance is the least expensive per MB of storage, disk duplexing or disk striping with parity? Explain your answer.
23. Does RAID 0 provide fault tolerance? Explain your answer.
24. Which Windows OS does not support any fault-tolerant method?
25. What is the term that Windows 2000 and Windows XP use for RAID 0?
26. Define and explain the differences between viruses, worms, logic bombs, and Trojan horses.
27. Where can viruses hide?
28. Name three ways that a virus can hide from antivirus software.
29. Are boot sector viruses limited to hard drives? Explain.
30. What is the most likely way that a virus will get access to your computer?

HANDS-ON PROJECTS

Using Windows 9x to Manage a Hard Drive

1. Using the chapter example of Windows 9x DriveSpace, practice disk compression by compressing two floppy disks. Use one newly formatted disk and one disk about half full of data. Compare the results of the two compressions.
2. With your instructor's permission, use the Defragmenter utility to defragment the hard drive of your computer. Don't use this utility if your disk has been compressed by a utility program other than Windows 9x. If you have used a program other than Windows 9x to compress the drive, look at the documentation for your compression software to see if it offers a defragmenting utility, and use that to defragment the drive.
3. If you are not using add-on utility software to compress your hard drive, use Windows9x ScanDisk to repair any cross-linked or lost clusters on the drive. If you are using utility software other than Windows 9x to compress your hard drive, use that software utility to scan for cross-linked or lost clusters.

Creating a Preventive Maintenance and Disaster Recovery Plan

Assume that you are a PC technician responsible for all of the 30 to 35 PCs of a small organization. The PCs are networked to a file server that is backed up each evening. No PC has power protection or line conditioning. Although some users make backups of data on their PC to tape drives or Zip drives, the company does not have a procedure to back up data or software. Your supervisor has asked you to submit a preventive maintenance and disaster recovery plan for these PCs and to estimate the amount of time you will spend each month for the next 12 months on preventive maintenance. She has also asked you to submit a suggested PC data backup plan for all users to follow, which will become a company policy. Do the following to create these plans and estimate your time:

1. List the possible causes of PC failures.
2. Using the list above, list what you can do to prevent these problems. Divide the list into two categories: what you plan to do one time for each PC or user, and what you plan to do on a routine or as-needed basis.
3. For each PC, estimate the amount of time you need to implement the one-time-only plan and the amount of time you need each year for ongoing maintenance.
4. Based on your answers to Question 3, how much time do you plan to spend, on average, each month for the next 12 months on preventive maintenance?
5. In response to the request for a recommended company policy to back up PC data, write a policy for users to follow to back up data on their PCs. Since all PCs are networked to the file server, suggest that company policy be that data on a PC should be backed up to the file server, where it will be backed up nightly in case of a file server failure. Write the backup policy and instructions on how to use it.

Using Windows to Back Up Files and Folders

This exercise lets you practice using Windows Microsoft Backup and see how the Backup utility manages several situations.

Part I

1. Using Windows Explorer, create a folder called **Backtest** on a hard drive.
2. Use Explorer to find a .txt file, and copy it to the new folder. Copy two other files to the Backtest folder. Make a subfolder called **Subfolder** in Backtest and copy a fourth file to C:\backtest\subfolder.
3. Right-click the **.txt** file and rename it **Overwrite.txt**. Right-click the second file and rename it Delete.txt. Rename the third file **NoChange.txt**. The fourth file can be left alone for now. Use Explorer and write down the file sizes before the backup.
4. Click **Start**, **Programs**, **Accessories**, **System Tools**, and **Backup**.
5. Use the directions provided in this book to back up the folder Backtest to a floppy disk. Use Explorer and compare the backup file size to the original file sizes. How are they different?
6. Delete the file **Delete.txt**. Edit and change the contents of the file Overwrite.txt. Make no changes to the file NoChange.txt. Delete **Subfolder**.

7. Using Windows Backup, restore the files from the backup to their original folder.
   a. What did Backup do with the Delete.txt file?
   b. What did Backup do with the Overwrite.txt file?
   c. What did Backup do with the NoChange.txt file?
   d. What did Backup do with the missing Subfolder and missing file?
   e. What is the name of the backup file on the floppy disk?
   f. What are the name and path to the error log created by Backup?
   g. Print the error log.

Part II

8. Use Windows Explorer to copy the Backtest folder to a second floppy disk.
9. Delete all the files in the Backtest folder on the hard drive.
10. Use Windows Explorer to copy the three files back to the Backtest folder.
11. Delete the files in the Backtest folder on the hard drive.
12. Open the Recycle Bin and restore the three files to the Backtest folder by highlighting the selected files and using the File, Restore option. Did they return to the correct folder
13. Once again, delete the files in the Backtest folder on the hard drive.
14. Highlight the three files in the Recycle Bin, and click **File**, **Delete**. Can you still restore the files?

Using the Internet to Learn About Viruses

One source of information about viruses on the Web is F-Secure Corporation. Go to the Web site *www.f-secure.com/v-descs*, shown in Figure 11-14, for information about viruses; the viruses are listed in alphabetical order with complete descriptions, including any known source of the virus. Print a description of three viruses from this Web site:

1. One virus that destroys data on a hard drive
2. One harmless virus that only displays garbage on the screen
3. One virus that hides in a boot sector

Download the Latest Update of AV Software

If you own antivirus software, download the latest antivirus definition list from the Internet. For example, for Norton AntiVirus, follow these directions:

1. Log on to the AV site: *www.symantec.com/downloads*
2. Click **Virus Definitions Updates**, and then click **Download Virus Definitions**. Select your Norton Antivirus product and operating system.

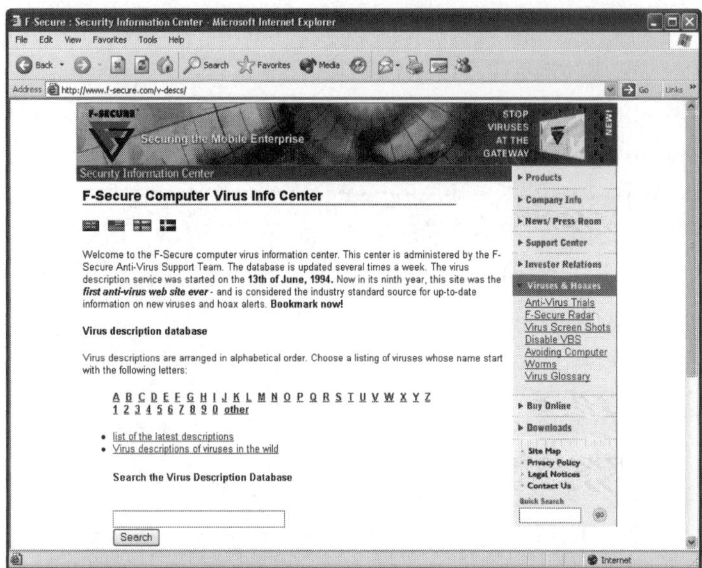

Figure 11-14 For complete virus information, see the Data Fellows web site

3. Follow the directions to download the latest update and signature list for the particular version of your AV software.
4. While online, see if the site offers information on virus hoaxes and create a list of hoaxes if it does.

CHAPTER

12

WINDOWS ON A NETWORK

In this chapter, you will learn:

- About the basics of networking
- About different types of addresses used on networks
- How to connect to and share resources over a local area network
- How to control a computer remotely

When PCs were first introduced, they had to contain and manage all the resources they needed to accomplish the tasks for which they were used. The development of networks enabled computers to share resources and data. This chapter introduces basic networking concepts, outlines the different levels of network communication, explains how computers are identified on a network, and shows how to share computer resources over a network. You also learn how to use one computer to remotely control another, for example, when you supply technical support. This information is explained in the context of a local network; Windows on the Internet, which is the largest network of all, is covered in the next chapter.

NETWORKING BASICS

A+ OS 4.1

As a system of interlinked computers, a network needs both software and hardware to work. Hardware on a network includes a **NIC (network interface card)**, designed for the physical network technology used, as well as external devices such as **hubs**, which are used to join or connect the nodes of a local network. (Physical network technologies and devices are not covered in this book.)

Software includes an operating system installed on each computer on the network and perhaps a **NOS (network operating system)** to control the entire network and its resources. If the network is small (fewer than 20 computers), it can be a **peer-to-peer network**, in which each computer on the network has the same authority as the other computers. Recall from Chapter 6, that a Windows peer-to-peer network is called a workgroup. Larger networks use the **client/server** model, in which access to a network is controlled by a NOS using a centralized database. A **client** computer provides a user ID and password to a **server** that validates the data against the security database. In a Windows network, this server is called the domain controller, and the network model is called a domain. Popular network operating systems are Windows NT/2000, Windows.NET, Novell NetWare, Unix, and Linux. Windows has client software built in for Windows and Novell NetWare servers. Alternately, for Novell NetWare, you can install Novell client software.

A network can have more than one workgroup or domain in operation, and some computers might not belong to any workgroup or domain. A computer joins a workgroup or domain in order to share resources with other computers and devices in the group or domain. Company policy controls how many workgroups or domains can exist within the company network based on user needs, security concerns, and administrative overhead required to manage the groups.

How Network Communication Works

When you mail a letter using the U. S. Postal Service, you most likely are not aware of the many different systems involved in its successful delivery. Figure 12-1 shows a simple view of those systems. A sender drops a letter in the mail and therefore is communicating indirectly (virtually) with the recipient by way of the letter. The systems that take the letter from the mailbox to the hand of the receiver are the direct (physical) means of communication.

On any network (including the Internet, which you will learn more about in the next chapter), you will see many similarities with this analogy. Communication between two computers can be broken down into separate systems or layers. There are protocols for communication between the layers of the system. Each layer must communicate directly with the layers above it and below it through these established protocols. Virtual communication also takes place as one layer on the originating side communicates with its counterpart layer on the destination side.

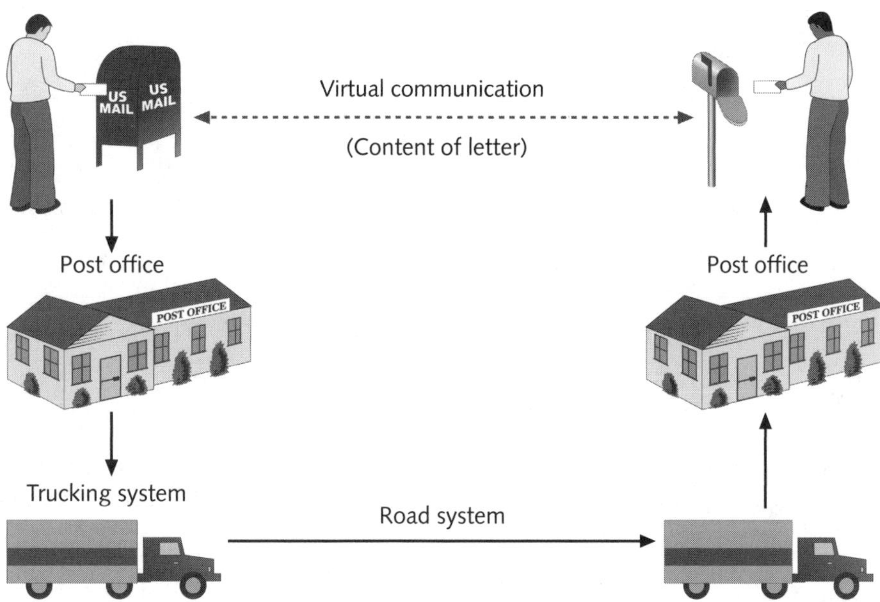

Figure 12-1 Communication is virtual between sender and receiver, but direct between adjacent systems in the Postal Service

Understanding Network Layers

12

When networks first began to be developed in the 1970s, there was little or no standardization in how communication between computers and other devices was to be accomplished. In an effort to identify and standardize all the levels of communication needed in networks, the **ISO (International Organization for Standardization)** developed a networking model called the **OSI (Open Systems Interconnect) reference model**, which is illustrated in Figure 12-2. The OSI reference model provides a universally accepted conceptual model of how data is transmitted on a network or between two or more networked devices. This model separates communication into seven layers that describe what happens within the operating system (top five layers) and the network card (lower two layers) so that two applications (such as a browser and a Web server) can communicate over a network. Each layer communicates directly with the layer just above it and the layer just below it. As with the postal system analogy of Figure 12-1, communication between adjacent layers is considered direct, but communication between matching layers is considered virtual because the matching layers are not directly connected (they have to communicate via the adjacent layers below them).

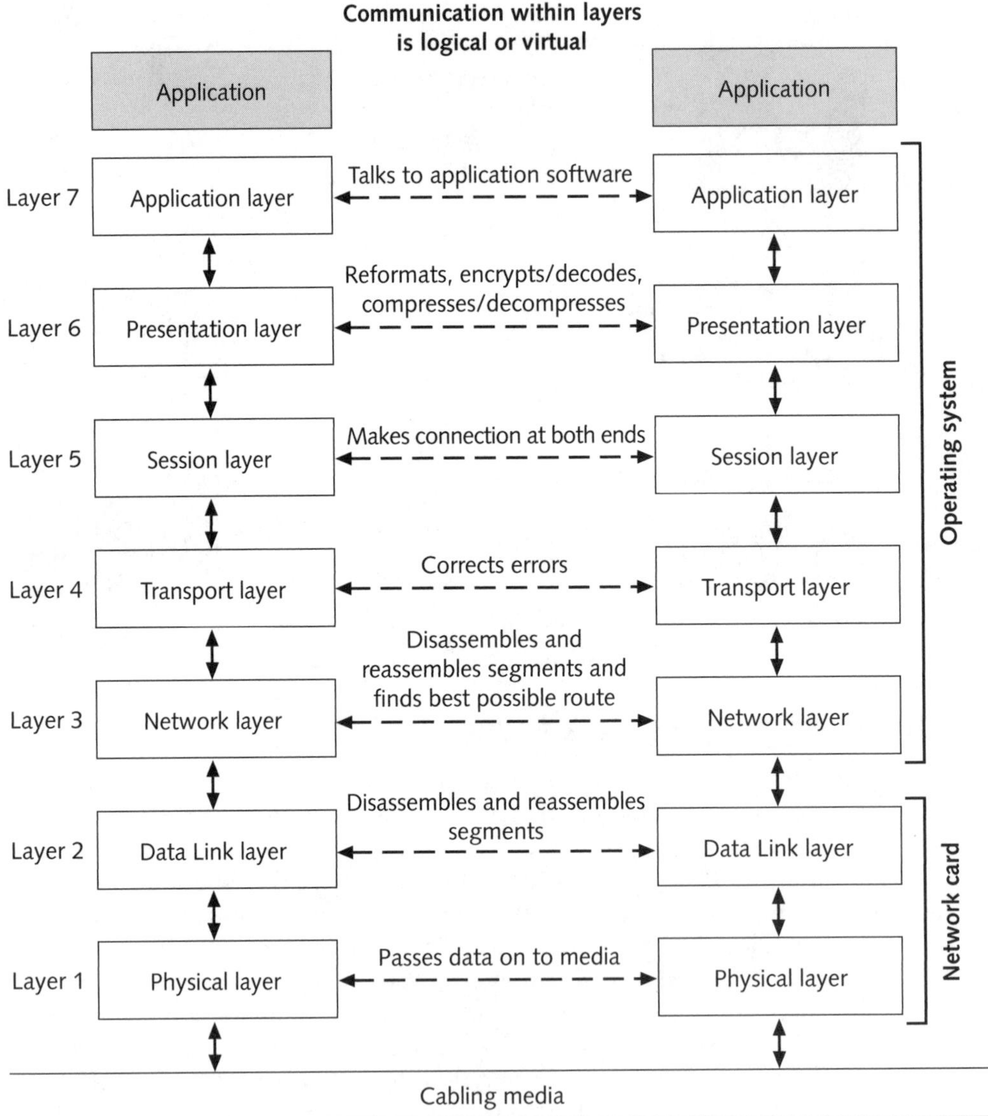

Figure 12-2 The OSI reference model identifies seven layers of network communication

Here is a short description of each layer in the OSI model.

- Application layer (Layer 7). The **Application layer** is responsible for interfacing with applications software such as word-processing programs or Web browsers.

- Presentation layer (Layer 6). The **Presentation layer** receives requests for files from the Application layer and presents the requests to the Session layer. The Presentation layer reformats, compresses, or encrypts data as necessary.
- Session layer (Layer 5). The **Session layer** is responsible for establishing and maintaining a session between two networked stations or hosts (covered in more detail later in the chapter).
- Transport layer (Layer 4). The **Transport layer** is responsible for error checking and for requesting retransmission of data if it detects errors. The Transport layer might or might not guarantee successful transmission or delivery of data, depending on how sensitive the transmission is to some loss of data.
- Network layer (Layer 3). The **Network layer** divides a block of data into segments that are small enough to travel over a network and finds the best possible route by which to send them. These segments of data are called **packets**, **data packets**, or **datagrams** and contain data, along with special identifying information in headers and trailers at the beginning and end of the packet called **frames**.
- Data Link layer (Layer 2). The **Data Link layer** is responsible for receiving packets of data from the Network layer and presenting them to the Physical layer for transport. If the packets are too large, the Data Link layer breaks them up into even smaller packets.
- Physical layer (Layer 1). The **Physical layer** passes data packets on to the cabling or the wireless media involved in data transmission. At this point, the data is just bits to be passed on; the Physical layer does not distinguish the frames from the data that constitutes the body of the transmission.

As you study the OSI model and network communication, remember that not all networks have a separate layer that matches each of the seven OSI model layers. In fact, no network today perfectly follows this model, but it does serve the networking industry as a reference point for discussing different levels or layers within a network.

The OSI Model Applied to a Local Network

A+ OS 4.1

When setting up a network, you have a lot of choices to make. Suppose you are setting up a small peer-to-peer network. Let's look at networking decisions in the context of the OSI model, as illustrated in Figure 12-3. The Data Link and Physical layers of the OSI model are determined by the physical network structure you use. For example, if you decide to use Ethernet, the most popular physical network technology for a LAN, then you will buy Ethernet NICs, cables, and hubs. A **LAN (local area network)** is a network that covers a fairly small geographical area, usually confined to one building or to a small group of buildings that are physically close to each other.

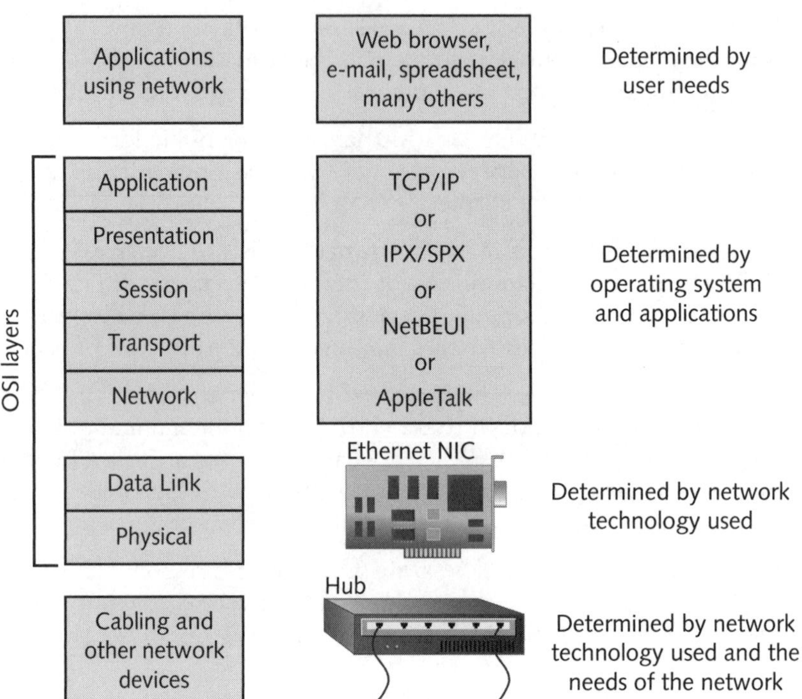

Figure 12-3 The applications, the operating system, and the network technology all determine how the OSI model is applied to a network

The top five layers are affected by choices about operating system, applications you need to support, and user needs. Which OS do you use? This decision is most likely driven by user needs and by what applications the network must support. Because so many applications are written for Windows, it is common to use Windows on computers connected to the network, and there is often a mix of several versions of Windows and other OSs on the same network. For example, a network might have a mix of computers using Windows 98, Windows NT, Windows 2000, Windows XP, Linux, and the Mac OS. As long as these operating systems can communicate using the same protocols, they can all coexist on the same network.

A+ OS 4.1

Windows supports three suites of protocols to be used at the top five layers of the OSI model, which are shown in Figure 12-3 and listed below. AppleTalk, which is shown in the figure but not listed here, is the default networking protocol for Macintosh computers.

- *TCP/IP (Transmission Control Protocol/Internet Protocol)* is the protocol suite used on the Internet and so should be your choice if you want to connect your network to the Internet, with each workstation having Internet access. Novell NetWare, Linux, Unix, and Mac OS also support TCP/IP.
- *IPX/SPX (Internetwork Packet Exchange/Sequenced Packet Exchange)* is a NW Link protocol suite designed for use with Novell NetWare NOS. It is somewhat similar to TCP/IP but is not supported on the Internet.

A+ OS 4.1

- *NetBEUI (Network BIOS Extended User Interface)* is a proprietary Windows protocol suite and is a good choice if your network is isolated from the Internet. NetBEUI is faster than TCP/IP but does not support routing to other networks and therefore is not supported on the Internet.

To use one of these protocols on a network, the first step is physically to connect the computer to the network by installing the NIC in the computer and connecting the network cable to the hub or other network device. The next step is to install the protocol in the operating system. Once the protocol is installed, it will automatically associate itself with any NICs it finds, which is called binding. **Binding** occurs when a higher-level protocol or OSI layer is associated with a lower-level protocol or layer. When the two protocols or layers are bound, communication continues between then until they are unbound, or released.

You can determine which protocols are installed in Windows by looking at the properties of a network connection. For example, for Windows 2000, from Control Panel, double-click the Network and Dial-up Connections icon. Then right-click the Local Area Connection icon (see Figure 12-4). The Local Area Connection Properties dialog box opens, as shown in the figure. In this figure, you can see that two of the three protocols provided with Windows 2000 are installed because they are checked. In this situation, this PC is using a TCP/IP network, but one network printer on the network uses IPX/SPX and does not support TCP/IP. Because this PC uses that printer, it must have IPX/SPX installed. (A **network printer** is a printer that is accessible by users on the network, either through its own network card and connection to the network, through a connection to a standalone print server, or through being connected to a computer as a local printer, which is shared on the network.) There is no problem with more than one networking protocol operating on the network at the same time.

You have just seen how an operating system uses TCP/IP or IPX/SPX to manage the network connection between applications and devices such as a network printer. The protocol used on a network is bound to the NIC, and more than one protocol can be bound to a NIC. The NIC uses the two lower layers of the OSI model, which are dependent on the network technology used, such as Ethernet or token ring. TCP/IP is the most popular networking protocol because it's the most universal and the one used by the Internet. In the rest of the chapter, we'll focus on TCP/IP, but also point out important differences between this protocol and NetBEUI.

A+ OS 4.1

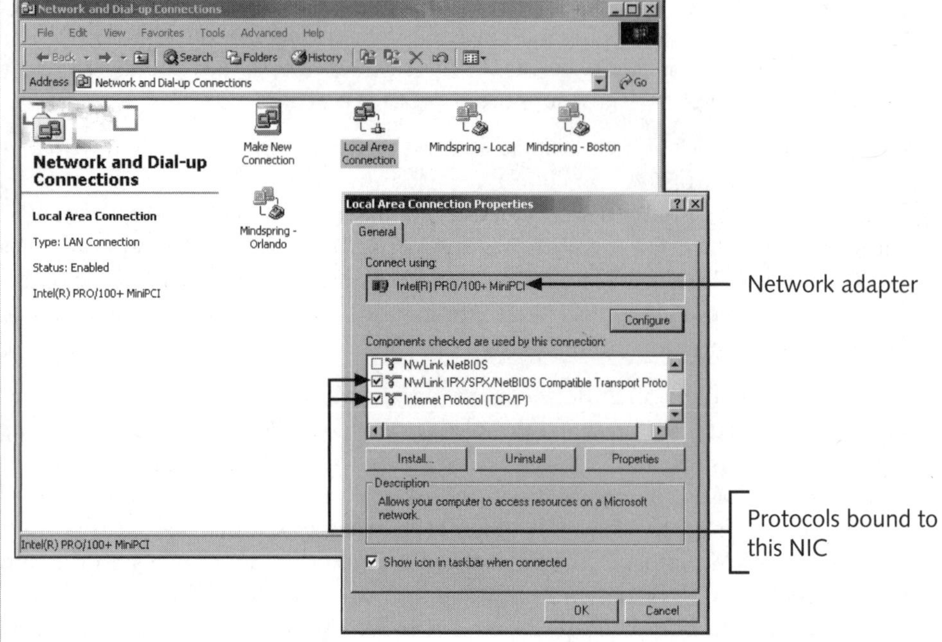

Figure 12-4 Two of three Windows 2000 network protocols are installed and bound to this network adapter

Addressing on a Network

Every device on a network has a unique address. Part of learning about a network is learning how a device (such as a computer or a printer) or a program (such as a Web server) is identified on the network. On a network, there are four methods used to identify devices and programs:

- A **MAC address (Media Access Control address)**, also known as a **physical address**, **adapter address**, or **hardware address**, is a unique address that is permanently embedded in a NIC and identifies a device on a LAN. A MAC address is a value that is expressed as six pairs of hexadecimal numbers and letters, often separated by hyphens. The MAC address is used only by hosts inside the local network and is not used outside the LAN. (A **host** is any computer or other device on a network that can be addressed on a network.)
- An **IP address** is a series of four numbers separated by dots that identifies a computer, printer, or other device on a TCP/IP network such as the Internet or an intranet. (An **intranet** is a company network that uses TCP/IP.) Each of the four numbers can be no larger than 255. An example of an IP address is 109.168.0.104. Consider a MAC address a local address and an IP address a long distance address.

A+ OS 4.1

- Character-based names, including domain names, host names, and **NetBIOS (Network Basic Input/Output System)** names, are used to identify a PC on a network with easy-to-remember letters rather than numbers. (**Host names** are used to identify hosts on a network.) In general, these character-based names are often called computer names.
- A port address is a number between 0 and 65,535 that identifies a program running on a computer. These port addresses are not the same as the I/O addresses discussed in previous chapters. Port addresses will be covered in the next chapter.

Figure 12-5 shows how each of these addresses relates to the OSI model. The sections that follow explain the different address types in more detail.

OSI model	Managing component	Identifying address
Application Presentation Session Transport Network	Operating system	Host name (joesmith.mycompany.com) NetBIOS name (joesmith) IP address (98.16.200.10)
Data Link Physical	Network card	MAC address (87-AA-17-D3-00-01)

Figure 12-5 How devices on a network are identified at different layers of the OSI model

12

MAC Addresses

A+ OS 4.1

A computer, network printer, or other device on a network connects to the network by way of a NIC. When a NIC is manufactured, it is assigned a MAC address at the factory that is unique to and most likely will never change for that card. No two MAC addresses are the same because of standards set by the **IEEE (Institute of Electrical and Electronics Engineers)**, which is a nonprofit organization that develops standards for the computer and electronics industries. The standard for MAC addresses was specified in RFC 802. An **RFC (Request for Comments)** begins as a suggestion for network specifications and may be developed into an accepted standard, as RFC 802 was for MAC addresses.

MAC addresses are used at the Data Link layer for computers on the same network to communicate. If a host does not know the MAC address of another host on the same network, it uses the higher-layer protocols to discover the MAC address. Because the Data Link layer protocols control traffic only on their own networks, computers on different networks cannot use their MAC addresses for communication. In order for the host to communicate with a host on another LAN across the corporate intranet or Internet, it must know the address of the host that is used by the TCP/IP protocols. These addresses are IP addresses (see Figure 12-6).

A+ OS 4.1

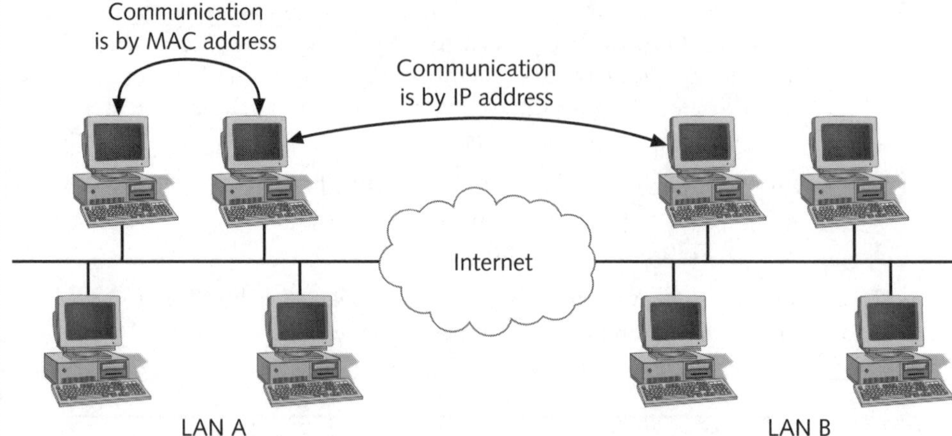

Figure 12-6 Computers on the same LAN use MAC addresses to communicate, but computers on different LANs use IP addresses to communicate over the Internet

If your PC is connected to the Internet or any other TCP/IP network, follow these directions to display the IP address and the NIC's MAC address in Windows 9x:

1. Click **Start**, **Run**. In the Run dialog box, type **winipcfg** and then press **Enter**. The IP Configuration window opens (see Figure 12-7).

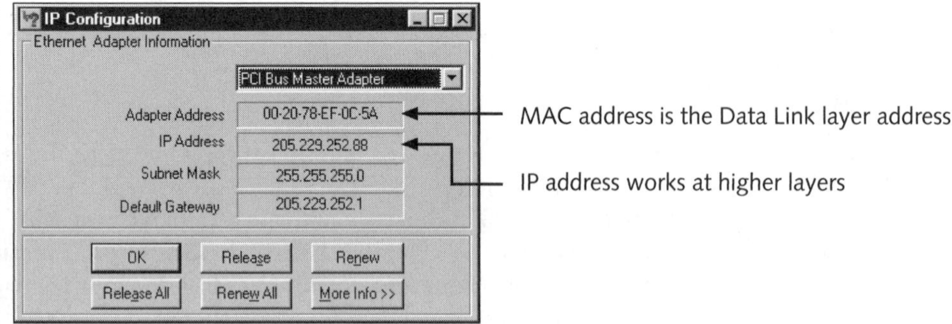

Figure 12-7 Use the Windows 9x Winipcfg utility to display a PC's IP address and MAC address

2. Click the NIC from the drop-down list of network devices. The Adapter Address displayed is the MAC address; in this case, it is 00-20-78-EF-0C-5A.
3. Click the **OK** button.

A+ OS 4.1 Windows NT, Windows 2000, and Windows XP use Ipconfig instead of Winipcfg. If you are using Windows 2000, follow these instructions to see your MAC address and IP address:

1. Click **Start**, **Programs**, **Accessories**, and then **Command Prompt**. A command prompt window is displayed.
2. At the command prompt, type **ipconfig/all |more**. The screen shown in Figure 12-8 is displayed.

```
Windows 2000 IP Configuration

Host Name ................................: JEAN2000
Primary DNS Suffix ....................:
Node Type.................................: Hybrid
IP Routing Enabled .....................: No
WINS Proxy Enabled..................: No
DNS Suffix Search List ...............: prestige.net

Ethernet adapter Local Area Connection:

Connection-specific DNS Suffix .: prestige.net
Description ................................: Intel(R) PRO/100+ MiniPCI
Physical Address .........................: 00-10-A4-90-1B-AA
DHCP Enabled...........................: Yes
Autoconfiguration Enabled ........: Yes
IP Address .................................: 192.168.1.101
Subnet Mask ..............................: 255.255.255.0
Default Gateway .........................: 192.168.1.1
DHCP Server ..............................: 192.168.1.1
DNS Servers...............................: 208.220.88.13
                                            64.8.16.13
Lease Obtained ..........................: Wednesday, August 01, 2001 2:14:06 AM
Lease Expires .............................: Tuesday, August 07, 2001 2:14:06 AM
```

Figure 12-8 Results of Windows 2000 Ipconfig/all |more command shows the current IP configuration including the subnet mask for this network

3. The |more option causes the results to appear one screen at a time instead of scrolling by too fast to read. Press **Enter** to see each screen.
4. To exit the command prompt window, type **Exit** at the command prompt.

IP Addresses

A+ OS 4.1 All the protocols of the TCP/IP suite identify a device on the Internet or an intranet by its IP address. An IP address is 32 bits long, made up of 4 bytes separated by periods, as in this address: 190.180.40.120. The largest possible 8-bit number is 11111111, which is equal to 255 in decimal, so the largest possible IP address in decimal is 255.255.255.255, which

A+ OS 4.1

in binary is 11111111.11111111.11111111.11111111. Each of the four numbers separated by periods is called an **octet** (for 8 bits) and can be any number from 0 to 255, making a total of 4.3 billion potential IP addresses (256 × 256 × 256 × 256). Because of the allocation scheme used to assign these addresses, not all of them are available for use.

The first part of an IP address identifies the network, and the last part identifies the host. It's important to understand how the bits of an IP address are used in order to understand how routing happens over interconnected networks such as the Internet and how the IP protocol is used to locate an IP address anywhere on the globe. When data is routed over interconnected networks, the network portion of the IP address is used to locate the right network. Once the data has arrived at the local network, the host portion of the IP address is used to identify one computer on the network that is to receive the data. Finally, the IP address of the host must be used to identify its MAC address so the data can travel on the host's LAN to that host. The next section explains this in detail.

Classes of IP Addresses

When a business, college, or some other organization applies for IP addresses, a range of addresses appropriate to the number of hosts on the organization's networks is assigned. IP addresses that can be used by companies and individuals are divided into three classes: Class A, Class B, and Class C, based on the number of possible IP addresses in each network within each class. IP addresses are assigned to these classes according to the scheme outlined in Table 12-1.

You can determine the class of an IP address and the size or type of company to which an address is licensed by looking at the address. More importantly, you also can determine what portion of an IP address is dedicated to identifying the network and what portion is used to identify the host on that network.

Table 12-1 Classes of IP addresses

Class	Network Octets (Blanks in the IP address stand for octets used to identify hosts.)	Total Number of Possible Networks or Licenses	Host Octets (Blanks in the IP address stand for octets used to identify networks.)	Total Number of Possible IP Addresses in Each Network
A	0.__.__.__ to 126.__.__.__	127	__.0.0.1 to __.255.255.254	16 million
B	128.0.__.__ to 191.155.__.__	16,000	__.__.0.1 to __.__.255.254	65,000
C	192.0.0.__ to 223.255.255.__	2,000,000	__.__.__.1 to __.__.__.254	254

Figure 12-9 shows how each class of IP address is divided into the network and host portions. A Class A address uses the first octet (leftmost) for the network address and the remaining octets for host addresses. A Class A license assigns a single number that is used in the first octet of the address, which is the network address. The remaining three octets of the IP address can be used for host addresses that uniquely identify each host on this

A+ OS 4.1 4.2 network. The first octet of a Class A license is a number between 0 and 126. For example, if a company is assigned 87 as its Class A network address, then 87 is used as the first octet for every host on this one network. Examples of IP addresses for hosts on this network are 87.0.0.1, 87.0.0.2, and 87.0.0.3. (The last octet does not use 0 or 255 as a value, so 87.0.0.0 would not be valid). In the example's address 87.0.0.1, the 87 is the network portion of the IP address, and 0.0.1 is the host portion of the address. Because three octets can be used for Class A host addresses, one Class A license can have approximately 256 × 256 × 254 host addresses, or about 16 million IP addresses. Only very large corporations with heavy communication needs can get a Class A license.

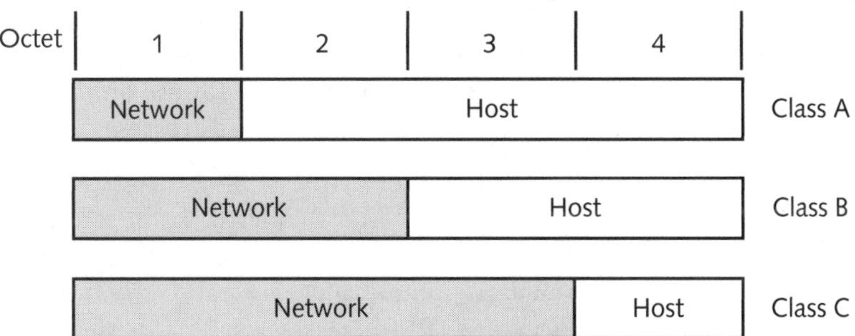

Figure 12-9 The network portion and host portion for each class of IP addresses

A Class B address uses the first two octets for the network portion and the last two for the host portion. A Class B license assigns a number for each of the first two leftmost octets, 12
leaving the third and fourth octets for host addresses. How many host addresses are there in one Class B license? The number of possible values for two octets is about 256 × 254 (some IP addresses are reserved, so these numbers are approximations), or about 65,000, host addresses in a single Class B license. The first octet of a Class B license is a number between 128 and 191, which gives about 63 different values for a Class B first octet. The second number can be between 0 and 255, so there are approximately 63 × 256, or about 16,000, Class B networks. For example, suppose a company is assigned 135.18 as the network address for its Class B license. The first two octets for all hosts on this network are 135.18, and the company uses the last two octets for host addresses. Examples of IP addresses on this company's Class B network are 135.18.0.1, 135.18.0.2, and 135.18.0.3. In the first example listed, 135.18 is the network portion of the IP address, and 0.1 is the host portion.

A Class C license assigns three octets as the network address. With only one octet used for the host addresses, there can be only 254 host addresses on a Class C network. The first number of a Class C license is between 192 and 223. For example, if a company is assigned a Class C license for its network with a network address of 200.80.15, some IP addresses on the network would be 200.80.15.1, 200.80.15.2, and 200.80.15.3.

Class D and Class E IP addresses are not available for general use. Class D addresses begin with the octet 224 through 239 and are used for **multicasting**, in which one host sends messages to multiple hosts, such as when it is transmitting a video conference over the Internet. Class E addresses begin with 240 through 254 and are reserved for research.

A+ OS 4.1

Different Ways of Assigning IP Addresses

When a small company is assigned a Class C license, it obtains 254 IP addresses for its use. If it has only a few hosts (say, less than 25 on a network), many IP addresses go unused, which is one of the reasons that there is a shortage of IP addresses. But suppose that the company grows and now has 300 workstations on the network and is running out of IP addresses. There are two approaches to solving this problem: (1) use private IP addresses, and (2) use dynamic IP addressing. Many companies use a combination of both methods. Following is an explanation of each of these solutions.

Public, Private, and Reserved IP Addresses

When a company applies for a Class A, B, or C license, it is assigned a group of IP addresses that are different from all other IP addresses and are available for use on the Internet. These IP addresses available to the Internet are called **public IP addresses**.

One thing to consider, however, is that not all of these 300 workstations need to have access to the Internet, even though they may be on the network. So, while each workstation may need an IP address to be part of the TCP/IP network, those not connected to the Internet don't need addresses that are unique and available to the Internet and therefore can use private IP addresses. **Private IP addresses** are IP addresses that are used on private intranets that are isolated from the Internet. Because the hosts are isolated from the Internet, no conflicts arise.

In fact, a small company most likely will not apply for a license of public IP addresses at all but instead solely rely on private IP addresses for its internal network. A company using TCP/IP can make up its own private IP addresses to use on its intranet. RFC 1918 recommends that the following IP addresses be used for private networks:

- 10.0.0.0 through 10.255.255.255
- 172.16.0.0 through 172.31.255.255
- 192.168.0.0 through 192.168.255.255

When assigning these isolated IP addresses, also keep in mind that a few IP addresses are reserved for special use by TCP/IP and should not be used. They are listed in Table 12-2.

Table 12-2 Reserved IP addresses

IP address	How it is used
255.255.255.255	Broadcast messages
0.0.0.0	A currently unassigned IP address
127.0.0.1	Indicates your own workstation

A+ OS 4.1 4.2

All IP addresses on a network must be unique for that network. A network administrator may assign an IP address to a standalone computer (for example, if someone is testing networking software on a PC that is not connected to the network). As long as the network is a private network, the administrator can assign any IP address he or she desires. On an isolated private network, the administrator is free to make up his or her own private IP addresses, although a good administrator avoids using the reserved addresses.

Dynamically Assigned IP Addresses

If an administrator must configure each host on a network manually, assigning it a unique IP address, the task of going from PC to PC to make these assignments and keeping up with which address is assigned to which PC can be an administrative nightmare. The solution is to have a server automatically assign an IP address to a workstation each time it comes onto the network. Instead of IP addresses being permanently assigned to workstations (called **static IP addresses**), an IP address is assigned for the current session only (called **dynamic IP addresses**). When the session is terminated, the IP address is returned to the list of available addresses. Because not all workstations are online at all times, fewer IP addresses than the total number of workstations can satisfy the needs of the network. Also, you can use private IP addresses for the range of IP addresses that can be assigned to workstations. When a workstation has an IP address assigned to it, it is said that the workstation is leasing the IP address. **Internet service providers (ISPs)**, organizations through which individuals and businesses connect to the Internet, use dynamic IP addressing for their subscribers.

The server that manages these dynamically assigned IP addresses is called a DHCP **(Dynamic Host Configuration Protocol)** server. In this arrangement, workstations are called DHCP clients. DHCP software resides on both the client and the server to manage the dynamic assignments of IP addresses. DHCP client software is built into Windows 9x and Windows NT/2000/XP.

When you configure a DHCP server, you specify the range of IP addresses that can be assigned to clients on the network. Figure 12-10 shows the configuration window for a DHCP server that is embedded as firmware on a router. The configuration window is accessed by using a Web browser on the network and entering the IP address of the router into the Web browser address box. In the figure, you can see that the router's IP address is 192.168.1.1, and the starting IP address to be assigned to clients is 192.168.1.100. Because the administration has specified that there can be up to 50 clients, the range of IP addresses is therefore 192.168.1.100 to 192.158.1.149. Also shown in the figure is a list of currently assigned IP addresses and the MAC address of the computer that currently leases that IP address.

A+ OS 4.1

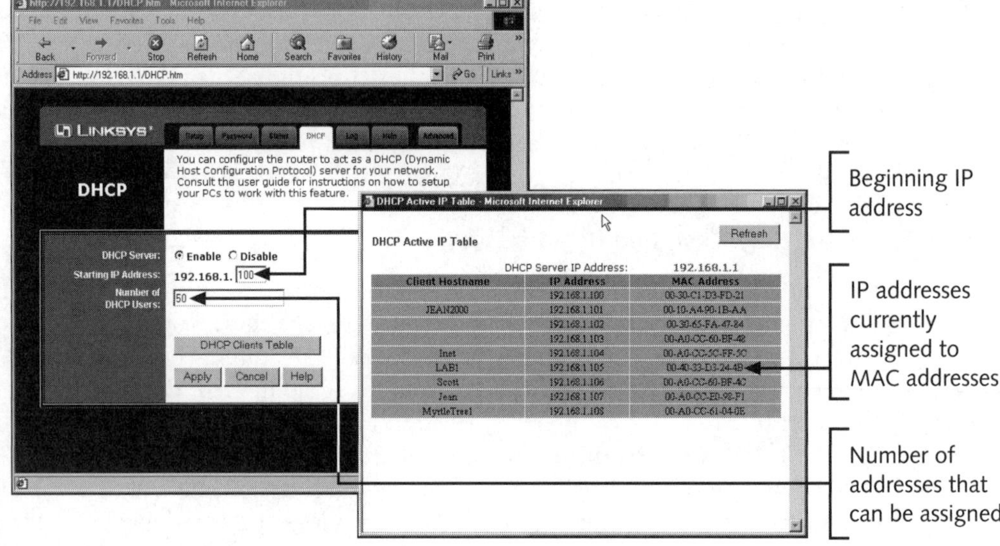

Figure 12-10 A DHCP server has a range of IP addresses it can assign to clients on the network

Network Address Translation

If the hosts on a network using private IP addresses need to access the Internet, a problem arises because the private IP addresses are not allowed on the Internet. The solution is to use **NAT (Network Address Translation)**, which uses a single public IP address to access the Internet on behalf of all hosts on the network using other IP addresses. When a computer on the network tries to access the Internet, it must go through a server, router, or other device that substitutes its own IP address for that of the computer requesting the information. Because the device is standing in proxy for the other hosts that want Internet access, it is called a **proxy server**. Figure 12-11 shows how a proxy server stands between the network and the Internet. This proxy server has two network cards installed. One card connects to the LAN, and the other card connects to a cable modem and on to the ISP and the Internet.

Because a proxy server stands between a LAN and the Internet, it often does double duty as a firewall. A **firewall** is software or hardware that protects a network from illegal entry. Because networks are so often attacked by worms and hackers from the Internet, even a small LAN will often have a device that stands between the LAN and the Internet serving as a proxy server, DHCP server, and firewall. As a firewall, it filters out any unsolicited traffic coming from the Internet.

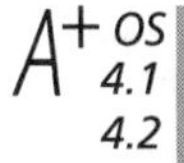
OS 4.1 4.2

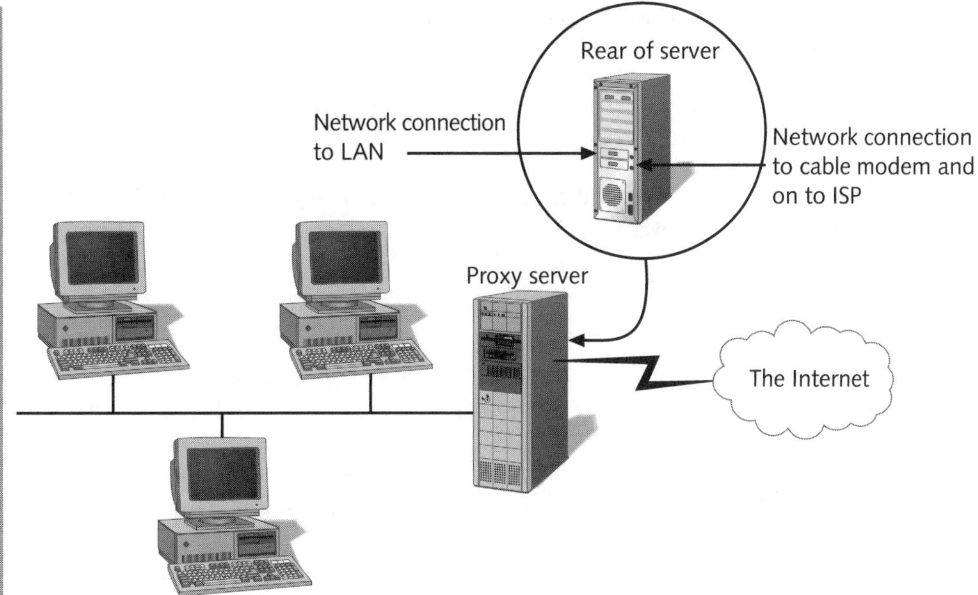

Figure 12-11 A proxy server stands between a private network and the Internet

> TIP: Windows 98 SE, Windows Me, Windows 2000, and Windows XP offer a NAT service called Microsoft Internet Connection Sharing (ICS). With it, two or more PCs on a home network can share the same IP address when accessing the Internet. Under ICS, one PC acts as the proxy server for other PCs on the home network.

12

Host Names and NetBIOS Names

OS 4.1 4.2

Each computer on a TCP/IP network is assigned an IP address, but these numbers are hard to remember. Host names and NetBIOS names use characters rather than numbers to identify computers on a network and are easier to remember and use than IP addresses. In addition, a company might have a **domain name** that can be used to identify the network. An example of a domain name is amazon.com. Domain names are covered in the next chapter.

How Host Names and NetBIOS Names Are Related

Recall that NetBEUI is a proprietary Windows network protocol used for Windows LANs not connected to the Internet. NetBEUI supports NetBIOS, which is a protocol used by applications to communicate. Before TCP/IP became such a popular protocol, Windows assumed that the protocol of choice would be NetBEUI and assumed that all computers on a network would be assigned a NetBIOS name such as *joesmith* or *Workstation12*. These names usually are assigned when the operating system is installed. In contrast, TCP/IP identifies computers by IP addresses, but TCP/IP also allows a computer to be assigned a character-based host name such as *joesmith*. The host name can also have a domain name

A+ OS 4.1 4.2 that identifies the network attached like this: *joesmith.mycompany.com*. On a TCP/IP network, the NetBIOS name or host name must be associated with an IP address before one computer can find another on the network. This process of associating a character-based name to an IP address is called **name resolution**.

There are two name resolution services that track relationships between character-based names and IP addresses: **DNS** (**Domain Name System**, also called **Domain Name Service**) and **Microsoft WINS** (**Windows Internet Naming Service**). DNS tracks host names, and WINS tracks NetBIOS names. Windows networks sometimes use a combination of DNS and WINS.

Windows 98 assumes that a computer name is a NetBIOS name, which can have only 15 characters, but Windows 2000 and Windows XP assume that the computer name is a host name, which uses the TCP/IP convention for host names. If the name is 15 characters or fewer, it will work as a NetBIOS name or a TCP/IP name on either a NetBEUI network or a TCP/IP network. If a host name is used, it can be up to 63 characters including letters, numbers and hyphens, as long as the computer is not part of a workgroup. If the computer is part of a workgroup, the host name should not exceed 15 characters. Microsoft is slowly abandoning NetBIOS as the default naming convention in favor of TCP/IP host names.

Remember that applications that use NetBEUI use NetBIOS API calls to communicate with other applications on the network. Applications that are using TCP/IP to communicate over the network use a type of API call known as **WinSock (Windows Sockets)**. WinSock is a part of the TCP/IP utility software installed with TCP/IP.

An application can make a NetBIOS API call to another computer on a network and identify the remote computer by its NetBIOS name even though the network is using TCP/IP. When dealing with these hybrid networks, you should know that the NetBIOS name of the remote computer must be related to an IP address before TCP/IP can make the connection.

Assigning or Changing a Computer Name

A+ OS 4.1 4.2 During the Windows installation process, if Windows Setup recognizes that a NIC is present, it gives you the opportunity to assign a name to the computer. Also, after the installation, you can give the computer a name or change its existing name. To assign a NetBIOS name to a Windows 9x computer, follow these directions:

1. Access the Control Panel and double-click the **Network** icon.
2. Click the **Identification** tab. See Figure 12-12.

A+ OS 4.1

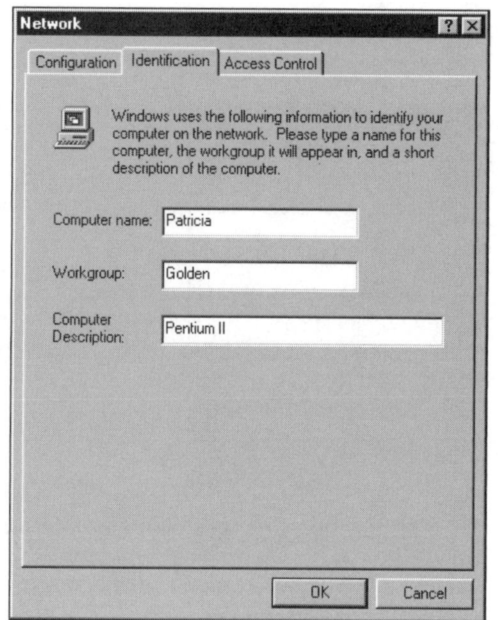

Figure 12-12 Each computer in a workgroup must be assigned a name that other users on the network will see in their Network Neighborhood window

3. Enter the name of the workgroup (Golden in this example). All users in the workgroup must have the same name entered in the window on their PC.
4. Enter the NetBIOS name of the computer (Patricia in this example). Each computer name must be unique within the workgroup.
5. Click **OK** to exit the window.

12

A+ OS 1.1

For Windows 2000, follow these directions to give a host name to a computer:

1. On the Windows 2000 desktop, right-click on **My Computer** and select **Properties** from the shortcut menu. The System Properties window appears.
2. Click the **Network Identification** tab, and then click the **Properties** button. The Identification Changes window appears (see Figure 12-13).
3. Enter the Computer name (Jean2000 in this example).
4. For a workgroup, select workgroup and enter the Workgroup name (Golden in this example). If the PC is to join a domain, you would enter the name of the domain here, such as mycompany.com.
5. Click **OK** to exit the Identification Changes window, and then click **OK** to exit the System Properties window.

A+ OS 4.1 4.2

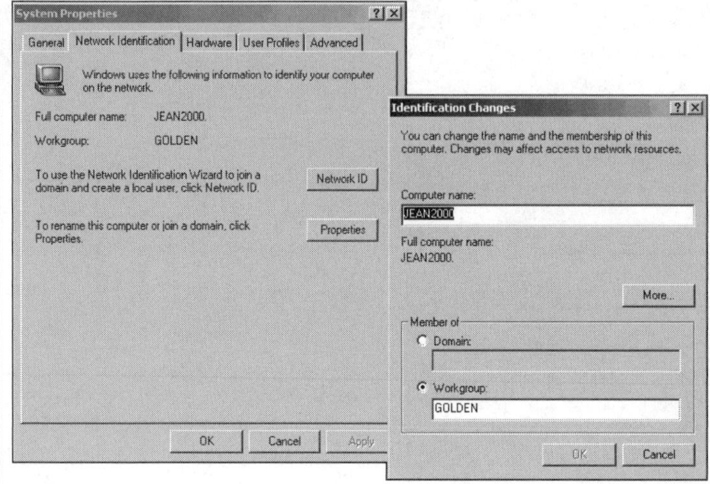

Figure 12-13 Windows 2000 uses the Identification Changes dialog box to assign a host name to a computer on a network

Before a computer can connect to a network, a network card must be installed and a network cable connected to the card and some other device such as a hub. Then, one or more network protocols must be installed and configured. How to install and configure a network protocol is covered next.

CONNECTING TO A NETWORK AND SHARING RESOURCES

A+ OS 4.1

In this section, you will learn how to install two network protocols, **NetBEUI (NetBIOS Extended User Interface)** and **TCP/IP (Transmission Control Protocol/ Internet Protocol)**, and how to configure both. You will then learn how to configure each PC to share resources on the network, including files, folders, and printers. Procedures for Windows 98 and Windows 2000 are covered.

Connecting to a NetBEUI Network

A+ OS 4.1

To use NetBEUI to connect to a network using Windows 98, do the following:

1. Access the Control Panel and double-click the **Network** applet. The Network window opens. (You can also access the applet by right-clicking on the Network Neighborhood icon on the desktop and selecting Properties from the shortcut window.)

For Windows 9x, if you don't see the Network Neighborhood icon on the desktop, then a network protocol has not been installed or is giving errors.

A+ OS 4.1

2. Click **Add** to display the Select Network Component Type window, as shown in Figure 12-14.

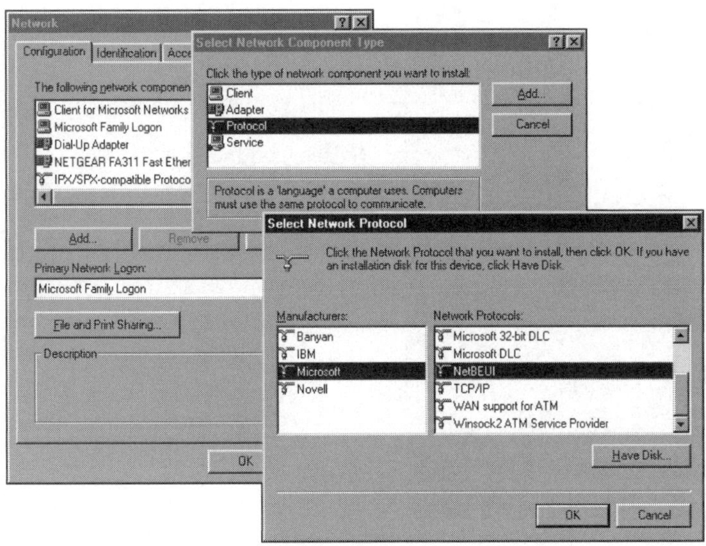

Figure 12-14 Install a network protocol in Windows 98 using the Network applet in Control Panel

3. Select **Protocol**, and then click **Add**. The Select Network Protocol window opens. Select **Microsoft** on the left and **NetBEUI** on the right. See Figure 12-14. Click **OK**.

12

When you return to the Network window, notice that NetBEUI is automatically bound to any network cards or dial-up adapters that it finds installed. (Recall that when a network protocol is associated with a network card or modem, the process is called binding.) For example, in Figure 12-15 the two adapters already installed are a network card (NetGear FA311 Fast Ethernet PCI Adapter) and Dial-Up Adapter. The dial-up adapter is a modem card that has been configured to use Dial-up Networking so that it can dial up and connect to a network such as that provided by an ISP to connect to the Internet.

The only configuration that NetBEUI requires is that the computer be given a NetBIOS name, which you have already learned how to do. If the Network Neighborhood icon was not on your desktop, it should be there now that a network protocol is installed. Open the icon and you should be able to see this and other computers on the network. Figure 12-16 shows an example of Windows 98 Network Neighborhood.

A+ OS 4.1

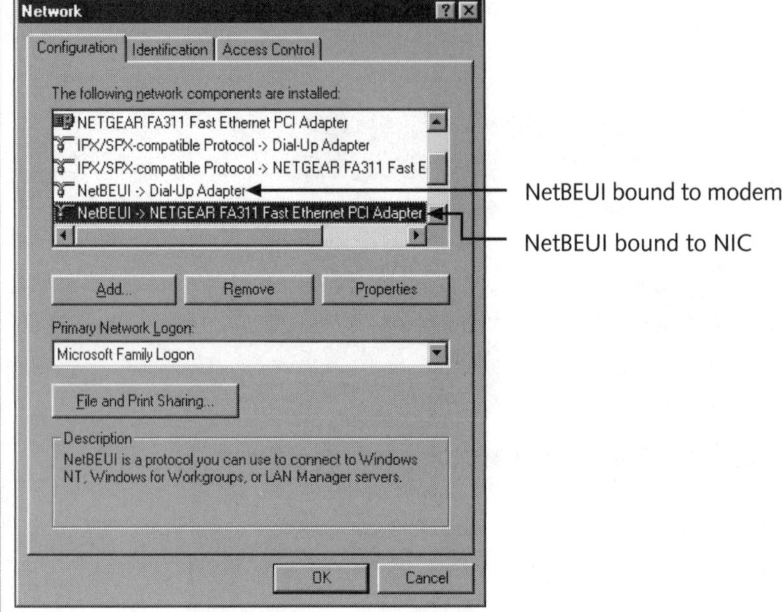

Figure 12-15 A network protocol automatically binds itself to any network adapter or dial-up adapter it finds installed

A+ OS 1.1 4.1

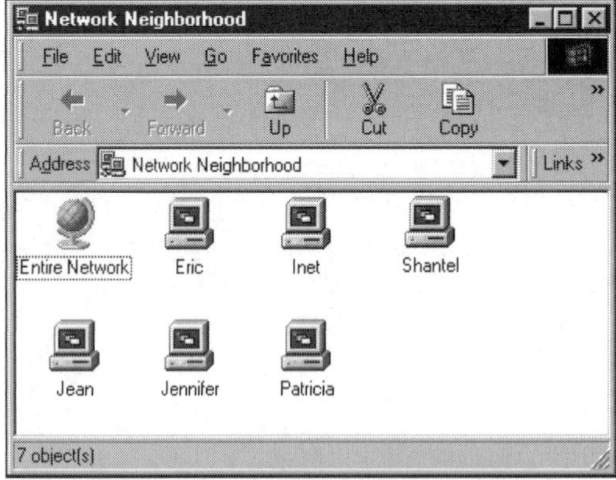

Figure 12-16 Windows 98 Network Neighborhood shows all computers on the LAN in a common workgroup

Network Neighborhood and My Network Places can be viewed on the desktop and in Windows Explorer. By default, Windows 98 puts Network Neighborhood in both places, Windows 2000 puts My Network Places in both places, and Windows XP puts My Network Places only in Windows Explorer.

A+ OS 4.1

You will not be able to access resources on the other computers on the network until a computer has been configured to share its resources. How to share resources is covered later in the chapter.

To connect to a network using NetBEUI on a Windows 2000 computer, do the following:

1. Access the Control Panel and open the **Network and Dial-up Connections** applet.
2. Right-click the **Local Area Connection** icon and select **Properties** from the shortcut menu. The Local Area Connection Properties window opens (see Figure 12-17).

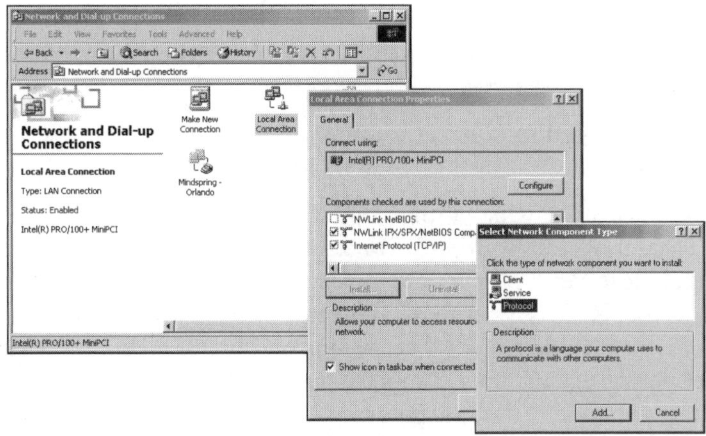

Figure 12-17 Use the Network and the Dial-up Connections applet in Control Panel to install a network protocol using Windows 2000

3. From this window, you can uninstall and install network components. Click **Install**. The Select Network Component Type windows opens, which is also shown in Figure 12-17. Select **Protocol**, and then click **Add**.
4. The Select Network Protocol window appears. Select **NetBEUI Protocol** from the list of uninstalled protocols, and then click **OK**.
5. When you return to the Local Area Connection Properties window, you should see NetBEUI Protocol checked as an installed component. Click **Close**. Windows 2000 does not automatically bind NetBEUI to an installed dial-up adapter, but will bind it to the network adapter providing this local network connection.
6. On the Windows 2000 desktop, double-click the **My Network Places** icon and view this and other computers on the network.

12

Connecting to a TCP/IP Network

A+ OS 4.1 4.2

NetBEUI works as long as you don't need to connect to the Internet or route requests to other networks. (For these reasons, NetBEUI is known as a nonroutable protocol.) For these situations, TCP/IP is needed. This section describes how to install and configure TCP/IP using Windows 98 and Windows 2000.

To install and configure TCP/IP, you will need to know the answers to these questions, which are supplied by your network administrator:

1. Will the PC use dynamic or static IP addressing?
2. If static IP addressing is used, what are the IP address, subnet mask, and gateway for this computer?
3. How is DNS to work? Do you enable or disable it? If enabled, what are the IP addresses of your DNS servers?
4. Is a proxy server used to connect to other networks (including the Internet)? If so, what is the IP address of the proxy server?

Here is a quick explanation of what all these questions mean. You will learn more about them in the next chapter. Recall from earlier in the chapter that in dynamic addressing the computer asks a DHCP server for its IP address each time it connects to the network. The server will also give the PC its subnet mask and gateway so that the computer will know how to communicate with other hosts that are not on its own network. A **gateway** is a computer or other device that allows a computer on one network to communicate with a computer on another network. A **default gateway** is the gateway a computer uses to access another network if it does not have a better option. A **subnet mask** is a group of four numbers (dotted decimal numbers) that tells TCP/IP if a remote computer is on the same or a different network. A **DNS server** is a computer that can find an IP address for another computer when only the domain name is known.

Install and Configure TCP/IP Using Windows 98

If TCP/IP is not already installed, you must install it. For Windows 98, do the following:

1. Access the Control Panel and double-click the **Network** icon. The Network window opens.
2. Click **Add** to display the Select Network Component Type window, as shown in Figure 12-18.
3. Select **Protocol**, click **Add**, and the Select Network Protocol window opens. Select **Microsoft** on the left and **TCP/IP** on the right. See Figure 12-18. Click **OK**. The system asks for the Microsoft Windows 98 CD and requests that you reboot the system.
4. When you return to the Network window, notice that TCP/IP is automatically bound to any network cards or modems that it finds installed.

A+ OS 4.1 4.2

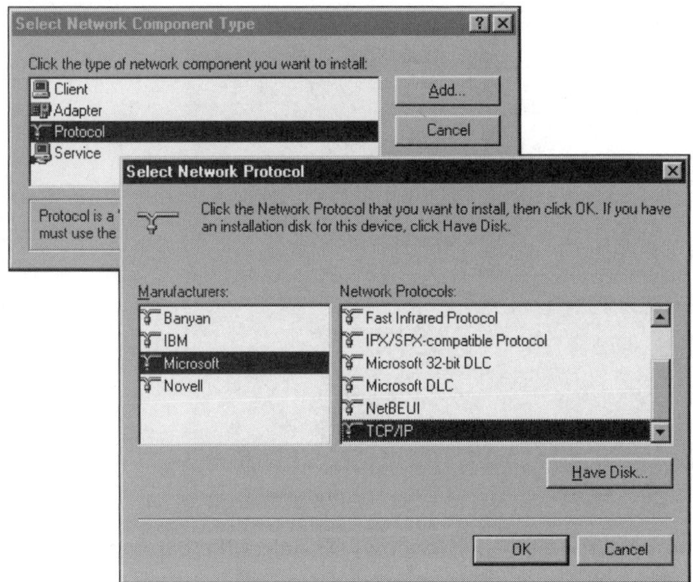

Figure 12-18 To install TCP/IP in Windows 98, use the Select Network Protocol dialog box

The next step is to configure TCP/IP for each of the bindings listed that you will use. Most likely, you will be using dynamic IP addressing and the DNS service is initially disabled (later the DHCP server will tell the PC to enable it). The DHCP server might also act as the proxy server so that computers inside the network can make connections to computers outside the network using the proxy server's public IP address. In Windows 98, to configure TCP/IP bound to a NIC to communicate over a local network, do the following: 12

1. In the Network window, select the item where TCP/IP is bound to the NIC. (In Figure 12-19, that item is TCP/IP->NETGEAR FA311 Fast Ethernet PCI Adapter.) Then, click **Properties**. The TCP/IP Properties window appears.
2. If static IP addressing is used, then click **Specify IP address**, and then enter the IP Address and Subnet Mask as supplied by your administrator. If dynamic IP addressing is used, click **Obtain an IP address automatically**. This will most likely be your selection.
3. Click the **DNS Configuration** tab and chose to enable or disable DNS (see Figure 12-20). If you enable DNS, enter the IP addresses of your DNS servers. If your network administrator has given you other specific values for the TCP/IP configuration, you will find the tabs for these settings on this window. But, in most cases, this is all that is needed to configure TCP/IP.

A+ OS 4.1 4.2

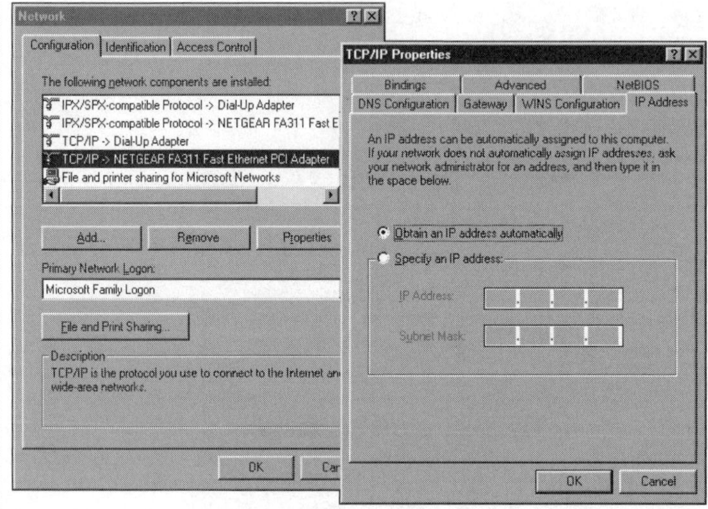

Figure 12-19 To configure TCP/IP in Windows 98, select the binding and click Properties to view the TCP/IP Properties window

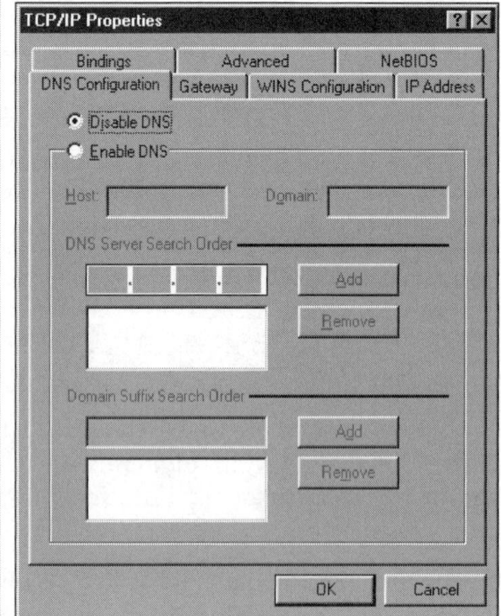

Figure 12-20 Configure DNS service under TCP/IP for Windows 98

4. When finished, click **OK** to exit the Properties window, and then **OK** to exit the Network window.

A+ OS 4.1 4.2

5. On the desktop, verify that you can see your and other computers on the network in Network Neighborhood on the desktop. If you don't see others on the network, reboot the PC.

Install and Configure TCP/IP using Windows 2000

For Windows 2000/XP, when a network card is installed, TCP/IP is installed by default. However, if TCP/IP has been uninstalled or is giving you problems, you can install it again. Use the same procedure given earlier to install NetBEUI under Windows 2000, this time selecting TCP/IP as the network protocol to install.

To set the TCP/IP properties for the connection follow the steps below.

1. Using Control Panel, open the **Network and Dial-up Connection** applet. Right-click the **Local Area Connection** icon, and then select **Properties** from the shortcut menu. See Figure 12-21.

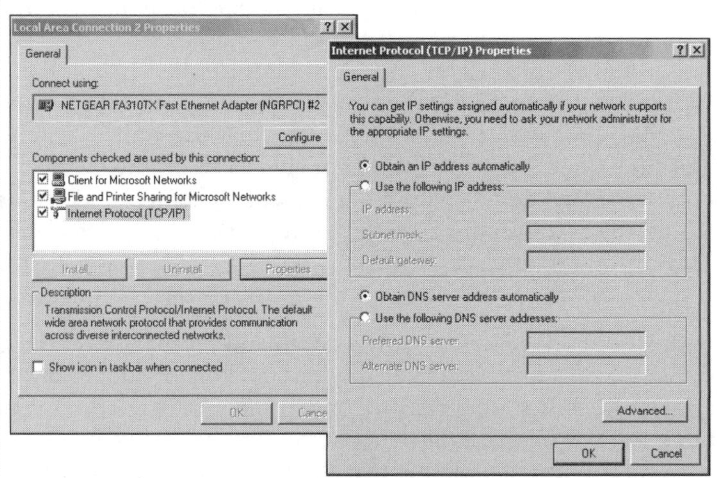

Figure 12-21 Configure a TCP/IP connection using Windows 2000

2. Select **(Internet Protocol) TCP/IP** from the list of installed components, and then click the **Properties** button. The TCP/IP Properties dialog box opens, which is also shown in Figure 12-21.

3. For dynamic IP addressing, select **Obtain an IP address automatically**. For static IP addressing, select **Use the following IP address** and enter the IP address, Subnet mask, and Default gateway.

4. To disable DNS until the DHCP server gives the computer the DNS server address, select **Obtain DNS server address automatically**. If you have the IP addresses of the DNS servers, click **Use the following DNS server addresses** and enter the IP addresses. Click **OK** twice to close both windows.

12

A+ OS 4.1 4.2

5. On the desktop, click **My Network Places** and verify that your computer and other computers on the network are visible. If you don't see other computers on the network, reboot the PC.

A+ OS 3.3 4.1

Troubleshooting TCP/IP Connections

Windows TCP/IP includes several diagnostic tools useful in troubleshooting problems with TCP/IP. You will learn about several of these in the next chapter. The most useful is **Ping (Packet Internet Groper)**, which tests connectivity and is discussed here. Ping sends a signal to a remote computer. If the remote computer is online and hears the signal, it will respond. Ipconfig under Windows NT/2000/XP and Winipcfg under Windows 9x test the TCP/IP configuration. Try these things to test TCP/IP configuration and connectivity:

- For Windows NT/2000/XP, at the command prompt, enter *Ipconfig /all*, or, for Windows 9x, click Start, Run, enter *Winipcfg* in the Run dialog box, and then click OK. If the TCP/IP configuration is correct and an IP address is assigned, the IP address, subnet mask, and default gateway appear along with the adapter address. For dynamic IP addressing, if the PC could not reach the DHCP server, then it will assign itself an IP address. This is called IP autoconfiguration. The Winipcfg window and the results of the Ipconfig command both show the IP address as the IP Autoconfiguration Address, and the address will begin with 169. In this case, suspect that the PC is not able to reach the network or the DHCP server is down. Try to release the current IP address and lease a new address. To do this with Winipcfg, with the network card selected, click the Release button, and then click the Renew button. For Ipconfig, first use the *Ipconfig /release* command, and then use the *Ipconfig /renew* command.
- Next, try the loopback address test. At a command prompt, enter the command *Ping 127.0.0.1* (with no period after the final 1). This IP address always refers to your local computer. It should respond with a reply message from your computer. If this works, TCP/IP is likely to be configured correctly. If you get any errors up to this point, then assume that the problem is on your PC. Check the installation and configuration of each component such as the network card and the TCP/IP protocol suite. Remove and reinstall each component and watch for error messages, writing them down so that you can recognize or research them later as necessary. Compare the configuration to that of a PC that is working on the same network.
- Next, Ping the IP address of your default gateway. If it does not respond, then the problem may be with the gateway or with the network to the gateway.
- Now try to Ping the host computer you are trying to reach. If it does not respond, then the problem may be with the host computer or with the network to the computer.
- If you have Internet access and substitute a domain name for the IP address in the Ping command, and the Ping works, then you can conclude that DNS works. If an IP address works, but the domain name does not work, the problem lies with DNS. Try this command: *ping microsoft.com*.

Sharing Resources on the Network

A+ OS 1.1 4.1

If users on a LAN are working on a common project and need to share applications and files or need to share printers, then all these users must be assigned to the same workgroup or domain on the LAN. Recall that Windows 9x makes shared resources available by way of Network Neighborhood, and Windows 2000/XP uses My Network Places. Open either icon to see the names of all computers on the network. Figure 12-22 shows My Network Places. Drill down to see shared files, folders, and printers in your workgroup. Using Network Neighborhood or My Network Places, you can copy files from one computer to another, use shared applications installed on one computer from another computer, and share printers.

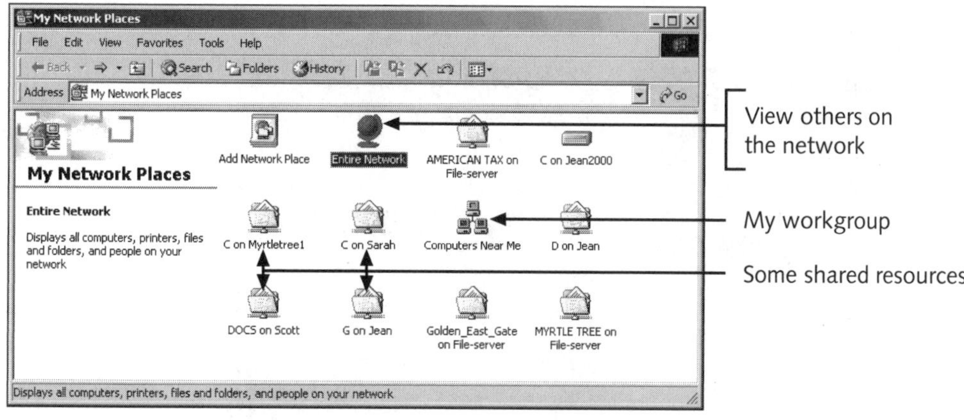

Figure 12-22 View and access shared resources on the network using My Network Places in Windows 2000

Workgroups can be effective when several people work on a common project. For example, if a group of people are building a Web site, sharing resources on the LAN can be an effective method of passing Web pages around as they are built. Or one computer on the LAN can be designated as the file server. The user of this computer makes a portion of hard drive space available for the Web site files. All users have access to this one resource, and the Web site files are neatly kept in a single location. When using workgroups, it is the responsibility of each user to protect the resources being shared by using password protection for read and write privileges to files and folders.

To share resources over a peer-to-peer network, you must first install Client for Microsoft Networks and File and Printer Sharing. Client for Microsoft Networks is the Windows component that allows you to use resources on the network made available by other computers, and File and Printer Sharing allows you to share resources on your computer with others in your workgroup. After these components are installed, the last thing to do is to share the folders, files, or printers that you want others to be able to access. All these steps are covered in this section.

A+ OS 4.1

Installing Windows 98 Components Needed to Share Resources

For Windows 98, to install Client for Microsoft Networks and File and Printer Sharing:

1. Use the Control Panel to access the Network applet. In the Network window, click **Add**. The Select Network Component Type dialog box opens.
2. Select **Client**, and click then **Add**. The Select Network Client window opens. See Figure 12-23.

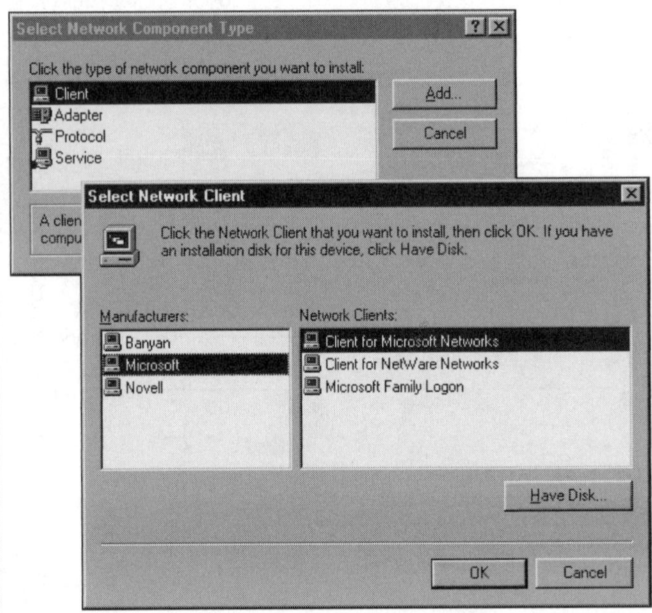

Figure 12-23 In Windows 98, install Client for Microsoft Networks so users on the LAN can connect to other PCs to share files, folders, and printers

3. Select **Microsoft** on the left and **Client for Microsoft Networks** on the right. Click **OK** and insert the Windows 98 CD.
4. Install the service for sharing files and printers with others on the Microsoft network. In the Network window, click **Add**. The Select Network Component Type dialog box opens.
5. Click **Service**, and then click **Add**. The Select Network Service window opens. See Figure 12-24.
6. Select **File and printer sharing for Microsoft Networks**, and then click **OK**. Insert the Windows 98 CD.
7. The next step is to turn on file and printer sharing. In the Network window, click **File and Print Sharing**. The File and Print Sharing window opens. See Figure 12-25. Check both options to share both files and printers, and then click **OK**.

A+ OS 4.1

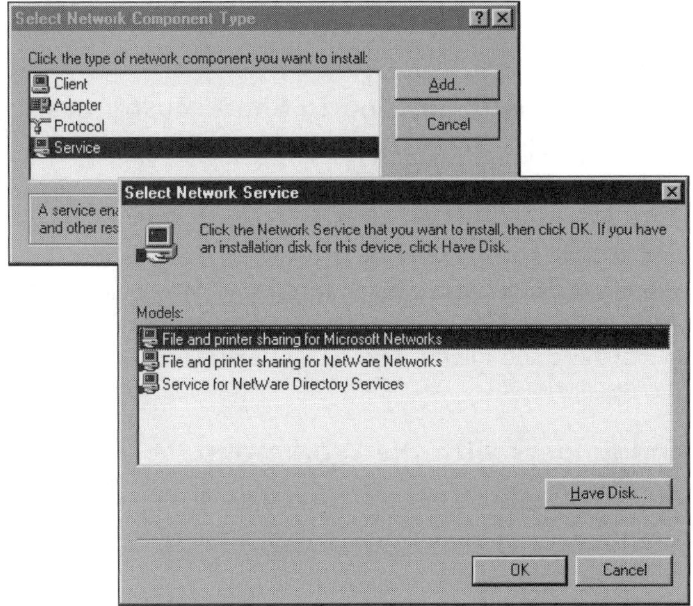

Figure 12-24 Install Windows 98 file and printer sharing for Microsoft Networks to be used to share files and printers on a LAN

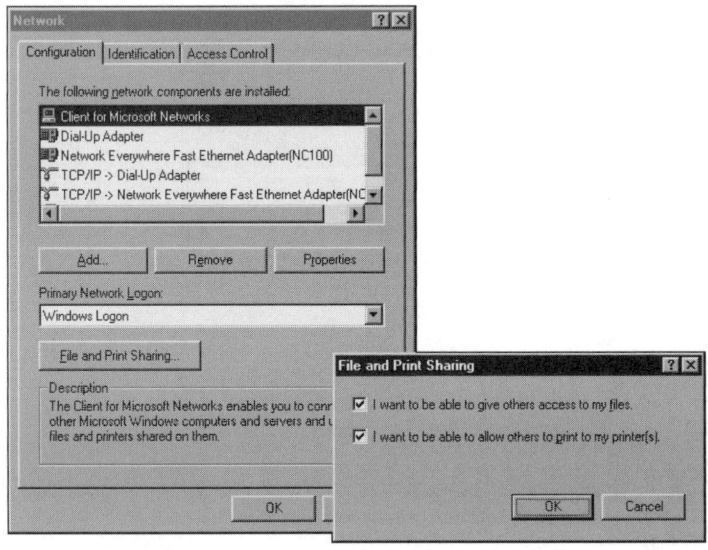

Figure 12-25 Turn on Windows 98 file and printer sharing so others on the LAN can access resources on this PC

When they are installed, Client for Microsoft Networks and File and Printer Sharing should automatically bind themselves to the TCP/IP protocol. You can verify this by

A+ OS 4.1

accessing the TCP/IP Properties window and clicking the Bindings tab. Verify that Client for Microsoft Networks and File and Printer Sharing are checked.

Windows 2000 Components Needed to Share Resources

Client for Microsoft Networks and File and Printer Sharing are installed by default during a Windows 2000 installation. However, if you are having a problem sharing resources on a LAN, you can try to uninstall and reinstall them. Both of these actions are performed using the Local Area Connection Properties window accessed earlier by way of the Network and Dial-up Connections applet in Control Panel. Refer back to Figure 11-17. Click Install. The Select Network Component Type window appears, which is also shown in Figure 12-17. Select Client and then click Add. You will need the Windows 2000 CD or other access to the installation files.

Sharing Files and Folders with the Workgroup

After the computer has been configured for file and printer sharing, using Windows 98 or Windows 2000, follow these example directions to make a folder on drive C named \data available to others on the LAN:

1. Using Windows Explorer, select the folder **C:\data**. Right-click the folder name. If the system is configured for file and printer sharing, the shortcut menu lists Sharing. Select **Sharing**. See Figure 12-26. The data Properties dialog box opens, as shown in Figure 12-27.

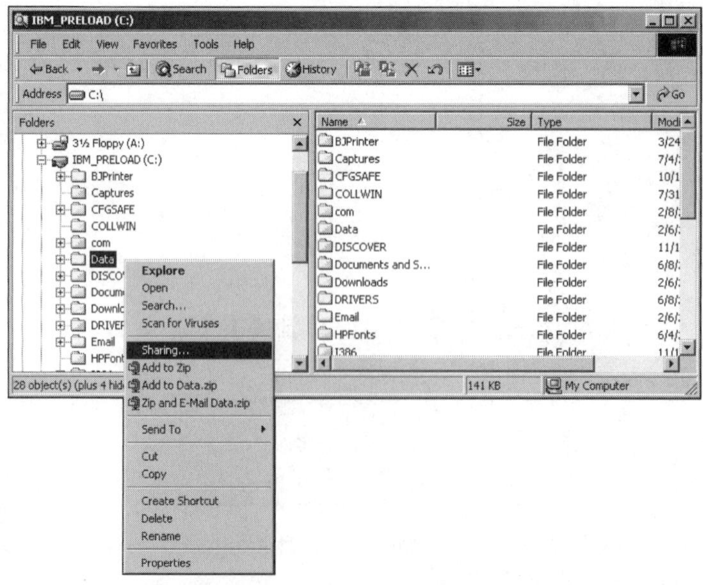

Figure 12-26 In Windows 98, use Windows Explorer to password protect a file or folder shared on a network

A+ OS 4.1

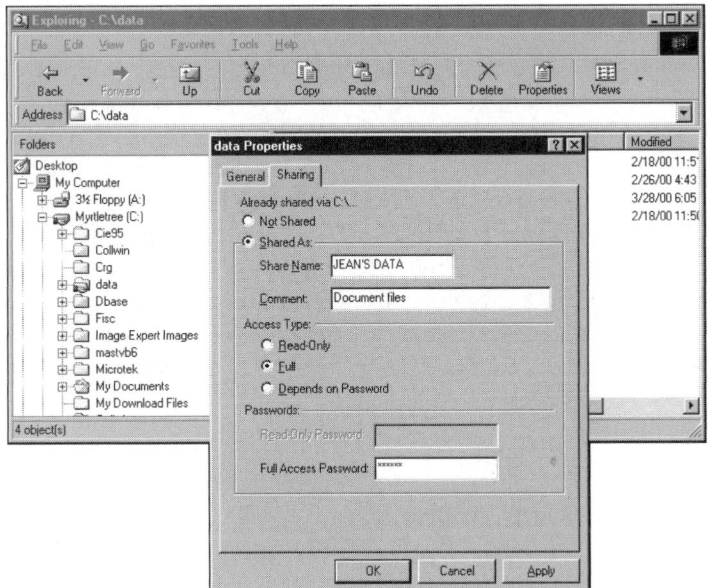

Figure 12-27 Using Windows 98, a user on a network can share a folder with others on the network

2. Click the **Shared As** option button and enter a name for the shared folder. In the figure, the name is JEAN'S DATA. This action makes the folder available to others on the network. They can see the folder when they open Network Neighborhood on their desktop.

3. In the section labeled Access Type, click the **Depends on Password** option button.

4. To allow others the right to make changes to the folder, enter a password under **Full Access Password**. For read-only access, enter a different password. Click **OK** to exit the window.

5. For added security when using Windows 2000, set up a user account and password for each user who will have access to shared resources. This added security requires that a user give a valid password before accessing shared files, folders, or printers on the Windows 2000 PC.

When using the option Depends on Password, be sure to enter a password in both fields. With this option, if a password field is empty, then no password is required to have that type of access to the folder. Distribute the two passwords to those people who need to access the folder. You control the access rights (permissions) by selecting which password(s) you give.

Applications can also be shared with others in the workgroup. If you share a folder that has a program file in it, a user on another PC can double-click the program file in Network Neighborhood and execute it remotely on their desktop. This is a handy way for several users to share an application that is installed on a single PC.

A+ OS 4.1

Installing and Sharing a Printer

A printer can be connected to a port on a computer and then the computer can share the printer with others on the network. There are also network printers that have Ethernet ports that can be used to connect the printer directly to the network. Each computer on the network that uses the printer must have printer drivers installed so the OS on each computer can communicate with the printer and provide the interface between applications it supports and the printer. This section covers how to install a local printer, how to share that printer with others on the network and how a remote computer on the network can use a shared printer. A printer connected to a computer by way of a port on the computer is a **local printer**, and a printer that is accessed by way of a network is a network printer. A computer can have several printers installed. Windows designates one printer to be the **default printer**, which is the printer Windows prints to unless another is selected.

Install a Local Printer

Follow these steps to install a local printer:

- Physically attach the printer to the computer by way of a parallel port, serial port, USB port or wireless access point. For a parallel port connection, use an IEEE 1284-compliant printer cable.
- Install the printer drivers. There are two approaches to do this. You can have Windows install the driver or you can use the printer manufacturer's installation program. In most cases, it is best to use the printer manufacturer's method. The exception to this is if you have several printers installed that are similar because Windows does a better job of preventing files used by one printer installation from being overwritten by files from another installation. To use the manufacturer's installation process, insert the printer driver CD that comes bundled with the printer in the CD-ROM drive and follow directions on screen to install the printer.
- Alternately, you can use the Windows Printer window to install the printer. For Windows 98 and Windows 2000 click Start, Settings, and Printer to open the Printer window. For Windows XP, to open the Printer window, click Start, Printers and Faxes. From the Printer window, click Add Printer and follow the Add Printer wizard to install the printer.
- Once the printer drivers are installed, test the printer. To do this, open the Printer window and right click the printer. Select Properties from the shortcut menu. Click the General tab and then click the Print Test Page button.

From the Printer window you can also delete printers, change the Windows default printer, purge print jobs in order to troubleshoot failed printing, and perform other printer maintenance tasks. If a printer is giving problems or you want to upgrade the printer drivers in order to add new functionality, search the printer manufacturer's Web site for the latest drivers for your printer and operating system. Download the drivers to a folder on the hard drive such as C:\Downloads\Printer, and then double click on the driver file to extract files and launch the installation program to update the printer drivers.

A+ OS 4.1

Share a Printer with the Workgroup

To share a local printer with others in the workgroup connected to a Windows 9x or Windows 2000/XP computer, do the following:

1. Click **Start**, point to **Settings**, and then click **Printers**. The Printers window opens.
2. Right-click the printer you want to share. From the shortcut menu, select **Sharing**. (This Sharing option is grayed out if File and Printer Sharing is not installed.)
3. The Properties dialog box opens with the Sharing tab selected (see Figure 12-28).

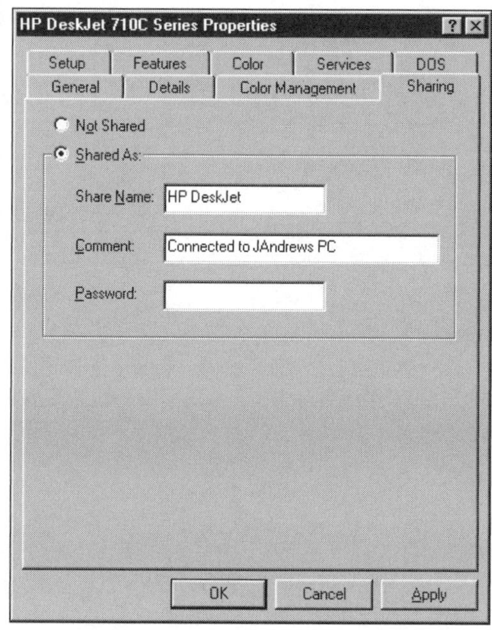

Figure 12-28 When using Windows 98, use the printer Properties window to share a connected printer with other computers on the network

4. Select **Shared As** and give the printer a **Share Name**. Click **OK** to exit.
5. The printer is listed in the Network Neighborhood group of other computers on the network.

To allow a remote PC to use a local printer connected to a Windows 2000 workstation, do the following:

1. On the Windows 2000/XP PC, allow print sharing: open the Printers window. Right-click the printer you want to share, and select **Sharing** from the shortcut menu. The printer's Properties dialog box opens, as seen in Figure 12-29 for Windows 2000, but Windows XP is similar. Select **Shared as** and enter a name for the printer.

12

A+ OS 4.1

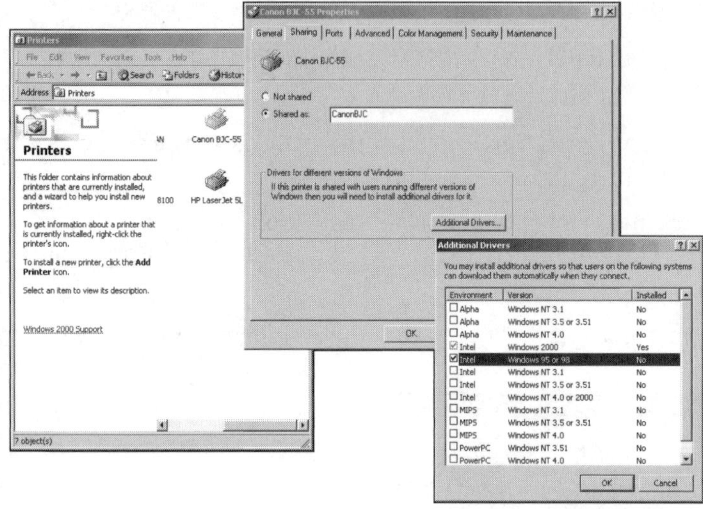

Figure 12-29 Sharing a printer on a Windows 2000 PC

2. If you want to make drivers for the printer available to remote users that are using an operating system other than Windows 2000/XP, then click **Additional Drivers**.
3. The Additional Drivers window appears, as also shown in Figure 12-29. Select the OS. In Figure 12-29, Windows 95 or 98 is selected so that those using these OSs will have the printer drivers they need. Click **OK** twice to close both windows. You might be asked for the Windows 2000/XP CD or other access to the installation files. A shared printer shows a hand icon under it in the Printer window.

Using a Shared Printer

There are two approaches to installing a shared network printer on a remote PC. You can perform the installation using the printer drivers installed on the host PC or you can perform the installation using the drivers on CD (either the Windows CD or printer manufacturer's CD). The installations work about the same way for Windows 98 and Windows 2000/XP. The Windows 98 installation is shown here.

To use a printer on the network that is shared, using printer drivers from CD, do the following using Windows 98:

1. Add a new printer: click **Start**, point to **Settings**, and click **Printers**. Double-click **Add Printer**. The Add Printer Wizard window opens. Click **Next**.
2. In response to the question, "How is this printer attached to your computer?", select **Network printer**. Click **Next**. The wizard window in Figure 12-30 opens.
3. Enter the host computer name and printer name. Begin with two backslashes and separate the computer name from the printer name with a backslash. Or you can click **Browse** and search the list of shared printers on the network, selecting the printer to install. Click **Next**. (If your network is using static IP addressing and you know the IP address of the host PC, you can enter the IP address instead of the host name in this step.)

A+ OS 4.1

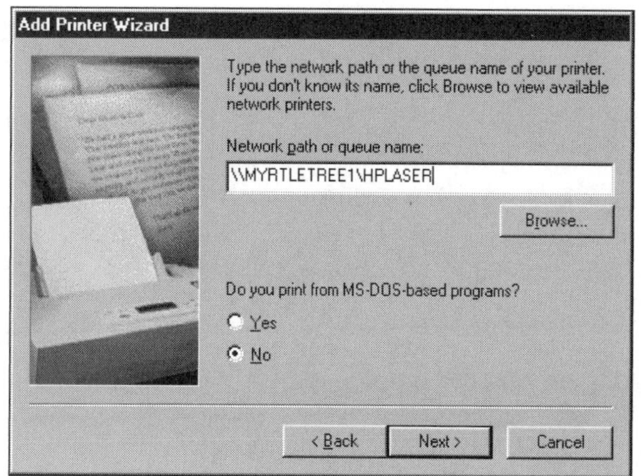

Figure 12-30 To use a network printer under Windows 98, enter the host computer name

4. Select the printer manufacturer and then the printer model from the list of supported printers. Click **Next** when you are finished.
5. Enter a name for the printer. You might include the location of the printer, such as 3rd Floor Laser or John's Laser. In response to the question, "Do you print from MS-DOS based programs?" Answer **Yes** if you have any intention of ever doing that, and then click **Next**.
6. Sometimes a DOS-based program has problems printing to a network printer. You can choose to associate the network printer with a printer port such as LPT1 to satisfy the DOS application. To do that, click **Capture Printer Port**. The Capture Printer Port dialog box appears (see Figure 12-31). Select the port from the drop-down menu, and then click **OK**.
7. Click **Next** to continue.
8. Choose to print a test page, and then click **Finish**. The network printer is now available for use.

12

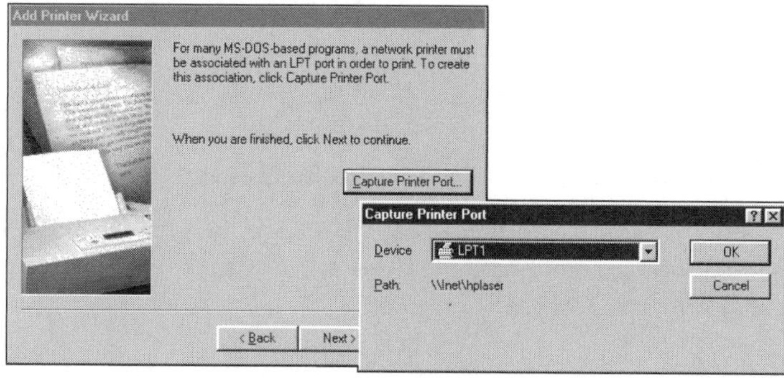

Figure 12-31 Associate a network printer with a printer port in order to help DOS applications in Windows 98

A+ OS 4.1

A quicker way to install a shared printer is to use the printer drivers already installed on the host PC. To do that using Windows 98 or Windows 2000/XP do the following:

1. On the host PC, share the \Windows folder so that printer drivers in this folder are available to others on the network.
2. On the remote PC, click **Network Neighborhood** and find the printer. Right-click the printer and select **Install** from the shortcut menu. See Figure 12-32. (For Windows 2000/XP, click **My Network Places** and find the printer. Right-click the printer and select **Connect**.)

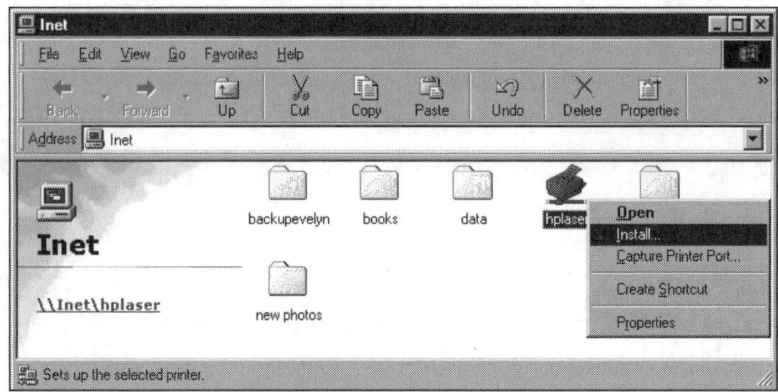

Figure 12-32 Install a shared printer in Windows 98 using drivers on the host computer

3. If the host computer is using the same OS as you are, or, in the case of a Windows NT/2000/XP host computer, if the additional drivers for your OS have been installed, you can use those drivers for the installation. If Windows cannot find the right drivers, it will give you an error message and give you the opportunity to install the drivers from your Windows CD or the printer manufacturer's CD.
4. Enter a name for the printer, decide how to handle printing from DOS applications, and print a test page to complete the installation.

If you must install the shared printer on several PCs in the workgroup, it's easier and faster to use the last method because each PC does not need to read from a CD, and you don't need to carry the CD from PC to PC. After the installations are complete, be sure to remove the shared permission on the host computer's \Windows folder so that this important folder will be more secure.

Other Methods of Sharing Printers over a Network

You have just seen how a printer can be installed as a local printer on one PC and then shared with others in a workgroup. There are three ways to make a printer available on a network, which are summarized here:

- A regular printer can be attached to a PC using the PC's parallel port, and then that PC can share the printer with the network (you just saw this method).
- A network printer with embedded logic to manage network communication can be connected directly to a network with its own NIC.

A+ OS 4.1

- A dedicated device or computer called a print server can control several printers connected to a network. For example, HP has software called HP JetDirect, designed to support HP printers in this manner. For more information, see the HP Web site at *www.hp.com*.

If printers are available on the network using one of the last two methods, follow the directions of the printer manufacturer to install the printer on each PC. If you don't have these directions, do the following: Download the printer drivers from the printer manufacturer's Web site and, if necessary, decompress the downloaded file. Open the Printers window and start the wizard to add a new printer. Select the option to install a local printer but do not ask Windows to automatically detect the printer. When given the opportunity, choose to create a new port rather than use an existing port (such as LPT1: or LPT2:). Choose to create a standard TCP/IP port. To create the port, you will need the IP address of the printer or the name of the printer on the network. When given the opportunity, click Have Disk so that you can point to and use the downloaded driver files that will then be used to complete the printer installation.

A+ OS 3.3

Troubleshooting Problems with Network Printers

Before we list the steps to take to troubleshoot problems with network printers, it is helpful to understand how Windows manages print jobs using one of three methods:

- For Windows applications using a non-PostScript printer, the print job data is converted to **Enhanced Metafile Format (EMF)**. This format embeds print commands in the data to help speed up printing.
- For Windows applications using a PostScript printer, the print job data is converted to the PostScript language. (A PostScript printer is a printer that uses a special language for data communication called PostScript, commonly used by the Mac OS.)
- Text data that contains no embedded control characters is sent to the printer as is. When DOS applications use this type printing, the data is called raw data and the print job is sent directly to the printer, bypassing the printer queue.

Normally, when Windows 9x receives a print job from an application, it places the job in a queue and prints from the queue, so that the application is released from the printing process as soon as possible. Several print jobs can accumulate in the queue, which you can view in the Printer window. This process of queue printing jobs is called **spooling**. (The word "spool" is an acronym for simultaneous peripheral operations on line.) Most printing from Windows 9x uses EMF spooling.

If the parallel port, printer cable, and printer all support bidirectional communication, the printer can communicate with Windows. For example, Windows 9x can ask the printer how much printer memory is available and what fonts are installed. The printer can send messages to the OS such as an out-of-paper or paper jam message.

Printing problems can be caused by the printer, the PC hardware or OS, the application using the printer, the printer cable, or, in the case of a printer installed on a network, the network. Follow the steps in Figure 12-33 to isolate the problem to one of the following areas:

- The application attempting to use the printer
- The OS and printer drivers

A+ OS 3.3

- Connectivity between the PC and the printer
- The printer

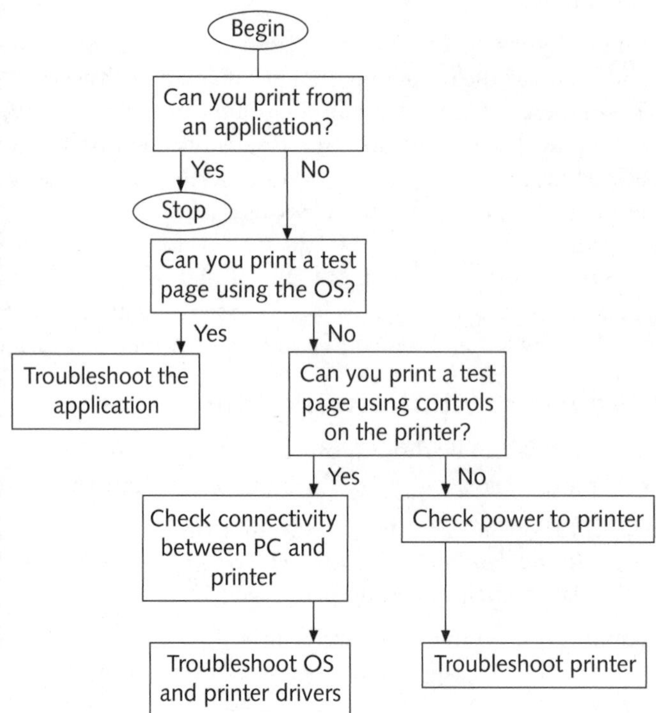

Figure 12-33 How to isolate a printer problem

When troubleshooting problems with connectivity between a PC on the network and a network printer, try these things:

- First check that you can print from the computer that has the printer attached to it locally by printing a test page using the Printer window. Right-click the printer you want to test, and choose Properties from the shortcut menu. Click the Print Test Page button to send a test page to the printer. Verify the correct default printer is selected.
- The print spool might be stalled. Try deleting all print jobs in the printer's queue. Double-click the printer icon in the Printers window. Select Printer, Purge Print Documents. (Note that it may take a moment for the print jobs to disappear.)
- If you still cannot print, verify that you can print from the computer that has the printer attached locally. Try printing a test page, purging the print queue, and rebooting the PC. Try removing and reinstalling the printer driver. To uninstall the printer driver, right-click the printer icon in the Printers window, select Delete to remove the printer, and then reinstall the printer.

A+ OS 3.3

- Check the configuration of the USB, serial, or parallel port in CMOS setup that the printer is using.
- Try another printer driver. It may not print graphics correctly, but if another driver does work at all, then you can conclude that you have a faulty driver. For example, if you have an HP LaserJet 5L, try using the HP LaserJet III driver.
- In the printer's Properties dialog box, click Disable bidirectional support for this printer. The PC and printer might have a problem with bidirectional communication.
- Check the resources assigned to the printer port. Open Device Manager, select LPT1, and click Properties. Verify that the resources are assigned correctly for LPT1 (I/O addresses are 0378 to 037B) and that Device Manager reports "No conflicts."
- In the printer Properties dialog box, try disabling "Check Port State Before Printing."
- Verify printer properties. Try lowering the resolution.
- If you can print from DOS, but not from Windows, try disabling printer spooling. Go to the printer Properties dialog box and select Print Directly to the Printer. Spooling holds print jobs in a queue for printing, so if spooling is disabled, printing from an application can be slower.
- If you are having trouble printing from an application, it may be incompatible with Windows. One way to try to solve this problem is to click Start, Run, and type mkcompat.exe. This utility enables you to troubleshoot and solve problems that may make an application incompatible with a certain version of Windows.
- If you are having trouble printing from an application, you can also bypass spooling by selecting Print from the File menu in the application, selecting the option to print to a file, and then dragging that file to the icon representing your printer.
- Try the printer on another PC. Try another power cable and another printer cable.
- Once you know you can print from the local computer, return to the remote computer, and, using the Printers window, delete the printer, and then, using Windows 9x Network Neighborhood or Windows 2000/XP My Network Places, reconnect the printer.

How Computers Find Each Other on a LAN

A+ OS 3.2

When an application using NetBIOS or WinSock wants to communicate with another computer on the same TCP/IP LAN, the requesting computer knows the name of the remote computer. Before TCP/IP communication can happen between the two computers, the first computer must discover the IP address of the remote PC. For Windows 98 using NetBIOS names, the computer runs through the following checklist in order shown to discover the IP address. (A Windows 2000 computer that is using just TCP/IP and not

A+ OS 3.2

NetBEUI uses DNS to resolve the name, not WINS, and begins at Step 5 below. If NetBEUI is running on this Windows 2000 computer, it tries DNS first, beginning at Step 5, and then turns to NetBEUI Steps 1 through 4 to resolve the name.)

1. The computer checks the NetBIOS name cache. This cache is information retained in memory from name resolutions made since the last reboot.
2. If the computer has the IP address of a WINS server, it queries the server. A WINS server is a Windows NT/2000 server on the network that maintains a database of NetBIOS names and IP addresses.
3. The computer sends a broadcast message to all computers on the LAN asking for the IP address of the computer with the broadcast NetBIOS name.
4. The computer checks a file named LMHosts, which is stored in the \Windows folder on the local computer. This file, called a host table, contains the NetBIOS names and associated IP addresses of computers on the LAN if someone has taken the time to manually make the entries into the file.
5. If the IP address is still not discovered, the computer assumes that the network is using DNS instead of WINS, so it checks the file in the \Windows folder named Hosts. The Hosts file is another host table that contains host names and associated IP addresses that is similar to the information kept by DNS servers.
6. If the computer has the IP address of a DNS server, it queries the DNS server.

Both the LMHosts and Hosts files are in the \Windows folder and are called host tables. **LMHosts** serves as a local table of information similar to that maintained by a WINS server for NetBIOS names, and **Hosts** serves as a local table of information similar to that kept by a DNS server.

If you look in the \Windows folder of a Windows 9x computer or the \Winnt\System32\drivers\etc folder of a Windows 2000/XP computer, you will see a sample of each file named LMHosts.SAM and Hosts.SAM, where the SAM stands for "sample." Open each file with Notepad to examine it. Entries in a host table file that begin with the # symbol are comments and are not read by the name resolution process. There are many commented lines in the sample files. You can add your entries to the bottom of the file without the # symbol. An example of a Hosts file is shown in Figure 12-34. It tells this computer what the IP address of the domain name apache.test.com is. Recall that a domain name is a name of a network. In the example, apache is the host name, and the domain name is test.com. The **fully qualified domain name (FQDN)** is apache.test.com, which is often loosely called the domain name.

A+ OS 3.2

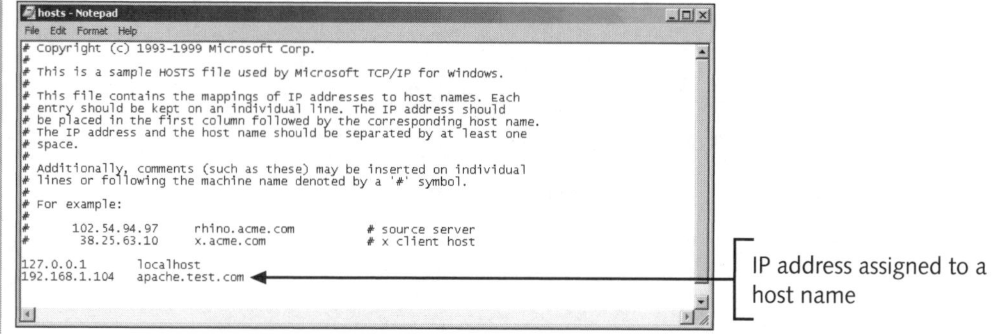

Figure 12-34 An entry in your client Hosts file will tell the client the IP address of an intranet Web site when no DNS service is running in Windows 98

In this example, the computer named apache.test.com is used as a Web server for a private network. In order for those on the network to use this domain name, the hosts file on each PC must have the entry in Figure 12-34, and the Web server must have the same IP address at all times. One way to accomplish this is to assign a static IP address to the server. Alternately, if your DHCP server supports this feature, you can configure it to assign the same IP address to your Web server each time if you tell the DHCP server your Web server's MAC address.

Network Drive Maps

A+ OS 4.1

A **network drive map** is one of the most powerful and versatile methods of communicating over a network. By using network file service (NFS) client/server software, the network drive map makes one PC (the client) appear to have a new hard drive, such as drive E, that is really hard drive space on another host computer (the server). Even if the host computer is using a different OS, such as Unix, the drive map still functions. Using a network drive map, files and folders on a host computer are available even to network-unaware DOS applications. The path to a file simply uses the remote drive letter instead of a local drive such as drive A or drive C. To set up a network drive under Windows 98 or Windows 2000, follow these steps:

1. On the host computer, using directions given earlier in the chapter, share the drive or folder on a drive that you want to allow others to have access to.
2. On the remote computer that will use the network drive, while connected to the network, access **Windows Explorer**. Click the **Tools** menu shown in Figure 12-35. Select **Map Network Drive**.

A+ OS 4.1

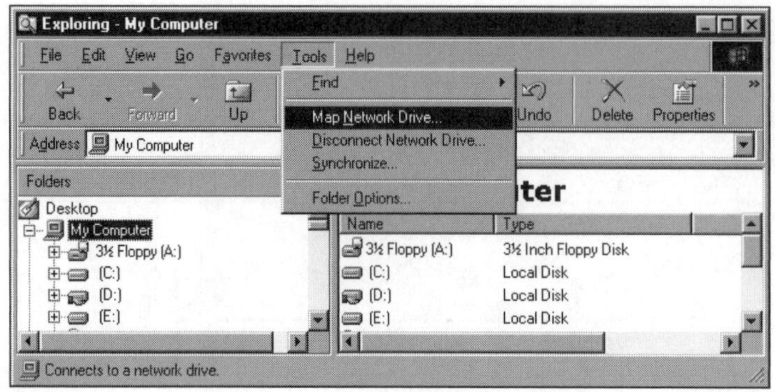

Figure 12-35 Mapping a network drive to a host computer in Windows 98, using Windows Explorer

3. The Map Network Drive dialog box appears, as in Figure 12-36. Select a drive letter from the drop-down list.

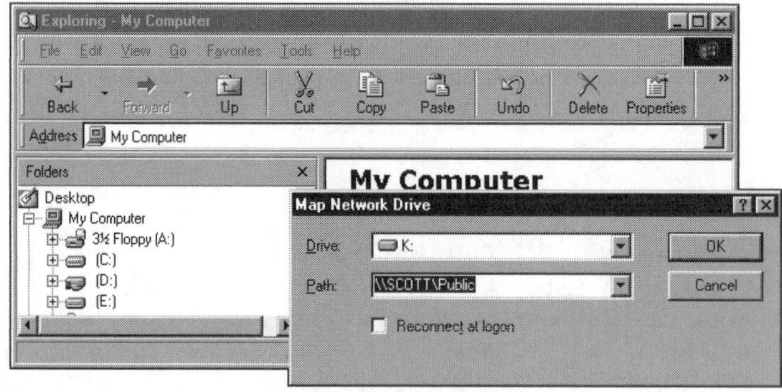

Figure 12-36 To map a network drive in Windows 98, enter a drive letter to use on your PC and the path to the host computer

4. Enter a path to the host computer. Use two backslashes, followed by the name of the host computer, followed by a backslash and the drive or folder to access on the host computer. For example, to access the folder Public on the computer named Scott, enter **\\Scott\Public**, and then click **OK**.

5. Figure 12-37 shows the results of the drive mapping. There is a new drive K displayed in Windows Explorer. Folders listed on the right side of the figure are on the host PC.

A+ OS 4.1

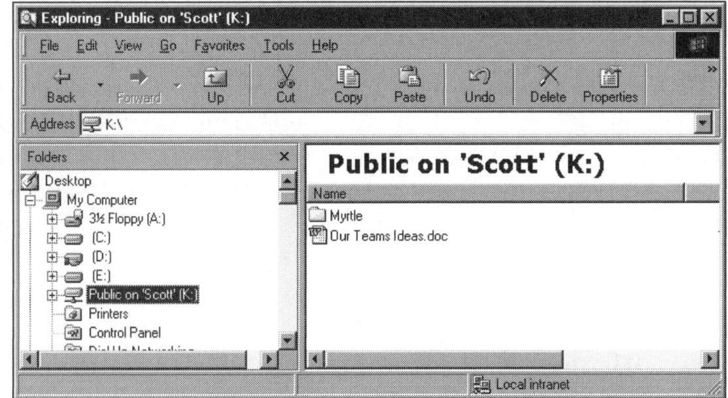

Figure 12-37 Content on the right side of Windows Explorer belongs to the host computer. This computer sees it as belonging to its drive K

If a network drive does not work, go to Network Neighborhood or My Network Places and verify that the network connection is still good.

Direct Cable Connection

A+ OS 4.1

Windows 9x and Windows NT/2000/XP offer a direct cable connection service that allows you to connect two PCs, using either a null modem cable (a cable that connects two PCs using their serial ports) or a parallel cable. Each end of the parallel cable must have a PC connector, not a printer connector. Buy a parallel cable with two DB-25 male/male connections, or buy an adapter for a printer cable. Direct Cable Connection is a handy utility when all you need to do is have two PCs share files or printers, and a cable can reach between them, or you want to allow a guest computer to access shared network resources that a host computer can access.

12

To set up a direct cable connection, set up both computers to share their resources and install the Direct Cable Connection component under Windows. Then run Direct Cable Connection on both computers (click Start, Programs, Accessories, Communications, and Direct Cable Connection). A Direct Cable Connection dialog box appears asking if you want to be the host or guest PC. Make one PC the host and the other the guest. Next, select a port for the connection, either a serial or parallel port. The host computer will then wait for the guest computer to initiate communication. Use Windows Explorer on the guest computer to view the shared folders on the host computer.

REMOTE ACCESS TO A NETWORK

Sometimes users need to dial in to a company network while at home or on the road. A computer on the network can act as a server for the inbound calls. Once dialed in, users can access the network just like any other user connected directly to it, except that access is slower. Remote access is also valuable when a user or support technician wants to control a computer from a remote location just as though he or she were sitting at the host computer. Allowing inbound connections to the network and remote control of a host computer are covered in this section.

Allowing Inbound Connections

You can configure a Windows computer to allow inbound calls so that remote users can access resources on the network. The remote user must have been set up with a user ID and password, and drives and/or folders must be shared. In Windows 95, install the Microsoft Plus utility; in Windows 98, install the Dial-Up Server component. In Windows NT, install the **Remote Access Service (RAS)**. Windows 2000/XP has the ability to allow incoming calls by default.

To allow inbound calls to a Windows 2000 computer, open the Network and Dial-up Connections applet in Control Panel. Click Make New Connection. The Network Connection Wizard window appears (see Figure 12-38). Select Accept incoming connections, and then click Next. The wizard will step you though the process of selecting the modem, user, and protocol for the connection and giving the connection a name.

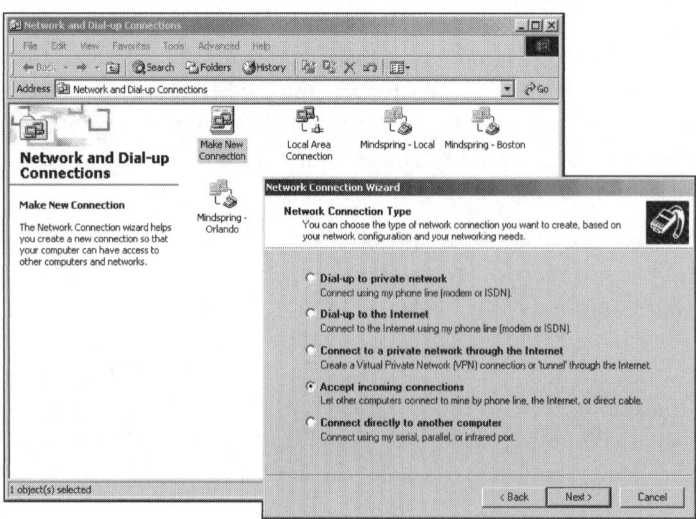

Figure 12-38 Use the Network and Dial-up Connections applet to allow incoming connections to your Windows 2000 PC

Remote Control

You have just seen how you can configure a Windows computer to allow a remote user to access the network through an inbound call. There is another use of a network called remote control. With remote control, you can be at one computer and control another host computer. If the remote control software is sophisticated enough, you can see the entire desktop of the host PC and every keystroke at your PC is directed to the other PC. Help-desk personnel find this kind of control very useful when supporting a user and PC at a remote location.

Using remote control, the remote PC sends commands to the host PC. The host PC uses these commands to execute software on the host PC and passes the results of the commands back to the remote PC. This method only passes commands from the remote PC to the host. The host PC cannot pass commands to the remote PC. To accomplish remote control over a network in Windows 9x and Windows 2000, use a third-party utility such as Symantec's pcANYWHERE (*www.symantec.com*). Figure 12-39 shows a remote PC desktop with the desktop of the host PC displayed by pcANYWHERE.

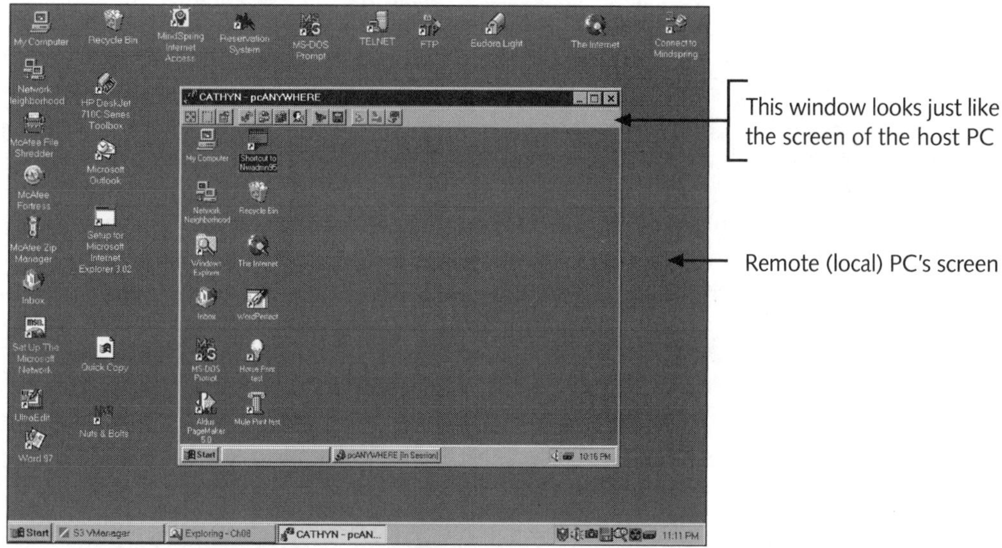

Figure 12-39 pcANYWHERE provides a window on the remote PC that replicates the screen on the host PC. From this window, the remote user can control the host PC

In Windows XP, you can accomplish remote control using a utility called Remote Assistance. This feature is designed to allow one user to send a request for help to another user, perhaps a technical support person, without the second person having physically to come to the first person's workstation.

There are three stages in using Remote Assistance in Windows XP:

1. The user on the host computer must send an invitation by clicking Start, Help and Support, Ask for Assistance, Invite a friend to connect to your computer with Remote Assistance, and Invite Someone to Help You.
2. The remote user (the helper) responds to the host user's request.
3. The host user accepts the remote user's assistance. When the remote user accepts the request for help, the Remote Assistance dialog box appears on the host computer, and the host user clicks **Yes** to enable the remote user to view the host computer screen and to send instant messages.

CHAPTER SUMMARY

- The OSI model describes network communication as consisting of seven layers: Application, Presentation, Session, Transport, Network, Data Link, and Physical. The top five, Application through Network, describe what happens within the operating system. The bottom two, Data Link and Physical, describe what happens on the network card.
- When you are setting up a network, decisions that you make about the operating system, applications you need to support, and user needs affect the top five layers of the OSI model, and decisions about the physical structure of the network affect the bottom two layers.
- The three protocols that Windows supports for use in the top five OSI layers are TCP/IP (which is the protocol suite for the Internet), IPX/SPX (which is designed for use with Novell NetWare), and NetBEUI (which is a proprietary Windows protocol for use on networks isolated from the Internet). Only TCP/IP is supported on the Internet.
- When a protocol is installed on a computer, it automatically binds itself to any NICs it finds. More than one protocol can be associated with a single NIC.
- The four types of addresses on a Windows network are MAC addresses, IP addresses, character-based names such as NetBIOS names, host names, domain names, and port addresses.
- MAC addresses are physical addresses for NICs that are assigned at the factory and generally do not change. They are used at the Data Link layer and can only be used for communication within a network.
- IP addresses identify devices on the Internet and other TCP/IP networks. They consist of four numbers separated by periods. The first part of an IP address identifies the network, and the last identifies the host. The class of an IP address determines how much of the address is used as the network identifier and how much is used for the host identifier.
- IP addresses can either be public or private. For private IP addresses to be able to access the Internet, they must go through NAT (network address translation) so that their requests all appear to be coming from a single public IP address for that network.
- Character-based names, such as fully qualified domain names, are used as an easy way to remember IP addresses.

- The IP address associated with a host name can change. DNS (Domain Name Service) and WINS (Windows Internet Naming Service) track the relationship between host names and IP addresses. DNS is more popular because it works on all platforms.
- Windows 98 assumes that a computer name is a NetBIOS name, which can have up to 15 characters. Windows 2000 and Windows XP assume that a computer name is a host name, which follows the TCP/IP convention and can have up to 63 characters.
- Applications that use TCP/IP for network communication use WinSock to make API calls to the OS.
- Using Network Neighborhood or My Network Places, you can copy files from one computer to another, use the applications installed on one computer from another computer, and share printers.
- In a workgroup, users on a LAN share control of resources, and in a domain, control of resources on the network is centralized.
- NetBEUI is a fast network protocol that can be used on an isolated network. For Internet access, use TCP/IP. TCP/IP requires that the PC be assigned an IP address.
- When configuring TCP/IP, you must know if IP addresses are statically or dynamically assigned.
- Ping is a useful TCP/IP utility to check network connectivity.
- Two other useful troubleshooting tools are Ipconfig (Windows NT, Windows 2000, and Windows XP) and Winipcfg (Windows 9x), which test TCP/IP configuration.
- Before users on a network can view or access resources on a PC, Client for Microsoft Networks and File and Printer Sharing for Microsoft Networks must be installed, and these resources must be shared.
- When troubleshooting printers, first isolate the problem. Narrow the source to the printer, cable, PC hardware, operating system including the device driver, application software, or network.
- Two files on a PC track IP addresses and related NetBIOS or host names. LMHosts tracks NetBIOS names on a NetBEUI network, and Hosts tracks host names on a TCP/IP network.
- Network drive mapping makes one PC appear to have a new hard drive when that hard drive space is actually on another host computer. Use Windows Explorer to map a network drive.
- Direct cable connection between two PCs using either a null modem cable or a parallel cable allows two PCs to share files or printers.
- Windows can accept inbound dial-up connections so that users can dial into a network from home or on the road.
- Remote control of a computer can be used to obtain technical support by allowing a user on a remote computer to control your computer, called the host computer. Two utilities for remote control are Remote Assistance on Windows XP and pcANYWHERE by Symantec.

KEY TERMS

adapter address
Application layer
binding
client
client/server
Data Link layer
data packets
datagrams
default gateway
default printer
DHCP (Dynamic Host Configuration Protocol) server
DNS (domain name) service or domain name system)
DNS server
domain name
dynamic IP address
Enhanced Metafile Format (EMF)
frame
fully qualified domain name (FQDN)
gateway
hardware address
host
host name
Hosts
hub
IEEE (Institute of Electrical and Electronics Engineers)
Internet service provider (ISP)
Intranet
IP address
IPX/SPX (Internetwork Packet Exchange/Sequenced Packet Exchange)
ISO (International Organization for Standardization)
ISP (Internet service provider)
LAN (local area network)
LMHosts
local printer
MAC address (Media Access Control Address)
multicasting
name resolution
NAT (Network Address Translation)
NetBEUI (NetBIOS Extended User Interface).
NetBIOS (Network Basic Input/Output System)
network drive map
Network layer
network printer
NIC (network interface card)
NOS (network operating system)
octet
OSI (Open Systems Interconnect) reference model
packets
peer-to-peer network
physical address
Physical layer
Ping
Presentation layer
private IP address
proxy server
public IP address
Remote Access Service (RAS)
RFC (Request for Comments)
server
Session layer
spooling
static IP address
subnet mask
TCP/IP (Transmission Control Protocol/Internet Protocol)
Transport layer
WINS (Windows Internet Naming Service)
WinSock (Windows Sockets)

Review Questions

1. Name the seven layers of the OSI model and give a short description of each.
2. Which OSI layers describe what happens in the operating system? Which layers describe what happens on the NIC?
3. What is the difference between a peer-to-peer network model and a client/server network model? In Windows, which model uses a workgroup and which uses a domain?
4. List the steps to change the NetBIOS name on a Windows 98 PC.
5. List the steps to change the host name on a Windows 2000 PC.
6. Describe the structure of an IP address. How is it different from a MAC address?
7. What organization set the standards for MAC addresses? What organization developed the OSI model?
8. At what OSI layer are MAC addresses used?
9. What is the Ipconfig command used for? Winipcfg? Ping?
10. How many potential IP addresses are there?
11. How many networks and addresses are available for Class A IP addresses? Class B? Class C?
12. Why are Class D and E addresses not available to individuals and companies?
13. Which octets are used for the network address and for host addresses in Class A? Class B? Class C?
14. In what class is the IP address 185.75.255.10?
15. In what class is the IP address 193.200.30.5?
16. Describe the difference between public and private IP addresses. If a network is using private IP addresses, how can the computers on that network access the Internet?
17. Why is it unlikely that you will find the IP address 192.168.250.10 on the Internet?
18. What are the two ways an IP address can be assigned to a PC? What is one advantage of each?
19. What two files in the \Windows folder are used to track IP addresses and computer names? Which file tracks NetBIOS names? Which file tracks host names?
20. List the steps to view the currently assigned IP address of a Windows 98 PC.
21. List the steps to view the currently assigned IP address of a Windows 2000 PC.
22. What are two ways to access the Network window of Windows 98?
23. List the steps to view the network protocols currently installed under Windows 2000.
24. Which applet in the Windows 2000 Control Panel is used to install network protocols?
25. Describe how WinSock is used.
26. What two Windows components are required to share resources on a network and access those shared resources?
27. What are two ways that printer drivers are installed on a remote computer accessing a printer shared by another computer on the network?
28. When would you want to enable Capture Printer Port when installing a network printer?

29. What must happen on the host computer before you can mount a network drive on a remote computer to the host?
30. What is the mkcompat.exe utility used for?
31. When you are isolating a printer problem, what are the four major possible sources of the problem?
32. List the steps to share a local printer with others in the workgroup.
33. Name and describe two utilities for remote control of a computer. When might you use them?

HANDS-ON PROJECTS

Investigating Your PC

If you are connected to the Internet or a network, answer these questions:

1. What is the hardware device that is used to make this connection (modem or network card)? List the device's name as Windows sees it.
2. If you are connected to a LAN, what is the MAC address of the NIC? Print the screen showing the address.
3. What is the IP address of your PC?
4. What Windows utilities did you use to answer the first three questions?
5. Print the screen showing which network protocols are installed on your PC.

Researching IP Address Classes

Use the Web site *www.f/umps.org/ip* by Paul Rogers to answer these questions:

1. List three companies that have a Class A IP address.
2. List three companies that have a Class B IP address.
3. Who is the owner of IP address class license 9.x.x.x?
4. Find another Web site on the Internet that gives similar information. How does the information on the new site compare with the information on the www.f/umps.org/ip site?

Using Windows Help

Using Windows Help as a resource, list the steps to allow inbound calls to your Windows 2000 computer.

Making a Direct Cable Connection

Using either a null modem cable or a parallel cable, connect two computers using a direct cable connection under Windows. After the connection is made, use Explorer on the guest computer to copy a file from the host computer. Next, reverse roles, making the host the guest computer, and the guest the host computer. Copy a file from the host to the guest computer.

Practicing Networking Skills

Do the following to practice networking skills using either Windows 98 or Windows 2000:

1. On a PC connected to a network, write down the TCP/IP configuration settings for the network.
2. Uninstall, reinstall, and configure TCP/IP.
3. Share a folder on the hard drive.
4. Mount a network drive to a folder shared by someone else on the network.
5. If you have a local printer, share it on the network.
6. Install a printer shared by someone else on the network. Verify that you can print to the printer.

CHAPTER

13

WINDOWS ON THE INTERNET

In this chapter, you will learn:

- How the OSI model applies to TCP/IP networks, such as the Internet
- How to connect to the Internet using a dial-up connection, cable modem or DSL
- About supporting some common Internet clients

In earlier chapters, you learned how different versions of Windows work on a single PC. In Chapter 12, you learned how Windows works on a LAN. This chapter takes the next logical step by discussing connections to the Internet using Windows. You will learn how the OSI model applies to TCP/IP (the Internet protocol suite), how to create and troubleshoot a dial-up connection to the Internet, and how to support some applications that use the Internet, such as Web browsers, e-mail clients, and FTP software.

THE OSI MODEL APPLIED TO A TCP/IP NETWORK

Recall from the last chapter that the OSI model is a universally accepted model describing the layers of communication over a network. You saw how this model applies to communication over a local network. You saw how the top five layers of the model work within the OS and the bottom two with the NIC. This section shows how the OSI model applies to a TCP/IP network such as the Internet or an **intranet** (a local network that uses TCP/IP as its networking protocol).

On a TCP/IP network, TCP/IP is managed by the operating system and covers the top five layers of the OSI model. Figure 13-1 shows the OSI model applied to TCP/IP, which is handling a request from a Web browser to a Web server. Recall that computers are identified by their IP addresses on a TCP/IP network. When a browser wants to access a Web server, it identifies the server by its IP address and uses the TCP/IP protocols of the OS to make the request.

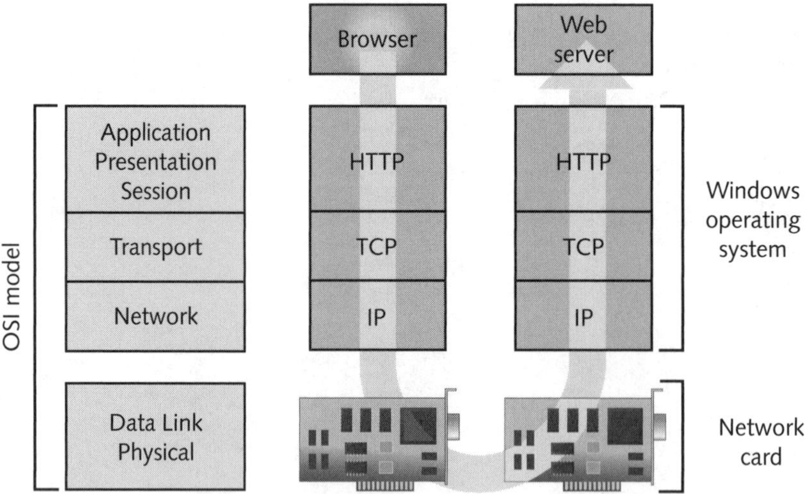

Figure 13-1 When a browser sends a request to a Web server, all layers of the OSI model are involved on both the client and the server

IP Address and Port Identifies a Service

A+ OS 4.2 A server on the Internet or an intranet might be running a Web server, an e-mail server, and an FTP server, all at the same time. (FTP is a quick and easy way to move files over a TCP/IP network.) Each service is an executable program running under the OS on that server. For example, one Web server is Apache.exe by the Apache Software Foundation *(www.apache.org)*, and an e-mail server is Ntmail.exe by Gordano LTD *(www.ntmail.co.uk)*. Both Apache.exe and Ntmail.exe can be running as background servers on a computer. How does a Web browser on a client PC say, "I want to speak with the Web server" and an e-mail program say "I want to speak with the e-mail server," each running on the same

A+ OS 4.2

computer using the same IP address? The answer is by using an identifying number, called a **port**, **port address**, or **port number**, that has been assigned to each service when it is started. A service is said to be listening at a certain port. (Don't confuse these port addresses with I/O addresses assigned to hardware devices, which were discussed in previous chapters.) A Web server is normally assigned port 80, and an e-mail server receiving mail is normally assigned port 25. Another example of a port number assigned to a common service is the use of port 119 for **NNTP (Network News Transfer Protocol)**, the protocol used for newsgroups. If a Web server is assigned a different port number, it can be entered in the address box of the Web browser following the IP address of the server and separated from it by a colon, like this: 138.60.30.5:80. A port number enables the server to determine which server software gets the request, as shown in Figure 13-2.

Figure 13-2 Each server running on a computer is addressed by a unique port number

A network administrator can assign any port number to a server, but there are established port numbers for common services and protocols, as listed in Table 13-1. Unless the administrator has a good reason to do otherwise, he or she uses these common assignments. (One reason not to use the default port assignments is if there is concern about security. Some malicious software targets systems using default port assignments.) Using these default port assignments, on the server in our example, the Web server would communicate at 138.60.30.5:80, and the e-mail server would communicate at 138.60.30.5:25.

13

A+ OS 4.2

Table 13-1 Common TCP/IP port assignments for well-known services

Port	Protocol	Service	Description
20	FTP	FTP	File transfer data
21	FTP	FTP	File transfer control information
23	Telnet	Telnet	Telnet, an application used by Unix computers to control a computer remotely
25	SMTP	E-mail	Simple Mail Transfer Protocol; send e-mail used by client to send e-mail
80	HTTP or HTTPS	Web browser	World Wide Web protocol
109	POP2	E-mail	Post Office Protocol, version 2; used by client to receive e-mail
110	POP3	E-mail	Post Office Protocol, version 3; used by client to receive e-mail
119	NNTP	News server	News servers
143	IMAP	E-mail	Internet Message Access Protocol, the newer protocol used by clients to receive e-mail

The Web browser initiates a request using an IP address and port, but is unaware of all that happens in order for the request to reach the Web server. In this next section, you'll see a quick rundown of each layer and the protocols used at each layer.

TCP/IP Protocols at Each Layer

A+ OS 4.2

Recall from Chapter 12 that TCP/IP covers the top five layers of the OSI model and is included in an operating system as a group of utilities called a stack. Figure 13-3 shows the four major groupings of the OSI model as applied to TCP/IP networks. Within these layers, several protocols operate, and the more significant ones are introduced in this section, but you should know that the TCP/IP protocol suite covers more protocols than just these.

Protocols at the Application, Presentation, and Session Layers

The top three layers of the OSI model are handled by the protocol specific to the application using it and are best treated as a single group rather than unique layers. Four of the most common applications that use the Internet are Web browsers, e-mail, chat rooms, and FTP.

When one of these applications wants to send data to another counterpart application on another host, it makes an API call to the operating system, which handles the request. The API call causes the OS to generate a request. For Web browsers, the request will be an HTTP request. **HTTP (Hypertext Transfer Protocol)** is the protocol used for the World Wide Web, and is used by Web browsers and Web servers to communicate. HTTP works at the OSI Application, Presentation, and Session layers as illustrated in Figures 13-1 and 13-3. In other words, HTTP formats the request, and encrypts and compresses it as necessary. It adds an HTTP header to the beginning of the data that includes the HTTP version being used and how the data is compressed and encrypted, if that was done. Later, when the response is received from the server, it decrypts and decompresses it as necessary before passing it on to the browser.

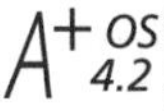

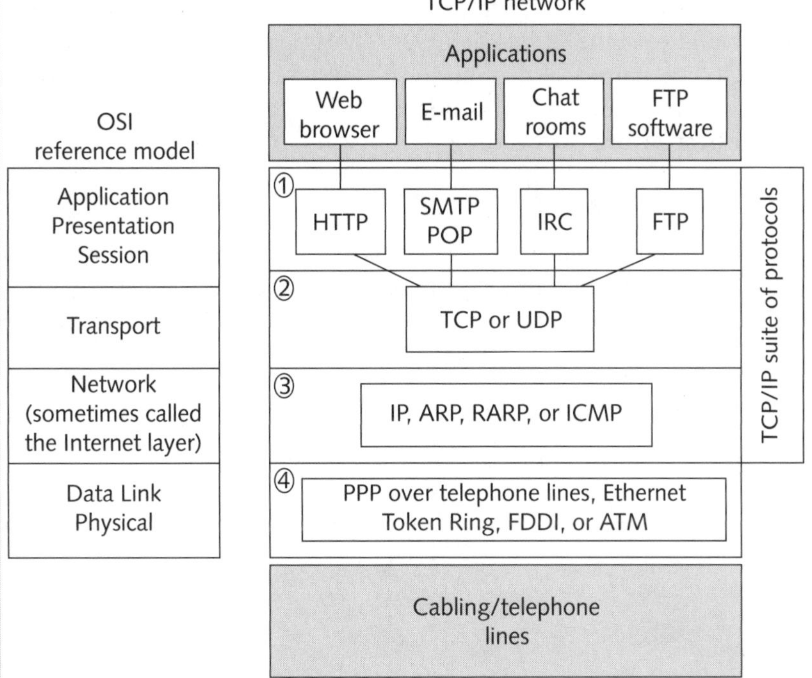

Figure 13-3 How software, protocols, and technology on a TCP/IP network relate to the OSI model

The Session layer is something of a hybrid layer. **Sessions** (established communication links between two software programs), sometimes called **sockets**, can be managed by one of the high-level application protocols such as HTTP, but a limited type of session is created and managed by TCP at the Transport layer. For this reason, sometimes you'll see the Session layer assigned to the high-level application protocols and sometimes assigned to TCP. Note in Figure 13-3 that the Session layer slightly overlaps into the TCP and UDP area (refer to the section labeled 2 in Figure 13-3).

13

Protocols at the Transport Layer

A network has two protocols that work at the Transport layer; one protocol guarantees delivery and the other does not. With TCP/IP, the protocol that guarantees delivery is **TCP (Transmission Control Protocol)**, and the protocol that does not guarantee delivery is **UDP (User Datagram Protocol)**. Recall that TCP is used for client and server requests and responses. Because TCP establishes a connection, it is called a **connection-oriented protocol**. When a TCP packet reaches its destination, an acknowledgment is sent back to the source. If the source TCP does not receive the acknowledgment, it will resend the data or pass an error message back to the higher-level protocol. TCP is used by applications such as Web browsers and e-mail. In our example of a Web browser request, HTTP hands the request off to TCP to guarantee delivery to the server.

A+ OS 4.2

UDP is primarily used for broadcasting and other types of transmissions, such as streaming video or sound over the Web, where best effort delivery will do and fast transmission is important. UDP is a protocol that sends data without checking whether or not the data is received. It does not establish a connection first; thus it is called a **connectionless protocol** or a **best-effort protocol.**

Network Layer Protocols

TCP and UDP communicate with the Network layer, which is sometimes called the Internet layer, passing a request to **IP (Internet Protocol)**, the governing protocol at this layer, which is responsible for breaking up and reassembling data into packets and routing them to their destination. See Figure 13-4.

Figure 13-4 TCP turns to IP to prepare the data for networking

Up to this point, the data with its header information is one long stream of bytes, sometimes too much data for transmission over a network. IP looks at the size of the data and breaks it into individual packets, which can be up to 4K in size. IP adds its own IP header, which includes the IP address of its host (source IP address) and that of the server (destination IP address), and then passes the packet off to the hardware.

Other protocols that operate at the Network layer include the following:

- **ARP (Address Resolution Protocol)**, which is responsible for locating a host on a local network
- **RARP (Reverse Address Resolution Protocol)**, which is responsible for discovering the Internet address of a host on a local network

A+ OS 4.2

- **ICMP (Internet Control Message Protocol)**, which is responsible for communicating problems with transmission (refer to the section labeled 3 in Figure 12-3). For example, if a packet has exceeded the number of routers (a device that routes packets over multiple networks) it can pass through on its way to its destination (called a hop count or a time to live), a router will kill the packet and return an ICMP message to the source, saying that the packet has been killed.

The Data Link and Physical Layer Protocols

When discussing communication over the Internet, the Data Link and Physical layers are generally treated as a single unit, because both of these layers are most often covered by the firmware on a single NIC or, for phone-line connections, by a modem and its drivers. The protocol used depends on the type of physical network that the data is traveling on. For example, for a regular phone line, the protocol is PPP (refer to the section labeled 4 in Figure 13-3) and the device managing that protocol is a modem. **PPP (Point-to-Point Protocol)** is used over phone lines, and allows a PC to connect to a network by using a modem. PPP is sometimes called a **line protocol** or, less commonly, a **bridging protocol**. An earlier version of a line protocol is **Serial Line Internet Protocol (SLIP)**, which does not support encrypted passwords and is seldom used today. PPP is the most popular protocol for managing network transmission from one modem to another. As you learned in the last chapter, Ethernet is the most popular network technology used for LANs, and its protocol is Ethernet. The Ethernet protocol is sometimes called the hardware protocol or the network protocol. Token ring is also used for LANs. FDDI and ATM technologies are used mostly for high-speed fiber-optic networking.

What Happens at the Destination Computer

13

When a Web browser sends a request to a Web server, HTTP, TCP, IP, and the hardware protocols all are involved before the packet leaves the source computer and is placed on the network or phone line. At its destination, these same layers are used in reverse order to pass the packet from the hardware up through the OS and on to the application.

At the destination computer, if the computer is connected to a network, the network protocol, most likely Ethernet, receives the packet. If the computer is connected to a phone line, the line protocol, most likely PPP, receives the packet. PPP or Ethernet will pass the packet up to the IP layer. IP on the destination computer regroups the packets into one continuous stream of data with header information for the higher layers, removing the IP header. IP then passes the one data and header stream on to the Transport layer, which removes the TCP header information and sends an acknowledgment back to the Transport layer on the client (see Figure 13-5). The HTTP server is listening at port 80. It receives the data, removes HTTP header information, decompresses and decrypts the data as necessary and passes the data on to the Web server.

Figure 13-5 TCP guarantees delivery by requesting an acknowledgment

TCP/IP Utilities

A+ OS 4.1

When TCP/IP is installed as a Windows 98 or Windows 2000/XP component, a group of utility tools are also installed that can be used to troubleshoot problems with TCP/IP. The most commonly used TCP/IP utilities are Ping, Winipcfg, and Ipconfig, which you learned about in the last chapter. Table 13-2 lists these and other TCP/IP utilities and gives a purpose for each. The program files are found in the \Windows or \winnt folder.

Table 13-2 Utilities installed with TCP/IP on Windows

Command	Description
ARP (arp.exe)	Manages the IP-to-Ethernet address translation tables that are used to find the MAC address of a host on the network when the IP address is known.
Getmac (getmac.exe)	A windows XP utility that displays the NIC's MAC address.
Ipconfig (ipconfig.exe)	Displays the IP address of the host and other configuration information. (A command similar to Ipconfig used by Unix is Ifconfig.) Some parameters are: `Ipconfig /all` Displays all information about the connection `Ipconfig /release` Releases the current IP address `Ipconfig /renew` Requests a new IP address `Ipconfig /?` Displays information about Ipconfig
FTP (ftp.exe)	Transfers files over a network.
Nbtstat (nbtstat.exe)	Displays current information about TCP/IP and NetBIOS when both are being used on the same network.
Netstat (netstat.exe)	Displays information about current TCP/IP connections.
Ping (ping.exe)	Verifies that there is a connection on a network between two hosts.

A+ OS 4.1

Table 13-2 Utilities installed with TCP/IP on Windows (continued)

Command	Description
Route (route.exe)	Allows you to manually control network routing tables.
Telnet (telnet.exe)	Allows you to communicate with another computer on the network remotely, entering commands to control the remote computer.
Tracert (tracert.exe)	Traces and displays the route taken from the host to a remote destination; Tracert is one example of a trace routing utility.
Winipcfg (winipcfg.exe)	Displays IP address and other configuration information in a user-friendly window (not available under Windows 2000). On the Winipcfg window, use Release and Renew to cause the system to release the current IP address and request a new one, which can sometimes solve TCP/IP connectivity problems when using a DHCP server.

When you have problems with connectivity, use Ping to test the connection. If Ping fails, use either Winipcfg (for Windows 9x) or Ipconfig (for Windows NT/2000/XP) to release and renew the IP address used by the PC. This can sometimes restore a connection.

Microsoft SNMP Agent

In addition to the utilities that are automatically installed with TCP/IP, another useful utility is Microsoft SNMP Agent. This utility can be installed after you install TCP/IP, and you can find it on the Windows 98 CD. **SNMP (Simple Network Management Protocol)** provides system management for networks. A system manager can monitor remote connections to computers running Windows clients with SNMP Agent. The manager will most likely use the utility sparingly because it can be a security risk. For more information about SNMP, see RFC 1156 (*www.rfc-editor.org*). 13

A+ OS 4.1

Using NSLookup

An interesting tool that lets you read information from the Internet name space is NSLookup, which requests information about domain name resolutions from the DNS server's zone data. Zone data is information about domain names and their corresponding IP addresses kept by a DNS server. The utility program is included in Windows 2000. For example, using Windows 2000, to retrieve what the DNS server knows about the domain name *www.microsoft.com*, follow these directions:

1. Open a command window: Click **Start**, **Programs**, **Accessories**, **Command Prompt**. A command window appears.
2. Enter the command: **Nslookup www.microsoft.com**. Figure 13-6 shows the results. Notice in the figure that the DNS server knows about three IP addresses that are assigned to www.microsoft.com. It also reports that this information is non-authoritative, meaning that it is not the authoritative, or final, name server for the www.microsoft.com name.

A+ OS 4.1

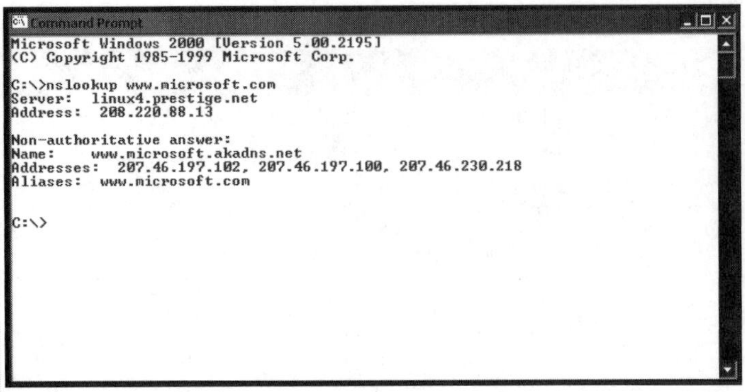

```
Command Prompt
Microsoft Windows 2000 [Version 5.00.2195]
(C) Copyright 1985-1999 Microsoft Corp.

C:\>nslookup www.microsoft.com
Server:  linux4.prestige.net
Address:  208.220.88.13

Non-authoritative answer:
Name:    www.microsoft.akadns.net
Addresses:  207.46.197.102, 207.46.197.100, 207.46.230.218
Aliases:  www.microsoft.com


C:\>
```

Figure 13-6 The Nslookup command reports information about the Internet name space

CONNECTING TO THE INTERNET USING A DIAL-UP CONNECTION

A+ OS 4.2 This section covers how to connect to the Internet over a phone line using a dial-up connection. To make such a connection, you need to have a modem installed on your PC, as well as drivers to control the modem. (Installing modems is a hardware task that is not covered in this book.) In the last chapter, you learned how to install TCP/IP and bind it to your NIC; the same procedure is used for binding TCP/IP to a modem. This section assumes that TCP/IP is installed and bound to the modem and covers how to connect to the Internet, beginning with how to install and configure the Dial-up Networking feature in Windows and continuing with how to create and test the connection to your ISP.

When a Windows PC connects to a network using a modem and regular phone line, the process is called **dial-up networking**. In effect, the modem on the PC acts like a network card, providing the physical connection to the network and the firmware at the lowest level of communication. After the dial-up connection is made, the PC's application software relates to the network as though it were directly connected to the network using a network card, but a network card is not needed. The modems and phone lines in between are transparent to the user, although transmission speeds with direct network connections are much faster than those of dial-up connections.

This section covers how to use dial-up networking utilities in Windows 9x and Windows 2000/XP. Note that in Windows 9x, Dial-up Networking and Network Connections are two different applets and are located under My Computer. In Windows 2000, there is a single applet in the Control Panel called Network and Dial-up Connections that combines both functions, and in Windows XP, this single Control Panel applet is called Network Connections.

How Dial-up Networking Works

A+ OS 4.2 Dial-up networking works by using PPP to send packets of data over phone lines. The network protocol packages the data, making it ready for network traffic, and then PPP adds its own header and trailer to these packets. Figure 13-7a shows how this works. The data

A+ OS 4.2

is presented to the network protocols, either TCP/IP, NetBEUI, or IPX/SPX, which add their header information. Then the packet is presented to the line protocol, PPP, which serves as the Data Link layer in the OSI model. A PPP header and trailer is added to the packet and then presented to the modem for delivery over phone lines to a modem on the receiving end.

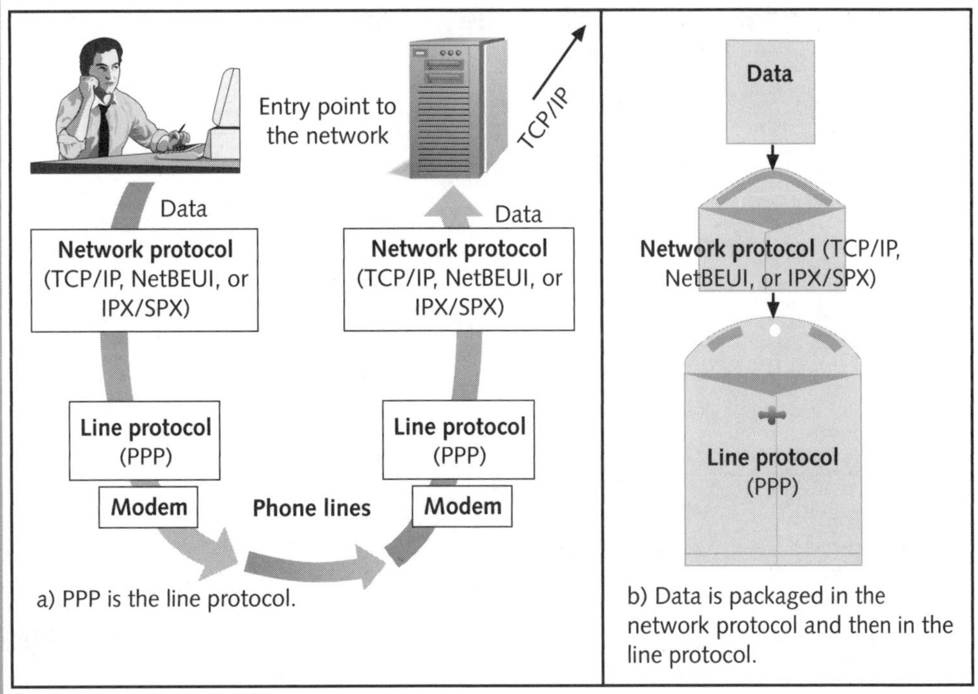

Figure 13-7 PPP allows a PC to connect to a network using a modem

13

The modem on the receiving end is connected to a PC or server. The receiving computer strips off the PPP header and trailer information and sends the packet on to the network still packaged in the TCP/IP protocols, or whatever other protocols the network is using. In Figure 13-7b, you can see how these two protocols act like envelopes. Data is put into a TCP/IP envelope for travel over the network. This envelope is put into a PPP envelope for travel over phone lines. When the phone line segment of the trip is completed, the PPP envelope is discarded.

Creating a Dial-up Connection in Windows 9x

A+ OS 4.2

To use Windows 9x or Windows NT to communicate with a network over phone lines, Dial-up Networking must be installed as an OS component on your PC using the Add/Remove Programs applet in Control Panel. (Network and Dial-up Connections in Windows 2000 and Network Connections in Windows XP are installed by default.)

When Windows 9x installs Dial-up Networking, it also "installs" a dial-up adapter. In terms of function, think of a dial-up adapter as a virtual network card. Remember that in

A+ OS 4.2

the last chapter, you learned how TCP/IP is bound to a network interface card. A dial-up adapter is a modem playing the role of a network card for dial-up networking. After Dial-up Networking is installed, open the Device Manager to see your "new" dial-up adapter listed under Network adapters, as in Figure 13-8. You can also see it listed as an installed network component in the Network window of the Control Panel.

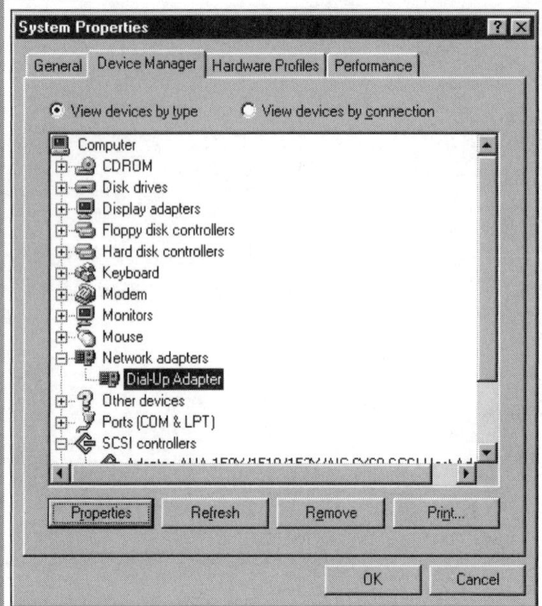

Figure 13-8 After Dial-up Networking is installed, a new virtual network device, a dial-up adapter, is listed as an installed hardware device

After installing Dial-up Networking, you create an icon in the Dial-up Networking group and then use the icon to make a connection. After you make the connection, you can use any Internet application, such as a Web browser or e-mail client, for which you have the software installed on your PC.

Make a New Connection

To create a new dial-up networking connection in Windows 98:

1. After Dial-up Networking is installed, click **Start**, point to **Programs**, **Accessories**, **Communications**, and then click **Dial-up Networking**. The Dial-up Networking dialog box appears, as in Figure 13-9.
2. Double-click **Make New Connection**. The Make New Connection Wizard appears, also shown in Figure 13-9. Click **Next** to move past the first screen.
3. Enter a name for the connection. When you are connecting to the Internet, you can use the name of your ISP and the city in which the server is located. An example would be Earthlink Boston. If your modem is already installed, it appears in the modem list.

A+ OS 4.2

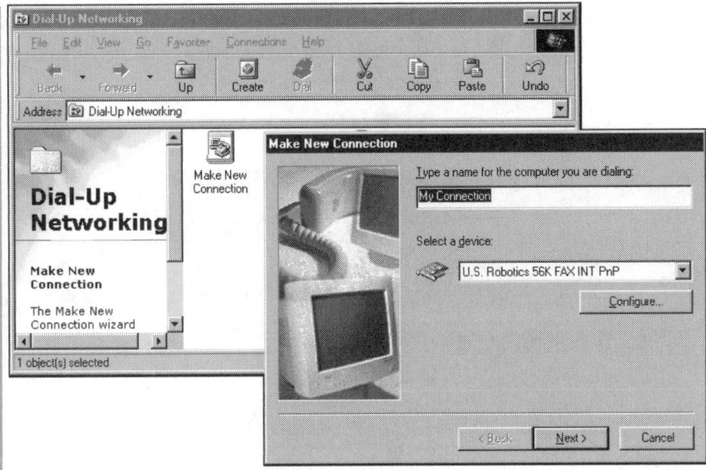

Figure 13-9 Creating a Windows 98 Dial-up Networking Connection icon

4. In the next dialog box, type the phone number to dial, and then click **Next** to continue.
5. Click **Finish** to build the icon. The icon is displayed in the Dial-up Networking window.

Set up a Connection to Your ISP

In order for your PC to connect to your ISP and use the Internet, you need answers to the following questions:

- What is the phone number of the ISP?
- What is your user ID and password for the ISP?
- Will DNS servers be assigned at connection? If not, what is the IP address of one or two DNS servers?
- How will your IP address be assigned (most likely dynamic)?

To set up an ISP connection, do the following:

1. Right-click the icon you created for the connection and select **Properties** from the drop-down menu.
2. Click the **General** tab. Verify that the correct phone number for your ISP is entered.
3. Click **Server Types**. Figure 13-10 shows the resulting dialog box. Verify that these selections are made:
   - Type of Dial-up Server: **PPP Internet, Windows NT Server, Windows 98**

A+ OS 4.2

- Advanced Options: Select **Enable software compression** (software compression is most likely to be enabled, but this option really depends on what the ISP is doing) and **Log on to network**.
- Allowed Network Protocols: **TCP/IP**

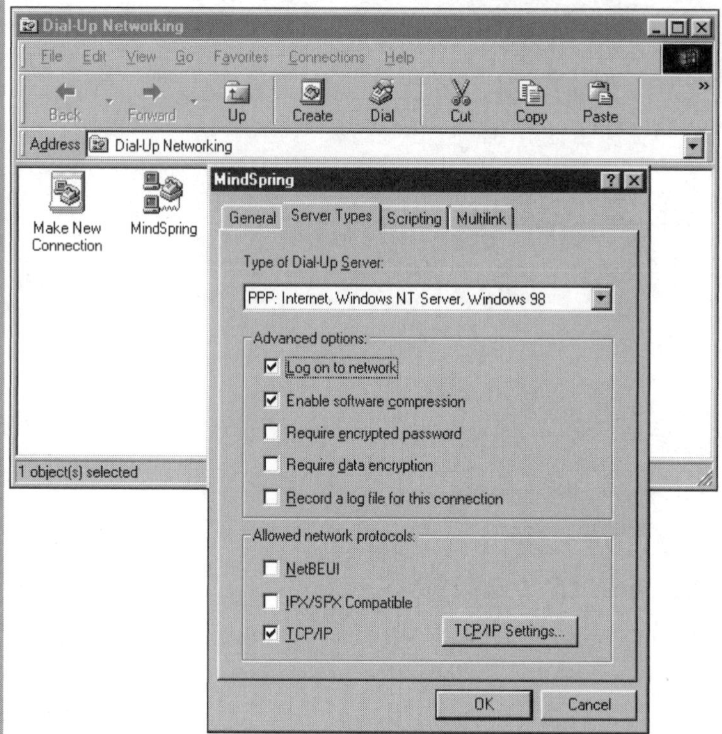

Figure 13-10 Configuring the server type for a connection to the Internet in Windows 9x

4. Click **TCP/IP Settings** to open the TCP/IP Settings dialog box, as shown in Figure 13-11. Verify that these settings (or other settings as specified by your ISP) are chosen:
   - **Server assigned IP address**
   - **Specify name server addresses**
   - **Use IP header compression**
   - **Use default gateway on remote network**
5. Enter the IP addresses of the primary and secondary DNS servers. (This information is provided by your ISP. If it is not provided, then select Server assigned name server addresses.)
6. Click **OK** two times to complete building the Dial-up Networking connection.

A+ OS 4.2

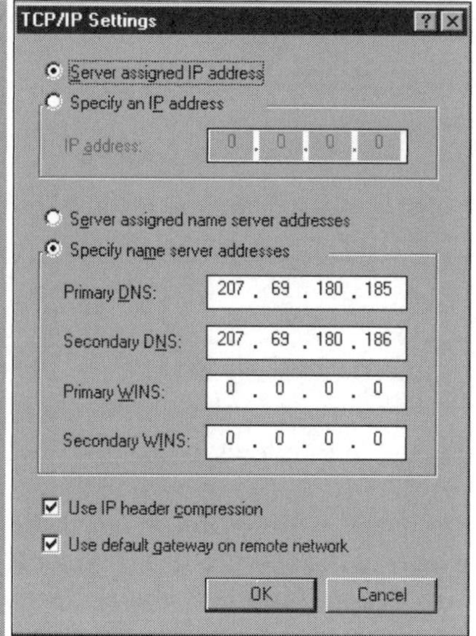

Figure 13-11 TCP/IP settings for a connection to the Internet in Windows 9x

7. To connect to your ISP, double-click the icon you created for it, which is now correctly configured. The first time you use the icon, you enter the user ID and password to connect to your ISP. Check the option to remember the user name and password if you don't want to have to enter it every time, but remember that this might not be wise if others who cannot be trusted have access to your PC.
8. Click **Connect**. You should now hear the modem making the connection.

Creating a Dial-up Connection in Windows 2000

A+ OS 4.2

Windows 2000 adds more wizards to make the configuration process easier than it was with Windows 9x. To create a new dial-up connection to the Internet in Windows 2000:

1. From the Start menu, click **Programs**, **Accessories**, **Communications**, and **Network and Dial-up Connections.**
2. The Network and Dial-up Connections window opens, as shown in Figure 13-12. Double-click the **Make New Connection** icon. If the Location Information screen opens, click **Next** to continue on to the Network Connection Wizard.
3. The Network Connection Wizard opens. Click **Next** to skip the welcome screen. On the next screen, select the second option, **Dial-up to the Internet**, and then click **Next**.
4. The Internet Connection Wizard opens. Select the option to configure an Internet connection manually, and then click **Next**.

A+ OS 4.2

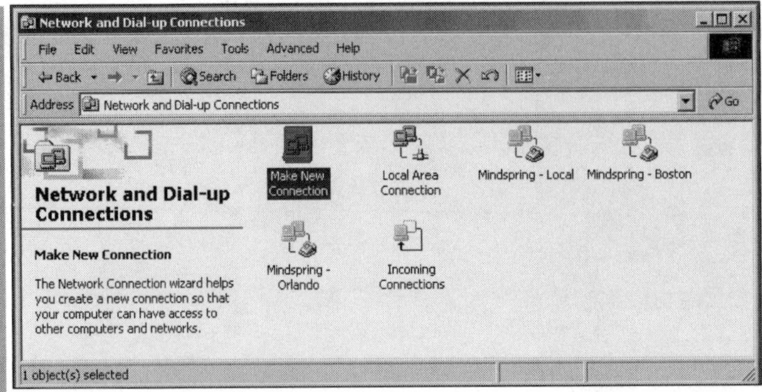

Figure 13-12 Network Dial-up connections applet in Windows 2000

5. Choose how you connect to the Internet. For this example, select the option **I connect through a phone line and a modem**, and then click **Next** (see Figure 13-13). Notice in Figure 13-13 that you can also choose to connect through a LAN at this point. (This option was not available through a wizard in Windows 9x.)
6. Follow the directions in the remainder of the wizard to enter the phone number to dial to connect to your ISP, your username and password, a name for the connection, and whether to set up a new e-mail account. (For this example, assume that you already have an e-mail account, and choose not to set up a new one.)
7. On the final screen of the wizard, which informs you that you have created the connection successfully and can access it through your browser, click **Finish** to close the wizard. Your new connection is shown in the Network and Dial-up Connections window.
8. If you want to create a shortcut to the dial-up connection on the desktop, right-click the icon in the Network and Dial-up Connections window and select **Create Shortcut** on the shortcut menu.
9. A message appears saying, "Windows cannot create a shortcut here. Do you want the shortcut to be placed on the desktop instead?" Click **Yes** to create a shortcut on the desktop.

The procedure for creating a dial-up networking connection from Windows XP is similar to the procedure in Windows 2000. Double-click the Network Connections icon from the Windows XP Control Panel, and in the resulting window, click the option to create a new dial-up connection, then follow the wizard's instructions.

A+ OS 4.2

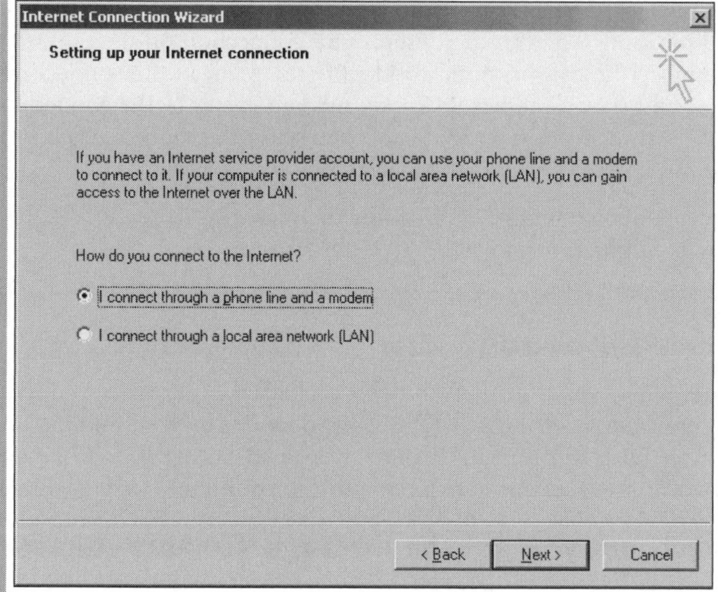

Figure 13-13 Using the Windows 2000 Internet Connection Wizard

Dial-up Networking Problems

A+ OS 4.2

In this section, you will learn about some of the most common problems and errors that you may encounter with dial-up networking and what to do about them. As always, check the simple things first before trying more difficult solutions.

13

You cannot make a connection

If you have a problem connecting to the Internet using a dial up connection, first find out what works and what doesn't work. Try the following:

- Find out the answers to these questions: At what point does the connecting process fail? Do you hear the modem hissing? If so, the problem is probably with the user ID and password. If not, then the problem might be the phone number, phone line, or modem. Is the phone line plugged in? Does the phone line work? Can you hear a dial tone?
- Check the Dial-up Networking connection icon for errors. Is the phone number correct? Does the number need to include a 9 to get an outside line? Has a 1 been added in front of the number by mistake?
- Try dialing the number manually from a phone. Do you hear beeps on the other end?
- Try another phone number.
- Does the modem work? Check Device Manager for reported errors about the modem.

A+ OS 4.2

- Print out the Modemlog.txt file from a successful connection on another computer and the same file from the unsuccessful connection on the problem computer. Compare the two printouts to identify the point in the connection at which an error occurs. (For Windows 9x, to log modem events to the Modemlog.txt file, double-click Modems in Control Panel, then select the modem, click Properties, Connection, Advanced, and turn on Recording to a log file.)
- Are all components installed? Check for the dial-up adapter and TCP/IP, and check the configuration of each.
- Reboot your PC and try again.
- Try removing and reinstalling each network component. Begin with TCP/IP.
- Sometimes older copies of the Windows socket DLL may be interfering with the current Windows 9x socket DLL. (Windows 9x may be finding and executing the older DLL before it finds the newer one.) Search for and rename any files named Winsock.dll except the one in the \Windows\System directory.

You can connect, but you get the message "Unable to resolve hostname..."

This error message means that TCP/IP is not able to determine how to route a request to a host. Right-click the Dial-up Networking connection icon, select Properties, and check for these things:

- Under Server Type, try making TCP/IP the only network protocol allowed.
- Under TCP/IP settings, check the IP addresses of the DNS servers.
- Make sure *Using the default gateway* is selected.
- Try *not* selecting IP header compression.

After connecting, you get the error message "Unable to establish a compatible set of network protocols"

This error is most likely to be caused by a problem with the installation and configuration of Dial-up Networking or TCP/IP. Try these things:

- Verify that the dial-up adapter and TCP/IP are installed and configured correctly.
- Remove and reinstall TCP/IP. Be sure to reboot after the installation.
- For Windows 9x, try putting the PC in a different workgroup.
- Windows 9x can write the events that occur when PPP processes a call to a log file. Create the Ppplog.txt file on a PC that makes a successful connection, and compare it to the log file of your bad connection to see exactly when the problem began. To turn on the logging of events to the file, double-click the Network icon in Control Panel. Click Dial-up Adapter, click Properties, select the Advanced tab, and then select Record a log file. On the Value list, click Yes, then click OK. Reboot the PC. The file Ppplog.txt is created in the Windows folder as the connection is made and used.

A+ OS 4.2

When you double-click the Web browser, the modem does not dial automatically

When this occurs, right-click the browser icon and select Properties from the drop-down menu. Under the Connection tab, check Connect to the Internet as needed.

DSL AND CABLE MODEM CONNECTIONS

A+ OS 4.2

When using cable modem, DSL, ISDN, wireless, LAN, or satellite, if you are connecting a single PC to the Internet using an ISP, then the TCP/IP settings are no different from those used by a modem-to-phone line connection. Cable modem, DSL and a LAN all use a network card in the PC for the physical connection. The network card provides a network port for a network cable. For cable modem service to the Internet, the other end of the network cable connects to a cable modem. For DSL, the other end of the cable connects to a DSL box and, for a satellite, the other end connects to a satellite converter box. For a LAN, the other end of the network cable connects to a network hub. The connection between the NIC and the broadband device most likely uses the **PPPoE (Point-to-Point Protocol over Ethernet)** protocol, a protocol specifically designed to support broadband connections and is included in Windows XP.

For each of these types of Internet connections, generally the installation goes like this:

1. Install the network card and the drivers to control the card.
2. Use a network cable to connect the PC to a cable modem, DSL box or network hub. For wireless, position the PC within range of a wireless access point.
3. Install TCP/IP and bind TCP/IP to the card.
4. Configure TCP/IP to connect to the Internet or LAN.
5. Install the applications software (for example, a browser) to use the connection.

In the following section, you'll learn about the different ways to connect to the Internet using these faster-than-phone line connections and the details of installing these services.

13

Cable Modem

A+ OS 4.2

The cable modem uses a regular TV cable cord to connect to a TV cable wall outlet. Figure 13-14 illustrates what the arrangement looks like. The cable modem also has an electrical connection to provide power to the box. A cable modem connects to your PC by way of a network port or a USB port using either a network cable or a USB cable from the modem to the PC. Your cable modem company will provide you with the TCP/IP settings to use to configure TCP/IP. For a home installation, some cable modem companies will do the entire installation for you. You might need to purchase the cable modem and NIC or they might be included in the installation fee. A service technician will come to your home, install the network card, and configure your PC to use the service.

A+ OS 4.2

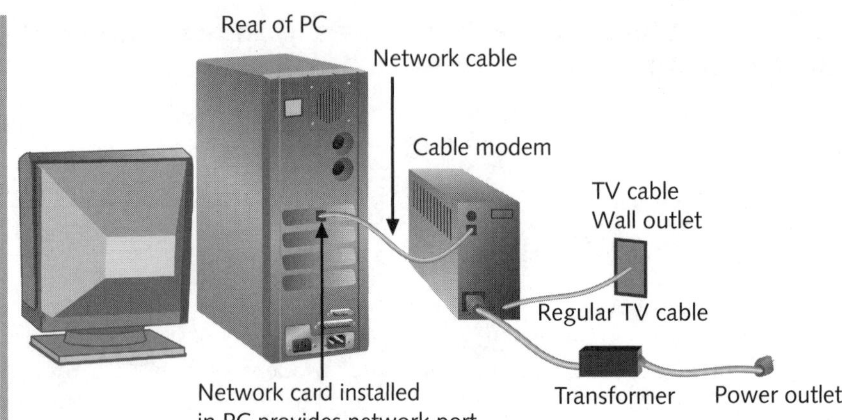

Figure 13-14 Cable modem connects to a PC through a network card installed on the PC

If you don't have on-site service from the cable modem company, follow these instructions to install cable modem when using a network card:

1. Install the network card and drivers. The cable modem company records the MAC address of the cable modem or the NIC in your PC into an online list of valid addresses that identifies your system as a subscriber to the cable modem service. The MAC address of the cable modem is written somewhere on the modem. If the cable company wants the MAC address of the NIC, use WinIPcfg or Ipconfig to obtain the address. Call the cable company help desk and give the technician the address. Also find out how to configure TCP/IP to use their service. Most likely an IP address, subnet mask, IP address of the default gateway and IP address of a domain name server are all dynamically assigned when the PC connects to the service.
2. Configure TCP/IP to use the network card, using the TCP/IP configuration information provided by the cable modem company.
3. Shut down the PC and connect one end of the network cable to the network port on the back of the PC. Connect the other end of the cable to the cable modem. Be sure the cable modem is plugged in and turned on. There is usually a switch on the back of the box. Connect the TV cable from the TV cable outlet to the cable modem. (Refer back to Figure 13-14.) Turn on the PC.
4. When the PC starts up, you should immediately be connected to the Internet. Test the connection using your web browser or e-mail client. If you are not connected, try the following:
   - For Windows 9x, use WinIPcfg or, for Windows 2000/XP, use Ipconfig to release the IP address and renew it. Check for Internet connectivity again.
   - If the above did not work, turn off the PC and the cable modem. Wait a full five minutes until all connections have timed out at the cable modem company.

A+ OS 4.2

Turn on the cable modem and then turn on the PC. After the PC boots up, again check for connectivity.

- If this doesn't work, call the cable modem help desk. The technician there can release and restore the connection at that end, which should restore service.

DSL

A+ OS 4.2

DSL is provided by the local telephone company. The telephone company's responsibility for the phone system ends at your house. Inside your house, you are responsible for your home phone network. A DSL connection uses a DSL converter box that is sometimes combined with a router as a single device so that more than one PC can use the DSL line. The device connects to the PC by way of a network cable and card.

As with cable modem, a technician from the phone company most likely will do an ISDN or DSL installation for you. The installation process on the PC works the same as that of cable modem.

Sharing Internet Connections

A+ OS 4.2

There are several ways that computers on a LAN can share an Internet connection. Here are a few options:

- If one computer on the LAN has a direct connection to the Internet by way of a phone line, cable modem or DSL, it can serve as a host computer for others on the LAN. Windows 98 and Windows XP Internet Connection Sharing (ICS) is designed to mange this type of connection. Using ICS, the host computer uses NAT and acts as the proxy server for the LAN. Windows XP ICS also includes a firewall.
- For broadband connections (cable modem and DSL), the broadband converter box can connect to a network device such as a router that manages the connection for the entire network. The router has a network connection to the converter box and one or more network ports for devices on the network. In this situation, the router is likely to also have firewall software embedded in it and is controlled by way of a Web browser. A user on any computer on the network can enter the IP address of the router in a Web browser window and bring up the software on the router to configure the router. The router can serve as a DHCP server, a NAT proxy server and a firewall.
- The router can also serve as a wireless access point for computers to connect wirelessly to the Internet. An example of a router that is also a wireless access point is the AirPlus D1-714P+ by D-Link (www.d-link.com) showing in Figure 13-15. It has one port for the converter box, four ports for computers on the network and a parallel printer port designed to manage a network printer. The router can also support several computers with wireless adapters.

A+ OS 4.2

Figure 13-15 This D-Link router allows computers on a LAN to share a broadband Internet connection and also is an access point for computers with wireless adapters

Windows Internet Connection Sharing

Windows XP and Windows 98 offers Internet Connection Sharing that allows others on a small office or home LAN to share an Internet connection with a host computer. To use Internet Connection Sharing, the computer that has a direct connection to the Internet by way of a phone line, cable modem or DSL is the host computer. Follow these general directions to configure the LAN for Internet Connection Sharing using Windows XP:

1. Following directions earlier in the chapter, install and configure the hardware (modem, cable modem or DSL) to connect to the Internet and verify the connection is working.
2. Open the Network Connections window in the Windows XP Control Panel and click on the link to **Set up a home or small office network**. The Network Setup Wizard opens. Click **Next**.
3. Select the connection method for your host computer, which is **This computer connects directly to the Internet. The other computers on my network connect to the Internet through this computer.** Click **Next**.
4. The wizard will look at your hardware connections (NIC or modem) and select the one that it sees as a "live" connection. Verify it selected correctly and then follow the wizard to enter a description for your computer, your computer name and workgroup name.
5. The next screen of the wizard offers you the option of creating a Network Setup Disk that you can use to quickly configure every other computer on the LAN that is to use the Internet connection (see Figure 13-16). Select the option to **Create a Network Setup Disk**, insert a blank floppy disk in the drive and click **Next**.

A+ OS 4.2

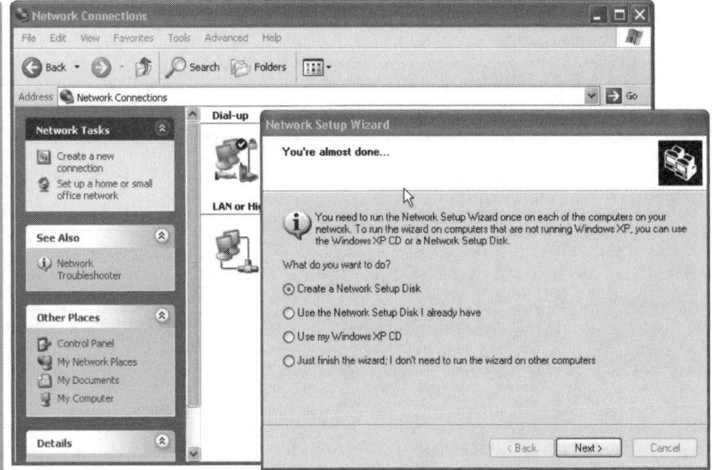

Figure 13-16 Create a Network Setup Disk to configure other computers on the LAN

6. The next screen gives you the option to format the disk. If it needs formatting, click **Format Disk**. Otherwise, click **Next**.
7. The wizard tells you that to use the disk, insert it into the next computer on the network and run the program on the disk named Netsetup.exe. Click **Next** and then click **Finish**.
8. Recall from Chapter 10 that you can enable Internet Connection Firewall to protect the connection to your ISP against unsolicited activity from the Internet. On the host computer only, to enable Internet Connection Firewall, in the Network Connections widows, right click on the network connection and select **Properties** form the shortcut menu. On the Properties box, click the **Advanced** tab and select **Protect my computer and network by limiting or preventing access to this computer from the Internet**.
9. Use the Network Setup Disk on each computer on the LAN that is to use the shared connection.

SUPPORTING INTERNET CLIENTS

A+ OS 4.2

Now that you've learned how to connect to the Internet and how to troubleshoot connections with it, let's look at some ways of using it. Earlier in the chapter in Table 12-1, you saw a list of applications that use the Internet. These applications are also called Internet clients. In this section, you will learn how to support some of the most common: Web browsers, e-mail, and FTP.

Supporting Web Browsers

A+ OS 4.1 4.2

A Web browser is a software application on a user's PC that is used to request Web pages from a Web server on the Internet or an intranet. A Web page is a text file that has an .htm or .html file extension. It can include text coded in **HTML (Hypertext Markup Language)** that can be interpreted by a Web browser to display formatted text and graphics, as well as play sounds. If the HTML code on the Web page points to other files used to build the page such as a sound file or a photograph file, these files are also downloaded to the browser. In this section, you will learn about the addresses that Web browsers use to locate resources on a Web server and how to troubleshoot common problems that occur with Web browsers.

How a URL Is Structured

Earlier in the chapter you saw that a Web browser requests a Web page by sending an IP address followed by an optional port number. This works well on an intranet, but on the Internet, a more user-friendly URL is preferred. A **URL (Uniform Resource Locator)** is an address for a Web page file or other resource on the Internet. Figure 13-17 shows the structure of a URL.

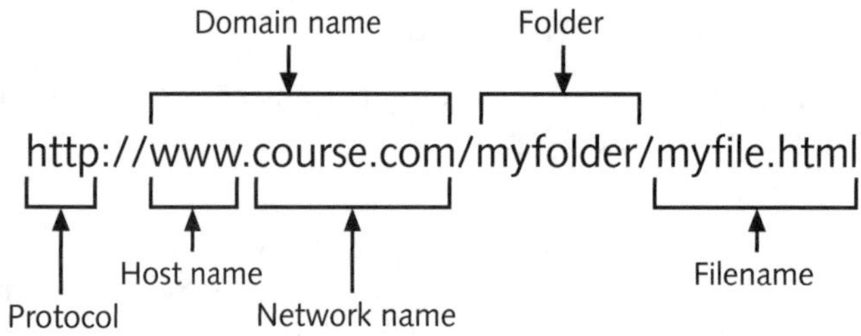

Figure 13-17 A URL contains the protocol used, the host name of the Web server, the network name, and the path and filename of the requested file

The first part of the URL shown in Figure 13-17 indicates the protocol, which in this case is HTTP. If secure HTTP were used to encrypt the data being transmitted, the protocol shown would be **HTTPS (HTTP secure)** and the secure protocol being used is SSL (secure socket layer). The protocol part of the URL specifies the rules, or protocol, the Web server should use when transmitting the page to the browser. Recall that rules of communication are called protocols and that although the browser can use several different protocols, HTTP is the one used for Web pages. A Web server is sometimes called an HTTP server.

Recall from Chapter 12 that a host name identifies a server or another computer within a network. In this example, the host name is *www* (a Web server), and *course.com* is the name of the Course Technology network, sometimes called the domain name. A name that contains not only the network name (in this case, course.com) but also the host on that network is, as you learned in the last chapter, called a fully qualified domain name (FQDN) (in this case, *www.course.com*). The Web page requested is located in the folder *myfolder* on the www server, and the file within that folder is named *myfile.html*. The FQDN must be resolved to an IP address before the request can happen.

A+ OS 4.1 4.2

The last segment, or suffix, of a domain name is called the **top-level domain** (.com in our example) and tells you something about the organization or individual that owns the name. Some domain names in the United States end in the suffixes listed in Table 13-3. There are other endings as well, including codes for countries, such as .uk for the United Kingdom. With the growth of the Internet, there has been a shortage of available domain names; because of this shortage, additional suffixes are being created.

Table 13-3 Suffixes used to identify top-level domain names

Domain Suffix	Description
.air	Aviation industry
.biz	Businesses
.com	Commercial institution
.coop	Business cooperatives
.edu	Educational institution
.gov	Government institution
.info	General use
.int	Organizations established by international treaties between governments
.mil	U.S. military
.museum	Museums
.name	Individuals
.net	Internet provider or network
.org	Nonprofit organization
.pro	Professionals

Domain names stand for IP addresses and provide an easy way to remember them, but domain names and IP addresses are not necessarily permanently related. A host computer can have a certain domain name and can be connected to one network and assigned a certain IP address, and then be moved to another network and assigned a different IP address. The domain name can stay with the host while it connects to either network. It is up to a name resolution service, such as DNS or WINS, to track the relationship between a domain name and the current IP address of the host computer. Using Internet Explorer, you can control support options such as how scripts are handled by clicking Tools, Internet Options. The Internet Options window opens. Click the Advanced tab.

A+ OS 4.1 4.2

Solving Browser Performance Problems

If you notice poor browser performance, use the tools you have seen in earlier chapters, such as Defrag, ScanDisk, and System Information, to make sure that you have enough free hard drive space, that the hard drive is clean, and that the virtual memory settings are optimized. If you perform these tasks and the browser is still slow, try the procedures given below using the most popular browser, Internet Explorer.

A+ OS 4.2

Internet Explorer If Internet Explorer (IE) is slow even after you have taken steps to optimize your system, do the following:

1. Right-click the **Internet Explorer** icon on the desktop and then click **Properties** on the shortcut menu. The Internet Properties window opens, as shown in Figure 13-18. (If the icon is not on the desktop, double-click on the **Internet** icon in Control Panel.)

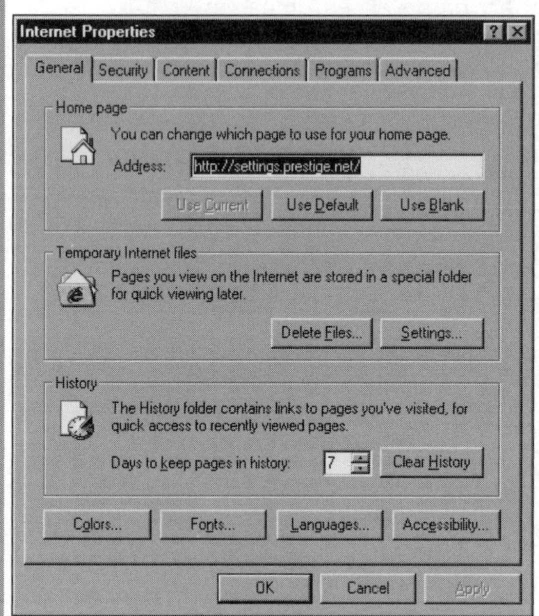

Figure 13-18 Use the Internet Properties dialog box to control the Internet Explorer environment

2. Click **Delete Files** under the Temporary Internet files heading to clean out the IE cache. The Delete Files dialog box appears asking you to confirm the deletion. Click **OK**. IE must search the entire cache each time it accesses a Web page. If the cache is too big, performance is affected.
3. Click **Clear History** under the History heading to clean out the shortcuts cache. The Internet Options dialog box appears asking you to confirm the deletions. Click **OK**. If this cache gets too big, performance can be slowed down. Also, if you reduce the days that Internet Explorer keeps pages in the history folder, performance might improve because there will be less material for Internet Explorer to search. For example, change the days to keep pages in history from the default value of 20 to 7.
4. Click **OK** to close the window.

Suppress the Downloading of Images Slow browser performance can be caused by a slow Internet connection. In this case, one thing you can do is to suppress the downloading

A+ OS 4.1 4.2

of images. Image files can be large and account for most of the downloaded data from Web sites. For Internet Explorer 5.x, you can download and install Web Accessories for Internet Explorer 5.x, which can be used to suppress the downloading of images from Web sites. If the Microsoft site has been updated since the writing of this book, you may need to search for the Web Accessories for Internet Explorer. Follow these directions:

1. Go to this Microsoft Web site: *www.microsoft.com/windows/ie/downloads/archive/default.asp*
2. Scroll down and click the heading **Web Accessories from Microsoft**, and then scroll down click the **Download it now** link.
3. Another page opens, with more information about the Internet Explorer 5.x Web Accessories. On the right side of the page, in a box labeled Download, click the link to the file **ie5wa.exe.**
4. Click **OK** to save the file to disk. When the download window opens, choose to download it to a location on your hard drive, and then click **Save**. Remember where you have saved the file.
5. After you have downloaded the file ie5wa.exe, double-click it, then click **Yes** to install accessories.
6. Close the IE browser window and reopen it.
7. To use the IE Web Accessories to suppress downloading images, right-click the IE menu bar. If Favorites is already checked and is already on your menu bar, you can move on to Step 8. If it is not, click **Links** on the shortcut menu. This action adds the Links menu to the menu bar items.
8. Click **Favorites** on the menu bar, then click **Links**, and then click **Toggle Images**. Web pages should now download without their images. You may have to click the **Refresh** button on your toolbar for the changes to take effect on an open page.
9. To reset the browser to download images, click **Favorites**, then **Links**, and then click **Toggle Images** again.

13

IE version 6 includes the option to suppress images, sound, animation, and video. Use the following procedure:

1. Open the **Tools** menu, and then click **Internet Options**.
2. The Internet Options window opens. Click the **Advanced** tab.
3. Scroll down to the multimedia section of the check box list and clear the check box or boxes for the feature or features that you do not wish to display (**Show pictures**, **Play animations**, **Play videos**, or **Play sounds**).

To display an individual video or picture when you have cleared the related check boxes, right-click the icon with which it has been replaced on the Web page.

A+ OS 4.1 4.2

Browser Updates and Patches

Browser manufacturers are continually improving their products, and generally speaking, you should be using the most current version of the browser on your PC to take advantage of the latest features and fixes to known problems. However, if you have an older computer or operating system, you might not want to update a browser that requires a lot of system resources, because your older PC might not be able to support it. In this case, it's better to keep an older version on your PC unless you are having problems with the version.

If you are using Internet Explorer, check the Windows support Web site at *support.microsoft.com* for specific problems with Internet Explorer. Search on the product and the error message for articles that describe the problem and possible solutions. Also check the Windows update Web site at *windowsupdate.microsoft.com* for updates or patches for known Internet Explorer problems. Download the patch and install it following the same general instructions you have seen in earlier chapters.

If you are not using the latest version of Internet Explorer, try downloading the latest version. If you use your browser for banking on the Internet, be sure to download the version of Internet Explorer for 128-bit encryption in order to get better security features. If the new version creates problems on your system, you can revert to your original version by uninstalling the new version.

Supporting E-Mail

A+ OS 4.2

E-mail is a client/server application that is used to send text messages to individuals and groups of individuals. When you send an e-mail message, it travels from your computer to your e-mail server. Your e-mail server sends the message to the recipient's e-mail server. The recipient's e-mail server sends it to the recipient's PC, but not until the recipient asks that it be sent by logging in and downloading e-mail. Different parts of the process are controlled by different protocols.

Figure 13-19 shows the journey made by an e-mail message as well as the protocols that control the different parts of the journey. The sender's PC and e-mail server both use **SMTP (Simple Mail Transfer Protocol)** to send an e-mail message to its destination. Once the message arrives at the destination e-mail server, it remains there until the recipient requests delivery. The recipient's e-mail server uses one of two protocols to deliver the message: either **POP (Post Office Protocol)** or **IMAP4 (Internet Message Access Protocol, version 4)**, a newer e-mail protocol. The current version of POP is version 3, often abbreviated as POP3.

A+ OS 4.2

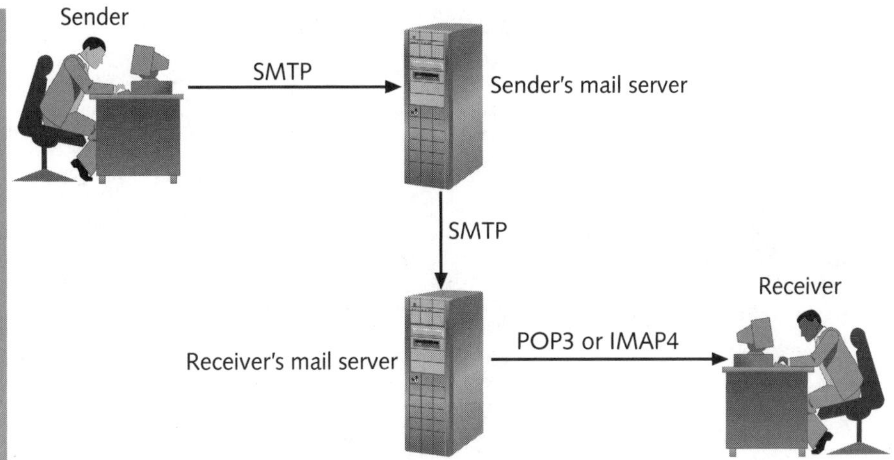

Figure 13-19 The SMTP protocol is used to send e-mail to a recipient's mail server, and the POP3 or IMAP4 protocol is used to download e-mail to the client

SMTP is defined in RFC821 and RFC822. When e-mail experts speak of error messages created during e-mail transactions, they sometimes call these messages 822 messages.

E-mail client software communicates with an e-mail server when it sends and receives e-mail. Two of the most common e-mail clients are Eudora and Microsoft Outlook Express. Figure 13-19 shows a user with one e-mail server. In fact, it's possible to have two e-mail servers, one for sending e-mail and the other for receiving e-mail. Figure 13-20 shows this arrangement.

13

The e-mail server that takes care of sending e-mail messages (using the SMTP protocol) is often referred to as the SMTP server. The e-mail server from which you collect messages that were sent to you is often referred to as the POP server, because it uses the POP protocol.

When you configure your e-mail client software for the first time, you need to enter the addresses of your e-mail servers. If you are connecting to e-mail via an Internet service provider, the ISP can tell you these addresses. For example, if your ISP is MyISP.net, you might have an outgoing mail server address of *smtp.myISP.net,* and an incoming mail server address of *pop3.myISP.net.*

In most e-mail client software, you enter the addresses of your POP server and your SMTP server in a dialog box when setting up the program. Look for menus or icons labeled Options, Preferences, Configuration, Setup, or similar names. After you have entered the addresses, the software saves this and other configuration information in an initialization file, the Windows registry, or some other location.

A+ OS 4.2

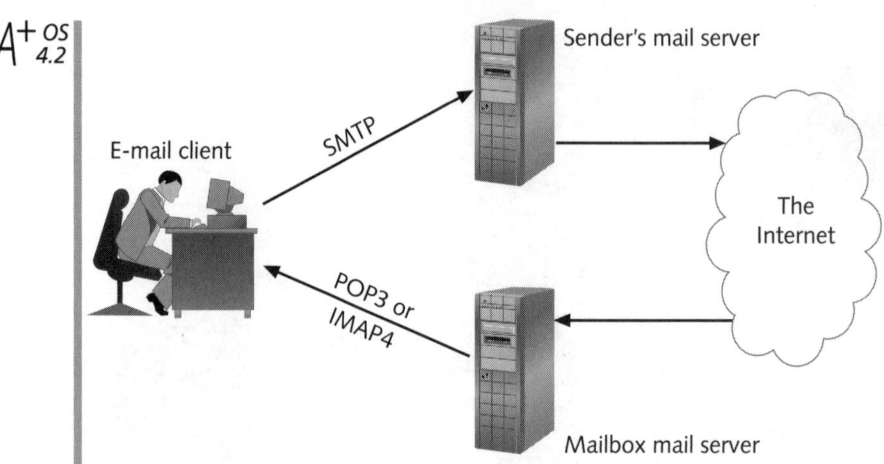

Figure 13-20 An e-mail client can use one server to send e-mail and another to receive e-mail

Supporting FTP

A+ OS 4.2

A common task of communications software is file transfer, the passing of files from one computer to another. For file transfer to work, the software on both ends must be using the same protocol. The most popular way to transfer files over the Internet is with the **File Transfer Protocol (FTP)**, which is used to transfer files between two computers using the same or different operating systems. A popular use of the Internet for companies is to provide files for customers to download to their PCs, for example, when new upgrades for software become available. This service is commonly provided by Windows NT, 2000, or Unix servers that offer access to files using FTP and are called FTP servers or FTP sites. These commercial FTP sites only provide the ability to download a file to your PC. However, FTP offers more power than just that. A user who has first logged on to a remote computer can use FTP utility software to copy, delete, and rename files, make directories, remove directories, and view details about files and directories.

Most communications applications provide an FTP utility that has a unique look and feel, but the basics of file transfer are the same from one utility to another. If you don't have graphical FTP software installed on your PC, you can use FTP commands from a command prompt.

File Transfer from a Command Prompt

FTP can be initiated at a DOS, Windows 9x, or Windows NT/2000/XP command prompt, if a connection is established to a network or the Internet. The FTP commands work like the dialog in Table 13-4.

A+ OS 4.2

Table 13-4 A sample FTP session from a command prompt

Command Entered at the Command Prompt	Description
FTP	Execute the FTP program, ftp.exe.
OPEN 110.87.170.34	Open a session with a remote computer having the given IP address.
LOGIN: XXXXXX	The host computer provides a prompt to enter a user ID for the computer being accessed.
PASSWORD: XXXXXX	The host computer requests the password for that ID. Logon is then completed by the host computer.
CD /DATA	Change directory to the /DATA directory.
GET YOURFILE.DAT	Copy the file YOURFILE.DAT (or whatever file you want) from the remote computer to my computer.
PUT MYFILE.DAT	Copy the file MYFILE.DAT (or whatever file you want) from your computer to the remote computer.
BYE	Disconnect the FTP session.

File Transfer Using FTP Software

FTP client software can be downloaded from the Internet or directly from your ISP. This example looks at how to execute FTP using such software:

1. Start the FTP utility software. In this example we are using WS_FTP Pro by Ipswitch (*www.ipswitch.com*). The FTP utility screen appears similar to the one in Figure 13-21.

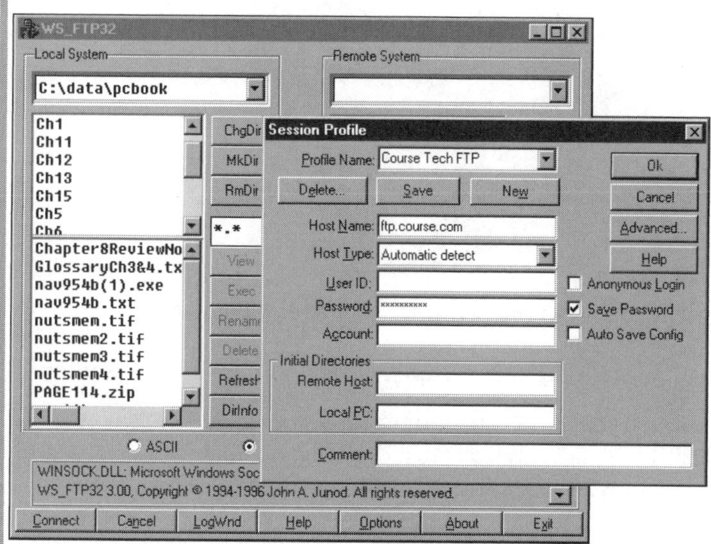

Figure 13-21 A typical FTP utility provided by an Internet service provider

A+ OS 1.4 4.2

2. Click **Connect** to log on to an FTP site. A Session Profile dialog box appears, similar to the one in Figure 12-18.
3. Enter the Host Name, for example ftp.course.com. Enter the User ID and Password for this host computer, and then click **OK**.
4. The connection is made, and your ID and password are passed to the host. After you have been authenticated by the host computer, a screen similar to that in Figure 13-22 is displayed.
5. The files on the left belong to you, and the files on the right belong to the remote host computer. You can drag and drop files either to or from the other computer, or you can use the commands at the bottom of the window. Notice in Figure 12-19 the choices toward the bottom of the window: ASCII, Binary, or Auto. These choices refer to the format that is to be used to transfer the files. Use ASCII only for text files, and use Binary for all others. If you are not sure which to use, choose **Auto**.

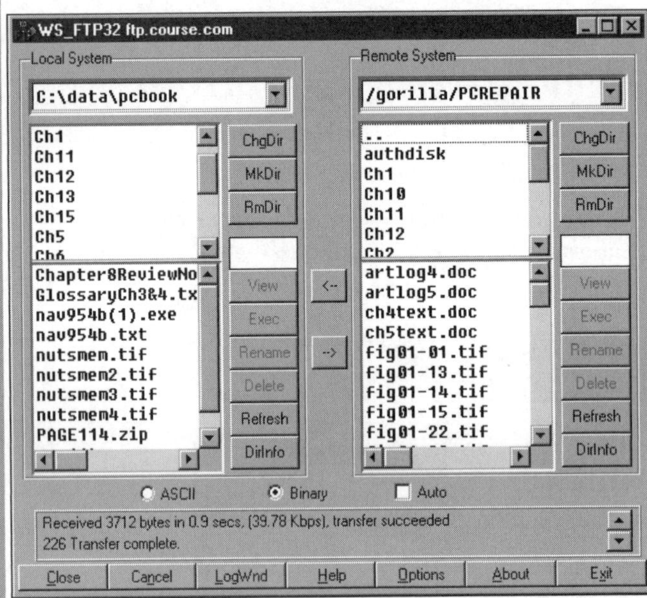

Figure 13-22 An FTP utility screen showing local and remote files

6. When the transfer of files is complete, click **Exit** to leave the utility.

Many Web pages provide a link on the page offering to you the ability to download a file. Click on the link to download the file. It is likely that this file is not being downloaded from the Web server but rather is downloaded from an FTP server. When you click the filename on the Web page, the program controlling the page executes FTP commands to the FTP server to download the file to you. If you receive an error, you can sometimes solve the problem by going directly to the company's FTP server and using an FTP utility (such as the one used above) to download the file or even see a list of other files that you might also like to download.

A+ OS 4.2

TIP

A Web browser can also serve as an FTP client. Enter the URL of the FTP server in the address box (for example, ftp.course.com). The browser changes menu options to become an FTP client. For Internet Explorer, to log onto the FTP server, on the menu bar, click File, and then click Login As. The Log On As dialog box appears for you to enter a user ID and password. Files and folders on the FTP server then display in the browser window.

CHAPTER SUMMARY

- Ports are used to address particular software or services, such as protocols, running on a computer. Common port assignments are port 80 for HTTP, port 25 for SMTP, port 110 for POP3, and port 20 for FTP.
- Generally, an API call is a way for an application to ask an operating system to do something. A browser uses an API call to access a Web server and make its request for information.
- HTTP works at the Application, Presentation, and Session OSI layers.
- TCP guarantees that a packet reaches its destination and so is called a connection-oriented protocol. UDP does not guarantee delivery and so is called a connectionless or best-effort protocol. Both operate at the Transport layer.
- IP is responsible for breaking data into packets and passing it from TCP or UDP to the hardware. It is the governing protocol at the Network layer.
- When data is sent, each layer adds header information, and the Data Link layer adds a trailer. On the receiving side, each layer removes its header and trailer information and passes the data to the layer above it.
- PPP is used in dial-up networking to send packets of data over phone lines. It operates at the Data Link and Physical layers and manages network transmission from one modem to another.
- Before you can create a dial-up connection to the Internet, you need to have a modem installed along with the drivers to run it as well as TCP/IP installed and bound to the modem.
- The Windows Dial-up Networking utility is used to connect to a network using a modem and a phone line. When a dial-up connection is made, a PC's application software relates to the network as though the computer were directly connected to the network using a network card.
- You can create a new dial-up networking connection in Windows 9x and Windows NT through the Dial-up Networking applet in My Computer, through the Network and Dial-up Connections applet in the Control Panel of Windows 2000, and through the Network Connections applet in the Control Panel of Windows XP.
- When experiencing problems with dial-up networking, make sure the modem is working, all necessary components are installed, and the phone number to dial and other settings are configured correctly.

- Winipcfg and Ipconfig both report configuration information about the current TCP/IP connection for a device and can release and restore the IP address. Winipcfg is not supported in Windows NT/2000/XP.
- Other TCP/IP utilities useful in solving networking problems are Tracert, Ping, and Nbtstat.
- DSL and cable modem are broadband Internet connections that use a converter box that connects to a PC by way of a network USB Port. The connection can use the PPPoE protocol.
- Computer can share an Internet connection. Windows 98 and Windows XP uses Internet Connection Sharing (ICS) to manage the connection on the host computer, or you can use a router that stands between the converter box and the network.
- Use a firewall on the host computer or router to protect the network from unsolicited activity from the Internet.
- A URL consists of a protocol, a host name, a network or domain name, and a top-level domain extension. Common top-level domains include .com for commercial institutions, .gov for divisions of government, and .org for nonprofit organizations.
- When you experience poor browser performance, try cleaning up your hard drive and making sure your system settings are optimized. If that doesn't work, try clearing your browser cache, clearing the Web page history, suppressing image downloads, or downloading updates.
- E-mail uses SMTP to send messages and POP to receive messages. POP is being replaced by IMAP. Your ISP will provide you with the server types and addresses that it uses to send and receive e-mail.
- FTP is used to transfer files from one computer to another, whether or not the computers are using the same operating system. Both computers must have FTP installed. It can be executed from user-friendly GUI software or from a command prompt.

Key Terms

ARP (Address Resolution Protocol)
best-effort protocol
bridging protocol
connectionless protocol
connection-oriented protocol
dial-up networking
FTP (File Transfer Protocol)
HTML (HyperText Markup Language)
HTTP (HyperText Transfer Protocol)
HTTPS (HTTP secure)
ICMP (Internet Control Message Protocol)
IMAP4 (Internet Message Access Protocol version 4)
intranet
IP (Internet Protocol)
line protocol
NNTP (Network News Transfer Protocol)
POP (Post Office Protocol)
port
port address
port number
PPP (Point-to-Point Protocol)
PPPoE (Point-to-Point Protocol over Ethernet)
RARP (Reverse Address Resolution Protocol)
session
SLIP (Serial Line Internet Protocol)
SMTP (Simple Mail Transfer Protocol)
SNMP (Simple Network Management Protocol)
socket
TCP (Transmission Control Protocol)
top-level domain
UDP (User Datagram Protocol)
URL (Uniform Resource Locator)

Review Questions

1. Explain how a single physical computer can be a Web server and an e-mail server at the same time.
2. Give the service and protocol for the following ports: port 21, port 25, port 80, and port 110.
3. At what OSI layer (or layers) does IP operate? TCP? HTTP? PPP?
4. What are API calls used for? Why are they necessary?
5. Which protocol used by Web browsers and Web servers is responsible for guaranteeing delivery? For breaking data into packets? For decrypting and decompressing data as necessary?
6. Why is the Session layer sometimes assigned to the high-level application protocols and sometimes to TCP?
7. Explain the difference between a connection-oriented protocol and a connectionless protocol, and give an example of each.
8. What layer of the OSI model is responsible for routing? What protocols operate at this layer?
9. What TCP/IP utility would you use to display the route taken over the Internet by a communication between a Web browser and Web server?
10. What utility would you use to display information about the name space information kept by a DNS server for a particular domain name?

11. What must you do to get your system ready for creating a dial-up networking connection?
12. If TCP/IP is bound to a modem on your system, does it also need to be bound to a network card? Why, or why not?
13. Explain how PPP is used by dial-up networking.
14. Place these stages of creating a dial-up networking connection in Windows 9x in the correct order: creating a new connection, verifying installation of the dial-up adapter, installing the Dial-up Networking feature, entering configuration information for your ISP.
15. How is the process for creating a new dial-up connection in Windows 2000 different from the process for Windows 9x?
16. Explain at least four different things you can try if you cannot make a connection to the Internet using a dial-up networking connection.
17. What should you try if you can connect but you get the error message "Unable to resolve hostname..."? If you get the error message "Unable to establish a compatible set of network protocols"?
18. Explain the functions of the following TCP/IP utilities: NSLookup, Winipcfg, Ipconfig, and Microsoft SNMP agent.
19. What is the full command line to use Ipconfig to release the current IP address?
20. Label the component parts of this URL: *http://www.companyabc.com/Reports/december2001.doc*
21. Give the type of organization that would use the following top-level domains: .mil, .net, .air, .com, .org, .gov.
22. What are three things you can do to improve slow browser performance?
23. What protocol is used for sending e-mail? For receiving it?
24. Explain what FTP is used for.
25. What is defined in RFC1156? RFC822?

HANDS-ON PROJECTS

Practicing Dial-up Networking Skills with Windows 9x

This project requires you have a modem installed and working.

1. Open My Computer and open the Dial-up Networking folder.
2. Double-click the **Make New Connection** option.
3. Enter the name **TEST** for the name of the computer that you are dialing. Click **Next**.
4. Enter your home phone number. Click **Next**.
5. Click the **Finish** button to create the Test dial-up.
6. Double-click the newly created Test dial-up icon, and confirm that it dials out correctly. Describe what happens.

Practicing TCP/IP Networking Skills

While connected to the Internet or another TCP/IP network, answer these questions:

1. What is your current IP address?
2. Release and renew your IP address. Now what is your IP address?
3. Are you using dynamic or static IP addressing? How do you know?
4. What is your adapter address used for this connection?
5. What is your default gateway IP address?
6. What response do you get when you Ping the default gateway?

Using a Browser Help Utility

Using your browser's help utility, print instructions for changing the size of the browser cache and cleaning out the cache.

Solving Browser Problems

Follow these instructions to solve problems with Netscape Navigator:

1. List the steps to access the Netscape Web site and search for information about a problem. Search the site for information about Error 403.6, IP Restriction error. Print any information you find about the error.
2. Print the Netscape Web site page that allows you to use SmartUpdate to download the latest fixes for Netscape Navigator. Download the update and apply it to your browser.
3. Perform the procedures to clean out the browser cache.

Now do the same three steps above for Microsoft Internet Explorer:

1. List the steps to access the Microsoft Web site and search for information about a problem. Search the site for information about Error 403.6, IP Restriction error. Print any information you find about the error.
2. Print the Microsoft Web site page that allows you to use the Update Wizard to download the latest fixes for Internet Explorer. Download the update and apply it to your browser.
3. Perform the procedures discussed in the chapter to clean out the browser cache.

Using Web Accessories for Internet Explorer

Download and install Web Accessories for Internet Explorer using this URL: *http://www.microsoft.com/windows/ie/downloads/archive/default.asp*. Use the tool to display and print the links on this Web page: *www.foxnews.com*.

CHAPTER

14

LINUX, MACS, AND NOTEBOOKS

In this chapter, you will learn:

- About starting up, using, and supporting hardware in the Mac OS
- About the file structure of the Linux OS and how to use some Linux commands
- How to support notebooks

So far in this book we have focused on Microsoft operating systems, because they are the most popular OSs for the desktop. However, as a software technician, you will need to be familiar with a variety of operating systems, including the Mac OS and Linux. In addition, this chapter covers the specific concerns of supporting operating systems installed on notebook computers.

Introducing the Mac OS

Recall from Chapter 1 that Mac OS X is the latest version of the proprietary OS for Apple Macintosh computers. This section covers the basic file and folder organization and startup process for the Mac OS. It is not intended to qualify you to support Macs but rather to give you a passing familiarity with them so that you will recognize some of the main features of the OS and know where to go for more information.

Starting Up a Mac

When the Mac starts up, you see a graphical illustration of some of the events occurring in the startup process, such as the loading of the desktop and system applets, including the **Finder window** (which is used to explore the Mac system). Most of the startup process, however, is hidden from the user. Here are the main steps in the process:

1. Self-test controlled from ROM
2. PRAM (parameter RAM) settings retrieved
3. System folder located
4. Mac OS ROM file loaded
5. Smiling Mac icon and welcome screen displayed
6. Enablers loaded
7. Disk First Aid runs if the Mac was not shut down properly
8. Other System folder contents located
9. Mac desktop displayed
10. Finder and startup programs located

Each of these steps is described in more detail below, and major differences between Mac OS X and Mac OS 9 are noted.

1. *Self-test is controlled from ROM.* When you press the power button on a Mac and power is sent to the motherboard, the ROM signals the Mac to perform a self-test. Components tested include the hard drive, the processor, ports, controllers, and expansion cards. The self-test ensures that they are operating correctly. Once this is confirmed, the Mac tests its RAM and halts the startup process if major damage or incorrect installations of RAM modules are detected. Minor damage to RAM may not be detected during the startup test of RAM and may manifest itself in system malfunctions later.
2. *PRAM settings are retrieved.* In the Mac, **PRAM**, or **parameter RAM**, stores configuration information for the Mac OS. After tests of components and RAM are completed, the Mac looks at the PRAM for settings that tell the system which drive is presently designated as the bootable drive (the startup disk). If it looks in that drive and does not find the Mac OS, it keeps looking in drives

until it finds a bootable drive. If it cannot find one, the system displays a flashing question mark and pauses the startup process.

3. *The System folder is located.* After the Mac locates a bootable disk, it looks for an active **System folder**, which is the folder that the system designates as the one from which the Mac OS is to be loaded. A System folder is required for a disk to be bootable. In Mac OS 9, the System folder is named System Folder, and in Mac OS X, the System folder is named System. See Figure 14-1.

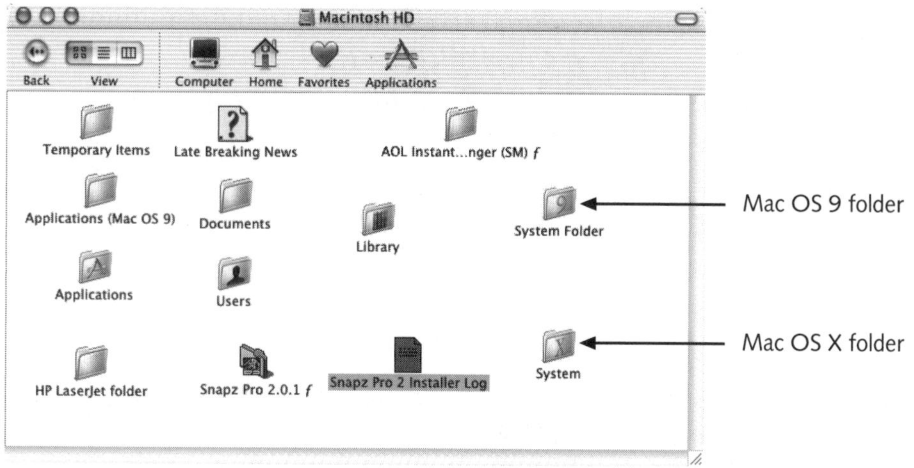

Figure 14-1 Mac OS 9 is stored in the System Folder, but Mac OS X uses System

4. *The Mac OS ROM file is loaded.* The first item that the Mac loads into memory from the System folder is the **Mac OS ROM file**, which contains commands required for interaction with hardware and the lower levels of the Mac OS. Before the iMac, these commands were stored in ROM on the motherboard in the Mac.

14

5. *The smiling Mac icon and welcome screen are displayed.* When the smiling Mac icon is displayed, the system is loading the OS into RAM, beginning with the **System file** containing the libraries and commands that make up the core of the OS.

6. *The system loads enablers for hardware components.* If Mac hardware is put on the market before the instructions to control it are included with the OS, an **enabler file** will be included with it that will enable it to function with the version of Mac OS being used on the computer. The enabler files are loaded after the System file. Generally, each revision of the Mac OS incorporates information included in enabler files that were necessary with the previous version.

7. *Disk First Aid runs if the system was not shut down properly.* If the system is not shut down properly, the next time the computer starts up the system will run **Disk First Aid**, a free Mac disk utility, to search for and repair any problems that it finds with the hard drive. Disk First Aid runs after the System file and any enabler files are loaded.

8. *Other contents of the System folder are loaded.* In Mac OS 9, in addition to the System file and enabler files, the System folder also contains the Control Panels and Extensions folders (see Figure 14-2). The **Control Panels folder** controls system settings such as time and date, speaker volume, and the configuration of the Finder window and the desktop. The **Extensions folder** contains add-ons to provide new features to a Mac, as well as shared libraries and icons. These no longer exist in Mac OS X; their functions are incorporated into a single **Library** folder, which is shown in Figure14-3.

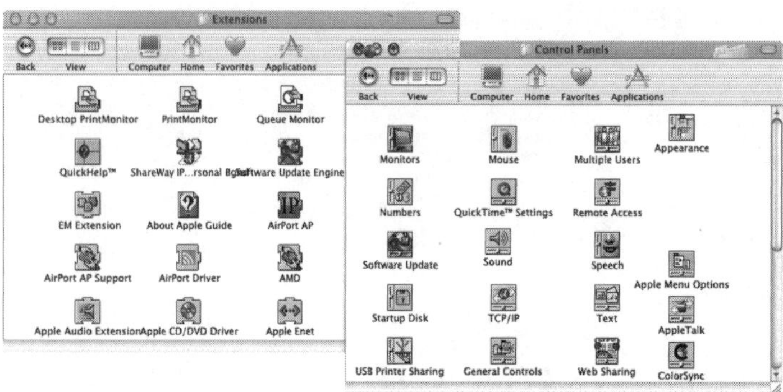

Figure 14-2 In OS 9, the Control Panel and Extensions folders are used to contain OS and applications utilities

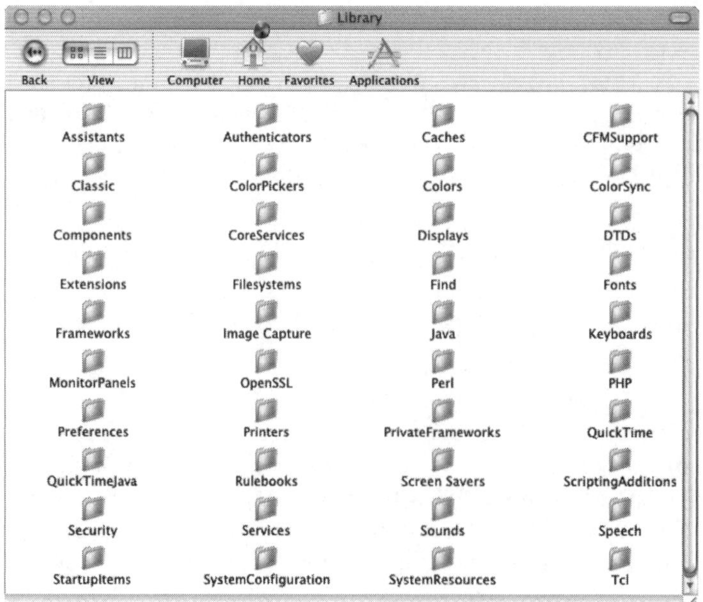

Figure 14-3 In OS X, the Library folder replaces the Control Panel and Extensions folders of OS 9

9. *The Mac desktop is displayed.* The Mac desktop is displayed after the necessary contents of the System folder have been loaded. All the required components of the Mac OS have been loaded at this point.

10. *The Finder window and startup programs are loaded.* After the Mac OS is completely loaded, the Finder window launches so that the user can access programs and files. The Finder itself is an application that is loaded automatically during the startup process, not a part of the OS. When the Finder window has been loaded, the system loads items in the Startup Items folder, which contains items that the user wants to open immediately upon startup. In Mac OS 9, it also opens the Launcher, which provides easy access to commonly used folders, programs, and files, if the Launcher control panel has been installed.

Using the Mac

Now that you've had an overview of the Mac OS startup process, let's look at some major features of the Mac interface and learn some important procedures and hints for using the Mac. In this section, you'll learn about the Finder window, the Apple menu, and procedures to help you work with files and applications in a Mac environment.

The Mac Desktop

The Mac OS X desktop, with its major components labeled, is shown in Figure 14-4. The Finder application is open and active. Because it is the currently active application, the menu bar for the Finder window is displayed at the top of the screen. The menu bar provides pull-down menus that contain options for working with applications, files, and the interface. A new feature in the Mac OS X user interface is the **dock** that appears at the bottom of the desktop. It contains icons that provide access to frequently used applications. When you click the minus button to minimize a window, an icon representing that window appears in the dock. To open an application from its icon in the dock, just click it once. The icons in the dock that represent open applications have a small triangle underneath them. The Mac OS X desktop also includes shortcut icons that are usually located on the right side of the screen and provide quick access to files, folders, and programs.

The Mac OS X interface has been redesigned, and it does not use its own interface to run applications that were written for OS 9. Instead, it stores the Mac OS 9 applications in a separate folder and launches the OS 9 interface, which it calls the classic interface, whenever a user wants to use one of those applications. In this way, a user can still use older Mac applications with the newer Mac interface. In Figure 14-4 you can see the icon on the right side of the screen to launch the Desktop (Mac OS 9) classic interface.

Using the Finder

The Mac's Finder window functions something like Explorer or My Computer in Windows, enabling the user to navigate and access the Mac's files and applications. The Finder window at the computer level, which is the top level of the Mac OS X's hierarchical file structure,

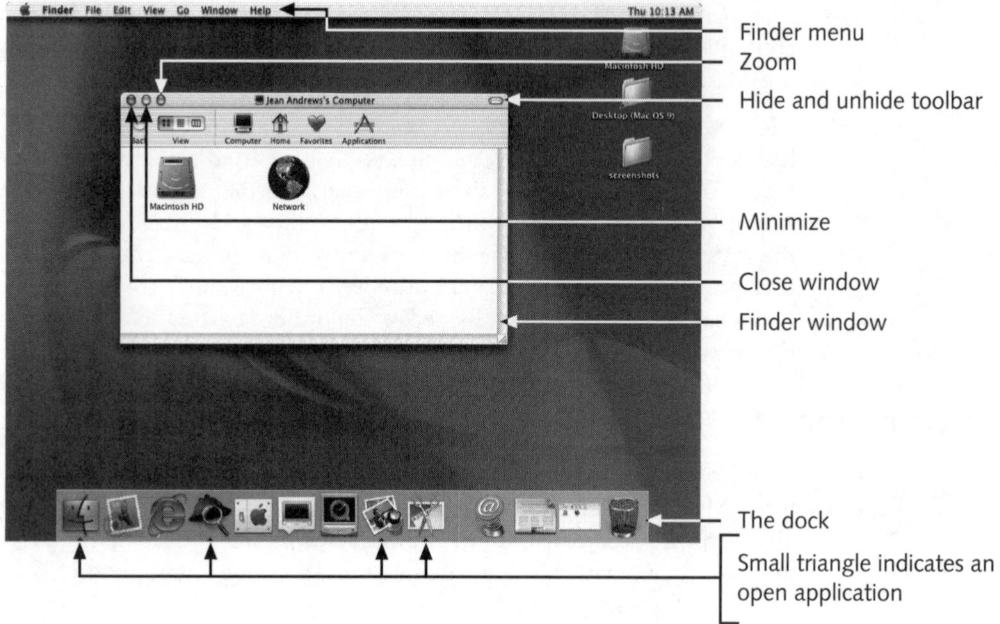

Figure 14-4 The Mac OS X desktop with a Finder window showing

shows an icon for the computer's hard drive as well as a Network icon to provide access to any other workstations that the computer is connected to. The Finder window and other windows contain a toolbar that appears at the top of the window and contains buttons that function much like the buttons in a Web browser, such as Back, Home, and Favorites. The Home button on the Mac OS X window toolbar takes the user back to the computer level.

If you use a folder frequently, such as the Documents folder, you can keep it open all the time without having it in your way. In Mac OS 9, drag it down to the bottom of the screen until it becomes a tab on the title bar. In Mac OS X, drag it down to the dock, and it will become an icon on the dock.

Besides allowing you to access programs, files, and folders, the Finder window provides you with a way to organize and manage them. For instance, to create a new folder, locate the folder in which you want to create the new folder using the Finder. When you've reached the desired folder, go to the File menu and click New Folder. The new folder will appear with its name highlighted. Type its new name and press the Return key to rename the folder.

It is easier to locate a file or folder in the Finder window if you know exactly where it is, especially if there are several levels of folders inside each other. If you don't know the location of the file or folder you want to find, use the Sherlock utility to search for it. By default, the dock in Mac OS X contains an icon for Sherlock; it looks like a hat and a magnifying glass. The search screen for Sherlock is shown in Figure 14-5. Type the name of the file, folder, or text you want to find, click the check box next to the location you want to search, and then click the green magnifying glass button to begin the search. In the figure, you are searching the hard drive for a file that is named Myfile.

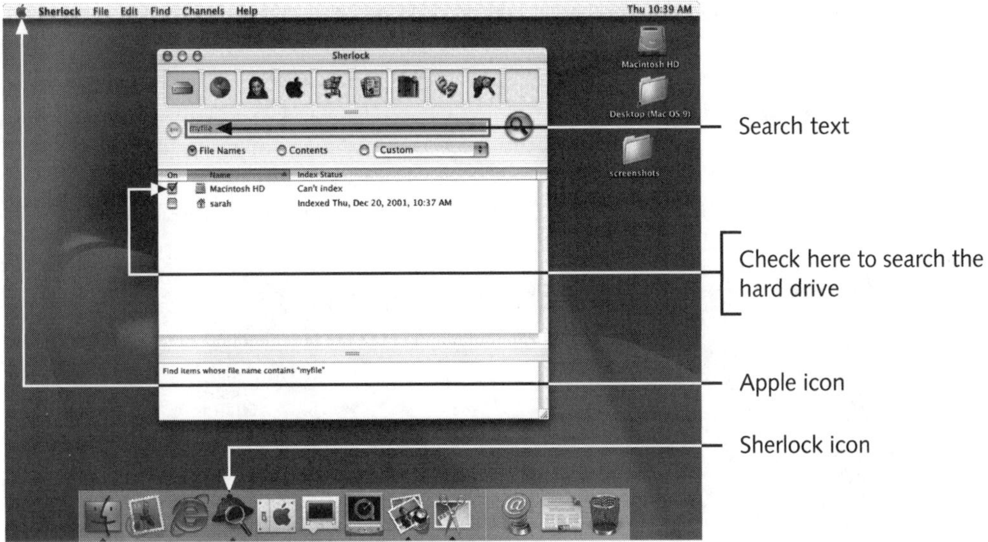

Figure 14-5 Use Sherlock to search for files and folders

When you don't need a file or folder any more, just drag its icon to the Trash Can until the Trash Can is highlighted, and release the mouse button. Note that this is the only way you can delete icons from the Finder window. When an item is moved to the Trash Can, you can still recover it by double-clicking the Trash Can and locating the item. Items are not actually removed from the system until you chose File, Empty Trash from the menu.

Using the Apple Menu

The menu at the top of the Mac OS screen changes with each application that is active except for the Apple icon, which is always shown at the far left of the menu bar. The **Apple menu**, which opens when you click the Apple icon, and is similar to the Microsoft Windows Start menu, is present and is constantly accessible no matter what folder, window, or application you are using. It contains accessories to help you manage system tasks as well as programs such as media players, a calculator, search programs, and word-processing programs. The Mac OS X Apple menu is shown in Figure 14-6.

Figure 14-6 The Apple menu is always available no matter what application is active

System Preferences on the Apple menu contains options for customizing the Mac interface. Click Apple and then click System Preferences to open the System Preferences window, shown in Figure 14-7. Control Panels, which you learned about earlier in the chapter, are also accessible from the Apple menu in OS 9. In Mac OS 9, you can customize the Apple menu to contain anything you want by adding items to or removing items from the Apple folder, which is located in the System folder. You can create up to five levels of submenus under the Apple menu. In Mac OS X, the Apple menu is no longer customizable.

Figure 14-7 The System Preferences window is used to customize the Mac interface

In Mac OS 9, there are three submenus on the Apple menu, called Recent Applications, Recent Documents, and Recent Servers. To customize these submenus, from the Apple menu, select Control Panels, Apple Menu Options. From this control panel, you can select whether or not to use recent menus and how many items to include on them. In Mac OS X, the Recent Items submenu on the Apple menu (shown in Figure 14-8) gives you access to recently accessed documents and applications.

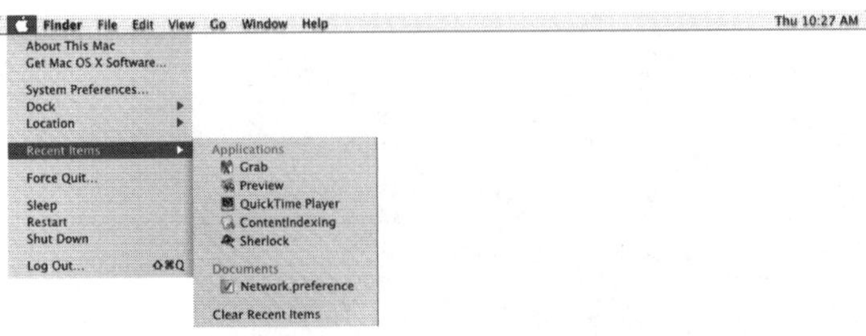

Figure 14-8 Using Mac OS X, the Recent Items menu under the Apple menu lists recently accessed documents and applications

Launching an Application

There are four ways to access applications on the Mac:

- Double-click the icon for the application from the Finder window or another window or from the desktop.
- Choose the application from the Recent Applications submenu on the Apple menu.
- Double-click the icon of a file associated with that application, such as a text file saved from the Notepad application.
- Drag to the application's icon the icon of a document that you want to open with it.

The first two methods have already been discussed. The last option works well if you want to open a document with an application other than the one in which it was originally saved.

As you work with applications on the Mac, you may find that you want to have more than one open at a time. In Mac OS 9, the Applications menu, which you can access from the upper right-hand corner of your screen, allows you to switch between open applications easily. The menu will show the icon and name of the currently active application. To access other open applications, click the menu and choose the name of the application you want to access. Recall that in Mac OS X, open applications are shown as icons in the dock with a small triangle under them.

Supporting Hardware

In addition to working with files and applications, you will also need to know how to support hardware in a Mac system, such as monitors and hard drives, and including changing settings for video, understanding the file system used on the hard drive, and using system maintenance tools. Again, this section will not give you all you need to know to work with Mac hardware; it is simply intended to show you some important tools for working with the system. For more information specific to working with Mac hardware, study books devoted specifically to the Mac, documentation and manuals that come with your system or with specific components, and the Apple Computer, Inc. Web site (*www.apple.com*).

Adjusting Display Settings

To change display settings such as color depth and resolution, double-click the Display icon under System Preferences. The Displays window appears, as seen in Figure 14-9. You can change the following settings in the Displays window:

- *Resolution*. The **resolution** of a display affects how many **pixels** are shown on-screen. A resolution of 1,024 × 768 means that there are 1,024 columns of pixels and 768 rows of pixels. When you change the resolution of your monitor, remember that the size of the items on the screen will change; the more pixels there are, the smaller items will be. This can be good if you want to see more items and space on your screen at one time, but it can be a drawback if you have vision problems. Two advantages to an 800 × 600 resolution are that it will produce a view close to what you will actually see in a printed document and that many Web pages are designed to be viewed at this resolution. A Web page optimized at 800 × 600 will look cramped at a lower resolution such as 640 × 480.

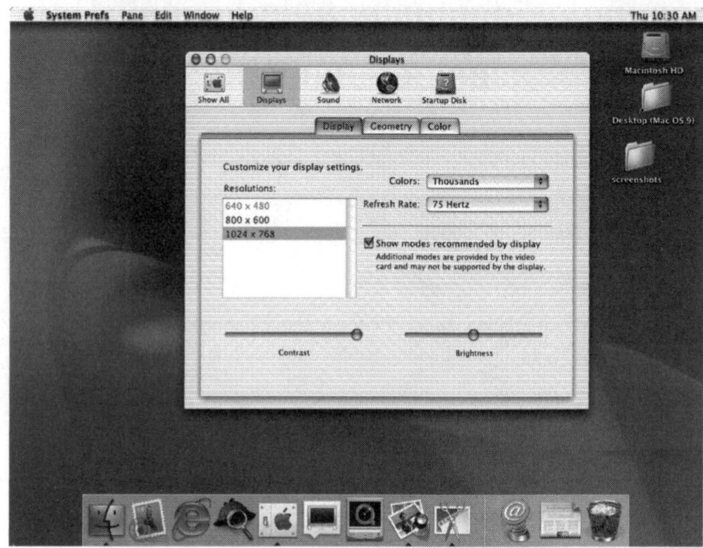

Figure 14-9 The Displays icon in System Preferences window is used to adjust the display settings

- *Contrast and brightness.* The sliders on the bottom of the Display tab of the Displays window enable you to control how much contrast there is between colors on your screen and how bright the overall display is. It is not a good idea to set a monitor to the highest brightness setting, because this can burn out the monitor prematurely.
- *Color depth.* Click the Color tab on the Displays window to view and change the settings for depth of color. The Color Depth box allows you to change how many colors can be shown on the screen: either 256, thousands, or millions. More colors mean a more realistic and more detailed picture. Sometimes a picture will have been created using a certain setting and will not be displayed correctly in a different setting. If a picture appears blurred or too gray, change the color depth until it appears correctly.
- *Display geometry.* Click the Geometry tab in the Displays window to reach options for changing the shape of the display on the screen. On most monitors, the display area is actually slightly smaller than the screen size, and you may see some black space around the display area. Use the Geometry settings to change the height, width, position, and shape of the display area.

A+ OS 1.2

Supporting the Hard Drive

As with other OSs, the Mac OS supports IDE and SCSI drive technologies and, for hard drives, there is a choice of file systems to use.

Drive Technologies: IDE and SCSI Recall from earlier chapters that IDE drives follow an interface standard that allows for up to four IDE drives in a system. SCSI drives are faster than IDE drives, and there can be up to 15 SCSI devices on a system. It is possible to mix IDE and SCSI devices on a system.

The terms IDE and SCSI refer not only to hard drives but also to other devices such as CD-ROM drives, Zip drives, and DVD drives.

In the mid-1990s, IDE became the main technology for connecting internal devices in a Mac, partially because it is less expensive than SCSI and is more widely used in the computer industry. However, because it is faster and can support more devices, SCSI can be a better choice for complex multimedia and graphics work. If you have a Mac that uses IDE technology and want to convert to SCSI, you can purchase a SCSI host adapter for that purpose. Choose a drive technology according to your needs, your budget, and what technology your system supports.

File Systems on the Mac Recall from Chapter 2 that a file system is the overall structure that an OS uses to name, store, and organize files on a disk. The two main choices for a file system on a Mac hard drive are **HFS (Hierarchical File System)**, also called **Mac OS Standard Format**, and **HFS+**, also called the **Mac OS Extended Format**. HFS was the format used for Mac disks before 1998, when drives larger than 1 GB started to become more common. HFS limited the number of allocation units on a disk to 65,536; how big each allocation unit was depended on the total size of the drive. These allocation units are called **allocation blocks** or simply **blocks**, and are similar to the Microsoft Windows file system's clusters; they are sets of hard drive sectors where the Mac's file system stores files. Files smaller than the size of a block still take up an entire block, which can cause a significant amount of space to be wasted; this wasted space is called slack.

In 1998, with the release of Mac OS 8.1, HFS was updated to HFS+, which allows for smaller blocks and can format drives up to 2,048 GB. Any drive larger than 1GB should be formatted with HFS+. Hard drives or removable media disks (such as floppy disks) smaller than 1 GB should be formatted with HFS, as should any hard drive that you plan to use with a Mac running Mac OS 8.1 or earlier.

In Mac OS 9, the File Exchange control panel is a component that can be installed to allow the Mac to use Microsoft Windows FAT16 and FAT32 partitions. Macs can read some NTFS or Linux/Unix file systems using utilities specially designed for that purpose. Mac OS X includes the ability to mount FAT drives but does not include a utility to format them as Mac OS 9 did.

The formatting of a hard drive with a file system creates blocks. It also creates a **directory structure** that allows the OS to access the drive. Some important elements of the directory structure are listed below.

- **Boot blocks** are the first two allocation blocks on the hard drive. They are initially empty, but once a System folder is installed on a computer, the boot blocks contain the location of the System folder so that the system can find and load the OS. You can correct damage to the boot blocks or replace erased boot blocks by installing a new System folder.
- Right after the boot blocks comes the **volume information block**, which holds information about the drive, including its format, name, number of files and folders, and allocation block size. This information must be present for a Mac to be able to access a drive. Because of the importance of the volume information block, a copy of it is stored in the next to last allocation block on the drive.
- A map of the allocation blocks on a hard drive is contained in the **volume bit map**, which uses a 1 to indicate that a block is storing files and a 0 to indicate that it is empty and is available for use. Damage to or corruption of the volume bit map does not prevent the Mac from being able to access the drive. However, when the Mac cannot determine from the volume bit map which allocation blocks are used, it might write new information to blocks that are full, overwriting the existing information. Regular disk maintenance (including use of the tools described in the next section) can help guard against this problem.
- The **catalog tree** is a database of the folders and files on a Mac hard drive, including information such as filenames and extensions, the application used to open a file, the creator of the file or folder, and the date the file or folder was created.
- The **extents tree** contains information about where the allocation blocks are located for files that take up more than one allocation block. When a file is larger than one allocation block, it is broken up into pieces called **extents**. One extent is stored in one allocation block. If a large proportion of the space on a hard drive is being used, the extents that make up a file might not be stored next to each other. The catalog tree and the extents tree work together and are both necessary for the Mac to be able to access data stored on the hard drive. They are the closest thing in the Mac to the FAT and the root directory in Windows.

Drive Maintenance Tools

Now that you've learned about some of the components and structures created when a Mac hard drive is formatted, let's look at some utilities you can use to format, maintain, and repair hard drives on a Mac. This is not an exhaustive list but rather points you to a few common tools used for typical hard drive tasks.

In Mac OS 9, disk maintenance tools were accessed as separate applications. In Mac OS X, the Utilities folder (shown in Figure 14-10) contains various system tools, including Disk Utility (shown in Figure 14-11), which combines the functions of the Mac OS 9 tools Drive Setup and Disk First Aid.

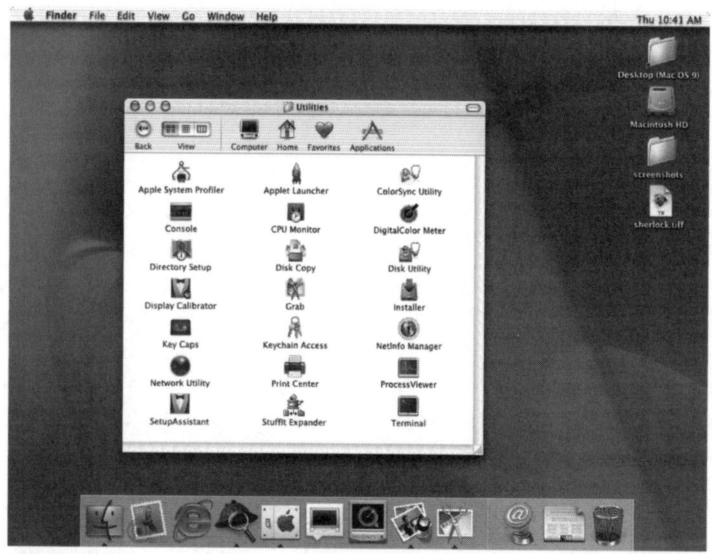

Figure 14-10 The Mac OS X Utilities folder contains several utilities, including those to manage a hard drive

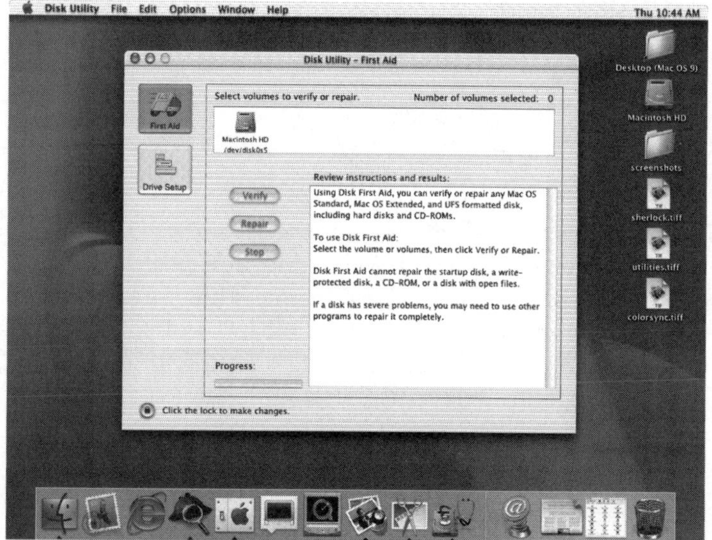

Figure 14-11 The Mac OS X Disk Utility is in the Utilities folder and can be used to set up and repair a hard drive

Drive Setup The **Drive Setup** function can be used to format a hard drive when it is initially installed or to reformat a damaged hard drive. Remember that reformatting a drive erases all data and programs on it because the format process creates new allocation blocks and directory structures. When you format a drive, you can choose whether or not to create partitions on it. Partitioning a drive is not required, but can be done to divide the drive into one or more logical drives. Drive Setup can format most IDE and SCSI drives. To use Drive Setup, on the Disk Utility window, click Drive Setup, select the disk you want to partition, and then click Partition. When you repartition a drive, all data on the current partitions is erased, and you cannot partition a drive that is currently used as the startup drive.

Defragmentation Utilities Third-party software, such as Norton Utilities (*www.symantec.com*) or TechTool Pro, which is specifically designed for use with Macs, (*www.micromat.com*) can be used to defragment your hard drive. These utilities copy the extents that make up a file into RAM on the Mac, reassemble the file, and save the complete file back onto the hard drive. One danger with these tools is that if a power failure occurs while they are running, any extents stored in the Mac's RAM will be lost. An alternate method, which is safer but much more time-consuming and cumbersome, is to back up the hard drive, reformat it, and then copy the files back onto the drive. You should always have a backup of your hard drive in case of any type of system failure.

Disk First Aid As you learned earlier in the chapter, Disk First Aid is a disk repair tool that checks for errors on the hard drive and runs automatically on reboot when a Mac is not shut down properly. You can also run this tool manually as a preventive maintenance measure or as an attempt to address poor hard drive performance. Disk First Aid is part of the free Apple utility Disk Utility and is less powerful than third-party disk repair utilities such as Norton Disk Doctor, which is part of Norton Utilities, or Alsoft's Disk Warrior (*www.alsoft.com*). There are some problems that these utilities can repair that Disk First Aid can only detect.

INTRODUCING LINUX

Generally, the Mac OS is very user-friendly and is ideal for many desktop computer uses. Linux is more often used as a file server, Web server, or e-mail server than as a desktop OS; therefore, our approach to it will be different. This introduction to Linux is designed to give you a behind-the-scenes look at what a system administrator must know in order to manage the Linux OS in a corporate setting. In this section, you will learn about root and user accounts, file structure, some common commands, and how to use the vi editor.

Recall from Chapter 1 that there are several different distributions of Linux. There are different versions within each distribution as well. The material in this section is meant as a general introduction to the OS. The organization of files and folders, the desktop's appearance, and the way each command works might be slightly different with the distribution and version of Linux you are using.

Root Account and User Accounts

Recall that an operating system is composed of a kernel, which interacts with the hardware and other software, and a shell, which interacts with the user and the kernel. Linux is a Unix-like operating system, and, just as with other versions of Unix, can use more than one shell. The default shell for Linux is the Bash shell. The name stands for "Bourne Again Shell" and takes the best features from two previous shells, the Bourne and the Korn shells.

For a Linux or Unix server, the system administrator is the person who installs updates to the OS (called patches), manages backup processes, supports the installation of software and hardware, sets up user accounts, resets passwords, and generally supports users. The system administrator has **root privileges**, which means that he or she can access all the functions of the OS and the principal user account called the **root account**. The administrator protects the password to the root account because this password gives full access to the system. When the administrator is logged on, he or she is logged on as the user root. You can use the *who* command to show a list of all users currently logged on to the system. In the example shown below, typing *who* shows that three users are currently logged on: the root, james, and susan.

```
who
root     tty1  Oct 12 07:56
james    tty1  Oct 12 08:35
susan    tty1  Oct 12 10:05
```

The Linux command prompt for the root is different from the command prompt for ordinary users. The root command prompt is #, and other users have the $ command prompt.

Directory and File Layout

The main directory in Unix and Linux is the **root directory** and is indicated with a forward slash. (In Unix and Linux, directories in a path are separated with forward slashes, in contrast to the backward slashes used by DOS and Windows.) Use the *ls* command, which is similar to the DOS Dir command, to list the contents of the root directory. The command (*ls -l /*) and its results are shown in Figure 14-12. Notice that the *-l* parameter is added to the command, which displays the results using the long format, and that there are spaces included before and after the parameter of the command. Also notice in the figure the format used to display the directory contents. The *d* at the beginning of each entry indicates that the entry is a directory, not a file. The other letters in this first column have to do with the read and write privileges assigned to the directory and the right to execute programs in the directory. The name of the directory is in the last column. The rights assigned the directory can apply to the owner of the directory, to other users, or to an entire group of users.

Table 14-1 lists directories that are created in the root directory during a typical Linux installation. The actual list of directories for a Linux computer that you work with may be a little different, because the directories created in the root directory depend on what programs have been installed.

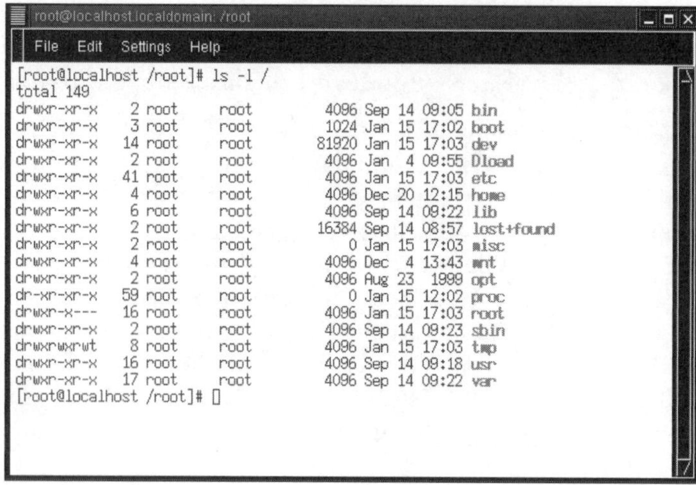

Figure 14-12 A directory listing using the ls command

Table 14-1 Directories in a typical Linux root directory

Directory	Description
/bin	Contains programs and commands necessary to boot the system and perform other system tasks not reserved for the administrator, such as shutdown and reboot.
/boot	Consists of components needed for the boot process, such as boot loaders.
/dev	Holds device names, which consist of the type of device and a number identifying the device. Actual device drivers are located in the /lib/modules /[kernel version]/ directory.
/etc	Contains system configuration data, including configuration files and settings and their subdirectories. These files are used for tasks such as configuring a user account, changing system settings, and configuring a domain name resolution service.
/home	Contains user data. Every user on the system has a directory in the /home directory, such as /home/jean or /home/scott, and when a user logs on, that directory becomes the current working directory.
/lib	Stores common libraries used by applications so that more than one application can use the same library at one time. An example is the library of C programming code, without which only the kernel of the Linux system could run.
/lost+found	Stores data that is lost when files are truncated or when an attempt to fix system errors is unsuccessful.
/opt	Contains installations of third-party applications such as Web browsers that do not come with the Linux OS distribution.
/root	The home directory for the root user; contains only files specific to the root user. Do not confuse this directory with the root directory, which contains all the directories listed in this table.

Table 14-1 Directories in a typical Linux root directory (continued)

Directory	Description
/sbin	Stores commands required for system administration.
/tmp	Stores temporary files, such as the ones that applications use during installation and operation.
/usr	Constitutes the major section of the Linux file system and contains read-only data.
/var	Holds variable data such as e-mail, news, print spools, and administrative files.

Linux Commands

This section describes some basic Linux and Unix commands, together with simple examples of how some are used. As you read along, be aware that all commands entered in Linux or Unix are case sensitive, meaning that uppercase and lowercase matter. Table 14-2 shows some common commands for Linux and Unix. This is not meant to be a comprehensive list of commands but simply to list some that might be useful to you in working with files, directories, network connections, and system configuration. In the rest of the section, you will learn how to use a few common commands. For all of these procedures, assume that you are in your home directory (which would be /home/<*yourname*>/).

Table 14-2 Some common Linux and Unix commands

Command	Description
cat	Lets you view the contents of a file. Many Linux commands can use the redirection symbol > to redirect the output of the command. For example, use the redirection symbol with the cat command to copy a file: `cat /etc/shells > newfile` The contents of the shells file are written to newfile.
cd	Change directory. For example, `cd /etc` changes the directory to /etc.
chmod	This command changes the attributes assigned to a file and is similar to the DOS Attrib command. For example, to grant read permission to the file myfile: `Chmod +r myfile`
clear	Clears the screen. This command is useful when the screen has become cluttered with commands and data that you no longer need to view.
cp	Used to copy a file: `cp <source> <destination>`
date	Entered alone, this command displays the current system date setting. Entered in the format `date <mmddhhmmyy>`, this command sets the system date. For example, to set the date to Dec 25, 2002 at 11:59 in the evening: `Date 1225235902`
echo	Displays information on the screen. For example, to display which shell is currently being used, enter this command: `echo $SHELL`
fdisk	Creates or makes changes to a hard drive partition table: `fdisk <hard drive>`
grep	Searches for a specific pattern in a file or in multiple files: `grep <pattern> <file>`

Table 14-2 Some common Linux and Unix commands (continued)

<table>
<tr><th>Command</th><th>Description</th></tr>
<tr><td>hostname</td><td>Displays a server's FQDN: hostname</td></tr>
<tr><td>ifconfig</td><td>Used to troubleshoot problems with network connections under TCP/IP. This command can disable and enable network cards and release and renew the IP addresses assigned to these cards. For example, to show all configuration information:
ifconfig -a
To release the given IP address for a TCP/IP connection named en0 (the first Ethernet connection of the system): ifconfig en0 -168.92.1.1</td></tr>
<tr><td>kill</td><td>Kills a process instead of waiting for the process to terminate:
kill <process ID></td></tr>
<tr><td>ls</td><td>The ls command is similar to the DOS Dir command, which displays a list of directories and files. For example, to list all files in the /etc directory, using the long parameter for a complete listing use: ls -l /etc</td></tr>
<tr><td>man</td><td>Displays the online help manual called the man pages. For example, to get information about the echo command: man echo
The manual program displays information about the command. To exit the manual program, type q.</td></tr>
<tr><td>mkdir</td><td>This command makes a new directory: mkdir <directory></td></tr>
<tr><td>|more</td><td>Appended to a command to display the results of the command on the screen one page at a time. For example, to page the ls command: ls |more</td></tr>
<tr><td>mv</td><td>Moves a file or renames it, if the source and destination are the same directory: mv <source> <destination></td></tr>
<tr><td>netstat</td><td>Shows statistics and status information for network connections and routing tables: netstat</td></tr>
<tr><td>nslookup</td><td>Queries domain name servers to look up domain names: nslookup</td></tr>
<tr><td>ping</td><td>Used to test network connections by sending a request packet to a host. If a connection is successful, the host will return a response packet. ping <host></td></tr>
<tr><td>ps</td><td>Displays the process table so that you can identify process IDs for currently running processes (Once you know the process ID, you can use the kill command to terminate a process): ps</td></tr>
<tr><td>pwd</td><td>Shows the name of the present working directory: pwd</td></tr>
<tr><td>reboot</td><td>Reboots the system: reboot</td></tr>
<tr><td>rm</td><td>Removes the file or files that are specified: rm <file></td></tr>
<tr><td>rmdir</td><td>This command removes a directory: rmdir <directory></td></tr>
<tr><td>route</td><td>Entered alone, this command shows the current configuration of the IP routing table. Entered in the format route [options], it configures the IP routing table.</td></tr>
<tr><td>traceroute</td><td>Shows the route of IP packets; used for debugging connections on a network:
traceroute <host></td></tr>
<tr><td>useradd</td><td>Adds a user to a system: useradd [option] <user></td></tr>
<tr><td>userdel</td><td>Removes a user from a system: userdel <user></td></tr>
</table>

Table 14-2 Some common Linux and Unix commands (continued)

Command	Description
vi	Launches a full-screen editor that can be used to enter text and commands: `vi <file>`
whatis	Displays a brief overview of a command. For example, to get quick information about the echo command: `whatis echo`
who	Displays a list of users currently logged in: `who`

Editing Commands

When you add options and file or directory names to a command, it can get quite long, and if you make a mistake while typing the command, you will want to edit it. Also, once the command has been entered, you can retrieve it, edit it, and press Enter to reissue the command. Some shells allow you to use the arrow, Backspace, Insert, and Delete keys to edit command lines, and other shells do not allow you to use these keys. Instead, use the following keystrokes to edit a command line:

- Alt+D Delete a word
- Ctrl+K Delete from the current position to the end of the line
- Ctrl+A Move the cursor to the beginning of the command line
- Alt+B Move the cursor left one word
- Alt+F Move the cursor right one word

For example, follow these steps to edit a command line:

1. Type **who is this** but DO NOT press Enter.
2. To move one word to the left, press **Alt+B** so that your cursor is positioned on the word "is."
3. To delete the word "is," press **Alt+D**.
4. To delete the portion of the command line that follows the current cursor position, press **Ctrl+K**.
5. To move the cursor to the beginning of the command line, press **Ctrl+A**.

14

Viewing the Shells File

The shells file in the /etc directory contains a list of available shells to use on a Linux system. Each shell incorporates slightly different support for programming and scripting languages. Additionally, different Linux shells may use keystrokes other than the ones you just learned in supporting command line editing; the keystrokes in the procedure in the last section work in Bash, the default Linux shell. To determine whether you are using the Bash shell, type `echo $shell` and press Enter. If you see the output /bin/bash, you are using the Bash shell. If you are not using the Bash shell, type `bash` and press Enter to change to the Bash shell.

To view a list of available shells:

1. Type **cat /etc/shells**, and then press **Enter**.
2. A list of available shells appears. This list may include the entries /bin/bash, /bin/bsh, /bin/csh, /bin/sh, /bin/tcsh, and /bin/zsh. Notice that all these shells are stored in the /bin directory. Type **clear**, and then press **Enter** to clear the screen.
3. Type **cat –n /etc/shells**, and then press **Enter**. Notice that this time, the same list of shells is displayed with a number before each line because you used the –n option. (See Figure 14-13.) Notice in the figure that the current user is root.

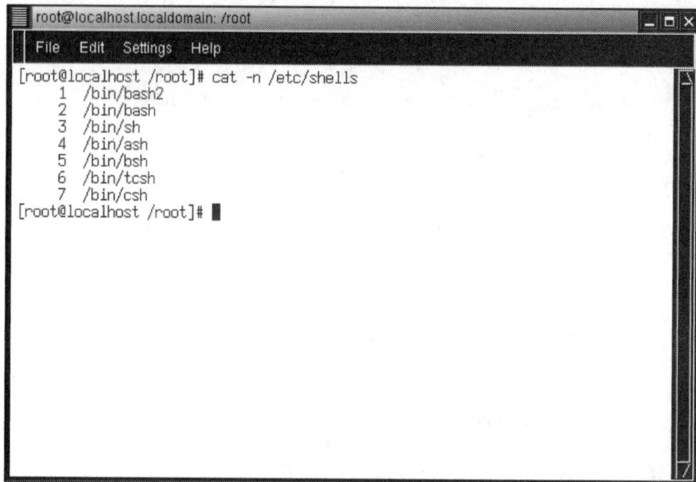

Figure 14-13 Use the Cat command to display a list of shells

Redirecting Output

Recall the list of available shells that you created using the `cat` command. When you entered the command `cat /etc/shells`, the list, which is the output of that command, was sent to the screen. What if you wanted to save that list? You would use the **redirection symbol**, which is the greater-than (>) sign, to direct the output to a file, perhaps with the name available_shells. Use these steps:

1. Go to the root directory by typing **cd /** and pressing **Enter**.
2. Type **cat /etc/shells > available_shells**, and then press **Enter**.
3. Notice that no command output appears on the screen, because the output has been saved to the new file available_shells (the file is created when the command is entered). To view the contents of the file, type **cat available_shells**, and then press **Enter**.

The file was created in the current directory which is the root directory.

Creating a Directory

It is not a good idea to store data files in the root directory, so let's create a new directory to which to move the new file available_shells:

1. Type **mkdir myfiles**, and then press **Enter**. This creates a new directory named myfiles under the current directory, which is root.
2. Type **cd myfiles** to change from the current directory to the new directory.
3. Type **mv /available_shells .** and then press **Enter** (don't overlook the period at the end of the command line; type it, too). This copies the file from the root directory to the current directory, which is /myfiles. The source directory is the root and the destination directory is /myfiles. The period in a command line means the current directory.
4. Type **ls** to see the contents of the myfiles directory. The available_shells file is listed. (See Figure 14-14.)

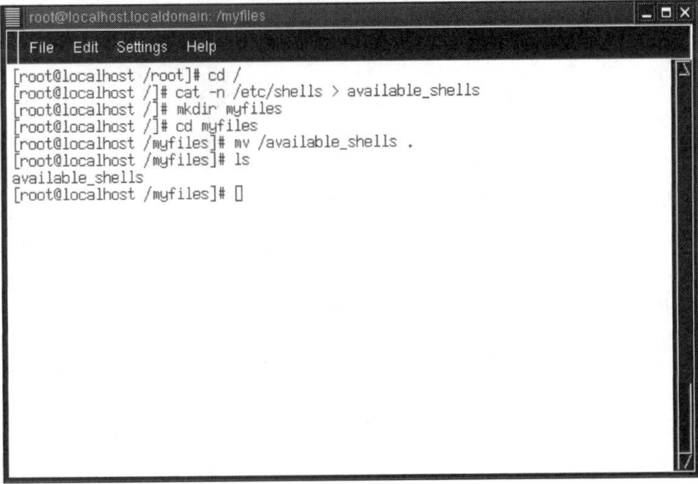

Figure 14-14 Creating and moving files to a directory

Using the vi Editor

Recall that you were introduced to the vi command in Table 14-2 earlier in the chapter. This command launches the **vi editor**, which got its name because it is a visual editor that was, at one time, the most popular Unix text editor. It is still used with shells that don't allow the use of the arrow, Delete, or Backspace keys. The editor can be used in **insert mode**, in which you can enter text, or **command mode**, which allows you to enter commands to perform editing tasks to move through the file. In this section, you will learn how to create and use commands on a text file in the vi editor. All of these commands are case sensitive.

Let's create and work with a file called mymemo.

1. To open the vi editor and create a file at the same time, type the command followed by the file name, as follows: **`vi mymemo`**
2. The vi editor screen is shown in Figure 14-15. Notice that the filename is shown at the bottom of the screen and that the cursor is at the top of the screen.

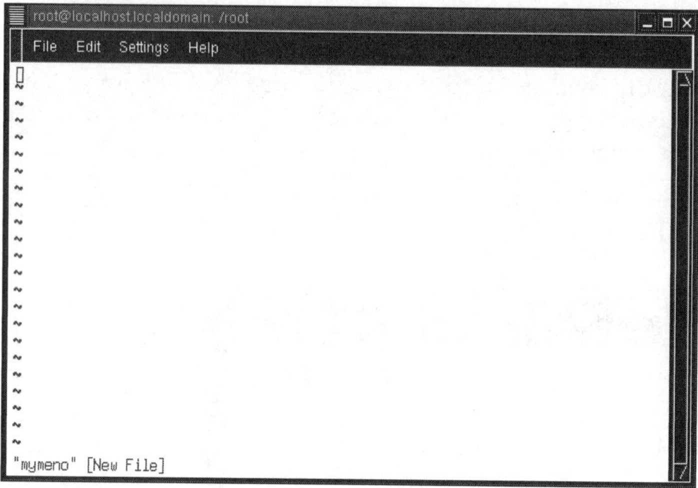

Figure 14-15 The vi text editor

3. At this point, when you first open the vi editor, you are in command mode, which means that anything you type will be interpreted as a command by the vi editor. Type **i** to switch to insert mode. You will not see the command on the screen, and you do not need to press Enter to execute it. The command automatically switches you to insert mode. When you are in insert mode, the word INSERT will be shown at the bottom of the screen.
4. Type the first two sentences of Step 3 as the text for your memo. If your shell supports it, practice using the arrow keys to move the cursor through the text, up, down, left, and right, one character at a time. You will see the keystrokes used to perform the same movements in Table 14-3; they can be used if the arrow keys are not supported.
5. To switch back to command mode, press the **Esc** key. Now you are ready to enter commands to manipulate your text. Type **H** to move the cursor to the upper-left corner of the screen. You must use an uppercase H, because all these commands are case sensitive.
6. Type **w** repeatedly until you reach the beginning of the word "first."

7. Type **dw** to delete the word "first." To delete one character at a time, you would use x; to delete an entire line, you would use dd.
8. To save the file and exit the vi editor, type **:x** and press **Enter**. This will save the file and close the editor.

Table 14-3 lists the vi editor commands to move the cursor. There are many more commands to manipulate text, set options, cancel, or temporarily leave a vi editor session. For a more complete list of vi editor commands, see a reference dedicated to Linux.

Table 14-3 vi editor commands

Command	Alternate	Description
Ctrl+B	Pg up	Back one screen
Ctrl+F	Pg down	Forward one screen
Ctrl+U	--	Up half a screen
Ctrl+D	--	Down half a screen
k	Up arrow	Up one line
j	Down arrow	Down one line
h	Left arrow	Left one character
l	Right arrow	Right one character
W	--	Forward one word
B	--	Back one word
0 (zero)	--	Beginning of the current line
$	--	End of current line
NG	--	Line specified by number *n*
H	--	Upper left corner of screen
L	--	Last line on the screen

Window Managers

Because many users prefer a Windows desktop, several applications have been written to provide a GUI for Unix and Linux. These GUIs are called window managers. You saw a typical window manager screen for Linux in Chapter 1. One popular desktop environment software is GNU Network Object Model Environment (GNOME). GNOME (pronounced "guh-nome") provides a desktop that looks and feels like Windows 98, and is free software designed to use a Linux kernel. The major components of a GNOME window are shown in Figure 14-16. For more information about GNOME, see the organization's Web site at *www.gnu.org*.

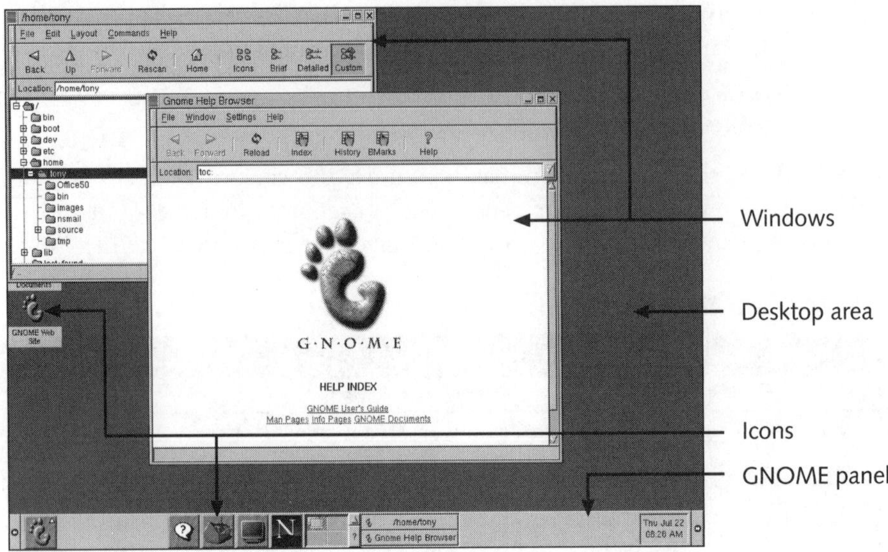

Figure 14-16 GNOME is popular desktop environment software used on Linux systems

SUPPORTING NOTEBOOKS

Supporting notebook computers is another essential task of a PC technician. This section discusses the special requirements for supporting notebooks, including changing power management options, understanding and supporting PC Cards, and using special Windows components available for supporting notebooks. Notebooks use the same technology as PCs do but with modifications so as to use less power, take up less space, and work when on the move.

A **notebook** or **laptop computer** is a computer designed for portability (see Figure 14-17). Notebooks use thin LCD panels instead of CRT monitors for display, compact hard drives that can withstand movement even during operation, and small memory modules and CPUs that require less power than regular components. Notebook LCD panels use one of two technologies. Active matrix (sometimes called thin film transistor or TFT) technology generally provides better quality than does passive matrix (sometimes called dual-scan twisted nematic, or DSTN) technology.

Notebooks cost more than PCs with similar features, because components are designed to be more compact and to endure movement when in use. The types and features of notebooks vary widely as they do for PCs. However, notebooks are generally purchased as a whole unit, including both hardware and software, and you are not as likely to upgrade a notebook's hardware and OS as you might be with a PC. In fact, some notebook manufacturers no longer support a notebook that has had the OS upgraded or new hardware components added. In contrast, recall that PCs are highly modular, letting you easily interchange, upgrade, and enhance components. In fact, PCs are often assembled from components purchased from various vendors and manufacturers. Notebook computers, on the other hand, are designed

Figure 14-17 A notebook is a computer designed for travel

with a different goal in mind and can be very proprietary in design, which means that the skills needed to support them are brand specific. In this chapter, we'll look at some universal support issues, but remember that procedures can vary from one notebook brand to another.

The LCD panels on notebooks are fragile and can be damaged. Take precautions against damaging the notebook's LCD panel through rough use.

When supporting any notebook, pay careful attention to the stipulations on the warranty that accompanies it. Some warranties are voided if you open the notebook case or install memory, batteries, or a hard drive that was not made by, or at least authorized by, the notebook's manufacturer. Almost all operating system installations on notebooks are customized by the manufacturer, and a floppy disk comes with the notebook that contains data and utilities specific to the configuration. Read the supporting documentation for the notebook before you consider upgrading or reinstalling the OS.

Windows 98 Notebook Features

A+ OS 1.1

The Windows 98 features designed to support notebooks include:

- Multilink Channel Aggregation, a feature that allows you to use two modem connections at the same time to speed up data throughput when connected over phone lines. It works on both regular analog phone lines and ISDN. To use the feature, you must have two phone lines and two modem cards that are physically designed to connect two phone lines at the same time.
- ACPI (Advanced Configuration and Power Interface) developed by Intel, Microsoft, and Toshiba to control power on a notebook and other devices. ACPI

A+ OS 1.1

allows a device to turn on a notebook or allows a notebook to turn on a device. For example, if you connect an external CD-ROM drive to the notebook, it can turn on the notebook, or the notebook can cycle up and turn on an external CD-ROM drive. The BIOS of the notebook and the device must support ACPI for it to work.

- Several improvements over Windows 95 for managing power consumption for notebooks. Windows 98 automatically powers down a PC Card modem when its not in use, supports multiple battery packs, and lets you create individual power profiles. Power profiles are described in the next section.
- Improved support for PC Cards, adding several new drivers.
- Microsoft Exchange lets a user select what e-mail to download when traveling with a notebook. Downloading large e-mail messages with attachments takes a long time over a modem. You might prefer to leave this e-mail to download when you are later connected directly to the network.

When returning from a trip with a notebook, you might want to update your desktop PC with all e-mail documents and other files created or updated during the trip. To do this, use Windows 9x **Briefcase**, a system folder used to synchronize files between two computers. Briefcase automatically updates files on the original computer to the most recent version. You can use a null modem cable, disk, or network for the file transfer.

Windows 2000 Notebook Features

A+ OS 1.1

Windows 2000 Professional has several features designed to support notebooks. When choosing between Windows 98 and Windows 2000 Professional for a notebook OS, use Windows 98 for low-end notebooks and Windows 2000 for high-end notebooks that are used in a business environment in which security is important. Windows 2000 has stronger power management and security features. The features new to Windows 2000 include:

- Offline Files, which replaces Briefcase, stores shared network files and folders in a cache on the notebook hard drive so you can use them offline. When you reconnect to the network, Offline Files synchronizes the files in the cache with those on the network.
- Hibernate mode, support for ACPI and APM (Advanced Power Management) have been improved.
- Improved battery support includes the ability to use two batteries and to monitor battery performance with greater control.
- Hot swapping of IDE devices and floppy disk external drives is a new feature.
- Folder redirection lets you point to an alternate location on a network for a folder. This feature can make the location of a folder transparent to the user.

Windows XP Notebook Features

Windows XP includes several features to make mobile computing easier, including power management features that build on similar capabilities in earlier versions of Windows. It also includes the ability to create **hardware profiles**, which specify which devices are to be loaded on startup for a particular user or set of circumstances. For example, you might set two different hardware profiles for a notebook computer, one for when it is connected to a port replicator and one for when it is not. A **port replicator** provides a means to connect a notebook to a power outlet and to the same external peripherals as are available to a desktop PC. A **docking station** does that and also provides additional secondary storage.

To create a hardware profile for a mobile user, follow these steps:

1. From the Start menu, open the **Control Panel**.
2. Double-click the **System** icon.
3. The System Properties dialog box opens. Click the **Hardware** tab.
4. Click the **Hardware Profiles** button at the bottom of the Hardware tab.
5. The Hardware Profiles dialog box opens (Figure 14-18). Click **Profile1 (Current)**, and then click the **Copy** button.

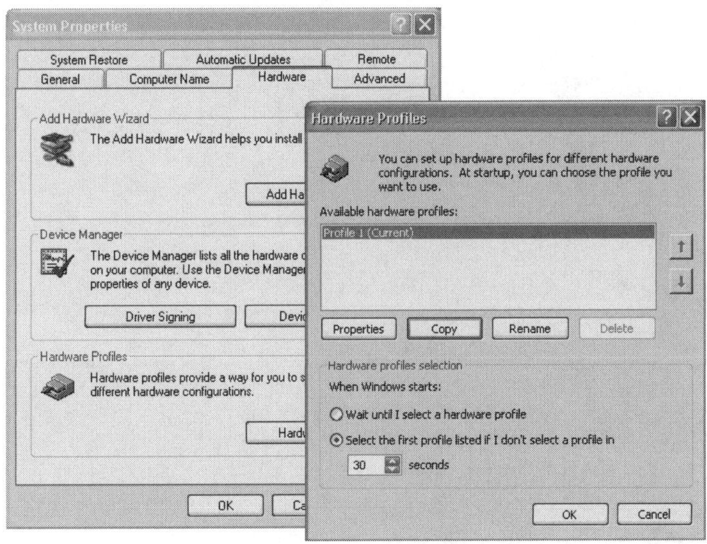

Figure 14-18 Windows XP allows you to set a hardware profile for each user

6. Type a new name for the profile, and then click **OK**.
7. Under When Windows starts, select either the option for Windows XP to wait for you to select a hardware profile or the option for Windows XP to start with the first profile listed if you don't select one in the specified number of seconds.
8. Restart the computer and, when prompted, select the new hardware profile.

14

9. Open the System Properties window. Click the **Hardware** tab, click **Device Manager**, and then double-click the icon for a device that you want to be enabled or disabled in the new profile.
10. Click the **General** tab in the Properties window for the device and in the area for device usage, select the option to enable the device, disable it for the current profile, or disable it for all hardware profiles.

Power Management

A notebook can be powered by a battery pack or an AC adapter connected to a power source. The length of time that a battery pack can power the notebook before being recharged varies according to the quality of the battery, the power consumption as determined by the devices being used, and how power is being managed.

Windows 98 and Windows 2000/XP have features to help manage power consumption. The goal is to minimize power consumption to increase the time before a battery pack needs recharging. Using Windows 98, to access the power management window, click Start, point to Settings, click Control Panel, and double-click the Power Management icon. Figure 14-19 shows the Power Management Properties dialog box for one notebook. (Other brands of notebooks may have different tabs in their Properties dialog box.) Use this dialog box to create, delete, and modify multiple power management schemes to customize how Windows 98 manages power consumption.

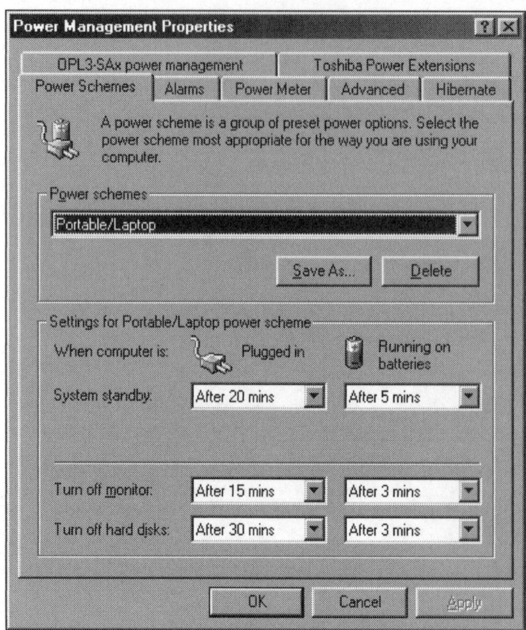

Figure 14-19 The Power Management Properties box of Windows 98 allows you to create and manage multiple power schemes

For example, one power-saving feature of Windows 98 puts a notebook into hibernation. When a computer hibernates, it stores whatever is currently in memory and then shuts down. When it returns from hibernating, it restores everything to the way it was before the shutdown. When hibernating, the notebook is using only a very small amount of power. When you step away from the notebook for a few minutes, direct the notebook to hibernate in order to save power. Before you direct a notebook to hibernate, make sure you know which keystrokes or buttons are required to restore the system to an active state without turning the computer off.

If the notebook supports hibernating, to configure Windows 98 to cause the notebook to hibernate when you close the lid of the notebook, do the following:

1. In the Power Management Properties dialog box, click the **Hibernate** tab (see Figure 14-20) and verify that hibernate support is enabled.

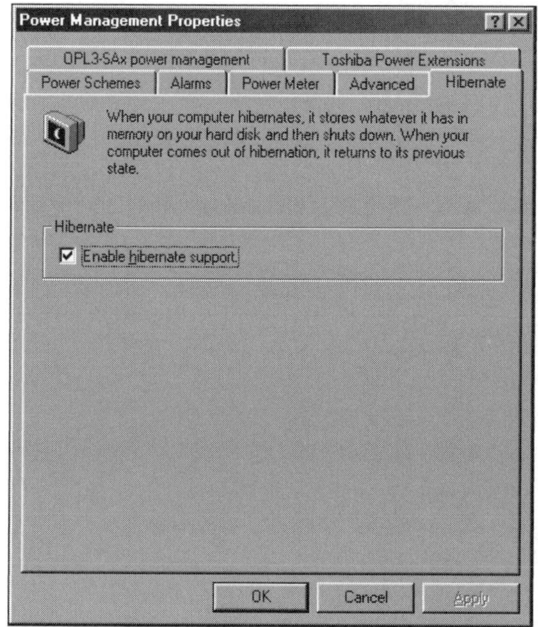

Figure 14-20 Verify that hibernate support is enabled

2. Click the **Advanced** tab. Figure 14-21 shows the Advanced page, which you use to control what happens when you press the shutdown button or close the lid of the notebook.

3. Click the list arrow for "When I close the lid of my portable computer" and select **Hibernate**. See Figure 14-22.

4. Click **Apply** and **OK** to close the Properties dialog box, saving your changes.

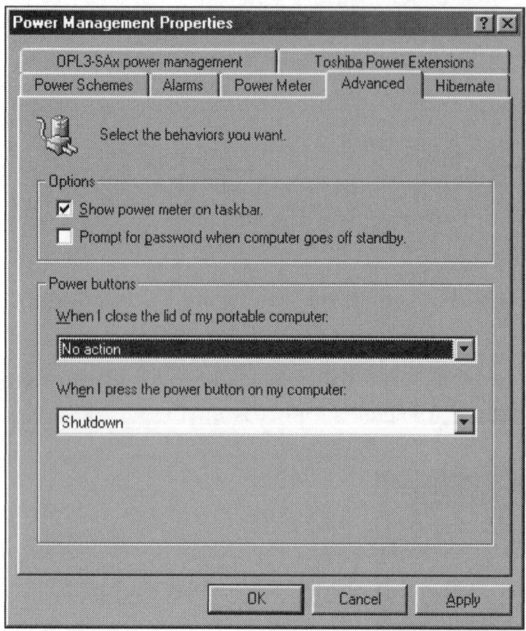

Figure 14-21 The Advanced tab of Power Management allows you to control the behavior of the power button and what happens when you close the lid of your notebook

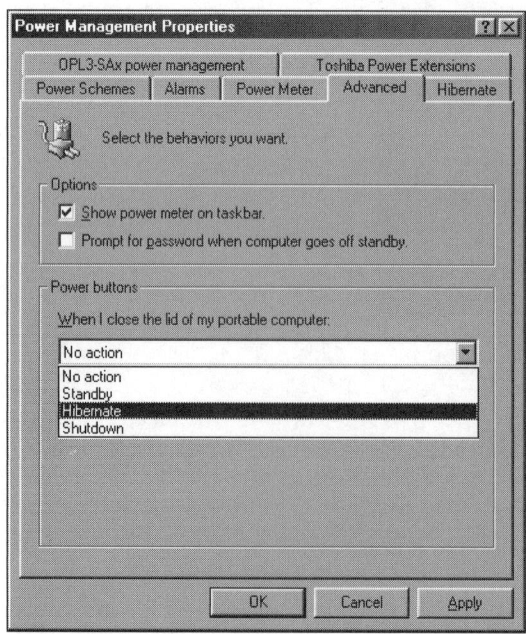

Figure 14-22 Choices of action when you close the lid of your notebook

If you need to use the notebook for extended periods away from an electrical outlet, you can use extra battery packs. When the notebook signals that power is low, remove the old battery and replace it with a charged one. See the notebook's user guide for directions. Here is an example of directions for exchanging the battery pack for one notebook:

1. Save your work and turn off the notebook.
2. Remove all cables connected to the notebook.
3. Set the notebook on its back, (as in Figure 14-23).
4. Slide the battery release panel to the left to expose the battery.
5. Lift the battery out of the computer.
6. Before placing a new battery in the slot, clean the edge connectors of the battery with a clean cloth.

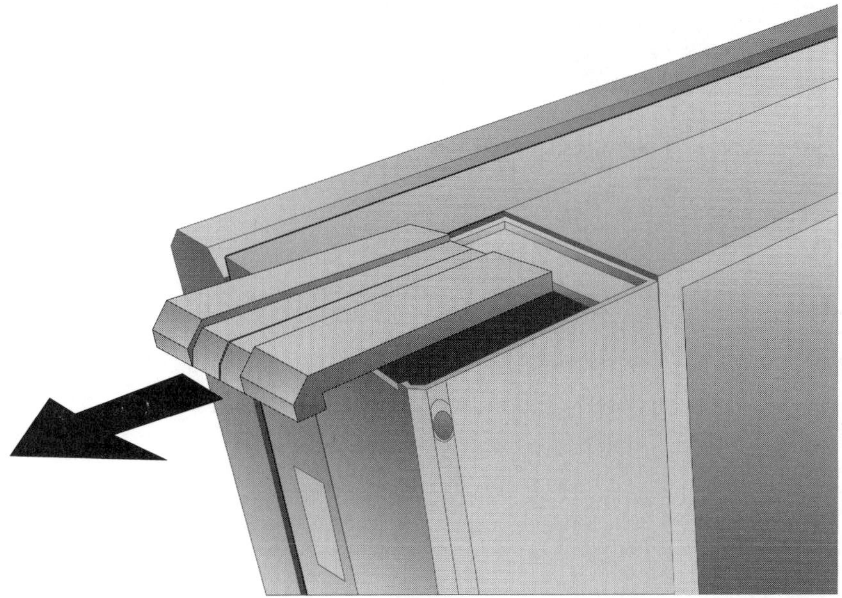

Figure 14-23 Slide the battery release panel to the left to expose the battery pack

To extend the life of your battery, don't leave the battery in the notebook while the notebook is turned on and it's connected to an electrical outlet. When using the notebook while it is connected to an electrical outlet, remove the battery from the case. To recharge the battery, leave the notebook turned off while it is connected to an electrical outlet with the battery inserted. Some older battery types required that to keep the battery operating at optimum performance, you allowed the battery to almost completely discharge before recharging it and then completely recharge it before using it again. Some newer battery types do not require this. Check the documentation for your particular notebook and battery, and never use a battery charger on a battery type other than the one for which it was designed.

Windows 2000 improves the power management features of Windows 98, including, as you have learned, adding ACPI and APM. In Windows 2000, you can monitor and manage batteries on notebooks that are ACPI- and APM-enabled. You can access the battery meter directly by adding the battery status icon to the taskbar (see Figure 14-24). Follow these steps:

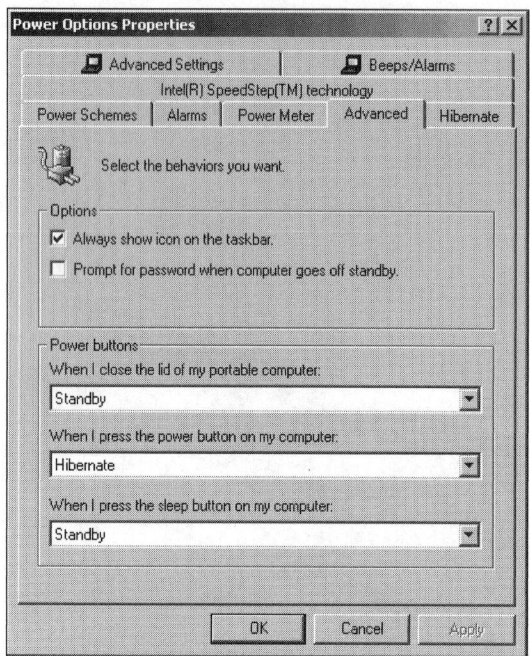

Figure 14-24 Use the Power Options Properties window to tell the Notebook what to do when you close the lid, press the power button, or press the sleep button

1. On the Start menu, click **Settings**, **Control Panel**.
2. Double-click **Power Options** to open the Power Options Properties dialog box.
3. Click the **Advanced** tab.
4. Click the check box labeled **Always show icon on the taskbar**.

Note that the Power Options box also offers tabs on which you can create power profiles and set alarms to alert you when battery power is low or critical.

Windows XP also includes power management features for notebooks, including support for ACPI and ACM. You can access these features from the Power Options icon in Control Panel. In the Power Options window, click the Power Schemes tab to select a **power scheme**, which is a collection of settings for a particular set of circumstances, such as for home/office desk use or portable/laptop use.

Online Resources for Notebooks

Except for the differences discussed in this section, notebooks work identically to desktop PCs, and the troubleshooting guidelines in previous chapters also apply to notebooks. When troubleshooting notebooks, be especially conscious of warranty issues; know what you can do within the guidelines of the warranty. The documentation that comes with a notebook is much more comprehensive than what comes with a PC and most often contains troubleshooting guidelines for the notebook. Remember that the loaded OS and the hardware configuration are specific to the notebook, so you can rely on the notebook's manufacturer for support more than you can for a desktop PC. Sometimes a notebook is designed so that the hard drive can be replaced or upgraded without violating warranties. See the notebook documentation for details. For questions about supporting a notebook that are not answered in the documentation, see the Web site of the notebook manufacturer. Some popular manufacturers of notebooks and their Web sites are listed in Table 14-4.

Table 14-4 Notebook manufacturers

Manufacturer	Web site
Acer America	*global.acer.com*
ARM Computer	*www.armcomputer.com*
Compaq Computer	*www.hp.com*
Dell Computer	*www.dell.com*
Gateway	*www.gateway.com*
Hewlett-Packard	*www.hp.com*
IBM	*www.ibm.com*
Micron PC	*www.micronpc.com*
PC Notebook	*www.pcnotebook.com*
Sony	*www.sonystyle.com/vaio*
Toshiba America	*www.csd.toshiba.com*
WinBook	*www.winbook.com*

Chapter Summary

- The Finder Window in the Mac OS functions somewhat like Explorer or My Computer in Microsoft Windows. It allows you to navigate through the Mac's hierarchical file structure.
- The Mac OS boot process begins with ROM-initiated self-test of hardware components and ends with the loading of the interface after necessary components, including the Mac OS ROM file, enablers, and System folder contents, are loaded.
- The dock at the bottom of the Mac desktop is new to Mac OS X. It provides access to frequently used applications.

- The Apple menu contains options that are accessible no matter what application you are in. It is customizable in Mac OS 9 but not in Mac OS X.
- There are four ways to launch an application on the Mac: double-click its icon, choose it from Recent Applications under Recent Items on the Apple menu, double-click the icon of a file associated with it, and drag a document icon to the application icon.
- Use the Display window, accessible from the System Preferences window, to change and monitor settings such as resolution, contrast, brightness, and geometry. Other system settings can also be accessed from System Preferences.
- The Drive Setup and Disk First Aid utilities, which are separate in Mac OS 9, have been combined into the Disk Utility in Mac OS X. This utility and other system tools are accessible in the Utilities folder, which is located under Applications.
- Macs can recognize, format, and support most IDE (Integrated Device Electronics) and SCSI (Small Computer System Interface) hard drives.
- The main file systems available for Mac are HFS and HFS+, but you can also mount FAT16, FAT32, and NTFS volumes on a Mac.
- Linux is based on Unix and uses many of the same commands.
- The default shell for Linux is the Bash shell.
- The system administrator for a Linux computer has root privileges and can access all the functions of the OS, support installations, manage backups, and make changes to system configuration.
- The root directory is the top level in the Linux file structure. The directory for each user is their /home directory, and unless a user has the root account, he or she is automatically in his or her home directory after logging on to the system.
- All commands in Linux and Unix are case sensitive. For example, in some of the text-editing commands, the same letter in lowercase and in uppercase can mean two different things.
- The vi editor is a text editor in Linux that runs in insert mode and command mode, allowing you to enter text and enter commands to manipulate that text.
- GUI interfaces for Linux are called window managers. One popular Linux window manager is GNOME.
- Notebook computers are designed for travel. They use the same technology as PCs, with modifications for space, portability, and power conservation. A notebook will generally cost more than a PC with the same specifications.
- When supporting notebooks, pay careful attention to what the warranty allows you to change on the computer.
- Windows 98 notebook computer features include Multilink Channel Aggregation, ACPI and APM, improved support for and management of PC cards, and the Briefcase.
- Windows 2000 notebook features support high-end notebooks better than Windows 9x and include offline files, improved battery support, hot-swapping, and folder redirection.
- A notebook can be powered by its battery pack or by an AC adapter connected to a power source.

- Windows XP notebook support includes the ability to create hardware profiles and power schemes that manage the computer's attached devices and its power settings differently depending on whether the computer is connected to a port replicator or not.
- Notebook settings and procedures vary more widely from model to model than with desktop computers. Check the manufacturer's documentation and Web site for information specific to your notebook model.

Key Terms

allocation blocks
Apple menu
block
boot blocks
Briefcase
catalog tree
command mode
Control Panels folder
directory structures
Disk First Aid
Disk Utility
dock
docking station
Drive Setup
enabler file
Extensions folder
extents
extents tree
Finder window
hardware profiles
HFS (Hierarchical File System)
HFS+
insert mode
laptop
Library
loopback device
Mac OS extended format
Mac OS ROM file
Mac OS standard format
notebook
pixel
port replicator
power scheme
PRAM (parameter RAM)
redirection symbol
resolution
root account
root directory
root privileges
System file
System folder
vi editor
volume bit map
volume information block
window manager

Review Questions

1. List at least five differences between Mac OS 9 and Mac OS X.
2. List the steps of the Mac OS startup process.
3. What role does the Mac OS ROM file play in the startup process?
4. Explain the four ways to access an application on a Mac.
5. Can you run Mac OS 9 applications from the Mac OS X interface? Explain.
6. How are open applications shown in Mac OS 9? In Mac OS X?
7. What is screen geometry, and how do you change it on a Mac?
8. Why is it a good idea to set your monitor's resolution to 800 x 600?
9. Name the two major hard drive technologies that Macs support.
10. What is the file system for the Mac? Name other, non-native file systems that Macs can support.

11. How did HFS+ improve on HFS?
12. If you do not have any third-party defragmentation utilities available, what is one way that you can defragment your Mac hard drive?
13. What is the default Linux shell? What were the two shells that preceded it?
14. List some of the responsibilities of a system administrator for a Linux machine.
15. Explain the difference between the Linux root account and a regular user account.
16. What is contained in the Linux /etc directory? /opt? /sbin?
17. Under which directory are applications installed using Linux?
18. Which Linux command is used to copy a file? To clear the screen? To kill a process? To list the contents of a file with a number in front of each line?
19. What is the vi editor? Explain how to open it and close it. When might you use it?
20. What are the two modes available in the vi editor? How do you switch between them?
21. Give two examples of background processes in Linux.
22. Explain what a Linux window manager is and give an example.
23. How are notebooks different from desktop PCs?
24. List notebook support features available in Windows 98, Windows 2000, and Windows XP.
25. Why is understanding the warranty on notebooks so important?

Hands-on Projects

Researching Mac Cross-compatibility

Using the Apple Web site (*www.apple.com*) and other Web sites as necessary, research whether you can do the following on a Mac:

1. Read Microsoft Word documents
2. Mount a volume that is using FAT32
3. Send documents to a Linux computer
4. Use applications that were designed for Mac OS 8.1 when Mac OS X is installed

Print the Web page showing the source of your information and instructions for accomplishing each task.

Using Mac Applications

On a Mac computer, locate the TextEdit application. Write a short memo and save it as myfile. Use this file and the instructions in this chapter to practice the four ways of accessing an application on the Mac.

Researching Linux

Recall from Chapter 1 that popular distributions of Linux include SuSE (*www.suse.com*), RedHat (*www.redhat.com*), and Caldera (*www.caldera.com)*. For each distribution, find out the following:

1. Latest version number
2. File systems supported
3. Availability of free downloads and cost of any paid versions
4. Whether you can read Microsoft Word and Microsoft Excel documents, and if so, how

Practicing Linux Commands

From Linux without a GUI or from a terminal within a Linux window manager, create a text file using the vi editor. Save it to your home directory and then execute the commands to move it to another user's home directory. Refer to Table 14-2 in this chapter as necessary.

Comparing Notebooks

From a site such as *www.cnet.com*, select three different notebooks in high, medium, and low price ranges. Using the comparison site and the Web site of the manufacturer of each notebook (you can refer back to Table 14-4), write down the following:

1. Price
2. Manufacturer
3. Display type, hard drive space, and RAM
4. Software included with the computer, including the OS
5. Whether hardware and software upgrades affect the warranty or the manufacturer's support of the product (if this information is available)

ERROR MESSAGES AND THEIR MEANINGS

A+ OS 3.1

The following table of error messages and their meanings can help you when you are diagnosing computer problems. For other error messages, consult your motherboard or computer documentation.

Error Message	Meaning of the Error Message and What to Do
Bad sector writing or reading to drive	Sector markings on the disk may be fading. Try ScanDisk or reformat the disk.
Bad command or file not found	The OS command just executed cannot be interpreted, or the OS cannot find the program file specified in the command line. Check the spelling of the filename and, for DOS or when working from a Windows startup disk, check that the path to the program file has been given to the OS.
Beeps during POST	Before the video is checked, during POST, the ROM BIOS communicates error messages with a series of beeps. Each BIOS manufacturer has its own beep codes, but the following are examples of some BIOS codes. For specific beep codes for your motherboard, see the Web site of the motherboard or BIOS manufacturer.
One single beep followed by three, four, or five beeps	Motherboard problems, possibly with DMA, the CMOS setup chip, timer, or the system bus.
Two beeps	The POST numeric code is displayed on the monitor.
Two beeps followed by three, four, or five beeps	First 64K of RAM has errors.
Three beeps followed by three, four, or five beeps	Keyboard controller has failed or video controller has failed.
Four beeps followed by two, three, or four beeps	Problem with serial or parallel ports, system timer, or time of day.
Continuous beeps	Problem with power supply.
Configuration/CMOS error	Setup information does not agree with the actual hardware the computer found during the boot. May be caused by a bad or weak battery or by changing hardware without changing setup. Check setup for errors.
Insufficient memory	This error happens under Windows when too many applications are open. Close some applications. A reboot may help.

A+ OS 3.1

Error Message	Meaning of the Error Message and What to Do
Hard drive not found	The OS cannot locate the hard drive, or the controller card is not responding.
Fixed disk error	The PC cannot find the hard drive that setup told it to expect. Check the cables, connections, power supply, and setup information.
Incorrect DOS version	When you execute a DOS external command, the OS looks for a program file with the same name as the command. It finds that this file belongs to a different version of the OS than the one that is now running. Use the Setver command in Autoexec.bat.
Invalid drive specification	The PC is unable to find a hard drive or a floppy drive that setup tells it to expect. Look for errors in setup, or for a corrupted partition table on the hard drive.
Invalid or missing Command.com	This may be caused by a nonbooting disk in drive A. Remove the disk and boot from drive C. Command.com on drive C may have been erased, or the path could not be found.
No boot device available	The hard drive is not formatted, or the format is corrupted, and there is no disk in drive A. Boot from a floppy and examine your hard drive for corruption.
Non-system disk or disk error	Command.com or one of two OS hidden files is missing from the disk in drive A or the hard drive. Remove the disk in drive A and boot from the hard drive. Use the SYS command to restore system files.
Not ready reading drive A: Abort, Retry, Fail?	The disk in drive A is missing, is not formatted, or is corrupted. Try another disk.
Numeric codes during POST	Sometimes numeric codes are used to communicate errors at POST. Some examples for IBM XT/AT error codes include:
Code in the 100 range	Motherboard errors
Code in the 200 range	RAM errors
Code in the 300 range	Keyboard errors
Code in the 500 range	Video controller errors
Code in the 600 range	Floppy drive errors
Code in the 700 range	Coprocessor errors
Code in the 900 range	Parallel port errors
Code in the 1100–1200 range	Async (communications adapter) errors
Code in the 1300 range	Game controller or joystick errors
Code in the 1700 range	Hard drive errors
Code in the 6000 range	SCSI device or network card errors
Code in the 7300 range	Floppy drive errors

A+ OS 3.1

Error Message	Meaning of the Error Message and What to Do
Track 0 bad, disk not usable	This usually occurs when you attempt to format a floppy disk using the wrong format type. Check the disk type and compare it to the type specified in the format command.
Write-protect error writing drive A:	Let the computer write to the disk by setting the switch on a 3½-inch disk or removing the tape from a 5¼-inch disk.
Missing operating system, error loading operating system	The MBR is unable to locate or read the OS boot sector on the active partition or there is a translation problem on large drives. Boot from a floppy and examine the hard drive file system for corruption.
Unknown error at POST	See the Web site of the system BIOS manufacturer: • AMI BIOS: *www.ami.com* • Award BIOS and Phoenix BIOS: *www.phoenix.com* • Compaq: *www.compaq.com* • Dell: *www.dell.com* • IBM: *www.ibm.com*
Error in Config.sys line *xx*	There is a problem loading a device driver or with the syntax of a command line. Check the command line for errors. Verify the driver files are in the right directory. Reinstall the driver files.
Himem.sys not loaded, missing or corrupt Himem.sys	Himem.sys is corrupted, not in the right directory, or not the right version for the currently loading OS. Verify Himem.sys.
Device not found	Errors in System.ini, Win.ini, or the registry. Look for references to devices or attempts to load device drivers. Use Device Manager to delete a device or edit System.ini or Win.ini.

APPENDIX

B

ASCII CHARACTER SET AND ANSI.SYS

ASCII (American Standard Code for Information Interchange) is a coding system that is used by personal computers to store character data, such as letters of the alphabet, numerals, some symbols, and certain control characters. There are 128 characters defined by the standard ASCII character set. Each ASCII character is assigned an 8-bit code that converts to a decimal number from 0 to 127, although in the standard set, the first bit is always 0. The first 31 values, which are nonprintable codes, are used for control characters and can be used to send commands to printers or other peripheral devices. Files that store data as ASCII characters are sometimes called ASCII files, ASCII text files, or simply text files. ASCII can be read by most editors and word processors and is considered the universal file format for personal computers. Autoexec.bat is one example of an ASCII file.

In addition to the standard ASCII character set, some manufacturers use an extended ASCII character set that is specific to their equipment and is not necessarily compatible with other computers. The extended ASCII character sets use the codes 128 through 255.

The American National Standards Institute (ANSI), an organization responsible for many computer standards, developed an extended character set using codes 128 through 255 that includes special characters such as letters in an international alphabet and accents, currency symbols, and fractions. ANSI has also defined a series of control codes that can be used to control monitors. For example, a sequence of control codes can clear a monitor, cause characters to be displayed upside down, or put color on a DOS screen. Ansi.sys is a device driver that, when loaded in a DOS environment, provides these monitor and keyboard functions. Ansi.sys is loaded from the Config.sys file with this command:

```
Device=C:\DOS\Ansi.sys
```

Some DOS programs need Ansi.sys loaded in order to interpret the extended character set entered from the keyboard, display these characters on the screen, and control the monitor in other ways.

Table B-1 lists the standard ASCII character set. Note that items 2 through 32, the control characters, and the extended ASCII character set are not included.

Table B-1 Standard ASCII character set

Item Number	Symbol	Meaning	ASCII in Decimal Representation	ASCII in Binary Representation	ASCII in Hex Representation
1	.	Null	0	0000 0000	0
33	b/	Space	32	0010 0000	20
34	!	Exclamation point	33	0010 0001	21
35	"	Quotation mark	34	0010 0010	22
36	#	Number sign	35	0010 0011	23
37	$	Dollar sign	36	0010 0100	24
38	%	Percent sign	37	0010 0101	25
39	&	Ampersand	38	0010 0110	26
40	'	Apostrophe, prime sign	39	0010 0111	27
41	(	Opening parenthesis	40	0010 1000	28
42	)	Closing parenthesis	41	0010 1001	29
43	*	Asterisk	42	0010 1010	2A
44	+	Plus sign	43	0010 1011	2B
45	,	Comma	44	0010 1100	2C
46	-	Hyphen, minus sign	45	0010 1101	2D
47	.	Period, decimal point	46	0010 1110	2E
48	/	Slant	47	0010 1111	2F
49	0		48	0011 0000	30
50	1		49	0011 0001	31
51	2		50	0011 0010	32
52	3		51	0011 0011	33
53	4		52	0011 0100	34
54	5		53	0011 0101	35
55	6		54	0011 0110	36
56	7		55	0011 0111	37
57	8		56	0011 1000	38
58	9		57	0011 1001	39
59	:	Colon	58	0011 1010	3A
60	;	Semicolon	59	0011 1011	3B

Table B-1 Standard ASCII character set (continued)

Item Number	Symbol	Meaning	ASCII in Decimal Representation	ASCII in Binary Representation	ASCII in Hex Representation
61	<	Less than sign	60	0011 1100	3C
62	=	Equals sign	61	0011 1101	3D
63	>	Greater than sign	62	0011 1110	3E
64	?	Question mark	63	0011 1111	3F
65	@	Commercial at sign	64	0100 0000	40
66	A		65	0100 0001	41
67	B		66	0100 0010	42
68	C		67	0100 0011	43
69	D		68	0100 0100	44
70	E		69	0100 0101	45
71	F		70	0100 0110	46
72	G		71	0100 0111	47
73	H		72	0100 1000	48
74	I		73	0100 1001	49
75	J		74	0100 1010	4A
76	K		75	0100 1011	4B
77	L		76	0100 1100	4C
78	M		77	0100 1101	4D
79	N		78	0100 1110	4E
80	O		79	0100 1111	4F
81	P		80	0101 0000	50
82	Q		81	0101 0001	51
83	R		82	0101 0010	52
84	S		83	0101 0011	53
85	T		84	0101 0100	54
86	U		85	0101 0101	55
87	V		86	0101 0110	56
88	W		87	0101 0111	57
89	X		88	0101 1000	58
90	Y		89	0101 1001	59
91	Z		90	0101 1010	5A
92	[	Opening bracket	91	0101 1011	5B
93	\	Reverse slant	92	0101 1100	5C
94	]	Closing bracket	93	0101 1101	5D

Table B-1 Standard ASCII character set (continued)

Item Number	Symbol	Meaning	ASCII in Decimal Representation	ASCII in Binary Representation	ASCII in Hex Representation
95	^	Caret	94	0101 1110	5E
96	_	Underscore	95	0101 1111	5F
97	`	Acute accent	96	0110 0000	60
98	a		97	0110 0001	61
99	b		98	0110 0010	62
100	c		99	0110 0011	63
101	d		100	0110 0100	64
102	e		101	0110 0101	65
103	f		102	0110 0110	66
104	g		103	0110 0111	67
105	h		104	0110 1000	68
106	i		105	0110 1001	69
107	j		106	0110 1010	6A
108	k		107	0110 1011	6B
109	l		108	0110 1100	6C
110	m		109	0110 1101	6D
111	n		110	0110 1110	6E
112	o		111	0110 1111	6F
113	p		112	0111 0000	70
114	q		113	0111 0001	71
115	r		114	0111 0010	72
116	s		115	0111 0011	73
117	t		116	0111 0100	74
118	u		117	0111 0101	75
119	v		118	0111 0110	76
120	w		119	0111 0111	77
121	x		120	0111 1000	78
122	y		121	0111 1001	79
123	z		122	0111 1010	7A
124	{	Opening brace	123	0111 1011	7B
125	|	Split vertical bar	124	0111 1100	7C
126	}	Closing brace	125	0111 1101	7D
127	~	Tilde	126	0111 1110	7E
128	Δ	Small triangle	127	0111 1111	7F

APPENDIX

C

The Hexadecimal Number System and Memory Addressing

Fundamental to understanding how computers work is understanding the number system and the coding system that computers use to store data and communicate with each other. Early attempts to invent an electronic computing device met with disappointing results as long as inventors tried to use our own decimal number system, with the digits 0–9. Then John Atanasoff proposed using a coding system that expressed everything in terms of different sequences of only two numerals: one represented by the presence of a charge and one represented by the absence of a charge. The numbering system that can be supported by the expression of only two numerals is the base 2, sometimes called binary, numbering system, invented by Ada Lovelace many years before, using the two numerals 0 and 1. Under Atanasoff's design, all numbers and other characters would be converted to this binary number system, and all storage, comparisons, and arithmetic would be done using it. Even today, this is one of the basic principles of computers. Every character or number entered into a computer is first converted into a series of 0s and 1s. Many coding schemes and techniques have been invented to manipulate these 0s and 1s, called **bits** for **bi**nary dig**its**.

The most widespread binary coding scheme for microcomputers, which is recognized as the microcomputer standard, is called the ASCII (American Standard Code for Information Interchange) coding system. (Appendix B lists the binary code for the basic 127-character set.) In ASCII, each character is assigned an 8-bit code called a **byte**. Table C-1 lists the terms used in the discussion of how numbers are stored in computers. The byte has become the universal single unit of storage for data in computers everywhere.

Table C-1 Computer terminology

Term	Definition
Bit	A numeral in the binary number system: a 0 or a 1
Byte	8 bits
Kilobyte	1,024 bytes, which is 2^{10}, often rounded to 1,000 bytes
Megabyte	Either 1,024 kilobytes or 1,000 kilobytes, depending on what has come to be standard practice in different situations. For example, when calculating floppy disk capacities, 1 megabyte = 1,000 kilobytes; when calculating hard drive capacity, traditionally, 1 megabyte = 1,024 bytes.
Gigabyte	1,000 megabytes or 1,024 megabytes, depending on what has come to be standard practice in different situations
ASCII	American Standard Code for Information Interchange coding scheme used for microcomputers, which assigns a 7- or 8-bit code to all characters and symbols. See Appendix B for more information.
Hex	Short for hexadecimal. A number system based on 16 values (called base 16), which is explained in detail below. Uses the sixteen numerals 0, 1, 2, 3, 4, 5, 6, 7, 8, 9, A, B, C, D, E, and F. Hex numbers are often followed by a lowercase h to indicate they are in hex (example: 78h).

Computers convert binary data into the hexadecimal number system (shortened to hex system) because it is much less complex for computers to convert binary numbers into hex numbers than into decimal numbers, and it is much easier for human beings to read hex numbers than to read binary numbers. This way, even though the actual processing and inner workings of computers use the binary system, they often display information using the hex system.

Learning to "Think Hex"

One skill a knowledgeable computer support person must have is the ability to read hex numbers and convert hex to decimal and decimal to hex. Once you understand one numbering system (decimal), you can understand any numbering system (including binary and hexadecimal), because they all operate on the same basic principle: place value. So we begin there.

Place Value

A key to understanding place value is to think of a number system as a method of grouping multiple small units together until there are enough of them to be packed into a single larger group, then grouping multiple larger groups together until there are enough of them to form an even larger group, and so on. In our (decimal) number system, once there are 10 units of any group, that group becomes a single unit of the next larger group. So, groups of 10 units are packed into groups of tens; groups of ten tens are packed into groups of hundreds; groups of 10 hundreds are packed into groups of thousands, and so forth.

An easy way to understand number systems is to think of the numbers as being packaged for shipping, into boxes, cartons, crates, truckloads, and so on. For the decimal numbering system, consider packing widgets (units) into boxes (tens) which are packed into cartons (100s) which are packed into crates (1000s), and so forth. The same analogy works for binary, decimal, and all other number systems.

Our friend Joe, in Figure C-1, is a widget packer in the shipping department of the ACE Widget Co. Joe can ship single widgets, or he can pack them in boxes, cartons, crates, and truckloads. He can fit three, and only three, widgets to a box; three, and only three, boxes into one carton ($3 \times 3 = 9$ widgets); three, and only three, cartons into one crate ($3 \times 9 = 27$ widgets); and three, and only three, crates into one truck ($3 \times 27 = 81$ widgets). He is not allowed to pack more widgets into boxes, cartons, crates, or truckloads than those specified. Neither is he allowed to send out a box, carton, crate, or truckload that is not completely filled.

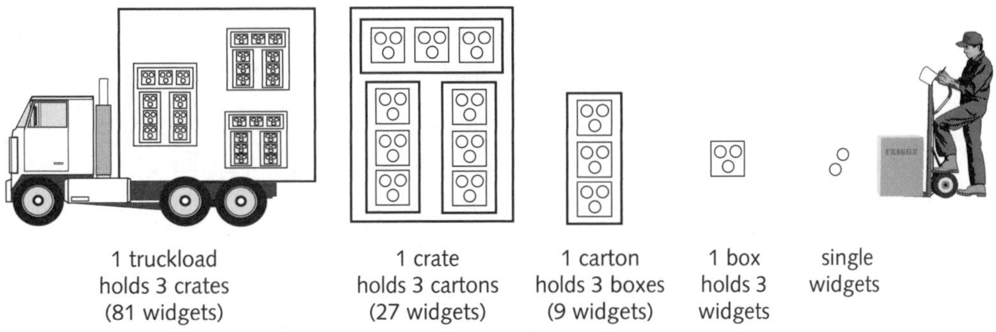

Figure C-1 Joe in the shipping department groups widgets in singles, boxes, cartons, crates, and truckloads—all in groups of three

Joe receives an order to ship out 197 widgets. How does he ship them? The answer is shown in Figure C-2. Joe sends out 197 widgets grouped into 2 truckloads ($2 \times 81 = 162$ widgets), 1 crate (27 widgets), no cartons, 2 boxes ($2 \times 3 = 6$ widgets), and 2 single widgets. We can write this grouping of widgets as 21022, where the "place values" from left to right are truckloads, crates, cartons, boxes, and units, which in this case are (in decimal) 81 widgets, 27 widgets, 9 widgets, 3 widgets, and single widgets. Notice that each "place value" in our widget-packing system is a multiple of 3, because the widgets are grouped into three before they are packed into boxes; the boxes are grouped into three before they are packed into cartons, and so on. By grouping the widgets into groups of 3s in this manner, we converted the decimal number (base 10) 197 into the ternary number (base 3) 21022. Joe's widget-packing method is a base three, or ternary, system. The numerals in the ternary number system are 0, 1, and 2. When you get to the next value after 2, instead of counting on up to 3, you move one place value to the left and begin again with 1 in that position, which represents 3. So, counting in base 3 goes like this: 0, 1, 2, 10, 11, 12, 20, 21, 22, 100, 101 and so on. This is the same as Joe's never shipping out 3 of any one group unless they are packed together into one larger group. For example, Joe wouldn't ship 3 individual boxes, he would ship one carton.

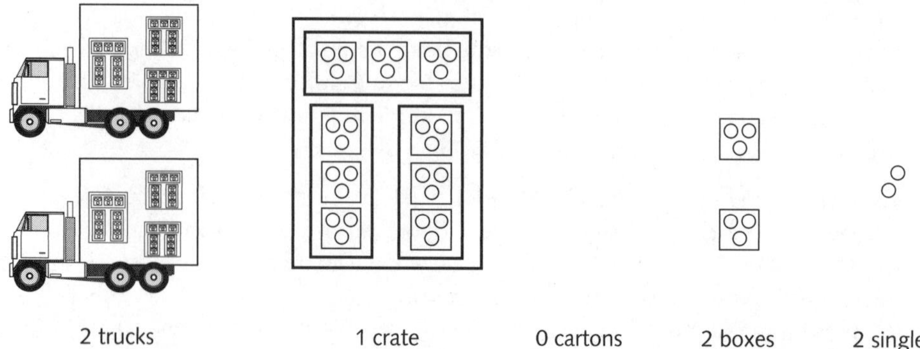

Figure C-2 Joe's shipment of 197 widgets: 2 trucks, 1 crate, 0 cartons, 2 boxes, and a group of 2 singles

You can easily apply the widget-packing analogy to another base. If Joe used 10 instead of three, he would be using base ten (decimal) rules. So, numbering systems differ by the different numbers of units they group together. In the hex number system, we group by 16. So, if Joe were shipping in groups of 16, as in Figure C-3, single widgets could be shipped out up to 15, but 16 widgets would make one box. Sixteen boxes would make one carton, which would contain 16 × 16, or 256, widgets. Sixteen cartons would make one crate, which would contain 16 × 256, or 4,096, widgets.

Suppose Joe receives an order for 197 widgets to be packed in groups of 16. He will not be able to fill a carton (256 widgets), so he ships out 12 boxes (16 widgets each) and 5 single widgets:

$12 \times 16 = 192$, and $192 + 5 = 197$

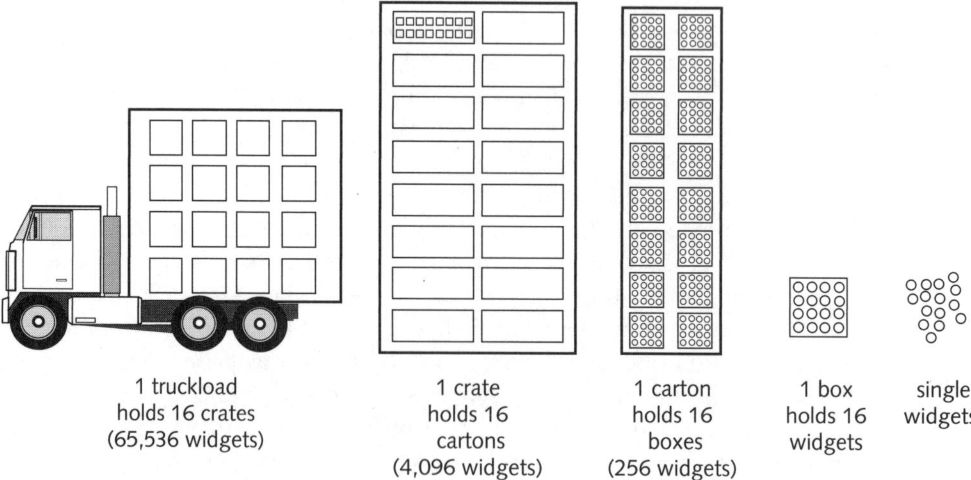

Figure C-3 Widgets displayed in truck loads, crates, cartons, boxes, and singles grouped in 16s

You approach an obstacle if you attempt to write the number in hex. How are you going to express 12 boxes and 5 singles? In hex, you need single numerals in hex to represent the numbers 10, 11, 12, 13, 14, and 15 in decimal. Hex uses letters for these numerals. A, B, C, D, E, and F are used for the numbers 10 through 15. Table C-2 shows values expressed in the decimal, hex, and binary numbering systems. In the second column in Table C-2, you are counting in the hex number system. For example, 12 is represented with a C. So you say that Joe packs C boxes and 5 singles. The hex number for decimal 197 is C5 (see Figure C-4).

Table C-2 Decimal, hex, and binary values

Decimal	Hex	Binary	Decimal	Hex	Binary	Decimal	Hex	Binary
0	0	0	14	E	1110	28	1C	11100
1	1	1	15	F	1111	29	1D	11101
2	2	10	16	10	10000	30	1E	11110
3	3	11	17	11	10001	31	1F	11111
4	4	100	18	12	10010	32	20	100000
5	5	101	19	13	10011	33	21	100001
6	6	110	20	14	10100	34	22	100010
7	7	111	21	15	10101	35	23	100011
8	8	1000	22	16	10110	36	24	100100
9	9	1001	23	17	10111	37	25	100101
10	A	1010	24	18	11000	38	26	100110
11	B	1011	25	19	11001	39	27	100111
12	C	1100	26	1A	11010	40	28	101000
13	D	1101	27	1B	11011			

Figure C-4 Hex C5 represented as C boxes and 5 singles = 197 decimal

For a little practice, calculate the hex values of the decimal values 14, 259, 75, and 1,024 and the decimal values of FFh and A11h.

How Exponents Are Used to Express Place Value

If you are comfortable with using exponents, you know that writing numbers raised to a power is the same thing as multiplying that number times itself the power number of times. For example, $3^4 = 3 \times 3 \times 3 \times 3 = 81$. Using exponents in expressing numbers can also help us easily see place value, because the place value for each place is really the base number multiplied by itself a number of times, based on the place value position . For instance, look back at Figure C-1. A truckload is really $3 \times 3 \times 3 \times 3$, or 81, units, which can be written as 3^4. A crate is really $3 \times 3 \times 3$, or 27, units. The numbers in Figure C-1 can therefore be written like this:

Truckload = 3^4 Crate = 3^3 Carton = 3^2 Box = 3^1 Single = 3^0

(Any number raised to the 0 power equals 1.) Therefore, we can express the numbers in Figure C-2 as multiples of truckloads, crates, cartons, boxes, and singles like this:

	Truckloads	Crates	Cartons	Boxes	Singles
21022 (base 3)	2×3^4	1×3^3	0×3^2	2×3^1	2×3^0
Decimal equivalent	162	27	0	6	2

When we sum up the numbers in the last row above, we get 197. We just converted a base 3 number (21022) to a base 10 number (197).

Binary Number System

It was stated earlier that it is easier for computers to convert from binary to hex or from hex to binary than to convert between binary and decimal. Let's see just how easy. Recall that the binary number system only has two numerals, or bits: 0 and 1. If our friend Joe in shipping operated a "binary" shipping system, he would pack like this: 2 widgets in a box, 2 boxes in one carton (4 widgets), two cartons in one crate (8 widgets), and two crates in one truckload (16 widgets). In Figure C-5, Joe is asked to pack 13 widgets. He packs 1 crate (8 widgets), 1 carton (4 widgets), no boxes, and 1 single. The number 13 in binary is 1101:

$$(1 \times 2^3)+(1 \times 2^2)+(0 \times 2^1)+(1 \times 2^0)= 8 + 4 + 0 + 1 = 13$$

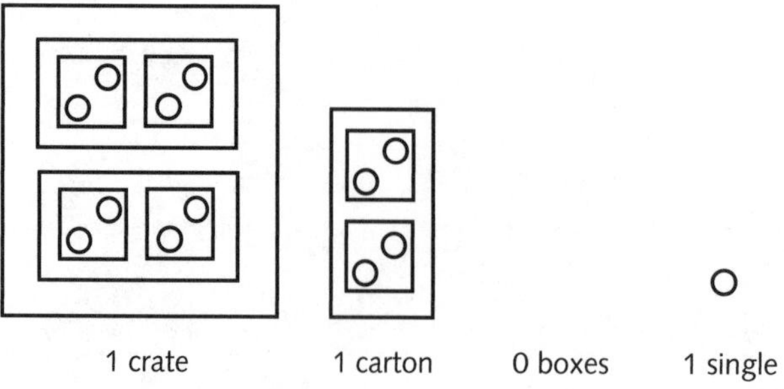

Figure C-5 Binary 1101 = 13 displayed as crates, cartons, boxes, and singles

Now let's see how to convert binary to hex and back again. The largest 4-bit number in binary is 1111. This number in decimal and hex is:

```
binary 1111 = 1 group of 8 = 8
             1 group of 4 = 4
             1 group of 2 = 2
                 1 single = 1

                 TOTAL = 15 (decimal)
Therefore, 1111 (binary) = 15 (decimal) = F (hex)
```

This last calculation is very important when working with computers: F is the largest numeral in the hex number system and it only takes 4 bits to write this largest hex numeral: F (hex) = 1111 (binary). So, every hex numeral (0, 1, 2, 3, 4, 5, 6, 7, 8, 9, A, B, C, D, E, and F) can be converted into a 4-bit binary number. Look back at the first 16 entries in Table D-2 for these binary values. Add leading zeroes to the binary numbers as necessary.

When converting from hex to binary, take each hex numeral and convert it to a 4-bit binary number and string all the 4-bit groups together. Fortunately, when working with computers, you will almost never be working with more than 2 hex numerals at a time. Here are some examples:

1. To convert hex F8 to binary, do the following: F = 1111, and 8 = 1000. Therefore, F8 = 11111000 (usually written 1111 1000).
2. To convert hex 9A to binary, do the following: 9 = 1001, and A = 1010. Therefore, 9A = 1001 1010.

Now try converting from binary to hex:

1. To convert binary 101110 to hex, first group the bits in groups of 4, starting at the right and moving left, adding leading zeros as necessary: 0010 1110.
2. Then convert each group of 4 bits in binary to a single hex numeral: 0010 = 2, and 1110 = E. The hex number is 2E.

Writing Conventions

Sometimes when you are dealing with hex, binary, and decimal numbers, it is not always clear which number system is being used. If you see a letter in the number, you know the number is a hex number. Binary numbers are usually written in groups of four bits. This book follows the convention of placing a lowercase h after a hex number, like this: 2Eh.

Memory Addressing

Computers often display memory addresses in the hex number system. You must either "think in hex" or convert to decimal. It's really easier, with a little practice, to think in hex. Here's the way it works:

Memory addresses are displayed as two hex numbers. An example is C800:5

The part to the left of the colon (C800) is called the *segment address*, and the part to the right of the colon (5) is called the *offset*. The offset value can have as many as four hex digits. The actual memory address is calculated by adding a zero to the right of the segment address and adding the offset value, like this: `C800:5 = C8000 + 5 = C8005`

The first 640K of memory is called conventional memory. Look at how that memory is addressed, first in decimal and then in hex (assuming 1 kilobyte = 1,024 bytes):

```
640K = 640 × 1,024 = 655,360
```

There are 655,360 memory addresses in conventional memory, where each memory address can hold 1 byte, or 8 bits, of either data or program instructions. The decimal value 655,360 converted to hex is A0000 (10×16^4). So, conventional memory addresses begin with 00000h and end with A0000h minus 1h or 9FFFFh. Written in segment-and-offset form, conventional memory addresses range from 0000:0 to 9FFF:F.

Recall that upper memory is defined as the memory addresses from 640K to 1,024K. The next address after 9FFF:F is the first address of upper memory, which is A0000, and the last address is FFFFF. Written in segment-and-offset terms, upper memory addresses range from A000:0 to FFFF:F.

Here is one way to organize the conversion of a large hex value such as FFFFF to decimal (remember F in hex equals 15 in decimal).

FFFFF converted to decimal:

$$
\begin{array}{llr}
15 \times 16^0 = & 15 \times 1 = & 15 \\
15 \times 16^1 = & 15 \times 16 = & 240 \\
15 \times 16^2 = & 15 \times 256 = & 3,840 \\
15 \times 16^3 = & 15 \times 4096 = & 61,440 \\
15 \times 16^4 = & 15 \times 65,536 = & 983,040 \\
 & \text{TOTAL} = & 1,048,575
\end{array}
$$

Remember that FFFFF is the last memory address in upper memory. The very next memory address is the first address of extended memory, which is defined as memory above 1 MB. If you add 1 to the number above, you get 1,048,576, which is equal to 1024 × 1024, which is the definition of 1 megabyte.

Displaying Memory with DOS DEBUG

In Figure C-6 you see the results of the beginning of upper memory displayed. The DOS DEBUG command displays the contents of memory. Memory addresses are displayed in hex segment-and-offset values. To enter DEBUG, type the following command at the C prompt and press Enter:

```
C:\> DEBUG
```

Type the following dump command to display the beginning of upper memory (the hyphen in the command is the DEBUG command prompt) and press Enter:

```
-d A000:0
```

Memory is displayed showing 16 bytes on each line. The A area of memory (the beginning of upper memory) is not used unless the computer is using a monochrome monitor or this area is being used as an upper memory block. In Figure C-6, the area contains nothing but continuous 1s in binary or Fs in hex. The ASCII interpretation is on the right side. To view the next group of memory addresses, you can type *d* at the hyphen and press Enter. DEBUG displays the next 128 addresses.

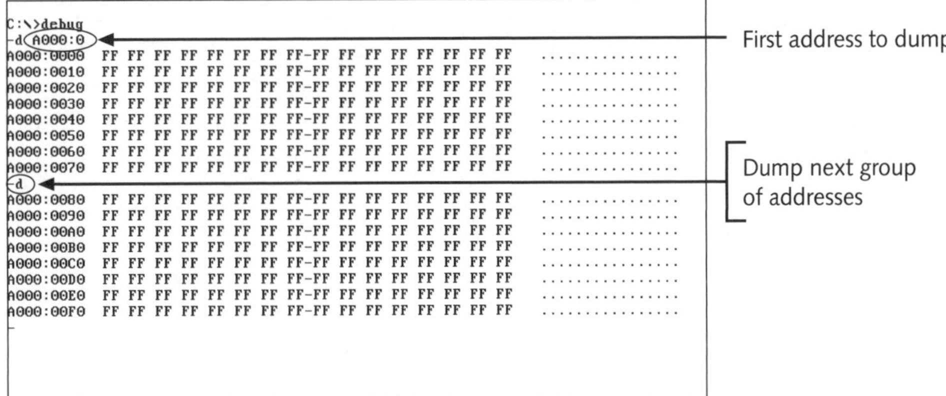

Figure C-6 Memory dump: `-d A000:0`

The A and B ranges of upper memory addresses (upper memory addresses that begin with A or B when written in hex) are used for monochrome monitors. The C range contains the video BIOS for a color monitor. Figure C-7 shows the dump of the beginning of the C range.

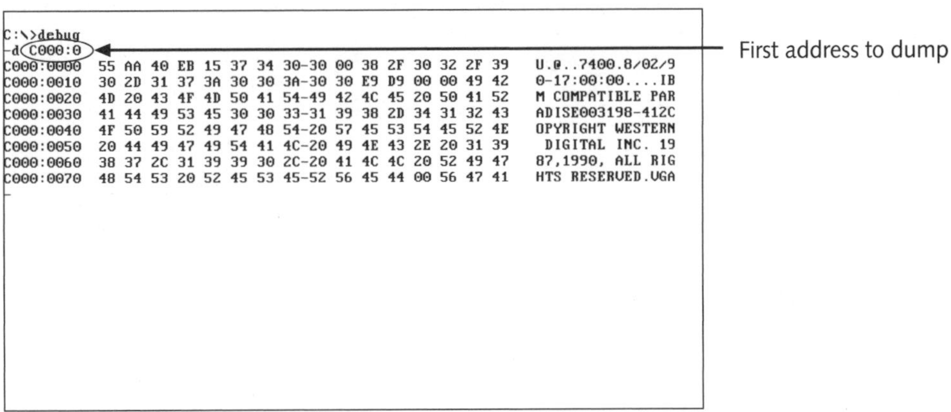

Figure C-7 Memory dump: `-d C000:0`

There is more than one way—in fact there are many ways—to identify the same segment-and-offset value. Try these commands to display the same upper memory addresses:

```
-d C000:0
-d BFF1:00F0
-d BFFF:0010
-d BEEE:1120
```

In summary, reading and understanding binary and hex numbers are essential skills for managing computers. All data is stored in binary in a computer and is often displayed in hex. Memory addresses are often displayed in hex segment-and-offset terms. An address in memory can be written in a variety of segment-and-offset values. The actual memory address is calculated by placing one zero to the right side of the segment address and adding the resulting value to the offset value. To exit DEBUG, type *q* for quit at the hyphen prompt.

APPENDIX

D

THE PROFESSIONAL PC TECHNICIAN

As a professional PC technician, you can manage your career by staying abreast of new technology and striving for top professional certifications. In addition, you should maintain excellent customer relationships, behave with professionalism, and seek opportunities for joining professional organizations. As you know, PC technicians provide service to customers over the phone, in person on-site, and sometimes in a shop where they have little customer contact. While each setting poses specific challenges, almost all of the recommendations made in this appendix apply across the board.

WHAT CUSTOMERS WANT: BEYOND TECHNICAL KNOW-HOW

Probably the most significant indication that a PC technician is doing a good job is that his or her customers are consistently satisfied. You should provide excellent service and treat customers as you would want to be treated in a similar situation. One of the most important ways to achieve customer satisfaction is to do your best by being prepared, both technically and nontechnically. Being prepared includes knowing what customers want, what they don't like, and what they expect from a PC technician.

Your customers can be "internal" (you both work for the same company) or "external" (your customers come to you or your company for service). Customers can be highly technical or technically naive, represent a large company or simply own a home PC, be prompt or slow at paying their bills, want only the best (and be willing to pay for it) or be searching for bargain service, be friendly and easy to work with or demanding and condescending. In each situation, the key to success is always the same: don't allow circumstances or personalities to affect your personal commitment to excellence.

Listed below are some traits that distinguish one competent technician from another in the eyes of the customer.

- *Have a positive and helpful attitude.* A positive and helpful attitude helps to establish good customer relationships.
- *Be dependable.* Customers appreciate those who do as they say. If you promise to be back at 10:00 the next morning, be back at 10:00 the next morning. If you cannot keep your appointment, never ignore your promise. Call, apologize, let the customer know what happened, and reschedule your appointment.

- *Be customer-focused.* When you're working with or talking to a customer, focus on him or her. Make it your job to satisfy this person, not just your organization, your boss, your bank account, or the customer's boss.
- *Be credible.* Convey confidence to your customers. Being credible means being technically competent and knowing how to do your job well, but a credible technician also knows when the job is beyond his or her level of expertise and when to ask for help.
- *Maintain integrity and honesty.* Don't try to hide your mistakes, not with your customer or with your boss. Everyone makes mistakes, but don't compound them by a lack of integrity. Accept responsibility and do what you can to correct the error.
- *Know the law with respect to your work.* For instance, observe the laws concerning the use of software. Don't use or install pirated software.
- *Act professionally.* Customers want a technician to look and behave professionally. Dress appropriately for the environment. Consider yourself a guest at the customer's site.
- *Perform your work in a professional manner.* If a customer is angry, allow the customer to vent, keeping your own professional distance. (You do, however, have the right to expect a customer not to talk to you in an abusive way.)

Support Calls: Providing Good Service

Customers want good service. Even though each customer is different and might expect different results, the following characteristics consistently constitute good service in the eyes of most customers.

- The technician responds and completes the work within a reasonable time.
- For on-site visits, the technician is prepared for the service call.
- The work is done right the first time.
- The price for the work is reasonable and competitive.
- The technician exhibits good interpersonal skills.
- If the work extends beyond a brief on-site visit or phone call, the technician keeps the customer informed about the progress of the work.

Planning for Good Service

Whether you support PCs on the phone, on-site, or in a shop, you need a plan to follow when you approach a service call. This section surveys the entire service situation, from the first contact with the customer to closing the call. Follow these general guidelines when supporting computers and their users:

- Almost every support project starts with a phone call. Follow company policies to obtain the specific information you should take when answering an initial call.

- Don't assume that an on-site visit is necessary until you have asked questions to identify the problem and asked the caller to check and try some simple things while on the phone with you. For example, the customer can check cable connections, power, and monitor settings, and can look for POST error messages.
- Be familiar with your company's customer service policies. You might need to refer questions about warranties, licenses, documentation, or procedures to other support personnel or customer relations personnel. Your organization might not want you to answer some questions, such as questions about upcoming releases of software or new products, or questions about your personal or company experience with supporting particular hardware or software.
- After reviewing your company's service policies, begin troubleshooting. Take notes, and then interview the customer about the problem so you understand it thoroughly. Have the customer reproduce the problem, and carefully note each step taken and its results. This process gives you clues about the problem and about the technical proficiency of the customer, which helps you know how to communicate with the customer.
- Search for answers. If the answers to specific questions or problems are not evident, become a researcher. Learn to use online documentation, expert systems, and other resources that your company provides.
- Use your troubleshooting skills. Isolate the problem. Check for user errors. What works and what doesn't work? What has changed since the system last worked? Reduce the system to its essentials. Check the simple things first. Use the troubleshooting guidelines throughout this book to help you think of approaches to test and try.
- If you have given the problem your best, but still haven't solved it, ask for help. You learn when to ask for help from experience. Once you have made a reasonable effort to help, and it seems clear that you are unlikely to be successful, don't waste a customer's time.
- After a call, create a written record to build your own knowledge base. Record the initial symptoms of the problem, the source of the problem you actually discovered, how you made that discovery, and how the problem was finally solved. File your documentation according to symptoms or according to solutions.

Making an On-site Service Call

When a technician makes an on-site service call, customers expect him or her to have both technical and interpersonal skills. Prepare for a service call by reviewing information given you by whoever took the call. Know the problem you are going to address; what computer, software, and hardware need servicing, and the urgency of the situation. Arrive with a complete set of equipment appropriate to the visit, which might include a tool kit, flashlight, multimeter, grounding strap and mat, and bootable disks that have been scanned for viruses.

Set a realistic time for the appointment (one that you can expect to keep) and arrive on time. When you arrive at the customer's site, greet the customer in a friendly manner. Use

Mr. or Ms. and last names rather than first names when addressing the customer, unless you are certain that the customer expects you to use first names. The first thing you should do is listen; save the paperwork for later.

As you work, be as unobtrusive as possible. Don't make a big mess. Keep your tools and papers out of the customer's way. Don't use the phone or sit in the customer's desk chair without permission. If the customer needs to attend to his or her own work while you are present, do whatever is necessary to accommodate that.

Keep the customer informed. Once you have collected enough information, explain to the customer what the problem is and what you must do to fix it, giving as many details as the customer wants. When a customer must make a choice, state the customer's options in a way that does not unfairly favor the solution that makes the most money for you as the technician or for your company.

After you have solved the problem:

- Allow the customer time to be fully satisfied that all is working before you close the call. Does the printer work? Print a test page. Does the network connection work? Can the customer log on to the network and access data on it?
- If you changed anything on the PC after you booted it, reboot one more time to make sure that you have not caused a problem with the boot.
- Review the service call with the customer. Summarize the instructions and explanations you have given during the call. This is an appropriate time to fill out your paperwork and explain to the customer what you have written.
- Explain preventive maintenance to the customer (such as deleting temporary files from the hard drive or cleaning the mouse). Most customers don't have preventive maintenance contracts for their PCs and appreciate the time you take to show them how they can take better care of their computers.

Phone Support

When someone calls asking for support, you must control the call, especially at the beginning. Follow these steps at the beginning of a service call:

- Identify yourself and your organization. (Follow the guidelines of your employer as to what to say.)
- Ask for and write down the name and phone number of the caller. Ask for spelling if necessary. If your helpdesk supports businesses, get the name of the business that the caller represents.
- Your company might require that you obtain a licensing or warranty number to determine if the customer is entitled to receive your support free of charge, or that you obtain a credit card number, if the customer is paying by the call. Get whatever information you need at this point to determine that you should be the one to provide service, before you start to address the problem.
- Open up the conversation for the caller to describe his or her problem.

Providing phone support requires more interaction with customers than any other type of PC support. To give clear instructions, you must be able to visualize what the customer is seeing at his or her PC. Patience is required if the customer must be told each key to press or command button to click. Help-desk support requires excellent communication skills, good phone manners, and lots of patience. As your help-desk skills improve, you will learn to think through the process as though you were sitting in front of the PC yourself. Drawing diagrams and taking notes as you talk can be very helpful.

If you spend many hours on the phone at a help desk, use a headset instead of a regular phone to reduce strain on your ears and neck. If you are accidentally disconnected, call back immediately. Don't eat or drink while on the phone. If you must put callers on hold, tell them how long it will be before you get back to them. Don't complain about your job, your company, or other companies or products to your customers. A little small talk is okay and is sometimes beneficial in easing a tense situation, but keep it upbeat and positive. As with on-site service calls, let the user make sure that all is working before you close the phone call. If you end the call too soon and the problem is not completely resolved, the customer can be frustrated, especially if it is difficult to contact you again.

When the Customer Is Not Knowledgeable

A help-desk call is the most difficult situation to handle when a customer is not knowledgeable about how to use a computer. When on-site, you can put a PC in good repair without depending on a customer to help you, but when you are trying to solve a problem over the phone, with a customer as your only eyes, ears, and hands, a computer-illiterate user can present a very challenging situation. Here are some tips for handling this situation:

- Don't use computer jargon while talking. For example, instead of saying, "Open Windows Explorer," say, "Using your mouse, right-click on the Start button and select Explore from the menu."
- Don't ask the customer to do something that might destroy settings or files without first having him or her back them up carefully. If you think the customer can't handle what you need done, then ask for some on-site help.
- Frequently ask the customer what he or she sees on the screen to help you track the keystrokes and action.
- Follow along at your own PC. It's easier to direct the customer, keystroke by keystroke, if you are doing the same things.
- Give the customer plenty of opportunity to ask questions.
- Compliment the customer whenever you can, to help the customer gain confidence.
- If you determine that the customer cannot help you solve the problem without a lot of coaching, you may need to tactfully request that the caller have someone with more experience call you.

When solving computer problems in an organization other than your own, check with technical support instead of working only with the PC user. The user may not be aware of policies that have been set on the PC to prevent changes to the OS, hardware, or application software.

When the Customer Is Overly Confident

Sometimes a customer is proud of what he or she knows about computers. This type of customer may want to give advice, take charge of a call, withhold information that he or she thinks you don't need to know, or execute commands at the computer without letting you know, so that you don't have enough information to follow along. A situation like this must be handled with tact and respect for the customer. Here are a few tips:

- When you can, compliment the customer concerning his or her knowledge, experience, or insight.
- Ask the customer's advice. Say something like, "What do you think the problem is?" (However, don't ask this question of customers who are not confident because they most likely don't have the answer and might lose confidence in you.)
- Slow the conversation down. You can say, "Please slow down. You're moving too fast for me to follow. Help me understand."
- Don't back off from using problem-solving skills. You must still have the customer check the simple things, but direct the conversation with tact. For example, you can say, "I know you've probably already gone over these simple things, but could we just do them again together?"
- Be careful not to accuse the customer of making a mistake.
- Use technical language in a way that conveys that you expect the customer to understand you.

When the Customer Complains

When you are on-site or on the phone, a customer might complain to you about your organization, products, or service, or the service and product of another company. Consider the complaint to be helpful feedback that can lead to a better product or service and better customer relationships. Here are a few suggestions on how to handle complaints and customer anger:

- Be an active listener, and let the customer know that he or she is not being ignored. Look for the underlying problem. Don't take the complaint or the anger personally.
- Give the customer a little time to vent, and apologize when you can. Then start the conversation from the beginning, asking questions, taking notes, and solving problems. If this helps, don't spend a lot of time finding out exactly whom the customer dealt with and what exactly happened to upset him or her.

- Don't be defensive. It's better to leave the customer with the impression that you and your company are listening and willing to admit mistakes.
- If the customer is complaining about a product or service that is not from your company, don't start off by saying, "That's not our problem." Instead, listen to the customer complain. Don't appear as though you don't care.
- If the complaint is against you or your product, identify the underlying problem if you can. Ask questions and take notes. Then pass these notes on to whoever in your organization needs to know.
- Sometimes simply making progress or reducing the problem to a manageable state for the customer reduces his or her anxiety. As you are talking to a customer, summarize what you have both agreed on or observed so far in the conversation.
- Point out ways that you think communication could be improved. For example, you might say, "I'm sorry, but I'm having trouble understanding what you want. Could you please slow down, and let's take this one step at a time."

When the Customer Does Not Want to End a Phone Call

Some customers like to talk and don't want to end a phone call. In this situation, when you have finished the work and are ready to hang up, you can ease the caller into the end of the call. Ask if there is anything that needs more explanation. Briefly summarize the main points of the call, and then say something like, "That about does it. Call if you need more help." Be silent about new issues. Answer only with "yes" or "no." Don't take the bait by engaging in a new topic. Don't get frustrated. As a last resort, you can say, "I'm sorry, but I must go now."

When You Can't Solve the Problem

You are not going to solve every computer problem you encounter. Knowing how to escalate a problem to those higher in the support chain is one of the first things you should learn on a new job. When escalation involves the customer, generally follow these guidelines:

- Before you escalate, first ask knowledgeable coworkers for suggestions for solving the problem, which might save you and your customer the time and effort it takes to escalate it.
- Know your company's policy as to how to escalate. What documents do you fill out? Who gets them? Do you remain the responsible "support" party, or does the person now addressing the problem become the new contact? Are you expected to still keep in touch with the customer and the problem, or are you totally out of the picture?
- Document the escalation. It's very important to include the detailed steps necessary to reproduce the problem, which can save the next support person lots of time.
- Pass the problem on according to the proper channels of your organization. This might mean a phone call, an online entry in a database, or an e-mail message.

- Tell the customer that you are passing the problem on to someone who is more experienced and has access to more extensive resources. In most cases, the person who receives the escalation will immediately contact the customer and assume responsibility for the problem. However, you should follow through, at least to the point where you know that the new person and the customer have made contact.
- If you check back with the customer only to find out that the other support person has not called or followed through to the customer's satisfaction, don't lay blame or point fingers. Just do whatever you can to help within your company guidelines. Your call to the customer will go a long way toward helping in the situation.

RECORDKEEPING AND INFORMATION TOOLS

If you work for a service organization, it will probably have most of the tools you will need to do your job, including forms, online recordkeeping, procedures, and manuals. In some cases, help-desk support personnel may have software to help them do their jobs, such as programs that support the remote control of customers' PCs (one example is pcAnywhere), an online help utility, or a problem-solving tool developed specifically for their help desk.

There are several types of resources, records, and information tools that can help you with your work supporting PCs, such as the following:

- Specific software or hardware that you support must be available to you to test, observe, and study, and to use to re-create a customer's problem whenever possible.
- You should have a copy of—and be familiar with—the same documentation that the user sees.
- Hardware and software products generally have more technical documentation than just a user manual. This technical documentation should be made available to you by a company when you support its product.
- Online help targeted specifically to field technicians and help-desk technicians is often available for a product. This online help will probably include a search engine that works by topics, words, error messages, and the like.
- Expert systems software is designed and written to help solve problems. It uses databases of known facts and rules to simulate human experts' reasoning and decision-making processes. Expert systems for PC technicians work by posing questions about a problem, to be answered either by the technician or by the customer. The response to each question will trigger another question from the software, until the expert system arrives at a possible solution or solutions. Many expert systems are "intelligent," meaning that the system will record your input and use it in subsequent sessions to select more questions to ask and approaches to try.

- Call tracking can be done online or on paper. Most organizations will have a call-tracking system that tracks (1) the date, time, and length of help-desk or on-site calls, (2) causes of and solutions to problems already addressed, (3) who did what, and when, and (4) how each call was officially resolved. Call-tracking software or documents can also be vehicles used to escalate calls when necessary and to track the escalation.

PROFESSIONAL ORGANIZATIONS AND CERTIFICATIONS

The work done by PC technicians has been viewed as a profession only within the past few years. The one most significant certifying organization for PC technicians is the Computing Technology Industry Association (CompTIA, pronounced "comp-TEE-a"). CompTIA sponsors the A+ Certification Program, and manages the A+ Service Technician Certification Examination, which measures the knowledge of job tasks and behavior expected of entry-level technicians. To become certified, you must pass two test modules: the A+ Core Hardware exam and the A+ Operating System Technologies exam. A+ Certification is gaining increasing industry recognition, so it should be your first choice for certification as a PC technician. As evidence of this industry recognition, these companies now include A+ Certification in their requirements for employment:

- Compaq Computer Corporation requires that all work done under its warranty agreements be done by A+ Certified personnel.
- Digital Equipment Corporation requires A+ Certification for all international and domestic warranty work.
- ENTEX Information Services requires that all service employees have A+ Certification.
- GE Capital Services requires that all service employees have A+ Certification one year after hire.
- Okidata requires that all field service technicians have A+ Certification.
- Packard Bell requires all employees to be A+ certified within 90 days of hire.

Some other organizations where A+ Certification is mandatory are Aetna U.S. Healthcare; BancTec, Inc.; Computer Data, Inc.; Computer Sciences Corp.; Delta Airlines; Dow Jones & Company; the FBI, the U.S. Department of Justice; Gateway 2000; New Horizons; Tandy Corporation; TSS IBM; US Airways; and Wang.

CompTIA has over 6,000 members, which include every major company that manufactures, distributes, or publishes computer-related products and services. For more information about CompTIA and A+ Certification, see the CompTIA Web site at *www.comptia.org*.

Other certifications are more vendor-specific. For example, Microsoft, Novell, and Cisco offer certifications to use and support their products. These are excellent choices for additional certifications when your career plan is to focus on these products.

Why Certification?

Many people work as PC technicians without any formal classroom training or certification. However, by having certification or an advanced technical degree, you prove to yourself, your customers, and your employers that you are prepared to do the work and are committed to being educated in your chosen profession. Certification and advanced degrees serve as recognized proof of competence and achievement, improve your job opportunities, create a higher level of customer confidence, and often qualify you for other training and/or degrees.

In addition to becoming certified and seeking advanced degrees, the professional PC technician should also stay abreast of new technology. Helpful resources include on-the-job training, books, magazines, the Internet, trade shows, interaction with colleagues, seminars, and workshops. Probably the best-known trade show is COMDEX and Windows World, where you can view the latest technology, hear industry leaders speak, and network with vast numbers of organizations and people. For more information about COMDEX and Windows World, see the Web site *www.comdex.com*.

Protecting Software Copyrights

As a computer support technician, you will be faced with the legal issues and practices surrounding the distribution of software. When someone purchases software from a software vendor, that person has only purchased a license for the software, which is the right to use the software, and does not legally *own* the software; he or she therefore does not have the right to distribute the software. The right to copy the work, called a copyright, belongs to the creator of the work or others to whom he or she has transferred this right.

As a PC technician you will be called upon to install, upgrade, and customize software. You need to know where your responsibility lies in upholding the law, especially as it applies to software copyrights. Copyrights are intended to legally protect the intellectual property rights of organizations or individuals to creative works, whether they be books, images, or, in the case of this discussion, software. While the originator of a creative work is the original owner of a copyright, the copyright can be transferred from one entity to another.

The Federal Copyright Act of 1976 was designed in part to protect software copyrights by requiring that only legally obtained copies of software be used; the law also allows for one backup copy of software to be made. Making unauthorized copies of original software violates the Federal Copyright Act of 1976, and is called software piracy, or, more officially, software copyright infringement. Making a copy of software and then selling it or giving it away is a violation of the law. Because it is so easy to do this, and because so many people do it, many people don't realize that it's illegal. Normally, only the person who violated the copyright law is liable for infringement; however, in some cases, an employer or supervisor is also held responsible, even when the copies were made without the employer's knowledge. The Business Software Alliance (a membership organization of software manufacturers and vendors) has estimated that 26 percent of the business software in the United States is obtained illegally.

Site licensing, whereby a company can purchase the right to use multiple copies of software, is a popular way for companies to provide software to employees. With this type of license, companies can distribute software to PCs from network servers or execute software directly off the server. Read the licensing agreement of any software to determine the terms of distribution.

One of two associations committed to the prevention of software piracy is the Software Information Industry Association, a nonprofit organization that educates the public and enforces copyright laws. Their Web address is *www.siia.net*, and their antipiracy hotline is 1-800-388-7478. Another organization is the Business Software Alliance, which manages the BSA Anti-Piracy Hotline at 1-888-NOPIRACY. The BSA can also be reached at their e-mail address: software@bsa.org. Their Web site is *www.bsa.org*. These associations are made up of hundreds of software manufacturers and publishers in North and Latin America, Europe, and Asia. They promote software raids on large and small companies, and, in the U.S., they receive the cooperation of the United States government to prosecute offenders.

What Does the Law Say?

The Federal Copyright Act of 1976 protects the exclusive rights of copyright holders. It gives legal users of software the right to make one backup copy. Other rights are based on what the copyright holder allows. In 1990, the United States Congress passed the Software Rental Amendment Act, which prevents the renting, leasing, lending, or sharing of software without the expressed written permission of the copyright holder. In 1992, Congress instituted criminal penalties for software copyright infringement, which include imprisonment for up to five years and/or fines of up to $250,000 for the unlawful reproduction or distribution of 10 or more copies of software.

What Are Your Responsibilities under the Law?

Your first responsibility as an individual user is to use only software that has been purchased or licensed for your use. As an employee of a company that has a site license to use multiple copies of the software, your responsibility is to comply with the license agreement. It is also your responsibility to purchase only legitimate software. Purchasers of counterfeit or copied software face the risk of corrupted files, virus-infected disks, inadequate documentation, and lack of technical support and upgrades, as well as the legal penalties for using pirated software.

GLOSSARY

16-bit mode — *See* real mode.

32-bit flat memory mode — A protected processing mode used by Windows NT/2000/XP to process programs written in 32-bit code early in the boot process.

32-bit mode — *See* protected mode.

822 messages — Error messages that occur during e-mail transactions. 822 messages are named after RFC 822, which is the RFC that defines them.

ACPI (Advanced Configuration and Power Interface) — Specification developed by Intel, Compaq, Phoenix, Microsoft, and Toshiba to control power on notebooks and other devices. Windows 98 and Windows 2000/XP support ACPI.

Active Directory — A Windows 2000 and Windows .NET directory database service that allows for a single point of administration for all shared resources on a network, including files, peripheral devices, databases, Web sites, users, and services.

active partition — The primary partition on the hard drive that boots the OS. Windows NT/2000/XP calls the active partition the system partition.

adapter address — *See* MAC address.

administrator account — In Windows NT/ 2000/XP, an account that grants to the administrator(s) rights and permissions to all hardware and software resources, such as the right to add, delete, and change accounts and to change hardware configurations.

Advanced Options menu — A Windows 2000/XP menu that appears when you press F8 when Windows starts. The menu can be used to troubleshoot problems when loading Windows 2000/XP.

AGP (Accelerated Graphics Port) bus — A bus or slot on the motherboard used for a single video card.

allocation blocks — Sets of hard drive sectors used by a Macintosh computer where the Mac's file system stores files.

answer file — A text file that contains information that Windows NT/2000/XP requires in order to do an unattended installation.

antivirus (AV) software — Utility programs that prevent infection or scan a system to detect and remove viruses. McAfee Associates' VirusScan and Norton AntiVirus are two popular AV packages.

API (Application Program Interface) — A method used by an application program to call another program or the OS to perform a utility task.

Apple menu — The Mac OS menu accessed by an apple icon in the upper-right corner of the desktop. The Apple menu contains options that are always available no matter what application you are in.

Application layer — The OSI layer responsible for interfacing with the application using the network.

application program interface (API) call — A request from software to the OS to access hardware or other software using a previously defined procedure that both the software and the OS understand.

ARP (Address Resolution Protocol) — A protocol that TCP/IP uses to translate IP addresses into physical network addresses (MAC addresses).

Autoexec.bat — A startup text file once used by DOS and used by Windows 9x to provide backward-compatibility. It executes commands automatically during the boot process and is used to create a 16-bit environment.

Automated System Recovery (ASR) — The Windows XP process that allows you to restore an entire hard drive volume or logical drive to its state at the time the backup of the volume was made.

backup domain controller (BDC) — In Windows NT, a computer on a network that holds a read-only copy of the SAM (security accounts manager) database.

Backup Operator — A Windows 2000/XP user account that can back up and restore any files on the system regardless of its having access to these files.

backward-compatible — Refers to new hardware and software that is able to support older, existing technologies. This is a common choice of hardware and software manufacturers.

baseline — The level of performance expected from a system, which can be compared to current measurements to determine what needs upgrading or tuning.

basic disk — A way to partition a hard drive, used by DOS and all versions of Windows, that stores information about the drive in a partition table at the beginning of the drive. Compare to dynamic disk.

batch file — A text file containing a series of OS commands. Autoexec.bat is a batch file.

best-effort protocol —*See* connectionless protocol.

binding — Associating an OSI layer to a layer above it or below it, such as when an IP address (Network layer) is associated with a network card and its MAC address (Data Link layer).

BIOS (basic input/output system) — Firmware that can control much of a computer's input/output functions, such as communication with the floppy drive and the monitor. Also called ROM BIOS.

block — *See* allocation block

blue screen — A Windows NT/2000/XP error that displays against a blue screen and causes the system to halt. Also called a stop error.

bootable disk — For DOS and Windows, a floppy disk that can upload the OS files necessary for computer startup. For DOS or Windows 9x, it must contain the files Io.sys, Msdos.sys and Command.com.

boot blocks — The first two allocation blocks on a Macintosh computer's hard drive. They are initially empty, but once a System folder is installed on a computer, the boot blocks contain the location of the System folder so that the system can find and load the OS.

booting — The process that a computer goes through when it is first turned on to get itself ready to receive commands.

boot loader menu — A startup menu that gives the user the choice of which operating system to load such as Windows 98 or Windows 2000 which are both installed on the same system creating a dual boot.

boot partition — The hard drive partition where the Windows NT/2000/XP OS is stored. The system partition and the boot partition may be different partitions.

boot record — The first sector of a floppy disk or logical drive in a partition; it contains information about the disk or logical drive. On a hard drive, if the boot record is in the active partition, then it is used to boot the OS. Also called boot sector.

boot sector — *See* boot record.

boot sector virus — An infectious program that can replace the bootstrap loader program with a modified, infected version of the program, often causing boot and data retrieval problems.

bootstrap loader — A small program at the end of the boot record that can be used to boot an OS from the disk or logical drive.

bridging protocol — *See* line protocol.

Briefcase — A system folder in Windows 9x that is used to synchronize files between two computers.

buffer — A temporary memory area where data is kept before being written to a hard drive or sent to a printer, thus reducing the number of writes to the devices.

built-in user account — An administrator account and a guest account that are set up when Windows NT/2000/XP is first installed.

bus — Wires or printed circuits used to transmit electronic signals or voltage on the motherboard to other devices.

bus enumerator — A component of Windows Plug and Play that locates all devices on a particular bus and inventories the resource requirements for these devices.

cabinet file — A file with a .cab extension that contains one or more compressed files and is often used to distribute software on disk. The Extract command is used to extract files from the cabinet file.

cache — A location in memory or some other place used to store frequently used data.

catalog tree — A database of the folders and files on a Macintosh computer's hard drive, including information such as filenames and extensions, the application used to open a file, the creator of the file or folder, and the date the file or folder was created. Works with the extents tree to allow the Mac to access hard drive data.

CD (change directory) command — A command given at the command prompt that changes the default directory, for example CD \Windows.

chain — A group of clusters used to hold a single file.

child directory — *See* subdirectory.

child, parent, grandparent backup method — A plan for backing up and reusing tapes or removable disks by rotating them each day (child), week (parent), and month (grandparent).

clean install — Installing an OS on a new hard drive or on a hard drive that has a previous OS installed, but without carrying forward any settings kept by the old OS including information about hardware, software, or user preferences. A fresh installation.

client — A software program or computer that requests information from another software program on another computer.

client/server — A computer concept whereby one computer (the client) requests information from another computer (the server).

cluster — One or more sectors that constitute the smallest unit of space on a disk for storing data (also referred to as a file allocation unit).

Cmd.exe — The 32-bit program that provides a command window.

CMOS configuration chip — *See* CMOS setup chip.

CMOS RAM chip — *See* CMOS setup chip.

CMOS setup chip — A microchip on the motherboard that contains a small amount of RAM, enough to hold the configuration information for a motherboard. Also called CMOS configuration chip, CMOS RAM chip.

cold boot — *See* hard boot.

Command.com — Along with Msdos.sys and Io.sys, one of the three files that are the core components of the real-mode portion of Windows 9x. Command.com provides a command prompt and interprets commands.

command mode — The Linux vi editor mode in which you can type commands to manipulate text or to change the status of the editor.

comment — A line or part of a line in a program that is intended as a remark or comment and is ignored when the program runs. A semicolon or an REM is often used to mark a line as a comment.

Compatibility mode — A Windows XP utility that provides an application with the older Microsoft OS environment it was designed to operate in.

compressed drive — A drive whose format has been reorganized in order to store more data. A compressed drive is really not a drive at all; it's actually a type of file, typically with a host drive called H.

Config.sys — A text file used by DOS and supported by Windows 9x that lists device drivers to be loaded at startup. It can also set system variables to be used by DOS and Windows.

Configuration Manager — A component of Windows Plug and Play that controls the configuration process of all devices and communicates these configurations to the devices.

connectionless protocol — A protocol such as UDP that does not require a connection before sending a packet and does not guarantee delivery. An example of a UDP transmission is streaming video over the Web. Also called a best-effort protocol.

connection-oriented protocol — In networking, a protocol that confirms that a good connection has been made before transmitting data to the other end. An example of a connection-oriented protocol is TCP.

console — A centralized location from which to execute commonly used tools.

Control Panels folder — In Mac OS 9, a folder that contains control panels for system settings such as time and date, speaker volume, and the configuration of the Finder window and the desktop. In Mac OS X, control panels no longer exist; their functions are incorporated into the Library folder.

conventional memory — Memory addresses between 0 and 640K. Also called base memory.

cooperative multitasking — A type of pseudo-multitasking whereby the OS switches back and forth between programs loaded at the same time. One program sits in the background waiting for the other to relinquish control. Also called task switching.

CPU (central processing unit) — The heart and brain of the computer, which receives data input, processes information, and executes instructions. Also called a microprocessor.

cross-linked clusters — Errors caused when files appear to share the same disk space, according to the file allocation table.

CVF (compressed volume file) — The file on the host drive of a compressed drive that holds all compressed data.

data bus — *See* data path

datagram — *See* packet.

Data Link layer — The OSI layer that disassembles packets and reassembles data into packets, preparing the packets to be passed on to the physical media.

data packet — *See* packet.

data path — That portion of a bus that carries data. A data bus is usually 32 or 64 bits wide. Also called a data bus.

default gateway —The gateway a computer on a network will use to access another network unless it knows to specifically use another gateway for quicker access to that network.

default printer — The printer Windows prints to unless another printer is selected.

defragment — To "optimize" or rewrite a file to a disk in one contiguous chain of clusters, thus speeding up data retrieval.

desktop — The initial screen that is displayed when an OS has a GUI interface loaded.

device driver — A program stored on the hard drive that tells the computer how to communicate with an input/output device such as a printer or modem.

DHCP (Dynamic Host Configuration Protocol) server — A service that assigns dynamic IP addresses to computers on a network when they first access the network.

dial-up networking — A Windows 9x and Windows NT/2000/XP utility that uses a modem and telephone line to connect to a network.

differential backup — Backup method that backs up only files that have changed or have been created since the last full backup. When recovering data, only two backups are needed: the full backup and the last differential backup.

digital certificate — *See* digital signature.

digital signature — Digital codes used to identify and authenticate the source of a file or document.

directory structure — Files created during formatting that allow a Macintosh computer to access its hard drive. Important directory include the boot blocks, the volume information block, the volume bit map, the catalog tree, and the extents tree.

directory table — An OS table that contains file information such as the name, size, time and date of last modification, and cluster number of the file's beginning location.

disk cache — A method whereby recently retrieved data and adjacent data are read into memory in advance, anticipating the next CPU request.

disk cloning — Making an exact image of a hard drive, including partition information, boot sectors, operating system installation, and application software to replicate the hard drive on another system or recover from a hard drive crash. Also called disk imaging.

disk compression — Compressing data on a hard drive to allow more data to be written to the drive.

Disk First Aid — A free Mac OS disk repair utility included with Mac OS 9. In Mac OS X, Disk First Aid and Drive Setup are combined into the single Disk Utility.

disk imaging — *See* disk cloning.

Disk Management — A Windows 2000/XP utility used to display and create and format partitions on basic disks and volumes on dynamic disks.

disk quota — A limit placed on the amount of disk space that is available to users. Requires a Windows 2000/XP NTFS volume.

disk thrashing — A condition that results when the hard drive is excessively used for virtual memory because RAM is full. It dramatically slows down processing and can cause premature hard drive failure.

Disk Utility — A Mac OS X utility that can be used to set up a drive, reformat a damaged drive, or detect and repair problems on it. It combines the functions of the Mac OS 9 tools Disk First Aid and Drive Setup.

distributions — Different versions of an OS by different vendors.

DLL (dynamic-link library) — A file with a .dll file extension that contains a library of programming routines used by programs to perform common tasks.

DMA (direct memory access) channel — Shortcut method whereby an I/O device can send data directly to memory, bypassing the CPU.

DNS (domain name service or domain name system) — A distributed pool of information (called the name space) that keeps track of assigned domain names and their corresponding IP addresses, and the system that allows a host to locate information in the pool. Compare to WINS.

DNS server — A computer that can find an IP address for another computer when only the domain name is known.

dock — A new feature of the Mac OS X interface that consists of icons representing frequently used and currently open applications on a bar at the bottom of the desktop.

docking station — A device that receives a notebook computer and provides additional secondary storage and easy connection to peripheral devices.

domain — In Windows NT/2000/XP, a logical group of networked computers, such as those on a college campus, that share a centralized directory database of user account information and security for the entire domain.

domain name — A unique, text-based name that identifies a network.

domain user account — An account for a user that has permission to access resources, folders, and files on a domain. A domain user can log on to a domain and access the network.

DOS box — A command window.

Dosstart.bat — A type of Autoexec.bat file that is executed by Windows 9x in two situations: when you select Restart the computer in MS-DOS mode from the shutdown menu or you run a program in MS-DOS mode.

Drive Setup — A Mac OS 9 tool that can be used to format a hard drive when it is initially installed or to reformat a damaged hard drive. In Mac OS X, Drive Setup and Disk First Aid are combined into the Disk Utility.

DriveSpace — A utility that compresses files so that they take up less space on a disk drive, creating a single large file on the disk to hold all the compressed files.

Dr. Watson — A Windows utility that can record detailed information about the system, errors that occur, and the programs that caused them in a log file. Windows 9x names the log file \Windows\ Drwatson\WatsonXX.wlg, where XX is an incrementing number. Windows 2000 names the file \Documents and Settings\user\Documents\ DrWatson\Drwtsn32.log.

Drwatson.log — The log file for the Dr. Watson utility in Windows XP.

dual boot — The ability to boot using either of two different OSs, such as Windows 98 and Windows 2000.

dump file — A file that contains information captured from memory at the time a stop error occurred.

dynamic disk — A way to partition one or more hard drives, introduced with Windows 2000, in which information about the drive is stored in a database at the end of the drive. Compare to basic disk.

dynamic IP address — An assigned IP address that is used for the current session only. When the session is terminated, the IP address is returned to the list of available addresses.

dynamic volume — A volume type used with dynamic disks for which you can change the size of the volume after you have created it.

dynamic VxD — A VxD that is loaded and unloaded from memory as needed.

EFS (Encrypted File System) — A way to use a key to encode a file or folder to protect sensitive data. Because it is an integrated system service, EFS is transparent to users and applications and is difficult to attack.

EIDE (Enhanced Integrated Drive Electronics) — A standard for managing the interface between secondary storage devices and a computer system. A system can support up to four IDE devices such as hard drives, CD-ROM drives, and Zip drives.

Emergency Repair Disk (ERD) — A Windows NT record of critical information about your system that can be used to fix a problem with the OS. The ERD enables restoration of the Windows NT registry on your hard drive.

Emergency Repair Process — A Windows 2000 process that restores the OS to its state at the completion of a successful installation.

emergency startup disk (ESD) — *See* rescue disk.

Emm386.exe — A DOS and Windows 9x utility that provides access to upper memory for 16-bit device drivers and other software.

enabler file — A file included with Macintosh hardware that is released before the instructions to control it are incorporated into the Mac OS. Enabler files allow a device to function with the version of Mac OS being used on the computer.

encrypting virus — A type of virus that transforms itself into a nonreplicating program in order to avoid detection. It transforms itself back into a replicating program in order to spread.

encryption — The process of putting readable data into an encoded form that can only be decoded (or decrypted) through use of a key.

enhanced metafile format (EMF) — A format used to print a document that contains embedded print commands. When printing in Windows 9x, EMF information is generated by the GDI portion of the Windows kernel.

environment — As related to OSs, the overall support that an OS provides to applications software.

executive services — In Windows NT/2000/XP, a group of components running in kernel mode that interfaces between the subsystems in user mode and the HAL.

extended memory — Memory above 1024K used in a DOS or Windows 9x system.

extended partition — The hard drive partition that can contain more than one logical drive.

Extensions folder — A Mac OS 9 folder that contains add-ons to provide new features to a Mac, as well as shared libraries and icons. Extensions no longer exist in Mac OS X; their functions are incorporated into the Library folder.

extents — On a Mac, the pieces into which a file is broken when it is larger than one allocation block.

extents tree — A Mac directory structure that contains information about where the allocation blocks are located for files that take up more than one allocation block.

external command — Commands that have their own program files.

FAT (file allocation table) — A table on a hard drive or floppy disk that tracks the clusters used to contain a file.

FAT12 — A file system used on floppy disks in which the width of each entry in the one-column table used to track clusters on the disk is 12 bits.

fatal system error — An error that prevents Windows from loading. An example is a damaged registry.

fault tolerance — The degree to which a system can tolerate failures. Adding redundant components, such as disk mirroring, is a way to build in fault tolerance.

file extension — A three-character portion of the name of a file that is used to identify the file type. In command lines, the file extension follows the filename and is separated from it by a period. For example, Msd.exe, where exe is the file extension.

filename — The first part of the name assigned to a file. In DOS, the filename can be no more than eight characters long and is followed by the file extension. In Windows, a filename can be up to 255 characters.

file system — The overall structure that an OS uses to name, store, and organize files on a disk. Examples of file systems are FAT16 and FAT32.

file virus — A virus that inserts virus code into an executable program and can spread wherever that program is accessed.

Finder window — A type of Mac window that allows a user to navigate the Mac OS hierarchical file structure. It functions something like My Computer or Explorer in Windows and includes buttons similar to those on a Web browser.

firmware — Programs permanently embedded on a microchip. The BIOS on a motherboard is an example of firmware.

folder — *See* subdirectory.

forgotten password floppy disk — A Windows XP disk created to be used in the event the user forgets the user account password to the system.

fragmentation — The distribution of data files such that they are stored in noncontiguous clusters.

fragmented file — A file that has been written to different portions of the disk so that it is not in contiguous clusters.

frame — The header and trailer information added to data to form a data packet to be sent over a network.

front-side bus — *See* system bus.

FTP (File Transfer Protocol) — The protocol used to transfer files over a TCP/IP network such that the file does not need to be converted to ASCII format before transferring.

full backup — A complete backup, whereby all of the files on the hard drive are backed up each time the backup procedure is performed. It is the safest backup method, but it takes the most time.

fully qualified domain name (FQDN) — A host name and a domain name such as jsmith.amazon.com. Sometimes loosely referred to as a domain name.

gateway — A computer or other device that connects networks.

GDI (Graphics Device Interface) — A Windows 9x component that controls screens, graphics, and printing.

global user account — Sometimes called a domain user account, the account is used at the domain level, created by an administrator, and stored in the SAM (security accounts manager) database on a domain controller.

group files — Windows 3.x files with the .grp file extension that contain information about a program group of Program Manager.

group profile — A group of user profiles. All profiles in the group can be changed by changing the group profile.

Guest user — A user who has limited permissions on a system and cannot make changes to it. Guest user accounts are intended for one-time or infrequent users of a workstation.

GUI (graphical user interface) — A user interface, such as the Windows interface, that uses graphics or icons on the screen for running programs and entering information.

HAL (hardware abstraction layer) — The low-level part of Windows NT/2000/XP, written specifically for each CPU technology, so that only the HAL must change when platform components change.

hard boot — Restart the computer by turning off the power or by pressing the Reset button. Also called a cold boot.

hardware address — *See* MAC address.

hardware cache — A disk cache that is contained in RAM chips built right on the disk controller.

hardware interrupt — An event caused by a hardware device signaling the CPU that it requires service.

hardware profile — A set of hardware configuration information that Windows keeps in the registry. Windows can maintain more than one hardware profile for the same PC.

hardware tree — A database built each time Windows 9x starts up that contains a list of installed components and the resources they use.

HCL (hardware compatibility list) — The list of all computers and peripheral devices that have been tested and are officially supported by Windows NT/2000/XP. (See *www.microsoft.com/hcl*)

HFS (Hierarchical File System) — The file system used for Macintosh computer disks before 1998, when drives larger than 1 GB started to become more common. HFS limited the number of allocation units on a disk to 65,536. Also known as Mac OS standard format.

HFS+ — The file system used for Mac disks since the release of Mac OS 8.1 in 1998. HFS+ is an update of HFS, and can format drives up to 2,048 GB. Also called Mac OS extended format.

hidden file — A file that is not displayed in a directory list. Whether to hide or display a file is indicated by one of the file's attributes kept by the OS.

Himem.sys — The DOS and Windows 9x memory manager extension that allowed access to memory addresses above 1 MB.

hive — Physical segments of the Windows NT/ 2000/XP registry that is stored in a file.

HMA (high memory area) — The first 64K of extended memory.

host — Any computer or other device on a network that has been assigned an IP address.

host drive — Typically drive H on a compressed drive. *See* compressed drive.

host name — A name that identifies a computer, printer, or other device on a network.

Hosts — A text file located in the Windows folder that contains host names and their associated IP addresses. This file is used for name resolution for a TCP/IP network using DNS.

HTML (HyperText Markup Language) — A markup language used for hypertext documents on the World Wide Web. This language uses tags to format the document, create hyperlinks, and mark locations for graphics.

HTTP (HyperText Transfer Protocol) — The protocol used by the World Wide Web.

HTTPS (HTTP secure) — A version of the HTTP protocol that includes data encryption for security.

hub — A network device or box that provides a central location to connect cables.

hypertext — Text that contains links to remote points in the document or to other files, documents, or graphics. Hypertext is created using HTML and is commonly distributed from Web sites.

I/O addresses — Numbers that are used by devices and the CPU to manage communication between them. Also called ports or port addresses.

ICMP (Internet Control Message Protocol) — Part of the IP layer that is used to transmit error messages and other control messages to hosts and routers.

IDE (Integrated Drive Electronics) — A standard governing hard drive technology and how secondary storage devices, such as hard drives, CD-ROM drives and Zip drives, relate to a system.

IEEE (Institute of Electrical and Electronics Engineers) — A nonprofit organization that develops standards for the computer and electronics industries.

IMAP4 (Internet Message Access Protocol version 4) — Version 4 of the IMAP protocol, which is an e-mail protocol that has more functionality than its predecessor, POP. IMAP can archive messages in folders on the e-mail server and can allow the user to choose not to download attachments to messages.

incremental backup — A time-saving backup method that only backs up files changed or newly created since the last full or incremental backup. Multiple incremental backups might be required when recovering lost data.

infestation — Any unwanted program that is transmitted to a computer without the user's knowledge and that is designed to do varying degrees of damage to data and software. There are a number of different types of infestations, including viruses, Trojan horses, worms, and logic bombs.

information (.inf) file — Text file with an .inf file extension, such as Msbatch.inf, that contains information about a hardware or software installation.

initialization files — Configuration information files for Windows. System.ini is one of the most important Windows initialization files.

insert mode — A Linux vi editor mode in which you can type text into the editor.

Installable File System (IFS) — A Windows 9x Plug and Play component that is responsible for all disk access.

internal command — Commands that are embedded in the Command.com file.

Internet Connection Firewall (ICF) — Windows XP software designed to protect a PC from unauthorized access from the Internet.

interrupt handler — A program (either BIOS or a device driver), that is used by the CPU to process a hardware interrupt. Also called request handler.

interrupt vector table — A table that stores the memory addresses assigned to interrupt handlers so the CPU can find one when needed. Also called a vector table.

intranet — A private network that uses the TCP/IP protocols.

Io.sys — Along with Msdos.sys and Command.com, one of the three files that are the core components of the real mode portion of Windows 9x. It is the first program file of the OS.

IP (Internet Protocol) — The rules of communication in the TCP/IP stack that control segmenting data into packets, routing those packets across networks, and then reassembling the packets once they reach their destination.

IP address — A 32-bit address consisting of four numbers separated by periods, used to uniquely identify a device on a network that uses TCP/IP protocols. The first numbers identify the network; the last numbers identify a host. An example of an IP address is 206.96.103.114.

IPX/SPX (Internetwork Packet Exchange/Sequenced Packet Exchange) — A networking protocol suite first used by Novell NetWare, which corresponds to the TCP/IP protocols.

IRQ (interrupt request number) — A line on a bus that is assigned to a device and is used to signal the CPU for servicing. These lines are assigned a reference number (for example, the normal IRQ for a printer is IRQ 7).

ISA (Industry Standard Architecture) — An 8-bit or 16-bit slot first used in the 1980s on motherboards and sometimes still used today.

ISO (International Organization for Standardization) — A standards organization composed of standards bodies from several countries. The ISO developed the OSI model.

ISP (Internet service provider) — A commercial group that provides Internet access for a monthly fee. AOL, Earthlink, and CompuServe are large ISPs.

kernel — The portion of an OS that is responsible for interacting with the hardware.

kernel mode — A Windows NT/2000/XP "privileged" processing mode that has access to hardware components.

key — (1) In encryption, a secret number or code used to encode and decode data. (2) In Windows, a section name of the Windows registry.

LAN (local area network) — A computer network that covers only a small area, usually within one building.

laptop — *See* notebook.

legacy — A term used to refer to older computer devices or software that does not use the most current technologies.

Library — The Mac OS X folder that takes over the functions of the Mac OS 9 control panels and extensions, which do not exist in Mac OS X. System settings and add-ons are controlled from the Library folder.

Limited user — Windows XP user accounts known as Users in Windows NT/2000, which have limited access to other users' data.

line protocol — A protocol used to send data packets destined for a network over telephone lines. PPP and SLIP are examples of line protocols.

LMHosts — A text file located in the Windows folder that contains NetBIOS names and their associated IP addresses. This file is used for name resolution for a NetBEUI network.

local bus — A bus that runs synchronized with the system bus and CPU.

local printer — A printer connected to a computer by way of a port on the computer.

local profile — User profile that is stored on a local computer and cannot be accessed from another computer on the network.

local user account — A user account that applies only to a local computer and cannot be used to access resources from other computers on the network.

logic bomb — Dormant code added to software that is triggered by a predetermined time or event.

loopback device — A virtual device, which consists of the local system and has the IP address 127.x.x.x. It is used to test the TCP/IP configuration on a computer.

lost allocation units — *See* lost clusters.

lost clusters — Lost file fragments that, according to the file allocation table, contain data that does not belong to any file. The command Chkdsk/F can free these fragments.

MAC address — A 6-byte hexadecimal hardware address unique to each NIC card and assigned by the manufacturer. The address is often printed on the adapter. An example is 00 00 0C 08 2F 35. Also called a physical address, an adapter address, or a hardware address.

Mac OS extended format — *See* HFS+.

Mac OS ROM file — The first item that the Mac loads into memory from the System folder during the startup process. This file contains commands required for interaction with hardware and the lower levels of the Mac OS.

Mac OS standard format — *See* HFS.

macro — A small sequence of commands, contained within a document, that can be automatically executed when the document is loaded, or executed later by using a predetermined keystroke.

macro virus — A virus that can hide in the macros of a document file. Typically, viruses do not reside in data or document files.

mandatory user profile — A roaming user profile that applies to all users in a group, and individual users cannot change that profile.

master file table (MFT) — The database used by the NTFS file system to track the contents of a logical drive.

MBR (Master Boot Record) — The first sector on a hard drive, which contains the partition table and a program the BIOS uses to boot an OS from the drive.

memory address — A number assigned to each byte in memory. The CPU can use memory addresses to track where information is stored in RAM. Memory addresses are usually displayed as hexadecimal numbers in segment/offset form.

memory bus — *See* system bus.

memory dump — The contents of memory saved to a file at the time an event halted the system. Support technicians can analyze the dump file to help understand the source of the problem.

memory extender — For DOS and Windows 9x, a device driver named Himem.sys that manages RAM giving access to memory addresses above 1 MB.

memory leak — Occurs when software unloads from memory but does not release the memory addresses that it was using for its data back to the OS.

memory paging — In Windows, swapping blocks of RAM memory to an area of the hard drive to serve as virtual memory when RAM is low.

memory-resident virus — A virus that can stay lurking in memory even after its host program is terminated.

microprocessor — *See* CPU.

Microsoft Management Console (MMC) — A utility to build customized consoles. These consoles can be saved to a file with a .msc file extension.

minifile system — In Windows NT/2000/XP, a simplified file system that is started so that Ntldr (NT Loader) can read files from any file system the OS supports.

mixed mode — A Windows 2000 mode for domain controllers used when there is at least one Windows NT domain controller on the network.

motherboard — The largest circuit board inside the computer; it holds the CPU, slots, connections, and ports for other devices and wires for communication called a bus. Also called system board.

Msdos.sys — In Windows 9x, a text file that contains settings used by Io.sys during booting. In DOS, the Msdos.sys file was a program file that contained part of the DOS core.

multicasting — A process in which a message is sent by one host to multiple hosts, such as when a video conference is broadcasted to several hosts on the Internet.

multipartite virus — A combination of a boot sector virus and a file virus. It can hide in either type of program.

multiprocessing — Having two or more CPUs in a system.

multitasking — Doing more than one thing at a time. A true multitasking system requires two or more CPUs, each processing a different thread at the same time. Compare to cooperative multitasking and preemptive multitasking.

multithreading — The ability to pass more than one function (thread) to the OS kernel at the same time, such as when one thread is performing a print job while another reads a file.

name resolution — The process of associating a NetBIOS name or host name to an IP address.

NAT (Network Address Translation) — A process that converts private IP addresses on a LAN to the proxy server's IP address before a data packet is sent over the Internet.

native mode — A Windows 2000 mode used by domain controllers when there are no Windows NT domain controllers present on the network.

NetBEUI (NetBIOS Extended User Interface) — A fast, proprietary Microsoft networking protocol used only by Windows-based systems, and limited to LANs because it does not support routing.

NetBIOS (Network Basic Input/Output System) — An API protocol used by some applications to communicate over a NetBEUI network. NetBIOS has largely been replaced by Windows Sockets over a TCP/IP network.

network drive map — Mounting a drive to a computer, such as drive E, that is actually hard drive space on another host computer on the network.

Network layer — The OSI layer responsible for routing packets.

network printer — A printer that is available to users on a network.

NIC (network interface card) — A expansion card that plugs into a computer's motherboard and provides a port on the back of the card to connect a PC to a network. Also called a network adapter.

NNTP (Network News Transfer Protocol) — The protocol used by newsgroup server and client software.

non-memory-resident virus — A virus that is terminated when the host program is closed. Compare to memory-resident virus.

NOS (network operating system) — An operating system that resides on the controlling computer in the network. The NOS controls what software, data, and devices a user on the network can access.

notebook — A portable computer that is designed for travel and mobility. Notebooks use the same technology as desktop PCs, with modifications for conserving voltage, taking up less space, and operating while on the move. Also called a laptop computer.

NTFS (NT file system) — The file system for the Windows NT/2000/XP operating systems. NTFS cannot be accessed by other operating systems such as DOS. It provides increased reliability and security in comparison to other methods of organizing and accessing files. There are several versions of NTFS that might or might not be compatible.

NTHQ (NT Hardware Qualifier) — A utility found on the Windows NT installation CD-ROM that examines your system to determine if all hardware present qualifies for NT.

Ntldr (NT Loader) — In Windows NT/2000/XP, the OS loader used on Intel systems.

NTVDM (NT virtual DOS machine) — An emulated environment in which a 16-bit DOS application resides within Windows NT/2000/XP with its own memory space or WOW (Win16 on Win32).

octet — Term for each of the four 8-bit numbers that make up an IP address. For example, the IP address 206.96.103.114 has four octets.

operating system — Software that controls a computer. An operating system controls how system resources are used and provides a user interface, a way of managing hardware and software, and ways to work with files.

OSI (Open Systems Interconnect) reference model — A network communication model that provides a universally accepted reference that illustrates how data is transmitted on a network or between two or more networked devices. This model separates communication into seven layers.

packet — Segment of network data that also include header, destination address, and trailer information that is sent as a unit. Also called data packet or datagram.

page fault — An OS interrupt that occurs when the OS is forced to access the hard drive to satisfy the demands for virtual memory.

page file — *See* swap file.

Pagefile.sys — The Windows NT/2000/XP swap file.

page-in — The process in which the memory manager goes to the hard drive to return the data from a swap file to RAM.

page-out — The process in which, when RAM is full, the memory manager takes a page and moves it to the swap file.

pages — 4K segments in which Windows NT/2000/XP allocates memory.

parallel port — A 25-pin female port on a computer that can transmit data in parallel, 8 bits at a time, and is usually used by a printer. The port is sometimes configured as LPT1 or LPT2.

partition table — A table at the beginning of the hard drive that contains information about each partition on the drive. The partition table is contained in the master boot record.

patch — An update to software that corrects an error, adds a feature, or addresses security issues. Also called an update or service pack.

path — (1) A drive and list of directories pointing to a file such as C:\Windows\command. (2) The OS command to provide a list of paths to the system for finding program files to execute.

PCI (Peripheral Component Interconnect) bus — A bus common on Pentium computers that runs at speeds of up to 33 MHz or 66 MHz, with a 32-bit-wide or 64-bit-wide data path. PCI-X, released in September 1999, enables PCI to run at 133 MHz. For some chip sets, it serves as the middle layer between the memory bus and expansion buses.

peer-to-peer network — A network of computers that are all equals, or peers. Each computer has the same amount of authority, and each can act as a server to the other computers.

physical address — *See* MAC address.

Physical layer — The OSI layer responsible for interfacing with the network media (cabling).

PIF (program information file) — A file used by Windows to describe the environment for a DOS program to use.

Ping — A program that allows one computer to send a packet to another computer and then receive a reply. Used as a method of testing connectivity.

pixel — Small spots on a fine horizontal scan line that are illuminated to create an image on a monitor.

Plug and Play (PnP) — A standard designed to make the installation of new hardware devices easier by automatically configuring devices to eliminate system resource conflicts (such as IRQ or I/O address conflicts). PnP is supported by Windows 9x, Windows 2000 and Windows XP.

Plug and Play BIOS — System BIOS that supports the Plug and Play standards and is designed to automatically recognize new devices when they are installed.

polling — A process by which the CPU checks the status of connected devices to determine if they are ready to send or receive data.

polymorphic virus — A type of virus that changes its distinguishing characteristics as it replicates itself. Mutating in this way makes it more difficult for AV software to recognize the presence of the virus.

POP (Post Office Protocol) — The protocol that an e-mail server and client use when the client requests the downloading of e-mail messages. The most recent version is POP3. POP is slowly being replaced by IMAP.

port — (1) As applied to services running on a computer, a number assigned to a process on a computer so that the process can be found by TCP/IP. Also called a port address or port number. (2) Another name for an I/O address. *See also* I/O address.

port address — *See* I/O address.

port number — *See* port.

port replicator — A device designed to connect to a notebook computer in order to make it easy to connect the notebook to peripheral devices.

POSIX (Portable Operating System Interface) — A set of standards for Unix and similar operating systems used to create applications to comply with standards used by federal agencies for their software.

POST (power-on self test) — A self-diagnostic program used to perform a simple test of the CPU, RAM, and various I/O devices. The POST is performed by startup BIOS when the computer is first turned on and is stored in ROM-BIOS.

power scheme — A feature of Windows XP support for notebooks that allows the user to create groups of power settings for specific sets of conditions.

Power User — *See* standard user.

PPP (Point-to-Point Protocol) — A protocol that governs the methods for communicating via modems and dial-up telephone lines. The Windows Dial-up Networking utility uses PPP.

PRAM (parameter RAM) — A small amount of RAM on a Mac that contains configuration information for the Mac.

preemptive multitasking — A type of pseudo-multitasking whereby the CPU allows an application a specified period of time and then preempts the processing to give time to another application.

Presentation layer — The OSI layer that compresses and decompresses data and interfaces with the Application layer and the Session layer.

primary domain controller (PDC) — In a Windows NT network, the computer that controls the directory database of user accounts, group accounts, and computer accounts on a domain. Also see backup domain controller.

primary partition — A hard disk partition that can contain only one logical drive.

primary storage — Temporary storage on the motherboard used by the CPU to process data and instructions. Memory is considered primary storage.

private IP address — An IP address that is used on a private TCP/IP network that is isolated from the Internet.

process — An executing instance of a program together with the program resources. There can be more than one process running for a program at the same time. One process for a program happens each time the program is loaded into memory or executed.

product activation — The process that Microsoft uses to prevent software piracy. For example, once Windows XP is activated for a particular computer, it cannot be installed on another computer.

program file — A file that contains instructions designed to be executed by the CPU.

protected mode — An operating mode that supports preemptive multitasking, the OS manages memory and other hardware devices, and programs can use a 32-bit data path. Also called 32-bit mode.

Protocol.ini — A Windows initialization file that contains network configuration information.

proxy server — A server that acts as an intermediary between another computer and the Internet. The proxy server substitutes its own IP address for the IP address of the computer on the network making a request, so that all traffic over the Internet appears to be coming from only the IP address of the proxy server.

public IP address — An IP address available to the Internet.

RAID (redundant array of inexpensive disks or redundant array of independent disks) — Several methods of configuring multiple hard drives to store data to increase logical volume size and improve performance, and to ensure that if one hard drive fails, the data is still available from another hard drive.

RAM (random access memory) — Memory modules on the motherboard containing microchips used to temporarily hold data and programs while the CPU processes both. Information in RAM is lost when the PC is turned off.

RAM drive — An area of memory that is treated as though it were a hard drive, but that works much faster than a hard drive. The Windows 98 startup disk uses a RAM drive. Compare to virtual memory.

RARP (Reverse Address Resolution Protocol) — A protocol used to translate the unique hardware NIC addresses (MAC addresses) into IP addresses (the reverse of ARP).

real mode — A single-tasking operating mode whereby a program has 1024K of memory addresses, has direct access to RAM, and uses a 16-bit data path. Using a memory extender (Himem.sys) a program in real mode can access memory above 1024K. Also called 16-bit mode.

Recovery Console — A Windows 2000/XP command interface utility and OS that can be used to solve problems when the Windows cannot load from the hard drive.

redirection symbol — The greater than (>) symbol used in OS commands to redirect output to a file or printer instead of to a screen.

registry — A database that Windows uses to store hardware and software configuration information, user preferences, and setup information.

Remote Access Service (RAS) — The Windows NT service used to configure a computer to allow inbound calls.

Remote Assistance — A Windows XP feature that allows a support technician at a remote location to have full access to the Windows XP desktop.

request handler — *See* interrupt handler.

rescue disk — A floppy disk that can be used to start up a computer when the hard drive fails to boot. Also called ESD or startup disk.

resolution — The number of pixels on a monitor screen that are addressable by software, such as 1024 × 768.

resource arbitrator — A Plug and Play component that decides which resources are assigned to which devices.

resource management — The process of allocating resources to devices at startup.

restore point — A snapshot of the Windows Me/XP system state, usually made before installation of new hardware or applications.

restricted user — *See* user.

RFC (Request for Comments) — A document that proposes a change in standards or protocols for the communications industry. An RFC can be presented by different organizations but is managed under the general guidance of the Internet Architecture Board (IAB).

roaming user profile — A user profile for a roaming user. Roaming user profiles are stored on a server so that the user can access the profile from anywhere on the network.

roaming users — Users who can move from PC to PC within a network, with their profiles following them.

root account — The principal user account in Linux, accessible by the system administrator. Only the owner of the root account has the ability to make certain alterations to the system and perform certain system tasks.

root directory — The main directory created when a hard drive or disk is first formatted. In Linux, indicated by a forward slash. In DOS and Windows, indicated by a backward slash.

root privileges — The privileges that the system administrator has on a Linux system, which allow the system administrator full access to the system.

run-time configuration — An ongoing Plug and Play process that monitors changes in system devices, such as the removal of a PC card on a notebook computer or the docking of a notebook computer to a docking station.

secondary storage — Storage that is remote to the CPU and permanently holds data, even when the PC is turned off, such as a hard drive.

sector — On a disk surface one segment of a track, which almost always contains 512 bytes of data.

security accounts manager (SAM) — A portion of the Windows NT/2000/XP registry that manages the account database that contains accounts, policies, and other pertinent information about local accounts.

serial port — A male 9-pin or 25-pin port on a computer system used by slower I/O devices such as a mouse or modem. Data travels serially, one bit at a time, through the port. Serial ports are sometimes configured as COM1, COM2, COM3, or COM4.

server — (1) A software program that interacts with client software in a client/server environment. (2) A computer that runs server software and responds to requests for information from client computers.

service pack — *See* patch.

session — An established communication link between two software programs. On the Internet, a session is created by TCP.

Session layer — The OSI layer that makes and manages an extended connection between two hosts on a network.

SFC (System File Checker) — A Windows tool that checks to make sure Windows is using the correct versions of system files.

shell — The portion of an OS that relates to the user and to applications.

shortcut — An icon on the desktop that points to a program that can be executed or to a file or folder.

Sigverif.exe — A Windows 2000/XP utility that allows you to search for digital signatures.

simple volume — A type of dynamic volume used on a single hard drive that corresponds to a primary partition on a basic disk.

single-tasking — When only one program is running at a time.

SLIP (Serial Line Internet Protocol) — A line protocol used by regular telephone lines that has largely been replaced by PPP.

SMARTDrive — A hard drive cache program that came with Windows 3.x and DOS and can be executed as a TSR from the Autoexec.bat file (for example, Device=Smartdrv.sys 2048).

SMTP (Simple Mail Transfer Protocol) — The protocol used by e-mail clients and servers to send e-mail messages over the Internet. *See* POP and IMAP.

snap-ins — Components added to a console using the Microsoft Management Console.

SNMP (Simple Network Management Protocol) — A protocol used to monitor and manage network traffic on a workstation. SNMP works with TCP/IP and IPX/SPX networks.

socket — *See* session.

soft boot — To restart a PC without turning off the power, for example, by pressing three keys at the same time (Ctrl, Alt, and Del). Also called warm boot.

software cache — Cache controlled by software whereby the cache is stored in RAM.

software interrupt — An event caused by a program currently being executed by the CPU signaling the CPU that it requires the use of a hardware device.

spanned volume — A type of dynamic volume used on two or more hard drives that fills up the space allotted on one physical disk before moving to the next.

spooling — Placing print jobs in a print queue so that an application can be released from the printing process before printing is completed. Spooling is an acronym for simultaneous peripheral operations online.

standard user — Also called power user. Standard users can read from and write to parts of the system other than their own local drive, install applications, and perform limited administrative tasks.

startup BIOS — Part of system BIOS that is responsible for controlling the PC when it is first turned on. Startup BIOS gives control over to the OS once it is loaded.

startup disk — *See* rescue disk.

static IP address — An IP address permanently assigned to a workstation.

Static VxD — A VxD that is loaded into memory at startup and remains there for the entire OS session.

stealth virus — A virus that actively conceals itself by temporarily removing itself from an infected file that is about to be examined, and then hiding a copy of itself elsewhere on the drive.

stop error — An error severe enough to cause the operating system to stop all processes.

striped volume — A type of dynamic volume used for two or more hard drives that writes to the disks evenly rather than filling up allotted space on one and then moving on to the next. Compare to spanned volume.

subdirectory — A directory or folder contained in another directory or folder. Also called a child directory or folder.

subnet mask — A subnet mask is a group of four numbers (dotted decimal numbers) that tell TCP/IP if a remote computer is on the same or a different network.

subsystems — The different modules into which the Windows NT/2000/XP user mode is divided.

swap file — A file on the hard drive that is used by the OS for virtual memory. Also called page file.

Sysedit — The Windows System Configuration Editor, which is a text editor generally used to edit system files.

system BIOS — BIOS located on the motherboard.

system bus — The bus between the CPU and memory on the motherboard. The bus frequency in documentation is called the system speed such as 200 MHz. Also called the memory bus, front-side bus, local bus, or host bus.

system disk — Windows terminology for a bootable disk.

System file —The Mac OS file that contains the libraries and commands that make up the core of the OS.

System File Protection — A Windows Me feature that prevents system files from being deleted.

System folder — The folder that a Mac system designates as the one from which the OS is to be loaded.

System.ini — A text configuration file used by Windows 3.x and supported by Windows 9x for backward-compatibility.

system partition — The active partition of the hard drive containing the boot record and the specific files required to load Windows NT/2000/XP.

System Restore — A Windows Me/XP utility, similar to the ScanReg tool in earlier versions of Windows, that is used to restore the system to a restore point. Unlike ScanReg, System Restore cannot be executed from a command prompt.

system state data — In Windows 2000/XP, files that are necessary for a successful load of the operating system.

System Tray — An area to the right of the taskbar that holds the icons of small applets launched at startup.

task switching — *See* cooperative multitasking.

TCP (Transmission Control Protocol) — Part of the TCP/IP protocol suite. TCP guarantees delivery of data for application protocols and establishes a session before it begins transmitting data.

TCP/IP (Transmission Control Protocol/Internet Protocol) — The suite of protocols that supports communication on the Internet. TCP is responsible for error checking, and IP is responsible for routing.

Terminate-and-stay-resident (TSR) — A program that is loaded into memory and remains dormant until called on, such as a screen saver or a memory-resident antivirus program.

thread — Each process that the CPU is aware of; a single task that is part of a longer task or program.

top-level domain — The highest level of domain names, indicated by a suffix that tells something about the host. For example, .com is for commercial use and .edu is for educational institutions.

track — One of many concentric circles on the surface of a hard drive or floppy disk.

Transport layer — The OSI layer that verifies data and requests a resend when the data is corrupted.

Trojan horse — A type of infestation that hides or disguises itself as a useful program, yet is designed to cause damage at a later time.

UDP (User Datagram Protocol) — A connectionless protocol that does not require a connection to send a packet and does not guarantee that the packet arrives at its destination. UDP works at the Transport layer and is faster than TCP because TCP takes the time to make a connection and guarantee delivery.

UMB (upper memory block) — In DOS and Windows 9x, a group of consecutive memory addresses in RAM from 640K to 1MB that can be used by 16-bit device drivers and TSRs.

unattended installation — A Windows NT/ 2000/XP installation that is done by storing the answers to installation questions in a text file or script that Windows NT/2000/XP calls an answer file so that the answers do not have to be typed in during the installation.

upgrade install — The installation of an OS on a hard drive that already has an OS installed in such a way that settings kept by the old OS are carried forward into the upgrade, including information about hardware, software, and user preferences.

upper memory — In DOS and Windows 9x, the memory addresses from 640K up to 1024K, originally reserved for BIOS, device drivers, and TSRs.

URL (Uniform Resource Locator) — An address for a resource on the Internet. A URL can contain the protocol used by the resource, the name of the computer and its network, and the path and name of a file on the computer.

USB (universal serial bus) — A bus that is expected to eventually replace serial and parallel ports. USB is designed to make installation and configuration of I/O devices easy, providing room for as many as 127 devices daisy-chained together. The USB uses only a single set of resources for all devices on the bus.

user — In reference to Windows NT/2000/XP permissions, a restricted user who has read-write access only on his or her own folders, read-only access to most system folders, and no access to other users' data.

user account — The information, stored in the SAM database, that defines a Windows NT/ 2000/XP user, including username, password, memberships, and rights.

user component — A Windows 9x component that controls the mouse, keyboard, ports and desktop.

user mode — In Windows NT/2000/XP, a mode that provides an interface between an application and the OS, and only has access to hardware resources through the code running in kernel mode.

user profile — A personal profile about a user that enables the user's desktop settings and other operating parameters to be retained from one session to another.

User State Migration Tool (USMT) — A Windows XP utility that helps you migrate user files and preferences from one computer to another in order to help a user makes a smooth transition from one computer to another.

value data — In Windows, the name and value of a setting in the registry.

VCACHE — A built-in Windows 9x 32-bit software cache that doesn't take up conventional memory space or upper memory space as SMARTDrive did.

VDM (virtual DOS machine) — An environment that a 32-bit protected-mode OS provides for a real-mode program to operate in.

vector table — *See* interrupt vector table.

VFAT (virtual file allocation table) — A variation of the original DOS 16-bit FAT that allows for long filenames and 32-bit disk access.

vi editor — A text editor in Linux that operates in two modes: insert mode, in which you can type text into the editor, and command mode, in which you can enter commands to work with the text or change the status of the editor.

virtual device driver (VxD or VDD) — A Windows device driver that may or may not have direct access to a device. It might depend on a Windows component to communicate with the device itself.

virtual DOS machine (VDM) — Environment in which Windows runs a 16-bit DOS application. In a VDM, the application "thinks" it is running in real mode, but the OS is managing hardware resources using 32-bit drivers and providing virtual memory to the application.

virtual machine — One or more logical machines created within one physical machine by Windows, allowing applications to make serious errors within one logical machine without disturbing other programs and parts of the system.

Virtual Machine Manager (VMM) — A Windows 9x program that controls virtual machines and the resources they use including memory. The VMM manages the page table used to access memory.

virtual memory — A method whereby the OS uses the hard drive as though it were RAM. Compare to RAM drive.

virtual real mode — An operating mode that works similarly to real mode provided by a 32-bit OS for a 16-bit program to work.

virus — A program that often has an incubation period, is infectious, and is intended to cause damage. A virus program might destroy data and programs or damage a disk drive's boot sector.

virus signature — A set of distinguishing characteristics of a virus used by antivirus software to identify the virus.

volume bit map — On a Macintosh computer, a map of the allocation blocks on a hard drive. It uses a 1 to indicate that a block is storing files and a 0 to indicate that it is empty and is available for use.

volume information block — On a Macintosh computer, the directory structure that comes right after the boot blocks on a hard drive. It holds information about the drive, including its format, name, number of files and folders, and allocation block size.

VxD — *See* virtual device driver.

warm boot — *See* soft boot.

WDM (Win32 Driver Model) — The only Windows 9x Plug and Play component that is found in Windows 98 but not Windows 95. WDM is the component responsible for managing device drivers that work under a driver model new to Windows 98.

WFP (Windows File Protection) — A Windows 2000/XP tool that protects system files from modification.

Win.ini — The Windows initialization file that contains program configuration information needed for running the Windows operating environment. Its functions were replaced by the registry beginning with Windows 9x, which still supports it for backward compatibility with Windows 3.x.

Win386.swp — The name of the Windows 9x swap file. Its default location is C:\Windows.

window manager — A graphical user interface for a Linux computer. A popular window manager is GNOME.

WINS (Windows Internet Naming Service) — A Microsoft resolution service with a distributed database that tracks relationships between NetBIOS names and IP addresses. Compare to DNS.

WinSock (Windows Sockets) — A part of the TCP/IP utility software that manages API calls from applications to other computers on a TCP/IP network.

WIS (Windows Installer Service) — A feature new to Windows 2000 that standardizes the installation process for applications.

workgroup — In Windows, a logical group of computers and users in which administration, resources, and security are distributed throughout the network, without centralized management or security.

worm — An infestation designed to copy itself repeatedly to memory, on drive space or on a network, until little memory or disk space remains.

WOW (Win16 on Win32) — A group of programs provided by Windows NT/2000/XP to create a virtual DOS environment that emulates a 16-bit Windows environment, protecting the rest of the OS from 16-bit applications.

INDEX

Special Characters

* (asterisk), 138
? (question mark), 138

A

A+ Certification, 639
Accelerated Graphics Port (AGP) bus, 51
ACPI (Advanced Configuration and Power Interface), 27, 64–65
  Windows 2000 Professional support, 308
Active Directory, Windows 2000 Professional, 304
Active X control snap-in, 354
adapter addresses, 490, 491–493
Add Counters window, Windows 2000, 364–365
Add or Remove Programs, Windows XP, 428
address(es)
  I/O (port), 54–55, 56
  memory. *See* memory addresses
Address Resolution Protocol (ARP), 542
addressing on networks, 490–502
  assigning and changing computer names, 500–502
  host names, 491, 499–500
  IP addresses, 490, 493–499
  MAC (adapter; hardware; physical) addresses, 490, 491–493
  NetBIOS names, 491, 499–500
  port addresses, 491
Administrative Tools group, Windows 2000, 351
administrator account, 279
Advanced Configuration and Power Interface (ACPI), 27, 64–65
  Windows 2000 Professional support, 308
Advanced Options menu, Windows 2000, 336–338
Advanced Program Settings dialog box, 204
AGP (Accelerated Graphics Port) bus, 51
allocation blocks, Mac, 585
allocation units, lost, 248–249, 456
American Standard Code for Information Interchange (ASCII) character set, 617–620, 622
ANSI.sys file, 617
answer files, 309
antivirus (AV) software, 467, 470, 475–477
APIs (application programming interfaces), 24
  API calls, 161
Apple menu, Mac, 581–582
applets, Control Panel, 190
application(s)
  DOS. *See* DOS applications
  launching, 80–87
  Mac, launching, 583
  Windows. *See* Windows applications
Application layer, OSI model, 486
  TCP/IP protocols, 540
application log, Event Viewer, 358
application programming interfaces (APIs), 24
  API calls, 161
Applications tab, Task Manager, 361, 362
archive bit, 128
ARP (Address Resolution Protocol), 542
ASCII (American Standard Code for Information Interchange) character set, 617–620, 622
ASR. *See* Automated System Recovery (ASR)
asterisk (*), wildcard, 138
Attrib command, 144–145
  Windows 2000, 340
audio, Windows XP Professional, 396–398
Autoexec.bat file, 103
  editing, 109–110
  upgrade installation of Windows 9x, 169
Automated System Recovery (ASR), 389–391
  System Restore utility compared, 436
  Windows XP, 428, 437–439
Autoplay (Autorun) feature, 168, 194
AV (antivirus) software, 467, 470, 475–477

B

backing up hard drives, 457–465
  backup software, 461–464
  child, parent, grandparent method, 457–458
  differential backups, 458–459
  disk cloning software, 465
  full backups, 458
  incremental backups, 458
  planning for disaster recovery, 465
  scheduling backups, 459–461
backing up system state data
  Windows 2000 Professional, 318–319
  Windows XP Professional, 391
backup domain controllers (BDCs), 291
backup utility
  Windows 98/Me, 240
  Windows 95, 240
  Windows 9x, 461–463
  Windows 2000, 345, 463–464
  Windows XP, 428, 463–464
backward compatibility, 13

baseline, 360
basic disks
  Windows 2000, converting to dynamic disks, 353–354
  Windows 2000 Professional, 306–307
basic input/output system. *See* BIOS (basic input/output system)
Batch command, Windows 2000, 340
batch files, 103, 147–148
BDCs (backup domain controllers), 291
best-effort protocols, 542
binary number system
  converting between hexadecimal number system and, 626–627
  writing conventions, 627
binding, 489
BIOS (basic input/output system), 44, 64–66, 74–80
  ACPI, 64–65
  hard drive detection by Windows NT, 283
  OS use, 74–76
  PnP, 65, 197–198, 222
  startup, 64, 96–102
  Windows 9x startup, 222
bits, 621, 622
blocks, Mac, 585
boot loader menu, 284
Boot logging option, Windows XP, 428
boot partition, 276
boot record (boot sector), 125–126, 137–138
boot sector viruses, 130, 468–469
bootable disks, 105
  Windows NT, 296–298, 299
Bootcfg.exe file, Windows XP, 428
booting up, 55, 96–104
  BIOS, 96–102
  hard (cold) boots, 96
  POST, 97, 98–99
  system resource assignment, 98–99
  Windows 9x. *See* troubleshooting Windows 9x boot process; Windows 9x boot process
  Windows NT. *See* troubleshooting Windows NT boot process; Windows NT boot process
  Windows 2000, 332–335. *See also* troubleshooting Windows 2000 boot process
bootstrap loaders, 125
bridging protocols, 543
browsers, 560–564
  as FTP clients, 569
  performance problems, 561–563
  updates and patches, 564
  URLs, 560–561
buffers, 451
built-in user accounts, Windows NT/2000/XP, 410
bus enumerator, 197
buses, 48, 49–52
bytes, 621, 622

C

cable modem connections, 555–557
Cacls.exe file, Windows XP, 428
case sensitivity
  Unix, 69
  Windows, 69
cat command, Linux, 591
catalog tree, Mac, 586
CD(s)
  Autoplay feature, 168
  installing Windows 9x, 165–166, 168
CD (change directory) command, 83
cd command, Linux, 591
Cd command, Windows 2000, 340
CD-ROM drives
  installing with Windows 9x, 193–196
  optimizing cache, 196
  testing, 194
central processing unit (CPU), 4, 48
Certificates snap-in, 354
certification, PC technicians, 639–640
chains, 247
change directory (CD) command, 83
Chdir command, 144
child directories, 68
child, parent, grandparent backup method, 457–458
Chkdsk command, 145
  Windows 2000, 340
  Windows XP, 428
chmod command, Linux, 591
Cipher command
  Windows NT/2000, 420–421
  Windows XP, 420–421, 428
classes of IP addresses, 494–495
clean installs
  Windows 9x, 167–168
  Windows 2000 Professional, 310–311, 314–317
  Windows XP Professional, 380
clear command, Linux, 591
client computers, 484
client/server model, 484
cloaking techniques for viruses, 469–470
Cls command, Windows 2000, 340
clusters, 10
  cross-linked, 248–249
  lost, 248–249, 456
CMD.exe file, Windows 2000, 348
CMOS configuration (RAM; setup) chip, 66
CMOS setup windows, 76
cold boots, 96
COM assignments, 55, 57
command(s). *See also specific commands*
  external, 103
  file management, 138–147
  internal, 103
  Linux, 591–595
  repairing/recovering registry, 236
command mode, Linux, 595
command prompt(s)
  accessing, 96, 110–112
  adding icon to desktop, 348
  file transfer from, 566–567
  Windows NY, 22–23
Command Prompt Only option, Windows 9x startup menu, 231
command window, Windows 2000, 348
Command.com file, 100, 102, 103
command-driven interfaces, 5–6

Commit Charge frame, Performance tab of Task Manager, 363
Compact.exe file, Windows XP, 428
compatibility, Windows NT, 19
Component Services snap-in, 354
CompTIA (Computing Technology Industry Association), 639
computer infestations, 467–477
  damage causes by, 470
  protecting against, 474–477
  spread, 470–472
  virus hoaxes, 473
  viruses. *See* virus(es)
Computer Management snap-in
  Windows 2000, 350–354
  Windows XP, 428
computer names, assigning and changing, 500–502
Computing Technology Industry Association (CompTIA), 639
Config.sys file, 119
  editing, 109
  upgrade installation of Windows 9x, 169
Configuration Manager, 163
configuring
  PnP devices, 223
  run-time, 197
  TCP/IP using Windows 98, 506–509
  TCP/IP using Windows 2000, 509–510
  Windows 9x startup with Msdos.sys, 175–177
connecting to networks, 502–510
  direct cable connection, 527
  how computers find one another, 523–525
  NetBEUI networks, 502–505
  network drive maps, 527
  TCP/IP networks, 506–510
connectionless protocols, 542
connection-oriented protocols, 541
Control Panel, applets, 190
Control Panels folder, Mac, 578
conventional memory, 116–117
Convert.exe file, Windows XP, 428
converting between number systems, 58
cooperative multitasking, 9
Copy command, 142
  Windows 2000, 340
copying program files into memory, 86
copyrights, software, protecting, 640–641
corrupted registry, recovery, 235–236
cp command, Linux, 591
CPU (central processing unit), 4, 48
cross-linked clusters, 248–249
customizing
  MMC, 355–357
  setup, 173–175
  Windows XP Professional desktop, 393–396

D

data access problems, hard drives, 453–455
data buses (data paths), 48
Data Link layer, OSI model, 486, 487
  TCP/IP protocols, 543
data packets, 487
datagrams, 487
date command, Linux, 591
Debug command, 147
Debugging Mode, Windows 2000 Advanced Options menu, 338
default gateways, 506
default printer, 516
Defrag utility, 146
  Windows 9x, 246–248
  Windows XP, 429
defragmentation utilities, Mac, 588
Del command, 140–141
  Windows 2000, 340
deleting folders, 188–189
Deltree command, 143
Dependency Walker
  Windows 2000, 346
  Windows XP, 429
desktop, 6
  Mac, 579
  Windows 9x, managing, 182–186
  Windows NT, 22
  Windows 2000 Professional, 320–323
  Windows XP Professional, customizing, 393–396
device driver(s), 15
  hardware control, 76–80
  installing under Windows 9x, 190–191
  legacy, troubleshooting in Windows 9x, 255–256
  loading high, 121–122
  memory management with Windows 9x, 204–206
  16-bit, distinguishing from 32-bit drivers, 205
  sources, 77
  32-bit, distinguishing from 16-bit drivers, 205
  32-bit, Windows 9x, 163–164
  viewing and changing, 191–192
  Windows 9x, 77–79
  Windows 2000, 80
Device Driver Roll Back, Windows XP, 429
Device Manager
  bus resource management, 51
  Windows 9x, 250–251
  Windows 2000, 354
  Windows XP, 429
  Windows XP Professional, 399–401
DHCP (Dynamic Host Configuration Protocol), 497
dial-up networking, 546–555
  creating connections in Windows 9x, 547–551
  creating connections in Windows 2000, 551–553
  creating connections in Windows XP, 552
  functioning, 546–547
  problems, 553–555
differential backups, 458–459
Digital Signature Check, Windows 98/Me, 240
Digital Subscriber Line (DSL), 557
Dir command, 140
  Windows 2000, 340

direct cable connection, 527
direct memory access (DMA) channels, 59–60
directories
  child, 68
  creating using Linux, 595
  Linux, 589–591, 595
  representing, 69
  root, 67–68
  subdirectories, 68
Directory Services Restore Mode option, Windows 2000 Advanced Options menu, 337
directory structure, Mac, 586
directory tables, 67
DirectX Diagnostic Tool, Windows XP, 429
Disable command, Windows 2000, 340
disaster recovery, planning for, 465
disk caching, 449–451
  changing methods, 451
  hardware and software, 450–451
  Windows 9x, 451
  Windows NT/2000/XP, 451
  Windows 3.x, 451
Disk Cleanup tool, Windows XP, 429
disk cloning software, 465
disk compression, 446–449
  Windows 9x, 446–448
  Windows 2000 and Windows XP, 448–449
Disk Defragmenter
  Windows 2000, 354
  Windows XP, 429
Disk First Aid, Mac, 577, 588
disk imaging, 465
Disk Management
  Windows 2000, 351–354
  Windows XP, 429
disk operating system. *See* DOS (disk operating system)
Disk Properties window, Windows 2000, 349–350
disk quotas, Windows NT/2000/XP, 416–418
disk thrashing, 208
Diskcopy command, 141–142
Diskpart command
  Windows 2000, 340
  Windows XP, 429
display(s)
  Mac, adjusting settings, 583–584
  resolution, 583–584
Display Properties window, Windows 9x, 182, 183
displaying memory with DOS DEBUG, 628–630
distributions, 33
DLLs (dynamic link libraries), 258
DMA (direct memory access) channels, 59–60
DNS (Domain Name System [Service]), 500
DNS servers, 506
docking stations, 601
domain(s)
  Windows NT, 289, 290–292
  Windows XP Professional, 380
domain name(s), 561
Domain Name System [Service] (DNS), 500
DOS (disk operating system), 3, 12–13
  applications. *See* DOS applications; DOS applications under Windows 9x
  installing Windows 9x over, 178
  interface, 5–6
  memory management, 113
  Windows 9x compared, 15–16
DOS applications
  virtual machines, 162–163
  Windows 9x. *See* DOS applications under Windows 9x
DOS applications under Windows 9x, 200–204
  memory management, 201–202
  real mode vs. virtual real mode, 202–204
DOS boxes. *See* virtual DOS machines (VDMs)
DOS commands, under Windows 9x, caution regarding, 250
DOS DEBUG, displaying memory, 628–630
Dosstart.bat file, 200
DoubleSpace, 170
downloading
  images, suppressing to improve browser performance, 562–563
  updates, 180
Dr. Watson
  Windows 98/Me, 240, 251–252
  Windows 2000, 366–367
  Windows XP, 429
drive(s). *See* hard drives; logical drives
Drive Setup function, Mac, 587–588
Driver Signing and Digital Signatures tool, Windows XP, 429
DSL (Digital Subscriber Line), 557
dual boots, 284
  Windows 2000 Professional, 311–312
  Windows XP Professional, 386–387
dynamic disks
  Windows 2000, converting basic disks to, 353–354
  Windows 2000 Professional, 306–307
Dynamic Host Configuration Protocol (DHCP), 497
dynamic IP addresses, 497–498
dynamic link libraries (DLLs), 258
dynamic volumes, Windows 2000 Professional, 306
dynamic VxDs, 223

E

echo command, Linux, 591
Edit command, 147
editing
  Autoexec.bat file, 109–110
  Config.sys file, 109
  Linux commands, 593
  registry, Windows NT/2000/XP, 426–427
EFS (Encrypted File System), Windows NT/2000/XP, 418–421
EIDE (Extended Integrated Drive Electronics) connections, 67
e-mail, 564–566
emergency repair disks (ERDs), Windows NT, 298–299
Emergency Repair Process, Windows 2000, 342–344

emergency startup disks (ESDs), 105–112
  accessing command prompts, 110–112
  troubleshooting using, 232–233
  updating to include access to devices, 194–195
  Windows 9x, 105–110
  Windows XP, 436–437
EMF (Enhanced Metafile Format), 521
Emm386.exe file, 119, 120–122
Enable Boot Logging option, Windows 2000 Advanced Options menu, 337
Enable command, Windows 2000, 340
Enable VGA Mode option, Windows 2000 Advanced Options menu, 337
enabler files, Mac, 577
Encrypted File System (EFS), Windows NT/2000/XP, 418–421
encrypting viruses, 470
encryption, Windows NT/2000/XP, 418–421
Enhanced Metafile Format (EMF), 521
environment, 10
Erase command, 140–141
erased files, recovering, 457
ERDs (emergency repair disks), Windows NT, 298–299
error events, Event Viewer, 358
error messages, 613–615
  dial-up connections, 554
  loading Windows 9x, 225–226
  Windows XP, 439–440
Error Reporting tool, Windows XP, 429
ESCD (extended system configuration data), 65–66
ESDs. *See* emergency startup disks (ESDs)
Event Viewer
  Windows 2000, 354, 357–360
  Windows XP, 429
executive services, Windows NT, 272
Exit command, Windows 2000, 340
Expand command, Windows 2000, 340
expandability, Windows NT, 18
Expand.exe file, Windows XP, 429
Extended Integrated Drive Electronics (EIDE) connections, 67
Extended Integrated Drive Electronics (IDE) standards, 67
extended memory, 58, 118
extended partition, 130
extended system configuration data (ESCD), 65–66
Extensions folder, Mac, 578
extents, Mac, 586
extents tree, Mac, 586
external commands, 103
Extract command, 147

F

FAT (file allocation table) file system, 10, 69–70, 126, 138. *See also* FAT16; FAT32; FAT12
FAT16, 132
  NTFS compared, 278–279
  operating system support, 309
  upgrade installation of Windows 9x, 169
FAT32, 133
  access by Windows NT, 284
  operating system support, 309
  upgrade installation of Windows 9x, 169–170
FAT12, 126
fault tolerance, 466–467
Fax Service Management snap-in, 354
Fdisk command, 135–136, 139
fdisk command, Linux, 591
file(s). *See also specific filenames*
  answer, 309
  attributes, changing using Windows Explorer, 189
  corruption on hard drives, 455–457
  enabler, Mac, 577
  fragmented, 126
  group, 169
  hidden, 102
  hypertext, 200
  information, 173
  initialization, 5
  policy, 245
  program, 68
  sharing with workgroup, 514–515
  swap (page), 72
  user, transferring to new PC, 388–389
file allocation table (FAT) file system, 10, 69–70, 126, 138. *See also* FAT16; FAT32
File Exchange control panel, Mac, 585
file extensions, 68
file headers, corrupted, 456
file organization, 69
file systems, 67
  FAT. *See* FAT16; FAT32; file allocation table (FAT) file system
  Mac, 585–586
  upgrade installation of Windows 9x, 169–170
  Windows NT, 158, 277–279
  Windows 2000 Professional, 308–309
  Windows XP Professional, 379
File Transfer Protocol (FTP), 566–569
  browsers as FTP clients, 569
  FTP from command prompt, 566–567
  FTP software, 567–568
file viruses, 469
filenames, 68
  conventions, 68–69
  wildcards, 138
Finder window, Mac, 576, 579–581
firewalls, 421–422, 498–499
FireWire, 51
firmware, 64
Fixboot command, Windows 2000, 341
Fixmbr command, Windows 2000, 341
floppy disks
  forgotten password, 413
  formatting process, 124–128
  logical storage, 123–124
  managing using Windows Explorer, 186–189
floppy drives, commands for managing, 138–147
folder(s), 68
  creating using Windows Explorer, 188
  deleting using Windows Explorer, 188–189
  Mac, keeping open all the time, 580

sharing with workgroup, 514–515
viewing and changing properties using Windows Explorer, 189
Folder snap-in, 354
forgotten password floppy disk, 413
Format command, 139–140
Windows 2000, 341
formatting floppy disks, 124–128
boot record, 125–126
creating tracks and sectors, 125
FAT, 126
root directory, 126–128
formatting logical drives, 137–138
FQDNs (fully qualified domain names), 524
fragmentation of hard disks, 246–248
fragmented files, 126
front-side buses, 50
Fsutil tool, Windows XP, 429
FTP. *See* File Transfer Protocol (FTP)
full backups, 458
fully qualified domain names (FQDNs), 524

G

gateways, 506
GDI (Graphics Device Interface), 160
gigabytes, 622
global user accounts, Windows NT/2000/XP, 410
graphical user interfaces (GUIs), 6
Graphics Device Interface (GDI), 160
grep command, Linux, 591
group files, 169
Group Policies
Windows NT/XP, 416
Windows 2000, 354, 416
Windows XP, 429
group profiles
Windows 9x, 245
Windows NT/2000/XP, 411
.grp file extension, 169
GUIs (graphical user interfaces), 6

H

HAL (hardware abstraction layer), 18
Windows NT, 272–273
hard boots, 96
hard drives, 445–478
backing up. *See* backing up hard drives
batch files for managing, 147–148
commands for managing, 138–147
defragmenting, 246–248
disk caching, 449–451
disk compression, 446–449
DOS commands under Windows 9x, caution regarding, 250
formatting logical drives, 137–138
high-level formatting, 128
infestations. *See* computer infestations; virus(es)
installing Windows NT as second OS on, 283–284
logical organization, 128–135
low-level formatting, 128
Mac, 585–588
managing using Windows Explorer, 186–189
managing using Windows 9x, 246–250
partitioning. *See* partitioning hard drives
ScanDisk utility, 248–249
troubleshooting. *See* troubleshooting hard drives
volume types and fault tolerance, 466–467
Windows 2000 Professional, 306–307
hardware. *See also specific types of hardware*
device drivers. *See* device driver(s)
legacy. *See* legacy hardware
Mac support, 583–588
troubleshooting in Windows 9x, 253–256
hardware abstraction layer (HAL), 18
Windows NT, 272–273
hardware addresses, 490, 491–493
hardware caches, 450
Hardware Diagnostic tool, Windows 98/Me, 239
hardware interrupts, 54, 60–61, 62
hardware profiles, Windows XP, 601
hardware tree, 197
hardware/operating system relationships, 44–70
BIOS, 44, 64–66
buses on motherboard, 49–52
CMOS setup chip, 66
CPU, 48
hard drives and other secondary storage devices, 66–70
motherboard, 46–47
RAM, 48–49
system resources on motherboard. *See* system resources on motherboard
Help and Support tool, Windows XP, 429
Help command, Windows 2000, 341
Help system, Windows 9x, 252, 253
hex, 622
hexadecimal number system, 621–630
converting between binary number system and, 626–627
displaying memory with DOS DEBUG, 628–630
exponent use to express place value, 626
memory addressing, 627–628
place value, 622–626
writing conventions, 627
HFS (Hierarchical File System), 585
HFS+, 585
hidden files, 102
Hierarchical File System (HFS), 585
high memory area (HMA), 116, 118
Himem.sys file, 112, 119
HMA (high memory area), 116, 118
host names, 491, 499–500
Hosts table, 524
HTML (Hypertext Markup Language), 560
HTTP (Hypertext Transfer Protocol), 540
HTTP secure (HTTPS), 560
hypertext files, 200
Hypertext Markup Language (HTML), 560
Hypertext Transfer Protocol (HTTP), 540

I

ICFs (Internet Connection Firewalls), 421–422
ICMP (Internet Control Message Protocol), 543
icon(s)
  command prompt, adding to desktop, 348
  managing in Windows 9x, 185–186
icon-driven interfaces, 6–7
IDE drives, 585
IDE (Extended Integrated Drive Electronics) standards, 67
IE (Internet Explorer), performance problems, 562
IEEE (Institute of Electrical and Electronics Engineers), 491
IEEE 1394, 51
ifconfig command, Linux, 592
IFS (Installable File System), 163
images, suppressing downloading to improve browser performance, 562–563
IMAP4 (Internet Message Access Protocol version 4), 564
incremental backups, 458
Indexing Service snap-in, 354
Industry Standard Architecture (ISA) slots, 50, 51
.inf file extension, 173
infestations. *See* computer infestations; virus(es)
information events, Event Viewer, 358
information files, 173
information tools, PC technicians, 638–639
initialization files, 5
insert mode, Linux, 595
Installable File System (IFS), 163
installing
  applications. *See* installing applications; installing applications in Windows 9x
  CD-ROM drives with Windows 9x, 193–196
  hardware. *See* installing hardware; installing hardware with Windows 9x
  local printers, 516
  updates, 180
  Windows 98 components needed to share resources, 512–514
  Windows 9x. *See* installing Windows 9x
  Windows NT. *See* installing Windows NT
  Windows 2000 components needed to share resources, 514
  Windows 2000 Professional. *See* installing Windows 2000 Professional
  Windows XP Professional. *See* installing Windows XP Professional
installing applications
  Windows 9x. *See* installing applications in Windows 9x
  Windows NT, 286, 288–289
  Windows 2000 Professional, 325–326
  Windows XP Professional, 401–404
installing applications in Windows 9x, 198–204
  preparation, 198–199
  supporting DOS applications, 200–204
  troubleshooting installations, 199–200
installing hardware
  Windows 9x. *See* installing hardware with Windows 9x
  Windows NT, 286–288
  Windows 2000 Professional, 323–325
  Windows XP Professional, 398–401
installing hardware with Windows 9x, 190–198
  CD-ROM drives, 193–196
  device drivers, 190–192
  PnP, 196–198
installing Windows 9x
  clean installation, 167–168
  configuring setup with Msdos.sys, 175–177
  contents of CD, 165–166
  customizing setup, 173–175
  downloading and installing updates, 180
  network installation, 168
  over DOS and Windows 3.x, 178
  preparation for installation, 166–167
  problems and solutions, 174–175
  process from setup screen, 171–177
  upgrade installation, 167, 168–170, 178–179
installing Windows NT, 275–284
  file systems, 277–279
  hard drive partitions, 276
  as only OS, 281–283
  preparation, 279–281
  as second OD on hard drive, 283–284
installing Windows 2000 Professional, 307–319
  ACPI support, 308
  backing up system state, 318–319
  clean installation, 314–317
  file system selection, 308–309
  network installations, 309–310
  planning installations, 307–314
  upgrade installation, 317–318
  upgrades from Windows 9x, 312–313
  upgrades from Windows NT, 313–314
  upgrades versus clean installs, 310–312
installing Windows XP Professional, 377–387
  dual boot, 386–387
  file systems, 379
  final checklist, 380–381
  hard drive partitions, 379
  installation process, 381–387
  joining workgroups or domains, 380
  minimum requirements and hardware compatibility, 377–379
  planning installation, 377–381
  upgrade versus clean install, 380
Institute of Electrical and Electronics Engineers (IEEE), 491
interfaces, 5–7
  command-driven, 5–6
  icon-driven, 6–7
  menu-driven, 6, 7
internal commands, 103

International Organization for Standardization (ISO), 485
Internet, 537–570
  cable modems, 555–557
  dial-up connections. *See* dial-up networking
  DSL, 557
  e-mail, 564–566
  FTP, 566–569
  OSI model. *See* Open Systems Interconnection (OSI) reference model
  sharing connections, 557–559
  Web browsers, 560–564
Internet Connection Firewalls (ICFs), 421–422
Internet Connection Sharing, 558–559
Internet Control Message Protocol (ICMP), 543
Internet Explorer (IE), performance problems, 562
Internet Message Access Protocol version 4 (IMAP4), 564
Internet Protocol (IP), 542
  addresses, ports, 538–540
Internet Service Providers (ISPs), 497
  setting up connections in Windows 9x, 549–551
Internetwork Packet Exchange/ Sequenced Packet Exchange (IPX/SPX), 488
interrupt handler, 60
interrupt request numbers (IRQs), 54, 56
interrupt vector table, 61
intranets, 490, 538
I/O addresses, 54–55, 56
I/O.sys file, 102, 122–123
IP (Internet Protocol), 542
  addresses, ports, 538–540
IP addresses, 490, 493–499
  classes, 494–495
  dynamically assigned, 497–498
  NAT, 498–499
  private, 496
  public, 496
  reserved, 496–497
IP Security Policy Management snap-in, 354
IPX/SPX (Internetwork Packet Exchange/Sequenced Packet Exchange), 488
IRQs (interrupt request numbers), 54, 56
ISA (Industry Standard Architecture) slots, 50, 51
ISO (International Organization for Standardization), 485
ISPs (Internet Service Providers), 497
  setting up connections in Windows 9x, 549–551

K

kernel, 5
kernel(s), 5
Kernel Memory frame, Performance tab of Task Manager, 363
kernel mode, Windows NT, 272–273, 274–275
keys
  encryption, 418
  Windows 9x registry, 234–235
keystroke shortcuts, Windows 9x, 180–182
kill command, Linux, 592
kilobytes, 622

L

Label command, 140
LANs (local area networks), 16
  how computers find one another, 523–525
  OSI model, 487–490
laptop computers. *See* notebook computers
Last Known Good Configuration
  Windows NT, 295–296
  Windows XP, 429
Last Known Good Configuration option, Windows 2000 Advanced Options menu, 337
launching applications, 80–87
  Windows desktop, 86–87
launching program files, 83–85
layers, networks, 485–487
legacy hardware, 12
  troubleshooting in Windows 9x, 255–256
legacy software, 12
  installing in Windows XP Professional, 402–404
line protocols, 543
Link to Web Access snap-in, 354
Linux, 3, 33–34, 588–598
  commands, 591–595
  directory and file layout, 589–591
  root account, 589
  user accounts, 589
  vi editor, 595–597
  window managers, 597–598
Listsvc command, Windows 2000, 341
LMHosts table, 524
loading
  device drivers, high, 121–122
  MS-DOS core of Windows 9x, 102–104
  operating systems, 99–102, 222–223
  Windows applications at startup, 224
local area networks (LANs), 16
  how computers find one another, 523–525
  OSI model, 487–490
local buses, 50
local printers
  installing, 516
  sharing with workgroup, 517–518
local user accounts, Windows NT/ 2000/XP, 410
Local Users and Groups snap-in, 355
Logged option, Windows 9x startup menu, 227–228
logging on, Windows NT/ 2000/XP, 414
logic bombs, 468
logical drives, 67, 128–135
  FAT16, 132
  FAT32, 133
  formatting, 137–138
  number, 133–134
  partitioning, 134–135
  size, 134
  VFAT, 132–133

Logon command, Windows 2000, 341
lost allocation units, 248–249, 456
lost clusters, 248–249, 456
LPT assignments, 55, 57
ls command, Linux, 592

M

MAC (Media Access Control) addresses, 490, 491–493
Mac OS, 3, 34–36, 576–588
  Apple menu, 581–582
  desktop, 579
  Finder window, 576, 579–581
  hardware support, 583–588
  launching applications, 583
  starting up Macs, 576–579
Mac OS Extended Format, 585
Mac OS ROM file, 577
Mac OS Standard Format, 585
macro(s), 469
macro viruses, 469
man command, Linux, 592
mandatory user profiles, Windows NT/2000/XP, 411
Map command, Windows 2000, 341
Master Boot Record (MBR), 100
  boot sector viruses, 130
master file table (MFT), 277
MBR (Master Boot Record), 100
  boot sector viruses, 130
MD command, 143
Md command, Windows 2000, 341
Media Access Control (MAC) addresses, 490, 491–493
megabytes, 622
memory
  conventional, 116–117
  copying program files into, 86
  displaying with DOS DEBUG, 628–630
  extended, 58, 118
  RAM, 10–11, 48–49, 116
  upper. *See* upper memory entries
  virtual, 72, 163
  Windows NT, 285
memory addresses, 49, 57–59, 114–115
  assignment, 58–59
  hexadecimal number system, 627–628
  use, 59
memory buses, 50
memory caches, CD-ROM, optimizing, 196
memory dumps, Windows 2000, 366–367
memory extenders, 71
memory management, 112–123
  memory map areas, 115–118
  operating system evolution, 113
  physical memory and memory addresses, 114–115
  utilities, 119–122
  Windows 9x. *See* memory management with Windows 9x
memory management with Windows 9x, 112, 113, 204–208
  default settings, 122–123
  device drivers, 204–206
  DOS applications in Windows 9x, 201–202
  swap file, 206
  VMM, 207–208
memory paging, 207
memory-resident viruses, 471
menu-driven interfaces, 6, 7
MFT (master file table), 277
microprocessors. *See* central processing unit (CPU)
Microsoft Management Console (MMC), Windows 2000, 354–360
  customizing, 355–357
  Event Viewer, 357–360
Microsoft support for Windows 9x, 208–209
Microsoft System Information
  Windows 98/Me, 239
  Windows 95, 239
Microsoft Web site, Windows 9x support, 252
Microsoft WINS, 500
minifile systems, 293
Mkdir command, 143
  Windows 2000, 341
mkdir command, Linux, 592
MMC. *See* Microsoft Management Console (MMC), Windows 2000
modes
  operating. *See* protected mode; real mode
  32-bit flat memory mode, 293
  Windows NT, 272–275
modular concept, Windows NT, 268–271
More command, Windows 2000, 341
| more command, Linux, 592
motherboard, 46–47
  system resources. *See* system resources on motherboard
MSD utility, 53
Msdos.sys file, 100, 102
  configuring Windows 9x startup, 175–177
multicasting, 495
multipartite viruses, 469
multiple logins, Windows XP Professional, 398
multiprocessing, 9
multitasking, 8–9
  cooperative, 9
  preemptive, 9–10
multithreading, 274
mv command, Linux, 592
My Computer, 186, 187

N

name resolution, 500
NAT (Network Address Translation), 498–499
native mode, Windows 2000 Professional, 304
NetBEUI (NetBIOS Extended User Interface), 489
  connecting to networks, 502–505
NetBIOS (Network Basic Input/Output System) names, 491, 499–500
netstat command, Linux, 592
network(s), 483–531
  addressing. *See* addressing on networks
  connecting to. *See* connecting to networks
  functioning, 484–485
  installing Windows 9x, 168

installing Windows 2000 Professional, 309–310
layers, 485–487
local. *See* local area networks (LANs)
peer-to-peer, 484
remote access. *See* remote access to networks
sharing resources. *See* network printers; sharing resources on networks
Windows NT, 289–292

Network Address Translation (NAT), 498–499
Network Basic Input/Output System (NetBIOS) names, 491, 499–500
network drive maps, 525–527
network interface cards (NICs), 484
Network layer, OSI model, 486, 487
TCP/IP protocols, 542–543
Network Neighborhood
Windows 9x, 502, 504
Windows 2000, 504
network operating systems (NOSs), 484
network printers, 489
newsgroups, Windows XP, 433
NICs (network interface cards), 484
non-memory-resident viruses, 471
Normal option, Windows 9x startup menu, 227
Norton Utilities, 452
NOSs (network operating systems), 484
notebook computers, 598–607
online resources, 607
power management, 602–606
Windows 98 features, 599–600
Windows 2000 features, 28, 600
Windows XP features, 601–602
NsLookup, 545–546
nslookup command, Linux, 592
NT file system (NTFS), 26
FAT16 compared, 278–279
features supported, 309
operating system support, 309
NT Hardware Qualifier (NTHQ), 280
NT Loader (Ntldr) program, 288
NT virtual DOS machines (NTVDMs), 273–274, 389
NTFS. *See* NT file system (NTFS)
NTHQ (NT Hardware Qualifier), 280
Ntldr (NT Loader) program, 288
NTVDMs (NT virtual DOS machines), 273–274, 389
number systems, converting between, 58

O

octets, 494
Open Systems Interconnection (OSI) reference model, 485–490, 538–546
IP address and port, 538–540
LANs, 487–490
layers, 485–487
TCP/IP protocols at layers, 540–544
TCP/IP utilities, 544–546
operating modes. *See* protected mode; real mode
operating systems (OSs)
commands, 103
comparison, 7–12
components, 4–5
DOS. *See* DOS (disk operating system)
functions, 2–12
hardware/operating system relationships. *See* hardware/ operating system relationships
launching applications, 80–87
Linux. *See* Linux
loading, 99–102, 222–223
media access control (MAC) OS. *See* Mac OS
OS/2, 2, 3, 34
software/operating system relationships. *See* software/ operating system relationships
Unix. *See* Unix
Windows. *See specific versions of Windows*
OS/2, 3, 34
OSI. *See* Open Systems Interconnection (OSI) reference model

P

packet(s), 487
Packet Internet Groper (Ping), 510
page(s), 285
page faults, 207
page files, 72
Pagefile.sys, 285
page-ins, 207
page-outs, 207
parallel ports, 46, 47
parameter RAM (PRAM), Mac, 576–577
Partition magic, 453
partition tables, 100
partitioning hard drives, 128, 129–131, 134–136
Fdisk, 135–136
Windows NT, 276
Windows XP Professional, 379
passwords, screen saver, 246
patches, 178
browsers, 564
path(s), 68
Path command, 84, 145
PC technicians, 631–641
professional organizations and certifications, 639–640
recordkeeping and information tools, 638–639
satisfying customers, 631–632
software copyright protection, 640–641
support calls. *See* support calls
PCI (Peripheral Component Interconnect) bus, 50
PDCs (primary domain controllers), 291
peer-to-peer networks, 484
performance
browsers, 561–563
Windows NT, 19
Performance Logs and Alerts snap-in, 355
Performance Monitor, Windows XP, 429
performance monitoring, Windows 2000, 361–367

performance optimization, Windows 2000, 360–361
performance problems, Windows 9x, troubleshooting, 259
Performance tab, Task Manager, 361, 362, 363
Performance window, Windows 2000, 364
Peripheral Component Interconnect (PCI) bus, 50
phone support, 634–637
  customer complaints, 636–637
  knowledgeable customers, 635–636
  overly confident customers, 636
  terminating calls, 637
physical addresses, 490, 491–493
Physical layer, OSI model, 486, 487
  TCP/IP protocols, 543
Physical memory frame, Performance tab of Task Manager, 363
PIFs (program information files), 200
Ping (Packet Internet Groper), 510
ping command, Linux, 592
pixels, 583
place value, hexadecimal number system, 622–626
Plug and Play (PnP), 65, 196–198
  BIOS, 197–198, 222
  components, 197
  configuration, 223
Point-to-Point Protocol (PPP), 543
Point-to-Point Protocol over Ethernet (PPPoE) protocol, 555
.pol file extension, 245
policy files, 245
polling, 54
polymorphic viruses, 470
POP (Post Office Protocol), 564, 565
port(s) (port addresses; port numbers)
  IP addresses, 538–540
  parallel, 46, 47
  serial, 46, 47
  USB, 46, 47, 51, 433
port addresses, 54–55, 56, 491
port replicators, 601
portability, Windows NT, 18
Portable OS Interface (POSIX), 268
POSIX (Portable OS Interface), 268
POST (Power-on Self Test), 97, 98–99
Post Office Protocol (POP), 564, 565
power management, notebook computers, 602–606
power use, Windows 2000, 27–28
Power-on Self Test (POST), 97, 98–99
PPP (Point-to-Point Protocol), 543
PPPoE (Point-to-Point Protocol over Ethernet) protocol, 555
PRAM (parameter RAM), Mac, 576–577
preemptive multitasking, 9–10
Presentation layer, OSI model, 486, 487
  TCP/IP protocols, 540
Previous Version of MS-DOS option, Windows 9x startup menu, 231
primary domain controllers (PDCs), 291
primary partition, 130
primary storage, 66
printers
  default, 516
  local, 516–518
  sharing on network. *See* sharing printers
private IP addresses, 496
processes, 274
product activation, Windows XP Professional, 387–388
professional organizations for PC technicians, 639
Program Compatibility Wizard, Windows XP, 429
program files, 68
  copying into memory, 86
  launching, 83–85
program information files (PIFs), 200
protected mode, 10, 48, 71, 72–74
  software, 73–74
  use by OS, 73
  Windows 9x startup, 223
protocols
  ARP, 542
  connectionless (best-effort), 542
  connection-oriented, 541
  ICMP, 543
  IMAP4, 564
  IP, 542
  IPX/SPX, 488
  line (bridging), 543
  OSI model, 488–490
  POP, 564, 565
  PPP, 543
  PPPoE, 555
  RARP, 542
  SLIP, 543
  SMTP, 564, 565
  SNMP, 545
  TCP/IP. *See* TCP/IP (Transmission Control Protocol/Internet Protocol)
proxy servers, 498–499
ps command, Linux, 592
public IP addresses, 496
pwd command, Linux, 592

Q

question mark (?), wildcard, 138

R

RAID (redundant array of independent disks), 466–467
RAM drives, 103
random access memory (RAM), 10–11, 48–49, 116
RARP (Reverse Address Resolution Protocol), 542
RAS (Remote Access Service), 528
Rd command, Windows 2000, 341
Readiness Analyzer, Windows XP Professional, 378
real mode, 10, 48, 71–72, 73–74
  with DOS applications in Windows 9x, 202–204
  software, 73–74
  use by OS, 73
  virtual, 74
reboot command, Linux, 592
recordkeeping, PC technicians, 638–639
Recover command, 141
recovering erased files, 457
Recovery Console
  Windows 2000, 338–342
  Windows XP, 430

redirecting output, Linux, 594
redirection symbol, Linux, 594
redundant array of independent disks (RAID), 466–467
registry, 5, 78
  Windows 9x. *See* registry, Windows NT/2000/XP
  Windows NT/2000/XP. *See* registry, Windows NT/2000/XP
Registry Checker
  Windows 98/Me, 239
  Windows 95/Me, 235–236
Registry Editor, Windows XP, 430
registry, Windows 9x, 233–238
  corrupted, recovering from, 235–236
  keys, 234–235
  modifying, 237–238
  organization, 234–235
registry, Windows NT/2000/XP, 422–427
  components, 422, 423
  editing, 426–427
  local organization, 422–424
  physical organization, 425–426
  restoring using Recovery Console, 341–342
reliability of Windows NT, 19
Remote Access Service (RAS), 528
remote access to networks, 528–530
  allowing inbound connections, 528
  remote control, 529–530
Remote Assistance
  Windows XP, 430
  Windows XP Professional, 398
Remote Desktop, Windows XP, 430
Removable Storage Management snap-in, 355
Ren command, Windows 2000, 341
Rename command, Windows 2000, 341
request handler, 60
rescue disks. *See* emergency startup disks (ESDs)
reserved IP addresses, 496–497
resolution of displays, 583–584
resource arbitrator, 197
resource management, 197
Reverse Address Resolution Protocol (RARP), 542
rm command, Linux, 592
Rmdir command, 144
  Windows 2000, 341
rmdir command, Linux, 592
roaming user profiles, Windows NT/2000/XP, 411
root accounts, Linux, 589
root directory, 67–68, 126–128, 138
  Linux, 589
  representing, 69
root privileges, Linux, 589
route command, Linux, 592
Runas.exe file, Windows XP, 430
run-time configuration, 197

S

Safe Mode, Windows XP, 430
Safe Mode Command Prompt Only option, Windows 9x startup menu, 231
Safe Mode option
  Windows 9x startup menu, 228–230
  Windows 2000 Advanced Options menu, 336–337
Safe Mode with Command Prompt option, Windows 2000 Advanced Options menu, 337
Safe Mode with Network Support option, Windows 9x startup menu, 230
Safe Mode with Networking option, Windows 2000 Advanced Options menu, 337
SAM (security accounts manager), 291
Scandisk command, 146
ScanDisk utility, 248–249
Scanreg command, 146
Sc.exe file, Windows XP, 430
Scheduled Task Wizard
  Windows 98/Me, 240
  Windows 95, 240
scheduling backups, 459–461
screen saver passwords, 246
SCSI drives, 585
secondary storage, 66–70
sectors, 10
  creating, 125
security
  screen saver passwords, 246
  user profiles, 245
  Windows 9x, 245–246
  Windows NT, 19. *See also* security using Windows NT/2000/XP
  Windows 2000, 26. *See also* security using Windows NT/2000/XP
security accounts manager (SAM), 291
Security Configuration and Analysis snap-in, 355
security log, Event Viewer, 358
security using Windows NT/2000/XP, 19, 410–422
  disk quotas, 416–418
  EFS, 418–421
  firewalls, 421–422
  user accounts and profiles, 410–416
Select Network Protocol dialog box, 506, 507
Serial Line Internet Protocol (SLIP), 543
serial ports, 46, 47
servers, 484
service packs, 178
Services snap-in, 355
Services tool, Windows XP, 430
session(s), 541
Session layer, OSI model, 486, 487
  TCP/IP protocols, 541
Set command, Windows 2000, 341
Setup command, switches, 173–174
setup screen, installation process from, 171–177
SFC. *See* System File Checker (SFC)
Shared Folders snap-in, 355
sharing Internet connections, 557–559
sharing printers, 516–523
  installing local printers, 516
  methods of sharing, 520–521
  sharing with workgroup, 517–518
  troubleshooting problems, 521–523
  using shared printers, 518–520
sharing resources on networks, 511–523
  files and folders, 514–515
  printers. *See* network printers

- Windows 98 components needed for, 512–514
- Windows 2000 components needed for, 514

shells, 4
shells file, Linux, 593–594
shortcut(s)
- keystroke. *See* keystroke shortcuts
- Windows 9x, 184–185
- Windows 2000 Professional, 320
- Windows XP Professional, 393–394

shortcut menus, Windows Explorer, 187–188
Simple Mail Transfer Protocol (SMTP), 564, 565
Simple Network Management Protocol (SNMP), 545
simple volumes, Windows 2000 Professional, 306
single-tasking, 8
16-bit device drivers, memory management with Windows 9x, 205–206
16-bit mode. *See* real mode
16-bit software, 73–74
SLIP (Serial Line Internet Protocol), 543
SMARTDrive, 451
SMTP (Simple Mail Transfer Protocol), 564, 565
snap-ins, 354–355
SNMP (Simple Network Management Protocol), 545
sockets, 541
soft (warm) boots, 96
software
- antivirus, 467, 470, 475–477
- application. *See* application(s)
- backup, 461–464
- disk cloning, 465
- FTP, 567–568
- legacy. *See* legacy software
- operating systems. *See* operating systems (OSs); *specific operating systems*
- problems, troubleshooting hard drives, 453–457
- protecting copyrights, 640–641
- 16-bit, 73–74
- third-party, troubleshooting hard drives, 452–453
- 32-bit, 73, 74
- uninstalling, 258–259

software caches, 450–451
software interrupts, 61, 63–64
software/operating system relationships, 71–80
- BIOS, 74–76
- device drivers, 76–80
- operating modes, 71–74

spanned volumes, Windows 2000 Professional, 306
SpinRite, 453
spooling, 521
Start menu
- Windows 2000, 27
- Windows 2000 Professional, 320–322

startup BIOS, 64
startup disks. *See* emergency startup disks (ESDs)
startup menu, Windows 9x, troubleshooting boot process using, 231–232
startup, Windows 9x, 218–224
- files used to customize, 218–220

static IP addresses, 497
static VxDs, 223
stealth viruses, 470
Step-by-Step Confirmation option, Windows 9x startup menu, 230
striped volumes, Windows 2000 Professional, 306
subdirectories, 68
subnet masks, 506
subsystems, Windows NT, 272
support calls, 632–638
- escalating problems, 637–638
- on-site, 633–634
- phone support, 634–637
- planning for good service, 632–633

support tools, Windows 2000, 345–346
swap files, 72
- Windows 9x, 206

Sys command, 145
System applet in Control Panel, Windows 9x, 239, 242–243
system BIOS, 44
system bus, 50
System Configuration Utility
- Windows 98/Me, 239, 243–245
- Windows XP, 430

system disks, 105
System file, Mac, 577
system file(s), WFP to protect, 347–348
System File Checker (SFC)
- Windows 98/Me, 239
- Windows 2000, 347–348
- Windows XP, 430

System folder, Mac, 577
System Information tool
- Windows 2000, 355
- Windows XP, 430

system log, Event Viewer, 358
System Monitor
- Windows 98/Me, 240, 243, 244
- Windows 2000, 363–365

system partition, 276
system performance tools, Windows 9x. *See* Windows 9x system performance and troubleshooting tools
System Recovery, Windows 98/Me, 240
system resources
- assignment, 98–99
- motherboard. *See* system resources on motherboard
- viewing, 53

system resources on motherboard, 52–64
- COM assignments, 55, 57
- DMA channels, 59–60
- hardware interrupts, 54, 60–61, 62
- I/O addresses, 54–55, 56
- IRQ, 54, 56
- LPT assignments, 55, 57
- memory addresses, 57–59
- software interrupts, 61, 63–64

System Restore utility
- ASR compared, 436
- Windows XP, 430, 435–436

system state data
  backing up in Windows 2000 Professional, 318–319
  backing up in Windows XP Professional, 391
system tray, Windows XP Professional, 395
Systemroot command, Windows 2000, 341

T

Task Killing Utility, Windows XP, 430
Task Lister tool, Windows XP, 430
Task Manager
  Windows 9x, 240
  Windows 2000, 361–363
  Windows XP, 430
task switching, 9
taskbar
  Windows 2000 Professional, 322–323
  Windows XP Professional, 395
Taskbar Properties window, Windows 9x, 183
TCP (Transmission Control Protocol), 541
TCP/IP (Transmission Control Protocol/Internet Protocol), 488, 502
  connecting to networks, 506–510
  installing and configuring using Windows 98, 506–509
  installing and configuring using Windows 2000, 509–510
  OSI model. *See* Open Systems Interconnection (OSI) reference model
  ports, 538–540
  troubleshooting connections, 510
  utilities, 544–546
technicians. *See* PC technicians
telephone support. *See* phone support
terminate-and-stay-resident (TSR) programs, 78
  upgrade installation of Windows 9x, 169
1394 (IEEE 1394), 51
32-bit mode. *See* protected mode
32-bit drivers, Windows 9x, 163–164
32-bit flat memory mode, 293
threads, 7, 274
.386 file extension, 205
top-level domain, 561
Totals frame, Performance tab of Task Manager, 363
traceroute command, Linux, 592
tracks, 10
  creating, 125
Transmission Control Protocol (TCP), 541
Transmission Control Protocol/Internet Protocol. *See* TCP/IP (Transmission Control Protocol/Internet Protocol)
Transport layer, OSI model, 486, 487
  TCP/IP protocols, 541–542
Trojan horses, 468, 472
troubleshooting
  applications in Windows 9x, 256–259
  hard drives. *See* troubleshooting hard drives
  hardware in Windows 9x, 253–256
  network printer problems, 521–523
  software installations, 199–200
  TCP/IP connections, 510
  Windows 9x. *See* Windows 9x system performance and troubleshooting tools
  Windows 9x boot process. *See* troubleshooting Windows 9x boot process
  Windows 9x performance problems, 259
  Windows NT. *See* troubleshooting Windows NT; troubleshooting Windows NT boot process
  Windows 2000. *See* Windows 2000 maintenance and troubleshooting tools
  Windows 2000 boot process. *See* troubleshooting Windows 2000 boot process
  Windows XP boot process. *See* troubleshooting Windows XP boot process
troubleshooting hard drives, 451–457
  software problems, 453–457
  third-party software, 452–453
troubleshooting Windows 9x boot process, 224–233
  error messages, 225–226
  startup disk use, 232–233
  startup menu options, 226–232
troubleshooting Windows NT, 294–299
  boot process. *See* troubleshooting Windows NT boot process
troubleshooting Windows NT boot process, 295–299
  boot disks, 296–298, 299
  ERD, 298–299
  Last Known Good Configuration, 295–296
troubleshooting Windows 2000 boot process, 335–344
  Advanced Options menu, 336–338
  Emergency Repair Process, 342–344
  Recovery Console, 338–342
troubleshooting Windows XP boot process, 433–440
  ASR, 437–439
  error messages, 439–440
  startup disk, 436–437
  System restore, 435–436
TSR (terminate-and-stay-resident) programs, 78
  upgrade installation of Windows 9x, 169
Type command, Windows 2000, 341

U

UDP (User Datagram Protocol), 541
UMAs (upper memory addresses), conflicts with, 255–256
UMBs (upper memory blocks), creating and using, 120–121
unattended installations, 309, 310
Undelete command, 141
Unformat command, 145
Uninstall Windows XP Professional tool, 430
uninstalling
  devices in Windows 9x, 192
  software in Windows 9x, 258–259
Universal Resource Locators (URLs), structure, 560–561

Universal Serial Bus (USB) ports, 46, 47, 51
  Windows XP, 433
Unix, 3, 32
  case sensitivity, 69
  directory representation, 69
  interface, 5
update(s)
  browsers, 564
  downloading and installing, 180
  Windows XP, 431–433
Update Device Driver Wizard, 192
upgrading
  to Windows Me, 179
  to Windows 98, 178–179
  Windows 98, 16–17, 179
  Windows 95, 178–179
  to Windows 9x, 167, 168–170, 178–179
  to Windows 2000 Professional. *See* upgrading to Windows 2000 Professional
  Windows XP Professional, 380
upgrading to Windows 2000 Professional, 311–312, 317–318
  from Windows 9x, 312–313
  from Windows NT, 313–314
upper memory, 116, 117–118
upper memory addresses (UMAs), conflicts with, 255–256
upper memory blocks (UMBs), creating and using, 120–121
URLs (Universal Resource Locators), structure, 560–561
USB (Universal Serial Bus) ports, 46, 47, 51
  Windows XP, 433
user accounts
  Linux, 589
  Windows NT/2000/XP, 410–411, 412–413
user component, 160
User Datagram Protocol (UDP), 541
user files, transferring to new PC, 388–389
user groups, Windows NT/2000/XP, 414–416
user mode, Windows NT, 272, 273–274
user profiles, 245
  Windows NT/2000/XP, 411–416
User State Migration Tool (USMT), 388
useradd command, Linux, 592
userdel command, Linux, 592
USMT (User State Migration Tool), 388
utilities
  memory management, 119–122
  TCP/IP, 544–546

V

value data, 234
VCACHE, 451
VDMs (virtual DOS machines), 5–6, 110–111, 113
  Windows NT, 273–274, 389
vector table, 61
Ver command, 146
Version Conflict Manager, Windows 98/Me, 240
VFAT (virtual file allocation table), 132–133
vi command, Linux, 593
vi editor, Linux, 595–597
video, Windows XP Professional, 396–398
viewing, system resources, 53
virtual device drivers (VxD drivers), 205
  static, 223
virtual DOS machines (VDMs), 5–6, 110–111, 113
  Windows NT, 273–274, 389
virtual file allocation table (VFAT), 132–133
virtual machine(s), 161–163
Virtual Machine Manager (VMM), 163, 207–208
virtual memory, 72, 163
  management, Windows 2000, 365–366
virtual real mode, 74
  with DOS applications in Windows 9x, 202–204
virus(es)
  boot sector, 130, 468–469
  cloaking techniques, 469–470
  definition, 468
  encrypting, 470
  file, 469
  memory-resident, 471
  multipartite, 469
  non-memory-resident, 471
  polymorphic, 470
  replication, 471–472
  responding to, 475–476
  stealth, 470
  symptoms, 474–475
virus hoaxes, 473
virus signatures, 469
VMM (Virtual Machine Manager), 163, 207–208
volume(s), 67
  types, 466–467
  Windows 2000 Professional, 306
volume bit map, Mac, 586
volume information block, Mac, 586
VxD drivers (virtual device drivers), 205
  static, 223
.vxd file extension, 205

W

warm boots, 96
warning events, Event Viewer, 358
WDM (Win32 Driver Model), 163
Web browsers. *See* browsers
WFP (Windows File Protection), Windows 2000, 347–348
whatis command, Linux, 593
who command, Linux, 593
wildcards, 138
window managers, Linux, 597–598
Windows
  case sensitivity, 69
  directory representation, 69
Windows applications
  installing in Windows 9x. *See* installing applications in Windows 9x
  loading at startup, 224
  32-bit, Windows 9x, 163–164

troubleshooting in Windows 9x, 256–259
virtual machines, 163
Windows desktop, loading applications, 86–87
Windows Explorer, 186–189
Windows File Protection (WFP)
Windows 2000, 347–348
Windows XP, 430
Windows Internet Naming Service (WINS), 500
Windows Me, 16–17, 159
boot process, Windows 95 boot process compared, 224
Registry Checker, 235–236
system performance and troubleshooting tools. *See* Windows 9x system performance and troubleshooting tools
upgrading from Windows 98, 179
Windows Media Player, 396–398
Windows Messenger, Windows XP Professional, 396
Windows 98
boot process, Windows 95 boot process compared, 224
components needed to share resources, 512–514
installing and configuring TCP/IP, 506–509
Network Neighborhood, 504
notebook features, 599–600
Registry Checker, 235–236
system performance and troubleshooting tools. *See* Windows 9x system performance and troubleshooting tools
upgrades, 16–17
upgrading from Windows 95, 178–179
upgrading to Windows Me, 179
Windows 95 compared, 158–159
Windows 2000 compared, 26–29
Windows 98 SE, 16
Windows 95
boot process, Windows 98/Me boot process compared, 224
registry backup, 235
system performance and troubleshooting tools. *See* Windows 9x system performance and troubleshooting tools
upgrading to Windows 98, 178–179
Windows 98 compared, 158–159
Windows 9x, 3, 13–17, 157–212. *See also specific versions of Windows*
architecture, 160–164
backup utility, 461–463
booting. *See* troubleshooting Windows 9x boot process; Windows 9x boot process
components, 163–164
desktop management, 182–186
device drivers, 77–79
dial-up connections, 547–551
differences from Windows 3.x and DOS, 15–16
disk caching, 451
disk compression, 446–448
drive management, 186–189
hardware requirements, 14
icons, 185–186
installing. *See* installing Windows 9x
installing applications. *See* installing applications in Windows 9x
installing hardware. *See* installing hardware with Windows 9x
keystroke shortcuts, 180–182
loading MS-DOS core of, 102–104
memory management. *See* memory management with Windows 9x
Microsoft support, 208–209
Network Neighborhood, 502, 504
registry. *See* registry, Windows 9x
shortcuts, 184–185
startup disks, 105–110
startup menu options, 226–232
system performance tools. *See* Windows 9x system performance and troubleshooting tools
troubleshooting. *See* Windows 9x system performance and troubleshooting tools
troubleshooting hardware, 253–256
upgrading to Windows 2000 Professional, 312–313
Windows 98 upgrades, 16–17
Windows NT compared, 19–24
Windows 9x boot process, 218–224
files used to customize startup process, 218–220
loading applications at startup, 224
startup process, 220–224
troubleshooting. *See* troubleshooting Windows 9x boot process
Windows 9x system performance and troubleshooting tools, 239–253
Device Manager, 250–251
Dr. Watson, 240, 251–252
hard drive management, 246–250
Microsoft Web site, 252
security management, 245–246
System applet in Control Panel, 239, 242–243
System Configuration Utility, 239, 243–245
System Monitor, 240, 243, 244
Windows Help, 252, 253
Windows NT, 3, 17–24, 267–300
boot process, 292–294
command prompt, 22–23
compatibility with software, 19
desktop, 22
disk caching, 451
expandability, 18
file system, 158
hardware supported, 21–22
installing. *See* installing Windows NT
installing hardware devices, 286–288
installing software, 286, 288–289
memory, 285
modes, 272–275
modular concept, 268–271
networking, 289–292
performance, 19
portability, 18
reliability, 19
security. *See* security using Windows NT/2000/XP
troubleshooting, 294–299
upgrading to Windows 2000 Professional, 313–314
Windows 9x compared, 19–24

Windows NT boot process, 292–294
  troubleshooting. *See* troubleshooting Windows NT boot process
Windows Sockets (WinSock), 500
Windows 3.x
  disk caching, 451
  installing Windows 9x over, 178
  memory management, 113
  Windows 9x compared, 15–16
Windows 2000, 3, 24–29, 331–369
  backup utility, 463–464
  boot process, 332–335. *See also* troubleshooting Windows 2000 boot process
  components needed to share resources, 514
  device drivers, 80
  dial-up connections, 551–553
  disk caching, 451
  disk compression, 448–449
  installing and configuring TCP/IP, 509–510
  maintenance and troubleshooting tools. *See* Windows 2000 maintenance and troubleshooting tools
  Network Neighborhood, 504
  notebook computer features, 28
  notebook features, 600
  registry. *See* registry, Windows NT/2000/XP
  security. *See* security using Windows NT/2000/XP
  updates, 367
  Windows 98 compared, 26–29
  Windows NT compared, 29
Windows 2000 Advanced Server, 25
Windows 2000 Datacenter Server, 25
Windows 2000 maintenance and troubleshooting tools, 344–367
  Backup tool, 345
  command window, 348
  Computer Management, 350–354
  Disk Properties window, 349–350
  Dr. Watson, 366–367
  memory dumps, 366–367
  MMC, 354–360
  performance monitoring and optimization, 360–365
  SFC, 347–348
  support tools, 345–346
  virtual memory management, 365–366
  WFP, 347–348
  Windows updates, 367
Windows 2000 Professional, 24–25, 303–327
  architecture, 304–307
  basic disks, 306
  dynamic disks, 306–307
  installing. *See* installing Windows 2000 Professional
  installing applications, 325–326
  installing hardware, 323–325
  new features, 304–305
  shortcuts, 320
  Start menu, 320–322
  taskbar, 322–323
Windows 2000 Server, 25
Windows 2.x, memory management, 113
Windows Update
  Windows 98/Me, 239
  Windows 95, 239
  Windows 2000, 367
Windows Upgrade tool, Windows XP, 430
Windows XP, 3, 29–32
  backup utility, 463–464
  dial-up connections, 552
  disk caching, 451
  disk compression, 448–449
  help on Web, 431–433
  maintenance and troubleshooting tools, 428–433
  newsgroups, 433
  notebook features, 601–602
  registry. *See* registry, Windows NT/2000/XP
  security. *See* security using Windows NT/2000/XP
  troubleshooting boot process. *See* troubleshooting Windows XP boot process
  update, 431–433
Windows XP Professional, 373–405
  architecture, 376
  audio, 396–398
  backing up hard drive, 389–391
  features, 374–375
  installing. *See* installing Windows XP Professional
  installing applications, 401–404
  installing hardware, 398–401
  multiple logins, 398
  product activation, 387–388
  remote assistance, 398
  shortcuts, 393–394
  system tray, 395
  taskbar, 395
  transferring user files and preferences to new PC, 388–389
  video, 396–398
  Windows Messenger, 396
WINS (Windows Internet Naming Service), 500
Win16 on Win32 (WoW) environment, 273
WinSock (Windows Sockets), 500
Win32 Driver Model (WDM), 163
Win386.swp file, 206
workgroups
  sharing local printers, 517–518
  Windows NT, 289, 290–292
  Windows XP Professional, 380
worms, 468
WoW (Win16 on Win32) environment, 273

X

Xcopy command, 142–143

THOMSON
COURSE TECHNOLOGY™

A+ PC Repair Total Solution